Strategies and Solutions for Public Sector Burnout

Kenny A. Hendrickson
University of the Virgin Islands, US Virgin Islands

Kula A. Francis
University of the Virgin Islands, US Virgin Islands

IGI Global
Scientific Publishing
Publishing Tomorrow's Research Today

Vice President of Editorial	Melissa Wagner
Director of Acquisitions	Mikaela Felty
Director of Book Development	Jocelynn Hessler
Production Manager	Mike Brehm
Cover Design	Jose Rosado

Published in the United States of America by
IGI Global Scientific Publishing
701 East Chocolate Avenue
Hershey, PA, 17033, USA
Tel: 717-533-8845
Fax: 717-533-7115
Website: https://www.igi-global.com E-mail: cust@igi-global.com

Library of Congress Cataloging-in-Publication Data

Names: Hendrickson, Kenny A., 1976- editor http://id.loc.gov/authorities/names/n2025026921 http://id.loc.gov/rwo/agents/n2025026921 | Francis, Kula A., 1979- editor http://id.loc.gov/authorities/names/n2023036759 http://id.loc.gov/rwo/agents/n2023036759
Title: Strategies and solutions for public sector burnout / edited by: Kenny A. Hendrickson and Kula A. Francis.
Description: Hershey, PA : IGI Global Scientific Publishing, [2026] | Includes bibliographical references and index. | Summary: "By engaging with diverse perspectives (i.e., Business, Criminal Justice, Education, Political Science, Psychology, Public Administration, Public Health, Leadership, Social Work, Sociology, Medicine, Nursing, Education, Military), this book offers insights into the causes, challenges and potential consequences of public sector burnout around the world"-- Provided by publisher.
Identifiers: LCCN 2025004494 (print) | LCCN 2025004495 (ebook) | ISBN 9798337301693 hardcover | ISBN 9798337301709 paperback | ISBN 9798337301716 ebook
Subjects: LCSH: Burn out (Psychology) http://id.loc.gov/authorities/subjects/sh85018150 | Public administration http://id.loc.gov/authorities/subjects/sh85108611 | Psychology, Industrial http://id.loc.gov/authorities/subjects/sh85108476
Classification: LCC BF481 .S858 2026 (print) | LCC BF481 (ebook) | DDC 158.7/23--dc23/eng/20250623
LC record available at https://lccn.loc.gov/2025004494
LC ebook record available at https://lccn.loc.gov/2025004495

British Cataloguing in Publication Data
A Cataloguing in Publication record for this book is available from the British Library.

Table of Contents

Detailed Table of Contents

In recent decades, studies have continued to explore burnout syndrome within various professions. However, there are limited studies on occupational burnout syndrome as an epidemic. Occupational burnout epidemic considers burnout syndrome as a large-scale spread of an occupational disease that impacts employees' health, welfare and performance at a particular period. In the realm of the public sector, there is a need for epidemiological studies on occupational burnout epidemics, specifically in the scope of disasters and crises and US territorial governments. Therefore, this chapter presents a research study on a burnout epidemic that affected the government workforce of the US Virgin Islands (USVI) during COVID-19. An exploratory mixed method design was used to gather empirical evidence. Data was collected from 201 participants working in nine departments/agencies of USVI government. The findings of this research uncovered identifiable symptoms of burnout syndrome experienced by USVI government workers during COVID-19 pandemic.

This chapter explores the significant issue of public sector burnout in the public sector through the lens of the Job Demands-Resources Theory. The chapter highlights the essential role of effective leadership and professional development in mitigating burnout and enhancing employee motivation and satisfaction. Key leadership theories

Burnout in health professionals can impact therapeutic outcomes in patients. Improving health outcomes for marginalized populations and bridging the gap in health disparities requires a concerted effort among all major stakeholders. The Workgroup Enhancing Community Advocacy & Research Engagement (WE-CARE) program at the University of South Florida is a pharmacy-led cross collaboration of multiple stakeholders who serve as an integrated network of academia, researchers, and community to improve health disparities by increasing minority enrollment and participation in research and building trust and mutual respect between the community and researchers. To do this effectively WE-CARE uses a 360-degree community engagement model that maximizes the efforts of all involved. This chapter explains the mission, community-engaging activities, collaborations, and research-supporting efforts that WE-CARE employs to fulfill its mission and describes how it has tried to mitigate burnout in health professionals through its activities.

First-responder and emergency healthcare workers face a higher risk of burnout than most occupations. Drawing upon the effort-reward imbalance model we examine how the growing effort required from them is increasingly met with diminishing reward. As a result, there are global shortages of workers in these occupations and the workers who remain are at greater risk of burnout. These front-line workers deal with significant occupational stressors but using the challenge-hindrance model of workplace stress we highlight the potentially greater significance for burnout of organizational stressors i.e. stressors created less by the work itself and more by the organization. Using a case study of firefighters in the UK we show how organizational change can increase both stress levels and the risk of burnout.

Teaching is an emotionally demanding profession, especially in the Philippines, where public school teachers must manage large class sizes, limited resources, and extensive administrative duties. This chapter explores emotional labor in teaching, emphasizing how Filipino educators navigate their emotions through surface and deep acting strategies. It also examines compassion fatigue, which results from prolonged exposure to students' struggles, leading to emotional exhaustion and reduced empathy. Teachers in low-income communities or those working with students with disabilities are particularly at risk. The chapter highlights significant factors contributing to compassion fatigue and proposes evidence-based interventions, such as mindfulness programs, peer support groups, and institutional reforms. Addressing emotional labor and compassion fatigue is essential for maintaining teacher well-being and enhancing the quality of education in the Philippines.

A review of burnout in the social work profession is presented in the chapter. The focus is on social workers' experience of burnout in the pre-pandemic and COVID-19 pandemic eras. Human service professionals have a high probability of experiencing burnout. Burnout has been described as the cost of caring for human service professionals and often occurs when workers are exposed to stressful situations. Having compassion fatigue, secondary trauma, vicarious trauma, shared trauma, collective trauma and trauma trigger fatigue are all situations that can lead to social worker burnout. Social worker burnout can include feelings of exhaustion, depersonalization and professional inefficacy. The purpose of the chapter is to define social work burnout, explore assessments for burnout, review social work job circumstances associated with burnout and present research on prevention/intervention for social work burnout in the pre-pandemic and COVID-19 pandemic eras.

This study examines the effectiveness of leadership strategies in mitigating burnout among public sector employees by fostering resilience, enhancing morale, and promoting organizational wellness. Using a mixed-methods approach, data were collected from 300 employees through surveys and 30 leaders via semi-structured interviews. Findings indicate that transformational leadership significantly reduces burnout by fostering psychological safety, motivation, and engagement, while transactional leadership exacerbates stress. Resilience emerged as a key protective factor, mediating the relationship between leadership and burnout. Additionally, organizational wellness initiatives, such as mental health support and flexible work policies, complement leadership efforts in burnout mitigation. The study underscores the need for leadership development programs and policy reforms to enhance workplace well-being in the public sector.

Stress is a multifaceted n from psychologists, medical professionals, and researchers due to its profound effects on mental and physical well-being. Stress refers to the body's response to any demand or challenge, often perceived as a threat or strain on an individual's resources. It can be caused by external factors, This article explores the definitions, causes, and consequences of stress, emphasizing its complexity and pervasive impact. Definitions changes that require adjustment or action. Hans Selye, a pioneering endocrinologist, described stress as the "nonspecific response of the body to any demand." This definition highlights that stress is not inherently negative; instead, it is a general reaction, such as preparing for an important exam or competing in a sports event. Conversely, distress, or "negative stress," occurs when demands exceed an individual's coping abilities, potentially leading to harmful consequences.

This chapter aims to explore the impact of organizational climate on teacher burnout and explore the mediating role of family conflict in this relationship. The study was done by using the survey method followed by quantitative analysis and the cross-sectional method. The researchers used the Organizational Climate Scale, Maslach Burnout Inventory, and Family Conflict Sale for data collection from 200 teachers from 10 government secondary schools. Multiple regression analyses were conducted to assess the effect of organizational climate on teachers' burnout. The mediating role of family conflict in the link between organizational climate and teacher burnout was investigated using Bootstrap methodology. The findings highlighted that organizational climate significantly contributes to burnout, corroborating prior

Preface

Around the globe, public sector systems stand as the pillars of social welfare, justice, education, health, and safety. Yet, in recent years, these essential systems and their workforces have been increasingly strained by an escalating tide of crises—ranging from public health emergencies to political instability and natural disasters. The result has been a surge in burnout among those tasked with serving the public good. This edited volume, *Strategies and Solutions for Public Sector Burnout*, is our response to that global challenge.

Public sector burnout is not merely an individual mental health and wellness concern— it is a structural and institutional issue that affects governments, nonprofit organizations, and public enterprises across nations. It impacts the well-being of civil servants, educators, healthcare providers, emergency responders, administrators, and countless others who keep public systems functioning. As burnout persists, its consequences reverberate outward: weakening institutions, eroding trust, decreasing productivity, and impairing the quality of vital services.

This book was conceived as both a scholarly intervention and a practical resource. It presents interdisciplinary research, lived experiences from practitioners, and innovative institutional responses that illuminate the depth and complexity of public sector burnout. Through the lens of diverse disciplines—including Public Administration, Psychology, Political Science, Sociology, Public Health, Criminal Justice, Nursing, Military Studies, Education, and more—contributors examine burnout's origins, manifestations, and solutions. These perspectives underscore that burnout is a multifaceted issue that requires multifaceted strategies.

Our collective aim is not only to diagnose the problem but to contribute meaningfully to its resolution. To this end, this volume explores critical strategies for promoting wellness, productivity, resilience, and long-term sustainability in public sector institutions. We seek to foster dialogue and action that transcends academic boundaries and reaches those on the frontlines of public service.

The global audience for this work includes researchers, educators, practitioners, policymakers, and students committed to enhancing the efficacy and humanity of public service. Whether in government, education, nonprofit leadership, or healthcare, our readers will find valuable insights, evidence-based solutions, and reaffirmed purpose.

It is our hope that this book will serve as both a mirror and a map: a mirror reflecting the current realities of burnout, and a map pointing toward pathways of recovery, renewal, and resilience.

ORGANIZATION OF THE BOOK

Chapter 1: Crisis Epidemiology of Burnout Syndrome in the US Virgin Islands' Government: The Consequences of COVID-19

This chapter offers an urgent and novel epidemiological approach to understanding public sector burnout by framing it as an occupational epidemic. Through an exploratory mixed-method study of 201 employees across nine government agencies in the U.S. Virgin Islands, the authors document the profound toll COVID-19 took on public workers. The research identifies clear symptoms of burnout and reinforces the need to treat burnout as a systemic phenomenon, especially during crises. This study makes a critical contribution to underrepresented regions in burnout literature and elevates the importance of disaster-responsive public workforce support.

Chapter 2: Reviving the Public Sector: Leadership's Key Role in Managing Burnout

Leadership emerges as a central antidote to public sector burnout in this chapter, which applies the Job Demands-Resources Theory to explore how professional development and supportive leadership can restore public service vitality. The authors offer a roadmap for embedding core leadership competencies—such as adaptability, communication, and continuous learning—into organizational culture. They advocate for institutionalizing leadership development to build resilience and retain motivated teams, while also providing actionable principles for public sector leaders striving to create more sustainable and satisfying workplaces.

Chapter 3: Prevention Strategies of Emergency Management and Disaster Professionals Battling Burnout

Emergency and disaster professionals often navigate two taxing operational realities—planning in calm periods and responding in chaos. This chapter dissects the paradox of stress under both "blue sky" and "gray sky" conditions. It calls attention to the occupational hazards and resource limitations these professionals face and outlines actionable strategies for prevention and recovery. Grounded in evidence-based practices, the authors provide insights that can inform jurisdictional policy, workforce protection strategies, and long-term sustainability of emergency management personnel.

Chapter 4: WE-CARE: Closing the Gap of Health Disparities Through Community Collaborations

In this chapter, burnout among healthcare professionals is addressed within the context of collaborative community engagement. The WE-CARE initiative at the University of South Florida exemplifies a pharmacy-led model of integrated stakeholders working to eliminate health disparities. By fostering trust between researchers and underrepresented communities, WE-CARE not only addresses systemic health inequities but also mitigates professional burnout through shared purpose and relational equity. This chapter highlights how community-engaged models can both elevate outcomes and support the well-being of public health professionals.

Chapter 5: How Organizational Change Impacts Burnout for First-Responders and Emergency Healthcare Workers: Firefighters as a Case Study

Using a case study of UK firefighters, this chapter explores how organizational change—rather than field conditions alone—can be a primary source of burnout. Through the lens of the effort-reward imbalance and challenge-hindrance stress models, the authors illustrate that increased job demands paired with diminishing support contribute significantly to emotional exhaustion and attrition. The findings underscore the necessity of aligning organizational structures with the realities of emergency service work and advocate for reforms that center worker wellness during periods of institutional transition.

Chapter 6: Caring at a Cost: Exploring Compassion Fatigue, Emotional Labor, and Well-Being Among Filipino Teachers

Educators in the Philippines, especially those serving marginalized or high-needs communities, face emotional burdens that can lead to compassion fatigue. This chapter delves into the emotional labor required in teaching, including surface and deep acting, and its toll on well-being. It introduces a set of evidence-based interventions—such as mindfulness, peer support, and institutional policy reform—to safeguard teacher health. By addressing both individual coping mechanisms and systemic reform, the chapter lays a foundation for improving teacher retention and educational quality.

Chapter 7: Burnout in the Social Work Profession: Now, Then, and with Planning, Maybe Never Again

Social workers, historically vulnerable to burnout due to their empathetic and high-stress roles, are the focus of this chapter. The authors provide a timeline analysis of burnout pre- and post-pandemic, explore common burnout-related phenomena such as vicarious trauma and compassion fatigue, and present diagnostic tools and prevention strategies. The chapter offers a well-researched, practical guide for social workers and human services institutions committed to addressing the deep-rooted issues that threaten workforce sustainability.

Chapter 8: Leadership Strategies to Mitigate Public Sector Burnout: Fostering Resilience, Employee Morale, and Organizational Wellness

This data-rich study emphasizes how leadership style and organizational policies shape burnout outcomes. Through surveys and interviews with over 300 public sector employees and leaders, the chapter finds transformational leadership and wellness initiatives to be powerful buffers against burnout. Psychological safety, motivation, and flexible work arrangements emerge as critical components. The research reinforces the urgency for leadership development programs and structural reforms aimed at promoting resilience and organizational health across the public sector.

Chapter 9: Citizen Satisfaction with the Quality of Public Administrative Services: Public Administration Reform in Vietnam

Administrative efficiency and citizen satisfaction are explored in this chapter as indirect but critical factors in mitigating public sector burnout. Drawing on data from Vietnam's Satisfaction Index of Public Administration Services, the authors identify key determinants—such as transparency, accountability, and digital access—that influence public perception. The findings show how poorly functioning systems not only frustrate citizens but also burden employees. Practical policy recommendations are provided to improve service quality and, by extension, reduce stress on public servants.

Chapter 10: The Invisible Load: Identity Struggles and Burnout in the Public Sector

Burnout is not a one-size-fits-all experience, and this chapter brings to light how identity-based inequities intensify burnout risks for marginalized public sector employees. Applying Social Identity Theory and Intersectionality, the authors analyze how race, gender, and sexuality intersect with workplace dynamics to create unique vulnerabilities. Recommendations include equity audits, inclusive leadership training, mentorship, and flexible work options. This chapter is a powerful call to action for inclusive reform that acknowledges and addresses the hidden burdens carried by diverse employees.

Chapter 11: Job-Related and Life-Related Stress

Broadening the conversation, this chapter examines stress as a dual phenomenon—one rooted in both professional and personal realms. Drawing from historical and contemporary psychological research, it differentiates between eustress and distress, offering a nuanced understanding of how stress affects physical and mental well-being. The authors stress that not all stress is inherently harmful, but unmanaged or chronic stress can catalyze burnout. This chapter provides foundational insights into stress management for both public employees and organizational leaders.

Chapter 12: Impact of Organizational Climate on Teacher Burnout: Family Conflict as a Mediating Factor

This empirical study explores how workplace culture (organizational climate) and personal life dynamics (family conflict) converge to influence burnout among public school teachers. Using survey data from 200 teachers in government schools, the authors show how key factors—such as autonomy, control, and involvement—significantly impact teacher stress levels. Family conflict was found to mediate these relationships, highlighting the need for holistic wellness strategies that address both work and home life. This chapter reinforces that supporting educators requires attention to the environments they inhabit—both in and beyond the classroom.

CONCLUSION

As editors of *Strategies and Solutions for Public Sector Burnout*, we recognize that burnout is not a passing concern but a persistent, global crisis—one that affects the vitality of public institutions and the well-being of the individuals who serve in them. The chapters within this volume reflect the complexity, scope, and urgency of this issue, while offering diverse and evidence-based insights that span disciplines, regions, and sectors.

From frontline responders to administrative leaders, educators, healthcare professionals, and policy-makers, the contributors to this book underscore the human cost of systemic stress and the institutional shifts needed to reverse it. These chapters illuminate the multi-layered causes of burnout—ranging from organizational culture and identity-based inequities to global crises and local governance challenges—and point to practical interventions grounded in research and lived experience.

Importantly, the solutions presented here are not only reactive but proactive. They challenge us to reimagine leadership, invest in employee resilience, embrace community collaboration, and implement policies that prioritize well-being as foundational to effective public service. Our contributors call for a cultural and structural shift in how we view and support those who work in service of the public good.

We hope this book serves as a vital resource for academics, practitioners, and students alike, encouraging continued dialogue, research, and reform. Burnout may be widespread, but it is not insurmountable. By working across disciplines and sectors, we can foster healthier institutions, empower public servants, and build sustainable systems that value care, resilience, and humanity.

Acknowledgement

We gratefully acknowledge the authors who contributed to this book. Their valuable insights and thoughtful writing have been instrumental in bringing this work to life. We extend special thanks to the Natural Hazards Center at the University of Colorado Boulder and the College of Liberal Arts and Social Sciences at the University of the Virgin Islands for their generous support of our work on public-sector burnout. We are also deeply appreciative of the reviewers who participated in the peer-review process, offering their time and expertise to strengthen this work.

Above all, we express our profound gratitude to the public sector workforce. Their unwavering dedication, resilience, and commitment to serving the public often go unrecognized. Yet, it is their tireless service that upholds effectual governance and ensures the welfare and well-being of our societies and communities.

Chapter 1

Crisis Epidemiology of Burnout Syndrome in the US Virgin Islands' Government:
The Consequences of COVID-19

Kula A. Francis
https://orcid.org/0000-0002-7977-1769
University of the Virgin Islands, US Virgin Islands

Kenny A. Hendrickson
University of the Virgin Islands, US Virgin Islands

ABSTRACT

In recent decades, studies have continued to explore burnout syndrome within various professions. However, there are limited studies on occupational burnout syndrome as an epidemic. Occupational burnout epidemic considers burnout syndrome as a large-scale spread of an occupational disease that impacts employees' health, welfare and performance at a particular period. In the realm of the public sector, there is a need for epidemiological studies on occupational burnout epidemics, specifically in the scope of disasters and crises and US territorial governments. Therefore, this chapter presents a research study on a burnout epidemic that affected the government workforce of the US Virgin Islands (USVI) during COVID-19. An exploratory mixed method design was used to gather empirical evidence. Data was collected from 201 participants working in nine departments/agencies of USVI government. The findings of this research uncovered identifiable symptoms of burnout syndrome experienced by USVI government workers during COVID-19 pandemic.

DOI: 10.4018/979-8-3373-0169-3.ch001

INTRODUCTION

As the COVID-19 pandemic engulfed the world, every government was burdened by guaranteeing societal survivability, resilience and stability (Mazzucato & Kattel, 2020). Globally, governments shared in the Herculean task of designing, operationalizing and implementing effective emergency public health responses (i.e., access to vaccine, diagnostics, dissemination of information, and quarantining), in tandem with providing necessary public services to citizens. However, the carrying out effective COVID responses and public services fell into the hands of the government employees to achieve. Government employees were put in a position of "self-sacrifice" and "extraordinary humanness" in their workplaces (Park & Ahn, 2022, p. 15). Unfortunately, the pandemic took a severe toll on all government employees. Park and Ahn (2022) confirmed government employees' susceptibility to COVID pandemic and the shocking death rates. COVID also created greater work, socioeconomic and emotional hardships (Barboza-Wilkes et al., 2024).

Specifically, COVID-19 placed this important workforce in the direct cross hairs of burnout. Burnout is often viewed simply as a simple stress of work environments. It is regularly mistaken as specific to frontline professional fields and specialties (i.e., Medical and Health). Burnout is also repeatedly examined solely on a case-by-case basis. However, burnout is a complex and concerning occupational phenomenon that can severely impact all government employees, regardless of position, profession, field or levels of government. To this matter, burnout should be conceptualized as an epidemiological topic. From an epidemiological standpoint, burnout should be studied as a large-scale occurrence or epidemic within the public sector, especially at the local levels of government amid disasters and crises. Specifically, research on burnout as an epidemic within territorial governments is crucial. Territorial governments and its employees are often overlooked by research and excluded by scholarly and governmental discussions. However, territorial governments have greater responsibilities to provide adequate and immediate direct response to their citizens in instances of remoteness, isolation and inaccessibility.

This chapter provides literary context to public sector occupational burnout syndrome as an epidemic of crisis. This work also explores burnout epidemic within a territorial government based on real experiences of government employees in the US Virgin Islands (USVI) during the COVID pandemic. The USVI is a territory of the United States. It is located in the Caribbean region. It consists of four islands (i.e., St. Thomas, St. John, St. Croix and Water Island). It is roughly 2700 km from the US mainland. Due to its geographic location, the USVI government faces the sole responsibility of providing immediate emergency responses. COVID-19 was a prime instance of this. COVID-19 greatly threatened the health, well-being and overall safety of citizens living on these islands as the territory's economy (VIOMB,

2024). Furthermore, the USVI was recovering from Hurricanes Irma and Maria that devastated the islands in 2017, when COVID-19 occurred (Francis, Clavier & Hendrickson, 2021). The USVI government was challenged with providing an effective frontline public health emergency response, especially during difficult periods of imposed quarantines, lockdowns and travel restrictions (2021).

In this chapter, details are shared about a survey-based research study conducted by researchers working at the University of the Virgin Islands in the Social Sciences department. The study was employed to address the research question: Did burnout affect US Virgin Islands' government employees during the COVID pandemic? The study sought to explore government burnout based on modified versions of Maslach Burnout Inventory (MBI) and Professional Quality of Life (ProQol). Finally, this work offers findings that could offer epidemiological understanding of burnout epidemics experienced within territorial governments.

LITERATURE REVIEW

While many of the COVID-19 publications spotlighted the plight of first responders, the lives of all employees working in government and in the public sector were at risk during the pandemic (Headley etal., 2023; Park & Ahn, 2022; Ehrlich, McKenney, & Elkbuli, 2020). COVID-19 severely impacted on the quality of not just their home lives but also work lives. Even with occupational safeguards in place, there were no jobs within the government that were considered safe from exposure to COVID. Due to the pandemic, government employees faced the challenges of ever-changing and conflicting work conditions, higher workloads and daily threats to safety, health and overall well-being. Barboz-Wilkes et al. (2022) found that government employees also suffered from extremely high job demands, extremely limited job resources, isolation and overwork. In fact, Lee and Na (2023) identified that the challenges of government employees were because of greater demands and expectations placed on public services. Depending upon departments, position and closeness to the frontlines, government employees, especially State, Local and Territorial, also faced high levels of emotional turmoil, prolonging occupational stress and extreme psychological weariness (Barboz-Wilkes et al., 2022).

Sever et al. (2021) noted that although COVID-19 was a biological disaster, it also created issues that gave rise to burnout within government. Government work conditions, because of COVID-19, caused or magnified existing professional or occupational burnout of local government employees (Łaskawiec-Żuławińska et al., 2024). Though not a commonly referred to as a medical condition, burnout is classified as an occupational occurrence that can affect the health of employees by the International Classification of Diseases of the World Health Organization

(WHO) (Li et al., 2023). Grzebyk et al. (2018) stated that government work has "high psychological labor costs" (p. 131). Gembalska-Kwiecień (2019) mentioned that occupational burnout can affect "almost every second employee" (p. 31). Grzebyk et al. (2018) also offered that occupational burnout is often associated with human centered and client- and service-oriented professional and prolonged hazardous environments. Occupational burnout of government employees can impact their interactions within the institution. Interaction involves their relationships between colleagues, subordinates, superiors, clients and/or citizens.

Occupational burnout is the consequence or the cause of work strain, chronic negative behaviors and bad habits. Occupational burnout of government employees involves prolonged exposure of occupational or work stress that affects the performance and well-being of government employees (Meeusen et al., 2023). In fact, Flueren et al. (2023) believed that the magnitude of burnout is the result of occupational stressors. Occupational stressors are socio-physical issues in work settings that negatively impact the organization and its employees (Zou et al., 2022). Zou and colleagues (2022) also revealed that occupational stressors may cause varying health problems for employees (i.e., headaches, anxiety, depression, low self-esteem). More significantly, occupational stressors can greatly lower employees "job satisfaction, performance, and commitment" (Pallewaththa & Wijesiri, 2021, p. 150). It can also lead to absenteeism, lower productivity, employee termination and turnover (2021).

Furthermore, occupational burnout can manifest as a syndrome. Carlotto and Camara (2019) presented that persistent occupational stressors can create burnout syndrome. Saed, Raheemah & Shaalan (2019) affirmed that recent scholars and researchers have deemed occupational burnout syndrome to be a major concern of the public sector and government. Occupational burnout syndrome can be described as an increase and accrual of psycho-social problems within occupational performance (Andruszkiewicz, 2019). Seo et al. (2022) asserted that Occupational burnout syndrome is a result of employees being "overwhelmed", diminished or compromised by highly stressful work environments (p. 2).

Significantly, syndrome means that burnout can be diagnosed with a few specific symptoms. WHO identified exhaustion (physical, mental and emotional), depersonalization and inefficacy as common symptoms of burnout (Bianchi & Schonfeld, 2023). Exhaustion can be considered as an energy depletion, tiredness, and weariness that often lead to apathy, indifference and dissatisfaction (López-Cabarcos etal., 2019). Depersonalization is a mental state of detachment, disinterest and dispassion (Fardous & Afzal, 2022. Lastly, inefficacy is employees' feelings of under- or non- achievement, unfulfillment and failing (Vagni et al., 2020). Vagni et al. (2020) offered that the three key symptoms of burnout are symbiotic; they reinforce each other. Maslach's theory of burnout establishes that as exhaustion and depersonalization increase, then personal accomplishment decreases (Eckleberry-

Hunte, Kirkpatrick & Barbera, 2018). Personal accomplishment is the attainment of significant achievements during an experience that signifies success or personal growth.

Although burnout syndrome has been commonly diagnosed based on three symptoms, emotional exhaustion is the primary element of burnout (2018). In addition, Tavella et al. (2021) and likeminded scholars also revealed a diagnostic ambiguity to burnout. They sought to redefine, discover more symptoms and means of studying occupational burnout, (2021). Thus, consideration can be given to other ways of assessing occupation burnout. Another method of measuring burnout is Professional Quality of Life (ProQol). ProQol can be viewed as quality (i.e., positive and negative) feelings that employees have about their work (Monroe, Morose & Price, 2020). ProQol is inclusive of features such as compassion satisfaction and compassion fatigue (Zakeri et al., 2020). Compassion satisfaction is positive feelings based on job performance (Kishimoto, & Asano, 2024). It can also be described as self-satisfaction of caring for others. Opposingly, compassion fatigue is adverse effect of caring from others (Garnett et al., 2023). cognitive depletion based on work conditions (Rauf, & Saba, 2024). Compassion fatigue is the product of secondary traumatic stress (duress caused by experience the trauma of others) and burnout (stress that weakens occupational performance).

Tavella et al. (2021) affirmed the need for understanding burnout nosologically (disease classification) and etiologically (casual assignment). These diagnostic ideologies open burnout to be considered as an occupational disease. In fact, Noorollahi et al. 2022 noted that occupational burnout syndrome is a "serious career disease" (p. 26). Occupational diseases are illnesses caused by harmful elements, such as risks and levels of toxic exposure within work environments, and occupations (Wiszniewska etal., 2023. The toxicity in the workplace, that cultivates burnout, can be biological, chemical, physical, social, technological, psychological, cultural or even institutional (Yurt, 2023). Emmons (2019) offered the belief that burnout is a moral injury to support the causality of toxicity in the workplace.

While most of the classic scholars focused on a micro-perspective to burn out, case specific or endemic, the COVID pandemic gave root to a more macro-exploration. COVID pandemic signaled the existence of burnout syndrome as a secondary or underlying pandemic. Sousa (2021) referred to burnout syndrome "as a silent pandemic" (p. 22). Sousa (2021) stated that burnout syndrome can be considered a pandemic due to the severe outbreak of burnout that affected many societal sectors and professionals in all continents. Neal and Lyons contented that the burnout pandemic was not just specific to "specialties and geographical areas". From the global context, burnout syndrome pandemic could be a large-scale epidemic "spreads across multiple populations or even worldwide" (Calcaterra et al., 2022, pp. 1346 & 1347).

Even before the COVID pandemic, Penz et al. (2018) and Schaufeli, Enzmann, & Girault (2017) brought attention to the need to study burnout syndrome as an epidemic. An epidemic is a spatial or temporal designation for a significant increase in an infectious disease. Abdallah and colleagues (2024) described it as "rapid rise in the number of instances of a particular disease within a defined geographic area or community" (p. 203). Specifically, burnout is an epidemic of a psychosocial disease or disease like socio-cognitive disorders. Prosen (2020) offered that psycho-epidemics can be considered as resultant or offshoot of a biological epidemic. He identified that the psychosocial epidemic can either follow a similar track or have an alternate social course from the originating infectious disease (2020).

To study occupational burnout as an epidemic, this work proposes epidemiology. Found in the work of Frérot et al. (2018), epidemiology can be viewed as studying "distribution and determinants of health-related states or events (including disease)" (p. 14). They also shared that the purpose of epidemiology is not just to study epidemics. It can be used to discover ways to track and control outbreaks. Although there are limited studies on the epidemiology of burnout syndrome, it can be considered as a form of occupational epidemiology (Bang, 2022). Occupational epidemiology includes an exploration of the institutional and professional dimensionality of the burnout syndrome epidemic. Thus, epidemiological knowledge of burnout provides practical and novel understanding to create and implement preventive institutional and performance measures for future outbreaks of burnout (Treluyer & Tourneux, 2021). More importantly, epidemiological knowledge can be used in syndromic surveillance and monitoring of burnout in populations, especially identify those that are at-risk (Hughes et al, 2020).

RESEARCH

At the beginning and throughout the pandemic, the local news and media coverage in the USVI kept citizens informed about the spread and impact of COVID, as well as the government's response to it (quarantine orders, vaccination mandates). However, there were limited news articles, research and publications on the psychosocial health and welfare of government workers. During COVID-19, the US Virgin Islands government employed roughly 10, 904 employees working in government (USVIBER, 2024). That number dropped to 10, 654 employees. As the largest workforce in the USVI, the recorded loss of roughly 2% indicated a consequence of COVID-19.

Our colleagues, working at the University of the Virgin Islands in the Social Sciences Department of the College of Liberal Arts and Social Sciences, were concerned about these issues and the possibility of government workers experiencing burnout. We decided to submit a proposal to the Natural Hazard Center at the University of Colorado (NHC). The NHC is an initiative at the University of Colorado that provides training and funding to support disaster research. The NHC posted a call that was geared to provide support for research on US territorial public health preparedness and response to recent disasters. The NHC research award was funded by the Center for Disease Control and Prevent (CDC) and the National Science Foundation (NSF).

Our proposed study centered on possibilities of burnout and the quality of work life of government employees in the USVI during COVID-19 (Hendrickson, Clavier & Hendrickson, 2021). We hoped to examine as many departments and agencies as possible, given the time constraints of the research award. We proposed the gathering of empirical evidence through exploratory mixed-method research. As an exploratory investigation, our study sought to study burnout epidemic as a unique phenomenon of the USVI government workforce during a crisis. Our mixed method research design combined elements of quantitative and qualitative research. This provided a rare opportunity to gain a comprehensive understanding of the experiences of USVI government employees in research.

Upon receiving approval for our research by NHC and in the process of receiving approval from our university's Institutional Review Board (IRB), we set out to contend with the biggest obstacle of the project, gaining access to government employees. The gatekeepers of access were the various department and agency heads. We would like to say that we got approval from everyone. However, that would not be a true depiction of completing research in government. Our request was denied by a few of them. There were some that never returned our calls or emails. In one of our email correspondences with a department head, the main reason for the denial of our request was made clear. The department head wrote in his response to our request:

> *"I will revisit the proposal again with my leadership. The issue is that when I presented initially to my Team, the feedback was not good as it was looked at as it would stir up more issues for us in the Department at this time. The climate in the department is one thing that I have to keep a steady pulse on as staff has been showing signs of fatigue for some time now. However, our culture is currently all over the place as some staff are not dealing well with the pressure of this pandemic especially on the heels of Irma and Maria. So, it has been very challenging to say the least.*
>
> *However, I will revisit with the Team, but I need to be able to highlight the benefits to the Department as I know that I will not get the support. We are so entrenched in processing and auditing right now in addition to all of the public scrutiny, I would not be able to ensure participation without the support of my Team."*

This was a learning moment for our research team. The correspondence revealed that government administrators and their leadership teams are often quite aware of existing and pervasive issues and crises facing their employees. They are often hesitant about or dismissive of external research, as can be viewed as stirring up institutional and public scrutiny. Thus, the obstacle of gaining access to employees through departments and agencies became ensuring that department/agency heads understood the clear intent of our research, providing them with assistance and expertise at no cost. We also shared that our research was intended to contribute to the welfare and sustainability of the USVI government and community. Lastly, it was also important that we made the connection between ourselves as residents of the Virgin Islands and government employees.

There were nine departments that allowed their employees to participate. The departments were the Bureau of Motor Vehicle (BMV), Department of Human Services (DHS), Department of Consumer and Licensing Affairs (DCLA), Department of Planning and Natural Resources (DPNR), Virgin Islands Fire Services (VFS), Virgin Islands Police Department (VIPD), Schneider Regional Hospital, Juan Luis Regional Hospital and Virgin Islands Territorial Emergency Management Agency (VITEMA). The administrative leaders of these departments were welcoming and had a deep concern for the health and welfare of their employees.

Due to our university's Institutional Review Board's suspension of in person or face to contact with participants during COVID-19, we were forced to use an e-survey strategy. This entailed recruiting participants via their government email addresses and their completion of an online survey. Our survey consisted of demographic items, a modified version of the Maslach Burnout Inventory (MBI) and Professional Quality of Life (ProQol), as well as open-ended questions geared towards discovering employee experiences during COVID. To obtain the highest quality of data, we chose to utilize Qualtrics to build and disseminate our survey and manage the data. Qualtrics was extremely user-friendly. It also allowed us to properly monitor the data collection. Each department and agency had their own security protocols. We were either provided an email listing by the entity or required to go through IT to send an e-blast through their messaging systems.

Notably, we did not offer any recruitment, enrollment or completion incentives to the participants. The practice of offering incentives (i.e. monetary/financial, gift cards) for recruitment or/and tokens of appreciation (e.g., Thank you" gifts and prizes) is a common practice used to boost response rates. However, if applied improperly, incentives can raise concerns of "undue inducement, exploitation and biased enrollment" (Resnik, 2015, p. 38). Our team weighed the pros and cons of using incentives in our research. We decided to rely solely on participants understanding the purpose of the research and willingness to participate. While this may have reduced the number of responses that were received. It did provide us with more unbiased responses.

The data collection process took roughly two months of dissemination. A sample of 201 employees participated in the study. As seen in Table 1, the largest number of responses was received from Governor Juan F. Luis Hospital and Medical Center & Schneider Regional Medical Center (28.36%) and Department of Human Services (26.37%). 90% of the respondents were women. The age distribution of survey respondents varied with 18–35 years at 18.41%, 36–45 at 50%, 46–55 at 38.81%, and 56 or older was 17.91%. A total of 77% of respondents identified as "African American or Black" and 23% identified as white, Latino or Hispanic. Level of education varied among survey respondents: 16.42% had a high school diploma; 34.33% had an undergraduate college degree, 22.39% had completed some college and 26.87% had a master's degree, doctorate or professional degree, including juris doctorates, MD, or PhD. The marital status of participants showed 39.8% as single, 34.33% as married, 11.94% as divorced, 11.94% in a relationship but not married. The majority (79.46 percent) of survey respondents lived in a one child household.

Table 1. Distribution of government agencies

Government Agencies	n	(%)
Department of Human Services	53	26.37
Department of Planning and Natural Resources, Department of Licensing and Consumer Affairs, and BMV	25	12.44
Governor Juan F. Luis Hospital and Medical Center & Schneider Regional Medical Center	57	28.36
VI Police Department & Department of Fire Services	40	19.90
VITEMA	26	12.94
Total	**201**	**100**

Once the data was collected. My colleagues and I went through the process of cleaning and formatting quantitative data to be analyzed. Overall, the survey responses indicated that most government workers report high levels of burnout and emotional exhaustion based on scoring of the Maslach Burnout Inventory. Professional Quality of Life responses yielded similar responses with respondents scoring high on the Compassion Satisfaction scale, while also scoring high on the Compassion fatigue scale. These findings are typical for governmental employees experiencing levels of distress following traumatic events.

SPSS or Statistical Package for Social Sciences is a commonly used program that allows for the completion of various statistical analysis. In analyzing the data, we decided to complete psychometric and bivariate analyses to explore burnout and professional quality of life of the participating. We utilized psychometric analysis to determine the internal strength of the data collected based on Maslach Burnout Inventory (MBI) and Professional Quality of Life Scale (ProQoL). We also completed bivariate analysis to explore the relationships between MBI and ProQol.

Burnout was assessed using a modified version of Maslach Burnout Inventory (MBI). The modified inventory used nineteen items rated on a five-point Likert scale, "Never" to Very often". Each item began with the phrase, "While performing my job-related duties during COVID-19". There were three components to the MBI: Emotional exhaustion (EE), Depersonalization (DP), and Personal Accomplishment (PA). EE consisted of eight items used to measure feelings of emotional depletion or exhaustion. Depersonalization consisted of five items. These items were used to assess feelings of detachment, dehumanization, inconsequentiality and insignificance da Silva Menguer et al. (2024). The last component of the MBI, personal accomplishment, consisted of 6 items geared measure feelings of competence and successful achievement in one's work or lack thereof.

Normally, burnout is measured based on summative MBI score. However, we decided to assess psychometric properties, internal consistency and intercorrelations of the three dimensions of MBI data, as seen in Table 2. Based on our analysis a strong relationship (0.801) was found between EE and DP. The Cronbach's alpha for the MBI dimensions were all within acceptable range (EE α score = 0.94; DP α score = 0.71; PA α score = 0.71). Acceptable scores for the MBI α scores are 0.60 or greater (Kokkinos, 2006).

Table 2. Psychometric properties, internal consistency, and intercorrelations of the three subscales of the MBI (n=201) during COVID-19

	Emotional Exhaustion (EE)	Depersonalization (DP)	Personal Accomplishment (PA)
Mean	3.15	1.99	3.57
SD	1.05	0.77	0.60
Alpha	0.94	0.71	0.71
DP	0.801***		
PA	-0.458***	-0.394***	

* $p < 0.05$, ** $p < 0.01$, *** $p < 0.001$

The Cronbach's alpha for the MBI subscales were all within acceptable range (EE α score = 0.92; DP α score = 0.65; PA α score = 0.71). Acceptable scores for the MBI α scores are 0.60 or greater (Kokkinos, 2006).

Quality of work life of US Virgin Islands government employees during COVID 19 were assessed using a modified version of the Professional Quality of Life Scale (ProQoL) (Stamm, 2010). It consists of eighteen items rated on a five-point Likert scale, "Never" to Very often". Each item began with the phrase, "While performing my job-related duties during COVID-19". rated on a five-point Likert scale, "Never" to Very often". The items evaluate quality of life in two dimensions: compassion satisfaction and compassion and compassion fatigue. The two dimensions are composed of three subscales that are comprised based on a summative score. Compassion satisfaction scale (CSS) consisted of five items used to determine the pleasure derived from performing well on the job. Compassion fatigue (CF) is composed of two scores, burnout and secondary traumatic stress scale. Burnout scale (BS) consisted of 8 items used to measure feelings of hopelessness and difficulty working. Secondary trauma stress scale (STS) consisted of 5 items used to measure indirect trauma caused by stressful events related to work.

To understand the professional quality of life of participants (ProQoL), we assessed psychometric properties, internal consistency and intercorrelations of the three dimensions. As seen in Table 3, there was a strong relationship (0.739) between BS and CSS. the Cronbach's alpha for the ProQoL dimensions were within normal range (CSS α score = 0.64; BS α score = 0.68; STS α score = 0.73).

Table 3. Psychometric properties, internal consistency, and intercorrelations of the three subscales of the Professional Quality of Life dimensions (n=201) during COVID-19

	Secondary Traumatic Stress (STS)	Burnout (BS)	Compassion Satisfactions (CSS)
Mean	3.46	3.57	2.88
SD	0.54	0.44	0.87
Alpha	0.64	0.68	0.73
Burnout	0.739***		
Compassion Satisfaction	0.052***	0.156	

* $p < 0.05$, ** $p < 0.01$, *** $p < 0.001$

The Cronbach's alpha for the ProQL subscales after covid-19 were within normal range (STS α score = 0.64; BS α score = 0.68; CSS α score = 0.73). Acceptable scores for the ProQ0L are from 0.65 or greater (Di Tella et al., 2020).

The resulting psychometrics showcased the reliability of both MBI and ProQoL. These elements of our study provide insight into burnout and the quality of life experienced by the participating government workers during COVID- 19. Thus, we further explored the relationship between burnout and quality of life. We proposed the following hypothesis:

H_0: There is no relationship between USVI government employees' burnout and professional quality of life during COVID-19.
H_1: There is a relationship between USVI government employees' burnout and professional quality of life during COVID-19.

Bivariate regression was employed to test the hypothesis. Bivariate regression can be used to correlate the magnitude and direction of two response variables. The results of the analysis indicated that EE is positively correlated with BS ad STS subscale scores (see Table 4). Employees reporting higher relationship between of EE and STS (.76) (Di Tella et al., 2020).

Table 4. Relationship between USVI frontline workers MBI and ProQol scores during COVID-19

Variables	EE	DP	PA
CSS	-0.10	-0.04	0.48***
BS	0.30*	-0.07	0.48***
STS	0.76***	0.35***	-0.16***

****p<.01, **p<.05, *p<.1*

The findings presented in Tables 2, 3 and 4 were used to model burnout of USVI government employees during COVID-19, as seen in Figure 1. The model presents the outcome of integrating dimensions of MBI and ProQol in understanding occupational burnout syndrome in USVI government. Thus, the model spotlights that our analysis found that emotional exhaustion has a strong relationship with depersonalization and secondary trauma stress. Emotional exhaustion was found to have a stronger relationship with depersonalization. While this may be the result of both subscales are primary components of MBI, our model displays all three dimensions. The model identifies symptoms of the occupational burnout syndrome faced by the participating USVI government workforce during COVID-19. The model also identifies emotional exhaustion as a key symptom of the experienced burnout syndrome. In addition, Secondary trauma stress could be considered a dual symptom identifier of burnout syndrome and quality of life experienced by the participating government workers. The model also pointed to the fact that compassion fatigue (i.e., burnout and secondary trauma stress) impacted the professional quality of life experienced by the participating USVI government employees during COVID-19.

Table 5. Themes and subthemes of burnout

MBI Subscale Item	Theme	Subthemes
Emotional Exhaustion n = 248)	- Exhaustion - Emotionally drained - Fatigue - Mental/Emotional strain - Burn out - Frustration	- Fatigue - Inadequate mental health support - Low morale - Excessively long hours - Limited or inadequate supplies - Inadequate support from superiors - Lack of information - Poor communication channels - No crisis support - Inadequate PPE - No post storm support - Lack of information - Poor communication
Personal accomplishment (n = 62)	- Need appreciation - Helpful - Success as a team -	- Morale boosters - Adequate support - Supportive coworkers helped with coping

The quantitative analysis provided us with an opportunity to identify three strongly associated symptoms of burnout syndrome based MBI and ProQol (see Figure 1). However, our research also provided an opportunity for obtaining the view of participants in their own words. We achieved this by including open-ended questions in the survey. Participants were asked to respond to the following open-ended questions:

1. Thinking back on your experiences after COVID-19, what support could have been provided by your supervisor(s), department, or Virgin Islands Government?

2. Please add any comments or experiences you had which may not have been captured based on the questions asked.

Thematic content analysis was used to interpret the data collected from the open-ended questions. Thematic content analysis is a research technique that allows for identifying, coding, structuring, categorizing and presenting of patterns in qualitative data based specific descriptors or themes. Eder and Meyer (2022) observed thematic analysis is "data driven" which encompasses "words and sentences" that were included in the participants' responses (p. 38). In this study, data was inductively coded based on the primary identifying feature of the utilized MBI and ProQoL subscales. The data was analyzed using MaxQDA. This qualitative software program has the capacity to greatly assist in the completion of thematic and content analysis (i.e., coding, managing and categorizing). The resulting findings of MAxQDA were identifiable patterns of burnout and professional quality of life. To ensure confirmability, a sample of 20% of data was analyzed for interrater reliability. A Cohen's kappa was calculated using MaxQDA and the highest observed agreement was 78%. Previous social science research scholars have published work with adequate agreement between coders ranging between 75% to 100% agreement among two coders (Shanahan, Jones, & McBeth, 2018).

Our analysis resulted in over 500 coded statements, which were obtained from themes and subthemes of MBI and Proqol features. These codes were then examined and the themes and subthemes they represented were named and defined. Participant responses were indexed to determine the number of participants that referenced each theme. Participants did not explicitly discuss themes corresponding to all of the features of MBI and Proqol. The resulting themes and subthemes are displayed in Tables 5 and 6.

Within the qualitative analysis, emotional exhaustion as the most identifiable MBI theme (as seen in Table 5). Overall, exhaustion was the most frequently nominated feature, with 43% of the sample describing feelings of exhaustion in relation to emotional fatigue, mental strain, and generally frustrated. Our analysis also found that the root causes of frustration were limited: a.) information sharing about the pandemic, b.) training and information to inform pandemic response activities, c.) flexible working hours and conditions (e.g., flex schedules or work from home options), d.) access to technology to support working from home, consideration for individuals with children, alternative childcare options, "a lack of manpower" and e.) access to personal protective equipment (PPE). In support, the following are comments by participants:

Comment 1: Parents and grandparents [that were] forced to choose between coming to work or risk losing their jobs because daycares and schools weren't open. Supervisors without children or independent children were not amenable to those who have young children.
Comment 2: Very lax in providing protective gear for the workers to get the job done.
Comment 3: Only when going before the senate for a hearing or when we had exposure on the job did it seem important to provide PPE gear. We were supposed to receive these supplies on a regular basis, and we should not have to ask.

Regarding emotional exhaustion, participants attributed mental and emotional strain to working extremely long hours: sometimes without any or adequate compensation. One participant summarized this frustration as a need for "additional staff to assist with job functions", because this participant and many others described "function[ing] in 2 roles during that time." Participants stated that the increase in demand following both events created mental and emotional distress for employees. The desire to receive "counseling [and] morale boosting activities" was demonstrated prominently throughout the sample. For example, one participant stated that there was a need to provide group counseling to "allow those on the frontline the ability to talk through and share the experiences that were bottled up. The feeling of being emotionally and physically overwhelmed was not discussed."

Another feature of MBI that had several numbers of coded statements was personal accomplishment. Ten percent of the coded statements expressed feelings of personal accomplishment. Most of these comments described negative personal accomplishment. Negative personal accomplishment is the absence of appreciation or compassion that would lead to job satisfaction or the absence of an environment that promotes employee morale and satisfaction. However, some participants did describe positive personal accomplishment. Participants stated that personal accomplishments as a team and co-worker support helped with the coping with the stress during disasters. As one participant remarked, "the teamwork of our staff is what carried us through". Significantly, these coded comments were all associated with the following agencies that were greatly impacted and at the frontline of COVID-19 public health response in the USVI: Governor Juan F. Luis Hospital and Medical Center & Schneider Regional Medical Center.

Table 6. Themes and subthemes of professional quality of life

ProQoL Subscale Item	Theme	Subthemes
Burnout (n = 195)	- Hopeless - Burdened - Overwhelmed - Bogged down - Anxiety/Depression	- Limited display of compassion for employees - Change is unlikely - Flexible work schedules - Consideration for those with children - Offer childcare options - Work from home options - Technology and support to work from home
Secondary Traumatic Stress (n = 72)	- Difficulty balancing home and work - Anxiety - Depression	- Crisis support for service professionals - Anxiety from interactions with anxious clients - Verbally abusive clients

As seen in Table 6, Burnout and Secondary Trauma Stress were found to be identifiable ProQol themes in the qualitative data. Burnout was one of the most frequently nominated features, with 34% of the sample describing their experiences as feeling overly burdened by both disasters. Issues related to flexible work options and childcare were the most dominant issue. For example, one participant stated that employees would have experienced less burnout if there were options for "more flexible work schedules, especially for those of us with very young children that are doing distance learning".

In addition, we found that described feelings of anxiety and depression during both events stating that "the range of emotions went from happy to sad, scared, uncertain of the future for myself and my children". Thus, secondary traumatic stress (STS) was nominated by 13% of the sample. While some simply listed feelings of anxiety, stress, and depression endured by the disasters, many others specified that anxiety was specifically related to their work. During the pandemic, secondary trauma was described in relation to the lack of consideration by employers. This viewpoint was summarized by one participant stating that "there was no consideration that we were also experiencing the stresses of COVID -the program operated "business as usual".

Figure 1. USVI government occupational burnout during COVID-19

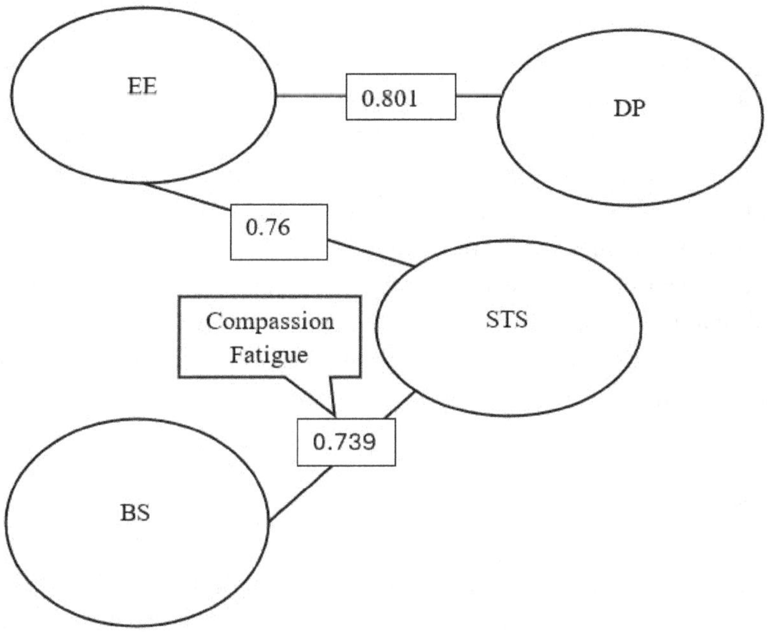

Figure 1. USVI Government Occupational Burnout During COVID-19

Our study offered exploratory evidence to support the existence of burnout syndromes in the nine participating departments in the USVI during COVID-19. Our mixed method design also identified specific symptoms of burnout syndrome (i.e., emotional exhaustion, depersonalization and secondary traumatic Stress). However, there were limitations to our study. First, the small sample size and demographic makeup of our study limited our ability to generalize our findings. We were able to identify or assert the existence of burnout syndrome in certain USVI government departments and agencies during COVID-19. But we were unable to identify the existence in all of the departments and agencies (i.e. Department of Education, Department of Labor, Bureau of Correction and National Guard). We were also unable to discern pre-existing symptoms of burnout, prior to COVID-19. We also acknowledge that participants may suffer from healthy worker survivor bias. This type of bias arises due to participants' feelings of guilt from being healthy or less exposed to work conditions or occupational diseases (Eisen, Elser & Picciotto,

2022). Healthy worker survivor bias cause participants to be untruthful or false in their completion of the survey.

Moreover, we acknowledge limitations in our study's design and methodology. While using e-surveys provided anonymity and easy means of widespread disseminating to participants, there was an uncertainty in determining if subjects received the e-survey. There is also concern that participants properly understood the items within the survey. Lastly, the limitations of this study can be found in the analysis. There are limitations to using bivariate regression and MaxQDA. Bivariate analysis cannot identify the direction or causality between variables. We were unable to understand the accurate relationship between symptoms of burnout syndrome and professional quality of life. In the case of MaxQDA, this form analysis allows for relies on researcher interpretations of themes and may be affected by their personal biases or subjectivity.

CONCLUSION

Within disasters and crises, territorial governments were forced to rely heavily on their workforce to provide necessary and effective responses. These employees were overwhelmingly challenged to fulfill their duties and obligations to citizens, communities and ultimately their families. While the dedication and self-sacrifice of frontline workers are periodically given media attention, there have been limited "unanswered questions" and accounts about the health, work conditions, welfare, hardships and life experiences of all Territorial government employees, regardless of their position, rank, type, place of employment (Park & Ahn, 2022, p. 15). One of the most understudied hardships that affect Territorial government employees during and in the aftermath of a disaster or crisis is occupational burnout syndrome. Occupational burnout syndrome is an occupational disease, which manifests because of "psychosomatic, psychological, and social symptoms" (Rodrigues et al., 2024, p. 2). Especially during disasters, burnout syndrome in the government and the public sector could be explored as a wide spreading disease or epidemic resulting from a chronic and pervasive occurrence of severe hardship and adversity in the work environment.

Unfortunately, the studies of burnout epidemics in government prior to or during disasters are limited. Likewise, research on burnout epidemic impacting US territorial government workforce during disasters and crises is almost non-existent. Unexpectedly, our research revealed apprehensions of some department and agency leaders' apprehension and unwillingness to allow their employees to participate in external research of burnout due to fear of internal institutional and public scrutiny. However, understanding, surveilling and monitoring the spread and propagation of burnout as an epidemic provides necessary realization for public sector leaders that burnout during a disaster should not just be viewed as an individual case by case matter. There is a need for government and its administrative leaders to prioritize collecting and utilizing data on employee burnout to develop and apply intervention, mitigation, prevention and preparedness strategies across government.

This chapter showcased the potential of epidemiological research on burnout epidemic of USVI government workforce during COVID-19. We were only able to gain participation of a modest number of participants employed in nine departments and agencies. However, participants provided us with significant data in identifying vital symptoms of burnout syndrome (i.e. emotional exhaustion and depersonalization) and compassion fatigue (secondary traumatic stress and burnout). Our findings confirm the existence of burnout syndrome in the USVI government workforce during COVID-19 and an overall need for addressing emotional exhaustion.

Further studies are needed to investigate burnout epidemics based on bio-psycho-socio-spirito-cultural symptoms, an entirety of the government workforce, diverse disasters and crises, as well as other impacted territories (Listopad et al., 2021). Within the vein of this current research, future studies are also needed to investigate the possibilities of a syndemic nature to burnout syndrome. Sharifi et al. (2021) discussed that burnout syndrome, as an epidemic, can synergistically interact with other epidemics. This results in synergistic growth and sustenance of clustering and intermingling epidemics (Mendenhall, Newfield, & Tsai, 2021). Epidemiology that incorporates syndemic theory can help to better understand burnout syndrome, as an epidemic, associated with other epidemics, disasters and crises. This type of research will facilitate the development of effective, preventive and supportive strategies that can mitigate and reduce burnout and promote general wellness in US government workforces, especially those within US Territories.

REFERENCES

Abdallah, R., AbdelGaber, S. A., & Sayed, H. A. (2024, March). Disease Outbreak/Epidemic in Public Health Sector. In *2024 6th International Conference on Computing and Informatics (ICCI)* (pp. 203-216). IEEE.

Andruszkiewicz, F. (2019). Professional burnout as a source of an early school education teachers' career destabilization. *Szkoła-Zawód-Praca*, (18), 111–121.

Bang, K. M. (2022). Occupational epidemiology. *Modern Occupational Diseases: Diagnosis, Epidemiology, Management and Prevention*, 25-40.

Barboza-Wilkes, C., Gonzalez, E., Resh, W., & Wong, S. (2024). The emotional toll of the COVID-19 crisis on local government workers. *Review of Public Personnel Administration*, *44*(1), 60–85. DOI: 10.1177/0734371X221108501

Bianchi, R., & Schonfeld, I. S. (2023). Examining the evidence base for burnout. *Bulletin of the World Health Organization*, *101*(11), 743–745. DOI: 10.2471/BLT.23.289996 PMID: 37961064

Calcaterra, G., Bassareo, P., Barilla, F., Romeo, F., de Gregorio, C., Mehta, P., & Mehta, J. L. (2022). Syndemic: A Synergistic Anthropological Approach to the COVID-19 Pandemic. *Encyclopedia*, *2*(3), 1344–1356. DOI: 10.3390/encyclopedia2030090

Carlotto, M. S., & Câmara, S. G. (2019). Burnout syndrome in public servants: Prevalence and association with occupational stressors. *Psico-USF*, *24*(3), 425–435. DOI: 10.1590/1413-82712019240302

da Silva Menguer, L., Pereira, E. V., da Silva, A. C. R., & de Farias, J. M. (2024). Burnout syndrome and job satisfaction in community health workers. *Revista Brasileira de Medicina do Trabalho : Publicacao Oficial da Associacao Nacional de Medicina do Trabalho-ANAMT*, *21*(4), e2021903. PMID: 39132269

Di Tella, M., Tesio, V., Bertholet, J., Gasnier, A., Del Portillo, E. G., Spalek, M., & Franco, P. (2020). Professional quality of life and burnout among medical physicists working in radiation oncology: The role of alexithymia and empathy. *Physics and Imaging in Radiation Oncology*, *15*, 38–43. DOI: 10.1016/j.phro.2020.07.001 PMID: 33458324

Eckleberry-Hunt, J., Kirkpatrick, H., & Barbera, T. (2018). The problems with burnout research. *Academic Medicine*, *93*(3), 367–370. DOI: 10.1097/ACM.0000000000001890 PMID: 28817432

Eder, L. L., & Meyer, B. (2022). Self-endangering: A qualitative study on psychological mechanisms underlying nurses' burnout in long-term care. *International Journal of Nursing Sciences*, *9*(1), 36–48. DOI: 10.1016/j.ijnss.2021.12.001 PMID: 35079603

Ehrlich, H., McKenney, M., & Elkbuli, A. (2020). Defending the front lines during the COVID-19 pandemic: Protecting our first responders and emergency medical service personnel. *The American Journal of Emergency Medicine*, *40*, 213–214. DOI: 10.1016/j.ajem.2020.05.068 PMID: 32513453

Eisen, E. A., Elser, H., & Picciotto, S. (2022). Working: The role of occupational epidemiology. *American Journal of Epidemiology*, *191*(2), 237–240. DOI: 10.1093/aje/kwab243 PMID: 34613355

Emmons, R. S. (2019). Burnout No More: How to Push Back Against the Toxic Medical Workplace. *Journal of American Physicians and Surgeons*, *24*(4), 114–119.

Fardous, N., & Afzal, M. T. (2022). Contribution of emotional exhaustion towards depersonalization among teachers. *Journal of Positive School Psychology*, *6*(8), 5265–5274.

Fleuren, B. P., Nübold, A., Uitdewilligen, S., Verduyn, P., & Hülsheger, U. R. (2023). Troubles on troubled minds: An intensive longitudinal diary study on the role of burnout in the resilience process following acute stressor exposure. *European Journal of Work and Organizational Psychology*, *32*(3), 373–388. DOI: 10.1080/1359432X.2022.2161369

Francis, K., Clavier, N., & Hendrickson, K. (2021). *Frontline Government Workers: Assessing Post-Disaster Burnout and Quality of Life* (Natural Hazards Center Public Health Disaster Research Report Series, Report 8). Natural Hazards Center, University of Colorado Boulder. https://hazards.colorado.edu/public-health-disaster-research/frontline-government-workers-assessing-post-disaster-burnout-and-quality-of-life

Frérot, M., Lefebvre, A., Aho, S., Callier, P., Astruc, K., & Aho Glélé, L. S. (2018). What is epidemiology? Changing definitions of epidemiology 1978-2017. *PLoS One*, *13*(12), e0208442. DOI: 10.1371/journal.pone.0208442 PMID: 30532230

Garnett, A., Hui, L., Oleynikov, C., & Boamah, S. (2023). Compassion fatigue in healthcare providers: A scoping review. *BMC Health Services Research*, *23*(1), 1336. DOI: 10.1186/s12913-023-10356-3 PMID: 38041097

Gembalska-Kwiecień, A. (2019). *Occupational burnout-characteristics of the phenomenon and methods of counteracting*. Zeszyty Naukowe. Organizacja i Zarządzanie/ Politechnika Śląska. DOI: 10.29119/1641-3466.2019.134.3

Grzebyk, M., Pierścieniak, A., & Ohimor, J. (2018). PROFESSIONAL BURNOUT OF EMPLOYEES IN LOCAL PUBLIC ADMINISTRATION–KNOWLEDGE, CAUSES AND PREVENTION. *ZESZYTY NAUKOWE POLITECHNIKI CZĘSTOCHOWSKIEJ RESEARCH REVIEWS OF CZESTOCHOWA UNIVERSITY OF TECHNOLOGY*, 131.

Headley, A. M., Remington, C., Witkowski, K., Contreras, S. L., & Ganapati, N. E. (2023). The impact of COVID-19 on first responders in the United States of America. *International Journal of Emergency Services*, *12*(2), 243–251. DOI: 10.1108/IJES-12-2022-0071

Hughes, H. E., Edeghere, O., O'Brien, S. J., Vivancos, R., & Elliot, A. J. (2020). Emergency department syndromic surveillance systems: A systematic review. *BMC Public Health*, *20*(1), 1–15. DOI: 10.1186/s12889-020-09949-y PMID: 33298000

Kishimoto, K., & Asano, K. (2024). The relationships among factors affecting compassion fatigue, compassion satisfaction, and burnout in Japanese nurses: A cross-sectional study. *Japan Journal of Nursing Science*, *21*(4), e12617. DOI: 10.1111/jjns.12617 PMID: 39148343

Kokkinos, C. M. (2006). Factor structure and psychometric properties of the Maslach Burnout Inventory-Educators Survey among elementary and secondary school teachers in Cyprus. *Stress and Health*, *22*(1), 25–33. DOI: 10.1002/smi.1079

Krishnapriya, R. B. (2023). BURN OUT AMONG NURSES DURING COVID-19 PANDEMIC.

Łaskawiec-Żuławińska, D., Grajek, M., Krupa-Kotara, K., Szlacheta, P., Karacan, H., Roszak, M., Łabuz-Roszak, B., & Korzonek-Szlacheta, I. (2024). Burnout and Life Satisfaction among Healthcare Workers Related to the COVID-19 Pandemic (Silesia, Poland). *Behavioural Neurology*, *2024*(1), 9945392. DOI: 10.1155/2024/9945392 PMID: 38725562

Li, H., Chen, J., Wei, Q., & Chen, H. (2025). Knowledge, attitudes, and practices of vocational college teachers towards occupational burnout. *Frontiers in Public Health, 13*, 1513170. López-Cabarcos, M. Á., López-Carballeira, A., & Ferro-Soto, C. (2019). The role of emotional exhaustion among public healthcare professionals. *Journal of Health Organization and Management*, *33*(6), 649–655.

Listopad, I. W., Michaelsen, M. M., Werdecker, L., & Esch, T. (2021). Bio-psycho-socio-Spirito-cultural factors of burnout: A systematic narrative review of the literature. *Frontiers in Psychology*, *12*, 722862. DOI: 10.3389/fpsyg.2021.722862 PMID: 34925130

López-Cabarcos, M. Á., López-Carballeira, A., & Ferro-Soto, C. (2019). The role of emotional exhaustion among public healthcare professionals. *Journal of Health Organization and Management, 33*(6), 649–655. DOI: 10.1108/JHOM-04-2019-0091 PMID: 31625822

Mazzucato, M., & Kattel, R. (2020). COVID-19 and public-sector capacity. *Oxford Review of Economic Policy, 36*(Supplement_1), graa031. Advance online publication. DOI: 10.1093/oxrep/graa031 PMID: 40504220

Meeusen, V., Gatt, S. P., Barach, P., & van Zundert, A. (2023). Occupational well-being, resilience, burnout, and job satisfaction of surgical teams. In Sanchez, J. A., Higgins, R. S., & Kent, P. S. (Eds.), *Handbook of perioperative and procedural patient safety* (pp. 205–229). Elsevier.

Mendenhall, E., Newfield, T., & Tsai, A. C. (2021). Syndemic theory, methods, and data. *Social Science & Medicine (1982), 295*, 114656.

Monroe, M., Morse, E., & Price, J. M. (2020). The relationship between critical care work environment and professional quality of life. *American Journal of Critical Care, 29*(2), 145–149. DOI: 10.4037/ajcc2020406 PMID: 32114615

Noorollahi, A., Pordelan, N., Khalijian, S., Koohi, A. H., & Abbasi, M. (2022). Investigating the Relationship between Sleep Quality and Career Adaptability with Occupational Burnout among Employees. *Journal of Sleep sciences.*

Pallewaththa, P., & Wijesiri, B. (2021). Occupational health: The impact of occupational stressors on job productivity. *Sri Lanka Journal of Social Sciences, 44*(2), 149–164. DOI: 10.4038/sljss.v44i2.8229

Park, J., & Ahn, Y. (2022). Government employees' experience and expectation of COVID-19 hardships: The moderating role of gender and race in the United States. *American Review of Public Administration, 52*(1), 15–35. DOI: 10.1177/02750740211049280

Penz, M., Wekenborg, M. K., Pieper, L., Beesdo-Baum, K., Walther, A., Miller, R., Stalder, T., & Kirschbaum, C. (2018). The Dresden Burnout Study: Protocol of a prospective cohort study for the bio-psychological investigation of burnout. *International Journal of Methods in Psychiatric Research, 27*(2), e1613. DOI: 10.1002/mpr.1613 PMID: 29611872

Prosen, M. (2020). Social stigma in the time of coronavirus (COVID-19): an epidemic we must not remain silent about. Obzornik zdravstvene nege, 54(2), 100-103.

Rauf, Z., & Saba, M. (2024). Compassion fatigue and professional quality of life among health professionals: Moderating role of professional resilience. *Wah Academia Journal of Social Sciences, 3*(2), 427–449.

Resnik, D. B. (2015). Bioethical issues in providing financial incentives to research participants. *Medicolegal and Bioethics,* •••, 35–41. DOI: 10.2147/MB.S70416 PMID: 26807399

Rodrigues, L. A., Rodrigues, A. M., Brunetti, M. N., Michels, M., Abatti, M., Indalecio, A., Rocha, L. B., & Dal Pizzol, F. (2024). Association between occupational stress, markers of inflammation, and oxidative stress in intensive care unit workers: A cross-sectional study. *Revista Brasileira de Medicina do Trabalho : Publicacao Oficial da Associacao Nacional de Medicina do Trabalho-ANAMT, 22*(2), 1–11. DOI: 10.47626/1679-4435-2022-1049 PMID: 39371284

Saaed, H. K., Raheemah, S. H., & Shaalan, U. H. (2019). The Effect of Organizational Silence on Occupational Burnout. *Opción: Revista de Ciencias Humanas y Sociales*, (22), 875–891.

Schaufeli, W. B., Enzmann, D., & Girault, N. (2017). Measurement of burnout: A review. *Professional burnout*, 199-215.

Seo, E., Kim, H., Sim, Y., Ha, M.-S., Kim, U., & Kim, H. (2022). Burnout, Presenteeism and Workplace Conditions of Korean Taekwondo Coaches of High-Performance Athletes. *International Journal of Environmental Research and Public Health, 19*(10), 5912. DOI: 10.3390/ijerph19105912 PMID: 35627449

Sever, M. S., Ortiz, A., Maggiore, U., Bac-García, E., & Vanholder, R. (2021). Mass disasters and burnout in nephrology personnel: From earthquakes and hurricanes to COVID-19 pandemic. *Clinical Journal of the American Society of Nephrology; CJASN, 16*(5), 829–837. DOI: 10.2215/CJN.08400520 PMID: 33414153

Sharifi, Y., Ebrahimpur, M., Payab, M., & Larijani, B. (2022). The Syndemic Theory, the COVID-19 Pandemic, and The Epidemics of Non-Communicable Diseases (NCDs). *Medical Journal of the Islamic Republic of Iran, 36*, 177. DOI: 10.47176/mjiri.36.177 PMID: 36919009

Sousa, J. (2021). A new and old pandemic–the burnout syndrome. *MOJ Gerontol Geriatr, 6*(1), 22–26. DOI: 10.15406/mojgg.2021.06.00262

Stamm, B. H. (2010). The Concise ProQOL Manual. 2010. Pocatello, ID: ProQOL.org. http://ProQOL.org/uploads/ProQOL_Concise_2ndEd_12-2010.pd

Tavella, G., Hadzi-Pavlovic, D., & Parker, G. (2021). Burnout: Redefining its key symptoms. *Psychiatry Research, 302*, 114023. DOI: 10.1016/j.psychres.2021.114023 PMID: 34052460

Thamrin, S., Sariwulan, T., Suryatni, M., Ridlo, M., Qamarius, I., & Capnary, M. C. (2022). The impact of work from home (WFH) during covid-19 pandemic period on job expectations: The case of the state civil apparatus. *Journal of Management Information and Decision Sciences, 25*(S2).

Treluyer, L., & Tourneux, P. (2021). Burnout among paediatric residents during the COVID-19 outbreak in France. *European Journal of Pediatrics, 180*(2), 627–633. DOI: 10.1007/s00431-020-03907-x PMID: 33410942

VIBER. (2024). 2023 U.S. VIRGIN ISLANDS ECONOMY. https://usviber.org/wp-content/uploads/2024/10/ECON-REVIEW-9-16-24.pdf

VIOMB. US Recovery Plan. https://arpa.vi.gov/wp-content/uploads/2024/08/USVI-2024-Recovery-Plan-1.pdf

VIOMB (2024). United States Virgin Islands Recovery Plan. Microsoft Word - DRAFT_USVI 2024 Recovery Plan_7.25.2024.docx

Wiszniewska, M., Rybacki, M., Lipińska-Ojrzanowska, A., Szkiela, M., & Walusiak-Skorupa, J. (2023). Recognition COVID-19 as an occupational disease in Poland–definition, criteria and recommendation. *Medycyna Pracy, 74*(5), 435–442. DOI: 10.13075/mp.5893.01427 PMID: 38104343

Yurt, Y. (2023). Work-Related and Occupational Liver Diseases. *EURASIAN JOURNAL OF MEDICAL ADVANCES, 3*(2), 51–55. DOI: 10.14744/ejma.2023.74046

Zakeri, M. A., Bazmandegan, G., Ganjeh, H., Zakeri, M., Mollaahmadi, S., Anbariyan, A., & Kamiab, Z. (2021). Is nurses' clinical competence associated with their compassion satisfaction, burnout and secondary traumatic stress? A cross-sectional study. *Nursing Open, 8*(1), 354–363. DOI: 10.1002/nop2.636 PMID: 33318843

Zou, Y., Lu, Y., Zhou, F., Liu, X., Ngoubene-Atioky, A. J., Xu, K., Hong, L., Shen, G., Wu, H., Cai, Z., Liu, Y., Chen, L., & Bao, D. (2022). Three Mental Health Symptoms of Frontline Medical Staff Associated With Occupational Stressors During the COVID-19 Peak Outbreak in China: The Mediation of Perceived Stress and the Moderation of Social Support. *Frontiers in Psychology, 13*, 888000. DOI: 10.3389/fpsyg.2022.888000 PMID: 35712133

KEY TERMS AND DEFINITIONS

Burnout: a state of high levels stress, exhaustion, depersonalization, and inefficacy.

Compassion satisfaction: positive and caring feelings within job performance.

Compassion fatigue: adverse effect of caring from others.

Depersonalization: mental state of detachment, disinterest and dispassion.

Epidemic: is a spatial or temporal designation for a significant increase in an infectious disease.

Epidemiology: the study of health-related states or events (including diseases) in a defined population.

Emotional exhaustion: experienced excessive emotional stress and fatigue.

Exhaustion: energy depletion, tiredness, and weariness resulting in apathy, indifference and dissatisfaction.

Inefficacy: feelings of under- or non- achievement, unfulfillment and failing.

Maslach's burnout: as exhaustion and depersonalization increase, then the personal accomplishment decreases.

Occupational burnout: burnout caused by work strain, chronic negative behaviors and bad habits.

Occupational burnout syndrome: advanced accumulation of psychosocial issues that negatively impact job performance.

Occupational disease: an illness caused by harmful elements, such as risks and levels of toxic exposure within work environments, and occupations.

Professional quality of life (ProQol): feelings (i.e., positive and negative) that employees have about their work experience.

Personal accomplishments: the attainment of significant achievements during work experience that signify success or personal growth.

Syndemic: two or more epidemics synergistically interact with each other.

Chapter 2
Reviving the Public Sector:
Leadership's Key Role in Managing Burnout

Summyr Burton
https://orcid.org/0000-0002-3004-0711
Celia Scott Weatherhead School of Public Health and Tropical Medicine, Tulane University, USA

Savannah Baus
Celia Scott Weatherhead School of Public Health and Tropical Medicine, Tulane University, USA

Stephen A. Murphy
https://orcid.org/0000-0001-9143-600X
Celia Scott Weatherhead School of Public Health and Tropical Medicine, Tulane University, USA

ABSTRACT

This chapter explores the significant issue of public sector burnout in the public sector through the lens of the Job Demands-Resources Theory. The chapter highlights the essential role of effective leadership and professional development in mitigating burnout and enhancing employee motivation and satisfaction. Key leadership theories and core competencies are discussed, emphasizing the need for communication, continuous learning, adaptability, and the creation of supportive environments. The chapter calls for systematically integrating leadership and professional development into public sector practices to build resilient, engaged, and motivated teams, ultimately improving public service delivery and employee retention. To conclude, it provides key considerations and guiding principles to consider when developing

DOI: 10.4018/979-8-3373-0169-3.ch002

a public sector leadership and professional development program to be used by any leader in their practice.

REVIVING THE PUBLIC SECTOR: LEADERSHIP'S KEY ROLE IN MANAGING BURNOUT

Sarah, a highly competent and committed program manager for a city's department for urban development, starts her day like any other, pouring over project files and coordinating with her team. Sarah has always been passionate about urban development, believing in its power to transform communities. Despite her dedication and consistent performance for over eight years, Sarah notices that promotions and professional development opportunities often bypass her. But her manager, Mr. Hargrove, seldom provides constructive feedback or acknowledges the efforts of his team; Sarah has not even had a performance review for almost two years. Sarah is increasingly confused and frustrated on how she can position herself as an ideal candidate for promotion. After all, Sarah is already completing the work of three full-time employees since her colleagues quit months ago and no replacements have been found.

As her day progresses, Sarah finds herself in various perfunctory meetings, relaying the latest findings in a report she disseminated to leadership last week. She poses several challenges uncovered in her report and even went the extra mile to highlight several low-cost solutions to implement. Unfortunately, Mr. Hargrove swiftly dismisses Sarah's ideas and tells her he will come up with another solution to these problems. Sarah leaves the meeting knowing that Mr. Hargrove will not follow through on his promise, since it is well known that he prefers to keep the department running "the same way it always has been". She is even more upset that her efforts went unrecognized, and she wasted time brainstorming innovative solutions hoping that Mr. Hargrove would acknowledge her contributions and hard work.

Feeling dejected, Sarah goes back to work tackling day-to-day tasks that she can complete with her eyes closed. She decides that it's not worth her time or effort to go above and beyond in her role, since she doesn't see how it benefits her or leads to change. Her work performance, once stellar, begins to suffer as she struggles to concentrate and meet deadlines. Sarah is not surprised when Mr. Hargrove doesn't even seem to notice, let alone ask her if she needs support.

Over the next few months, Sarah starts to experience chronic fatigue, finding it increasingly difficult to get out of bed each morning. Her enthusiasm for work diminishes, replaced by a sense of dread and disengagement. She starts to suffer from headaches and insomnia, symptoms she initially dismisses but which begin to impact her daily life. The final straw comes when a less experienced and skilled colleague is promoted over her, solely because of their closer personal relationship with Mr. Hargrove. This unfair decision and recognizing the toll her job is taking on her mental and physical health, Sarah makes the difficult decision to resign. She leaves her position not because she doesn't care about her work, but because she realizes her well-being and professional growth cannot continue in such an environment.

She takes a sabbatical to focus on her health and eventually finds a new role in a nonprofit organization where her efforts are appreciated, and her career aspirations are supported. Her experience highlights the critical need for effective leadership that fosters employee development and wellness, reminding organizations of the real cost of employee burnout.

Sarah's journey echoes the real-world experiences of many public sector workers who have left their roles due to burnout. Many more have left due to the high stress and long-term overload of work demands required by the COVID-19 pandemic response, particularly in chronically under resourced and understaffed sectors. In the contemporary landscape of the public sector, burnout among public sector employees is a critical issue with far-reaching consequences on workforce sustainability, organizational effectiveness, and public trust.

Research into public sector burnout has consistently found a relationship between burnout, attrition, and a lack of or inadequate leadership and professional development opportunities within their workplace. This chapter proposes that developing leadership capacity is essential to addressing burnout in the public sector and discusses actionable strategies to combat burnout, focusing on two broad and interconnected areas: leadership development and professional advancement. Together, these initiatives work in tandem address the root causes of burnout by enhancing organizational resilience and equipping employees with the tools to thrive in high-pressure roles (Linos & Ruffini, 2019).

This book chapter seeks to achieve the following objectives:

1. To explore the role of leadership and professional development in reducing burnout and enhancing employee well-being.
2. To examine strategies and considerations for mitigating public sector burnout, including training, mentoring, peer support, and career development programs.
3. To provide actionable insights and recommendations for implementing professional advancement and leadership development programs effectively and sustainably within public sector settings.

UNDERSTANDING BURNOUT IN THE PUBLIC SECTOR

Burnout, characterized by emotional exhaustion, depersonalization, and a diminished sense of accomplishment, disrupts productivity, diminishes morale, and compromises the quality of public services (Awashreh & AlGhunaimi, 2024). Perhaps unsurprising to those who have experience working in the public sector, burnout was conceptualized and refined by observing the contexts of human and public services.

Though the term was already in existence, Herbert Freudenberger is recognized for linking the term with the context of how it is understood today. While working as a psychologist in 1974, he used burnout to describe symptoms he observed in healthcare volunteers at a New York City free clinic including reduced emotional capacity, motivation, and commitment (Schaufeli, 2017). Another name may be more familiar for those who have been exposed to literature on burnout: Christina Maslach. Maslach, a professor of social psychology, discovered the term at nearly the same time as Freudenberger as she studied the ways by which human services workers cope on the job (Maslach & Schaufeli, 1993; Schaufeli, 2017).

Burnout did not truly garner America's attention until the 1970s, evidenced by the onslaught of magazine articles and journals directed at practitioners (as opposed to academics) in a slew of people-oriented public services: medicine, education, criminal justice, and social services, to name a few (Maslach & Schaufeli, 1993). Although a definitive rationale as to why this reaction occurred specifically in the mid-1970s is still up for debate, Farber (1983) argues that it is an amalgamation of several social, political, and economic factors, including:

- Disconnection and alienation from non-workplace communities;
- Increased expectations for personal attainment and gratification from the workplace; and
- A change in human services work becoming more "professionalized, bureaucratized, credentialized, and isolated" (Maslach & Schaufeli, 1993, p. 3).

Since then, governmental cost-cutting measures in many human service agencies has meant higher workloads pushed on few workers, with little incentive or reward (e.g., adequate salary). Our present climate remains this way in many public sector environments, further challenged by significant increases in population size, frequency and severity of crises and disasters, and political polarization. As we well know, the COVID-19 pandemic wreaked havoc on the workplace, creating a massive global surge of burnout.

Although this may seem like an insurmountable issue incapable of fixing, there exists a strong force of individuals, teams, institutions, organizations, and entire governments committed to developing, implementing, and sustaining effective, evidence-based solutions to mitigate and prevent burnout within the public sector and beyond. Since the 1980s, when empirical methods to study burnout truly began, research exploded with studies on risk factors, individual and organizational impacts, frameworks and assessments, and so on. A large and ever-growing list of variables have been studied to understand how burnout develops to establish effective interventions. Still, none have been found to be more strongly related to burnout than factors related to their job and workplaces (Maslach & Schaufeli, 1993). Leiter and Maslach (1999) suggest six indicators of burnout within the workplace: unsustainable workload, lack of control, insufficient reward for effort, lack of supportive community, mismatch between values and skills, and unfair practices. With this in mind, we suggest the best way to review burnout's impact and contributing factors through the Job Demands-Resources theory lens.

Job Demands-Resources Theory

The Job Demands-Resources (JD-R) Theory offers a comprehensive framework for understanding employee well-being and performance within organizations. The theory suggests that a balance between job demands and resources is crucial for maintaining employee motivation and preventing burnout. When resources are ample, employees are more likely to be engaged, motivated, and productive. Conversely, when demands outweigh resources, employees may experience stress and burnout, leading to decreased performance and well-being. Understanding the mechanisms outlined in this framework allows organizations to optimize work environments to enhance employee engagement and reduce burnout, ultimately driving organizational success. The JD-R theory's main components include job demands and job resources.

Job Demands

Job demands are aspects of the workplace that require sustained effort and are therefore associated with physiological and psychological costs (Tummers & Bakker, 2021). These can include aspects of an individual's standard role and responsibilities but also include interpersonal and organizational demands. At the individual-level, job demands include any aspects in the workplace that cost physical, mental, and emotional energy (Bakker & Demerouti, 2018). This includes items such as workload or complex tasks and projects. Interpersonal demands can include things like experiencing conflicting demands from managers and clients, bullying, or handling workplace conflicts with colleagues.

Organizational demands may be the most impactful demand type on burnout, including things such as high workloads, staff shortages, reassignment to assist under-resourced departments, or mandatory overtime to cover absenteeism. Employees impacted by any of these demands cause employees to feel unsupported by leadership as well as extreme frustration towards institutional policies, poor communication, or inaction by their leadership (Hofmeyer et al., 2020). Government workers have reported increased work demands, such as workload and staffing shortages, are main causes of burnout and turnover intention (Asplund & Tatel, 2023; Newhouse, 2024; Orr & Leider, 2023).

When job demands are high, an employee may develop job strain, characterized by exhaustion, job-related anxiety, and health complaints (Bakker & Demerouti, 2018). Job strain negatively impacts motivation and job performance as exhaustion causes an inability to focus, difficulties with communication, and increases in mistakes and conflicts. Exposure to daily workload transforms into chronic overload over a long period of time, leading to a health-impairment process defined by chronic exhaustion manifesting as physical health problems (Bakker & Demerouti, 2018). Physical health problems include common afflictions such as headaches and sleeping issues (e.g., insomnia) but can also include serious issues such as h as substance misuse, particularly alcohol and painkillers, and cardiovascular diseases (e.g., coronary artery disease) (Kristensen et al., 2007; Linos et al., 2022).

Job Resources

Job resources are aspects of the job that help the workforce achieve their work goals, overcome draining job demands, and stimulate personal growth and development (Bakker & Demerouti, 2018). When workplace environments ensure ample availability of resources, motivation and work engagement will also increase, shown by employees who are energetic, enthusiastic, and immersed in their work (Tummers & Bakker, 2021). At the organizational-level, high motivation is showcased by improved job performance shown through increased financial returns, decreased absenteeism, and higher client satisfaction (Bakker & Demerouti, 2018).

Resources are further broken down into job and personal resources. Job resources include factors such as feedback, social support, and opportunities for personal growth or promotion. Feedback helps employees understand their work and provides guidance on how to improve in the future, removing role uncertainty and refining their skills. It also strengthens the relationship between leader and employee, building trust and a perception that their leader is available and a part of their team.

Social support, actual or perceived, has been firmly established as a protective factor for mental health and burnout by impacting an individual's sense of belonging, value, self-esteem, and self-worth (Linos et al., 2022). Additionally, social support allows co-workers and teams to successfully process and cope with adversity or highly stressful events by reappraising them together to reduce the adverse psychological impacts on each individual (Linos et al., 2022; Prati & Pietrantoni, 2010; Wills & Shimar, 2000). Strong social support among teams is particularly vital in sectors dealing with high-intensity situations such as healthcare, law enforcement, and emergency management.

Unsurprisingly, workers have a strong desire to work hard in their roles to hone their skills in effort to advance within their workplace via promotions and recognition. Interestingly, public health employees who were less than 35 years of age or held tenure of less than five years were disproportionately more likely to have left their roles between 2017 and 2021, when nearly half of all public health agency employees left the sector (Kolman, 2024; Leider et al., 2023). Large-scale surveys of public sector workers help explain this phenomenon, reporting significantly high rates of employees intent on vacating their positions cite a lack of career development or professional advancement opportunities as their main reason (de Beaumont, 2022; Choi et al., 2023).

Stagnation and lack of career direction primarily contribute to employee dissatisfaction and emotional exhaustion (Linos & Ruffini, 2019). In workplaces that provide feedback, social support, and skill variety, employees are able to identify their work as meaningful while meeting basic psychological needs such as feeling competent, relatable, and in control of their environment (Deci & Ryan, 1985).

Personal resources relate to an individual's perceptions and beliefs regarding the control they have over their environment (Tummers & Bakker, 2021). It involves having the freedom to make choices and the ability to act in accordance with one's own values and interests. In the workplace, autonomy can lead to higher job satisfaction and engagement, as employees feel empowered to take initiative and contribute meaningfully to their roles. Perceptions of autonomy do change in accordance with job demands and organizational practices, such as requiring employees to return to office rather than allowing employees to decide, personal resources such as self-efficacy and optimism can also influence autonomy.

Bandura's (1977) concept of self-efficacy describes how an individual's confidence in their ability to succeed increases through mastery experiences and vicarious learning. This perception affects how people approach goals, tasks, and challenges. Higher self-efficacy can lead to greater motivation and persistence when facing obstacles, as individuals feel more capable of influencing their outcomes. Optimism is the expectation that good things will happen in the future and that negative events are temporary and manageable. Optimistic individuals generally have a positive outlook on life and believe that they have control over their future. This mindset can enhance resilience against adversities and is associated with better physical and mental health. Aspects of self-efficacy and optimism have been shown to decrease burnout, such as employees reminding themselves that they can succeed, reframing situations as challenges, and finding positive aspects of their work (Asplund & Tatel, 2023).

A Case Study: COVID-19 and the Public Health Sector

The COVID-19 pandemic showed the fragility of the public health sector, which has been chronically underfunded and under-resourced for decades. A late 2021 report estimated the public health workforce would need to expand by 80%, or 80,000 full-time employees, to provide the minimum level of services for the public, services like substance misuse prevention, family planning services, and violence prevention (de Beaumont, 2021). This number does not include the public health emergency response needs to combat the pandemic, such as contact tracers, disaster behavioral health providers, or vaccinators.

To meet the demands, many health departments relied on reassigning employees from their regular duties, hiring staff on temporary contracts, and partnering with public health and nursing schools. Eight out of ten local health departments, historically impacted the hardest by limited funding and stretched capacities, were forced to reassign employees to bolster the pandemic response workforce. The National Council on County and City Health Officials (NACCHO), (2022) found that by March of 2021, state, tribal, local, and territorial public health agencies had onboarded nearly 55,000 employees to meet the demands of the pandemic response. Hundreds of volunteers from the Medical Reserve Corps, American Red Cross, and AmeriCorps were called upon to operate call centers, alternate care sites, and sites for testing and vaccination. These efforts, while impactful for pandemic mitigation, were not as positive for the public health workforce.

The pandemic response initiatives in the public health sector involved significant cognitive, mental, and emotional challenges and frequently included physical demands due to the risk of viral exposure. The burden of this work was increased further as the response became politicized, resulting in hundreds of reports of bullying and harassment from the general public (NACCHO, 2022). Reassignment led to burnout by adversely impacting employee workload, autonomy, self-efficacy, and optimism. Although reassignment was necessary to ramp up the pandemic response workforce, basic public health service needs continued, meaning many employees were tasked with maintaining their current responsibilities while taking on additional pandemic-related tasks. Reassigned employees often lacked the skills necessary to be effective in these roles and likely did not share the same passion for their pandemic response duties as they show for their hired roles. Moreover, the prolonged timeframe of the pandemic required reassignment periods expected to last a few weeks yet often extended for months and in some cases, years (Office of the Assistant Secretary for Planning and Evaluation (ASPE), 2023).

Onboarding and training of reassigned or new staff and volunteers created additional burdens on public health emergency response staff. While necessary and beneficial to curb the pandemic, these efforts were not long-lasting; new staff returned to their assigned duties or left when their contracts expired, bringing staffing back to pre-pandemic levels (ASPE, 2023). Adding to this, the utilization of external, short-term resources denies team-building and social cohesion opportunities to the core staff. These high, chronic job demands and low job and personal resources caused substantial burnout to the entire public health workforce.

LEADERSHIP AND PROFESSIONAL DEVELOPMENT

Concepts of leadership have evolved significantly since the dawn of civilized society, with substantial movement over the past hundred years. Table 1. captures the evolution of leadership since the 1900s, highlighting the central focus and key concepts associated with each time period. This was certainly not the inception of discussions on what leaders are and what they do.

As far back as 100 A.D., figures such as Theseus, Mohandas Gandhi, and Napoleon Bonaparte were believed to encompass certain traits, characteristics, and qualities that position them as 'natural born leaders' (Plutarch, 1770; Northouse, 2022). In the early 20th century, traditional theories, such as the "Great Man" theory, emerged to describe these beliefs. Despite research quickly abandoning these theories given lack of empirical support, these beliefs still persist in our global society, particularly related to inherent traits like masculinity, dominance, and confidence. McChrystal et al., 2018).

These theories remained prevalent until the mid-20th century when research shifted outside of the individual leader to focus on followers and situational contexts leaders find themselves in. This initially focused on democratic leadership aspects, including human relations, collaboration, and communication. Later, at the turn of the century, leadership became increasingly focused on motivation, engagement, and inspiration.

As the public sector advanced into the 21st century, leadership was again forced to evolve as it faced challenges such as globalization, technological advancements, and an increasing visibility of successes and failures. The scope of leadership that persists today maintains the democratic and visionary underpinnings solidified in earlier eras but with key refinements. It is now understood as a social process involved in enabling others to achieve collective outcomes in collaborative, inclusive, and ethical ways.

Currently, certain areas of the public sector continue to rely on traditional, command-and-control leadership styles as exemplified by the Incident Command System and National Incident Management System, often provided as core trainings during onboarding processes (Owen et al., 2015). Though helpful, even vital, in contexts such as disaster response, overreliance on this approach's strict seniority systems and inflexible processes create power gradients that disempower subordinates and curb the two-way communication needed to refine plans, overcome challenges, and foster innovation (Owen et al., 2015). Team members working under these conditions are uncomfortable speaking up about concerns, ideas, and even mental health issues; the perfect conditions for burnout.

Table 1. Perceptions of leadership across time from early 1900s to present

Time Period	Definition Focus	Key Concepts
Early 1900s	Those with the authority to make decisions and direct others in achieving specific tasks.	Control Power Centralization Authority
1920s-30s	Leaders are born with inherent characteristics and qualities that made someone a leader. Leaders cannot be made.	Traits Inherent Qualities "Great Man" theory
1940s-50s	Leadership viewed as a process of social interaction rather than merely a set of personal traits; Leaders have the ability to influence others.	Group Dynamics Social Interaction Influence Processes
1960s-70s	Leadership viewed as the role of leaders in motivating and engaging their followers. Research focused on styles and behaviors that inform roles.	Leadership Styles Leadership Behaviors Transformational-Transactional Theory
1980s-90s	Leadership is the ability to inspire and create a vision for the future while mobilizing people towards achieving that vision.	Vision Change Inspiration Visionary Leadership
2000s-Present	Leadership is a social process that involves enabling individuals and groups to achieve collective outcomes.	Social Process Inclusivity Collaboration Ethical Practices

Leadership Approaches and Core Competencies

In today's rapidly evolving organizational landscape, leadership theories serve as foundational frameworks that guide the development and execution of effective leadership practices. These theories, which have been rigorously developed and refined over decades, provide invaluable insights into the diverse styles, attributes, and behaviors that constitute successful leadership. As organizations navigate the complexities of globalization, technological advancements, and shifting societal expectations, the need for adaptable and robust leadership models has never been more crucial.

In the public sector, where the stakes involve public trust, transparency, and the efficient delivery of services, leadership theories play an essential role in shaping the approaches and strategies that leaders adopt. Unlike the private sector, public sector leaders must often balance a myriad of challenges, including bureaucratic constraints, limited resources, and overseeing public health crises. Therefore, understanding and applying relevant leadership theories can significantly enhance the ability of public sector leaders to inspire their teams, drive innovation, and meet the growing demands of the communities they serve.

The application of these theories not only helps in aligning leadership practices with organizational goals but also fosters a culture of continuous improvement and accountability. By embracing theories such as transformational, situational, and ethical leadership, the public sector can cultivate leaders who are equipped to address contemporary challenges with empathy, integrity, and strategic foresight.

In his 2018 article, Emmanuel Mango highlights the existence of 66 leadership theories, presenting challenges in discussing them comprehensively and determining which are most suitable for integration into practice. As such, we will focus solely on the specific contexts of cultivating public sector leadership in such a way as to reduce burnout in the workforce. However, the leadership theories discussed below will improve much more than attrition rates to affect entire teams, systems, and organizations. We will discuss the significance of several leadership theories, offering insights into how they can be harnessed to develop effective leadership programs and nurture a new generation of public sector leaders prepared to navigate the complexities of the modern world.

Public Service Leadership Model

The Public Service Leadership Model serves as a framework designed to guide and enhance leadership within the public sector. It emphasizes public service leaders' unique challenges and responsibilities, focusing on fostering a culture of integrity, accountability, and service excellence.

The model highlights two core values every government leader should embody: stewardship of public trust and commitment to public good. Both values hold that public sector leaders must be held to the highest of standards and showcase integrity given their influence, power, and government-provided resources (Partnership for Public Service (PPS), n.d.a). Four key competencies complete the model: becoming self-aware, engaging others, leading change, and achieving results.

Becoming Self-Aware. Self-awareness requires reflecting on your core values, motivations, and thought patterns (PPS, n.d.a). Only by building self-awareness are leaders able to develop and refine leadership traits, communicate effectively, and provide the highest service to the public. Sub-competencies include:

- Self-reflection
- Authenticity
- Emotional intelligence
- Integrity
- Continuous learning

Engaging Others. Leaders should strive to cultivate strong collaborative foundations within their team by providing evaluative and constructive feedback, recognizing their employees for jobs well done, and offering professional development opportunities for themselves and their employees (PPS, n.d.c). Five subcompetencies for engagement include:

- Relationship building
- Empowering others
- Collaboration
- Conflict management
- Fostering engagement

Leading Change. Being a leader of change requires taking initiative to sponsor and/or implement innovative solutions to the ever-changing public sector environment (PPS, n.d.a). Effective leaders must also manage and support others through changes that are rife with uncertainty and upheaval of normal routine. Subcompetencies that allow leaders to lead change include:

- Vision setting
- Influence
- Innovation and creativity
- Embracing risk and uncertainty
- Adaptability

Achieving Results. Every workplace has goals and standards to meet. Leaders must harbor the skills to manage effectively, including strategic thinking and strong decision-making (PPS, n.d.a). These skills will allow the leader to provide measurable outcomes of their team's work, showcasing their efforts for the public good. Sub-competencies for achieving results are:

- Accountability
- Evidence-based decision-making
- Systems thinking
- Tech savviness
- Customer experience

A significant aspect of the Public Service Leadership Model is its recognition of the polytomy of leaders, such as emerging leaders, leaders of teams, leaders of leaders, and leaders of organizations (PPS, n.d.a). This model denotes that while each leadership core value, competency, and sub-competency is relevant across all leadership types, the application will depend on the characteristics of the leadership role. By promoting these principles and recognizing the diversity of needs between distinct leader types, the model seeks to create a responsive and resilient public service capable of addressing emerging challenges and opportunities.

Transformational Leadership

Transformational leadership theory emerged as a compelling framework that revolutionized the understanding of leadership's impact on organizations and their members. Introduced by James MacGregor Burns in his 1978 book *Leadership*, this theory redefined leadership by shifting the focus from mere transactional exchanges to inspiring transformative change within followers and organizations.

At the heart of transformational leadership lies inspiration and motivation, effective tools to empower individuals to exceed their self-interests for the greater good. Public sector leaders who adopt transformational behaviors are more adaptable in chaotic situations, able to meet the growing expectations of the public they serve, and mobilize their team to improve services and meet community needs. This approach emphasizes the development of a shared vision, fostering an environment where creativity, innovation, and personal growth can flourish. Transformational leaders are characterized by their ability to articulate a compelling vision of the future, instill pride, communicate high expectations, and provide personalized support to their followers.

The introduction of transformational leadership concepts into the organizational world brought with it a new understanding of the profound influence leaders can have on their teams. By emphasizing the "Four I's" - charisma, inspirational motivation, intellectual stimulation, and individualized consideration - transformational leadership spurred a paradigm shift that encouraged leaders to become agents of change, capable of inspiring profound shifts in organizational culture and performance. Descriptions and key concepts for each of the "I's" can be found in Table 2.

Table 2. Descriptions and key concepts of transformational leadership's four I's

Four I's	Description	Key Concepts
Idealized Influence (Charisma)	Leaders act as role models for their followers, inspiring them through their behavior and ethical standards. Leaders demonstrate high moral and ethical conduct, which earns them trust and respect. They embody the values and principles they wish to instill in their teams, creating a deep sense of loyalty and admiration.	Role Model Ethical Standards Trust Respect Integrity
Inspirational Motivation	Leaders use inspirational motivation to articulate a compelling vision of the future. They communicate with enthusiasm and optimism, motivating followers to pursue ambitious goals. By fostering a sense of purpose and meaning, leaders galvanize their teams to overcome challenges and attain collective objectives.	Clear Vision Optimism Enthusiasm Productivity Sense of Purpose Encouragement
Intellectual Stimulation	Leaders encourage innovation and creativity by challenging assumptions and encouraging new perspectives. They foster an environment where followers feel safe to explore new ideas and question the status quo. They promote critical thinking and problem-solving, stimulating followers to develop innovative solutions.	Innovation Creativity Goals Challenge Problem-Solving Critical Thinking
Individualized Consideration	Leaders demonstrate individualized consideration by providing personalized support and attention to each follower's needs and development. They recognize the unique strengths and aspirations of each team member, offering mentorship and coaching tailored to individual growth. Personalized approaches help foster a supportive and nurturing environment, enhancing follower engagement and satisfaction.	Mentorship Empathy Purpose Skills Inclusion Supportive Environment Tailored Development

Through the lens of burnout mitigation, transformational leaders focus on enhancing job satisfaction and engagement. Indeed, this leadership style has been linked to increases in job satisfaction, employee motivation, work attitudes, and job performance (Bakker & Demerouti, 2018; Fernet et al., 2015; Judge & Piccolo, 2004). Transformational behaviors also protect against work periods with higher workloads, cognitive work demands, and role conflict (Breevaart & Bakker, 2018). Transformational behaviors act as motivation for followers to utilize their own personal strengths to overcome work challenges (Bakker & Demerouti, 2018). Strengthening worker self-efficacy and autonomy are not the only resources transformational leaders achieve; others include higher quality relationships, decision-making, and job recognition (Fernet et al., 2015).

Importantly, Fernet and colleagues (2015) noted that transformational practices such as these act by shaping an employee's perception of their job, not by actually changing the job itself. This finding is particularly important for public sector settings where leaders are often limited in their capacity for organizational change by bureaucracy, funding, or staffing issues. In sum, transformational leadership is relatively easy to adopt in practice and offers a wealth of benefits for entire teams in spite of public sector obstacles related to cultivating organizational change.

Adaptive Leadership

The adaptive leadership framework encompasses the ability to lead and manage change in complex environments. Developed by Ronald Heifetz and Marty Linsky in the 1990s, it emphasizes the behaviors leaders must showcase to support employees and teams through changing circumstances by addressing adaptive challenges—problems that require new learning and changes in behavior. Adaptive leaders provide opportunities and space for workers to overcome challenges on their own, cultivating supportive learning experiences and expanding individual's capacities to overcome real-world changes in attitudes, perceptions, and behaviors (Northouse, 2021). This theory is highly relevant given the public sector's sensitivity to these changes. The model posits that when situational challenges arise, particularly those adaptive in nature, specific leadership behaviors will provide the necessary components for adaptive work to occur.

Situational challenges are grouped into technical, adaptive, and those with dimensions of both technical and adaptive challenges. Technical challenges are problems that have clear definitions and achievable solutions engrained within existing organizational structures and procedures (Northouse, 2021). Adaptive challenges, the primary focus of this leadership style, are issues that lack clear definitions, achievable solutions, and built infrastructures available to support the solution. Technical and adaptive challenges have characteristics of both dimensions, meaning they may have straightforward and clear definitions but a dearth of available solutions.

Adaptive leaders leverage these complex challenges to provide their followers with the developmental experiences to define the issue and identify effective solutions. To do this, leaders must demonstrate six behaviors:

1) Get on the Balcony: The leader must rise above, or step away from, the current situation to assess the challenge with clarity and a broad perspective.
2) Identify the Adaptive Challenge: The leader analyzes the situation, diagnosing challenges as technical, adaptive, or both. Then, if adaptive in nature, determine the challenge's impacts on their team's emotions, beliefs, values, and attitudes.
3) Regulate Distress: Adaptive challenges require innovative solutions that often mean change, which can be dysregulating and distressful for individuals. Leads must monitor levels of distress and take action on rising stress by regulating personal distress, creating a supportive holding environment, and providing direction, protection, orientation, conflict management, and productive norms.
4) Maintain Disciplined Attention: By regulating distress, adaptive leaders create an environment where individuals are capable of confronting change to solve the adaptive challenge. They must manage the stress and emotions that come with change, providing support while maintaining momentum towards adaptation.
5) Give the Work Back to the People: Leaders must build and maintain awareness of their team, providing support and taking control in some instances or dropping back and empowering others to actively participate in problem-solving activities.
6) Protect Leadership Voices from Below: Adaptive leaders must be equitable when demonstrating all adaptive behaviors, meaning they remain vigilant and focused on listening to the voices of those who may be marginalized, disempowered, or part of an out-group.

Only once leaders have effectively demonstrated each of the six behaviors and built a safe, supportive environment can adaptive work take place. Adaptive work is a social process in which non-leaders lead the charge to experiment, innovate, and develop new solutions and overcome challenges (Northouse, 2021).

Compared to the private sector, the public sector is constantly exposed to intricate and rapidly changing issues, such as changes in policy, technology, and societal needs. These environments necessitate leadership capable of handling the complexities of adaptive challenges while navigating the public sector constraints that limit innovation and change. When the approach is integrated properly in practice, leaders unlock the ability to respond more effectively to emerging challenges and building resilient teams and organizations.

Importantly, many behaviors of this approach reduce burnout and build psychological safety and an environment of continuous learning and development for employees. Distributing leadership responsibilities and involving team members in problem-solving builds trust, shared responsibility, social support, and cohesion among the group. Adaptive work reduces burnout by spreading the workload equitably, ensuring emerging challenges do not increase job demands or job strain in leaders or followers. The focus on building safe, supportive environments for two-way communication, emotional support, and space to brainstorm and experiment innovative solutions allows team members to develop skills while feeling supported, valued, and understood.

Essential Public Sector Leadership Competencies

James MacGregor Burns, a pioneer of leadership research who is credited with forming the Transformational Leadership Theory, said in his 1978 book *Leadership*:

> *"If we know all too much about our leaders, we know far too little about leadership. We fail to grasp the essence of leadership that is relevant to the modern age and hence we cannot agree on the standards by which to measure, recruit, and reject it. ... Leadership is one of the most observed and least understood phenomena on earth."*

Burns' words are no less true today, where a quick Internet search will populate thousands of conflicting articles touting the top skills every leader should encompass (or gain) to be effective in the workplace. Even scholars have been unable to fully agree on any one set group of competencies that make a great leader. However, this is not necessarily true within the public sector as the U.S. Office of Personnel Management (OPM) (n.d.b) identified five standards in 1997, called executive core qualifications (ECQs), that largely inform leadership development initiatives for public servants. Table 3 provides a breakdown of ECQs, describing their core competencies and fundamental qualities.

Table 3. U.S. office of personnel management's executive core qualifications and competencies

Core Qualification	Definition	Competencies
Leading Change	the ability to bring about strategic change, both within and outside the organization, to meet organizational goals. Inherent to this ECQ is the ability to establish an organizational vision and to implement it in a continuously changing environment.	Creativity and Innovation External Awareness Flexibility Resilience Strategic Thinking Vision
Leading People	the ability to lead people toward meeting the organization's vision, mission, and goals. Inherent to this ECQ is the ability to provide an inclusive workplace that fosters the development of others, facilitates cooperation and teamwork, and supports constructive resolution of conflicts.	Conflict Management Leveraging Diversity Developing Others Team Building
Results Driven	the ability to meet organizational goals and customer expectations. Inherent to this ECQ is the ability to make decisions that produce high-quality results by applying technical knowledge, analyzing problems, and calculating risks.	Accountability Customer Service Decisiveness Entrepreneurship Problem Solving Technical Credibility
Business Acumen	the ability to manage human, financial, and information resources strategically.	Financial Management Human Capital Management Technology Management
Building Coalitions	the ability to build coalitions internally and with other Federal agencies, State and local governments, nonprofit and private sector organizations, foreign governments, or international organizations to achieve common goals.	Partnering Political Savvy Influencing/ Negotiating
Fundamental Competencies		
Interpersonal Skills	Treats others with courtesy, sensitivity, and respect. Considers and responds appropriately to the needs and feelings of different people in different situations.	
Oral Communication	Makes clear and convincing oral presentations. Listens effectively; clarifies information as needed.	
Integrity & Honesty	Behaves in an honest, fair, and ethical manner. Shows consistency in words and actions. Models high standards of ethics.	
Written Communication	Writes in a clear, concise, organized, and convincing manner for the intended audience.	
Continual Learning	Assesses and recognizes own strengths and weaknesses; pursues self-development.	
Public Service Motivation	Shows a commitment to serve the public. Ensures that actions meet public needs; aligns organizational objectives and practices with public interests.	

Source: OPM (n.d.b)

Unsurprisingly, OPM's framework for leadership development encompasses many aspects of the transformational, adaptive, and public sector leadership theories we discussed above. Critiques of OPM's model highlight two main limitations. First, OPM established these ECQs in 1997 and have failed to routinely review and update them to maintain relevancy and utility in today's complex world (McDonald et al., 2020). Second, these leadership competencies are specifically geared towards the Senior Executive Service, a niche cohort of less than 10,000 individuals working under the executive branch and oversee federal programs and functions (Partnership for Public Service, n.d.b; OPM, n.d.c). This presents a limitation in the utility and scope for differing types of leaders and for public servants with vastly different roles and responsibilities.

The Leadership Action Cycle represents another set of core competencies. Arguably the most comprehensive, the LAC categorizes 35 competencies by traits, skills, and three sets of behaviors (task-oriented, people-oriented, and organizational) seen in Table 4 (Kapucu & Van Wart, 2008; Van Wart, 2003). These competencies integrate aspects of many leadership approaches and theories, including the transformational leadership theory (Crosby & Bryson, 2017). Like many other public sector leadership experts, Van Wart believes that no singular leadership approach or theory applies to all public sectors, nor all aspects of public sector work at a given time (Shawe & McAndrew, 2023). Perhaps the most poignant example relates to disaster response, characterized by highly chaotic, complex, and rapidly evolving situations. Leaders exhibiting transformational behaviors such as considering the needs of each individual team member before making a decision would likely delay pertinent mitigation measures, increasing economic costs as well as greater risk of injury and mortality to vulnerable communities.

Table 4. Leadership competencies of the leadership action cycle

Traits	Skills	Behaviors		
Self-confidence	**Communication**	**Task-Oriented**	**People-Oriented**	**Organizational**
Decisiveness*	Social skills	Monitor and assess work	Consult	Scan the environment*
Resilience	Influencing and negotiating	Operations planning	Plan and organize personnel*	Strategic planning*
Energy	Analytic skills	Clarify roles	Develop staff	Articulate mission and vision
Need for achievement	Technical skills	Inform*	Motivate*	Network and partner*

continued on following page

Table 4. Continued

Traits	Skills	Behaviors		
Willingness to assume responsibility	Continual learning	Delegate	Manage teams / team building*	Perform general management functions
Flexibility*		Problem-solving*	Manage personnel conflict	Decision-making*
Service motivation		Manage innovation and creativity*	Manage personnel change	Manage organizational change
Personal integrity				
Emotional maturity				

Cross-Cutting Themes

You likely noticed several overarching themes across the various models, theories, frameworks, and competencies that constitute effective leadership. Some themes, such as inspiration, ethics, and personal growth, have already been discussed for their benefits within this chapter. However, one theme, change and adaptability, offers yet another benefit for the public sector.

Change and Adaptability. Leadership in contemporary workplaces is characterized by change—driven by technological innovation, shifting employee expectations, and dynamic external pressures – and failing to adapt to hybridized work environments may lead to employee disengagement and burnout (Microsoft, 2022). Leaders who remain open to learning—by seeking new ideas, engaging in reflective practices, and systematically gathering feedback—are more adept at identifying emerging stressors and devising timely, context-specific solutions (Jacobs, 2021). Self-efficacy increases with continuous learning, with leaders becoming more adaptable and self-assured in managing high-stress scenarios and influencing how they address employee concerns, distribute workloads, and communicate organizational changes (Dandalt, 2024).

Over time, these learning-focused leaders foster a culture that prioritizes professional growth at every level, alleviating the stagnation and role ambiguity that often trigger burnout (Allison, 2024). Furthermore, continuous learning spurs innovation in managerial practices, which is necessary to address the multifaceted issue of burnout. Organizations frequently rely on standardized, one-size-fits-all solutions for a challenge that is inherently complex and dynamic. However, leaders who remain curious and open-minded are more likely to develop new approaches—such as flexible scheduling, participatory decision-making, or digital collaboration platforms—that effectively reduce work-related stress (Pladdys, 2024). When these initiatives are supported by ongoing feedback loops, employees feel both valued and engaged in the organization's evolution, thereby strengthening their commitment and reducing cynicism (Vranjes, Notelaers, & Salin, 2021).

Adapting to change also involves reevaluating leadership styles. Managers who initially adopt transactional approaches may, with experience, incorporate elements of transformational leadership, such as encouraging intellectual stimulation and offering individualized consideration (Bennis & Nanus, 2012). By embracing ongoing learning as a personal practice and organizational imperative, leaders can tackle burnout on multiple fronts, cultivating resilient teams well-equipped to cope with evolving workplace demands.

Case Study: Leadership Approaches in Action

John's Approach: Supportive & Collaborative Leadership. John has served as the environmental program director at a Department of Environmental Protection regional office for the past eight years. When tasked with rolling out a new sustainability initiative, John must figure out the best way to motivate and rally his staff in support of this new work. John begins by meeting with his team and presenting clear, fact-based evidence on the benefits of the initiative and how this initiative aligns with the department's mission, vision, and values. He provides data on environmental impacts, budget forecasts, and potential community benefits, ensuring that the team understands the importance and feasibility of the project. In the following weeks, John encourages two-way communication by organizing workshops, brainstorming sessions, and one-on-one meetings with all members of the team to discuss potential barriers and solutions.

By leveraging rational persuasion, consulting all team members, and making inspirational appeals, John fosters a sense of ownership and collective responsibility for the initiative. His team remains motivated, engaged, and committed, resulting in a successful project launch and high job satisfaction.

Christine's Approach: Authoritarian & Pressure-Based Leadership. As the Director of a State Emergency Management Agency, Christine has been responsible for disaster preparedness and response coordination for the past twenty years. While overseeing a new disaster preparedness initiative, she adopts a more rigid approach to building team motivation and engagement. Christine starts by convening a small, select group of the team to make key decisions. Shortly after, she emails her entire team outlining the initiative and providing strict deliverable deadlines. When employees raise concerns about the feasibility of the timeline, Christine responds that the deadlines are non-negotiable and warns of disciplinary action for non-compliance. Over the following weeks, she closely monitors progress but provides little additional support.

While Christine's team ultimately meets the deadlines, their work quality suffers due to time constraints and lack of engagement. The pressure-based approach fosters low morale, increased stress, and eventually leading to high burnout and turnover among employees.

Key Takeaways

- **John's leadership approach** fosters engagement, high performance, and resilience by ensuring employees feel valued and included.
- **Christine's leadership approach** increases stress, lowers motivation, and results in burnout, even if deadlines are met.

Professional Development

Naturally, not every individual in a workplace can hold a leadership title, but nearly all will benefit from leadership development for several reasons. As we discussed earlier, many individuals, particularly those new to their roles, leave or intend to leave as they cannot see pathways to progress within themselves or their organizations. Some employees may not have the necessary skills to lead or do their jobs effectively, also contributing to career stagnation. To combat this, leaders can build employee morale by implementing and encouraging opportunities for professional advancement, a key job resource that plays a role in burnout reduction while retaining a competent, skilled workforce.

Professional development is a continuous process of acquiring new skills, knowledge, and experiences to enhance one's career and personal growth. In the public sector, professional development is crucial as it equips employees with the necessary tools to meet the evolving demands of their roles, thereby improving the delivery of public services. It encompasses a wide range of activities, including training programs, workshops, mentorship, and formal education, all tailored to address the specific needs of public sector employees.

The benefits of professional development in the public sector are manifold. It fosters a more competent and efficient workforce capable of adapting to new technologies, regulations, and societal needs. By investing in the development of their employees, public sector organizations not only enhance service delivery but also boost employee morale and job satisfaction. Employees who feel supported in their career growth are more engaged, motivated, and committed to their roles, which in turn leads to better outcomes for the communities they serve.

The public sector often faces challenges such as high workloads, limited resources, and bureaucratic constraints, which can lead to stress and job dissatisfaction. By providing opportunities for career advancement and skill enhancement, professional development helps mitigate these stressors. Employees who see a clear path for advancement and feel equipped to handle their responsibilities are less likely to experience burnout. They are also more likely to remain in their positions longer, reducing turnover rates and the associated costs of recruiting and training new staff.

LEADERSHIP'S ROLE IN PREVENTING BURNOUT

So far, we have discussed a plethora of factors contributing to burnout, including many facets of leadership. We have also examined the role of leadership and professional development within the public sector. Leaders can either exacerbate burnout through restrictive, bureaucratic measures or alleviate it by modeling supportive, empowering behaviors that enhance engagement and resilience (Allison, 2024; Pladdys, 2024). The leadership approach used within an organization influences employee morale, work satisfaction, and long-term retention, ultimately determining organizational outcomes (Jacobs, 2021). Leadership, therefore, is not merely a managerial function but a transformative force that shapes organizational culture, fosters trust, and mitigates stress (Awashreh & AlGhunaimi, 2024). If effective leaders are trained in strategies grounded in emotional intelligence, adaptability, and clear communication, they can identify and address the early signs of burnout (Linos & Ruffini, 2019).

Before we move forward, it is important to separate the concept of leadership from our actual managers, leaders, and supervisors. The intent of this book chapter is to recognize the impact of leadership on burnout and explore the ways that leadership may be leveraged to reduce the prevalence and substantial impact burnout continues to cause within public offices, departments, and agencies. Indeed, public servants in leadership roles disproportionately suffer from burnout compared to non-leaders. For example, a recent Gallup poll estimates that approximately 35% of state, municipal, and federal workforce managers were experiencing burnout compared to 23% of "individual contributors" (Petrucelli & Ritz, 2024). Further, efforts must be made to avoid vilification of leaders who may be suffering from burnout as opposed to actively making decisions (or not making them) to create poor work environments that fuel the issue. Effectively combatting burnout in the public sector must be inclusive of all public servants.

How Leadership Can Mitigate Burnout

At its most basic level, leadership oversees the operations of an identified group of individuals to ensure activities are completed and goals are achieved. Therefore, the quality of the leader dictates the group's efficiency, and can influence the efficiency by providing workplace standards of conduct, defining the goals and values of the group, and ensuring collective harmony and group cohesion (Bodjrenou & Xu, 2018).

Earlier, we introduced the JD-R theory to conceptualize burnout within the public sector. Now, we can again look towards this theory to elucidate the role of the leader in each of these relationships. This insight will provide clarity on simple, strategic actions teams, departments, and even entire organizations can make to retain a healthy, engaged, and motivated workforce. The JD-R theory suggests that leadership plays a crucial role in balancing job demands and resources for employees.

Leaders Decrease Job Demands

As noted above, chronic work overload and staffing shortages are leading risk factors for burnout in government employees. Leaders and leadership both hold substantial capacity to mitigate these effects. In practice, leaders may:

- Implement two-way communication methods to identify employee's workplace issues, concerns, and obstacles.
- Provide opportunities for individuals and teams to share their stressful experiences and decompress from high job demands.
- Encourage healthy work-life balances.
- Develop robust conflict-management skills and processes.

Leaders have the ability to provide structure within the workplace, creating a more stable, less uncertain environment for their employees. Leaders can build structure by setting team goals, prioritizing projects and activities, setting deadlines, and providing feedback (Trummers & Bakker, 2021). Naturally, effective communication practices must be integrated into these processes for them to have a positive effect on employees. As we learned from John and Christine's leadership approaches, projects may be prioritized and deadlines may be set, but without effective two-way communication, leaders may exacerbate job demands rather than mitigate them. Dollard and Bailey (2021) found that training middle managers to foster psychological safety and reduce job stressors improved communication, commitment, and psychological safety even during the chaotic COVID-19 pandemic.

Leaders Increase Job Resources

Effective leadership acts as a key resource that influences the well-being and productivity of employees within the JD-R framework. Leaders have the organizational power to provide job resources such as support, feedback, and opportunities for development, assuaging job strain by reducing job demands (e.g., workload, pressure). Increasing job resources has been positively associated with work engagement, performance, and attitudes in public schools and the military (Breevaart et al., 2014a; Breevaart et al., 2014b; Fernet et al., 2015). Specifically, leaders can increase resources by:

- Provide opportunities in safe and supported environments for employees to tackle challenges and brainstorm innovative solutions.
- Meet one-on-one with employees to provide evaluative feedback, discuss goals, and assess psychological well-being related to the workplace.
- Offer opportunities for shadowing, mentoring, and other professional advancement opportunities.
- Implement or advocate for changes in organizational policies, structures, and processes to increase job resources (e.g., hiring more staff, reducing redundant/ineffective meetings).

Support from leaders can take many forms. Consideration of all employees via checking in, being responsive to concerns, or providing recognition of work achievements is one example of support (Trummers & Bakker, 2021). Cultivation of high-quality relationships between leaders and followers increases trust, job satisfaction, and performance while mitigating stress and turnover intentions (Ilies et al., 2007). Building support mechanisms between staff members and between leaders and staff members is an efficient, low-cost strategy that is often overlooked by leaders when looking for burnout mitigation strategies. Opportunities for training and development are significant job resources leaders can leverage as a retainment strategy. In fact, career development and advancement cited as one of the most important drivers of both employee attrition and retention (De Smet et al., 2022).

Essential Leadership Skills to Reduce Burnout

Burnout is not solely an individual issue—it is a structural and cultural challenge within organizations that stems from poor leadership strategies. Leaders who employ emotionally intelligent, transparent, and adaptable methods create environments where employees feel psychologically safe and supported. Effective leadership reduces burnout through key behaviors such as emotional intelligence, effective communication, strategic delegation, and boundary management.

Emotional Intelligence. One of the key leadership skills in burnout mitigation is emotional intelligence. Leaders who are adept at recognizing and regulating both their own emotions and those of their team members foster a climate of psychological safety, where employees feel comfortable sharing challenges and seeking help (Goleman, 1998; Jacobs, 2021). Such an environment is vital in preventing the sense of isolation that often precipitates burnout. Those who lead with empathy are also better able to encourage their subordinates to do the same (Gilin et al., 2023). By showing empathy, communicating attentively, and demonstrating genuine concern, emotionally intelligent leaders can reduce the stress and anxiety that come with high workloads and tight deadlines (Maslach et al., 2012).

Effective Communication. Effective communication requires more than just sending clear emails or conducting regular briefings. It involves transparency in decision-making, consistency in verbal and nonverbal cues, and a willingness to listen attentively to feedback from all levels of the organization (Pladdys, 2024). Through open dialogues about organizational changes, workload concerns, and potential stressors, leaders can engage employees in problem-solving and collaborative decision-making, strengthening their sense of autonomy and control (Allison, 2024). This enhanced autonomy has been linked to a reduction in emotional exhaustion and cynicism, both key components of burnout (Orgambídez-Ramos & Borrego-Alés, 2014).

Strategic Delegation. Overburdening high-performers while under-challenging less-experienced staff can create resentment and disengagement. Leaders who delegate tasks strategically—matching them to employees' strengths and professional growth needs—help prevent burnout and promote a learning culture that fosters innovation and engagement (Schaufeli & Buunk, 2003). By ensuring that responsibilities align with each team member's skill set, leaders help employees feel both supported and empowered, significantly lowering the risk of burnout.

Boundary Management. A significant contributor to burnout in today's workforce is the inability to disconnect from work. In an era of digital communication and remote or hybrid work environments, the lines between personal time and professional duties often blur. Leaders who set clear expectations about after-hours availability, encourage regular breaks, and model healthy boundary-setting are more likely to cultivate teams capable of sustaining energy and productivity (Microsoft, 2022; Truglia, 2024). Work environments that respect employees' personal time and well-being lead to higher satisfaction and reduced stress levels.

PROFESSIONAL ADVANCEMENT STRATEGIES FOR BURNOUT MITIGATION

Our journey thus far has clearly positioned leadership and professional development as some of the most effective long-term organizational strategies for mitigating burnout, enhancing workplace resilience, and cultivating a culture of sustained professional growth. They also represent initiatives that have not effectively been engrained into regular public sector processes. Despite the ongoing crisis caused by burnout and attrition, career development and leadership continue to be the only retention strategies lacking prioritization by State Chief Administrative Officers (National Association of State Chief Administrators & McKinsey & Company, 2023).

The lack of implementation of these strategies will continue to cause role stagnation, burnout, intent to leave, and attrition in employees, followed by work overload placed on those who remain, fueling the vicious cycle of burnout through entire teams and departments. As leadership demands evolve, organizations must implement structured training initiatives that not only equip individuals with the necessary skills to lead effectively but also contribute to long-term workforce well-being.

Leadership development within the public sector involves fostering the essential skills and competencies that empowers all public sector employees, from entry-level positions to managers and supervisors, to lead effectively and compassionately. By equipping leaders with the ability to inspire, motivate, and support their teams, organizations can create a work environment that prioritizes employee engagement and satisfaction. This, in turn, reduces the stress and dissatisfaction that often culminate in burnout. Moreover, leadership development programs promote a culture of continuous learning and adaptability, enabling public sector organizations to respond proactively to the dynamic challenges they face.

While leadership development programs are widely implemented, it must be understood that short-term interventions alone are insufficient in addressing burnout long-term. Studies show that effective burnout reduction requires ongoing leadership training, systemic workplace adjustments, and structured mentorship programs (Maslach et al., 2012; Truglia, 2024). Professional advancement opportunities create clear pathways for career growth and personal development. By offering training, mentorship, and diverse career trajectories, public sector organizations cultivate a sense of purpose and fulfillment, which in turn enhances employees' skillsets, motivation, and job satisfaction while reducing the incidence of burnout. Professional development provides employees with a sense of purpose and future orientation, fostering resilience and reducing turnover (Pijpker et al., 2019).

Additionally, strengthening both individual and organizational performance ensures the consistent delivery of high-quality public services that effectively meet community needs. However, persistent challenges in many public sectors continue to highlight a crucial yet unaddressed need for ongoing training and professional development. For instance, despite widespread acknowledgment of these gaps in health security and emergency management sectors, the failure to translate lessons learned into actionable improvements has created a cycle where the same shortcomings are repeatedly identified but never fully resolved. This lack of follow-through fosters frustration, disengagement, and declining morale among employees who see their professional growth neglected. Over time, the absence of meaningful investment in training and career development erodes institutional preparedness, weakens workforce resilience, and exacerbates burnout. Without a sustained commitment to professional advancement, public sector organizations risk not only losing experienced personnel to turnover but also diminishing their ability to respond effectively to crises, ultimately compromising the very communities they serve.

We have come to understand leadership, including its historical and theoretical underpinnings, and how leadership effectively overcomes burnout. We also discussed the need for organizational changes and professional advancement opportunities such as shadowing and mentoring. But what development tools can be used to build out a leadership development program? What about a professional development activity? To better understand how to establish an effective strategy, we must first understand the tools we can leverage and how they have been implemented to benefit the workplace.

Training

While some individuals may naturally possess strong leadership abilities, formal training is essential for ensuring that leaders are equipped with the tools to mitigate burnout effectively. Without proper training, leaders may inadvertently adopt authoritarian or disengaged leadership styles that increase stress and turnover. Comprehensive organizational change also often requires structured programs that integrate these skills into the broader workplace culture. Leadership training programs are foundational in this effort, equipping current and emerging leaders with the knowledge and competencies needed to recognize burnout risks and implement proactive interventions (Dandalt, 2024). According to Flaig, formal leadership development programs indicated an increase in confidence across many functions, including the ability to lead staff and manage projects. Further, these results suggest an increase in confidence, a new way of thinking, and increased adaptability (Flaig et al., 2020). This adaptability finding is pivotal to sustaining mental wellness and career growth while working in high-stress or emergency-related positions.

These initiatives may range from short-term immersive workshops focusing on emotional intelligence to more extended programs that integrate peer coaching, reflective assignments, and ongoing assessments of workforce well-being. Tailoring training modules to specific workplace environments is critical. For example, in a nonprofit human services agency, training might emphasize resource prioritization and self-care strategies for social workers dealing with high emotional labor. In contrast, a government agency, such as a municipal emergency management office, might focus on crisis decision-making, stakeholder negotiation, and public accountability (Allison, 2024). Public sector leadership training programs must address unique challenges, such as rigid bureaucratic structures, political pressures, and constrained budgets, to ensure they are practical and impactful. Organizations that invest in leadership development—particularly in emotional intelligence, communication, and work-life balance strategies—see lower burnout rates, higher job satisfaction, and improved organizational resilience. Leadership training programs should focus on:

- Recognizing early signs of burnout and addressing them proactively.
- Developing emotional intelligence and interpersonal skills to foster psychological safety.
- Creating transparent and inclusive communication channels.
- Implementing strategies for boundary-setting and work-life balance.

Effective Leadership Training Methods

Leadership training programs vary in structure and implementation, ranging from traditional classroom instruction to immersive, hands-on learning approaches. Historically, many organizations have relied on passive instructional methods, such as lectures and theoretical case studies, which often fail to translate into practical, long-term leadership effectiveness. However, research demonstrates that methodologies such as action learning, structured leadership workshops, and meta-analytic training frameworks offer more effective solutions for building leadership capacity and addressing workplace stressors (Lacerenza, Reyes, Marlow, Joseph, & Salas, 2017; Sogunro, 1997; Hess, 2020).

Action learning involves training leaders through real-world problem-solving, where they work on actual workplace challenges rather than hypothetical scenarios. In a public sector context, this could involve city planners and emergency managers developing a response plan for a major disaster, receiving structured feedback from mentors, and refining their approach in real time. Structured leadership workshops, such as those conducted in federal agencies like FEMA or the National Institutes of Health (NIH), provide immersive training experiences where participants engage in crisis simulations, policy negotiations, and strategic decision-making exercises (Skipton & Lang, 2010; Willgerodt et al., 2020).

Integrating Burnout Mitigation in Public Sector Training

Future leadership training initiatives should integrate digital tools, remote collaboration strategies, and resilience training to equip leaders with the skills necessary to manage the evolving workforce landscape. Research (Pladdys, 2024; Truglia, 2024) suggests that burnout mitigation must be a central component of leadership development. Programs incorporating mindfulness training, stress management techniques, and emotional intelligence development have demonstrated promise in reducing workplace stress and improving leadership effectiveness.

For example, public health departments implementing burnout prevention training can incorporate resilience-building strategies into their onboarding and ongoing professional development programs. One effective approach is peer-coaching circles, where leaders engage in guided discussions about workplace challenges and collaborate on solutions. This technique has been successfully implemented in healthcare leadership training to improve well-being and organizational performance. Similarly, emergency management agencies could introduce scenario-based resilience training, preparing leaders for high-pressure decision-making while reinforcing stress management techniques.

Training Success and Implementation Strategies

Sogunro (1997) conducted a comprehensive evaluation of a longstanding leadership training program, underscoring the importance of multi-method assessment approaches in evaluating training efficacy. His findings indicate that leadership programs yield optimal outcomes when they integrate:

- Pre-training preparation (assessing baseline leadership competencies),
- Structured workshops (using case studies, crisis simulations, and interactive problem-solving),
- Post-training evaluation (measuring leadership growth and workplace impact), and
- Ongoing follow-up assessments (mentorship, peer evaluations, and continued education).

For example, in government agencies managing public services, structured feedback loops could involve periodic performance evaluations, where trained leaders are assessed on their ability to manage stress, resolve conflicts, and implement strategic initiatives. In local emergency management agencies, iterative learning cycles—where participants apply training concepts in disaster response exercises and then refine their approaches through structured reflection have shown success in improving crisis leadership competency and reducing burnout rates.

Hess (2020) expands on this notion by addressing the challenges faced by technical professionals, such as engineers or emergency response coordinators, when transitioning into leadership roles. Many public sector leadership programs focus on high-level policy and decision-making but neglect interpersonal skills critical for team management, such as conflict resolution, delegation, and effective communication. Training models tailored for public sector leaders should integrate scenario-based learning, interactive problem-solving exercises, and personalized feedback mechanisms to ensure the simultaneous development of both technical expertise and managerial competencies.

Case Study: Boeing and Public Sector Applications

Boeing has long recognized leadership development as essential to both organizational success and employee well-being. The company integrated action learning into its leadership training framework, equipping employees with hands-on problem-solving capabilities in high-pressure environments. Through immersive learning experiences, emerging leaders collaborated with senior executives to address real-world organizational challenges, reinforcing a culture of accountability and strategic thinking (Leonard & Lang, 2010).

Public sector agencies can adapt Boeing's model to fit their own needs. For instance, a state emergency management office could implement an incident leadership development program, where emerging leaders work alongside senior crisis managers to develop response plans for simulated disasters. Participants would analyze real-world disaster data, design response strategies, and test their effectiveness in controlled exercises.

However, Boeing's experience also highlights a common pitfall: the lack of sustained reinforcement. Studies indicate that while initial improvements in leadership competency were significant, without ongoing mentorship and structured follow-up, the long-term benefits of training diminished over time. This underscores the necessity of embedding leadership training into an organization's broader talent development strategy, ensuring that leadership development is treated as a continuous learning journey rather than a one-time event.

Mentorship and Peer Support

In the public sector, mentorship and peer support play a crucial role in leadership development, knowledge transfer, and employee resilience. These programs go beyond informal guidance by offering structured, goal-oriented frameworks that help employees navigate high-pressure environments, complex bureaucratic systems, and leadership responsibilities. Public sector mentorship and peer support programs have been shown to improve decision-making, reduce burnout, improve employee retention, and strengthen leadership pipelines to create a more resilient workforce (Allison, 2024; Day et al., 2014; Orgambídez-Ramos & Borrego-Alés, 2014).

Public Sector Mentorship

Mentorship is a structured professional relationship where an experienced individual (mentor) provides guidance, feedback, and career support to a less experienced individual (mentee). Unlike casual workplace interactions, mentorship programs have defined objectives, scheduled check-ins, and clear accountability measures (Dandalt, 2024). These programs help mentees gain deeper insights into organizational culture, develop leadership skills, and prepare for career advancement.

Example: Federal Emergency Management Agency's Peer-to-Peer Mentoring Program. The Federal Emergency Management Agency (FEMA) operates a structured Peer-to-Peer Mentoring Program to help employees develop leadership skills, manage stress, and navigate the challenges of emergency management. This initiative pairs experienced FEMA professionals with newer employees, providing mentorship that enhances problem-solving abilities, professional resilience, and institutional knowledge (FEMA, 2020). FEMA's mentorship framework emphasizes:

- Regular one-on-one meetings – These scheduled sessions provide mentees with a structured space to discuss challenges, seek advice, and receive constructive feedback. Unlike informal workplace discussions, these meetings follow a strategic approach that ensures mentees are progressing toward professional growth and leadership readiness.
- Defined milestones and competency tracking – FEMA sets clear performance and leadership milestones to help mentees measure their progress. These could include mastering interagency collaboration, understanding FEMA's disaster response framework, or developing crisis communication skills. Progress tracking ensures that the mentorship is not just advisory but results-driven.
- Disaster response leadership development – Mentees receive firsthand insights into FEMA's incident command structures, disaster recovery operations, and coordination with local, state, and federal agencies. This practical exposure helps them build confidence and decision-making capabilities in high-pressure situations.

FEMA integrates mentorship into leadership development programs such as the Emergency Management Institute's (EMI) Advanced Leadership Series, where aspiring leaders are paired with seasoned professionals to gain hands-on leadership experience (FEMA, 2020).

Public Sector Peer Support

Peer support refers to employee-to-employee support systems where colleagues provide guidance, stress management strategies, and shared problem-solving. Unlike mentorship, which follows a hierarchical structure, peer support emphasizes mutual learning and collective resilience (Day et al., 2014). Strong peer networks serve as a buffer against workplace stress and help employees navigate challenging professional situations.

Example: FEMA's Peer Support Networks. FEMA has implemented formal peer support programs to help employees manage the emotional and psychological toll of disaster response work. These programs include:

- Crisis Peer Support Teams – Following major disaster deployments, FEMA organizes structured peer debriefings where employees discuss their experiences, process stress, and receive guidance from colleagues who have faced similar challenges. These debriefings provide a psychological outlet and help prevent long-term burnout (FEMA, 2020).
- FEMA Employee Assistance Program (EAP) – This peer-driven initiative offers confidential counseling, crisis intervention, and mental health resources to employees dealing with stress, trauma, or burnout. Unlike traditional HR-led mental health programs, EAP is designed to be easily accessible, reducing stigma around seeking help in high-pressure work environments (FEMA, 2020).
- Workplace Resilience Initiatives – FEMA's Workplace Resilience Program provides employees with self-care training, resilience-building exercises, and peer-led workshops focused on stress management. This program ensures that support structures extend beyond crisis events and are embedded into the agency's daily work culture (FEMA, 2020).

Career Development

In parallel, career development programs address another frequent contributor to burnout: the sense of stagnation that arises when employees perceive no viable pathways for advancement (Maslach et al., 2012). By outlining transparent progression trajectories and offering skill-building or rotation opportunities, organizations demonstrate a commitment to their employees' long-term success (Pladdys, 2024). These programs reinforce a sense of purpose and forward momentum, both of which counteract the disillusionment that can lead to exhaustion and cynicism. When public sector workers engage in structured professional development programs that provide hands-on experience, they are more likely to develop the confidence and skill sets necessary to manage workplace challenges effectively. In contrast, environments that lack such opportunities may leave employees feeling stagnant, disconnected, and ultimately more susceptible to burnout.

Continuous learning is another critical factor in burnout prevention. The ability to adapt to new challenges and expand one's competencies fosters a sense of growth and purpose in the workplace (Day et al., 2014). Public sector organizations can mitigate burnout by encouraging lifelong learning through training programs, leadership workshops, and cross-functional collaboration opportunities. Employees who perceive a clear trajectory for career advancement and professional enrichment are more likely to remain engaged and motivated in their roles.

Career Development Case Study. To illustrate the impact of career development programs, let's consider a hypothetical case in a state-level Emergency Preparedness and Response Department, which is responsible for disaster response coordination, crisis communication, and preparedness training across multiple jurisdictions. Recently, the department has seen an increase in employee turnover and declining morale, particularly among mid-career emergency planners who feel stuck in routine roles without clear advancement opportunities. Recognizing the need for structured career development, leadership within the department launches the Emergency Management Career Advancement Program (EMCAP): a professional development initiative designed to provide growth opportunities, skill expansion, and leadership preparation.

EMCAP focuses on three strategic components:

1. Skill-Building and Cross-Training: Employees gain experience in different emergency management functions, such as disaster logistics, hazard mitigation planning, and federal grant administration.
2. Professional Certification and Credentialing Support: SEMA provides financial and logistical assistance for employees pursuing the Certified Emergency Manager (CEM), FEMA Professional Development Series (PDS), and other industry-recognized credentials.
3. Leadership Pipeline Program: Mid-career professionals participate in a structured leadership track, where they receive mentorship, lead cross-agency projects, and engage in scenario-based decision-making exercises.

Emily, a disaster recovery specialist at SEMA, has spent the past five years conducting damage assessments and coordinating financial aid requests for disaster-stricken communities. While Emily is passionate about emergency management, she feels professionally stagnant and disconnected from other aspects of disaster response operations. Through EMCAP, Emily enrolls in a cross-training rotation that allows her to work with the disaster logistics division, where she assists in deploying resources to affected areas. During this rotation, she develops expertise in supply chain management for emergency response, a field she had little prior exposure to. Encouraged by this experience, Emily takes advantage of her department's certification support program and begins preparing for the Certified Emergency Manager (CEM) exam. With access to study resources, mentorship from senior emergency managers, and a financial stipend for exam fees, she successfully earns her credential—qualifying her for a new role overseeing logistics operations during major disasters.

Meanwhile, Chris, a mid-career hazard mitigation specialist, participates in the department's Leadership Pipeline Program. He is paired with a senior policy advisor who helps him develop the strategic and interpersonal skills needed for management positions. As part of the program, Chris leads a cross-agency initiative to improve floodplain management policies, gaining valuable leadership experience and policy expertise. By the end of the program, Chris is offered a promotion to Deputy Director of Hazard Mitigation, a position he once believed was out of reach. Through structured skill-building, credentialing support, and leadership development, EMCAP helps employees like Emily and Chris reignite their professional motivation while preparing them for career advancement.

This scenario demonstrates how career development programs can transform workplace culture by providing employees with meaningful opportunities for skill expansion and leadership growth. Through structured job rotations, certification support, and leadership preparation, public sector organizations can combat stagnation, reduce burnout, and improve employee retention. As illustrated by the department's Emergency Management Career Advancement Program, professional development initiatives empower employees to take ownership of their careers while ensuring that public sector agencies maintain a resilient, highly skilled workforce prepared to meet evolving challenges.

Considerations for Public Sector Strategies

In mission-driven settings such as public-sector agencies, the synergy of training, mentorship, and career development is particularly potent (Allison, 2024). Leaders in these environments must often reconcile efficiency mandates with humanitarian or community-focused objectives. By designing programs that emphasize both operational skills (e.g., financial management, policy adherence) and mission-oriented values (e.g., client satisfaction, public service ethics), organizations enable managers to balance competing demands without succumbing to chronic stress (Dandalt, 2024). This alignment between professional development and organizational identity not only buffers against burnout but also enhances employee loyalty and team cohesion.

Taken together, training, mentorship, and career development form an ecosystem that supports leaders in recognizing and mitigating burnout at multiple levels. When these initiatives are embedded into everyday organizational processes, rather than administered sporadically, leaders at all tiers become adept at identifying early burnout signs, managing role demands, and fostering a workplace culture where well-being is a continuous priority. By embedding mentorship and peer support structures into the workplace, agencies can ensure that employees at all levels are prepared to handle challenges effectively. Key strategies for strengthening mentorship and peer support include:

- Formalizing mentorship structures: Public sector organizations can follow FEMA's model by integrating mentorship into employee training programs. This includes setting clear expectations, training mentors, and ensuring that mentees receive consistent and constructive guidance (FEMA, 2020). Agencies should create a standardized mentorship framework that includes competency-based learning and career development roadmaps.
- Encouraging peer-led resilience initiatives: Agencies should develop structured peer support programs to address mental health challenges, stress management, and crisis fatigue. FEMA's success with its Crisis Peer Support Teams and EAP program demonstrates how public agencies can implement peer support systems that provide immediate and long-term emotional assistance (FEMA, 2020).
- Embedding self-reflection into professional development: Organizations can incorporate coaching sessions, leadership journaling, and periodic evaluations that emphasize both career growth and well-being (Dandalt, 2024). FEMA integrates self-reflection exercises into its leadership programs, helping employees assess their own leadership style, stress responses, and personal resilience strategies.

Through such systemic and sustained efforts, organizations cultivate leaders who are not only skilled and adaptable but also committed to preserving a mission-driven environment in which employees can thrive. Dandalt (2024) examines the implementation of governmental leadership training in the United States, emphasizing the need for leadership competency in high-pressure decision-making roles. Programs such as the Federal Executive Institute (FEI) and various state-run leadership academies focus on developing leaders capable of navigating complex bureaucratic challenges while maintaining workforce engagement. By incorporating structured mentorship, peer networking, and iterative training, these programs effectively prevent burnout among government employees, who often contend with high workloads and organizational stressors.

It is paramount to cultivate an approach that is both industry-specific and long-term in focus. Empirical research demonstrates that structured leadership programs, when designed with iterative learning, hands-on application, and tailored industry considerations, have the potential to significantly reduce workplace stress and foster resilience among leaders and their teams. Future policies should emphasize mandatory integration of leadership development into organizational frameworks, structured mentorship programs to reinforce learning beyond initial training, adaptive training modules that reflect industry-specific challenges, and continuous assessment and refinement of leadership initiatives based on employee feedback. Without sustained investment and continuous adaptation, even the most well-designed leadership programs risk obsolescence over time.

GUIDING PRINCIPLES FOR PROGRAM DEVELOPMENT

Throughout this chapter we have discussed the utility of leadership and how to leverage it to improve the public sector and mitigate burnout within its workforce. But how can the public sector develop a program that builds leaders, provides professional advancement opportunities, and reduces employee burnout? Consider Table 5's guiding principles and considerations when building out and overseeing any programs.

Table 5. Program development phases, key concepts, and actions

Program Development Phase	Concept	Action
Conceptualization	Needs Assessment	Examine the current workplace environment, employee needs, and organizational gaps.
Conceptualization	Strategic Alignment	Ensure that the program supports the organization's strategic goals and addresses specific leadership or professional development gaps.
	Definition of Clear Objectives	Set measurable goals for the program, such as improving leadership skills, enhancing team performance, or increasing employee engagement.
	Definition of Target Audience(s)	Choose participants based on potential and readiness for leadership development, not just current position or performance.
Program, Curricula, & Activity Development	Customize Learning Experiences	Tailor the program to address the needs of different leadership levels and learning styles.
	Integrate Multi-Level Strategy	Utilize training, mentoring, peer support, and career development activities to increase efficacy.
	Incorporate a Mix of Learning Modalities	Combine workshops, e-learning, on-the-job training, and mentoring to create a comprehensive program.
	Involve Leadership	Engage senior leaders as sponsors or mentors to provide real-world insights and support.
Program Implementation, Measurement, & Improvement	Measure Impact	Regularly assess the program's effectiveness through feedback, performance metrics, and business outcomes.
	Adaptability & Continuous Improvement	Be prepared to adjust the program based on feedback and changing organizational needs.

Conceptualization

A generic program generates generic leaders and results. You must rely on understanding why an intervention is needed and align its goals to these identified needs. This is formally known as a "needs assessment," described as a systematic process to determine and address gaps between current conditions and desired outcomes. A needs assessment can take many forms, including surveys, interviews, focus groups, and observations, among others. We encourage you to use evidence-based tools during this data-gathering phase to firmly establish your team needs. Mind Garden, a non-profit dedicated to developing products related to leadership and burnout and best known for their Maslach Burnout Inventory tool, offers an extensive tool inventory to measure individual, interpersonal, and organizational workplace indicators (Mind Garden, n.d.).

We would further recommend that the leadership program and curriculum be informed by practitioners both within the agency and across various partners. This would allow for a better understanding of the true needs in practice beyond the possible culture and limitations of a single department or agency. Again, this fosters trust and shows further investment in the personnel entering or being recommended to the program. From the needs assessment, you will be able to determine who would benefit from the program and in which ways they may benefit. Identification of these target audiences and a basic understanding of the needs will allow you to begin to tailor your objectives more appropriately. Informing your program based on the stated needs of your team and the results of these assessments will substantially improve its relevance and utility.

To build support and buy-in from higher ups, you must assess how the results of your needs assessment align with the strategic goals of your team, department, or organization. If there is no strategic alignment, the program will likely not be approved by leadership. Brainstorm how aspects of the program can influence burnout can be used to highlight the utility of a program. A few possible examples taken from this chapter include:

- Reduced absenteeism and attrition will reduce the costly process of hiring replacements while boosting performance and client satisfaction.
- Increased workforce competence and skills improve performance and provides succession planning by building the leadership pipelines.
- Cultivating effective leaders can improve workforce efficiency by inspiring employees, finding innovative solutions, and building team cohesion.

The next step involves defining clear objectives that will lay the groundwork for measuring your program's impact. These measurable outcomes should align with your strategic organizational goals identified in the previous step and encompass three distinct areas: learner experience, job performance, and organizational impact (Foster, 2024). We recommend taking time to develop each objective using the SMART goal framework, a well-known strategy to develop clear and achievable objectives. The SMART acronym encourages all objectives to be:

- Specific – Clearly define what is to be achieved, who is involved, where it will happen, and why it is important.
- Measurable – You will need to include criteria for tracking progress and determining when a goal has been accomplished. This will likely include quantitative or qualitative measures to assess programmatic success.

- Achievable – Consider all of your resources and constraints to determine what is realistic and attainable for your objective. Ideally, your objective should be challenging yet feasible to accomplish.
- Relevant – Your objective should a) align with the stated goals, gaps, and needs that will inform your program, and b) show significance to the target audience and organization. It must be worthwhile and have a clear purpose.
- Time-bound – The most straightforward piece, your objective should have a specified time frame for completion.

With a solid conceptual plan and support for the program, you will now be able to build out the activities, strategies, and interventions of your program curriculum.

Curriculum Development

When developing a program with a goal of burnout reduction, it is important to recognize burnout as a function of individual, team, and organizational factors acting on and influencing each other over time (Bakker & Demerouti, 2018). Therefore, we highly suggest any burnout reduction program driven by leadership development should not be siloed to impact just one level of the organizational system. A growing body of literature suggests that to improve the reach and sustainability of a leadership program, there must be an emphasis on developing the target audience as well as the key influencers that will impact the target audience (Raver et al., 2022), underscoring the importance of a mentorship element. Leadership training for the target audience alone has been shown to fail over time. As previously discussed, differing training modalities are useful for different sectors, and multiple methods should be employed for any program. Review the above section on methods to further refine your plans.

It is critical to receive support across the various levels of your agency – both horizontally and vertically – to ensure the training is positioned for success. If targeting the mid-level, emerging leader, then engaging supervisors overseeing them would not only be a crucial step to secure time within work hours to engage with the program activities while also eliciting mentorship opportunities beyond the current supervisory relationship. Professional development in this manner cannot be expected on the employees' own time; instead, consider having a window of protected time for the employee to participate fully and securely without interruption. This shows investment in them, trust in them, and support for their growth.

Program Implementation, Measurement, & Improvement

The work does not end once you begin the program. An effective program relies on continuous progress measurement and quality improvement processes. The goal should be routine data gathering and analysis to inform how to improve program relevance, utility, and efficacy. Aim to gather feedback from those taking the program on a consistent basis, using anonymous methods where needed.

Case Study: The Region 6 Public Health Leadership Institute

The Region 6 South Central Public Health Training Center launched the Region 6 Public Health Leadership Institute (R6-PHLI) in Fall 2023. The purpose of R6-PHLI remains to develop the next generation of leaders in public health by providing an opportunity for strategic professional growth for those interested in refining their leadership skills and advancing their career to the next level. The R6-PHLI decided the focus on mid-management emerging leaders, making applicants aware that the program is not intended for senior executives.

R6-PHLI was intentionally designed to create a learning community that would explore timely leadership topics and build core skills necessary to thrive as a leader. The sessions used interactive discussions with leaders in the field and were reinforced through practice activities led by seasoned experts each bi-weekly meeting. Each accepted member of the annual cohorts was required to provide the R6-PHLI team with letters from immediate superiors or supervisors indicating approval for the participating employee to join this critical professional development during work hours.

Importantly, because the R6-PHLI was established to strengthen the leadership of emerging leaders in U.S. HHS region 6 states (Arkansas, Louisiana, Oklahoma, New Mexico, and Texas), the curriculum was developed using annual focus groups and key informant interviews with senior leaders across these states to identify the leadership skills needed to thrive in the public health sector. Across the U.S., other regional institutes were established, each emphasizing adaptive leadership across the training program (Brandert et al., 2022). These programs conducted extensive evaluation based on Kirkpatrick's levels of evaluation and collected common metrics, resulting in demonstrable high levels of satisfaction from participants and home agency and among others, improvement of subject matter understanding (Brandert et al., 2022) and ability to implement.

Prior to the start of each cohort in the R6-PHLI, applicants complete a self-assessment for emotional intelligence (EI) to foster a better understanding of personal emotions and how they impact others, develop awareness of self-regulation and responses to emotions, improve motivation toward goals when facing negative emotions, increase empathy and appreciation for how others feel, and to improve social skills to elicit a positive response from others. Following this extensive assessment, each participant met one-on-one with a professional leadership counselor to interpret and discuss each participant's EI results. This element directly aligns with the current literature suggesting the need to become better aware of personal emotions and well-being in order to project effective leadership and improve decision-making, especially in high-stress incidents (Yemiscigil et al., 2022). The individual session allowed for the participants to learn more about themselves and how provided a launching point from which the remainder of the program could be viewed.

The curriculum for R6-PHLI continues to focus on timely issues and practical applications for current managers or team leads who are positioned to soon become leaders and decision-makers. These topics, while flexible across annual cohorts, included both crisis leadership and crisis communications. As Helm-Murtagh and Erwin posit, leading effectively in the current public health environment requires crisis leadership skills, including the ability to clearly articulate messaging in order to build trust and accountability (Helm-Murtagh and Erwin, 2024).

Public health cannot accomplish its mission alone. The United States spent $3.8 trillion on health in 2019 but only 2.6% was directed to public health and prevention and it is estimated that state and local health departments need an additional 80,000 full-time positions to provide essential services. Accounting for much of this gap, the state workforce declined by 10% and the local workforce declined by more than 15% from 2012-2022 (Brandert et al., 2022). Partnerships are required and remain paramount to success. However, forging, facilitating, and promoting partnerships at this level requires systems thinking, which DeSalvo and Kadakia included as one of the core dimensions of Public Health 3.0 (Helm-Murtagh & Erwin, 2024).

While curricula germane to the needs of the agency or area delivering the leadership development remains flexible and individualized as needed, it is important to recognize these elements as directly and peripheral to addressing burnout concerns.

SUMMARY

Burnout will remain a significant burden on the public sector until we create innovative solutions to combat its root causes. Providing opportunities for all levels of staff, employees and leaders alike, is one such solution that is low-cost and high-reward. Workplaces that continue to invest in their employees will reap the rewards of reduced staff turnover and enhanced work engagement, job performance, and public service. Implementing a leadership development program can (and should) take many forms to truly be effective within the public sector. Burnout does not have to continue its vicious cycle through the public sector; we have the tools to disrupt its destruction through the individuals we already employ.

REFERENCES

Allison, E. E. (2024). *Does Structural Empowerment Mitigate Organizational Burnout? A Qualitative Exploration of the Relationship Between Managerialism and Burnout Among Middle Managers in Two Nonprofit Human Service Agencies* (Order No. 31236335). [Doctoral dissertation, San Diego State University]. ProQuest Dissertations & Theses Global. http://libproxy.tulane.edu:2048/login?url=https://www.proquest.com/dissertations-theses/does-structural-empowerment-mitigate/docview/3040227374/se-2

Asplund, J., & Tatel, C. (2023, March 22). *Fighting burnout with strengths.* CliftonStrengths. https://www.gallup.com/cliftonstrengths/en/472067/fighting-burnout-strengths.aspx

Bakker, A. B., & Demerouti, E. (2018). Multiple levels in job demands-resources theory: implications for employee well-being and performance. In Diener, E., Oishi, S., & Tay, L. (Eds.), *Handbook of well-being*. DEF Publishers., https://research.tue.nl/files/116456879/Multiple_Levels_in_Job_Demands_Resources_Theory_Implications_for_Employee_Well_being_and_Performance.pdf

Bandura, A. (1977). Self-efficacy: Toward a unifying theory of behavioral change. *Psychological Review*, *84*(2), 191–215. DOI: 10.1037/0033-295X.84.2.191 PMID: 847061

Bennis, W., & Nanus, B. (2012). *Leaders: strategies for taking charge [Second edition]* 9780061762505, 0061762504. Dokumen.pub. https://dokumen.pub/leaders-strategies-for-taking-charge-second-edition-9780061762505-0061762504.html

Bodjrenou, K., & Xu, M. (2018). Review of recent developments in leadership theories. *Open Journal of Social Sciences*, *6*(7), 180–188. DOI: 10.4236/jss.2018.67014

Brandert, K., Alperin, M., Lloyd, L. M., Rose, B., Bekemeier, B., Rogers, M., & Grimm, B. (2022). Learning to lead: 3 Models to support public health leadership development. *Journal of Public Health Management and Practice*, *28*(S5), S203–S211. DOI: 10.1097/PHH.0000000000001519 PMID: 35867490

Breevaart, K., & Bakker, A. B. (2018). Daily job demands and employee work engagement: The role of daily transformational leadership behavior. *Journal of Occupational Health Psychology*, *23*(3), 338–349. DOI: 10.1037/ocp0000082 PMID: 28358569

Breevaart, K., Bakker, A. B., Demerouti, E., Sleebos, D. M., & Maduro, V. (2014a). Uncovering the underlying relationship between transformational leaders and followers' task performance. *Journal of Personnel Psychology, 13*(4), 194–203. DOI: 10.1027/1866-5888/a000118

Breevaart, K., Bakker, A. B., Hetland, J., Demerouti, E., Kjellevoldd-Olsen, O., & Espevik, R. (2014b). Daily transactional and transformational leadership and daily employee engagement. *Journal of Occupational and Organizational Psychology, 87*(1), 138–157. DOI: 10.1111/joop.12041

Choi, R., Chowdhary, S., Erdmann, D., & Ward, T. (2023, March 17). Bridging the talent gap in state government postpandemic. *McKinsey & Company*. https://www.mckinsey.com/industries/public-sector/our-insights/bridging-the-talent-gap-in-state-government-postpandemic

Crosby, B. C., & Bryson, J. M. (2017). Why leadership of public leadership research matters: And what to do about it. *Public Management Review, 20*(9), 1265–1286. DOI: 10.1080/14719037.2017.1348731

Dandalt, E. (2024). Government-level public leadership development in the United States. *Australian Journal of Public Administration*, 1467-8500.12670. Advance online publication. DOI: 10.1111/1467-8500.12670

Day, D. V., Fleenor, J. W., Atwater, L. E., Sturm, R. E., & McKee, R. A. (2014). Advances in leader and leadership development: A review of 25 years of research and theory. *The Leadership Quarterly, 25*(1), 63–82. DOI: 10.1016/j.leaqua.2013.11.004

De Smet, A., Dowling, B., Hancock, B., & Schaninger, B. (2022, July 13). The Great Attrition is making hiring harder. Are you searching the right talent pools? *McKinsey & Company*. https://www.mckinsey.com/capabilities/people-and-organizational-performance/our-insights/the-great-attrition-is-making-hiring-harder-are-you-searching-the-right-talent-pools

Deci, E. L., & Ryan, R. M. (1985). *Intrinsic motivation and self-determination in human behavior*. Plenum. DOI: 10.1007/978-1-4899-2271-7

Dollard, M. F., & Bailey, T. (2021). Building psychosocial safety climate in turbulent times: The case of COVID-19. *The Journal of Applied Psychology, 106*(7), 951–964. DOI: 10.1037/apl0000939 PMID: 34383511

Federal Emergency Management Agency. (2020). *Peer-to-Peer Mentoring at FEMA: The What, Why, and How of Getting Involved: Monday Minute for June 22, 2020*. https://content.govdelivery.com/accounts/USDHSFEMA/bulletins/2920b4e

Fernet, C., Trépanier, S.-G., Austin, S., Gagné, M., & Forest, J. (2015). Transformational leadership and optimal functioning at work: On the mediating role of employees' perceived job characteristics and motivation. *Work and Stress*, *29*(1), 11–31. DOI: 10.1080/02678373.2014.1003998

Foster, D. (2024). How to create a successful leadership development program. *Harvard Business Publishing*. https://www.harvardbusiness.org/how-to-create-a-successful-leadership-development-program/

Gilin, D. A., Anderson, G. G., Etezad, S., Lee-Baggley, D., Cooper, A. M., & Preston, R. K. (2023). Impact of a Wellness Leadership Intervention on the Empathy, Burnout, and Resting Heart Rate of Medical Faculty. *Mayo Clinic Proceedings. Innovations, Quality & Outcomes*, *7*(6), 545–555. DOI: 10.1016/j.mayocpiqo.2023.09.005 PMID: 38075429

Helm-Murtagh, P. C., & Erwin, P. C. (2024). Building a new generation of public health leaders forged in a public health crisis. *American Journal of Public Health*, *114*(6), 626–632. DOI: 10.2105/AJPH.2024.307633 PMID: 38603662

Hess, D. W. (2020, June 22-26). *Technical Leadership Skills Development Through Interactive Workshops* [Conference session]. ASEE Virtual Conference. https://peer.asee.org/35288

Hofmeyer, A., Taylor, R., & Kennedy, K. (2020). Fostering compassion and reducing burnout: How can health system leaders respond in the Covid-19 pandemic and beyond? *Nurse Education Today*, *94*, 104502. DOI: 10.1016/j.nedt.2020.104502 PMID: 32980180

Ilies, R., Nahrgang, J. D., & Morgeson, F. P. (2007). Leader-member exchange and citizenship behaviors: A meta-analysis. *The Journal of Applied Psychology*, *92*(1), 269–277. DOI: 10.1037/0021-9010.92.1.269 PMID: 17227168

Jacobs, M. (2021). *The influence of leadership development and psychological capital on burnout and turnover* [Doctoral dissertation, Liberty University]. https://digitalcommons.liberty.edu/cgi/viewcontent.cgi?article=4045&context=doctoral

Judge, T. A., & Piccolo, R. F. (2004). Transformational and transactional leadership: A meta-analytic test of their relative validity. *The Journal of Applied Psychology*, *89*(5), 755–768. DOI: 10.1037/0021-9010.89.5.755 PMID: 15506858

Kapucu, N., & Van Wart, M. (2008). Making matters worse: An anatomy of leadership failures in managing catastrophic events. *Administration & Society*, *40*(7), 711–740. DOI: 10.1177/0095399708323143

Kolman, S. (2024). State actions to bolster the public health workforce. *National Conference of State Legislatures*. https://www.ncsl.org/health/state-actions-to-bolster-the-public-health-workforce

Kristensen, T. S., Borritz, M., Villadsen, E., & Christensen, K. B. (2007). The Copenhagen Burnout Inventory: A new tool for the assessment of burnout. *Work and Stress*, *19*(3), 192–207. DOI: 10.1080/02678370500297720

Lacerenza, C. N., Reyes, D. L., Marlow, S. L., Joseph, D. L., & Salas, E. (2017). Leadership training design, delivery, and implementation: A meta-analysis. *The Journal of Applied Psychology*, *102*(12), 1686–1718. DOI: 10.1037/apl0000241 PMID: 28749153

Leider, J. P., Yeager, V. A., Kirkland, C., Krasna, H., Hare Bork, R., & Resnick, B. (2023). The state of the US public health workforce: Ongoing challenges and future directions. *Annual Review of Public Health*, *44*(1), 323–341. DOI: 10.1146/annurev-publhealth-071421-032830 PMID: 36692395

Leiter, M. P., & Maslach, C. (1999). Six areas of worklife: A model of the organizational context of burnout. *Journal of Health and Human Services Administration*, *21*(4), 472–489. PMID: 10621016

Linos, E., & Ruffini, K. (2019). Belonging affirmation reduces employee burnout and resignations in front line workers. *ResearchGate*. https://doi.org/DOI: 10.13140/RG.2.2.21546.36801

Linos, E., Ruffini, K., & Wilcoxen, S. (2022). Reducing burnout and resignations among frontline workers: A field experiment. *Journal of Public Administration: Research and Theory*, *32*(3), 473–488. DOI: 10.1093/jopart/muab042

Maslach, C., & Schaufeli, W. (1993). Historical and Conceptual Development of Burnout. In Schaufeli, W., Maslach, C., & Marek, T. (Eds.), *Professional Burnout: Recent Developments in Theory and Research* (pp. 1–16). Taylor & Francis.

McDonald, R., Conant, D., & Marshall, A. (2020, April 20). A non-partisan model for developing public-service leaders. *Harvard Business Review*. https://hbr.org/2020/04/a-nonpartisan-model-for-developing-public-service-leadership

Microsoft. (2022). *Hybrid Work Is Just Work. Are We Doing It Wrong?*https://www.microsoft.com/en-us/worklab/work-trend-index/hybrid-work-is-just-work

Mind Garden. (n.d.). *List of psychological assessments*. https://www.mindgarden.com/14-our-products

NACCHO. (2022). 2020 forces of change: The COVID-19 edition. https://www.naccho.org/uploads/downloadable-resources/2020-Forces-of-Change-The-COVID-19-Edition.pdf

Newhouse, S. M. (2024). Burnout among government workers is decreasing but still high, according to new pulse survey data. https://www.govexec.com/workforce/2024/06/burnout-among-government-workers-decreasing-still-high/397392/

Northouse, G. Peter. (2022). *Leadership: Theory and practice* (9th Edition). Thousand Oaks: SAGE Publications.

Orgambídez-Ramos, A., & Borrego-Alés, Y. (2014). Empowering employees: Structural empowerment as antecedent of job satisfaction in university settings. *Psychological Thought*, *7*(1), 28–36. DOI: 10.5964/psyct.v7i1.88

Orr, J. M., & Leider, J. P. (2023). Voluntary separations and COVID-19: A snapshot of turnover intention in the federal workforce in the first year of the pandemic. *Journal of Public Health Management and Practice*, *29*(4), 442–445. DOI: 10.1097/PHH.0000000000001720 PMID: 36693625

Owen, C., Scott, C., Adams, R., & Parsons, D. (2015). Leadership in crisis: Developing beyond command and control. *Australian Journal of Emergency Management*, *30*(3), 15–19. https://hdl.handle.net/102.100.100/541400

Partnership for Public Service. (n.d.a) *Public Service Leadership Model.* https://ourpublicservice.org/public-service-leadership-institute/public-service-leadership-model/

Partnership for Public Service. (n.d.b). *Senior Executive Service: Trends over 25 years.* https://ourpublicservice.org/fed-figures/senior-executive-service-trends-over-25-years/

Partnership for Public Service. (n.d.c). *Public Service Leadership Model: Engaging others.* https://ourpublicservice.org/public-service-leadership-institute/public-service-leadership-model/engaging-others/

Petrucelli, L., & Ritz, M. (2024, March 25). *What is driving federal government burnout?* Gallup. https://www.gallup.com/workplace/612518/driving-federal-government-burnout.aspx

Pladdys, J. (2024). Mitigating workplace burnout through transformational leadership and employee participation in recovery experiences. *HCA Healthcare Journal of Medicine*, *5*(3). Advance online publication. DOI: 10.36518/2689-0216.1783 PMID: 39015600

Prati, G., & Pietrantoni, L. (2010). The relation of perceived and received social support to mental health among first responders: A meta-analytic review. *Journal of Community Psychology*, *38*(3), 403–417. DOI: 10.1002/jcop.20371

Raver, C., Ledford, A., Norton, M. (2022). A strategic organizational approach to developing leadership developers. Journal of Character and Leadership Development, 10(1), 15-28. - http://dx.doi.org/DOI: 10.58315/jcld.v10.253

Schaufeli, W. B. (2017). Applying the Job Demands-Resources model: A 'how to' guide to measuring and tackling work engagement and burnout. *Organizational Dynamics*, *46*(2), 120–132. DOI: 10.1016/j.orgdyn.2017.04.008

Schaufeli, W. B., & Buunk, B. P. (2003). *Burnout: An Overview of 25 Years of Research and Theorizing*. https://www.wilmarschaufeli.nl/publications/Schaufeli/181.pdf

Shawe, R., & McAndrew, I. R. (2023). Theories of leadership and emergency management. *Modern Economy*, *14*(6), 738–750. DOI: 10.4236/me.2023.146040

Skipton, L. H., & Lang, F. (2010). Leadership Development via Action Learning. *Advances in Developing Human Resources*, *12*(2), 225–240. DOI: 10.1177/1523422310367800

Sogunro, O. A. (1997). Impact of training on leadership development. *Evaluation Review*, *21*(6), 713–737. DOI: 10.1177/0193841X9702100605

Truglia, H. (2024). *Testing the effectiveness of the ImpACT Me burnout intervention for leaders*. https://library2.smu.ca/bitstream/handle/01/31963/Truglia_Holly_MASTERS_2024.pdf

Trummers, L. G., & Bakker, A. B. (2021). Leadership and Job Demands-Resources theory: A systematic review. *Frontiers in Psychology*, *12*, 722080. Advance online publication. DOI: 10.3389/fpsyg.2021.722080 PMID: 34659034

Van Wart, M. (2003). A comprehensive model of organizational leadership: The Leadership Action Cycle. *International Journal of Organization Theory and Behavior*, *7*(2), 173–208. DOI: 10.1108/IJOTB-07-02-2004-B002

Vranjes, I., Notelaers, G., & Salin, D. (2021). Putting workplace bullying in context: The role of high-involvement work practices in the relationship between job demands, job resources, and bullying exposure. *Journal of Occupational Health Psychology*, *27*(1), 136–151. DOI: 10.1037/ocp0000315 PMID: 34968115

Willgerodt, M. A., Abu-Rish Blakeney, E., Summerside, N., Vogel, M. T., Liner, D. A., & Zierler, B. (2020). Impact of leadership development workshops in facilitating team-based practice transformation. *Journal of Interprofessional Care*, *34*(1), 76–86. DOI: 10.1080/13561820.2019.1604496 PMID: 31039647

Yemiscigil, A., Born, D., Snook, S., & Pate, E. (2022). Authentic leader(ship) development and leaders' psychological well-being: An outcome-wide analysis. *Leadership and Organization Development Journal*, *43*(8), 1287–1307. DOI: 10.1108/LODJ-11-2021-0525

Chapter 3

Prevention Strategies of Emergency Management and Disaster Professionals Battling Burnout

Kesley Richardson
https://orcid.org/0009-0003-8251-6800
Texas Southern University, USA

Colby Cavanaugh
Georgetown University, USA

ABSTRACT

Burnout in the world of public services, particularly in emergency and disaster management, can be a paradox. Two standard modes of operations often exist, including steady state (blue sky) operations of prevention and planning activities amid conflicting priorities and politizing events and the activation (grey sky) operations of responding to incidents, disasters, and crises. These two high-stress modes of operation, coupled with added pressure from leadership and resource limitations, increase undue stress in a first responder environment without the protections and resources afforded most first responders. This chapter will review and discuss the background and causal impacts of burnout in emergency and disaster management, provide recommendations and strategies for prevention and recovery and evidence-based practices, and leave you with additional considerations for your jurisdiction, policies, and/or practices.

DOI: 10.4018/979-8-3373-0169-3.ch003

INTRODUCTION

Burnout within the public sector is an important issue that impacts the functions of public services and the continuity of community work. The effects of personal and community circumstances are often stressed and reflected during natural and human-caused disasters such as hurricanes and cyber-attacks, which heavily influence burnout. This issue is further compounded by public sector workers being exposed to high-stress environments when directly or indirectly responding to an incident, including workers in fire, law enforcement, and the hub of operations and planning, "Emergency Management." Emergency management evolved from Civil defense in the wake of the 2001 terrorist attacks and now serves as a critical cornerstone of community resilience and sustainability within an American context. This chapter will explore the background of emergency management and disaster services, the standard effects practitioners experience working through various incidents without immediate access to their families, and the influence such exposure and limited support have on burnout levels as emergency management and disaster service workers support the larger community's efforts to establish a 'new normal' after the incident. More specifically, exposure to high-stress situations often impacts thousands, if not millions, of lives at the intersection of professional advancement and mental health. Encouraging working through stress without proper care, addressing the core challenges, and allowing enough recovery time from planned and unplanned events is commonplace within the professional emergency and disaster service field. The nature of emergency and disaster service work in the public sector is community-oriented, which translates to professionals often prioritizing the needs of the community and response efforts over their individual needs as responders. These two methods of 'profession first, professional second' negatively influence burnout. This was reflected by the mass exodus of professionals during and after the COVID-19 pandemic globally. The issue was highlighted by the Domestic Preparedness Journal (DomPrep) written by Dr. Kesley Richardson, sponsored by the Texas Division of Emergency Management (TDEM), and later mentioned by Sonny Patel, Kim Guevara, and other in the Journal of Emergency Management (JEM) at the International Association of Emergency Managers (IAEM) 2023 International Convention in Long Beach, CA (Richardson, 2022 & Patel, S. S., Guevara, K., Hollar, T. L., Richard A. DeVito, J., & Erickson, T. B. 2023). . These examples highlight the importance of preventing burnout within the public sector of emergency management and disaster services. However, imbalanced prioritizing and exposure to high-stress environments are not the only issues this profession faces.

An additional issue within the emergency management and disaster service space is that the public sector professionals working within this space often have differing job protection statuses and health resources with varying benefits associated based on their interal agency policies. Some also have pseudo statuses that fluctuate and limit the support given to the "uniformed responders." This status depends on whether the department can extend certain benefits to the professional with or without the ability to be tied to a union or similar supportive organization. Sometimes, this is tied to the city, county, state, or federal agency the professional supports within an American context. Some agencies do not have roles specifically designated as emergency management focused, so responsibilities of these roles become other duties assigned to public sector workers who may not have interest, training, or background in emergency and disaster service efforts. The gap between professional investment and professional competency can lead to a sharper increase in burnout felt by individuals trying to support a function that requires specialized training in more than one area from an interdisciplinary approach. This issue also has health implications for the professionals, their family, their community, and their overall quality of work, which can lead to cascading impacts on the overall public health of a community. For example, first responders such as law enforcement and firefighters may be considered emergency managers or equivalents in many parts of the world. Still, emergency managers in the U.S. don't often receive similar 'first responder' designation or status. This is especially evident in the leading professional association of emergency managers in the U.S., where the lead trainer for the Certified Emergency Manager Commission does not recognize emergency managers as first responders (Lee-Spiewak, 2012). However, this is not true of all communities, made especially evident when reviewing the complexities of disaster work involving terrorism, healthcare, judicial, public health, critical and cyberinfrastructure, utilities, engineering, and other intersectional professions. Training, education, and experience all influence how and where emergency management responsibilities are woven into various roles that support the efforts of prevention, response, recovery, and mitigation in all communities. Even though most of the examples presented in this chapter will be from an American context, international examples will be included based on the literature to support a more diverse perspective on the impact and the strategies that can be leveraged.

The governmental structure, governance utilized, and personal and professional cultural differences must be considered internationally. Do some wellness approaches apply to the common practice within other countries, provinces, or cities? Do the respective countries have access to the same resources or abilities to allow additional support to disaster professionals supporting their communities before, during, and after disasters, planned events, or incidents? Frequently, there are limitations when working from an American context. Yet still, on occasion, there are also lessons to be identified from other countries in their approach to combating workforce burnout, and the approach to benefits supersede the American approach to this chronic issue. Within an international context, resources play a significant role in the discussion around prevention strategies that can be employed for burnout (Carod-Artal, F. J., & Vázquez-Cabrera, C., 2013). While being well-resourced is preferred, experiencing a lack of resources is more common across public sector professions in the United States and their global equivalents. Drawing from international and domestic examples, lived experience, and literature, this chapter aims to share identified practices for professionals to employ in their personal and professional environments. Additionally, with equal importance, this chapter will identify areas for further research engagement and exploration to support the development of literature within the intersection of emergency management and disaster service burnout in the public sector.

Alongside the effects of burnout on public sector professionals, there have been strides to improve the retention and application of burnout prevention programs and strategies to support the recovery and wellness of public sector employees. Some of these programs include but are not limited to emotional intelligence development, wellness programs, paid time off (PTO), flextime, paid incentives, access to mental health support, and/or scaled-down time before and after incidents and disasters. The programs and information are available. The issue within the emergency management and first responder paradigm is the intervention application of these programs throughout the organizations to support the everyday public sector professional to utilize and benefit from burnout relief. Decision-making issues and other forms of fatigue are exacerbated without adequate intention for burnout prevention. Intentional burnout prevention may also include other ways to alleviate pressure on public sector employees in different areas, such as creating a recreational and open environment for stress relief or supporting healthy work practices and work-life balance. One approach to burnout prevention, favored in this chapter as a leading strategy, will be developing and maintaining a wellness culture within professional organizations and public sector departments. This strategy is more than platitudes and must be integrated within an organization's fabric for success. The approach also creates a safe space to ask for help, seek aid, and utilize resources for mental reprieve under the pressures of public service work, especially within the high-stress environment of the emergency operations center, which serves as the everyday working space for emergency management and disaster professionals within an American context.

BACKGROUND

This chapter will explore ***Employee Benefits***, defined as "Elective compensation resources employers offer to promote employee health and wellness, satisfaction, productivity, and retention." These benefits may be offered in the form of an official benefits package in which an employee can leverage options such as medical insurance, dental insurance, vision insurance, paid time off (PTO), discounts, holidays, or other official policy-based programs for the employee as a "perk" of the job. Other benefits may not be policy-based, like the autonomy of planning the day, organizational support with a culture of continued learning, and room for leadership growth and development within the organization, which improves the individual professional. A mixture of policy and non-policy benefits can support the prevention of burnout in small and large organizations throughout the public sector. The contribution of a balanced benefit approach can have positive effects in preventing burnout but can also contribute to burnout if not leveraged appropriately. The stress felt by any employee, especially in emergency, disaster, and crisis management professionals globally, can tip the scales multiple ways toward or away from burnout, depending on an individual's leader and organizational policies. All countries, jurisdictions, governments, and communities are not created equally or equitably, and this fact ties back to the direct impacts of benefits to communities in times of need where emergency management professionals would respond and support benefit distribution from the federal government within an American context.

The idea of *Wellness Culture is also important,* which we define as "an individual's ability to integrate multifaceted well-being (physical, mental, emotional, etc.) in all aspects of the professional environment, including practices and policies that prioritize individual well-being and healthy work-life balance." Though closely related, *Organizational Culture* can often contradict wellness culture within agencies in every part of the world. We define it as "The culture of practices conducted within an organization which may or may not be directly expressed in policy, guidelines, or practice that is otherwise identified as everyday procedures or preferences accepted and expected within the organization." Where wellness culture is focused on the individual's abilities, organizational culture is focused on the organization's abilities. This idea of organizational culture is also identified in the Journal of Emergency Management 2023 article on *Surveying Mental Health Stressors of Emergency Management Professionals,* which shared that the "24x7x365 nature of disaster response and emergency management" can add additional pressures when including technology, communication, the demand of instantaneous information in communication advances (Patel et al., 2023). This is one example of how culture can be impacted, where developing a healthy organizational culture starts with the people and can be shaped by the policy, procedure, and established practices. Still, the support leaders put behind developing and maintaining organizational culture, such as funding, freedoms, and intentional recovery times, can significantly influence an individual's career progression and overall satisfaction with their work and professional environments.

EMERGENCY MANAGEMENT BURNOUT FROM AN AMERICAN PARADIGM

Due in part to changing global conditions and increasingly complex, interrelated hazards, the scope of emergency management roles in the United States is expanding rapidly and leading to employee burnout. Professionals in these roles face increased pressures and stress to perform in unknown environments, without adequate professional support systems, often in the face of conflicting priorities, and with minimal resources to address the long-term impacts on individual well-being. The effect on personal well-being can and has been shown to impact team and organizational well-being and performance if untreated or unrecognized (Shi et al., 2024). Large-scale incidents that define generations, such as the COVID-19 Pandemic, and record more frequent hurricanes setting global records are causing overwhelming working conditions that most professionals are not prepared to handle and may leave the profession due to managing (Remington et al., 2024). As evident in the long days, extended emergency operations, shifting cultural expectations, generational differences, and the broadening scope of responsibilities all lead to increased burnout (*Burnout Epidemic: International SOS Data Highlights Urgent Need for Action*, 2024). This can be seen, for example, within the SOS Risk Outlook report of 2024, which reviews the impacts on the global workforce and its multiple generational stages of flux.

While emergency management is a high-stress occupation due to the nature of the emergency response and high political pressures, employers can implement multiple strategies and options in the professional environment to help invest in employees, reduce burnout turnover, and increase retention. Such investments are critical for the success of both the experienced and the organization. There are three key areas of investment/strategies:

Figure 1. Strategies to combat burnout

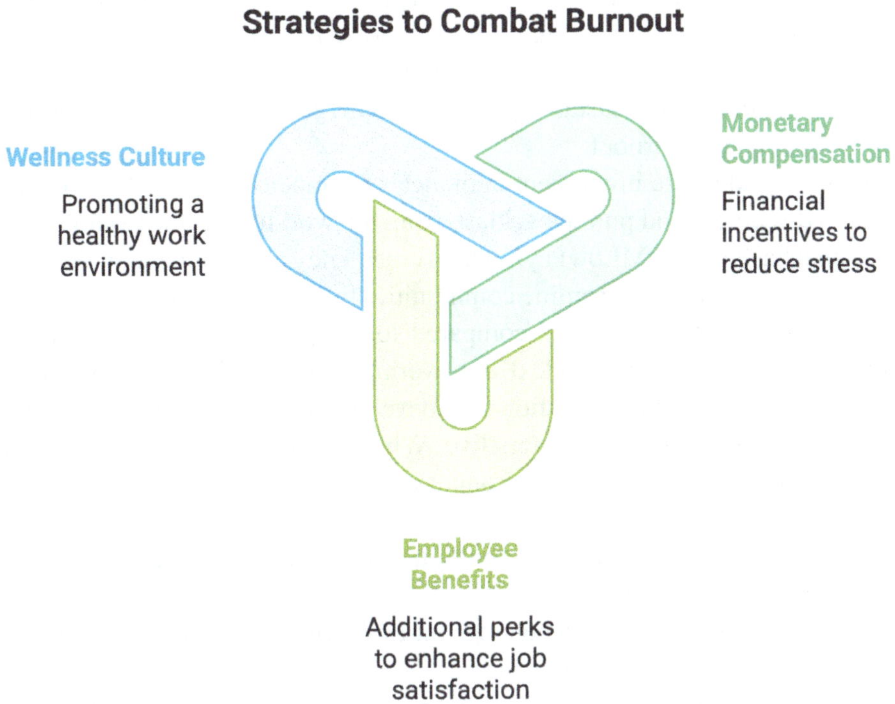

Monetary compensation focuses on the core principle that employees should be adequately paid for their work at a rate that allows them to thrive in the community. Without this foundational support, most employees' basic needs are not being met, which, according to Maslow, limits higher levels of fulfillment and happiness (Maslow, 1943). In most cases, monetary compensation refers directly to an employee's salary and or possibilities for overtime. Beyond simple payment, the key to positive investment in monetary compensation is ensuring employees are paid livable wages. "At its simplest, a living wage is what one full-time worker must earn hourly to help cover the cost of their family's minimum basic needs where they live while still being self-sufficient (Glasmeier, 2025)."

Paying a livable wage encourages employee job satisfaction while reducing external risk factors, such as housing instability, that may influence retention. The safety of stable housing and family support can only enhance the ability of the public service motivation theory to occur and allow good people to continue to do good work (Perry & Wise, 1990). Internal risk factors are mitigated by paying livable wages that promote housing stability. For example, emergency response efforts are time sensitive, and livable wages allow employees to live closer to the community they serve, thereby reducing response time and positively benefiting overall response efforts. Risks associated with fatigue after response concludes and traveling are also mitigated through livable wages that bring shorter commute times. Reducing overall risk factors is paramount to sustaining a healthy emergency management workforce capable of preventing burnout.

Moreover, inadequate investment in monetary compensation and livable wages can lead to discontent and public backlash from the workforce. One example is the international hashtag "#EMLowPay," which emergency management professionals use on social media and other online communities to share cautions about positions that do not pay adequate salaries compared to the position's requirements and/ or location. Even within the context of government or public service workers, a paycheck-to-paycheck living situation may develop without adequate pay to match the jurisdiction in which practitioners live. When this is the case, under-qualified staff often represent communities or cannot retain professionals with higher skills and experience. There is a growing trend of public service workers transitioning into the private workforce to provide for their families and alleviate # the financial stress incurred by #EMLowPay.

"For agencies advertising job postings on LinkedIn and other professional networking sites, having their posting shared with #EMLowPay amounts to a public callout that the agency does not value its emergency manager." The job postings that fall within this category have been left mainly to the individuals starting their careers, which adds another layer of stress and burnout to professionals early in their career. The equivalent of virtual caution tape or a glaring red flag makes the potential candidate pause and consider the position's value. The core purpose of the hashtag is to increase salary transparency and highlight postings that do not pay enough for the demanding responsibilities and high prerequisites of the job (Cavanaugh, 2024).

The interconnectivity of professionals is an opportunity employers can benefit from through shared positive reviews and advocacy for the organization. Employers also motivate their employees and promote positive performance by providing livable wages. They may also have greater chances of retaining employees and signaling to prospective candidates that they are invested in the success of both the personal and professional being. In a study of employee motivation and organizational performance, equitable wages and promotions were identified as among the core practices that help boost the morale of employees. Additionally, opportunities for promotion and equitable salaries for job responsibilities also encourage employee loyalty (Kalogiannidis, 2021).

Furthermore, monetary compensation in overtime pay during emergency response can help encourage loyalty while reducing burnout. Professionals want to be fairly compensated for their work while feeling supported and valued by their employers. Especially during disasters, the need for overtime pay that adequately compensates for the energy, time, emotion, skill, and overall work is evident. This form of compensation also ties directly into financial benefits, which will be discussed later in this chapter.

In addition to the monetary compensation, robust employee benefits packages can also be used to help recruit and retain emergency and disaster management professionals. Employee benefits often refer to elective compensation resources employers may offer to promote employee health and wellness, satisfaction, productivity, and retention. These benefits can include and are not limited to discounts, programs, events, or other resources directed toward employees. According to Forbes (2024), employee benefits can be categorized into four groups (Haan, 2022):

Figure 2. Comprehensive employee benefits overview

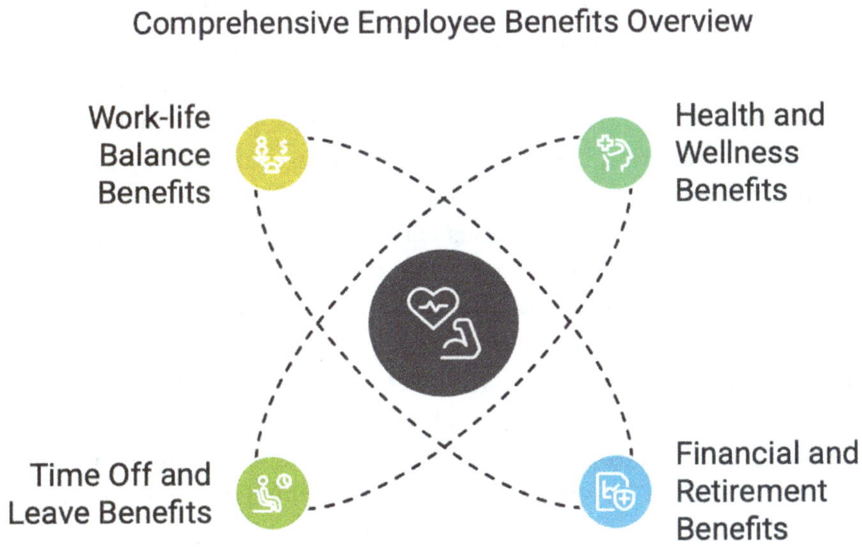

Health and wellness benefits are generally tailored to maintaining the physical well-being of an employee. In contrast, financial and retirement benefits focus primarily on the fiscal health of individuals and how they navigate the economic space around them. Time off and leave benefits generally focus on allowing and encouraging the employee to be temporarily out of work. In contrast, work-life balance benefits focus more on effectively prioritizing responsibilities and requirements of an individual's personal and professional environments on any given day. A healthy balance among the four listed benefit categories to support the culture of wellness in the employee's life and the employee's family can severely reduce the stress an individual feels. Not offering one or more of these benefit categories or even delivering all four without the support and championing from leaders to engage with the benefits can lead to underutilized resources and a toxic culture of fear surrounding their general use. This may also lead to misperceptions of professional weakness, disloyalty, and lack of commitment to the organization's mission or culture.

Health and wellness benefits refer to traditional insurance benefits such as health, dental, vision, and life and employee assistance programs. Insurance benefits help reduce employees' financial burden when experiencing health-related issues common in emergency management and the public sector. The snowball effects of stress, trauma, and burnout can wreak havoc on a person's health and are inextricably linked to resilience (Van Der Kolk, 2014), especially in professions with high trauma exposure, such as public safety and emergency management. Health benefits are critical to reducing such effects and caring for the individual. Beyond standard insurance benefits, employee assistance programs are also dynamic resources that help employees navigate the variable challenges of life. Benefits in this category may include counseling, crisis intervention resources, professional and personal development opportunities, legal assistance, and financial planning consultations. Overall, this bucket of benefits promotes positive health and wellness by providing resources to identify and address issues early that may directly impact employee performance, satisfaction, and burnout. In addition to reducing the financial burden of health-related problems through health and wellness benefits, employers can also invest in proactive financial health in their employees.

Financial and retirement benefits may include investment options and financial planning resources to stabilize employee finances further and encourage long-term financial health. As discussed in the chapter, they may also include overtime pay for emergency response. Examples of this benefit include financial counseling and investment planning, pension and deferred compensation plans, retirement planning, and employer matches. Where monetary compensation is intended to address the short-term financial health of an employee, this investment is for the long-term financial health of the employee. Financial stability is critical to preventing burnout and helping public sector employees feel valued (Sahin et al., 2024). However, employees also value exercising their financial freedom, so providing ample time off and leave benefits is equally important.

Time off and leave benefits may include traditional paid leave options such as vacation, sick days, and established holidays and nontraditional ones such as flextime, parental and family leave, floating holidays, and employee wellness days. There are also nontraditional forms of leave, such as flextime, and nontraditional benefits, such as seasonal early releases for staff at the end of the year. The need to take time off from work is as old as time itself. In the United States, vacation, sick days, and paid holidays are becoming standard leave options offered throughout the emergency management field and beyond. Vacation leave allows employees to schedule time off to enjoy their personal lives and address unexpected or unplanned disruptions.

Sick leave allows employees to prioritize their health and recovery while promoting health and wellness benefits. This type of leave takes many forms throughout the emergency management field. Still, it is primarily observed as leave intended to address seasonal illnesses and/or short-term emergencies that are not expected to go beyond a few days. It is common for this leave to be made available over some time based on how many hours an employee worked in each period. Health-related leave beyond the more routine illnesses may include short and long-term disability leave, which is intended to be used when an employee experiences an incident that disables them and prevents them from returning to work for multiple weeks or months, depending on the nature of the incident. Disability leave, while related to sick leave, is not as standard in US agencies and often requires external insurance to address the financial impacts of taking leave for extended amounts of time.

Another form of leave, like sick and disability leave, is family medical leave. In the United States, the Family Medical Leave Act is the federal government's principal policy that outlines minimum requirements and basic protections afforded to employees taking family medical leave. According to the Wage and Hour Division of the United States Department of Labor, "The FMLA entitles eligible employees of covered employers to take unpaid, job-protected leave for specified family and medical reasons with continuation of group health insurance coverage under the same terms and conditions as if the employee had not taken leave (*Family and Medical Leave Act*, 2025)." In short, where sick and disability leaves are structured to allow the employee to heal and recover, family medical leave gives the employee time to help their family member(s) heal and recover. It may also be applicable for employee use regarding emergencies that do not fall within the parameters set forth for sick and disability leaves on a case-by-case basis.

When an employee experiences sudden loss in the death of an immediate family member, bereavement leave may be offered. The purpose of bereavement leave is to provide time for an employee to grieve their loss and support relatives when needed without the stresses of work and requirements of being in the office or online. This leave is neither earned nor banked, and the duration depends on individual agency/organizational policies. While this type of leave benefits employees and may certainly reduce burnout during the applicable circumstances, its limitations and associated impacts due to the nature of the leave make it a less than desirable option to count on for year-round burnout reduction.

However, established holidays and their associated leave allow for 'reliable' leave throughout the year that can be used as calendar milestones, breaks from work-related stress, and opportunities for coordinated time with family and supporters. This should not be the only approach to using holidays within organizations. Holidays can also be extended as workflow indicators on how to (when possible) decrease the continual workload if increasing the workforce is not an option. While on holiday, professionals should not be contacted on holidays or after work hours unless a triggering event has taken place that requires the person(s) on call to respond or for the team to activate in the face of an incident. Leaders must set an example for this approach and respect it primarily in a 'blue sky' situation where it is the regular office day and eight-hour shifts. The triggering events are often determined by agency policy to transition to and from 'blue sky'. The consideration of and around holidays would be the bare minimum of burnout considerations for prevention that is often violated at all levels of practice.

The simple existence of leave options is not always enough to benefit efforts to reduce burnout. The United States Office of Personnel Management, in their Handbook on Pay and Leave Benefits for Federal Employees Affected by Severe Weather Conditions or Other Emergency Situations 2021, addresses the capacity to take these traditional leaves during emergencies may be dictated by the operating status of the organization and any potential emergency or incidents impacting response postures (Office of Personnel Management, 2021). The authors' personal experiences echo similar limitations regarding utilizing leave during emergencies. For example, emergencies can happen anytime, regardless of holiday status or other leave. While an employee may look forward to the extended break celebrating holidays in late December and early January, the reality of weather conditions and seasonal response needs may require them to forego their leave to participate in emergency response efforts. This uncertainty creates a gap in offering traditional leave and the practical ability to use it Duane Morris LLP., 2023).

To address this gap, many organizations are beginning to offer nontraditional leave options such as flextime, parental and family leave, floating holidays, and wellness days. Flextime is best described as fulfilling the hour requirements for work in a nonstandard or flexible period. In practice, this may include working extra hours during a workweek but taking time off the following week to address the overages in time rather than taking overtime pay. With well-established budget limitations in the public sector, flextime offers an affordable alternative that still prioritizes employee well-being. Flextime is especially critical during and following emergency response efforts, where operational shifts often extend beyond standard working hours.

Parental and family leave, more commonly referred to as Maternity/Paternity Leave(s), is intended to provide time for employees to address the needs of their growing family (U.S. Dept of Labor, 1993). In the United States, *The Family and Medical Leave Act* entitles parents to 12 work weeks of unpaid leave with protections for their position, pay, benefits, and status (U.S. Dept. of Labor, 1993). 12 weeks of unpaid leave to In its narrowest form, this type of leave may include caring for a mother after giving birth, caring for and bonding with a newborn child, and/or fostering or adopting a child. However, broader forms make leave more accessible to parents and guardians in nontraditional families in various circumstances. Additionally, this type of leave may expand beyond caring for children and youth and include all guardianship responsibilities, including elder care and caring for family members with disabilities. Guardianship can create higher stress levels and add to the level of responsibilities and pressure an individual is experiencing. For these reasons, parental and family leave can help reduce burnout by allowing employees to prioritize what matters without sacrificing their careers or overburdening their limited time to accomplish their responsibilities.

Floating holidays are less common but offer a few days a year to use however they see fit. In practice, they appear like vacation days. Still, they are often provided at the beginning of a year, in increments comparable to standard holidays (8 hours), and with a limited time to use. They offer flexibility in vacation with the reliability of the preloaded hours offered by holidays. Though not as common as the other leave types, additional flexibility can be provided through wellness days. Wellness days are intended to be used to promote the employee's wellness. Unlike sick days, they are most often offered as incentives for participating in organizational wellness programs, pre-banked like floating holidays, with the primary focus being to address the gap in what sick days do not cover (often mental health) or offered following major disruptions or projects. Incentivized wellness days encourage employees to engage in a wellness culture within an organization and create wellness accountability. Pre-banking wellness days are another way to signal to employees and prospective hires that their wellness is being prioritized at the organization. Offering wellness days during and after disasters in emergency management agencies reflects an organization's responsibility to care for their employees while building resilience and strengthening recovery. Being the least common in practice, the format of wellness days varies widely between organizations. Still, all have benefits, and an organization's mission and values should choose specific methods.

All forms of traditional and nontraditional leave and time off are key benefits organizations may offer to prevent and reduce burnout. A spectrum of these options should help reduce burnout in the emergency management and public sectors. Healthy leave options help invest in employees as persons and allow individuals to prioritize their time as necessary. In emergency management, we recognize that taking advantage of health and wellness, financial, and leave benefits is not always easy in the short term, especially when working in an area or organization with frequent incidents or high-stakes projects. When these options are not readily available and/or capable of being utilized, the importance of work-life balance benefits is even more highlighted.

Work-life balance benefits vary widely between organizations but may include flexible work arrangements, telecommuting, and assistance with child and eldercare. This bucket of benefits has the broadest potential for exploring and trying out new strategies based on the organization's needs. For emergency management, burnout is frequent following major emergencies requiring extensive coordination and response. During such emergencies, practitioners must balance and prioritize the needs of the community they serve, their organizational priorities, their personal lives, the requirements of their families, and the demanding requirements of the incident/emergency itself. This also adds to the potential that the emergency directly impacts the practitioner outside their job scope. For example, a practitioner in Florida responding to a major hurricane may need to balance and prioritize the many complexities mentioned in addition to worrying about their flooded home. Work-life balance benefits in this lens are intended to reduce the burden of the many hats emergency managers wear while maintaining cohesion and partnering with the personnel to maintain professionalism.

Examples of work-life balance benefits include flexible work arrangements such as schedules and locations, telecommuting options, and assistance with child and eldercare services. Flexible work arrangements help emergency managers maintain healthy personal lives without sacrificing critical time necessary for their jobs. Flexibility in standard working hours and locations allows professionals to accomplish their assigned tasks in their personal and professional lives. This flexibility helps reduce burnout by introducing time for the professional to prioritize what matters most at that moment, notwithstanding time and priorities bound by geographic considerations. Telecommuting options allow for physical and visual breaks from the stress of the office and/or Emergency Operations Center (EOC) environment(s). This option, amplified during the COVID-19 Pandemic, helps balance mental health and offers flexibility in location. Locational flexibility is beneficial during regular business and certain emergency operations where a combined physical location for emergency response may not provide the safest option (i.e., shelter in place, tornadoes, critical infrastructure attacks, etc.). Child and eldercare services are among the most impactful benefits to professionals with young or aging family members. Caring for family members can be a significant barrier and cause burnout when a professional does not have the resources to succeed in their professional and care roles. This benefit allows the professional to focus on their critical and often life-saving work while addressing their care responsibilities. While this option is essential during regular 'blue sky' days, the resource becomes significantly more important when attention and priorities may be unevenly split or focused primarily on emergency response, especially if other options for work-life balance benefits are not available.

The most fundamental task of emergency management professionals is to use the good days to prepare for the bad days so they do not become worse, and the community can recover quickly. Successfully fulfilling that task means that on any given day, emergency management professionals carry heavy weight in their jobs and are at increased risk of burnout. Burnout is not merely an emergency management issue. Burnout throughout the public sector is as much a personal issue as a business issue when public organizations incur costs and lose institutional knowledge (Izard-Carroll, 2016). To reduce this risk and prevent burnout, organizations must invest in their employees inside and outside the professional environment.

While monetary compensation and robust benefits packages are clear and tangible strategies to promote employee investment, building a Wellness Culture is the most effective for reducing burnout and increasing employee retention. Such building requires intentionality and consistency above simply using the term as a buzzy recruitment tactic. Building a wellness culture includes intentional and ongoing organizational efforts to encourage and promote, sometimes requiring health and well-being benefits. An example of this can be something as simple as wellness webinars, providing books for book clubs, and setting times to talk about the books to help produce a culture of wellness within an organization and its employees.

EVIDENCED-BASED BURNOUT PREVENTION STRATEGIES

Prevention Strategies that have been proven to combat professional burnout have a theme that resonates with the individual. Still, some high-level approaches help most people—for example, providing access to and/or creating mental health support and awareness throughout the organization for employees to utilize and leverage as they see fit (Pálfi et al., 2024). Employees' access to this mental health support and awareness can be used from access to the mental health services that might benefit the organization, mental health wellness webinars or events, and other resources that can provide mental health relief. The creative approaches to supporting mental health relief to employees enduring mental strain from political pressures, the weight of life safety, and extended shifts filled with adrenaline through 12+ hours of activation. These shifts and the lifestyle of first responders, public safety, emergency managers, and supporting agencies who have been activated can take a mental, physical, and emotional toll on those involved. The approach to the access and support of mental health within an organization can also support a work culture that benefits the entire organization.

Fostering a supportive work culture is only limited by resources, imagination, and creativity. However, it must be supported by organization leaders so that it is safe within the organization. Creating an air or aura of camaraderie can quickly be built amongst work in the field but can struggle across agencies and office workers, creating emotional support for all involved (Vaughn, 2023). Shared experiences, such as deployments or activations in an emergency operations center, can jumpstart the development of a supportive work culture. The nature of facing an obstacle and overcoming it together as a team promotes interpersonal relationships and reliance on others. Fieldwork is also attributed to more straightforward missions that offer more direct visibility into the outcome and positive impacts the work has on others.

Conversely, routine work environments may be siloed or less reliant on others for success and overcoming obstacles. It is up to individual employees to determine their motivation behind working in specific roles. In the routine environment, this motivation is less focused on the common mission and more on the benefit to the employee. Routine environments also exist within a competitive space where career advancement and professional development may come to mind before the team's needs overcome the obstacles. In this way, agencies struggle to promote interpersonal relationships and shared vision or buy-in throughout their teams, thus leading to a reduced sense of belonging and minimized efforts to build culture. In simple terms, an individual can be a part of an organization, or an organization can be part of individuals. A supportive work culture cannot exist if the individual employees cannot trust their colleagues and/or agency to support them or be responsive to their support needs. This takes investment from all involved parties and a clear focus on thriving together.

Where there is a supportive work culture, there is a more straightforward approach to work-life balance within organizations where employees can have balance, which makes retention easier and helps prevent burnout. Encouraging work-life balance is a constant struggle in all working professions and intersects throughout all industries. Work-life balance within the first responder, emergency management, and public safety community struggles with balancing work and life more than other sectors. There is often a response mentality where the family and personal life suffer. Still, some prevention strategies can be adopted from the planning phase to organizations' strategic planning. One example is where family prep time gets included in activation processes; in this, employees can go home and prepare their families before activation when there are planned events and when possible, or able to send people home when feasible within the battle rhythm cadence.

Figure 3. Cycle of burnout prevention strategies

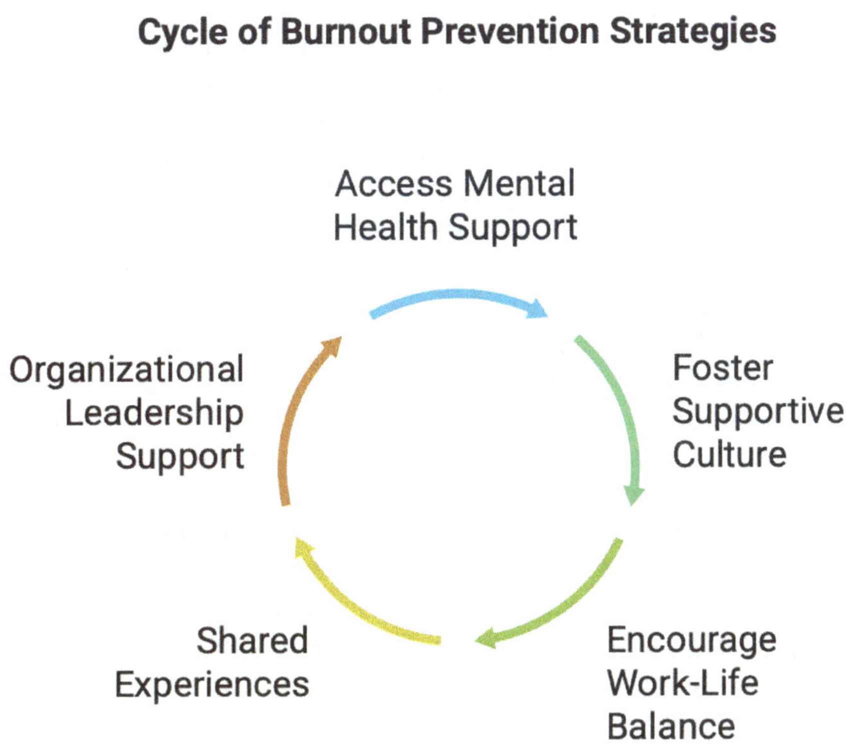

IMPLEMENTATION & RECOMMENDATIONS

Implementing burnout prevention tends not to get very far without the support of organizational leadership and intentionality. Leadership support can make or break the implementation and support needed to create and maintain a wellness or organizational culture that can limit professional burnout (Allan et al., 2023). As depicted in Figure 3 above, the cycle of burnout prevention strategies is as follows: access to mental health support, foster a supportive culture, encourage work-life balance, shared experiences, and organizational leadership support. After leadership support, some programs may require resources, whether it be an existing benefit that employees can use, a mechanism built into their health insurance, a benefit for the organization that employees can utilize, or something that may require funding or time. Identifying this resource is critical for enhancing or establishing preventive burnout strategies that align with any particular organization. Here are some implementation and further recommendations that can be included and incorporated into organizations battling burnout and aiming to prevent it before it happens. These recommendations have been curated to align with organizations in or adjacent to emergency management, disaster management, crisis management, public safety, and first responders.

One recommendation previously mentioned as an example in this chapter is to promote work-life balance and encourage this behavior with some flexibility in accordance with paid time off and/or time used after an activation demobilizes (Papazoglou, 2023). This can be done by policy modification, which allows for additional regular breaks and opportunities for leave with people working longer than an average eight-hour workday. This can also be done informally if the leader or director has flexibility regarding people management within their departments and on their teams to support a balance to allow for additional rest time for employees. This recommendation is the most straightforward approach, where it can be conducted formally and informally to support teams when they happen to work more than a traditional 40-hour work week or in addition to additional stresses on employees that may take place outside of blue sky (everyday nonactivated) situations.

The second recommendation is for emergency management professionals to enhance organizational support where it is needed to reduce burnout. This can be done with peer support groups, access to counseling, and additional services like partner organizations such as law enforcement, fire services, dispatch, and EMS (Vaughn, 2023). A supportive work environment can help resolve burnout where emergency management organizations and teams are treated as first responders and often the last ones out of activation, but operating without the perks of a first responder in most cases. This grey area is frequently treated as a pseudo-responder status informally, but it does not extend to the benefits, support, or appreciation that their official responder counterparts can leverage. One example can be establishing or adopting this professional population into a union, like how dispatch was adopted into fire or law enforcement unions. With emergency management teams often being small, underfunded, and under-resourced, there is often insufficient personnel to support a push for an independent union. Still, adoption into the emergency management department's organization (fire, law enforcement, etc.) can help facilitate that supportive environment in several areas.

Third, Recommendations are also under focus for emergency management personnel, such as implementing adaptive emotional regulation strategies. This can range from *Emotional Intelligence* to emotional identification and management, which can be utilized by all staff throughout the ranks, from the field worker and program coordinator to the agency director and department chief. To implement this strategy, mental and emotional health resources can be brought into an agency to educate employees and teach them strategies and techniques to develop emotional resilience. Additionally, supervisors and agency leadership can actively practice and encourage using adaptive emotional regulation strategies throughout routine and emergency work. Post-disaster counseling and trauma recovery services, such as chaplains, therapists, counselors, and peer support, can also promote emotional identification and management. This can be a great way to encourage the use of emotional regulation strategies to support stress management.

The last recommendation is to support regular mental health screenings, which have been done for public safety professionals previously. This can be done to catch burnout in the early stages to help with prevention by utilizing screening tools such as the Maslach Burnout Inventory (MBI) and providing immediate support to those identified as at risk, which is one method (Ugwu & Idemudia, 2024). Identifying mental health screening tools and burnout intervention methods can help maintain a stable, resilient, and sustainable approach to burnout prevention for professionals.

Figure 4. Strategies for preventing professional burnout

ADDITIONAL THOUGHTS FOR THE READER

Emergency management and disaster professionals build their careers in environments ripe for burnout. The stressful nature and perceived pressures of emergency and disaster response create a host of complexities and individual factors that all influence burnouts. No two situations or professional environments and experiences are the same, so no two strategies and tactics for burnout reduction are the same. Even with the complexities of disasters and activations, burnout indicators and stressors can be identified and approached accordingly for teams exposed to the stressors. Readers are encouraged to review the strategy and information presented in this chapter and then adapt them to their organization's and its professionals' needs. Interdisciplinary research and discussion are necessary to advance burnout mitigation thoughts and strategies.

Organizations and professionals should also work to identify future causes of burnout and consider external influences that may be out of their control. External influences include disaster frequency and its physical and psychological impacts on pathos and empathy. Emergency management and disaster professionals have been informally recruited to the field through disaster pathos, appealing to a professional's sense of service and duty for decades. This 'higher calling' approach capitalizes on the emotional disruption caused by periodic large disasters. However, the approach is less practical when 'once in a lifetime' incidents occur more frequently and with higher news coverage. In this regard, the rallying cry to join public sector emergency and disaster response roles after a disaster happens sounds more like rolling recruitment for positions listed as 'open until filled.' Like the general public's desensitization to disasters and the subsequent ask for donations and support, emergency management and disaster response workers are becoming desensitized to the calls to action. Furthermore, the increased frequency of disasters, skyrocketing recovery costs, and cross-border desensitization led to further resource reductions. It primes public sector agencies for high levels of burnout.

Disasters are interconnected now more than ever in both the professional and personal spheres. The cascading impacts of disasters cross geopolitical boundaries, climates, and populations. This interconnectivity is causing additional stress on the pathos mentioned above, resource availability, process, and policy development. For example, a catastrophic fire in one region may devastate a community, make news headlines, and bring forth calls to action for support. At the same time, cascading factors influence insurance and mitigation funding in another region due to the impacts of the fire. These impacts will affect the individual in multiple areas of their life. It will simultaneously impact the individual's professional life as they prepare for emergencies in their jurisdiction and look at their risks and vulnerability.

Another example is the COVID-19 pandemic, which has personally impacted all people across the globe in some form or another. Emergency and disaster management individuals responding to this emergency lived with 100% exposure to the incident through the saturation in their personal and professional lives. The lines between work and home were continuously blurred, as was the work-life balance. COVID-19 was not an anomaly, and disaster interconnectivity will continue to concern professionals. With the decrease in the ability to escape work, the risk for burnout is increasing, and the role of emergency and disaster management professionals is expanding.

Professionals are also being asked to go beyond their normal scope of operations and expertise as part of a broader pattern of requiring more with fewer resources across the emergency management and disaster response field. Disasters are dynamic and constantly changing, as are the expectations and requirements of the professionals responding to them. Organizations increasingly rely on a few select professionals to fill the gaps in the expertise of a multitude of many. The scope of emergency response is rapidly expanding as the threats, hazards, and impacts vary greatly. At the professional level, emergency management across the globe is evolving from traditional natural disaster response to take on more comprehensive emergency responses as well as homeland security efforts in certain areas. At the local level, a typical example is emergency managers needing to be comfortable in fire and law enforcement response processes, critical infrastructure and cybersecurity, and their expected coordination and incident management expertise. Scope creep is an increasing issue that will continue to influence burnout. It is also an issue that organizations can work to identify and mitigate in the short term to reduce potential consequences in the long term. The scope will depend on the agency's mission; however, organizations should complete internal and regional research to understand the capabilities, needs, and gaps.

Another consideration is the varying educational and experience requirements of similar positions and the lack of standardization. Where financial compensation is concerned, a gap in experience and pay requirements throughout the field can lead to rapid burnout in professionals. For example, professionals in certain regions may be hired into entry-level positions with minimal requirements but higher pay levels. The opposite also applies, where professionals with extensive experience are hired into managerial and leadership roles with lower pay. Additionally, many positions may require advanced degrees and higher education without adequate financial compensation for the educational requirements. This contradiction in requirements and compensation influences how professionals perceive being valued by their employers, which influences wellness culture and burnout. Further research is needed on this topic to better understand how to mitigate the risk while maintaining adequate requirements for role applicability.

One of the most common conversations within the emergency management and public safety space is the consideration of the fusion of academic findings and practical applications. This application can enhance workflow, lower cost, improve production quality, and utilize cutting-edge approaches to support our communities and jurisdictions. One consideration is the education and application of the theories noted in this chapter to battling burning and other emerging theories such as the *Innovative Structural Theory of Emergency Management (IST-EM),* which was created for emergency management and public administration use but can be applied to various areas of programmatic evaluation and enhancement (Richardson, 2023). By leveraging these evidence-based practices into working professionals' methodology and standard operating procedures, the evaluation and continued enhancement of burnout strategies can constantly be mitigated year by year.

Figure 5. Unpacking the innovative structural theory

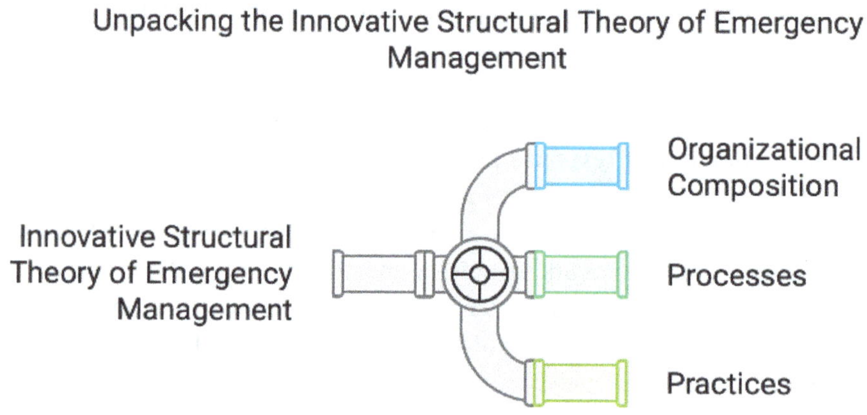

Dynamic mitigation is also necessary to address the internal challenges that may lead to more organizational burnout. In countries where government leadership rotates periodically through elections, there exists potential for fluctuation and uncertainty regarding support for emergency management and disaster service agencies and responsibilities in the public sector. Such uncertainty can lead to additional burnout throughout the public sector. The value of emergency response efforts is highly politicized due to their direct impacts on quality of life. Similarly, the value of the public sector workforce and its perceived size is also highly politicized. Changes in political leadership and their varying priorities, pressures, and direction can dramatically alter where, when, and how emergency management and disaster service roles are utilized. As evident in the United States Government's organizational workforce changes following the inauguration of President Donald Trump in January 2025 (White House, 2025), dynamic situations can arise when priorities change. While this example points to a federal level change, similar situations can occur throughout all levels of government in the United States and abroad. As discussed, adequate funding and resource allocation are pivotal to the success of emergency management and disaster services. While the full extent of such changes may take many years to understand, uncertainty of organizational support can decrease employee morale, increase burnout, and cause adverse impacts to wellness and organizational culture. Additional information and studies incorporating interdisciplinary research are needed to better understand the full extent of the complexities and influences associated with the adverse impacts of such changes on emergency management and disaster service workers in the public sector.

Finally, intergovernmental relationships and authorities also need additional research to better understand how regulatory authorities, unfunded mandates, and politics impact individual professionals in the emergency management and disaster service fields. For most public sector work, effective emergency management and disaster services rely heavily on intersectional training, coordination, resources, and information sharing. Emergency managers like to say, 'emergency management is a team sport', meaning the work should never be completed in a silo or a singular professional field. However, no level of organizational and wellness culture established at an agency is immune to the influences of underperforming teammates in response. An agency can support the organization and individual but may face external pressures and/or responsibilities that it cannot adequately address due to many factors. Ultimately, the 'team' success will rely on the individuals comprising the 'team', and its members may share the stresses. However, regulatory authorities and unfunded mandates are critical in determining who and how the 'team' engages. Burnout prevention in the public sector and high-stress professions such as emergency management and disaster services must be fully integrated into a comprehensive approach. Ongoing research is necessary to continue identifying impacts with each leadership transition and mitigate the changes brought on.

CONCLUSION

In the summary and conclusion of this chapter, there is a critical need for a comprehensive approach to address burnout among emergency management and disaster professionals globally. These identified methods are again to be utilized as tools to support organizations in an international context to navigate the consistent battle against burnout for public safety, emergency, disaster, and crisis management professionals. The first approach highlighted in this chapter leans heavily on a multifaceted approach to burnout prevention and taking lessons identified from practices inside and outside the disaster and public safety profession. This undertone throughout the chapter aims to leverage evidence-based practices and evaluation methods to not only prevent burnout but also to create a cycle of evaluation and growth within the culture, spaces, and methods of burnout prevention. This involves addressing various aspects of the professional environment, including monetary compensation, employee benefits, wellness culture, and evidence-based prevention strategies.

The second approach centers on adequate monetary and financial compensation for the professional as they try to maintain livable situations, whether with a family or alone. The two main concepts were around livable wages, which are needed for any professional to live in the jurisdiction upon which they work. Still, ideally, wages reflect the education gained, training obtained, certifications captured, and experience developed through work within this developing profession from internships, fellowships, volunteering, to full-time work experience. The other central concept was around overtime pay or the balance of working overtime in times of disaster and emergency operation center action (grey skies) shift. If overtime is not allowable, straight time or flextime should be the professional's opt-in choice. This, again, is where workdays go from traditional eight-hour to 12-16-hour workdays without leaving the office until it is safe to do so or the emergency is within a manageable scope.

The third approach is rooted in robust employee benefits that can help mitigate the burnout of highly stressful work where the weight of lives is at stake and communities hang in the balance. This, tied with political ramifications and conflicting priorities, needs additional balance outside monetary compensation. The pillars under this approach are the health and wellness of practitioners and employees, financial and retirement benefits, time off and leave (including the culture around using it), the practice of work-life balance, and the sustainable application and implementation of systems to support the person, the team, and the organization.

The fourth approach is to help foster and sustain a wellness culture within the organization or department where the professionals work and are exposed to the stressors that lead to burnout. Wellness culture is manifested through the intentional application of a people-centered approach to work-life balance and its resources, where the norm is to take care of yourself rather than work tirelessly. This culture has to have the policy and resources to support it, as well as the leadership and informal regularity where people care about individual sustainability and work rate. In a fast-paced and highly stressful line of work, it is easy to lose sight of wellness when communities are in danger, but self-care is still critical for a long-term positive impact on communities. This approach is supported by the Public Service Motivation theory (PSM), which states that the motivation to work in this profession is based on morality or the perceived attractiveness of the organization's mission. Still, it is not sustainable without the acknowledgment of the needs of the employees, where safety and psychological needs supersede the desire and motivation to help others. Without the need for psychological safety being considered, the need to help the community can become corrupted and add additional stress to the practitioners.

The fifth approach includes leadership support from the organization's supervisor, chief, director, and/or leader and intentional resource allocation to support programs and initiatives. This can range from regular mental health screening post-disaster, just for check-ins after stressful events, to the team and staff. This approach can also include the constant development of a supportive work culture, which will stem from teamwork, camaraderie, and trust to help develop peer-to-peer trust and coping support systems. Lastly, modeling the behavior and leading by example, showing the boss utilizing services, getting down and working with the team, or even utilizing policy and taking time off will help support the utilization of organizational strategies. Without leadership support, any adaptation of this chapter, even if it could be initiated, would not be sustainable as it would conflict with leadership direction. A champion for your cause and wellness will distinguish between a stress reliever and a stress builder. With a champion, the application of resource allocations, whether it be time, funding, or another resource, is more tangible where those in power and leadership support the wellness of the team.

The sixth and final approach highlighted throughout this chapter would have to be implementing, applying, and leveraging evidence-based strategies and methodologies implemented, maintained, and practiced within organizations at every level to help battle burnout pre-, during, and post-disaster. This includes and is not limited to the intersectional support from other departments exposed to the disaster-related stressors and families associated with this type of work, which can have a ripple effect across time and throughout families and communities. This final approach stems from the research realm and is to be transferred to the practical application realm for practitioners to use in an easy and adaptable manner. Without the direct application and even a step-by-step implementation guide, an organization can struggle to adapt where the "why" may not be clear. So, the applied research and support of champions, as stated above, can change the outcome of application strategies to support professionals in the field in all phases of emergency, disaster, and crisis management.

In closing, these six approaches—a multifaceted approach to burnout, consideration and action on adequate monetary compensation, building a robust employee benefits program, fostering and maintaining wellness culture, investment, and intentionality by leadership with resource allocations, and lastly, evidence-based practices—are the approaches and key prevention strategies for battling burnout.

These six approaches can be applied within an international context as they must be used and modified to the nuances of organizations, laws, cultural differences, and social norms. The approaches identified here are by no means the only approaches that can be taken to battle and support the prevention of burnout for the professional. Still, these six themes or approaches are consistent areas that continue to pop up through the literature and research on existing applications and practitioner-based experiences within the profession of emergency, disaster, and crisis management.

REFERENCES

Allan, J., Olcon, K., Everingham, R., Fox, M., Pai, P., Mackay, M., & Keevers, L. (2023). Leading wellness in healthcare: A qualitative study of leadership practices for wellness in hospital settings. *PLoS One*, *18*(7), e0285103. DOI: 10.1371/journal.pone.0285103 PMID: 37467299

Carod-Artal, F. J., & Vázquez-Cabrera, C. (2013). Burnout Syndrome in an International Setting. In Bährer-Kohler, S. (Ed.), *Burnout for Experts: Prevention in the Context of Living and Working* (pp. 15–35). Springer. [1], https://link.springer.com/chapter/10.1007/978-1-4614-4391-9_2 DOI: 10.1007/978-1-4614-4391-9_2

Cavanaugh, C. (2024). #EMLowPay: Is America Investing Enough In The Salaries Of Non-Federal Emergency Managers? National Emergency Management Advanced Academy. https://www.usfa.fema.gov/library/

Glasmeier, A. (2025). *Living Wage Calculator*. Https://Livingwage.Mit.Edu. https://livingwage.mit.edu./

Haan, K. (2022, November 22). *Employee Benefits In 2025: The Ultimate Guide*. Forbes Advisor. https://www.forbes.com/advisor/business/emp

Izard-Carroll, M. (2016). Public Sector Leaders' Strategies to Improve Employee Retention. *Walden Dissertations and Doctoral Studies*. https://scholarworks.waldenu.edu/dissertations/2157

Kalogiannidis, S. (2021). IMPACT OF EMPLOYEE MOTIVATION ON ORGANIZATIONAL PERFORMANCE. A SCOPING REVIEW PAPER FOR PUBLIC SECTOR. *Strategic Journal of Business & Change Management*, *8*(3). Advance online publication. DOI: 10.61426/sjbcm.v8i3.2064

Lee-Spiewak, D. (2012). *Core vs. Program Functions* [Professional Organization]. Https://Www.Iaem.Org/Certification/CEM_Corner/Core-vs-Program-Functions. https://www.iaem.org/certification/CEM_Corner/core-vs-program-functions

Maslow, A. H. (1943). A THEORY OF HUMAN MOTIVATION. *Psychological Review*, *50*(4), 370–396. DOI: 10.1037/h0054346

Office of Personnel Management. (2021). Handbook on Pay and Leave Benefits for Federal Employees Affected by Severe Weather Conditions or Other Emergency Situations.

Pálfi, K., Major, J., Horváth-Sarródi, A., Deák, A., Fehér, G., & Gács, B. (2024). Adaptive emotion regulation might prevent burnout in emergency healthcare professionals: An exploratory study. *BMC Public Health, 24*(1), 3136. DOI: 10.1186/s12889-024-20547-0 PMID: 39533222

Patel, S. S., Guevara, K., Hollar, T. L., Richard, A., DeVito, J., & Erickson, T. B. (2023). Surveying mental health stressors of emergency management professionals: Factors in recruiting and retaining emergency managers in an era of disasters and pandemics. *Journal of Emergency Management (Weston, Mass.), 21*(5), 375–384. DOI: 10.5055/jem.0820 PMID: 37932942

Perry, J. L., & Wise, L. R. (1990). The Motivational Bases of Public Service. *Public Administration Review, 50*(3), 367–373. DOI: 10.2307/976618

Remington, C. L., Witkowski, K., Ganapati, N. E., Headley, A. M., & Contreras, S. L. (2024). First Responders and the COVID-19 Pandemic: How Organizational Strategies Can Promote Workforce Retention. *American Review of Public Administration, 54*(1), 33–56. DOI: 10.1177/02750740231192968

Richardson, K. (2023). Quality Check: How Good is Your Emergency Management Program? [Dissertation]. West Chester University. https://digitalcommons.wcupa.edu/all_doctoral/229/

Sahin, E. B., Homberg, F., Sahin, E. B., & Homberg, F. (2024). *How to Reduce Burnout in Public Service Organizations during Times of Crisis? A Review of (Promising) Interventions*. IntechOpen., DOI: 10.5772/intechopen.1006691

Shi, L., Van Veldhoven, M., Kooij, D., Van De Voorde, K., & Karanika-Murray, M. (2024). High-performance work systems and individual performance: A longitudinal study of the differential roles of happiness and health well-being. *Frontiers in Psychology, 14*, 1261564. Advance online publication. DOI: 10.3389/fpsyg.2023.1261564 PMID: 38298369

The White House. (2025, February 11). *Fact Sheet: President Donald J. Trump Works to Remake America's Federal Workforce*. The White House. https://www.whitehouse.gov/fact-sheets/2025/02/fact-sheet-president-donald-j-trump-works-to-remake-americas-federal-workforce/

Ugwu, L. E., & Idemudia, E. S. (2024). Burnout and Post-traumatic Stress Disorders in Police Officers: Systematic Review and Meta-analysis. *Journal of Police and Criminal Psychology*. Advance online publication. DOI: 10.1007/s11896-024-09713-7

U.S. Dept of Labor. (1993). *The Family and Medical Leave Act of 1993*. The Family and Medical Leave Act of 1993. https://www.dol.gov/agencies/whd/laws-and-regulations/laws/fmla

Van Der Kolk, B. A. (2014). *The Body Keeps the Score*. https://www.penguinrandomhouse.com/books/313183/the-body-keeps-the-score-by-bessel-van-der-kolk-md/

Vaughn, T. (2023). *Reducing Burnout using Emergency Planning: A Literature Review*.

KEY TERMS AND DEFINITIONS

Emergency Management: can be described as crisis or disaster management depending on the country's practices. It is the practice and work of planning, developing prevention strategies, responding to, recovering from, or mitigating societal disruptions caused by man-made, natural, cyber, planned, or unplanned events.

Emergency Operations Center (EOC)-: The location upon which emergency management missions occur, whether an actual structure, base camp, or the back of a truck, but an area where leadership can make determinations in management crises.

Emotional Intelligence-: The ability to identify and be aware of emotional status, influence, and the emotional identification and management of self and the people around us.

Employee Benefits- Elective compensation resources employers offer to promote employee health and wellness: satisfaction, productivity, and retention.

Innovative Structural Theory (IST-EM) –: An evaluation theory that aligns with the continuous improvement models of the public safety space to identify, evaluate, and improve with evidence-based practices within a system.

Organizational Culture-: The culture of practices conducted within an organization which may or may not be directly expressed in policy, guidelines, or practice that is otherwise identified as everyday procedures or preferences accepted and expected within the organization.

Wellness Culture- An individual's ability to integrate multifaceted well-being (physical, mental, emotional, etc.) in all aspects of the professional environment: including practices and policies that prioritize individual well-being and healthy work-life balance.

Chapter 4

WE-CARE:
Closing the Gap of Health Disparities Through Community Collaborations

Angela M. Hill
https://orcid.org/0000-0001-8023-8470
University of South Florida, USA

Kevin B. Sneed
University of South Florida, USA

Deborah Austin
REACHUP Incorporated, USA

Deanna B. Wathington
REACHUP Incorporated, USA

Hiram B. Green
University of South Florida, USA

Michael B. Morgan
REACHUP Incorporated, USA

Janet B. Roman
University of South Florida, USA

Feng B. Cheng
University of South Florida, USA

John E. Clark
University of South Florida, USA

Natasha Rubie
https://orcid.org/0009-0000-4936-2254
University of South Florida, USA

Kristy Andre
University of South Florida, USA

Thea Moore
University of South Florida, USA

Antionette Davis
EnVision Resolution, USA

Feng Cheng
University of South Florida, USA

Karia Doreen MacAulay
University of South Florida, USA

Maisha Standifer
Morehouse School of Medicine, USA

DOI: 10.4018/979-8-3373-0169-3.ch004

Judette Louis
University of South Florida, USA

Kyaien Conner
University of Pittsburgh, USA

Joseph Diamond
https://orcid.org/0009-0002-8029-8056
University of South Florida, USA

Victor Obi
Victor & Hilda Obi Foundation, USA

Samantha Thompson
Florida A&M University, USA

ABSTRACT

Burnout in health professionals can impact therapeutic outcomes in patients. Improving health outcomes for marginalized populations and bridging the gap in health disparities requires a concerted effort among all major stakeholders. The Workgroup Enhancing Community Advocacy & Research Engagement (WE-CARE) program at the University of South Florida is a pharmacy-led cross collaboration of multiple stakeholders who serve as an integrated network of academia, researchers, and community to improve health disparities by increasing minority enrollment and participation in research and building trust and mutual respect between the community and researchers. To do this effectively WE-CARE uses a 360-degree community engagement model that maximizes the efforts of all involved. This chapter explains the mission, community-engaging activities, collaborations, and research-supporting efforts that WE-CARE employs to fulfill its mission and describes how it has tried to mitigate burnout in health professionals through its activities.

INTRODUCTION

Burnout Syndrome and job dissatisfaction is common in the healthcare sector. According to the Agency for Healthcare Research and Quality, burnout is common in <70% of nurses, half of physicians, nurse practitioners, and physician assistants. (Bridgeman, 2018) Some of the factors that contribute to burnout syndrome include, but are not limited to management pressure, reactivity to stress, relationship status, administrative work, routine, regretting decisions regarding patients, harassment at work, age of healthcare professional, gender, job category, and site of practice, experience of healthcare professional and sacrifice of personal time. (Taranu, 2022) Health professionals are expected to improve health outcomes in light of changes from fee-for-service to value-based care reimbursement practices. Global events, like the SARS-19-COVID pandemic also caused an exponential increase in burnout in frontline workers because of the health hazards, shortage of personnel, limited resources, and death and dying associated with the pandemic. Exhaustion from increased work demands and changes in roles led to increased prevalence of mental health issues in healthcare professionals, particularly nurses, pharmacists, intensive care workers, emergency department workers and other first line workers. (Gualano, 2021, Jalili 2021, Aras 2024)

Health disparities are another phenomenon that affects patients but also contributes to burnout in healthcare professionals. Health disparities are a global problem that affects marginalized groups disproportionately. (Rami, 2023). Health disparities result in a decrease in the quality of life, shortened lifespans, and increases the cost of health care particularly (Zavala, 2021). Health disparities are influenced by the social determinants of health, which includes factors like socioeconomic status, racism and discrimination, unequitable distribution of and access to resources, healthcare, and social injustice (Williamson, 2024; Mitchell, 2021). Efforts to improve health disparities can subsequently mitigate burnout in healthcare professionals.

Changing the trajectory of health outcomes and preventing burnout in health professionals can be mitigated through various measures. Some examples of strategies include, but are not limited to expanding education about health issues, increasing access to care, improving the social determinants of health, creating a diverse workforce, promoting cultural competence among the health professions, promoting social justice, and including the community on developing strategies to promote positive interventions that can change the trajectory of health outcomes in groups most affected by health disparities are needed to mitigate health disparities.

The healthcare system does not have the capacity to efficiently give attention to all of these areas, but community-engaged approaches can be meaningful tools to empower marginalized groups and break down barriers that promote health disparities (Dankwa-Mulan, 2021).

Universities with health programs are in a unique position to provide support in eliminating or impacting health disparities and healthcare professional burnout through use of clinical faculty and learners, clinical research, and clinical services. The University of South Florida (USF) is one such example. USF is a public university in the State of Florida (www.usf.edu) with > 240 undergraduate, graduate, specialist, and doctoral-level degree programs (USF Pocket Fact Book, 2022) including medicine, pharmacy, nursing, public health, physical therapy, physician assistant, social work, aging studies, health sciences, bioinformatics, computational biology, health informatics, biotechnology, and athletic training. USF also has an Academic Medical Center with more than 1,000 providers representing 30 specialties that serves patients through outpatient centers and works collaboratively with neighboring hospitals. The Taneja College of Pharmacy was established in 2010 and offers the Doctor of Pharmacy degree, and a Master of Science (MS) degree in Pharmaceutical Nanotechology and graduate certificates in drug discovery, nanopharmaceutics, and translational clinical research in pharmacy (https://health.usf.edu/pharmacy).

The health programs at USF work collaboratively with each other and the neighboring medical institutions, and prides itself on interdisciplinary training of its students. In 2009, the Dean for the Taneja College of Pharmacy led the University in establishing a Center for Health Equity through a federally-funded grant with H. Lee Moffitt Cancer Center (https://www.moffitt.org/cancers/), and the USF College of Public Health. The mission of the Center was to minimize disparities in cancer and clinical trial recruitment. Additional partnerships were developed with several community-based organizations such as REACHUP, Inc. (https://www.reachupincorporated.org/), USF Area Health Education Center (AHEC) (https://health.usf.edu/ahec/), and 50 Hoops (https://www.50hoopslegends.com/50-hoops). The Center for Health Equity successfully achieved its mission until 2015 when the funding period ended. In 2015, the College's Dean, established WE-CARE (**W**.orkgroup **E**.nhancing **C.**ommunity **A**.dvocacy & **R**.esearch **E**.ngagement) with an expanded mission from the Center of Health Equity to close the gap of health disparities with education and other collaborative initiatives to increase the recruitment and retention of marginalized and diverse populations in cancer and non-cancer-related areas of clinical research. WE-CARE is one component of the community outreach arm of the Taneja College of Pharmacy at the University of South Florida, and is the only known pharmacy-led community-engagement participatory research entity.

WE-CARE continues to work with REACHUP, Inc., Moffitt Cancer Center, AHEC, 50 Hoops, and collaborates with a host of other civic, social, Greek service organizations, professional and faith-based organizations to achieve its mission.

The mission of WE-CARE is two-fold, 1) to advocate for and oversee research activities within the community and 2) to close the gap of health disparities for marginalized populations through education. This mission empowers marginalized groups through expanding their knowledge about the protections and processes of various types of research. This mission also bridges the gap between the research community and the lay or non-scientific community, and repairs and expands the trust between the community, researchers and the clinical institutions. Figure 1 further outlines the mission of WE-CARE. WE-CARE's mission is in alignment with the National Institute of Health's 2001 goal to eliminate health disparities (Dankwa, 2021). Increasing both diversity and participation in clinical trials is also essential for the health and research community to provide optimal care and achieve optimal therapeutic outcomes. (Borell, 2021)

The primary way that WE-CARE supports researchers is through use of a Research Advisory Board (RAB) that is composed of various members from the community and the WE-CARE team. The RAB reviews research proposals from the University research community or the researchers in the community and provides suggestions on ways to market and recruit participants with a focus on local, regional contacts tight recruitment schedules. The RAB meets in bi-monthly or quarterly depending on the number of proposals received. The researchers submit information via an electronic portal to the RAB. The researcher is given 15-20 minutes to present the research AIMS to the RAB and explain the status of their recruitment success, timelines for recruitment, and eligibility criteria for participation. The RAB asks questions related to the research, and then information is provided to the researcher on ways to reach their target population for the study. In addition to assisting with recruitment the Research Advisory Board provides suggestions for retention and dissemination to the researchers when requested.

Researchers who submit proposals to the RAB are also offered additional training on the importance of cultural humility/competency, implicit bias, and other strategies that may mitigate the hesitancy of marginalized groups to participate in clinical research. Figure 2 describes the process for the Research Advisory Board review process.

The core members of WE-CARE include the Executive Director, Program Director, Assistant Program Director, the USF Health Community Outreach Director from USF. The Executive Director and Program Director are pharmacists. The Co-Founder & Retired Director of Community Engagement, Clinical Director and the Community Engagement and Outreach Manager for REACHUP, Inc. are also members of the core team. This group meets twice a month to plan events and conduct other WE-CARE activities. Community collaborators and students from across the health disciplines at USF are invited to these meetings as needed.

WE-CARE ACTIVITIES DURING THE PANDEMIC

The SARS- COVID-19 Pandemic uncovered many racial/ethnic, social, economic, and health disparities (Nana-Sinkam, 2021) and WE-CARE mobilized strategies to address the disparities, educate the public and support the healthcare community. Marginalized groups had the highest morbidity and mortality rates during the pandemic because of structural racism, occupational hazards, medical comorbidities, and preexisting social/racial, economic, and health inequities. (Borell, 2021). Anticipating the need to prepare these and other groups for the need for openness to immunization against COIVD-19 and wanting to make sure that these groups were included in clinical research trials, the WE-CARE team positioned itself as an educational resource by providing or participating in virtual workshops, Q&A sessions, town halls, panel discussions, and coordinating vaccine events to educate the community about COVID-19 (Dada, 2022). The workshops were held in collaboration with numerous faith-based, Greek-letter, social, and civic groups in the Tampa Bay region and beyond.

The WE-CARE Team utilized their clinical expertise to provide the educational events. The Executive Director for WE-CARE is an ambulatory care and metabolic syndrome clinical pharmacy specialist who has additional background training in microbiology. He provided key concepts on the pathogenesis and disease course for COVID infection, variants, and the nuances of the vaccines and supportive care for COVID. The Program Director is a neuropsychiatric pharmacy specialist with additional training in geriatrics. She provided similar insights on the disease pathogenesis and course, vaccines, variants and provided key concepts on the mental health consequences of COVID and Long-COVID. The community liaisons on the team provided information on community resources and were essential and instrumental in technologically arranging sessions and connecting the WE-CARE team to the community. REACHUP, Inc. hosted the majority of the virtual meetings, maintained an electronic library with recordings of the sessions, and took the lead on marketing events.

The first of many educational sessions offered by WE-CARE, was a four-part COVID education series that was launched at the beginning of the quarantining to mitigate myths about the disease. Table 1 provides a summary of the content covered in those sessions. After the first series of virtual workshops, numerous groups requested similar information be provided exclusively to their membership and or the public at large. As the vaccines became available, myths and other concerns started circulating about the vaccines, the intent of the research, and the agenda of the government. To mitigate the myths, the team broadened their educational efforts and provided several workshops on historical events like the Henrietta Lacks Story and the Tuskegee Study that influenced modification of research processes.

Table 1. Initial COVID Care Virtual Seminars

Session I	Pathogenesis, Symptoms, and Testing for COVID-19- Part 1
Session 2	Implications of COVID-19 Infection in Pregnancy and in Other Groups
Session 3	Strategies to Address the Mental Health Aspects of the Pandemic
Session 4	Community Resources

Upon the availability of vaccines, feedback from the community included concerns about the online requirements for registering online to get vaccinated being a barrier to aging individuals for getting vaccinated. Secondly, the positive uptake of getting vaccinated resulted in long wait lines at the department of health sites. Consequently, WE-CARE coordinated four vaccinations events with the Department of Health with and at churches targeting individuals > 65 who had hypertension and other chronic disease comorbidities to offset this challenge resulting in >600 elders being vaccinated at the four churches. Representatives from the Phi Beta Sigma Fraternity, Inc., and churches in the area identified individuals and community gatekeepers to assist with gathering the demographic information of the elders and registering them for the vaccination events at the churches. Two additional vaccination events were held at the University of South Florida Morsani Health Academic Center with assistance from local chapters of Delta Sigma Theta Sorority, Inc. and Zeta Phi Beta Sorority, Inc. in both recruitment and manpower for the event. Both sororities also provided financial support for these events which facilitated the marketing of educational materials and snacks.

WE-CARE was involved in also providing virtual education to pharmacy practitioners across the diaspora to Lagos, Nigeria as the result of a collaboration with the Pharmaceutical Society of Nigeria (PSN). The Pharmaceutical Society of Nigeria is composed of pharmacists who practice primarily in community practice, pharmaceutical industry or academia in Nigeria. The Nigerian American practitioners participate in their monthly meetings, and requested that the program director arrange for mini-educational sessions to keep the PSN abreast of ongoing developments with the disease and treatment in the US and Nigeria. The topics that were addressed with the PSN are noted in Table 2.

Table 2. Virtual Topics Provided by WE-CARE to the Pharmaceutical Society of Nigeria

ABCs of COVID-19 Variants	COVID Care During Pregnancy
An Update on the Astra Zeneca COVID Vaccine	COVID Care for Children
Importance of Managing Chronic Diseases During the Pandemic	Post Acute COVID Syndrome
Truths and Myths about the COVID-19 Vaccine	Long COVID: Symptoms and Management
Pain or Depression: A Closer Look at Various Pain Management Options	Medication Distribution System in the United States Part 2
COVID Vaccines Update: US and Nigeria Perspectives	Medication Distribution System in the United States Part 2

In light of the George Floyd murder in June of 2020, as the anxiety from the pandemic was at an emotional high, and global attention to the mental health impacts of social injustice and the mental health consequences of the pandemic were highlighted and birthed the Black Lives Matter Movement (Shim, 2021). WE-CARE included information on strategies for addressing the isolation that many community members were experiencing because of the physical isolation and quarantine requirements (Escalante, 2021).

The University of South Florida provided funding for faculty to do research on social justice issues consequent to the Black Lives Matter Movement. WE-CARE partnered in the production of the first National Alliance for Mental Illness (NAMI) This is My Brave: Voices of the African American community in 2020 with a faculty member in the Department of Aging Studies and assisted in marketing and coordinating content. The virtual program featured individuals who had various forms of mental illness share their stories artistically as they chose. Poems, music, dance, and other forms of storytelling were utilized by the individuals to share their stories. A survey was administered pre- and post-event that asked questions regarding the perceived stigma and prevalence associated with mental illnesses, definitions of discrimination, barriers to and opinions about seeking treatment for mental illness, and anti-racism beliefs and other attitudes toward mental health with a particular focus on African Americans. This event was the first-event to focus on the African-American community ever offered by NAMI (Conner, 2023; Conner, 2024).

WE-CARE also supported a Wellness and Burnout Prevention Study during the pandemic that was a funded project with faculty from the USF College of Nursing, Pharmacy, and Muma School of Business entitled " Improving Well-Being of Frontline Healthcare Practitioners and Identification of Burnout for Managers Early Intervention Study." The project was initiated based on research that showed that medical practitioners were suffering from mental health issues and ill-being while engaging in the treatment and care of patients with COVID-19 (Cai, 2020). The most noted suggestions of mental illness expressed more frequently by frontline healthcare workers were depression, anxiety, fear, trauma, and sense of incapacity (Song, 2020). The research team felt that finding and targeting effective ways to support the mental health of medical practitioners was an urgent need and subsequently developed the project that provided education and non-pharmacologic approaches to prevent burnout in frontline workers who dealt with death and dying issues more frequently compared to other frontline workers. The primary aim of this study was to evaluate the incidence depression, anxiety, and sleep disruption in hospice practitioners (nurses, physicians, social workers, chaplains, pharmacists, therapists) during the COVID-19 pandemic. A secondary aim of this study was to identify risks of burnout in hospice practitioners and provide this data to hospice managers for early intervention. The third aim was to evaluate the impact of a six-week wellness training program consisting of virtual educational workshops on resilience training, complementary and alternative approaches to mental health, physical wellness, spiritual wellness, and stress management. The study team hypothesized that a wellness training program would mitigate anxiety, depression and sleep disorders in hospice practitioners while providing risks of burnout data to managers for early intervention. Hospice workers and their managers were chosen as the intervention group because this group of frontline workers dealt with more death and dying consequent to the pandemic, and there was an extraordinary increase in workforce turnover during the pandemic.

The study provided six weeks of virtual training to the hospice workers who voluntarily signed up. The virtual educational workshops are listed in Table 3, and all were offered within an hour except for the third topic (Complementary and Alternative Approaches to Mental Health) which was offered over two hours. The impact of the educational workshops was not statistically finalized at the time of submission of this chapter, but the themes noted from the managerial interviews are included.

Table 3. Virtual Workshop Topics for Burnout Project

Topic 1: Resilience Training
Topic 2: Alternative Herbal Medication
Topic 3: Complementary and Alternative Approaches to Mental Health
Topic 4: Physical Wellness
Topic 5: Spiritual Wellness
Topic 6: Stress Management

The themes that were noted in the managerial interviews centered around staffing issues, personal protective equipment (PPE) testing, regulatory restrictions, communication stress/burnout and a sense of appreciation. Table 4 provides more details about the themes. The areas for improvement that the managers noted after the interviews were 1) there are too many different technologies and apps being used 2) open spaces for wellness and screening for wellness are needed, and 3) more opportunities for employees to express their feelings and needs should be made available to employees.

Table 4. Themes of Managerial Interviews

Themes	Managerial Comments
Staffing Issues	Decline in care Agency workers Flexible schedules
PPE/Testing	Changing regulations/limited supplies Not understanding all of the roles of employees
Regulatory Restrictions	Dealing with families and death
Communication	Limitations and isolations Huddle meetings in Zoom
Stress/Burnout	Strategies needed to help
Sense of Appreciation	Unaware of the impact

There were five leaders that were interviewed to learn about their experience during the pandemic. Participants were asked to talk about how they and their departments were impacted by COVID-19 as well as learn about the support structures that were in place for them as they tried to manage during these unprecedented times. Once the interviews were conducted and transcriptions were made, the content was organized in thematic themes.

The limited number of participants made it difficult to draw conclusions from the data, however, there were five themes that did arise from the transcripts that are worth exploring further in future research. The five themes included Staffing Issues, Care of Employees, Regulatory Restrictions, Communication, Stress, and Sense of Appreciation. Each of the themes provides some general insight for health care administrators and warrants future exploration in future studies.

Another project focusing on burnout examined the impact of the pandemic on pharmacy providers. The WE-CARE Program Director served as co-PI of a collaborative with faculty from Florida A&M University College of Pharmacy and their Institute of Public Health. This project was developed because workplace stress for pharmacists increased dramatically during the pandemic as a result of the compilation of additional tasks, including COVID-19 testing and immunization to their existing obligations, which included more drug information services, wellness screenings, prescription processing and verification (Goff, 2020; Austin, 2020; Jones, 2021). Feelings of fatigue among pharmacy practitioners, graduate pharmacists, pharmacy technicians, pharmacy residents and interns progressed from isolated grievances to widespread mental and physical health emergency. Pharmacy professionals' well-being declined while disengagement increased as a result of the new pressures in the work environment. Unfortunately, the expanded roles of pharmacy team members resulted in burnout and work dissatisfaction (Johnston, 2021; Phan, 2021; Coelho, 2021).

The Maslach Healthcare Burnout Inventory and a Resilience Scale was distributed via Qualtrics through email, text, messages, and social media to licensed pharmacists in Florida. There were 181 responses on the Maslach Burnout Inventory completed between July 2, 2022 and September 30, 2022. The pharmacists practiced in a variety of settings to include community practice (38%), in-patient care (14%), managed care (40%), academia (3%), long-term Care (2%), nuclear pharmacy (2%) and other (1%). Approximately 89.9% of the pharmacists were working between 40 and 60 or more hours per week. The results suggested that half of the pharmacists were experiencing dissatisfaction with their job every day or multiple days of the week. The respondents overwhelmingly felt that as the scope of pharmacists expanded, that mental health resources should be a priority to alleviate burnout.

WE-CARE is continuing to promote well being in hopes of preventing burnout in health professionals and the community. One project what is being developed is a Brain Health Toolkit which includes resources and information on mental illnesses, cognitive disorders and their respective treatment options. The Brain Health Toolkit is a collaborative with the National Alliance on Mental Health (NAMI), the Association of Black-Health Systems Pharmacists (ABHP), faith-based entities, health professionals from the community, and faculty with expertise in these areas. The Toolkit will be made available to churches, community pharmacies, community health workers, and other health professionals.

WE-CARE has additional projects that will allow it to carry out its mission, such as a mobile unit, and initiatives that engage and include community members and students with understanding research processes and address health disparities. WE-CARE is expanding its community footprint through employing a mobile unit focused on research and health education, clinical trial recruitment, and non-primary care clinical services like health counseling, vaccinations, and community screenings. The unit was previously used by the USF Neuroscience Byrd Alzheimer's Institute and utilized for clinical trial visits, clinical trial recruitment, research education, and memory screenings. This mobile unit will be a vital resource designed to enhance healthcare access and community engagement across underserved and underrepresented populations in the Tampa Bay region. By delivering these services, the mobile unit will advance healthcare services and health equity. The unit is equipped with an evaluation room, laboratory testing area, a reception area, bathroom, and a mini-conference room. WE-Care plans to move the unit around the Tampa Bay area and allow its community partners to use the unit for education, clinical trial recruitment or non-primary care clinical services.

One example of how WE-CARE will utilize the mobile unite to collaborate with community partners for non-primary care services is with the REACHUP, Inc.'s Doula program. The REACHUP, Inc. Doula program provides pregnant women with health education, prenatal support, mentoring, hospital labor and delivery assistance as well as breastfeeding and nutrition support. This program is available to expectant parents residing in Hillsborough County, Florida. REACHUP, Inc. has utilized an innovative method of providing doula care for over a decade – the Doula team are full-time employees with benefits and their services are offered to the community at no cost due to collaboration with respected and dedicated external funders. The Doula team also receives continuing education, in-service programming, and more via REACHUP, Inc. 's Doula Resource Center. This year will mark the launch of the REACHUP, Inc. Doula Training Program as the organization's next step in workforce development to meet the needs of the families and communities they serve. REACHUP, Inc. hires its staff from the communities it serves and believes that this practice strengthens their ability to provide services in a culturally aligned manner while also acknowledging and supporting the skills of trusted social service, health education and allied health professionals from their communities. REACHUP, Inc.

also provides services to mothers and fathers via linked programming of their doula service and services for dads.

WE-CARE would like to optimize on the well-established community engaging strategy being utilized to enhance the supportive efforts for researchers by developing a community or citizen science initiative. Community or citizen science can be an effective way to bridge trust between marginalized groups who have many reasons to distrust the medical community and academic research community. Engaging the community in all levels of research from development or the proposal to implementation and analysis of the methodology allows the community needs to be better addressed and the concerns of the community heard and appreciated. Inclusion of and collaborations with the "gatekeepers" of said communities also improve the public's trust. (Dave, 2018) The use of non-scientists in the research process affords the researcher the ability to increase the community member's knowledge about science, expand the amount of data collected, and possibly decrease the costs associated with data collection at the risk of concerns about the variances of the quality of the data being collected while increasing trust of the researcher in the community. (Kovaka, 2021) One additional benefit of citizen science is the opportunity to increase diversity in clinical trials. Based on a recent study by Sekar and associates, it was concluded that marginalized populations or others with adverse social determinants of health are least likely to consider, have access to, or be offered the opportunity to participate in clinical trials. (Sekar, 2024) It is postulated that over 85% of clinical researchers have difficulty meeting recruitment goals and often lead to delays in clinical trial processes. Engaging and educating the community through citizen science may improve the landscape of diversity in clinical trial participation. (Chesser, 2019)

The WE-CARE Community Science Initiative (CSI) is an expansion of research training for students and community members to broaden the capacity of researchers. The CSI will provide a certificate to participants who complete training in 1)research processes, 2) clinical trial recruitment strategies and 3) community-engaged participatory research methods. CSI participants will also be allowed to educate the public on research opportunities and participate in the research advisory board as needed.

As WE-CARE continues to work with various community groups, the need to provide education related to health, financial, and technology literacy is becoming more and more apparent. Health literacy is a critical component for eliminating health disparities. Health literacy can be defined as one's ability to read, translate, or understand health information that will assist in ensuring one's ability to make informed and appropriate decisions and behaviors to ensure good health outcomes. (Liu, 2020) Clear communications are required between patients and their providers, but education regarding health literacy can be the consequence of multiple sources, to include, but not be limited to socioeconomic status, cultural and generational practices, social media, access to care, and education in primary and secondary education. (Auld, 2020).

In 1990, The Human Health Services first identified subject matter experts across various health fields to develop a framework of national goals for achieving healthy outcomes. These goals are revised every ten years. (www.health.gov) For the first time in the initiative's history, the Committee specifically considered health literacy in its decisions throughout the development of Healthy People 2030. One of the initiative's overarching goals demonstrates this focus: "Eliminate health disparities, achieve health equity, and attain health literacy to improve the health and well-being of all." (Healthy People 2023/health.gov.) This project will hopefully improve the health literacy of those involved in the project, which can potentially reset health outcomes for future generations.

In alignment with Healthy People 2030, a health literacy program would be valuable in closing the gap of health disparities (https://odphp.health.gov/our-work/national-health-initiatives/healthy-people/healthy-people-2030#:~:text=Healthy%20People%202030%20includes%20355%20core%20%E2%80%94%20or,and%20prioritize%20the%20most%20pressing%20public%20health%20issues). The Health Communication and Health Information Technology Workgroup developed six Healthy Objectives specifically related to health literacy in its decisions throughout the development of Healthy People 2030. The six objectives include 1) increase the proportion of adults whose health care provider checked their understanding 2) decrease the proportion of adults who report poor communication with their health care provider 3) increase the proportion of adults whose health care providers involved them in decisions as much as they wanted 4)increase the proportion of people who say their online medical record is easy to understand 5) increase the proportion of adults with limited English proficiency who say their providers explain things clearly and 6) increase the health literacy of the population.

WE-CARE is currently working with the AHECs in the Tampa Bay region about remerging and modifying a program they provided to community health care workers in years past that would improve personal health literacy. They are also engaging literacy councils in the area who serve community members. The hope is to continue the mission of the AHECs by training healthcare professional trainees and healthcare professionals, while also training community members. The other hope is to educate healthcare professionals to drive system changes or organizational health literacy.

During the pandemic, the WE-CARE team launched a Wellness Program which was designed to circumvent repeating the morbidity and mortality in marginalized groups noted with the SARS-COVID-19 pandemic. The four pillars of the program include physical, mental, spiritual, and financial wellness. Individuals were invited to join the Wellness Club by simply providing their email address. Health information is emailed to club members on a monthly basis. The Wellness Club goals are to promote health awareness, healthy lifestyle practices, and to emphasize important health screenings. Because of the focus on getting the pandemic under control, the Wellness program did not offer much insight on financial wellness, but WE-CARE is developing a collaboration with financial planners and banking organizations to provide money management education to community members and students. The mobile unit will be utilized for community training with the goal of promoting and maintaining strong credit and promoting home ownership. The Taneja College of Pharmacy also has an Entrepreneurship Initiative with the USF Muma College of Business that can be used to provide certificates and training in small business ownership.

The WE-CARE Wellness Club inspired a Wellness Initiative in the Taneja College of Pharmacy that served faculty, staff, and was open to students during the pandemic. The focus of this program was mental well-being. Faculty and staff convened virtually to share ideas on how they were maintaining their mental well-being during the quarantining period and adjusting to work demands. Some of the ideas shared by the group included meditation, deep breathing exercises, yoga, and other complimentary practices. As the pandemic ended, this wellness initiative continued for students in the college.

WE-CARE is currently exploring a collaboration with the USF Center for Applied Lifestyle Medicine (CALM) which is led by the College of Public Health (https://health.usf.edu/publichealth/research/calm/overview). CALM seeks to advance multidisciplinary community-engaged lifestyle medicine to address chronic health conditions through an evidence-based approach to preventing, treating, and reversing the progression of chronic conditions via comprehensive lifestyle changes. Like the current WE-CARE Wellness Club, CALM is promoting physical activity, but it also is promoting better nutrition, sleep, stress management, social support, and avoiding risky substances. CALM is currently offering services targeting obesity, diabetes, hypertension, and mental health, which are all areas of interest for WE-CARE. This collaboration could allow for CALM to have a community presence through the WE-CARE mobile unit, as well as allow for a "community service lab" for College of Public Health and other health students.

The pride point of WE-CARE's work lies in it's involvement of health students with it's activities. The WE-CARE Student Ambassador Program empowers students to uplift its mission by serving as advocates and educators. Although students from all disciplines are encouraged to participate, students from the USF Health Colleges of Pharmacy, Public Health and Medicine have been most involved. Student Ambassadors play a crucial role in promoting public health awareness, delivering essential information on topics such as vaccinations, mental health, clinical research, and global health issues. Beyond education, they take on leadership responsibilities, guiding fellow ambassadors in the execution of impactful initiatives. These include social media campaigns aimed at raising awareness of diseases like cancer and organizing community-based events such as drive-thru COVID-19 vaccination clinics, which enhance vaccine accessibility. In addition to outreach, student ambassadors help assess community health needs by collecting demographic and medication-related information, which informs the development of targeted programs that address specific concerns. By combining education, leadership, and data-driven outreach, the WE-CARE Student Ambassador Program not only equips students with valuable skills in health advocacy and communication but also fosters a more informed and healthier community, aligning with the university's mission to improve healthcare access and outcomes for underserved populations.

The student ambassadors assist with the content development for the Wellness program and coordinated the first newsletter. Student organizations like The Student National Pharmacy Association (SNPhA) Chapter at USF has also been involved in serving as hosts for community-engaging events and marketing of events on campus. This year, the Student National Medical Association (SNMA) has committed to assisting with developing and organizing content for the Wellness Program and newsletter. The SNMA students have also attended and served as hosts/hostesses and analyzed the data from the breakout sessions for the Maternal Health program and provided information about participating in clinical trials at a healthfair.

Student Ambassadors are also given the opportunity to become Vaccine Ambassadors through a collaborative with a community-based organization called Project Link (https://www.project-link.org/). Project link provides back to school immunizations to uninsured school-aged kids across the Tampa Bay area. As Vaccine Ambassadors, the students are trained to educate community members about the importance of immunizations and taught strategies to address vaccination hesitancy. The student ambassadors also accompany Project Links staff to children's legislative day at the capital to lobby for laws and find funds to support immunization efforts. Project Link also has an eMerging Healthy Students initiative that WE-CARE supports which focuses on the healthy mental well-being of students.

Other activities that WE-CARE uses to minimize health disparities is to have community-facing events that focus on diseases that are seen predominantly in marginalized populations. One example is the Alzheimer's Community Forums which are a collaboration with the Alzheimer's Association, AARP, and other WE-CARE stakeholders. A second example is Community Conversations which focus on Maternal Health Issues. This event had been done in collaboration with REACHUP, Inc. and other community-based organizations that serve women of child-bearing age and their children. A third example is the *Barbershop Real Talk* events in which WE-CARE serves as a collaborative partner in workshops that are held in community barbershops that focus on wellness and financial health. Attendees not only learn about the health topics, but are encouraged to participate in clinical studies pertaining to these and other topics.

Table 5. Virtual Workshop Topics for Burnout Project

Topic 1: Resilience Training
Topic 2: Alternative Herbal Medication
Topic 3: Complementary and Alternative Approaches to Mental Health
Topic 4: Physical Wellness
Topic 5: Spiritual Wellness
Topic 6: Stress Management

CONCLUSION

WE-CARE was established to bridge the gaps in health disparities by leveraging community-driven advocacy and research engagement. The WE-CARE program at the University of South Florida exemplifies the power of collaboration between academic institutions and community stakeholders to address healthcare disparities and fuels the research enterprise by increasing the effectiveness of clinical trial recruiting. This can serve as a scalable model to empower individuals and improve healthcare outcomes.

REFERENCES

Aras, F. M., & Gümüssoy, S. (2024). Emotional burnout, job satisfaction, and intention to leave among pre-hospital emergency healthcare workers during the COVID-19 pandemic. *Work (Reading, Mass.)*, *79*(1), 47–59.

Auld, M. E., Allen, M. P., Hampton, C., Montes, J. H., Sherry, C., Mickalide, A. D., Logan, R. A., Alvarado-Little, W., & Parson, K. (2020). Health literacy and health education in schools: Collaboration for action. *NAM Perspectives*. Advance online publication. DOI: 10.31478/202007b

Austin, Z., & Gregory, P. (2020). Resilience in the time of pandemic: The experience of community pharmacists during COVID-19. *Research in Social & Administrative Pharmacy*, *17*(1), 1867.

Borrell, L. N., & Kapadia, F. (2021, August). Social Justice for Marginalized Communities. *American Journal of Public Health*, *111*(8), 1366. DOI: 10.2105. AJPH.2021.306426

Bridgeman, P. J., Bridgeman, M. B., & Barone, J. (2018). Burnout syndrome among healthcar professionals. *Bulletin - American Society of Hospital Pharmacists*, *75*(3), 147–152.

Cai, Q., Feng, H., Huang, J., Wang, M., Wang, Q., Lu, X., Xie, Y., Wang, X., Liu, Z., Hou, B., Ouyang, K., Pan, J., Li, Q., Fu, B., Deng, Y., & Liu, Y. (2020). The mental health of frontline and non-frontline medical workers during the coronavirus disease 2019 (COVID-19) outbreak in China: A case-control study. *Journal of Affective Disorders*. Advance online publication. DOI: 10.1016/j.jad.2020.06.031

Chesser, S., Porter, M. M., & Tuckett, A. G. (2019). Cultivating citizen science for all: Ethical considerations for research projects involving diverse and marginalized populations. *International Journal of Social Research Methodology*, *23*(5), 497–508. DOI: 10.1080/13645579.2019.1704355

Coelho, E., Amaral, A. P., Rocha, C., Cruz, R., & Brito-Costa, S. (2022). Burnout in pharmacy professionals during COVID-19 outbreak. *Acta Biomedica*, *93*(6), e2022281. DOI: 10.23750/abm.v93i6.13386

Conner, K. O., Abusuampeh, D. K., Kosyluk, K., Tran, J. T., Davis-Cotton, D., Hill, A. M., & Brown, A. P. (2024). Mitigating the stigma of mental illness: The impact of story telling in the black community. *International Journal of Environmental Research and Public Health*, *21*(11), 1473.

Conner, K. O., Kosyluk, K., Tran, J. T., Anderson, E., Davis-Cotton, D., & Hill, A. M. (2023). The impact of a culturally meaningful storytelling intervention on stigma and attitudes about mental health treatment. *The Journal of Nervous and Mental Disease*, *211*(6), 419–426.

Dada, D., Djiometio, J. N., McFadden, S. M., Demeke, J., Vlahov, D., Wilton, L., & Nelson, L. E. (2022). Strategies that promote equity in COVID-19 vaccine uptake for black communities: A review. *Journal of Urban Health*, *99*(1), 15–27.

Dankwa-Mullan, I., Pérez-Stable, E. J., Gardner, K. L., Zhang, X., & Rosario, A. M. (2021). *The Science of Health Disparities Research*. John Wiley & Sons., DOI: 10.1002/9781119374855

Dave, G., Frerichs, L., Jones, J., Kim, M., Schaal, J., Vassar, S., Varma, D., Striley, C., Ruktanonchai, C., Black, A., Hankins, J., Lovelady, N., Cene, C., Green, M., Young, T., Tiwari, S., Cheney, A., Cottler, L., Sullivan, G., & Corbie-Smith, G. (2018). Conceptualizing trust in community-academic research partnerships using concept mapping approach: A multi-CTSA study. *Evaluation and Program Planning*, *66*, 70–78. DOI: 10.1016/j.evalprogplan.2017.10.007

EREnvision Resolution A Wellness Movement. https://ermovement.com/

Escalante, E., Golden, R. L., & Mason, D. J. (2021). Social isolation and loneliness: Imperatives for health care in a post-COVID world. *Journal of the American Medical Association*, *325*(6), 520–521.

Escalante, L., & Maisonnave, H. (2021). The impact of the COVID-19 pandemic on women's welfare and domestic burdens in Bolivia. HAL Archives. hal-03118060.

Gillis, C., Montenigro, P., Nejati, M., & Maserejian, N. (2023). Estimating prevalence of early Alzheimer's disease in the United States, accounting for racial and ethnic diversity. *Alzheimer's & Dementia*, *19*(5), 1841–1848. DOI: 10.1002/alz.12822

Goff, D. A., Ashiru-Oredope, D., Cairns, K. A., Eljaaly, K., Gauthier, T. P., Langford, B. J., & Schellack, N. (2020). Global contributions of pharmacists during the COVID-19 pandemic. *Journal of the American College of Clinical Pharmacy: JAACP*, *3*(8), 1480–1492.

Gomez, S. L., Llera, A., Neuhausen, S. L., Newman, L., Nguyen, T., Palmer, J. R., Palmer, N. R., & Fejerman, L. (2021). Cancer health disparities in racial/ethnic minorities in the United States. *British Journal of Cancer*, *124*, 315–332. 10.1038s41416-020-01038-6

Gualano, M. R., Sinigaglia, T., Lo Moro, G., Rousset, S., Cremona, A., Bert, F., & Siliquini, R. (2021). The burden of burnout among healthcare professionals of intensive care units and emergency departments during the COVID-19 pandemic: A systematic review. *International Journal of Environmental Research and Public Health, 18*(15), 8172.

Jalili, M., Niroomand, M., Hadavand, F., Zeinali, K., & Fotouhi, A. (2021). Burnout among healthcare professionals during COVID-19 pandemic: A cross-sectional study. *International Archives of Occupational and Environmental Health, 94*, 1345–1352.

Johnson, H. A., & Goodhart, A. L. (2021). The pharmacists behind the front lines: One year later. *Journal of the American Pharmacists Association, 61*(6), 648.

Johnston, K., O'Reilly, C. L., Scholz, B., Georgousopoulou, E. N., & Mitchell, I. (2021). Burnout and the challenges facing pharmacists during COVID-19: Results of a national survey. *International Journal of Clinical Pharmacy, 43*(3), 716–725.

Jones, A. M., Clark, J. S., & Mohammad, R. A. (2021). Burnout and secondary traumatic stress in health-system pharmacists during the COVID-19 pandemic. *American Journal of Health-System Pharmacy, 78*(9), 818–824.

Kovaka, K. (2021). Evaluating community science. *Studies in History and Philosophy of Science, 88*, 102–109.

Liu, C., Wang, D., Liu, C., Jiang, J., Wang, X., Chen, H., Ju, X., & Zhang, X. (2020). What is the meaning of health literacy? A systematic review and qualitative synthesis. *Family Medicine and Community Health, 8*(2), e000351. DOI: 10.1136/fmch-2020-000351

Maslach, C., Leiter, M. P., & Schaufeli, W. (2009). Measuring Burnout. In Cartwright, S., & Cooper, C. L. (Eds.), *The Oxford Handbook of Organizational Well Being*. Academic., DOI: 10.1093/oxfordhb/9780199211913.003.0005

Mitchell, U. A., Nishida, A., Fletcher, F. E., & Molina, Y. (2021). The long arm of oppression: How structural stigma against marginalized communities perpetuates within-group health disparities. *Health Education & Behavior, 48*(3), 342–351.

Nana-Sinkam, P., Kraschnewski, J., Sacco, R., Chavez, J., Fouad, M., Gal, T., & Behar-Zusman, V. (2021). Health disparities and equity in the era of COVID-19. *Journal of Clinical and Translational Science, 5*(1), 99. DOI: 10.1017/cts.2021.23

Office of Disease Prevention. Healthy People 2030 https://odphp.health.gov/our-work/national-health-initiatives/healthy-people/healthy-people 2030#:~:text=Healthy%20People%202030%20includes%20355%20core%20%E2%80%94%20or,and%20prioritize%20the%20most%20pressing%20public%20health%20issues

Phan, H., Mills, A. R., & Fleming, J. (2021). Perceived wellness among pharmacy residents during COVID-19. *Journal of the American Pharmacists Association, 61*(6), e52–e59.

Rami, F., Thompson, L., & Solis-Cortes, L. (2023). Healthcare disparities: vulnerable and marginalized populations. In Searight, H. R. (Ed.), *Covid-19: Health Disparities and Ethical Challenges Across the Globe*. Springer., DOI: 10.1007/978-3-031-26200-5_6

Sekar, R. R., Herrel, L. A., & Stensland, K. D. (2024). Social Determinants of Health and the Availability of Cancer Clinical Trials in the United States. *JAMA Network Open, 7*(5), e2410162. DOI: 10.1001/jamanetworkopen.2024.10162

Shim, R. S., & Starks, S. M. (2021). COVID-19, structural racism, and mental health inequities: Policy implications for an emerging syndemic. *Psychiatric Services (Washington, D.C.), 72*(10), 1193–1198.

Song, X., Fu, W., Liu, X., Luo, Z., Wang, R., Zhou, N., Yan, S., & Lv, C. (2020). Mental health status of medical staff in emergency departments during the Coronavirus disease 2019 epidemic in China. Brain, behavior, and immunity, S0889-1591(20)30962-4. Advance online publication. https://doi.org/DOI: 10.1016/j.bbi.2020.06.002

Taranu, S. M., Ilie, A. C., Turcu, A. M., Stefaniu, R., Sandu, I. A., Pislaru, A. I., & Alexa-Stratulat, T. (2022). Factors associated with burnout in healthcare professionals. *International Journal of Environmental Research and Public Health, 19*(22), 14701.

University of South Florida. (n.d.) About USF overview, [Webpage]. Retrieved August 17, 2021 from https://www.usf.edu/about-usf/

University of South Florida Pocket Fact Book. (2022-23). [Infographic]. Retrieved December 9, 2022 from https://www.usf.edu/ods/documents/factbook-2022-23-final.pdf

University of South Florida Pocket Fact Book. (2019-20). [Infographic]. Retrieved from https:www.usf.edu/ods/documents/system-facts/usf-system-facts-2019-20.pdf

University of South Florida Taneja College of Pharmacy. https://health.usf.edu/pharmacy

USF College of Public Health. https://health.usf.edu/publichealth/research/calm/overview

What is preeminence and why it matters to you. (2020, September 17). In Wikipedia. https:admissions.usf.edu/blog/what-is-preeminence-and-why-it-matters-to-you

Williamson, G. (2024). Healthcare access disparities among marginalized communities. Global Perspectives in Health. *Medicine and Nursing*, *3*(1), 11–22.

Zavala, V.A., Bracci, P.M., Carethers, J.M., Carvajal-Carmona, L., Coggins, N.B., Cruz-Correa, M.R., Davis, M., de Smith, A.J., Dutil, J., Figueiredo, J.C., Fox, R., & Graves, K.D.,

KEY TERMS AND DEFINITIONS

Clinical Trials: research studies in humans that evaluate the efficacy, safety, and therapeutic impact on diseases by investigational or established therapeutic agents.

Collaboration: partnership between two or more entities focusing on a similar mission.

Community Engagement: process of allowing access to, input, feedback, and guidance from members of the non-scientist or health professional community.

Education: the exchange of information on a particular topic.

Research: the process of investigating the use, safety, efficacy, and other properties of a therapeutic product or device to establish factual information for future use. Research can also be the investigation of the perceptions, history, or characteristics of a group or a topic.

Wellness: the state of physical, mental, spiritual, financial, intellectual, environmental, social, and occupational balance for an individual.

Burnout: the state of psychological fatigue usually associated with caregiving or occupational tasks.

Ambassadors: Individuals who serve as liaisons between groups to assist in carrying out the mission of one of the groups.

Financial literacy: an individual's level understanding about saving, spending, and investing money.

Health literacy: an individual's level of understanding about issues pertaining to health diagnoses, use of medication and other treatment modalities, navigating healthcare systems and being able to effectively communicate, comply, and understand the perceptions and expectations of their healthcare providers.

Chapter 5
How Organizational Change Impacts Burnout for First-Responders and Emergency Healthcare Workers:
Firefighters as a Case Study

Angela Stephanie Mazzetti
https://orcid.org/0000-0002-1270-6735
Newcastle University, UK

Anniken Grønstad
https://orcid.org/0000-0001-8770-3814
Oslo New University College, Norway

John Blenkinsopp
https://orcid.org/0000-0002-1548-0583
Oslo New University College, Norway

ABSTRACT

First-responder and emergency healthcare workers face a higher risk of burnout than most occupations. Drawing upon the effort-reward imbalance model we examine how the growing effort required from them is increasingly met with diminishing reward. As a result, there are global shortages of workers in these occupations and the workers who remain are at greater risk of burnout. These front-line workers deal with significant occupational stressors but using the challenge-hindrance model of workplace stress we highlight the potentially greater significance for burnout of

DOI: 10.4018/979-8-3373-0169-3.ch005

organizational stressors i.e. stressors created less by the work itself and more by the organization. Using a case study of firefighters in the UK we show how organizational change can increase both stress levels and the risk of burnout.

INTRODUCTION

The concept of burnout has been widely researched over the past decades leading to an increased understanding of the negative impact of burnout on employees across a diverse range of occupations (Halbesleben & Buckley, 2004). Burnout is commonly understood as a chronic stress syndrome characterized by three primary symptoms: emotional exhaustion; depersonalization; and a reduced sense of personal accomplishment (Maslach, 1982; Maslach & Leiter, 1997; Maslach et al., 2001). Emotional exhaustion occurs when workers have used up their emotional resources in trying to cope with the demands they are facing (Freedy & Hobfoll, 1994). With depleted resources, workers no longer have the capacity to positively invest in their work, losing interest, and therefore unlikely to make a positive contribution (Bakker & de Vries, 2021). This leads to a process of depersonalization whereby workers disengage from and develop a cynicism towards their work, their coworkers, their clients and their organizations (Halbesleben & Buckley, 2004). Workers come to believe that they are no longer able to perform their work effectively, leading to a reduced sense of personal efficacy and a diminished sense of personal accomplishment (Bakker & de Vries, 2021).

Burnout has implications not only in terms of individual wellbeing but also in terms of organizational effectiveness (Halbesleben & Buckley, 2004). At the individual level, burnout has a detrimental impact on both physical and psychological health and wellbeing (Abareshi et al., 2022; Alves et al., 2023; Durand et al., 2019; Kim et al., 2020; Kumar & Narula, 2021; Tarcan et al., 2017). Additionally, this impact spills into an individual's family domain leading to family conflict and strained family relationships (Pluut et al., 2018). At the organizational level, burnout reduces productivity and performance whilst simultaneously increasing workplace errors, absenteeism, intention to quit and employee turnover (Bakker et al., 2014). Furthermore, there is a recognition that burnout can spread from one employee to others through a process of burnout contagion (Bakker et al., 2001). A wide range of organizational factors have been identified as triggers for burnout including the nature and content of job roles, the level of workload, the level of employee fit with their role, competing workplace demands, and strained workplace relationships (Edú-Valsania et al., 2022). Research conducted within public sector organizations has identified a range of organizational factors as contributing to employee burnout including, increasing work demands combined with decreasing work rewards (Bianchi & Schonfeld, 2024; Dudau and Brunetto, 2020; Kinman 2016; Restrepo & Lemos, 2021; Wilson & Britt, 2021), the emotion work inherent in human service work roles (Bianchi & Schonfeld, 2024; Humphrey, 2021; Dudau & Brunetto, 2020; Wilson & Britt, 2021); the scale and frequency of organizational change (Buttigieg et al, 2023; Dudau & Brunetto, 2020; Grønstad et al., 2019; Noblet et al., 2006; Rafferty, 2021); and staff shortages which increase the workload for other workers (Hetzel-Riggin et al., 2020).

In this chapter we explore organizational change as a trigger for employee burnout through the theoretical lens of the effort-reward imbalance (ERI) model (Siegrist, 1996). This theoretical framework allows examination of the impact of a disequilibrium between efforts and rewards and its potential impact on health. For example, Bakker et al. (2000) found nurses experienced their investments (working harder in response to higher demands) went unrewarded (no improvement in promotion prospects) and the study provided empirical support for a predictive effect of the ERI model on nurses' burnout. In this chapter, we explore the impact of organizational change on burnout through the theoretical lens of ERI, for a specific group of public sector workers; those who work in first response and emergency healthcare occupations. We include in this category police officers, firefighters, paramedics and emergency department nurses and emergency department physicians. These occupations work under extreme and risky conditions, requiring their members to deal quickly, efficiently and effectively with complex and shifting incidents of risk and danger (Hällgren et al., 2018). It is therefore vital that these groups of workers remain physically and psychologically fit to perform their roles whilst remaining emotionally engaged and committed to their work as they provide a vital function in protecting society (Dudau & Brunetto, 2020; Saud & Rice, 2024). In this chapter, we draw on a range of public sector burnout studies from across the globe, to explore how organizational change has the potential to disrupt the equilibrium between the personal investment, sacrifice and effort expended in performing these demanding roles, whilst simultaneously reducing the rewards for doing so for these occupations which disrupts their effort and reward equilibrium rendering these already high stressed occupations more susceptible to burnout.

This chapter is structured as follows. First, we set out the shifting landscape of the public sector globally, as over the past few decades, the sector has come under increased pressure to mimic private sector approaches to organizational efficiency which have impacted how public sector occupations are organized, funded and performance monitored (Dudau & Brunetto, 2020; Noblet et al., 2006; Saud & Rice, 2024). This has led to frequent large-scale changes being implemented within the public sector (Dudau & Brunetto, 2020; Rafferty, 2021). We discuss how it is not necessarily change *per se* that leads to adverse health outcomes (Rafferty, 2021; Wilson & Britt, 2021). Rather, change creates alterations in the working conditions which, in turn, lead to poor and straining working conditions (Grønstad et al., 2019) and these generate a taxing work environment that may take a toll on employees (Kinman 2016; Wilson & Britt, 2021). We distinguish between challenge stressors (workplace demands that require coping reserves but are stimulating and enhance performance) and hindrance stressors (workplace demands that constrain performance and deplete coping reserves) (Mazzola & Disselhorst, 2019). Within research on workplace stress in policing the classification of occupational and organizational stressors maps loosely onto this distinction (Rabbing et al., 2023). We highlight that as these occupations tend to attract those with a high level of vocational calling, their group members are prepared to make personal sacrifices because they gain a sense of personal achievement and reward through having made a positive contribution to society (Buttigieg et al., 2023; Wilson & Britt, 2021). However, we discuss why first responders and emergency healthcare workers are vulnerable to organizational changes that hinder how their roles are performed, increasing their workload and the hindrance stressors they have to cope with, thereby disrupting the effort- reward equilibrium (Buttigieg et al., 2023; Wilson & Britt, 2021).

Next, we present findings from a three-year ethnographic study undertaken with three fire and rescue services in England which explored the impact of occupational culture on stress and coping. The study adopted a range of ethnographic methods including participant observation, artefact analysis, and participant interviews. The section in this chapter, draws on one-to-one and focus group interviews undertaken with firefighters operating at varying levels of seniority within the service. Throughout the interviews, the impact of organizational change was regularly discussed. We set out how the wide-ranging UK New Public Management changes implemented in the service impacted the day-to-day working lives of this group of firefighters, resulting in a perceived effort-reward-imbalance. We explain how changes to working conditions not only disrupted their normalized working routines, increasing their exposure to risk, but fundamentally changed the nature of their role as a firefighter. The firefighters therefore perceived these changes as hindrance stressors, placing further demands on their workload. The lack of consultation with firefighters regarding change had also widened the gap between frontline firefighters and their more senior managers. The firefighters perceived that the lack of consultation had led to poorly conceived changes which drew attention to the fact that management did not understand what they did on a day-to-day basis. These changes at the organizational level were further compounded by a shift in public attitudes towards firefighters leaving the firefighters feeling that neither their management nor the public valued their contributions.

These insights presented in this chapter have major implications for practice as the risk of employee burnout is exacerbated for public sector emergency services personnel and first responders (Alden et al., 2021). This is due to these first responders having to cope with the challenges of organizational change stressors in addition to the cumulative impact of regular exposure to traumatic events, rendering them vulnerable to the depletion of coping resources (Alden et al., 2021; Regehr & Bober, 2005). Furthermore, the wellbeing of such occupations has come under increased scrutiny since the COVID-19 pandemic, as these workers experienced unprecedented changes to their working environments combined with an increased workload and risk to their personal health (Edú-Valsania et al., 2022; Mika-Lude et al., 2023; Saud & Rice, 2024). It is therefore vital that public sector organizations employing these groups of workers, understand how best to ameliorate the triggers of burnout and put in place health promoting working conditions (Restrepo & Lemos, 2021; Saud & Rice, 2024). This will not only protect the mental, physical and emotional health of these essential workers, but also go some way to stemming the tide of workers quitting these professions which has resulted in global shortages of these key workers (Kumar & Narula, 2021; Mika-Lude et al., 2023; Rozo et al., 2017). This is important given the contribution that these occupations make to the protection and safety of society (Galanis et al., 2021). These insights also have relevance for public sector healthcare and first response more broadly where work has become increasing more demanding, leading to higher burnout rates and increased staff turnover leading to global staff shortages (Derycke et al., 2010; Hetzel-Riggin et al., 2020; Mika-Lue et al. 2023). Furthermore, these staff shortages have been further compounded by recruitment challenges which may be due to negative public perceptions of working conditions for these occupations (Derycke et al., 2010; Mike-Lude et al., 2023).

LITERATURE REVIEW: PUBLIC SECTOR CHANGE AND BURNOUT

This literature review is structured as follows. First, we explain the theoretical framework underpinning this study, the efforts-rewards imbalance (ERI) model of stress. Second, we differentiate between workplace challenge and hindrance stressors. Next, we set out how the introduction of neoliberal policies have changed the global public sector landscape leading to large-scale change in this sector. Finally, we explore how the high-risk nature of first response and emergency healthcare work differentiates these occupations from other public sector workers making them more vulnerable to the impact of organizational change.

The Effort-Reward Imbalance Model

The efforts-reward imbalance (ERI) model is an acknowledged model for the study of chronic stress in occupations that involve a high degree of interaction with others (Buttigieg et al., 2023; Kinman, 2016; Nguyen Van et al., 2018; Restrepo & Lemos, 2021). The ERI model is based on the premise of contractual reciprocity whereby workers perceive that they will be comparatively rewarded for the efforts they put into performing their work (Siegrist, 1996, 2017; van Vegschel et al., 2005). Efforts encompass the demands of the job (such as workload, time pressures and level of responsibility) that are imposed by the employer (van Vegschel et al., 2005) as well as an individual's intrinsic motivation to match these demands (Siegrist, 2017). Contractual rewards encompass financial rewards (such as salary), status-related rewards (such as promotion opportunities and job stability) and esteem-related rewards (such as recognition) (Siegrist, 2017). Furthermore, workers' perceptions of reward may not always be employer related but may relate more broadly to society's recognition and appreciation for workers' efforts (van Vegschel et al., 2005).

Failed reciprocity occurs when individuals do not perceive that their efforts have been equivalently rewarded resulting in a high cost of effort spent versus a low gain or reward received (Siegrist, 2016, 2017; van Vegschel et al., 2005). Failed reciprocity elicits negative emotions such as anger and frustration, and recurrent exposure to high cost of effort versus low reward gain increases workers' risk of occupational stress (Siegrist, 2016, 2017) and burnout (Hetzel-Riggin et al., 2020; Kinman, 2016; van Vegschel et al., 2005). Siegrist (2017) states that effort-reward imbalance generally occurs under three specific situational conditions: dependency; strategic choice; and overcommitment. Dependency relates to there being a lack of alternative employment elsewhere either due to the worker profile (such as workers with skills deficits) or the labour market (such as a low demand for workers) (Siegrist, 2017; van Vegschel et al., 2005). In dependency situations, workers may be forced to put up with the low gain for the efforts exerted because they have no other alternative (Siegrist, 2017). Strategic choice relates to situations where workers perceive that the imbalance will get better and are therefore willing to put up with the imbalance in the hope of a brighter future (Siegrist, 2017). Finally, overcommitment refers to the tendency for some people to stive for high levels of achievement in their work generally because of an underlying personal need for esteem and recognition (Kinman, 2016; Siegrist, 2017). Overcommitment can stem from informal pressures imposed on employees by their work environment or from high levels of intrinsic motivation to perform (Siegrist, 2016).

Overcommitment is defined as "a set of attitudes, behaviours and emotions that reflect excessive striving in combination with a strong desire of being approved and esteemed" (Siegrist, 2001, p. 55). Overcommitted employees are more susceptible to the negative impact of perceived high effort versus low gain due to their tendency to both exaggerate their efforts and downplay their rewards (Derycke et al., 2010; Siegrist, 2016). Studies suggest that overcommitment can result in a "double-edged sword" with workers becoming more at risk of work-related stress and burnout (Wilson & Britt, 2021, p. 111). This is partly because highly committed workers are more prone to workaholism and therefore mental and physical fatigue (Abareshi et al., 2022; Hetzel-Riggin et al., 2020) as such, there are fewer 'recovery' opportunities for workaholics to recharge their batteries (Siegrist et al., 2004). Additionally, workaholism can spill over into the home domain creating work-family imbalances and conflict (Alves et al., 2023; Kim et al., 2020). For example, healthcare employees are especially prone to burnout (Shanafelt, 2011) as well as work-family conflict, reducing their vitality and increasing their intentions to leave healthcare (Blanco-Donoso et al., 2021). In this regard, the Conservation of Resources (COR) theory (Hobfoll, 1989) holds relevance to comprehend how workaholism may lead to work-family conflict (Shimazu et al., 2011) by arguing that stress surfaces in instances where workers' resources remain non-renewed (Halbesleben et al., 2014). In light of the COR framework, one may consider workaholism as mirroring an inadequate allocation of their (limited) resources which propels the risk of work-family conflict (Daniel et al., 2022).

Challenge and Hindrance Stressors

The challenge-hindrance model (CHM) of workplace stress was first developed by Cavanaugh et al. (2000) to explain why certain workplace stressors have greater physical and psychological impact than others. They split workplace stressors into two categories: challenge stressors and hindrance stressors. They defined challenge stressors as workplace demands such as high workload, high levels of responsibility and job scope. They suggested that whilst these types of workplace demands were inherently stressful, they created opportunities for personal growth and accomplishment "worth the discomfort that was involved" (p. 66). They defined hindrance stressors as workplace demands such as red tape, role ambiguity, bureaucracy and low level of job security. They suggested that hindrance stressors interfered with the achievement of personal goals and thwarted individual performance. They posited that the distinct categories of stressors had different impacts on workers with challenge stressors likely to be positively appraised and hindrance stressors likely to be negatively appraised by workers. As such, Cavanaugh et al. (2000) surmised that challenge stressors would lead to positive outcomes in terms of performance, such as job satisfaction whereas hindrance stressors would lead to negative outcomes of employee stress and strain.

The CHM has received some criticism for its simplistic approach to classifying workplace stress. In their meta-analysis of CHM, Mazzola & Disselhorst (2019) criticised the blanket approach to categorising one stressor as a challenge and another as a hindrance as stressors are likely to contain elements of both challenge and hindrance dependant on individual appraisal. They identified that challenge stressors are likely to have some element of hindrance and that workers' overall encounters with stress in the workplace, regardless of whether classified as challenge or hindrance, were likely to have an overall long-term negative impact in terms of their well-being. They suggested that this was likely due to challenge stressors still requiring energy in terms of coping resources in order to overcome workplace challenges. As such, although in the short-term, there is a potential for positive gain, in the longer-term, individual resources will become depleted leading to negative physical and psychological outcomes. This goes some way to explaining why both challenge and hindrance stressors have been linked to higher levels of exhaustion and burnout (Buttigieg et al., 2023; Hetzel-Riggin et al., 2020; Wilson & Britt, 2021). As we explore below, CHM may also help to explain why organizational change has the potential to disrupt the balance of challenge and hindrance stressors inherent in public sector job roles rendering these occupations more prone to burnout.

Public Sector Reform

Over the past thirty years, public sector workers globally have experienced significant organizational changes because of the introduction of neoliberal policies (Dudau & Brunetto, 2020; Noblet et al., 2006). This has resulted in the implementation of private sector style performance management practices to monitor the costs associated with delivering public services against the quality of the output they produce (Dudau & Brunetto, 2020; Ferlie et al., 2003; Hyndman & McGeough, 2008; Noblet et al., 2006). These organizational changes have presented "structural, procedural, and cultural" challenges for public sector workers (Noblet et al., 2006, p. 336). Structural changes have often been large scale, such as mergers, downsizing, and outsourcing which can lead to job cuts or the threat of job cuts and a reduction in finances and other work resources (Noblet et al., 2006; Rafferty, 2021). Procedural changes impact how work tasks are performed leading to role ambiguity, intergroup conflict and job insecurity (Buttigieg et al., 2023). Cultural change impacts how performance is perceived and measured (Noblet et al., 2006). Studies highlight the difficulties when implementing performance management systems which focus on quantifiable output into public sector services as attention needs to be given to the social and political contexts in which public sector organizations operate (Broadbent & Guthrie, 1992; Dudau & Brunetto, 2020; Hyndman & McGeough, 2008). The public sector is constrained by government policy setting, increased media criticism, government and public scrutiny, and ever-changing user expectations and demands (Dudau & Brunetto, 2020; Ferlie et al., 2003). In this context the concept of effectiveness is more complex as the delivery of the service is co-produced and therefore there is less of a tangible link between inputs and results (Derycke et al., 2010; Dudau & Brunetto, 2020; Ferlie et al., 2003; Hyndman & McGeough, 2008).

These changes have impacted working conditions for public sector workers by increasing the demands associated with performing their tasks whilst simultaneously reducing their access to resources to perform their tasks effectively (Buttigieg et al., 2023; Noblet et al., 2006). Studies therefore highlight that rather than enhancing public services, public sector reform has had unintended consequences leading to increased stress levels and burnout amongst workers, reduced organizational commitment and work satisfaction, increased work errors, mistakes and accidents, and increased absence levels and employee turnover (Derycke et al., 2010; Dudau & Brunetto, 2020; Noblet et al., 2006; Rafferty, 2021). For example, in their study of large-scale changes at a public hospital in Malta, Buttigieg et al. (2023) identified that change placed greater demands on workers who were already experiencing work overload. Through the lens of Conservation of Resources (COR) theory, they highlighted how this had led to employees disengaging from their work to preserve their already stretched coping reserves.

High-Risk Occupations

First responders (such as firefighters, police officers, and paramedics) and emergency healthcare workers (such as emergency department physicians and nurses) belong to a distinct group of occupations exposed to risky contexts (Hällgren et al., 2018). An occupation is defined as "a collection of work roles with similar goals that require the performance of distinctive activities as well as the application of specialized skills or knowledge to accomplish these goals (Dierdorff et al., 2009, p. 974). The nature of the work undertaken and the skills and knowledge base to conduct such work varies across occupations with some occupations having more stringent controls to entry and constraints in terms of behaviours (Dierdorff & Ellington, 2008; Dierdorff & Morgeson, 2007). Distinct occupations, such as those explored in this chapter, are distinguished from more indefinable occupations (such as 'managers') because they are characterized by group members having a shared understanding of what their job comprises, how best to complete the relevant tasks required to successfully undertake their job, complemented by training to develop the skills-set and a knowledge base to proficiently complete their tasks (Ford, 2012; Hällgren et al., 2018). As such, both those aspiring to enter those occupations and the wider public would have established perceptions of what the job entails, the archetypal occupational member, as well as the dominant values that underpin that occupation (Beyer & Hannah, 2002; Ford, 2012). Distinct occupations are important cultural groups within the workplace as their culture and membership do not coincide with organizational boundaries and therefore extend beyond organizational controls and influences (Alvesson, 2002; Hällgren et al., 2018).

Studies of first responders and emergency healthcare occupations highlight that these workers generally attract people who have a high level of vocational calling (Lee & Olshfski, 2002; Wilson & Britt, 2021). Dik & Duffy (2009, p. 427) define a 'calling' as a

> *transcendent summons, experienced as originating beyond the self, to approach a particular life role in a manner oriented toward demonstrating or deriving a sense of purpose or meaningfulness and that holds other-oriented values and goals as primary sources of motivation.*

The first dimension of this definition refers to the spiritual nature of one's calling which in some way transcends the individual, originating from some higher order drive and passion to pursue a particular career (Dik & Duffey, 2009; Wilson & Britt, 2021). The second dimension of a calling refers to the sense of purpose and meaning that one drives from undertaking their calling (Dik & Duffey, 2009). This sense of purpose is derived from performing the work itself, regardless of outcomes achieved (Wilson & Britt, 2021). Finally, the third dimension relates to the prosocial nature of a calling, working to benefit others and society (Dik & Duffey, 2009; Wilson & Britt, 2021).

Occupations that serve to protect the welfare of others, and face danger in doing so, internalise a favourable self-image of themselves as honourable professions due to the value they provide to society (Lee & Olshfski, 2002). Their motivation and commitment to their role therefore transcend organizational boundaries as they derive much of their sense of identity from their work, feeling a deep sense of belonging and connection to their occupational community (Dik & Duffey, 2009; Lee & Olshfski, 2002; Wilson & Britt, 2021). This connection can extend beyond the individual group member to include their family members. For example, Green et al. (2006) highlight that belonging is so strongly embedded in the firefighter culture that firefighters will not only do all they can to rescue a fellow firefighter in danger, but consider they have a moral obligation to support the family of firefighters killed in service.

First responders and emergency healthcare workers regularly encounter traumatic events, observing suffering and death whilst simultaneously facing the possibility of injury or death, in the performance of their work (Alves et al., 2023; Durand et al., 2019; Greene et al., 2006; Haslam & Mallon, 2003; Kim et al., 2020; Rozo et al., 2017; Scott & Myers, 2005; Sexton et al., 2021; Waters & Ussery, 2007).

Furthermore, these occupational group members will undoubtedly experience numerous traumatic events over the course of their working lives and therefore there is a cumulative impact of trauma experienced across multiple events (Abareshi et al., 2016; Alves et al., 2023; Durand et al., 2019; Gomes et al., 2022; Kim et al., 2020). This cumulative impact not only renders these occupations more vulnerable to burnout but may also render these workers more vulnerable to posttraumatic stress disorder (PTSD) (Del Ben et al., 2006; Galanis et al., 2021; Jahnke et al., 2016).

To enable normal operational functioning despite these working conditions, these occupations have developed highly practised work routines that enable members to act quickly, safely and efficiently even under highly emotive and challenging conditions (Geiger et al., 2021; Greene et al., 2006; Hällgren et al., 2018). The consistent enactment of these routines relies on regular rehearsal and training, high degrees of interdependent teamworking, as well as high levels of trust in the competencies of others to perform their routines correctly (Colquitt et al., 2011; Hällgren et al., 2018). For example, in their study of firefighters, Geiger at al. (2021) highlighted those clear lines of hierarchical decision making and communication combined with highly practised rhythms developed during training, enabled the firefighters to 'get ahead of time' and maintain control despite temporal and incident uncertainties.

These occupations also engage in highly contextualised emotion work that enables them simultaneously to display appropriate compassion to others whilst also remaining calm during chaos, and to take control of traumatic situations to protect the public (Durand et al., 2019; Gibbons, 2024; Gomes et al., 2022; Ivanić et al., 2017; Palazoğlu & Koç, 2019; Scott & Myers, 2005; Tuckey et al., 2012; Waters & Ussery, 2007). This requires that these workers develop strong efficacy beliefs about their levels of control and their ability to make life or death decisions under time pressured and emotionally charged situations (Alves et al., 2023; Durand et al., 2019; Galanis et al., 2021; Tuckey et al., 2012; Waters & Ussery, 2007). However, studies highlight that this suppression of emotion can result in workers having little opportunity to express their feelings with their peers or talk openly about their experiences (Adriaenssens et al., 2015; Gibbons, 2024; Haslam & Mallon, 2003; Schwab et al., 2016; Sexton et al., 2021; Tuckey et al., 2012; Waters & Ussery, 2007). For example, humour is a normalised coping mechanism for first responders who make jokes about situations which others would consider sacred and distasteful (Scott, 2007; Green et al., 2006). Humour serves not only as a 'safety valve' for the release of emotions and protection against psychological harm, but also as a means of building team camaraderie to help these professionals deal with the absurdities of their work (Haslam & Mallon, 2003; Scott, 2007). First responders develop a shared understanding of 'what constitutes funny and this implicit understanding is culturally defined' meaning that those outside of the culture may experience this humour as inappropriate (Scott, 2007, p. 352).

However, those whose work has extensive emotion work obligations are more vulnerable to burnout if they do not have the coping strategies to engage with emotion work or they do not have adequate time to recover and renew (Gomes et al., 2022; Humphrey, 2021). First responders and emergency healthcare workers generally demonstrate high levels of overcommitment partly because of their high levels of vocational calling and partly because of their commitment to protect others (Lee & Olshfski, 2002; Wilson & Britt, 2021). Furthermore, these occupations generally have demanding work schedules; they work long hours, they commit to being on 24-hour standby and they work shift patterns (Durand et al., 2019; Galanis et al., 2021; Gomes et al., 2022; Kim et al., 2020; Kumar & Narula, 2021; Navarro Moya et al., 2020). This can disrupt sleeping routines, lead to a lack of time for eating, and impact family life (LaFontaine, 2024; Navarro Moya et al., 2020; Palazoğlu & Koç, 2019). This lack of time to engage in basic functions can be compounded when there are staff shortages (Kumar & Narula, 2021; Navarro Moya et al., 2020; Palazoğlu & Koç, 2019). This can take its toll not only in terms of physical exhaustion but also in terms of mental exhaustion (Abareshi et al, 2016; Rozo et al., 2017). This vulnerability to both mental and physical exhaustion has been further compounded by the COVID-19 pandemic as recent studies have highlighted that due to the high levels of commitment, investment and workaholism required of first responders and emergency healthcare workers during the pandemic, levels of fatigue, exhaustion and work-family conflict increased, leaving these workers' coping reserves significantly depleted further exacerbating their risk of burnout (Dominic et al., 2021; Raudenská et al., 2020; Sagaltici et al., 2022; Saud & Rice, 2024; Soeker 2022; Tham et al., 2023).

Stress Management Interventions to Reduce Risk of Burnout

The various studies forming this review suggested a range of stress management interventions that might be introduced to ameliorate the risk of burnout and PTSD amongst first responders and emergency healthcare workers. Workplace stress management intervention strategies are generally categorised into primary interventions (interventions which are aimed at eliminating or mitigating the stressors); secondary interventions (which aim to make the individual more 'stress hardy'); and tertiary interventions (which provide support for individuals who have been exposed to stress) (Dewe et al., 2010). Studies recommended a range of primary interventions such as the removal of red tape and bureaucracy for these first line workers (Dominic et al., 2021); the provision of physical spaces for relaxation and decompression (Abareshi et al., 2016; Adriaenssens et al., 2015; Dominic et al., 2021; Salmela et al., 2020); creating an inclusive environment of social support (Adriaenssens et al., 2015; Gomes et al., 2022; Ivanić et al., 2017; Kim et al., 2020;

LaFountaine, 2024; Navarro Moya et al., 2020); job rotation to give workers more time to recharge (Abareshi et al., 2016); rethinking operational models such as shift work (Gomes et al., 2022); and more involvement of front line staff in decision making processes (Adriaenssens et al., 2015; Gomes et al., 2022; Ivanić et al., 2017; Sexton et al., 2021). Secondary interventions included: training and development to help workers recognise the early signs of stress and burnout (Adriaenssens et al., 2015; Gomes et al., 2022; LaFountaine, 2024; Sexton et al., 2021); and formal debriefing after traumatic events to help workers talk about their feelings (Adriaenssens et al., 2015; Haslam & Mallon, 2003; Schwab et al., 2016; Sexton et al, 2021). Tertiary interventions included the provision of counselling and trauma support for stressed workers (Adriaenssens et al., 2015; Haslam & Mallon, 2003; Schwab et al., 2016). However, many of the studies identified that putting in place robust stress management interventions would require significant investment from public administrations and governments to redress the effort-reward imbalances in the system as demand for public services continues to grow despite the pressures that these workers are already under (Dominic et al., 2021; LaFountaine, 2024; Navarro Moya et al., 2020; Sexton et al., 2021)

Furthermore, the studies highlighted that a 'one size fits all' approach may not be appropriate but rather interventions may need to be occupationally targeted at the different specialisms (Dominic et al., 2021). Individuals are embedded within their occupational cultures which inform attitudes to stress and coping: stress management interventions therefore need to be contextualised and matched to their cultural context (Noblet & LaMontagne, 2006: Nytrø et al., 2000). For example, in their study of physicians, Dominic et al. (2021) identified that physicians preferred to access support from outside services rather than in house services. This was due to a reluctance on their part to talk about their struggles in work as they perceived that this would have a negative impact on their careers. Similarly, in their review of the stress intervention strategies of the New York Police Department, Dowling et al. (2005) discuss the merits of the 'Cop 2 Cop' programme which provided confidential peer-based assistance to officers. Within a police culture where there is a reluctance to seek help from internal departments (as this may have a negative impact on the career of the officer), but also a reluctance to talk to those outside of the occupational culture, this kind of programme can provide an effective and targeted intervention. In their review of the New York Fire Department, Green et al. (2006) discussed the importance of informal strategies. They identified that the 'Brotherhood' provides a safe collective release for emotions. In the unpredictable environment of fire and rescue, they suggest that the time spent around the fire house 'kitchen table' is cherished for its stability and normality and in this context, firefighters can openly share feelings and emotions. However, they also suggest this close 'paramilitary' style connection, that provides a safe outlet for the sharing of traumatic experiences, also results in an embedded reluctance to accept help from those outside the 'Brotherhood', including health professionals. They suggest that stress intervention strategies therefore need to be delivered by those who have 'insider' knowledge of this close family network.

Reviews of stress management intervention strategies highlight the predominance of individual-focused strategies rather than wider organizational targeted interventions (Dewe et al., 2010; LaMontagne et al., 2007; Richardson & Rothstein, 2008). Inherent in the assumptions that underpin individually focused intervention strategies is the belief that individuals can modify and change their work environment. For example, Salmela et al. (2020) reported on the impact of a project to provide emergency department nurses with a restorative space to decompress after a traumatic event or when they felt overwhelmed. The initiative called the "serenity room" provided the nurses with safe and calming space to take some time out to gather their thoughts and regain focus. Their study found that the nurses who had used the room felt renewed. However, they also found that due to limited staffing and lack of time in their shift, many nurses had not been able to use the space. In addition, individuals can do little to change the views that society holds regarding the expected behaviour patterns associated with specific occupational groups. Using the media's attention on the New York Fire Department firefighters after 9/11 as an example, Greene et al. (2006) highlight the problem of living up to societal expectations. They describe how the media hype of being a 'hero' became too much for the firefighters who were struggling to come to terms with the loss of so many of their 'brothers' and as time passed, media attention started to focus on the misbehaviour of the firefighters with a shift from admiration to scandal which had a very negative impact on the self-esteem of the firefighters involved.

CASE STUDY: THE IMPACT OF ORGANIZATIONAL CHANGE ON FIREFIGHTERS

In this section, we present a case study of the impact of organizational change driven by public sector reform on perceptions of effort-reward imbalance for firefighters at three fire and rescue services in England. As part of a three-year ethnographic study exploring how occupational culture informed perceptions of stress, a series of one-to-one and focus group interviews were conducted with firefighters (of varying lengths of operational service and at varying levels of managerial rank) employed at the three fire departments. O'Reilly (2012) stresses that ethnographic interviews are not just for the purposes of data collection but are also an important relationship building mechanism. She further stresses however, that building relationships requires trust between the ethnographer and the participants. Trust is a key characteristic of the firefighter culture that underpins both their attitudes to themselves and also to others with a general mistrust amongst firefighters of those from outside the firefighter culture (Green et al., 2006). Issues of trust were further exacerbated in this study due to the sensitivity of the research topic (stress) combined with contextual sensitivities as the research was conducted during a period of significant austerity funding reforms and firefighter industrial action against these reforms. As such, the interviews were not video or audio recorded, with the researcher opting instead to rake notes during the interviews as a record of the issues discussed (Mazzetti, 2019). This enabled issues of confidentially to be handled more sensitively (Brewer, 2000) and facilitated the participants to open up and raise issues in a trusting environment (O'Reilly, 2012). These notes were written up as 'qualitative descriptions' after the interviews, a form of building interview discussions into a narrative resembling an interview transcript (Brewer, 2000). Relevant qualitative descriptions have been shared with the reader in this section to give insights into the issues discussed with the research participants. By its nature, organizational ethnography involves a small number of research settings and therefore there is a greater risk that the identity of the participants might be made visible (Murphy & Dingwall, 2001). Throughout this section neither the institutions nor the individuals participating in this research are identified.

During these interviews and focus groups the firefighters indicated that organizational change had become a major stressor impacting their everyday working lives. Over the past three decades, successive UK governments have implemented a series of New Public Management reforms across the UK public sector with the objective of improving service effectiveness and efficiency (Hyndman & McGeough, 2008). Government reform has impacted how fire and rescue services in England are funded and performance-managed with the level of funding from central government dependent on the achievement of several service delivery and corporate health performance outcomes (Penfold et al., 2009; Seifert & Sibley, 2005). Because of these efficiency and effectiveness reforms, the firefighters employed at the case organizations had experienced changes to their terms and conditions of employment (such as pension and pay reforms), changes to their role and responsibilities as firefighters (such as a greater focus on incident prevention tasks) and changes to their firefighter routines due to the introduction of cheaper safety equipment and clothing. Furthermore, they considered that these changes were taking place amidst increasingly hostile social, political and media discourses that downplayed the highly skilled and traumatic nature of their role. As such, the firefighters were experiencing effort and reward imbalance. The firefighters perceived that their workload effort had increased due to a government attitude of 'doing more with less' that resulted in changes to their terms and conditions of employment. Yet simultaneously their rewards had diminished as they were experiencing a loss of occupational identity and value assigned to the role of a firefighter; a loss of voice in decision making processes that impacted their wellbeing and safety; and loss of access to informal coping mechanisms. These reward losses will now be discussed in more detail below.

Loss of Firefighter Identity and Value

Firefighters derive much of their identity and status from their occupation (Green et al., 2006; Lee & Olshfski, 2002). They are a classic example of an occupational type described above, namely those who protect the safety and welfare of others and face danger in doing so, and therefore as with other occupations in this category they have internalised a favourable self-image of the value they provide to society as a means of coping with the risks associated with their role (Geiger et al., 2021; Hällgren et al., 2018). The New Public Management modernisation agenda in the UK has seen a shift in focus from the response activities of fire and rescue services to prevention activities with targets for prevention initiatives being set centrally and performance monitored at the level of individual fire and rescue services (Seifert & Sibley, 2005). The firefighters at the case organizations regularly highlighted that although they appreciated the importance of prevention initiatives, they had experienced a sense of loss of their identity as a firefighter. This was particularly significant for those who had been with the service for a long time and therefore had seen a shift in the expectations of their role. This is illustrated by a firefighter comment raised at one of the focus group interviews:

This change in focus has changed the role of a firefighter. We now spend more time on prevention duties like checking smoke alarms and doing talks in the community. For those that have been with the service for a while it has been difficult to adjust.

Firefighters have a high-level of vocational calling and therefore feel rewarded when helping others (Kim et al., 2020). However, the firefighters at the case organization, often stated that the refocus on prevention tasks was demeaning of their expertise as firefighters. Additionally, they highlighted that these activities failed to give them the adrenaline rush, the buzz of firefighting as these preventative tasks were less challenging. This had altered their perception of effort-reward balance, as they found these activities a hindrance that required effort but gave them little or no reward. Furthermore, studies of firefighters have indicated that lack of challenge can be a key contributor to burnout (Kim et al., 2020).

Seifert & Sibley (2005) highlight that to reinforce the importance of the preventive role of the service, targets to reduce the number of incidents and fatalities were introduced. This created a clash of ideologies between the government and fire and rescue services, as these services are measured against targets over which they have limited control – the public are responsible for creating incidents, not firefighters, and yet firefighters must risk their lives in response to incidents which are considered failures in performance management terms. This issue was eloquently illustrated by a station manager in a one-to-one interview at one of the case study organizations:

How do you tell your crews when they have risked their lives to save someone else's that they are a failure because they shouldn't have let the fire start in the first place?

In addition, firefighters across the case organizations considered that engaging in preventative safety awareness activities within the community had resulted in firefighters being put under unnecessary scrutiny from the public who have a different expectation as to the role and purpose of a firefighter. As one firefighter noted during a focus group interview:

When the public see a fire appliance turn up, they expect to see us responding to some emergency. If they don't see this, they think we are just hanging about with nothing to do, and they taunt us with 'have you not got any fires to put out?'

The firefighters therefore felt that the introduction of incident reduction targets had challenged the firefighter paradigm that they represent a highly valued emergency response occupation. This loss had been further exacerbated by an economic climate of money and job worries and increased public and media scrutiny regarding public expenditure. However, they also considered that the public had an out-dated view of the role of a modern-day firefighter. The firefighters gave numerous examples of the non-emergency calls they had to deal with and the pressure that the public would put firefighters under to enter fires, jump into rivers, or onto frozen lakes before the risks had been assessed or the necessary procedures put in place to mitigate risk. The firefighters considered that the public no longer valued the importance of their role or more significantly, no longer valued their lives as noted by a firefighter in one of the focus group interviews.

When you get to an incident, they are shouting at you to 'get in'. They don't understand that we have restrictions and procedures to follow. We have processes to follow to keep us safe, but they don't seem to care about us. They don't seem to have any respect for our lives.

As such, the firefighters at the case organizations were experiencing an imbalance in terms of their perceived increase in effort due to both the changes in their terms and conditions of employment and public discourses of 'doing more with less' combined with perceived losses of rewards related to the status and value assigned to their role of emergency response personnel. They considered that this imbalance would be further exacerbated as the importance of their role was consistently downplayed by the government who continued to enforce changes to their terms and conditions of employment, and a general public who no longer valued the role firefighters play in society. Public services are not delivered in a conventional sense and therefore managers' views of performance may be at odds with the public's view of performance (Ferlie et al., 2003). However, the firefighters also expressed the view that public expectations are unrealistic, and perceived that the public have scant regard for their safety.

Loss of Voice in Decision Making

Occupations that operate in risky contexts, such as firefighters, manage the risks associated with their role through high levels of interdependent trust and teamwork coupled with well-practised work routines (Colquitt et al., 2011; Dahles & Van Hees, 2004; Geiger et al., 2021; Hällgren et al., 2018). This point was illustrated by a firefighter participating in one of the focus groups:

We trust one another. This trust is built on competence and experience. You know that your colleagues can do the job and have your back.

Because they worked in close-knit teams that had generally been established for some time the firefighters were familiar with each other's skill set. They therefore trusted one another's competencies to perform their role. This trust was not only interdependent on other firefighters making up a crew but also interdependent on the trust they placed on their commanding fire officers. They highlighted the most experienced firefighters generally held the more senior roles and took command of the more complex incidents. The firefighters therefore had trust in their commanding officers' abilities to take reasoned and competent action.

However, the firefighters employed at the case organizations highlighted that efficiency initiatives had resulted in changes to their teamworking practices. For example, working across different crews and different services. One of the firefighters in the focus groups highlighted the significance of this on trust:

Although we are all trained to do the same job you get used to your own crew and the way they work. When you're with another team they do things differently and this can be stressful.

At one of the case organizations firefighters frequently referred to a new department that had been introduced to take control of the service's procurement to enhance efficiency savings, including the procurement of firefighter safety equipment and safety clothing. The firefighters noted that some of the new equipment and clothing was not fit for operational purpose, therefore increasing the risk to their wellbeing whilst at an incident. For example, a firefighter taking part in one of the focus groups noted:

It is important that when you attend an incident you have everything under control. Equipment that isn't fit for purpose just makes the job so much harder.

Firefighting is a high-reliability occupation and therefore trust in operating procedures, the performance of others, and trust in equipment is vital for effective functioning in an unpredictable and dangerous context (Colquitt et al., 2011). This study suggests that trust is a key resource which influences the appraisal of events and therefore any changes that alter trust reserves (for example faulty equipment, new team members, inexperienced managers) can result in an appraisal of loss or threat. Firefighters appraise in a multisensory way and therefore their senses are key coping resources. Any changes to equipment or clothing which reduce the effectiveness of their senses will therefore alter their appraisal of events.

The firefighters employed at the case organizations expressed their powerlessness to challenge these changes to routines and equipment, further devaluing their sense of status and importance:

You don't have any control over new equipment or new procedures that they bring in. No one listens to your opinions.

Additionally, the firefighters highlighted that organizational changes that impacted their work routines were generally implemented without their involvement or consultation resulting in a perceived loss of voice in the decisions that impacted their wellbeing and safety. This point is illustrated by a comment by a firefighter in one of the focus groups:

They say, 'the biggest asset is the workforce' and yet they implement systems that contradict this. They have lost touch with the grass roots and what is important. They are too far detached from reality.

This had resulted in cynicism and resistance to change even for those firefighters now operating in a management role. These operational managers had experienced significant conflict as they belonged to both the dominant occupational group (firefighters) but also the organization's 'administration' responsible for driving through change. This has led to a clash in ideologies for many managers, particularly those at the middle layers who did not consider that changes were always in the best interests of the service. For example, in a one-to-one interview, a middle level operational manager noted that:

All the changes have caused a lot of mistrust in the service. There is now a big gap between the crews on the ground and those at the top. This has made our roles very difficult as we are stuck in the middle trying to motivate our crews and at the same time trying to implement policy.

These middle level managers had become "unwilling brokers" oscillating between top down organizational pressures to implement change yet unable to perceive how the changes created value for service operatives and users (Dudau & Brunetto, 2020, p.12). This has implications for the success of organizational change initiatives as managers act as organizational change agents and as such, they influence their subordinates' attitudes towards change (Cinite el al., 2009). If managers do not embody their organization's values regarding change, they will not create a sense of readiness for change in their subordinates, and their subordinates will therefore continue to resist change (Cinite et al., 2009; Armenakis et al., 1993).

Loss of Access to Informal Coping Mechanisms

In addition to the formal stress management interventions (such as formal debriefing after traumatic incidents and access to counselling and trauma support services the firefighters employed at the case organizations also highlighted a number of informal coping mechanisms. They considered their camaraderie to be a key coping resource. They discussed how they worked in close-knit teams and how this family extended beyond their work duties as they regularly socialised together and engaged in sports teams and events. They discussed the importance of talking about an incident with their crew members as an important outlet for their ruminations. This was so important that even if an incident happened at the end of the shift, they would stay back to be together and take some time to decompress together. Haslam & Mallon (2003) noted that firefighters often ruminate on their actions and informal debriefing provides a mechanism to discuss the actions taken with those who had been through the same experience. However, the firefighters at the case organizations reflected on the impact on the higher ranks when they moved out of the family team structure. Indeed, the higher-ranking operational managers discussed the impact of not being part of such a close team had on their ability to cope. They used the term '*manager flu*' to describe how they struggled to cope with the demands of their work without the resource of a support network (the watch) as this key coping resource was lost upon moving up through the ranks.

The firefighters employed at the case organizations also referred to their use of '*gallows humour*' as a means of decompressing after an incident. Haslam & Mallon (2003) found that humour not only helped to break the ice and therefore acted as a safety-valve to relieve tension during difficult and emotion-laden situations, but that humour also acted as a means of sharing the emotion of the experience with colleagues, promoting closeness in the team and strengthening group membership. However, the firefighters employed at the case organizations, were increasingly aware that their humour was highly contextualised to their watch, and they discussed how new members could alter their use of humour. They were also increasingly concerned that those external to their environment would find the humour inappropriate or disrespectful which made them wary of engaging in this decompression activity.

Case Summary

For the firefighters employed at the case organizations, organizational change was experienced as a major stressor which created perceived effort reward imbalances, leading to cynicism and resistance to further organizational changes. Insights from the case organizations suggest that a lack of contextual awareness has led to flaws in the implementation of the various change initiatives, highlighting the paradoxes which can emerge when organizational change conflicts with the deeply embedded assumptions and values of a constituent occupational group such as firefighters. Crucially, when organizational leaders act in ways that increase the risk of burnout for their workforce they may be unaware of this, especially if they frame any concerns raised as illustrating workers' resistance to change rather than the voicing of legitimate and significant problems. Insights from the case organizations suggest that a lack of contextual awareness has led to flaws in the design and implementation of the various change initiatives, highlighting the paradoxes which can emerge when organizational change conflicts with the deeply embedded assumptions and values of a constituent occupational group such as firefighters. This has major implications for practice as the risk of employee burnout is exacerbated for public sector emergency services personnel, such as firefighters (Alden et al., 2020; Kim et al., 2020). This is due to these first responders having to cope with the challenges of organizational change stressors in addition to the cumulative impact of regular exposure to traumatic events, rendering them vulnerable to the depletion of coping resources (Alden et al., 2020; Kim et al., 2020; Regehr & Bober, 2005). This case study illustrates that the way in which change is managed and implemented, significantly influences how change will be perceived and experienced by those involved.

CONCLUSION

The fire service case study presented here captures in microcosm the macro trends which intersect to create the burnout challenge which is the focus of this chapter. The National Intelligence Council's "Global Trends 2040" report (Office of the Director of National Intelligence, 2021: 79) summarises these trends very neatly:

> *Governments in all regions will face mounting pressures from economic constraints and a mix of demographic, environmental, and other challenges. Meanwhile, populations will demand more, and they are empowered to push for their conflicting goals and priorities.*

The challenges driving governments to attempt to deliver more with less, coupled with the reluctance of governments to level with citizens about what these challenges might mean for public services, leave workers in public service occupations attempting to meet the unachievable demands of government and the unrealistic expectations of the public.

Experiencing a tension between organizational demands and customer expectations is hardly a novel experience for workers. But for frontline public service workers, especially in those occupations discussed here, the risk of it producing burnout is exacerbated by occupational norms and culture which reject self-protecting strategies such as disengagement (Afrahi et al., 2022) and push workers to deliver the service to the public despite chronic stressors. This is clearly unsustainable – given global shortages in these key occupations (e.g. Mika-Lude et al., 2023) we cannot afford to lose more of these workers to burnout. We see a key role for leaders in creating work environments which acknowledge the challenges of contemporary public service and provide workers with the support and resources to cope with the demands placed on them.

REFERENCES

Abareshi, F., Salimi, F., Farnia, F., Fallahi, M., & Rastaghi, S. (2022). The impact of mental workload, work-related and socio-demographic factors on job burnout among emergency medical staff. *Work (Reading, Mass.)*, *72*(4), 1269–1277. DOI: 10.3233/WOR-210001 PMID: 35723141

Adriaenssens, J., De Gucht, V., & Maes, S. (2015). Determinants and prevalence of burnout in emergency nurses: A systematic review of 25 years of research. *International Journal of Nursing Studies*, *52*(2), 649–661. DOI: 10.1016/j.ijnurstu.2014.11.004 PMID: 25468279

Afrahi, B., Blenkinsopp, J., de Arroyabe, J. C. F., & Karim, M. S. (2022). Work disengagement: A review of the literature. *Human Resource Management Review*, *32*(2), 100822. DOI: 10.1016/j.hrmr.2021.100822

Alden, L. E., Matthews, L. R., Wagner, S., Fyfe, T., Randall, C., Regehr, C., White, M., Buys, N., Carey, M. G., Corneil, W., White, N., Fraess-Phillips, A., & Krutop, E. (2021). Systematic literature review of psychological interventions for first responders. *Work and Stress*, *35*(2), 193–215. DOI: 10.1080/02678373.2020.1758833

Alves, L., Abreo, L., Petkari, E., & Pinto da Costa, M. (2023). Psychosocial risk and protective factors associated with burnout in police officers: A systematic review. *Journal of Affective Disorders*, *332*, 283–298. DOI: 10.1016/j.jad.2023.03.081 PMID: 36972850

Alvesson, M. (2002). *Understanding Organizational Culture*. SAGE Publications Ltd. DOI: 10.4135/9781446280072

Armenakis, A. A., Harris, S. G., & Mossholder, K. W. (1993). Creating Readiness for Organizational Change. *Human Relations*, *46*(6), 681–703. DOI: 10.1177/001872679304600601

Bakker, A. B., & de Vries, J. D. (2021). Job Demands–Resources theory and self-regulation: New explanations and remedies for job burnout. *Anxiety, Stress, and Coping*, *34*(1), 1–21. DOI: 10.1080/10615806.2020.1797695 PMID: 32856957

Bakker, A. B., Demerouti, E., & Sanz-Vergel, A. I. (2014). Burnout and work engagement: The JD–R approach. *Annual Review of Organizational Psychology and Organizational Behavior*, *1*(1), 389–411. DOI: 10.1146/annurev-orgpsych-031413-091235

Bakker, A. B., Killmer, C. H., Siegrist, J., & Schaufeli, W. B. (2000). Effort-reward imbalance and burnout among nurses. *Journal of Advanced Nursing*, *31*(4), 884–891. DOI: 10.1046/j.1365-2648.2000.01361.x PMID: 10759985

Bakker, A. B., Schaufeli, W. B., Sixma, H. J., & Bosveld, W. (2001). Burnout contagion among general practitioners. *Journal of Social and Clinical Psychology*, *20*(1), 82–98. DOI: 10.1521/jscp.20.1.82.22251

Beyer, J. M., & Hannah, D. R. (2002). Building on the past: Enacting established personal identities in a new work setting. *Organization Science*, *13*(6), 636–652. DOI: 10.1287/orsc.13.6.636.495

Bianchi, R., & Schonfeld, I. S. (2024). Beliefs about burnout. *Work and Stress*, •••, 1–19. DOI: 10.1080/02678373.2024.2364590

Blanco-Donoso, L. M., Moreno-Jiménez, J., Hernández-Hurtado, M., Cifri-Gavela, J. L., Jacobs, S., & Garrosa, E. (2021). Daily Work-Family Conflict and Burnout to Explain the Leaving Intentions and Vitality Levels of Healthcare Workers: Interactive Effects Using an Experience-Sampling Method. *International Journal of Environmental Research and Public Health*, *18*(4), 1932. DOI: 10.3390/ijerph18041932 PMID: 33671211

Brewer, J. D. (2000). *Ethnography*. Open University Press.

Broadbent, J., & Guthrie, J. (1992). Changes in the Public Sector: A Review of 'Alternative' Accounting Research. *Accounting, Auditing & Accountability Journal*, *5*(3), 3–31. DOI: 10.1108/09513579210011835

Buttigieg, S. C., Daher, P., Cassar, V., & Guillaume, Y. (2023). Under the shadow of looming change: Linking employees' appraisals of organisational change as a job demand and transformational leadership to engagement and burnout. *Work and Stress*, *37*(2), 148–170. DOI: 10.1080/02678373.2022.2120560

Cavanaugh, M. A., Boswell, W. R., Roehling, M. V., & Boudreau, J. W. (2000). An empirical examination of self-reported work stress among US managers. *The Journal of Applied Psychology*, *85*(1), 65–74. DOI: 10.1037/0021-9010.85.1.65 PMID: 10740957

Cinite, I., Duxbury, L. E., & Higgins, C. (2009). Measurement of Perceived Organizational Readiness for Change in the Public Sector. *British Journal of Management*, *20*(2), 265–277. DOI: 10.1111/j.1467-8551.2008.00582.x

Colquitt, J. A., Lepine, J. A., Zapata, C. P., & Wild, R. E. (2011). Trust in Typical and High-Reliability Contexts: Building and Reacting to Trust Among Firefighters. *Academy of Management Journal*, *54*(5), 999–1015. DOI: 10.5465/amj.2006.0241

Dahles, H., & Van Hees, E. (2004). Firefighters across frontiers: Two fire brigades cooperating in the Dutch–German borderland. *Culture and Organization*, *10*(4), 315–328. DOI: 10.1080/1475955042000313759

Daniel, C., Gentina, E., & Mesmer-Magnus, J. (2022). Mindfulness buffers the deleterious effects of workaholism for work-family conflict. *Social Science & Medicine*, *306*, 115118. Advance online publication. DOI: 10.1016/j.socscimed.2022.115118 PMID: 35696778

Del Ben, K. S., Scotti, J. R., Chen, Y.-C., & Fortson, B. L. (2006). Prevalence of posttraumatic stress disorder symptoms in firefighters. *Work and Stress*, *20*(1), 37–48. DOI: 10.1080/02678370600679512

Derycke, H., Vlerick, P., Burnay, N., Decleire, C., D'Hoore, W., Hasselhorn, H. M., & Braeckman, L. (2010). Impact of the effort-reward imbalance model on intent to leave among Belgian health care workers: A prospective study. *Journal of Occupational and Organizational Psychology*, *83*(4), 879–893. DOI: 10.1348/096317909X477594

Dewe, P., O' Driscoll, M., & Cooper, C. (2010). *Coping with Work Stress: A Review and Critique*. Wiley-Blackwell. DOI: 10.1002/9780470711712

Dierdorff, E. C., & Ellington, K. (2008). It's the nature of work: Examining behavior-based sources of work- family conflict across occupations. *The Journal of Applied Psychology*, *93*(4), 883–892. DOI: 10.1037/0021-9010.93.4.883 PMID: 18642990

Dierdorff, E. C., & Morgeson, F. P. (2007). Consensus in work role requirements: The influence of discrete occupational context on role expectations. *The Journal of Applied Psychology*, *92*(5), 1228–1241. DOI: 10.1037/0021-9010.92.5.1228 PMID: 17845082

Dierdorff, E. C., Rubin, R. S., & Morgeson, F. P. (2009). The milieu of managerial work: An integrative framework linking work context to role requirements. *The Journal of Applied Psychology*, *94*(4), 972–988. DOI: 10.1037/a0015456 PMID: 19594238

Dik, B. J., & Duffy, R. D. (2009). Calling and Vocation at Work: Definitions and Prospects for Research and Practice. *The Counseling Psychologist*, *37*(3), 424–450. DOI: 10.1177/0011000008316430

Dominic, C., Gopal, D. P., & Sidhu, A. (2021). 'It's like juggling fire daily': Well-being, workload and burnout in the British NHS - A survey of 721 physicians. *Work (Reading, Mass.)*, *70*(2), 395–403. DOI: 10.3233/WOR-205337 PMID: 34633337

Dowling, F., Genet, B., & Moynihan, G. (2005). A Confidential Peer-Based Assistance Program for Police Officers. *Psychiatric Services (Washington, D.C.)*, *56*(7), 870–871. DOI: 10.1176/appi.ps.56.7.870 PMID: 16020823

Dudau, A., & Brunetto, Y. (2020). Debate: Managing emotional labour in the public sector. *Public Money & Management*, *40*(1), 11–13. DOI: 10.1080/09540962.2019.1665912

Durand, A.-C., Bompard, C., Sportiello, J., Michelet, P., & Gentile, S. (2019). Stress and burnout among professionals working in the emergency department in a French university hospital: Prevalence and associated factors. *Work (Reading, Mass.)*, *63*(1), 57–67. DOI: 10.3233/WOR-192908 PMID: 31127745

Edú-Valsania, S., Laguía, A., & Moriano, J. A. (2022). Burnout: A review of theory and measurement. *International Journal of Environmental Research and Public Health,* 19 (1780), 1-27. https://doi.org/DOI: 10.3390/ijerph19031780

Ferlie, E., Hartley, J., & Martin, S. (2003). Changing Public Service Organisations: Current Perspectives and Future Prospects. *British Journal of Management*, *14*(s1), 1–14. DOI: 10.1111/j.1467-8551.2003.00389.x

Ford, M. T. (2012). Job-occupation misfit as an occupational stressor. *Journal of Vocational Behavior*, *80*(2), 412–421. DOI: 10.1016/j.jvb.2011.10.004

Freedy, J. R., & Hobfoll, S. E. (1994). Stress inoculation for reduction of burnout: A conservation of resources approach. *Anxiety, Stress, and Coping*, *6*(4), 311–325. DOI: 10.1080/10615809408248805

Galanis, P., Fragkou, D., & Katsoulas, T. A. (2021). Risk factors for stress among police officers: A systematic literature review. *Work (Reading, Mass.)*, *68*(4), 1255–1272. DOI: 10.3233/WOR-213455 PMID: 33867384

Geiger, D., Danner-Schröder, A., & Kremser, W. (2021). Getting Ahead of Time—Performing Temporal Boundaries to Coordinate Routines under Temporal Uncertainty. *Administrative Science Quarterly*, *66*(1), 220–264. DOI: 10.1177/0001839220941010

Gibbons, C. (2024). Stress, Coping, burnout and mental health in the Irish Police Force. *Journal of Police and Criminal Psychology*, *39*(2), 348–357. DOI: 10.1007/s11896-023-09638-7

Gomes, G. P., Ribeiro, N., & Gomes, D. R. (2022). The Impact of Burnout on Police Officers' Performance and Turnover Intention: The Moderating Role of Compassion Satisfaction. *Administrative Sciences*, *12*(3), 1–18. DOI: 10.3390/admsci12030092

Greene, P., Kane, D., Christ, G., Lynch, S., & Corrigan, M. (2006). *FDNY Crisis Counselling: Innovative Responses to 9/11 Firefighters, Families and Communities*. John Wiley & Sons.

Grønstad, A., Kjekshus, L. E., Tjerbo, T., & Bernstrøm, V. H. (2019). Organizational change and the risk of sickness absence: A longitudinal multilevel analysis of organizational unit-level change in hospitals. *BMC Health Services Research*, *19*(1), 895. DOI: 10.1186/s12913-019-4745-2 PMID: 31771576

Halbesleben, J. R. B., & Buckley, M. R. (2004). Burnout in Organizational Life. *Journal of Management*, *30*(6), 859–879. DOI: 10.1016/j.jm.2004.06.004

Halbesleben, J. R. B., Neveu, J.-P., Paustian-Underdahl, S. C., & Westman, M. (2014). Getting to the "COR": Understanding the Role of Resources in Conservation of Resources Theory. *Journal of Management*, *40*(5), 1334–1364. DOI: 10.1177/0149206314527130

Hällgren, M., Rouleau, L., & de Rond, M. (2018). A matter of life or death: How extreme context research matters for management and organization studies. *The Academy of Management Annals*, *12*(1), 111–153. DOI: 10.5465/annals.2016.0017

Haslam, C., & Mallon, K. (2003). A preliminary investigation of post-traumatic stress symptoms among firefighters. *Work and Stress*, *17*(3), 277–285. DOI: 10.1080/02678370310001625649

Hetzel-Riggin, M. D., Swords, B. A., Tuang, H. L., Deck, J. M., & Spurgeon, N. S. (2020). Work Engagement and Resiliency Impact the Relationship Between Nursing Stress and Burnout. *Psychological Reports*, *123*(5), 1835–1853. DOI: 10.1177/0033294119876076 PMID: 31510876

Hobfoll, S. E. (1989). Conservation of resources: A new attempt at conceptualizing stress. *The American Psychologist*, *44*(3), 513–524. DOI: 10.1037/0003-066X.44.3.513 PMID: 2648906

Humphrey, N. M. (2021). Emotional labor and employee outcomes: A meta-analysis. *Public Administration*, *101*(2), 422–446. DOI: 10.1111/padm.12818

Hyndman, N., & McGeough, F. (2008). NPM and performance measurement: A comparative study of the public sectors in Ireland and the UK. *Irish Accounting Review*, *15*(2), 5–46. DOI: 10.52399/001c.26982

Ivanić, D., Adam, V. N., Srzić, I., Stepić, A., & Pintarić, H. (2017). Burnout syndrome in emergency medicine. *Hong Kong Journal of Emergency Medicine*, *24*(6), 290–297. DOI: 10.1177/1024907917740094

Jahnke, S. A., Poston, W. S. C., Haddock, C. K., & Murphy, B. (2016). Firefighting and mental health: Experiences of repeated exposure to trauma. *Work (Reading, Mass.)*, *53*(4), 737–744. DOI: 10.3233/WOR-162255 PMID: 26890595

Kim, R., Hee Ha, J., & Jue, J. (2020). The moderating effect of compassion fatigue in the relationship between firefighters' burnout and risk factors in working environment. *Journal of Risk Research*, *23*(22), 1491–1503. DOI: 10.1080/13669877.2020.1738529

Kinman, G. (2016). Effort-reward imbalance and overcommitment in UK academics: Implications for mental health, satisfaction and retention. *Journal of Higher Education Policy and Management*, *38*(5), 504–518. DOI: 10.1080/1360080X.2016.1181884

Kumar, A., & Narula, S. (2021). Quantitative Demands, Burnout, and Applied Outcomes for Indian Police Officers. *Fortune Institute of International Business. Business Review*, *10*(1), 74–85. DOI: 10.1177/2319714521999136

LaFontaine, A. (2024). One element of the emergency department nurse burnout epidemic – who can help? Based on a qualitative exploratory case study. *International Journal of Healthcare Management*, *18*(1), 141-153, 1–12. DOI: 10.1080/20479700.2024.2405324

Lamontagne, A. D., Keegel, T., Louie, A. M., Ostry, A., & Landsbergis, P. A. (2007). A Systematic Review of the Job-stress Intervention Evaluation Literature, 1990–2005. *International Journal of Occupational and Environmental Health*, *13*(3), 268–280. DOI: 10.1179/oeh.2007.13.3.268 PMID: 17915541

Lee, S.-H., & Olshfski, D. (2002). Employee Commitment and Firefighters: It's My Job. *Public Administration Review*, *62*(s1), 108–114. DOI: 10.1111/1540-6210.62.s1.19

Maslach, C. (1982). *Burnout: The cost of caring*. Prentice Hall.

Maslach, C., & Leiter, M. P. (1997). *The Truth about Burnout*. Jossey-Bass.

Maslach, C., Schaufeli, W. B., & Leiter, M. P. (2001). Job Burnout. *Annual Review of Psychology*, *52*(1), 397–422. DOI: 10.1146/annurev.psych.52.1.397 PMID: 11148311

Mazzetti, A. S. (2019). *To Tape or Not to Tape? Reflections on the Complexities of Taping Ethnographic Interviews*. SAGE Research Methods., DOI: 10.4135/9781526477347

Mazzola, J. J., & Disselhorst, R. (2019). Should we be "challenging" employees? A critical review and meta-analysis of the challenge-hindrance model of stress. *Journal of Organizational Behavior*, *40*(8), 949–961. DOI: 10.1002/job.2412

Mika-Lude, K. M., Degges-White, S., & Isawi, D. (2023). Under fire: Meta-dehumanization and burnout among first responders. *Journal of Employment Counseling*, *60*(3), 144–158. DOI: 10.1002/joec.12208

Murphy, E., & Dingwall, R. (2001). The Ethics of Ethnography. In Atkinson, P., Coffey, A., Delamont, S., Lofland, J., & Lofland, L. (Eds.), *Handbook of Ethnography*. SAGE Publications Ltd. DOI: 10.4135/9781848608337.n23

Navarro Moya, P., Villar Hozb, E., & Gonzalez Carrasco, M. (2020). How medical transport service professionals perceive risk/protective factors with regard to occupational burnout syndrome: Differences and similarities between an Anglo-American and Franco-German model. *Work (Reading, Mass.)*, *67*(2), 295–312. DOI: 10.3233/WOR-203280 PMID: 33044211

Nguyen Van, H., Dinh Le, M., Nguyen Van, T., Nguyen Ngoc, D., Tran Thi Ngoc, A., & Nguyen The, P. (2018). A systematic review of effort-reward imbalance among health workers. *The International Journal of Health Planning and Management*, *33*(3), 674–695. DOI: 10.1002/hpm.2541 PMID: 29722057

Noblet, A., & LaMontagne, A. (2006). The role of workplace health promotion in addressing job stress. *Health Promotion International*, *21*(4), 346–353. DOI: 10.1093/heapro/dal029 PMID: 16880197

Noblet, A., Rodwell, J., & McWilliams, J. (2006). Organizational change in the public sector: Augmenting the demand control model to predict employee outcomes under New Public Management. *Work and Stress*, *20*(4), 335–352. DOI: 10.1080/02678370601050648

Nytr, Ø. (2000). An appraisal of key factors in the implementation of occupational stress interventions. *Work and Stress*, *14*(3), 213–225. DOI: 10.1080/02678370010024749

O' Reilly, K. (2008). *Key concepts in ethnography*. SAGE Publications Ltd.

Palazoğlu, C. A., & Koç, Z. (2019). Ethical Sensitivity, Burnout and Job Satisfaction in Emergency Nurses. *Nursing Ethics*, *26*(3), 809–822. DOI: 10.1177/0969733017720846 PMID: 28814140

Penfold, C., Lewis, J., & Tennant, R. (2009). *Attendance Management in the Fire and Rescue Service: Managing sickness absence and managing and supporting attendance*. National Centre for Social Research.

Pluut, H., Ilies, R., Curşeu, P. L., & Liu, Y. (2018). Social support at work and at home: Dual-buffering effects in the work-family conflict process. *Organizational Behavior and Human Decision Processes*, *146*, 1–13. DOI: 10.1016/j.obhdp.2018.02.001

Rabbing, L., Lau, B., Fostervold, K. I., Blenkinsopp, J., & Bjørkelo, B. (2023). Enhancing Self-Reported Assessment of Working Conditions in Policing: Revisiting the Psychometric Properties and Applications of the Police Stress Questionnaire. *Psychological Reports*, *0*(0), 00332941231207957. Advance online publication. DOI: 10.1177/00332941231207957 PMID: 37902227

Rafferty, A. E. (2021). Organizational Change and Employee Health and Well-Being: A Review and Recommendations for Future Research. In P. Brough, E. Gardiner & K. Daniels (Eds), *Handbook on Management and Employment Practices*. Handbook Series in Occupational Health Sciences. Springer. pp.1-21. https://doi.org/DOI: 10.1007/978-3-030-24936-6_11-1

Raudenská, J., Steinerová, V., Javůrková, A., Urits, I., Kaye, A. D., Viswanath, O., & Varrassi, G. (2019). Occupational burnout syndrome and post-traumatic stress among healthcare professionals during the novel coronavirus disease 2019 (COVID-19) pandemic. *Best Practice & Research. Clinical Anaesthesiology*, *34*(3), 553–560. DOI: 10.1016/j.bpa.2020.07.008 PMID: 33004166

Regehr, C., & Bober, T. (2005). *In the Line of Fire: Trauma in Emergency Services*. Oxford University Press. DOI: 10.1093/acprof:oso/9780195165029.001.0001

Restrepo, J., & Lemos, M. (2021). Addressing psychosocial work-related stress interventions: A systematic review. *Work (Reading, Mass.)*, *70*(1), 53–62. DOI: 10.3233/WOR-213577 PMID: 34511476

Richardson, K. M., & Rothstein, H. R. (2008). Effects of Occupational Stress Management Intervention Programs: A Meta-Analysis. *Journal of Occupational Health Psychology*, *13*(1), 69–93. DOI: 10.1037/1076-8998.13.1.69 PMID: 18211170

Rozo, J. A., Olson, D. M., Thu, H., & Stutzman, S. E. (2017). Situational Factors Associated With Burnout Among Emergency Department Nurses. *Workplace Health & Safety*, *65*(6), 262–265. DOI: 10.1177/2165079917705669 PMID: 28557637

Sagaltici, E., Saydam, R. B., Cetinkaya, M., Şahin, Ş. K., Küçük, S. H., & Müslümanoğlu, A. Y. (2022). Burnout and psychological symptoms in healthcare workers during the COVID-19 pandemic: Comparisons of different medical professions in a regional hospital in Turkey. *Work (Reading, Mass.)*, *72*(3), 1077–1085. DOI: 10.3233/WOR-210517 PMID: 35634831

Salmela, L., Woehrle, T., Marleau, E., & Kitch, L. (2020). Implementation of a "Serenity Room": Promoting Resiliency in the ED. *Nursing*, *50*(10), 58–63. DOI: 10.1097/01.NURSE.0000697160.77297.06 PMID: 32976304

Saud, J., & Rice, J. (2024). Stress, Teamwork, and Wellbeing Policies: A Synergistic Approach to Reducing Burnout in Public Sector Organizations. *Administrative Sciences*, *14*(319), 1–19. DOI: 10.3390/admsci14120319

Schwab, D., Napolitano, N., Chevalier, K., & Pettorini-D'Amico, S. (2016). Hidden Grief and Lasting Emotions in Emergency Department Nurses. *Creative Nursing*, *22*(4), 249–253. DOI: 10.1891/1078-4535.22.4.249 PMID: 29195538

Scott, C., & Myers, K. K. (2005). The Socialization of Emotion: Learning Emotion Management at the Fire Station. *Journal of Applied Communication Research*, *33*(1), 67–92. DOI: 10.1080/0090988042000318521

Scott, T. (2007). Expression of humour by emergency personnel involved in sudden deathwork. *Mortality*, *12*(4), 350–364. DOI: 10.1080/13576270701609766

Seifert, R., & Sibley, T. (2005). *'United They Stood': The Story of the UK Firefighters' Dispute, 2002-2004*. Lawrence and Wishart.

Sexton, B., Levine, L. K., & Flores, D. (2021). An Analysis of Nurse Burnout in the Emergency Department. *Journal of Business and Behavioral Sciences*, *33*(1), 94–108.

Shanafelt, T. (2011). Burnout in anesthesiology: A call to action. *Anesthesiology*, *114*(1), 1–2. DOI: 10.1097/ALN.0b013e318201cf92 PMID: 21139497

Siegrist, J. (1996). Adverse health effects of high effort–low reward conditions at work. *Journal of Occupational Health Psychology*, *1*(1), 27–41. DOI: 10.1037/1076-8998.1.1.27 PMID: 9547031

Siegrist, J. (2001). A theory of occupational stress. In Dunham, J. (Ed.), *Stress in the workplace: Past, present and future*. Whurr Publishers.

Siegrist, J. (2016). Effort-Reward Imbalance Model. In Fink, G. (Ed.), *Stress: Concepts, Cognition, Emotion, and Behavior* (pp. 81–86). Academic Press.

Siegrist, J. (2017). The Effort–Reward Imbalance Model. In Cooper, C. L., & Quick, J. C. (Eds.), *The Handbook of Stress and Health* (pp. 24–35)., DOI: 10.1002/9781118993811.ch2

Siegrist, J., Starke, D., Chandola, T., Godin, I., Marmot, M., Niedhammer, I., & Peter, R. (2004). The measurement of effort–reward imbalance at work: European comparisons. *Social Science & Medicine*, *58*(8), 1483–1499. DOI: 10.1016/S0277-9536(03)00351-4 PMID: 14759692

Soeker, M. S. (2022). Healthcare professionals' perceptions and experiences of the influence of the COVID-19 pandemic on their personal and work performance. *Work (Reading, Mass.)*, *73*(3), 787–798. DOI: 10.3233/WOR-211143 PMID: 35988253

Tarcan, G. Y., Tarcan, M., & Top, M. (2016). An analysis of relationship between burnout and job satisfaction among emergency health professionals. *Total Quality Management & Business Excellence*, *28*(11–12), 1339–1356. DOI: 10.1080/14783363.2016.1141659

Tham, T. L., Alfes, K., Holland, P., Thynne, L., & Vieceli, J. (2023). Extreme work in extraordinary times: The impact of COVID-stress on the resilience and burnout of frontline paramedic workers – the importance of perceived organisational support. *International Journal of Human Resource Management*, *35*(10), 1739–1762. DOI: 10.1080/09585192.2023.2237871

Tuckey, D., Winwood, P., & Dollard, M. (2012). Psychological culture and pathways to psychological injury within policing. *Police Practice and Research*, *13*(3), 224–240. DOI: 10.1080/15614263.2011.574072

Waters, J., & Ussery, W. (2007). Police stress: History, contributing factors, symptoms and interventions. *Policing*, *30*(2), 169–188. DOI: 10.1108/13639510710753199

Wilson, C. A., & Britt, T. W. (2021). Living to work: The role of occupational calling in response to challenge and hindrance stressors. *Work and Stress*, *35*(2), 111–131. DOI: 10.1080/02678373.2020.1743791

Chapter 6
Caring at a Cost:
Exploring Compassion Fatigue, Emotional Labor, and Well-Being Among Filipino Teachers

Marie Grace Avelino Gomez
https://orcid.org/0000-0003-0180-9875
University of the Philippines, Philippines

Kenith B Villaruel
https://orcid.org/0000-0002-2403-8252
Northern Iloilo State University, Barotac Viejo Campus, Philippines

ABSTRACT

Teaching is an emotionally demanding profession, especially in the Philippines, where public school teachers must manage large class sizes, limited resources, and extensive administrative duties. This chapter explores emotional labor in teaching, emphasizing how Filipino educators navigate their emotions through surface and deep acting strategies. It also examines compassion fatigue, which results from prolonged exposure to students' struggles, leading to emotional exhaustion and reduced empathy. Teachers in low-income communities or those working with students with disabilities are particularly at risk. The chapter highlights significant factors contributing to compassion fatigue and proposes evidence-based interventions, such as mindfulness programs, peer support groups, and institutional reforms. Addressing emotional labor and compassion fatigue is essential for maintaining teacher well-being and enhancing the quality of education in the Philippines.

DOI: 10.4018/979-8-3373-0169-3.ch006

INTRODUCTION

Most teachers show care and compassion toward their students as part of their dedication to their profession. Filipino teachers, particularly public school teachers, teach 40 to 80 students per class, with some even higher. While care and compassion are identified as promising constructs for promoting psychological well-being among learners (O'Toole & Dobutowitsch, 2023), they can cause compassion fatigue in the teacher (Fute et al., 2022). In the long run, these contribute to burnout and secondary traumatic stress (Oberg et al., 2023).

Teaching can include more than delivering instruction; it can consist of ensuring the competencies are met, assessing students, and grading them. It is considered a multitasking profession with cognitive and emotional components (Kariou et al., 2021). Teachers use emotional labor at work. Emotional labor refers to regulating, controlling, or managing emotional expressions with others as part of one's professional work role (Penn State, 2024). It is characterized by two main regulation strategies: surface-acting and deep-acting (Lu et al., 2019). Surface acting occurs when employees display emotions required for a job without changing what they feel, and deep acting refers to modifying internal feelings to be consistent with the display rules of the profession (Yang et al., 2019). A teacher must project enthusiasm, support, and happiness to the students, even under challenging circumstances, as they are expected to display positive emotions while teaching (Dreer, 2021; Keller et al., 2018). Too often, a teacher adheres to the display rules of the profession even when feeling sick, tired, irritated, or overwhelmed with his or her personal life to make the students feel comfortable in class (Zhang & Zhang, 2024; Eva, 2022) . Teachers are expected to adjust their teaching style so that the students can learn better.

Compassion fatigue can be experienced by teachers who need to show high empathy toward students. Teachers who are in schools that have high poverty incidences (Mason-Williams et al., 2022; Isenberg et al., 2021; DuBois & Mistretta, 2012) and those who handle students with disabilities can develop compassion fatigue (Darawsheh et al., 2023; Vučinić et al., 2020; Tuchinda, 2020). Compassion fatigue is a form of emotional and physical exhaustion that can arise from the chronic stress of caring for others, especially in helping professions like teaching (Yang et al., 2023; Bardach et al., 2022; Smith, 2021). As a developing country, public schools in the Philippines can have students coming from slum areas or those in poverty-stricken areas (ChildHope Philippines, 2023). Some students come to school without eating their meals or those without school materials (Basilio, 2024; Hartigan-Go et al., 2024). Given this situation, some teachers support students by giving them food or school supplies. In the process, they share their meager earnings with their students who are in need. For teachers of students with disabilities, they must constantly address the wide range of physical, emotional, behavioral, and intellectual challenges of their students. Teachers who teach students with disabilities usually display empathy and compassion towards them (Ginevra et al., 2022).

Teaching is an emotionally demanding profession, particularly in the Philippines, where educators face numerous challenges beyond instruction. Stressors happen when teachers try their best to integrate distinct aspects of their work to perform in an ever-changing environment with varying expectations (Abdul-Messie, 2023; De Clercq et al., 2022; Stang-Rabrig et al., 2022; Cui, 2022; Siekkinen et al., 2020). The lack of resources, overcrowded classrooms, teacher shortages, and insufficient infrastructure place immense pressure on teachers, forcing them to manage large groups of students with limited support (Cardarelli, 2023; Biyela, 2019). In addition, excessive administrative work—such as preparing reports, managing student records, and fulfilling government-mandated tasks—further drains their time and energy, leaving them with little room to focus on actual teaching and student engagement (Laurenio & Cabal, 2023; Ocbian & Dischoso, 2015). Despite all the difficulties, teachers must remain patient, compassionate, and dedicated to their students' well-being (Giray et al., 2023). This constant emotional investment and systemic challenges make teaching one of the country's most emotionally exhausting yet undervalued professions.

Chapter Objectives

This chapter aims to comprehensively explore emotional labor among Filipino teachers, highlighting an often invisible yet critical aspect of their profession. Emotional labor in teaching extends beyond instructional duties; it involves constantly regulating emotions to maintain a positive and supportive learning environment, often at the expense of personal well-being. Filipino educators, in particular, navigate a unique cultural landscape where *malasakit* (compassionate concern) informs their professional responsibilities, sometimes to their physical or emotional detriment. Teachers are expected to be strong academic pillars and emotional anchors for their students, frequently absorbing their learners' struggles and distress. Most Filipino teachers in the public school system do not merely teach; they also care for students facing family issues, food insecurity, and other financial challenges. This chapter illustrates teachers' daily experiences of this form of labor, revealing the depth of their emotional commitment and challenges. The discussion captures the lived realities of Filipino educators, emphasizing how their dedication to students, combined with systemic limitations, often results in exhaustion and emotional strain.

Further, the chapter seeks to identify the key circumstances that contribute to compassion fatigue among Filipino teachers. Compassion fatigue arises from prolonged exposure to others' suffering, leading to emotional depletion and a reduced capacity for Empathy. Many teachers, especially public school teachers, are expected to fulfill multiple roles—mentor, counselor, disciplinarian, and parental figure—without adequate resources. This section will delve into these contributing factors, critically analyzing how the Philippine education system inadvertently fosters conditions that make compassion fatigue more likely.

Recognizing the impact of emotional labor and compassion fatigue, this chapter will also recommend evidence-based wellness programs to help Filipino teachers mitigate stress and maintain emotional resilience. Effective interventions must go beyond superficial solutions, addressing individual coping strategies and institutional reforms. Proposed initiatives include mindfulness and self-care programs tailored to educators, structured peer support groups that provide emotional validation, and professional development opportunities focused on emotional regulation and resilience-building. Additionally, the discussion will highlight existing wellness efforts in Philippine schools, evaluating their effectiveness and identifying areas for improvement. Beyond individual strategies, systemic reforms must also be advocated, such as policy changes that promote work-life balance, access to mental health resources, and a shift toward a more supportive school culture that values teachers' well-being. It also identifies how educational institutions can reinforce existing laws and mandates to help address the concerns of emotional labor and compassion fatigue. Ultimately, this chapter argues that maintaining a sustainable and nurturing environment for educators is essential for their well-being and the quality of education they provide. By addressing teachers' emotional burdens, schools can create a more holistic and supportive framework that enables educators to thrive.

Compassion Fatigue Defined

Compassion fatigue is defined as an identifiable set of negative psychological symptoms experienced by helping professionals such as those in the medical, educational, and social work professions (Ondrejková & Halamová, 2022). It is said to be a conceptualized combination of burnout and secondary traumatic stress (Sinclaire et al., 2022). It is seen as a psychological and emotional condition that results from prolonged exposure to others' suffering, leading to emotional exhaustion, reduced empathy, and a sense of helplessness (Berger & Nott, 2023).

Compassion fatigue was originally conceptualized by Figley (1995) as a form of caregiver burnout among psychotherapists, and it is contrasted with simple burnout and countertransference (Figley, 2002).Compassion fatigue is a multi-factor model that emphasizes the costs of caring, empathy, and emotional investment in helping the suffering (Juárez & Becton, 2024; Barry, 2023; Yang et al., 2023; Cordaro, 2020; Pehlivan & Güner, 2018). Unlike burnout, which stems from excessive workloads and organizational stress, compassion fatigue arises from the emotional burden of supporting students' personal and academic struggles, often without adequate institutional support (Castro-Schepers, 2023; Jennings & Min, 2023; Henson, 2020). Compassion fatigue is also described as a diminished ability to empathize or maintain interest in clients, often reflected in behavioral and emotional responses to witnessing others' traumatic experiences (Stevens & Al-Abbadey, 2024).

COMPASSION FATIGUE AMONG HELPING PROFESSIONALS

Professionals working in emotionally demanding fields often experience compassion fatigue due to the constant exposure to others' trauma (Wozencroft & Scott, 2016). Doctors (Bhugra, 2025), nurses (Todaro-Franceschi, 2024), social workers (Stanley & Sebastine, 2024), teachers (Wu et al., 2023), legal professionals (Chlap & Brown, 2022), police officers (Ondrejková & Halamová, 2022), and emergency responders are particularly vulnerable to this condition (Renkiewicz & Hubble, 2021). Those who work with survivors of criminal victimization (Voth-Schrag et al., 2021) and lay trauma counselors (McGlinchey et al., 2024) are also at significant risk. Among these professions, child protection workers face an even greater likelihood of developing compassion fatigue and burnout due to the intensity of their responsibilities (Bowman, 2022; Pharris et al., 2022; Hinds & Giardino, 2020).

In education, secondary special education teachers are especially susceptible to compassion fatigue due to excessive workloads and a shortage of trained personnel to assist them (Floyd et al., 2024; Triviño-Amigo et al., 2022) . The challenges of working with students with disabilities, combined with demanding job expectations, high-stress levels, inadequate professional support, and a lack of self-care training, contribute to their emotional exhaustion (Costin et al., 2023). Similarly, childcare workers in residential treatment facilities for children with emotional and behavioral disorders face immense stress due to understaffing and the difficult behaviors they must manage, increasing their risk of compassion fatigue (Benveniste et al., 2024). Additionally, student affairs professionals, who constantly address urgent student concerns, also experience high levels of compassion fatigue (Perez & Bettencourt, 2023}.

CHALLENGES FACED BY REGULAR AND SPECIAL EDUCATION TEACHERS

In the Philippines, low salaries and challenging working conditions have led to declining interest in teaching, particularly among special education teachers, who seek better financial opportunities abroad (Arcay et al., 2024). Beyond financial constraints, organizational challenges and insufficient behavior management training further exacerbate stress levels among teachers working with students with language disabilities (Gilmour & Wehby, 2020). Teachers handling children with autism often face work hazards, as some students exhibit aggressive behaviors such as biting, hitting, and self-harm (Naparan et al., 2025). Special education teachers, however, make positive behavioral adjustments when a student gets aggressive. According to a teacher:

"A child facing behavioral challenges needs support and understanding from their teachers to have an opportunity for positive change in their behavior." (Illustrative text cited from Catubig et al., 2024)

Regular teachers in inclusive classrooms also struggle with managing students with attention deficit hyperactivity disorder (Gaastra et al., 2020; Paulsrud & Nilholm, 2020), while those teaching students with emotional and behavioral disorders frequently cite behavior management as a major challenge (Hirsch et al., 2021). Additionally, the lack of proper training in behavioral interventions, difficulties in engaging uncooperative parents, and the broader challenge of inclusive education contribute to stress among regular education teachers (Allam & Martin, 2021; Vučinić et al., 2020). One teacher admitted:

"I still have this fear that I will not be able to teach the lesson well despite the fact that this is no longer my first time to teach students with special needs and so I would always ask for suggestions from my colleagues how and or what materials can I use to teach my lesson." (Illustrative text cited from Ignacio & Allit, 2023)

Despite being unintentionally hurt by their students, special education teachers continue to care for them with all their capacity. As one special educator has expressed:

"You won't blame this child for being different because they are unique in their own way, and that's why I know you won't. You will have the ability to empathize with them despite the fact that they have caused you a great deal of physical damage." (Illustrative text cited from Cuadra, 2023)

In the Philippines, this is part of the cultural trait, *malasakit,* wherein one gives utmost care to the best of his or her ability. However, this act can also make the teacher suffer from compassion fatigue (Go et al., 2020; Mendoza, 2020). This is affirmed by another response from a special educator:

"If you want to be a teacher, you should be prepared to work with students with special needs because they are far more challenging and draining than other students. This is a difficult task but doing it will ultimately result in the sense of accomplishment. You must have a positive attitude about imparting your knowledge to others." (Illustrative text cited from Cuadra, 2023)

COMPASSION FATIGUE IN THE TEACHING PROFESSION

Teaching is widely recognized as one of the most stressful professions (Ormiston et al., 2022). The onset of the COVID-19 pandemic further intensified compassion fatigue among educators, leading to reduced work engagement (Fute et al., 2022). This condition is regarded as a specialized form of burnout unique to teachers (Yu, 2022). Many educators become deeply involved in addressing students' needs, often resulting in emotional exhaustion (Inbar & Shiri, 2021).

Special education teachers are particularly vulnerable to high levels of compassion fatigue due to the demanding nature of their work (Davis & Palladino, 2011). Teachers with strong social and emotional learning competencies tend to experience higher compassion fatigue as they invest more emotional energy in their students (Yang, 2021). Additionally, educators with longer years of service report higher levels of compassion fatigue than their less-experienced counterparts (Yang et al., 2021). Special education teachers, in particular, face more severe burnout and lower psychological well-being than their colleagues in regular education (Nnubia, 2022; Koenig et al., 2018). Moreover, teachers with a tendency toward self-criticism are more likely to develop compassion fatigue (Ondrejková & Halamová, 2022). Those who struggle to balance their professional and personal lives also experience greater emotional exhaustion (Levkovich & Gada, 2020). Furthermore, teacher-administrators report higher levels of compassion fatigue than classroom teachers due to the added responsibilities of leadership (Christian-Brandt, 2020). However, higher educational attainment has been linked to lower levels of compassion fatigue, suggesting that additional training and professional development may serve as protective factors (Banks et al., 2024; Ruiz-Fernández et al., 2020).

Compassion Fatigue Among Filipino Teachers

Philippine public school teachers face overwhelming workloads due to large class sizes, numerous non-teaching responsibilities, and their role as *in loco parentis* (acting as second parents to students). Teachers have heavy workloads (Dy-Zulueta, 2024). Most of the time, it causes them to experience stress. On some occasions, it is the lack of resources and support from the school administration, and lack of autonomy and control as their supervisors can be domineering (Villarejo et al., 2022; Sarabia & Collantes, 2020) . These teachers can have students in dire poverty, and some teachers may be compelled to help beyond the call of duty. With many classes often exceeding regular class size, teachers must cater to diverse learning needs while managing administrative tasks such as documentation, reports, and extracurricular duties (Tarraya, 2023; Arañas, 2023). Beyond academics, they are expected to provide emotional support, discipline, and guidance to students from disadvantaged backgrounds (Robosa et al., 2021; Nalipay et al., 2021) . The constant juggling of instructional and parental roles, coupled with inadequate resources and systemic challenges, leads to chronic stress and exhaustion (Malquisto et al., 2023; Fabelico & Afalla, 2020). Most teachers continue to provide extraordinary service as it is a cultural trait to care for children who need help, and those who need help the most. Over time, this emotional and physical strain contributes to compassion fatigue, where teachers struggle to maintain empathy and motivation, ultimately affecting their well-being and the quality of education they provide (Ching et al., 2025; Buriel et al., 2021).

In addition to this, the Filipino educational context, teachers are deeply embedded in a culture of *malasakit* (compassionate concern), *pakikiramay* (sympathy), and *utang na loob* (a sense of gratitude and obligation), which shape their professional roles (Redillas, 2020). These cultural expectations intensify emotional labor, as Filipino educators are often perceived as *pangalawang magulang* (second parents) who must provide academic instruction and moral and emotional guidance (Recede, 2025). Filipino teachers, frequently take on additional emotional responsibilities—mentoring students from economically disadvantaged backgrounds, addressing students' family issues, and even providing financial assistance—all of which contribute to emotional depletion over time.

Beyond professional duties, compassion fatigue takes a toll on teachers' mental health, often manifesting as anxiety, depression, and emotional numbness. This emotional exhaustion can negatively influence teacher-student interactions, as educators may become less patient, less empathic, or disengaged. Over time, the accumulation of stress and frustration may lead to increased attrition rates, with many teachers opting to leave the profession in search of less demanding and emotionally taxing careers. This exodus affects individual educators and weakens the public school system, exacerbating teacher shortages and further burdening those who remain.

Compassion fatigue significantly affects the performance of Filipino teachers, leading to decreased motivation, diminished instructional quality, and emotional exhaustion. Some teachers who are close to retirement not to feel the need for additional training or obligation. The overwhelming workload, large class sizes, and numerous non-teaching responsibilities drain teachers' energy, making it difficult to sustain enthusiasm and engagement in the classroom. Mentally and emotionally exhausted teachers may struggle to provide personalized attention to students, impacting learning outcomes. Furthermore, chronic stress can lead to burnout, characterized by cynicism, detachment, and a reduced sense of accomplishment, ultimately lowering overall job performance and effectiveness.

Emotional Labor in Teaching

The term "emotional labor" began when concepts of emotions started to surface in most sociological literature. It was attributed to Arlie R. Hochschild who wrote the book *The Managed Heart* (Wharton, 2009). The term, as it is highly associated in the organizational context, is defined by most literature as controlling one's emotions for the employee to deliver the task properly (Peat & Ridge 2024; Ashforth & Humphrey, 1993, Hochschild, 1983). Hochschild has described two major forms of emotional labor: 1.) surface acting and 2.) deep acting (Hochschild,1983). Surface acting focuses on how the employee would control the external displays of emotions. On the other hand, deep acting involves modifying emotions to serve the clientele better. Regardless of the type of emotional labor an employee espouses, it affects not only their health, but also the overall organizational efficacy (Remington, 2016).

Some earlier studies on this subject conceptualized emotional labor as a "professional feeling." How these professional feelings are managed could sometimes put the worker in a state of emotional dissonance as this creates confusion on the part of the employee as to whether they would reconcile these feelings on a personal level or they would subscribe to the rules set by the organization. In the Philippines, Hechanova (2011), initiated the discussion of emotional labor among customer service representatives (CSRs). The findings of her study revealed that those who showed commitment to their work as CSRs tend to practice deep acting. The study further highlights the need for the call center industry to develop training programs on how CSRs can enhance their skills in executing deep acting in dealing with customers. She claims that emotional labor should be given a second look by reconceptualizing its two dimensions (surface and deep acting) into "emotion management strategies with varying impacts" (Hechanova 2011).

Based on the studies mentioned earlier, those who commonly experience emotional labor are mainly in the service-oriented professions (Yang & Chen, 2021; Kim & Wang, 2018). More recently, developing interest among researchers to explore emotional labor was noticed among mental health service providers like school counselors (Lim et al., 2025; Lindstrom-Johnson et al., 2024; Hou & Zheng, 2021), psychologists (Clarke et al., 2024; Joffe & Peters, 2024; Clarke et al., 2021) and healthcare professionals like nurses (Feng et al., 2024; Xu & Fan, 2023; Zaghini et al., 2020).

Emotions shape teacher identity. These can be self-transformative and serve as a means to challenge the typical norms inside the classroom, resulting in reclaiming their sense of teacher agency (Herera & Martinez-Alba, 2022). Teachers apply emotional labor not only inside the classroom but also in fulfilling their administrative duties and functions as they serve the school's important internal and external stakeholders: the students, their fellow faculty, and the general public (Go et al., 2020). Bellas

(1999) also attempted gender differentiations by identifying women faculty as the one who mainly practices emotional labor compared to their male counterparts. This tends to put weight on some claims that females tend to occupy emotional labor-intensive careers, one of which is the teaching profession (Morgan, 2024).

Teaching remains a troubled profession (Cochran-Smith, 2021; Savellano, 1999). Moreso, at its very core, political (Walker, 2018). On a systematic level, teachers in the Philippines have to endure oppressive policies, perform irrelevant tasks, and receive very dismal support for funding in education, which, on a much bigger picture, has a domino effect on the learners (Sy & Hernandez, 2023; Palatino, 2023). So, how can teachers perform well inside the classroom if they are plagued with such concerns in the first place? How can they perform their classroom functions well if they do not have sufficient resources? In some public schools in the Philippines, even chalk to be used on blackboards has to be shouldered by the teacher. The debate about this and the search for feasible solutions remains a work in progress.

Despite inefficiencies in school governance and politically motivated expectations in order to meet institutional demands, a good teacher is fueled with positive emotions. They are not only competent and efficient, but in all aspects, should also be passionate in what they do in teaching students (Fabella & Paz-Aler, 2023).

Specific Emotional Labor Demands for Teachers and its Consequences

A typical K-12 teacher performs emotional labor while doing these professional responsibilities: delivery of instruction, promotion of a positive climate in the classroom, and doing collaborative work with other teachers (Brown et al., 2023). Known to others, teachers often engage with the same clientele, all throughout their productive hours which makes them different from other service-oriented professions whose interaction with other clients are brief and random (Stark & Bettini, 2021).

As what was previously mentioned, teachers in the Philippines have to deal with systemic, long-time, unresolved issues that are oftentimes affecting the execution of their mandated functions. These concerns also have a domino effect on students, especially in their classroom performance and performance in international assessments (Reyes, 2024).

Dealing with the high prevalence rate of bullying (Ombay, 2025), the rising mental health issues among students (Esguerra, 2025), and classroom management concerns could result in teachers feeling emotionally exhausted. On the "surface level" teachers try to be solution-focused and show that everything will be handled and managed properly (Auger & Formentin, 2021). This only shows that teachers are capable of regulating their feelings and emotions to suit professional and organizational standards of behavior when dealing with concerns related to student welfare and safety. The regulation of feelings and emotions could emanate demeanors of professionalism as teachers cautiously observe their emotional boundaries with students (Fortich & Jaspe, 2022). For some teachers, they use surface acting to regulate their emotions during undesirable classroom situations (Horner et al., 2020), however, this will put them at risk of increased burnout and job dissatisfaction (Lavy & Eshet, 2018). Meanwhile, teachers who practice emotional labor in deep acting, for example, can evoke positive emotions as they deliver their lessons. (Yin, 2006). Hence, seen as a beneficial type of emotional labor (Zhang & Zhu, 2008; Humphrey, 2023).

Relative to other studies mentioned in this chapter, the multitude of work of Filipino teachers in which they apply emotional labor in various situations (e.g., maintaining students' attention, dealing with behavioral issues of students) is also reflected in the qualitative study conducted by Asuncion (2021). She expressed that teachers are at risk of occupational hazards and stress (Asuncion, 2021). These findings tell us that teachers share collective concerns regarding practicing emotional labor in the classroom.

Differences in emotional labor between male and female teachers are also evident. Some studies show that female teachers tend to practice more emotional labor than their male counterparts (Naz et al., 2024; Xie et al.,2022; Noor & Zainuddin, 2011). Interestingly, in more recent studies and reports, male teachers practicing emotional labor are starting to be recognized in the literature (Fazackerley, 2024;Töre, 2022).

Constant practice of "surface acting" emotional labor is known to have health consequences among teachers. Well-being literatures pointed out that it could pose risk on teachers physical health (Karakus et al., 2024; Qi et al., 2017), can trigger emotional exhaustion (Kim, 2016), disengagement in teaching students (Sezen-Gultekin et al., 2021; Cheung & Lun, 2015) resulting to work underperformance (Geng et al., 2023; Acheson et al., 2016). On the contrary, those teachers who engage in deep acting were able to empathize with others (Lee & van Vlack, 2018). Since teaching is a profession that is highly invested in emotions, those teachers who are not effective in emotionally regulating inside the classroom might possibly put them at risk of considering leaving the profession (Heffernan et al., 2022).

Recommendations for Promotion of Teacher Well-Being

Given Filipino educators' challenges, well-being practices must be implemented to mitigate these problems. Filipino teachers are usually given free medical check-ups annually as stipulated in the Magna Carta for Teachers (Philippine Congress, 1966). However, this is not sufficient to address the issues that can result to high levels of stress or burnout. Wellness routines can provide the necessary breaks that teachers need from constant caregiving demands. Such practices may include mindfulness, relaxation exercises, sports, recreational activities, and other endeavors that enable them to produce positive emotions (Glickman & Burns, 2021). School administrations can develop evidence-based well-being programs to help alleviate the effects of stressors on teachers.

Teacher stress, burnout, and compassion fatigue stem from excessive workloads, emotional labor, and the expectation to go beyond teaching responsibilities. Many teachers struggle to balance their professional duties with their well-being, often working beyond the typical eight-hour workday. To address these challenges, the Philippine Department of Education, as the primary duty bearer, should implement policies that mitigate the emotional and psychological burdens of teaching.

One crucial step is adhering to Republic Act 7880, which stipulates that class sizes should not exceed 45 students (Philippine Congress, 1995). Effectively managing class sizes allows teachers to provide individualized attention without feeling overwhelmed. Furthermore, principals and school heads should ensure that teacher workloads are realistic and aligned with their primary role of educating students.

Recognizing that compassion fatigue and emotional labor significantly contribute to burnout, educational leaders must integrate psychosocial programs and mental health support into school policies. Occupational Safety and Health principles should be applied to safeguard teachers' well-being, including stress management training, self-care workshops, and mental health interventions. Implementing wellness initiatives, such as mindfulness sessions, peer support groups, and guided reflections, can help teachers process the emotional weight of their work.

The Philippine Department of Education should collaborate with the Department of Health and the Philippine Health Insurance Corporation to offer free consultations with mental health professionals for teachers exhibiting severe stress or burnout. The Mental Health Act of 2017 provides a legal basis for such support, emphasizing the importance of accessible mental health services for educators.

The enforcement of Occupational Safety and Health programs must be strengthened through the joint memorandum circular of the Civil Service Commission, Department of Health, and Department of Labor and Employment (This document is known as CSC-DOH-DOLE JMC No.1, 2020.). This mandates educational institutions to develop and disseminate stress management strategies via official communication channels, including school websites and social media platforms. Educational institutions should also ensure that teachers have access to regular mental health seminars, webinars, and practical discussions on coping mechanisms for emotional exhaustion.

Teachers should be encouraged to report stress-related concerns without fear of stigma or professional repercussions. School leaders can foster an open dialogue about mental health through Learning Action Cells sessions, where teachers can share experiences and support one another. Networking with mental health and wellness professionals can also provide targeted interventions to address teacher burnout.

Stress-reduction programs should be integrated into each school's Annual Work and Financial Plan to institutionalize well-being practices and included in the School Improvement Plan. Schools' Safety and Health Committees should lead in implementing these programs, alongside health education teachers who can advocate for stress management initiatives.

Labor unions and teacher organizations can also play a crucial role in promoting teacher wellness. These groups can advocate for fair workloads, reasonable working hours, and improved support systems within educational institutions. They can also negotiate for policies that protect teachers from excessive emotional labor and provide structured guidelines for handling parent consultations, which often extend beyond work hours.

Furthermore, pre-service teacher education should incorporate discussions on work-life balance, emotional regulation, and self-care strategies. Educational Psychology and Guidance courses should emphasize the importance of mental well-being, aligning their curriculum with Republic Act 4670 (The Magna Carta for Public School Teachers) and the Philippine Labor Code.

Ultimately, teachers must be empowered to advocate for themselves. Teacher labor groups should actively lobby for just working conditions, including manageable class sizes and fair workloads. Teachers can create a more sustainable and supportive work environment by collectively advocating for their rights.

Supporting teachers in coping with compassion fatigue, burnout, and emotional labor is crucial for maintaining a thriving educational system. When teachers receive the care and respect they deserve, they can continue shaping the future without sacrificing their well-being.

REFERENCES

Abdul-Messie, L. (2023). "Trying to feel the right feeling for the job": The emotional labour of English language teachers in state secondary schools in Italy. *Social Sciences & Humanities Open*, *8*(1), 100582. DOI: 10.1016/j.ssaho.2023.100582

Acheson, K., Taylor, J., & Luna, K. (2016). The burnout spiral: The emotion labor of five rural US foreign language teachers. *Modern Language Journal*, *100*(2), 522–537. DOI: 10.1111/modl.12333

Allam, F. C., & Martin, M. M. (2021). Issues and Challenges in Special Education: A Qualitative Analysis from Teacher's Perspective. *Southeast Asia Early Childhood*, 10(1), 37-49. https://eric.ed.gov/?id=EJ1296259

Arañas, J. Q. (2023). Tasks Beyond Instruction: A Case Study on Teachers' Ancillary Functions. *International Journal of Educational Innovation and Research*, *2*(2), 179–186. DOI: 10.31949/ijeir.v2i2.5740

Arcay, N.Jr, Rebucas, J. N., & Aparece, R. (2024). The Attrition and Migration of Bohol Association of Catholic Schools Teachers of The Diocese of Tagbilaran. *University of Bohol Multidisciplinary Research Journal*, *12*(1), 77–93. DOI: 10.15631/ppmzak16

Ashforth, B. E., & Humphrey, R. H. (1993). Emotional Labor in Service Roles: The Influence of Identity. *Academy of Management Review*, *18*(1), 88–115. DOI: 10.2307/258824

Asuncion, R. A. (2021). An Exploratory Study on Emotional Labor: The 'Invisible' Work of Teachers. *Philippine Journal of Labor and Industrial Relations*, *34*, 80–113. https://www.journals.upd.edu.ph/index.php/pjlir/article/view/ 7704/6712

Auger, G. A., & Formentin, M. J. (2021). This is depressing: The emotional labor of teaching during the pandemic spring 2020. *Journalism & Mass Communication Educator*, *76*(4), 376–393. DOI: 10.1177/10776958211012900

Banks, J., Lopez, V., Sahay, A., & Cleary, M. (2024). A scoping review of compassion fatigue among oncology nurses caring for adult patients. *Cancer Nursing*, *47*(4), E213–E225. DOI: 10.1097/NCC.0000000000001226 PMID: 36944157

Bardach, L., Klassen, R. M., & Perry, N. E. (2022). Teachers' psychological characteristics: Do they matter for teacher effectiveness, teachers' well-being, retention, and interpersonal relations? An integrative review. *Educational Psychology Review*, *34*(1), 259–300. DOI: 10.1007/s10648-021-09614-9

Barry, D. P. (2023). Self-Compassion practice to mitigate teachers' empathy fatigue and burnout. In *Developing Trauma-Informed Teachers: Creating* Classrooms That Foster Equity, Resiliency, and Asset-Based Approaches, 49-70. USA: Information Age Publishing.

Basilio, K. C. L. (2024). *Philippine Students are in Deep Trouble*. Retrieved from https://www.bworldonline.com/special-reports/2024/09/09/619447/philippin e-students-are-in-deep-trouble/

Bellas, M. L. (1999). Emotional labor in academia: The case of professors. *The Annals of the American Academy of Political and Social Science*, *561*(1), 96–110. DOI: 10.1177/000271629956100107

Benveniste, T., Smith, D. R., Gupta, C. C., Chappel, S. E., & Sprajcer, M. (2024). Compassion Fatigue in Out of Home Care Workers: A Systematic Review. *Residential Treatment for Children & Youth*, *42*(1), 51–79. DOI: 10.1080/0886571X.2024.2310583

Bhugra, D. (2025). Compassion fatigue: Result or cause of burnout? And do doctors get it? *Journal of the Royal Society of Medicine*, *118*(4), 138–140. DOI: 10.1177/01410768251320166 PMID: 39946213

Biyela, B. N. (2019). *Leading teaching and learning in an overcrowded* classroom: experiences of four teachers in two secondary schools. Unpublished Master's Thesis, University of Kwazulu-Natal, South Africa. Retrieved from https://researchspace.ukzn .ac.za/server/api/core/bitstreams/beea2023-cd42-4f49-83a2-b38a37375c02/content

Bowman, M. E. (2022). Child welfare worker wellness: An ethical imperative in the service of children. *Child Abuse Review*, *31*(5), e2758. DOI: 10.1002/car.2758

Brown, E. L., Stark, K., Vesely, C., & Choe, J. (2023). "Acting often and everywhere:" Teachers' emotional labor across professional interactions and responsibilities. *Teaching and Teacher Education*, *132*, 104227. Advance online publication. DOI: 10.1016/j.tate.2023.104227

Buriel, M. C., Cachero, K. C., Padua, S. G., Palmeda, M. A., & Vergara, E. M. (2021). A comparative study of compassion fatigue between selected public and private junior and senior high school educators.*GreenPrints*. https://greenprints .dlshsi.edu.ph/grade_12/242

Cardarelli, R. (2023). Challenges facing educators and displaced students during emergencies: Implications for higher education. In *Higher Education in Emergencies: Best Practices and Benchmarking* (pp. 67-81). Emerald Publishing Limited. https://doi.org/DOI: 10.1108/S2055-364120230000053005

Castro Schepers, O. (2023). Exploring the demographics of teachers who experience secondary traumatic stress. *BMC Psychology, 11*(1), 181. DOI: 10.1186/s40359-023-01217-z PMID: 37322560

Catubig, C. G. H., Alas, A. F. D., Danganon, A. C., & Cagape, W. E. (2024). Elementary Teachers Lived Experiences in Handling Learners with Behavioral Difficulties. *International Journal of Research Publications, 149*(1), 19–19. DOI: 10.47119/IJRP1001491520246548

Cheung, F. Y., & Lun, V. M. C. (2015). Relation between emotional labor and organizational citizenship behavior: An investigation among Chinese teaching professionals. *The Journal of General Psychology, 142*(4), 253–272. DOI: 10.1080/00221309.2015.1091764 PMID: 26649924

ChildHope Philippines. (2023). *Breaking the Cycle: Children Poverty in the Philippines.* Retrieved from https://childhope.org.ph/children-in-poverty/

Ching, G. S., Malabanan, J. C., & Canete, J. J. O. (2025). Adapting to online education: Social and emotional learning and teaching efficacy among Filipino teachers post-pandemic. *International Journal of Research, 14*(3), 1–16. DOI: 10.5861/ijrse.2025.25801

Chlap, N., & Brown, R. (2022). Relationships between workplace characteristics, psychological stress, affective distress, burnout and empathy in lawyers. *International Journal of the Legal Profession, 29*(2), 159–180. DOI: 10.1080/09695958.2022.2032082

Christian-Brandt, A. S., Santacrose, D. E., & Barnett, M. L. (2020). In the trauma-informed care trenches: Teacher compassion satisfaction, secondary traumatic stress, burnout, and intent to leave education within underserved elementary schools. *Child Abuse & Neglect, 110*, 104437. DOI: 10.1016/j.chiabu.2020.104437 PMID: 32151429

Clarke, J. J., Rees, C. S., Breen, L. J., & Heritage, B. (2021). The perceived effects of emotional labor in psychologists providing individual psychotherapy. *Psychotherapy (Chicago, Ill.), 58*(3), 414–424. DOI: 10.1037/pst0000351 PMID: 33271050

Clarke, J. J., Rees, C. S., Mancini, V. O., & Breen, L. J. (2024). Emotional labor and emotional exhaustion in psychologists: Preliminary evidence for the protective role of self-compassion and psychological flexibility. *Journal of Contextual Behavioral Science, 31*, 100724. DOI: 10.1016/j.jcbs.2024.100724

Cochran-Smith, M. (2021). Rethinking teacher education: The trouble with accountability. *Oxford Review of Education, 47*(1), 8–24. DOI: 10.1080/03054985.2020.1842181

Cordaro, M. (2020). Pouring from an Empty Cup: The Case for Compassion Fatigue in Higher Education. *Building Healthy Academic Communities Journal*, *4*(2), 17–28. DOI: 10.18061/bhac.v4i2.7618

Costin, A., Roman, A. F., & Balica, R. S. (2023). Remote work burnout, professional job stress, and employee emotional exhaustion during the COVID-19 pandemic. *Frontiers in Psychology*, *14*, 1193854. DOI: 10.3389/fpsyg.2023.1193854 PMID: 37325768

Cuadra, J. M. (2023). Uncovering the Complexities of Coping: A Qualitative Study on the Challenges Faced by Special Education Teachers in the Sandwich Generation. *Philippine Social Science Journal*, *6*(1), 41–51. DOI: 10.52006/main.v6i1.646

Cui, L. (2022). The role of teacher–student relationships in predicting teachers' occupational wellbeing, emotional exhaustion, and enthusiasm. *Frontiers in Psychology*, *13*, 896813. DOI: 10.3389/fpsyg.2022.896813 PMID: 35664194

Darawsheh, S. R., Asha, I. K. K., AbuSaif, R., Alhejoj, A. F., & Khasawneh, M. A. S. (2023). An Outline of the Professional Quality of Teachers who Teach Children with Special Needs. *Journal of Education and e-learning Research*, *10*(3), 358–363. https://eric.ed.gov/?id=EJ1408079. DOI: 10.20448/jeelr.v10i3.4711

Davis, K., & Palladino, J. (2011).*Compassion Fatigue among Secondary Special* Education Teachers: A Case Study about Job Stress and Burnout. Retrieved from https://eric.ed.gov/?id=ED522807

De Clercq, M., Watt, H. M. G., & Richardson, P. W. (2022). Profiles of teachers' striving and wellbeing: Evolution and relations with context factors, retention, and professional engagement. *Journal of Educational Psychology*, *114*(3), 637–655. DOI: 10.1037/edu0000702

Dreer, B. (2021). Teachers' well-being and job satisfaction: The important role of positive emotions in the workplace. *Educational Studies*, *50*(1), 61–77. DOI: 10.1080/03055698.2021.1940872

DuBois, A. L., & Mistretta, M. A. (2019). *Overcoming burnout and compassion fatigue in schools: A guide for counselors, administrators, and educators*. Routledge. DOI: 10.4324/9781351030021

Dy-Zulueta, D. (2024, January 5). *Filipino teachers overworked by 400 unpaid hours annually — Study*. PhilStar Global. Retrieved June 7, 2025, from https://www.philstar.com/lifestyle/on-the-radar/2024/01/05/2297929/filipino-t eachers-overworked-400-unpaid-hours-annually-study

Eastwood, C., & Ecklund, K. (2008). Compassion Fatigue Risk and Self-Care Practices among Residential Treatment Center Childcare Workers. *Residential Treatment for Children & Youth, 25*(2), 103–122. DOI: 10.1080/08865710802309972

Esguerra, D. J. (2024). *PBBM OKs law to arrest 'alarming' mental health concerns among youth.* Retrieved from https://www.pna.gov.ph/articles/1239528

Eva, A. L. (2022). *Surviving teacher burnout: A weekly guide to build resilience, deal with emotional exhaustion, and stay inspired in the classroom.* New Harbinger Publications.

Fabelico, F., & Afalla, B. (2020). Perseverance and passion in the teaching profession: Teachers' grit, self-efficacy, burnout, and performance. *Journal of Critical Reviews, 7*(11), 108–119. DOI: 10.31838/jcr.07.03.05

Fabella, F. E. T., & Paz-Aler, R. A. D. (2023). Optimism as a mitigator of burnout: The relationship between optimism and burnout among selected teachers. *International Research Journal of Modernization in Engineering Technology and Science, 5*(02), 414–420.

Fazackerley, A. (2024). *Schools in England boost maternity pay to stem exodus of female teachers in their 30s.* Retrieved from https://www.theguardian.com /teacher-network/2024/nov/02/uk-schools-boost-maternity-pay-to-stem-exo dus-of-female-teachers-in-their-30s

Feng, H., Zhang, M., Li, X., Shen, Y., & Li, X. (2024). The Level and Outcomes of Emotional Labor in Nurses: A Scoping Review. *Journal of Nursing Management, 2024*(1), 5317359. DOI: 10.1155/2024/5317359 PMID: 40224865

Ferrer, J. C. (2024). Academic Performance and Predictors of the Licensure Examination for Teachers of the Bachelor of Elementary Education. [MJSSH]. *Malaysian Journal of Social Sciences and Humanities, 9*(11), e003091–e003091. DOI: 10.47405/mjssh.v9i11.3091

Figley, C. R. (1995). Compassion fatigue: Toward a new understanding of the costs of caring. In Stamm, B. H. (Ed.), *Secondary traumatic stress: Self-care issues for clinicians, researchers, and educators* (pp. 3–28). The Sidran Press.

Figley, C. R. (2002). Compassion fatigue: Psychotherapists' chronic lack of self care. *Journal of Clinical Psychology, 58*(11), 1433–1441. DOI: 10.1002/jclp.10090 PMID: 12412153

Floyd, K. K., Horn, A., & Sherfinski, M. (2024). Compassion Fatigue, Resilience, and Endurance of Special Educators in Rural P–12 and Higher Education. *Rural Special Education Quarterly, 43*(2), 104–116. DOI: 10.1177/87568705241244576

Fortich, J., & Jaspe, M. (2022). Teachers' Emotional Labor in Relation to Classroom Management Practices of University of Bohol, Tagbilaran City, Bohol. *ACADEME University of Bohol, Graduate School and Professional Studies*, 20(1), 88-97.DOI: 10.15631/aubgsps.v20i1.181

Fute, A., Sun, B., & Oubibi, M. (2022). Assessing teaching compassion, work engagement, and compassion fatigue among teachers during the pandemic. *Psychology Research and Behavior Management, 15*, 2561–2571. DOI: 10.2147/PRBM.S383292 PMID: 36124334

Gaastra, G. F., Groen, Y., Tucha, L., & Tucha, O. (2020). Unknown, unloved? Teachers' reported use and effectiveness of classroom management strategies for students with symptoms of ADHD. In *Child & Youth Care Forum* (Vol. 49, pp. 1-22). Springer US.DOI: 10.1007/s10566-019-09515-7

Geng, F., Yu, S., & Yuan, R. E. (2023). Exploring L2 writing teachers' feeling rules, emotional labor and regulation strategies. *System, 119*, 103160. DOI: 10.1016/j.system.2023.103160

Gilmour, A. F., & Wehby, J. H. (2020). The association between teaching students with disabilities and teacher turnover. *Journal of Educational Psychology, 112*(5), 1042–1060. DOI: 10.1037/edu0000394

Ginevra, M. C., Di Maggio, I., Valbusa, I., Santilli, S., & Nota, L. (2022). Teachers' attitudes towards students with disabilities: The role of the type of information provided in the students' profiles of children with disabilities. *European Journal of Special Needs Education, 37*(3), 357–370. DOI: 10.1080/08856257.2021.1878658

Giray, L., Asuncion, M. K. C., Edem, J., Gumalin, D. L., Jacob, J., & Lucero, S. M. (2023). Positive and Negative Lessons from Hidden Curriculum at a Philippine State University.*Educational Process: International Journal*, 12(1), 71-93. https://www.ceeol.com/search/article-detail?id=1109519

Glickman, C., & Burns, R. W. (2021). Supervision and teacher wellness: An essential component for improving classroom practice. *Journal of Educational Supervision, 4*(1), 18.https://doi.org/https://doi.org/10. 31045/jes.4.1.3

Go, M. B., Golbin, R. A.Jr, Velos, S. P., & Bate, G. P. (2020). Filipino Teachers' Compartmentalization Ability, Emotional Intelligence, and Teaching Performance. *Asian Journal of University Education, 16*(3), 27–42. https://eric.ed.gov/?id=EJ1274296. DOI: 10.24191/ajue.v16i3.7912

Hartigan-Go, K., Castillo, A. F., & Prieto, M. L. (2024, January 28). *Hungry children do not make good students*. Rappler. Retrieved June 2, 2025, from https://www.rappler.com/voices/imho/opinion-hungry-children-do-not-make-good-students/

Hechanova, M. R. M. (2011). Deconstructing Emotional Labor. *Philippine Journal of Psychology*, *44*(1), 1–1.

Heffernan, A., Bright, D., Kim, M., Longmuir, F., & Magyar, B. (2022). 'I cannot sustain the workload and the emotional toll': Reasons behind Australian teachers' intentions to leave the profession. *Australian Journal of Education*, *66*(2), 196–209. DOI: 10.1177/00049441221086654

Henson, J. S. (2020). Burnout or compassion fatigue: A comparison of concepts. *Medsurg Nursing*, *29*(2).

Hinds, T. S., & Giardino, A. P. (2020). Compassion fatigue, burnout, and coping strategies among child-serving professionals. Child Sexual Abuse: Current Evidence, Clinical Practice, and Policy *Directions*, 95-102.DOI: 10.1007/978-3-030-52549-1_4

Hirsch, S. E., Bruhn, A. L., McDaniel, S., & Mathews, H. M. (2021). A Survey of Educators Serving Students With Emotional and Behavioral Disorders During the Covid-19 Pandemic. *Behavioral Disorders*, *47*(2), 95–107. DOI: 10.1177/01987429211016780

Hochschild, A. R. (1983). *The managed heart: Commercialization of human feeling*. University of California Press.

Horner, C. G., Brown, E. L., Mehta, S., & Scanlon, C. L. (2020). Feeling and acting like a teacher: Reconceptualizing teachers' emotional labor. *Teachers College Record*, *122*(5), 1–36. DOI: 10.1177/016146812012200502

Hou, Y., & Zheng, J. (2021). The Relationship Between Bob Burnout and Emotional Labor among College Counselors: Mediating Effect of General Self-Efficacy. *In7th International Conference on Social Science and Higher Education (ICSSHE 2021)* (pp. 616-621). Atlantis Press.DOI: 10.2991/assehr.k.211122.167

Humphrey, N. M. (2023). Emotional labor and employee outcomes: A meta-analysis. *Public Administration*, *101*(2), 422–446. DOI: 10.1111/padm.12818

Ignacio, T. D., & Allit, K. J. N. I. (2023). Attitudes of university faculty toward inclusion of students with special education needs. *Erudio Journal of Educational Innovation*, *10*(1), 1–11. DOI: 10.5281/zenodo.8105178

Inbar, L., & Shiri, S.-A. (2021). Managing the emotional aspects of compassion fatigue among teachers in Israel: A qualitative study. *Journal of Education for Teaching*, *47*(4), 562–575. DOI: 10.1080/02607476.2021.1929876

Isenberg, E., Max, J., Gleason, P., & Deutsch, J. (2021). Do Low-Income Students Have Equal Access to Effective Teachers? *Educational Evaluation and Policy Analysis*, *44*(2), 234–256. DOI: 10.3102/01623737211040511

Jennings, P. A., & Min, H. H. (2023). Transforming empathy-based stress to compassion: Skillful means to preventing teacher burnout. *Mindfulness*, *14*(10), 2311–2322. DOI: 10.1007/s12671-023-02115-6 PMID: 37362185

Joffe, A. D., & Peters, L. (2024). The association between emotional labour, affective symptoms, and burnout in Australian psychologists. *Australian Psychologist*, *59*(4), 1–13. DOI: 10.1080/00050067.2023.2299668

Juárez, S. W., & Becton, A. B. (2024). A Self-Care and Wellness Framework in Educator Preparation to Address Burnout, Compassion Fatigue, and Secondary Traumatic Stress. *Action in Teacher Education*, *46*(2), 168–186. DOI: 10.1080/01626620.2024.2319294

Karakus, M., Toprak, M., Caliskan, O., & Crawford, M. (2024). Teachers' affective and physical well-being: Emotional intelligence, emotional labour and implications for leadership. *International Journal of Educational Management*, *38*(2), 469–485. DOI: 10.1108/IJEM-07-2023-0335

Kariou, A., Koutsimani, P., Montgomery, A., & Lainidi, O. (2021). Emotional Labor and Burnout among Teachers: A Systematic Review. *International Journal of Environmental Research and Public Health*, *18*(23), 12760. DOI: 10.3390/ijerph182312760 PMID: 34886485

Keller, M. M., Becker, E. S., Frenzel, A. C., & Taxer, J. L. (2018). When teacher enthusiasm is authentic or inauthentic: Lesson profiles of teacher enthusiasm and relations to students' emotions. *AERA Open*, *4*(2), 2332858418782967. DOI: 10.1177/2332858418782967

Kim, S., & Wang, J. (2018). The Role of Job Demands⁻Resources (JDR) between Service Workers' Emotional Labor and Burnout: New Directions for Labor Policy at Local Government. *International Journal of Environmental Research and Public Health*, *15*(12), 2894. DOI: 10.3390/ijerph15122894 PMID: 30562995

Kim, Y. (2016). *Emotional labour and burnout among public middle school teachers in South Korea*. Unpublished Master's Thesis, University of Jyväskylä. https://urn.fi/URN:NBN:fi:jyu-201604262318

Koenig, A., Rodger, S., & Specht, J. (2018). Educator burnout and compassion fatigue: A pilot study. *Canadian Journal of School Psychology*, *33*(4), 259–278. DOI: 10.1177/0829573516685017

Lavy, S., & Eshet, R. (2018). Spiral effects of teachers' emotions and emotion regulation strategies: Evidence from a daily diary study. *Teaching and Teacher Education*, *73*, 151–161. DOI: 10.1016/j.tate.2018.04.001

Lee, M., & Van Vlack, S. (2018). Teachers' emotional labour, discrete emotions, and classroom management self-efficacy. *Educational Psychology*, *38*(5), 669–686. DOI: 10.1080/01443410.2017.1399199

Levkovich, I., & Gada, A. (2020). The weight falls on my shoulders": Perceptions of compassion fatigue among Israeli preschool teachers. *Asia-Pacific Journal of Research in Early Childhood Education*, *14*(3), 91–112. DOI: 10.17206/apjrece.2020.14

Lim, H., Lee, T. J., Weng, C., & Lee, S. M. (2025). Effects of surface acting on exhaustion of Korean school counselors. *Journal of Counseling and Development*, *103*(1), 49–59. DOI: 10.1002/jcad.12536

Lindstrom Johnson, S., Johnson, B., Meléndez Guevara, A. M., & Fillhouer, M. (2024). The Life of a School Mental Health Professional: A Daily Diary of School Counselor and Social Worker Tasks. *School Mental Health*, **•••**, 1–13. DOI: 10.1007/s12310-024-09733-y

Lu, Y., Wu, W., Mei, G., Zhao, S., Zhou, H., Li, D., & Pan, D. (2019). Surface Acting or Deep Acting, Who Need More Effortful? A Study on Emotional Labor Using Functional Near-Infrared Spectroscopy. *Frontiers in Human Neuroscience*, *13*, 419957. DOI: 10.3389/fnhum.2019.00151 PMID: 31133836

Malquisto, I. R., Casinillo, L. F., & Salabao, A. A. (2023). Burnout among secondary teachers amid the new normal: Case in Ormoc City, Philippines. Journal of Research, Policy & Practice of Teachers & Teacher. *Education*, *13*(2). Advance online publication. DOI: 10.37134/jrpptte.vol13.2.2.2023

Mason-Williams, L., Bettini, E., Morris Mathews, H., Boveda, M., & Rodgers, W. (2022). Disparities in Teachers' Access to Schools' Collective Social Assets Based on Role, Race, and Poverty. *Remedial and Special Education*, *44*(1), 3–15. DOI: 10.1177/07419325211068170

McGlinchey, D., Roebuck, B. S., Sakauye, P., Lalonde, C., Ferns, A., & Killian, K. (2024). "Increasing Demands and Competing Priorities": How Organizational Structure Affects Worker Well-Being in the Victim Services Field. *Human Service Organizations: Management, Leadership & Governance*, 49(2), 152–169.https:// doi.org/. 2024.2417785DOI: 10.1080/23303131

Mendoza, M. (2020). The Lived Experiences of Beginning Teachers: An Odyssey. *JPAIR Multidisciplinary Research, 41*(1), 1–15. DOI: 10.7719/jpair.v41i1.787

Morgan, K. (2024). *'The extra shift': The unpaid emotional labour expected of women at work*. Retrieved from https://www.bbc.com/worklife/article /20240313-invisible-emotional-labour-women-in-workplace

Nalipay, M. J. N., King, R. B., Haw, J. Y., Mordeno, I. G., & Rosa, E. D. D. (2021). Teachers who believe that emotions are changeable are more positive and engaged: The role of emotion mindset among in-and preservice teachers. *Learning and Individual Differences, 92*, 102050. DOI: 10.1016/j.lindif.2021.102050

Naparan, G., Deloria, O., & Naparan, J. (2025). Special Education Teachers' Challenges and Coping Mechanisms in Behavior Management of Learners with Autism. *International Journal of Social Sciences & Educational Studies, 12*(2), 37–53.

Naz, V., Raza, M. A., & Ali, R. (2024). An analysis of female teachers' emotional labor and work-life conflicts at the secondary level. *International Journal of Academic Research for Humanities, 4*(3), 85–95. https://jar.bwo-researches .com/index .php/jarh/article/view/438

Nnubia, U. I., & Nwobi, C. A. FO, O. F. O., & Eke, B. A. (2022). Assessment of Compassion Fatigue and Psychological Well-Being of Special Needs Children's Educators in Enugu State. *Journal For Family & Society Research*, 1(2).https://jfsr .afass.org.ng/index.php/JFSR/article/ view/18

Noor, N. M., & Zainuddin, M. (2011). Emotional labor and burnout among female teachers: Work–family conflict as mediator. *Asian Journal of Social Psychology*, 14(4), 283-293.https://doi.org/. 01349.xDOI: 10.1111/j.1467-839X.2011

O'Toole, C., & Dobutowitsch, M. (2023). The Courage to Care: Teacher Compassion Predicts More Positive Attitudes Toward Trauma-Informed Practice. *Journal of Child & Adolescent Trauma, 16*(1), 123–133. DOI: 10.1007/s40653-022-00486-x PMID: 36157295

Oberg, G., Carroll, A., & Macmahon, S. (2023, March). Compassion fatigue and secondary traumatic stress in teachers: How they contribute to burnout and how they are related to trauma-awareness. In *Frontiers in Education* (Vol. 8, p. 1128618). Frontiers Media SA.https://doi.org/. 1128618DOI: 10.3389/feduc.2023

Ocbian, M. M., & Dischoso, M. A. (2015). Empowering Secondary School Teachers through Administrative Tasks. *Asia Pacific Journal of Multidisciplinary Research, 3*(4), 19–27.

Ombay, G. (2025). *Bullying still a 'silent, persistent' problem in schools – EDCOM.* Retrieved from https://www.gmanetwork.com/news/topstories/nation/ 934485/ bullying-still-a-silent-persistent-problem-in-schools-edcom/story/

Ondrejková, N., & Halamová, J. (2022a). Prevalence of compassion fatigue among helping professions and relationship to compassion for others, self-compassion and self-criticism. *Health & Social Care in the Community, 30*(5), 1680–1694. DOI: 10.1111/hsc.13741 PMID: 35133041

Ondrejková, N., & Halamová, J. (2022b). Stressful factors, experiences of compassion fatigue and self-care strategies in police officers. *Journal of Police and Criminal Psychology, 37*(4), 892–903. DOI: 10.1007/s11896-022-09538-2 PMID: 35874902

Ondrejková, N., & Halamová, J. (2022c). Prevalence of compassion fatigue among helping professions and relationship to compassion for others, self-compassion and self-criticism. *Health & Social Care in the Community, 30*(5), 1680–1694. DOI: 10.1111/hsc.13741 PMID: 35133041

Ormiston, H. E., Nygaard, M. A., & Apgar, S. (2022). A systematic review of secondary traumatic stress and compassion fatigue in teachers. *School Mental Health, 14*(4), 802–817. DOI: 10.1007/s12310-022-09525-2 PMID: 35694002

Palatino, M. (2023). *The Philippines' Basic Education Crisis.* Retrieved from https:// thediplomat.com/2023/02/the-philippines-basic-education-crisis/

Paulsrud, D., & Nilholm, C. (2020). Teaching for inclusion – a review of research on the cooperation between regular teachers and special educators in the work with students in need of special support. *International Journal of Inclusive Education, 27*(4), 541–555. DOI: 10.1080/13603116.2020.1846799

Peat, A., & Ridge, E. (2023). Introduction: Imagining and Reimagining Emotional Labour. *Women a Cultural Review, 34*(4), 259–270. DOI: 10.1080/09574042.2023.2278261

Pehlivan, T., & Güner, P. (2018). Compassion fatigue: The known and unknown. Journal of Psychiatric Nursing/Psikiyatri Hemsireleri Dernegi, 9(2).DOI: 10.14744/phd.2017.25582

PennState. (2024). *What is Emotional Labor?* Retrieved from https://weld.la.psu.edu/what-is-emotional-labor/#:~:text=Emotional%20labor%20is% 20a%20workhanbooks%2C%20training%2C%20financial%20goals.

Perez, R. J., & Bettencourt, G. M. (2023). Exploring Compassion Fatigue and Community Care in Student Affairs. *Journal of Student Affairs Research and Practice, 61*(2), 266–278. DOI: 10.1080/19496591.2023.2176774

Pharris, A. B., Munoz, R. T., & Hellman, C. M. (2022). Hope and resilience as protective factors linked to lower burnout among child welfare workers. *Children and Youth Services Review, 136*, 106424. DOI: 10.1016/j.childyouth.2022.106424

Philippine Congress. (1966). Magna Carta for Public School Teachers. Retrieved from https://lawphil.net/statutes/repacts/ra1966/ ra_4670_1966.html

Philippine Congress. (1995).*Fair and Equitable Access to Education Act.* Retrieved from https://lawphil.net/statutes/repacts/ra1995/ra _7880_1995.html

Qi, X., Ji, S., Zhang, J., Lu, W., Sluiter, J. K., & Deng, H. (2017). Correlation of - emotional labor and cortisol concentration in hair among female kindergarten teachers. *International Archives of Occupational and Environmental Health, 90*(1), 117–122. DOI: 10.1007/s00420-016-1179-6 PMID: 27804039

Recede, R. A. A. (2025, April 29). *Restoring discipline and moral values among Filipino learners.* Philippine Daily Inquirer. Retrieved June 8, 2025, from https://opinion.inquirer.net/182799/restoring-discipline-and-moral-values-a mong-filipino-learners

Redillas, S. (2020). Filipino Teachers' Identity: Framed by Community Engagements, Challenges for Citizenship Education. *The Palgrave Handbook of Citizenship and Education*, 275-295. DOI: 10.1007/978-3-319-67828-3_11

Remington, C. L. (2016). Emotional Labor. In Farazmand, A. (Ed.), *Global Encyclopedia of Public Administration, Public Policy, and Governance*. Springer., DOI: 10.1007/978-3-319-31816-5_2779-1

Renkiewicz, G. K., & Hubble, M. W. (2021). Secondary Traumatic Stress in Emergency Services Systems (STRESS) Project: Quantifying and Predicting Compassion Fatigue in Emergency Medical Services Personnel. *Prehospital Emergency Care, 26*(5), 652–663. DOI: 10.1080/10903127.2021.1943578 PMID: 34128453

Reyes, R. O. (2024). *Overworked, underpaid Filipino teachers leaving for bigger paychecks abroad.* Retrieved from https://www.sunstar.com.ph/tacloban /overworked-underpaid-filipino-teachers-leaving-for-bigger-paychecks-abro ad

Robosa, J., Paras, N., Perante, L., Alvez, T., & Tus, J. (2021). The experiences and challenges faced of the public school teachers amidst the COVID-19 pandemic: A phenomenological study in the Philippines. *International Journal of Advance Research and Innovative Ideas in Education, 7*(1), 1342–1361.

Ruiz-Fernández, M. D., Pérez-García, E., & Ortega-Galán, Á. M. (2020). Quality of Life in Nursing Professionals: Burnout, Fatigue, and Compassion Satisfaction. *International Journal of Environmental Research and Public Health, 17*(4), 1253. DOI: 10.3390/ijerph17041253 PMID: 32075252

Sarabia, A., & Collantes, L. M. . (2020). Work-Related Stress and Teaching Performance of Teachers in Selected School in the Philippines. *Indonesian Research Journal in Education |IRJE|*, 4(1), 6–27. DOI: 10.22437/irje.v4i1.8084

Savellano, J. M. (1999). Teacher education in the Philippines. *Philippine Studies, 47*(2), 253–268. https://www.jstor.org/stable/42634316

Sezen-Gultekin, G., Bayrakcı, M., & Limon, I. (2021). The mediating role of organizational commitment on the relationship between emotional labor and work engagement of teachers. *Frontiers in Psychology, 12*, 648404. DOI: 10.3389/fpsyg.2021.648404 PMID: 34290645

Siekkinen, T., Pekkola, E., & Carvalho, T. (2020). Change and continuity in the academic profession: Finnish universities as living labs. *Higher Education, 79*(3), 533–551. DOI: 10.1007/s10734-019-00422-3

Sinclair, S., Raffin-Bouchal, S., Venturato, L., Mijovic-Kondejewski, J., & Smith-MacDonald, L. (2017). Compassion fatigue: A meta-narrative review of the healthcare literature. *International Journal of Nursing Studies, 69*, 9–24. DOI: 10.1016/j.ijnurstu.2017.01.003 PMID: 28119163

Smith, T. D. (2021). Teaching through trauma: Compassion fatigue, burnout, or secondary traumatic stress? In *Trauma And Resilience In Music Education* (pp. 49–63). Routledge. DOI: 10.4324/9781003124207-3

Stang-Rabrig, J., Brüggemann, T., Lorenz, R., & McElvany, N. (2022). Teachers' occupational well-being during the COVID-19 pandemic: The role of resources and demands. *Teaching and Teacher Education, 117*, 103803. DOI: 10.1016/j.tate.2022.103803 PMID: 35761972

Stanley, S., & Sebastine, A. J. (2024). Predictors of Compassion Fatigue and Compassion Satisfaction in Social Workers (A Quantitative Study from India). *Human Service Organizations: Management, Leadership & Governance*, 48(5), 540–554. https://doi.org/. 2319210DOI: 10.1080/23303131.2024

Stark, K., & Bettini, E. (2021). Teachers' perceptions of emotional display rules in schools: A systematic review. *Teaching and Teacher Education, 104*, 103388. Advance online publication. DOI: 10.1016/j.tate.2021.103388

Stevens, K., & Al-Abbadey, M. (2024). Compassion fatigue and global compassion fatigue in practitioner psychologists: A qualitative study. *Current Psychology (New Brunswick, N.J.), 43*(8), 7259–7274. DOI: 10.1007/s12144-023-04908-3

Stoves, D. (2014). *Compelled to Act: The Negotiation of Compassion Fatigue among Student Affairs Professionals*. Unpublished Doctor of Education Dissertation, University of Corpus Christi. Retrieved from https://www.proquest.com/openview/ec869e694e7be8574dbafa131e973fb 9/1?pq-origsite=gscholar&cbl= 8750

Sy, J. M., & Hernandez, R. A. (2023). *Teachers, Precarity and State Violence in the Philippines*. Retrieved from https://labourreview.org/teachers-precarity -violence/

Tarraya, H. (2023). Teachers' Workload Policy: Its Impact on Philippine Public School Teachers. *Puissant*, 4. https://puissant.stepacademic.net/

Todaro-Franceschi, V. (2024). *Compassion fatigue and burnout in nursing: Enhancing professional quality of life*. Springer Publishing Company. DOI: 10.1891/9780826155290

Töre, E. (2022). Investigation of Emotional Labor in Teaching. *International Journal of Psychology and Educational Studies*, *8*(3), 51–62. DOI: 10.52380/ijpes.2021.8.3.225

Triviño-Amigo, N., Mendoza-Muñoz, D. M., Mayordomo-Pinilla, N., Barrios-Fernández, S., Contreras-Barraza, N., Gil-Marín, M., Castillo, D., Galán-Arroyo, C., & Rojo-Ramos, J. (2022). Inclusive Education in Primary and Secondary School: Perception of Teacher Training. *International Journal of Environmental Research and Public Health, 19*(23), 15451. DOI: 10.3390/ijerph192315451 PMID: 36497523

Tuchinda, N. (2020). The imperative for trauma-responsive special education. *NYUL Rev., 95*, 766. Retrieved from https://heinonline.org/HOL/Landing Page?handle=hein.journals/nylr95&div=18&id=&page=

Villarejo, F. B., Mamburao, R. S., & Lumapenet, H. T. (2022). Work demands and occupational burnout among public school teachers in the Philippines. *International Journal of Advance Research and Innovative Ideas in Education*, *8*(3), 4923–4926.

Voth Schrag, R. J., Wood, L. G., Wachter, K., & Kulkarni, S. (2021). Compassion Fatigue Among the Intimate Partner Violence and Sexual Assault Workforce: Enhancing Organizational Practice. *Violence Against Women, 28*(1), 277–297. DOI: 10.1177/1077801220988351 PMID: 33596785

Vučinić, V., Stanimirovic, D., Gligorović, M., Jablan, B., & Marinović, M. (2020). Stress and Empathy in Teachers at General and Special Education Schools. *International Journal of Disability Development and Education, 69*(2), 533–549. DOI: 10.1080/1034912X.2020.1727421

Walker, T. (2018). *'Education is Political': Neutrality in the Classroom Shortchanges Students.* Retrieved from https://www.nea.org/nea-today /all-news-articles/education-political-neutrality-classroom-shortchanges-stu dents

Waller, S. N., Wozencroft, A. J., & Scott, J. L. (2016). Compassion fatigue among disability camp staff: An exploratory study. *Annals of Leisure Research, 20*(2), 206–221. DOI: 10.1080/11745398.2016.1162724

Wu, Q., Cao, H., & Du, H. (2023). Work Stress, Work-Related Rumination, and Depressive Symptoms in University Teachers: Buffering Effect of Self-Compassion. *Psychology Research and Behavior Management, 16*, 1557–1569. DOI: 10.2147/PRBM.S403744 PMID: 37151906

Xie, S., Liang, L., & Li, H. (2022). Emotional labor and professional identity in Chinese early childhood teachers: The gendered moderation models. *Sustainability (Basel), 14*(11), 6856. DOI: 10.3390/su14116856

Xu, Y. W., & Fan, L. (2023). Emotional labor and job satisfaction among nurses: The mediating effect of nurse–patient relationship. *Frontiers in Psychology, 14*, 1094358. Advance online publication. DOI: 10.3389/fpsyg.2023.1094358 PMID: 37342648

Yanay, N., & Shahar, G. (1998). Professional Feelings as Emotional Labor. *Journal of Contemporary Ethnography, 27*(3), 346–373. DOI: 10.1177/089124198027003003

Yang, C., & Chen, A. (2021). Emotional labor: A comprehensive literature review. *Human Systems Management, 40*(4), 479–501. DOI: 10.3233/HSM-200937

Yang, C., Chen, Y., & Zhao, X. (2019). Emotional Labor: Scale Development and Validation in the Chinese Context. *Frontiers in Psychology, 10*, 486277. DOI: 10.3389/fpsyg.2019.02095 PMID: 31620048

Yang, C., Greenstein, J. E., Manchanda, S., Golshirazi, M., & Yabiku, T. (2023). Preventing compassion fatigue among educators: an educator resiliency study during the COVID-19 pandemic. In *School Violence and Primary Prevention* (pp. 653–686). Springer International Publishing., DOI: 10.1007/978-3-031-13134-9_26

Yang, C., Manchanda, S., & Greenstein, J. (2021). Educators' online teaching self-efficacy and compassion fatigue during the COVID-19 pandemic: The dual roles of "connect". *School Psychology, 36*(6), 504–515. DOI: 10.1037/spq0000475 PMID: 34766814

Yin, H. (2016). Knife-like mouth and tofu-like heart: Emotion regulation by Chinese teachers in classroom teaching. *Social Psychology of Education, 19*(1), 1–22. DOI: 10.1007/s11218-015-9319-5

Yu, H., Jiang, A., & Shen, J. (2016). Prevalence and predictors of compassion fatigue, burnout and compassion satisfaction among oncology nurses: A cross-sectional survey. *International Journal of Nursing Studies, 57*, 28–38. DOI: 10.1016/j.ijnurstu.2016.01.012 PMID: 27045562

Yu, X., Sun, C., Sun, B., Yuan, X., Ding, F., & Zhang, M. (2022). The cost of caring: Compassion fatigue is a special form of teacher burnout. *Sustainability (Basel), 14*(10), 6071. DOI: 10.3390/su14106071

Zaghini, F., Biagioli, V., Proietti, M., Badolamenti, S., Fiorini, J., & Sili, A. (2020). The role of occupational stress in the association between emotional labor and burnout in nurses: A cross-sectional study. *Applied Nursing Research, 54*, 151277. DOI: 10.1016/j.apnr.2020.151277 PMID: 32650898

Zembylas, M. (2003). Emotions and teacher identity: A poststructural perspective. *Teachers and Teaching, 9*(3), 213–238. DOI: 10.1080/13540600309378

Zhang, Q., & Zhu, W. (2008). Exploring emotion in teaching: Emotional labor, burnout, and satisfaction in Chinese higher education. *Communication Education, 57*(1), 105–122. DOI: 10.1080/03634520701586310

Zhang, Y., & Zhang, L. J. (2024). "Good for me to leave it for good": A longitudinal study on how emotion labor in teaching contributes to a beginning EFL teacher's resignation. *TESOL Quarterly, 58*(4), 1460–1492. DOI: 10.1002/tesq.3289

Chapter 7
Burnout in the Social Work Profession:
Now, Then, and With Planning, Maybe Never Again

Carolyn Allen
https://orcid.org/0009-0000-8534-2605
University of the Virgin Islands, US Virgin Islands

ABSTRACT

A review of burnout in the social work profession is presented in the chapter. The focus is on social workers' experience of burnout in the pre-pandemic and COVID-19 pandemic eras. Human service professionals have a high probability of experiencing burnout. Burnout has been described as the cost of caring for human service professionals and often occurs when workers are exposed to stressful situations. Having compassion fatigue, secondary trauma, vicarious trauma, shared trauma, collective trauma and trauma trigger fatigue are all situations that can lead to social worker burnout. Social worker burnout can include feelings of exhaustion, depersonalization and professional inefficacy. The purpose of the chapter is to define social work burnout, explore assessments for burnout, review social work job circumstances associated with burnout and present research on prevention/intervention for social work burnout in the pre-pandemic and COVID-19 pandemic eras.

INTRODUCTION

From the pre-COVID-19 pandemic era to the pandemic era, social work professionals report experiencing burnout at an increased rate (Kranke, Kranke & Der-Martirosian, 2024). In the pre-pandemic era social workers rates of burnout are

DOI: 10.4018/979-8-3373-0169-3.ch007

recorded as 30-75% (Childs et al., 2024). However, during the pandemic era social workers burnout rate in the United States and United Kingdom is as high as 80 - 90% (Evans et al., 2021; McFadden et al., 2015). The finding of higher reported rates of burnout during the pandemic is not surprising. Individuals endured isolation, fear of contagion, and loss during the pandemic (Asakura et al., 2023). The pandemic has made life more stressful for everyone and social workers are no exception. Indeed, social workers have been exposed to the COVID-19 stress both in their personal lives and in their professional work (Holmes, 2021). The dual stress exposure social workers experience complicates their strain (Kranke et al., 2022).

Cherniss (1980) suggests burnout is a transactional process that occurs over time due to workers encountering intolerable workplace stress that is not alleviated. The stress which is not ameliorated leads to tension, fatigue and exhaustion in the worker, who in response to the strain may emotionally detach from work. According to Cherniss, the nature of human service work creates a workplace environment ripe for burnout. Social workers' passion for helping conflicts with the limited resources and bureaucracy found in the field. Essentially, social work professionals are attracted to their career based on a desire to serve. However, once in the profession, social workers find bureaucratic constraints, heavy paperwork demands, limited professional autonomy, seemingly intractable social problems and client recidivism and defensiveness (Leiter, 1991). The mismatch between the passion for social work and the day-to-day job duties lead to burnout (Kranke et al., 2024).

Additionally, Zerden (2024) explains that the expectation for social workers is to be "everything, everywhere, all at once". The social work job role is inclusive of case manager, resource specialist, advocate, therapist, community organizer and more (Kirst-Ashman & Hull, 2018). In other words, be everything. The social work tasks are performed in many settings, e.g., schools, hospitals, counseling centers, nonprofit organizations, governmental agencies, communities and more (Berg-Weger, 2019). Therefore, social workers must be everywhere. Social workers perform duties with people throughout the lifespan and in all situations of crisis and need (Birkenmaier & Berg-Weger, 2017). Consequently, social workers must perform disparate duties all at once.

The U.S. News listed two social work jobs in the top five of the most stressful jobs in the United States (Adam, 2024). Clinical social worker was the third most stressful job and Child and Family social worker was the fifth most stressful job. Stressful jobs can beget burnout. We know that social workers experience burnout during the pre-COVID-19 pandemic era through to the post pandemic era (Kranke & Der-Martirosian, 2024). Discussion in the chapter will explore the social work experience with burnout in the pre-pandemic and COVID-19 pandemic eras, the definition of burnout, the assessment of burnout, the circumstances associated with social workers experiencing burnout, and research on social work burnout prevention/ intervention in the pre-pandemic and COVID-19 pandemic eras.

HOW DID STRESS AND BURNOUT RELATE TO THE SOCIAL WORK PROFESSION DURING THE PANDEMIC?

During the pandemic, marginalized groups such as racial minorities, low-income populations, the LGBTQ community and people with disabilities experienced some of the harshest impacts (Asakura et al., 2023) and social workers were expected to respond with cultural and linguistic sensitivity. Additionally, the pandemic brought a rise in domestic violence and reports of child abuse (Sidpra et al., 2021; Swedo et al., 2020). Child welfare social workers faced several complicated case management issues at the time of the pandemic (Katz et al., 2021). Social work professionals were expected to respond to higher caseloads while working remotely (Axelrad-Levy et al, 2023). Further, the authors describe that many childcare residential facilities were closed due to COVID-19 restrictions. Simultaneously, the closure of schools and daycare facilities placed children who were at-risk for abuse in their home settings for more hours. Possibly predictably, Emergency Department visits connected to child abuse and neglect increased in the United States during the pandemic (Swedo et al., 2020).

During the pandemic, child welfare social workers toggled between trying to remotely manage a higher caseload with children who were at greater risk for abuse versus attempting to follow COVID-19 safety protocol for face-to-face service delivery for clients in need (Axelrad-Levy et al, 2023). A survey of 878 child welfare social workers was conducted to investigate the practitioners perceived stress and job performance (Axelrad-Levy et al, 2023). The social workers reported poorer job performance in the circumstances of the pandemic crisis. The perceived stress interrupted supervision and compromised autonomy. In prior research, the identified factors, disrupted supervision and less autonomy, have been associated with greater burnout for social workers (Maslach & Leiter, 2007).

Social workers were on the frontlines of helping clients manage their fear of COVID-19 and understand the COVID-19 restrictions (Tan & Yeap, 2022). During the pandemic, hospital social workers were found to experience higher levels of burnout than their counterparts who were employed as community social workers in the pandemic (Shinan-Altman et al., 2024). Hospital social workers could be tasked to communicate with family members of patients hospitalized by the coronavirus. The new job demands occurred simultaneously with social workers' managing the impacts of COVID-19 in their personal lives (Holmes et al., 2021). Given the exposure to job stress and personal stress, it is understandable that social workers experienced burnout.

HOW DID STRESS AND BURNOUT RELATE TO THE SOCIAL WORK PROFESSION PRE-PANDEMIC?

Social workers were no stranger to burnout before the COVID-19 pandemic occurred. Particularly in the pre-pandemic era, social workers described stressful job conditions related to working with survivors of natural disasters such as Hurricane Katrina (Findley et al., 2017) and working with immigrant communities (Negi, 2018). In the year 2000, the National Association of Social Workers (NASW) released a policy statement underlining that social workers were equipped to work with and advocate for clients impacted by natural disasters. Namely, the NASW six core values of Service, Social justice, Dignity and worth of the person, Importance of human relationships, Integrity and Competence make the profession well aligned with service delivery to those impacted by disasters whether natural or human caused (Findley et al., 2017). Further, social workers are trained in generalist practice and educated to use a systems framework while being mindful of the person in environment perspective (Cain, 2019). Social workers embrace diversity, empowerment and the strengths perspective. An orientation to work with individuals and communities which use these principles is well-suited to serving populations recovering from disasters.

Findley et al. (2015) find that social workers play a pivotal role in ameliorating the psychological impact of disasters and social workers have served populations displaced by natural disasters for decades. Social workers have provided services after natural disasters such as earthquakes, floods and hurricanes. The National Oceanic and Atmospheric Administration (NOAA) report 17 major hurricanes between 2001 and 2023 which impacted the United States and its territories. Charley (category 4), Ivan (category 3), Jeanne (category 3), Dennis (category 3), Katrina (category 3), Rita (category 3) Wilma (category 3), Superstorm Sandy special mention (category 1) Harvey (category 4), Irma (category 5), Maria (category 5), Michael (category 5), Laura (category 4), Zeta (category 3) Ida (category 4) Ian (category 4) and Idalia (category 3) all had devastating impacts on the populations they touched and social workers were present to assist with recovery efforts (*HURDAT Re-Analysis*, n.d.).

Hurricane Katrina delivered the harshest impacts to African Americans who earned less than $10,000 per year when the storm struck New Orleans in 2005 (Moyo & Moldovan, 2008). The population benefitted from social work intervention to help find resources and stabilize the situation (Manning & Kushma, 2016). Social work students' understanding of disaster recovery practice was so relevant post Hurricane

Katrina that Tulane University in New Orleans, Louisianna developed a disaster-related curriculum (Findley et al., 2017). Similarly, the Rutgers School of Social Work in New Jersey integrated a disaster response training program into the graduate social work curriculum immediately after experiencing impacts from Superstorm Sandy. Crawford (2021) reflects that Hurricane Harvey taught social workers important lessons about working with communities during disasters. Social workers have a set of skills which assist in communicating with vulnerable populations.

Although social workers are prepared and present in disaster recovery work, disaster recovery work brings job stress. Bride and Figley (2007) considered the work stress and emotional challenges social workers encounter when providing services to survivors of disasters. High caseloads, unrealistic paperwork demands, and lack of social work compensation are all job stressors social workers face with disaster work, natural or human-caused (Bride and Figley, 2007). So, job stress and burnout were familiar in the social work profession before the pandemic era.

WHAT IS BURNOUT?

The World Health Organization's International Statistical Classification of Diseases and Related Health Problems (11th ed.; ICD-11) defines burnout as "a syndrome conceptualized as resulting from chronic workplace stress that has not been successfully managed" (World Health Organization, 2019, para. 3). The workplace can create an environment where burnout flourishes. Working conditions where employees have little control of their time, low autonomy, high bureaucracy and limited job role clarity invite burnout (Wagaman et al., 2015). Further, lack of flexibility in job function can make the work tedious and contribute to burnout (Leiter, 1991).

Symptoms of Burnout

The list of burnout symptoms is long; however, burnout symptomatology can collapse into categories. Schaufeli and Enzmann (1998) suggest as many as 132 symptoms are associated with burnout and cleverly alphabetize the symptoms from anxiety to zeal. The Substance Abuse and Mental Health Services Administration [SAMHSA] (2022) notes the three dimensions of burnout are exhaustion, depersonalization, and professional inefficacy. Burnout can present with physical, emotional/mental, or behavioral indicators.

Exhaustion is a physical sign. Workers with burnout may complain of fatigue, weariness, tension, insomnia, gastrointestinal discomfort, muscle strain, and headaches (Lee & Ashforth, 1990; Maslach & Leiter, 2007; Wagaman et al., 2015; Zerden, 2024). Depersonalization can be considered an emotional/mental symptom where the person attempts to distance themselves from others as an action to protect the self (Lee & Ashforth, 1990). The human service professional may detach from the workplace and express pessimistic views of their organization (Childs et al., 2024) and cynical attitudes toward clients (Bakker & Demerouti, 2017). The worker experiencing burnout may manifest depression and anxiety (Tosone et al., 2012). Professional inefficacy is akin to reduced personal accomplishments. If self-efficacy bodes a sense of personal accomplishment, professional inefficacy represents the opposite (Lee & Ashforth, 1990). Professional inefficacy can present with behavioral signs such as absenteeism, tardiness, increased worker errors, and intention to leave employment (Maslach & Leiter, 2007; Wagaman et al., 2015).

Gradual Development of Burnout

Cherniss (1980) developed a three-stage model for burnout. In the first stage, the practitioner experiences stress based on the imbalance between resources and demands. Stage two describes strain, fatigue, and anxiety as the emotional response to the imbalance. In stage three the practitioner attempts to cope with the strain by detaching, withdrawing, or becoming more cynical. The signs and symptoms of burnout are abundant.

Further, burnout occurs over time where an individual gradually experiences a loss of energy (Schaufeli & Enzmann, 1998). Burnout is based on an accumulation of experience rather than being caused by a one-time event (Tosone et al., 2012). Powell (2019) argues that social workers are at high risk for burnout, as are all human service professionals. Kranke et al. (2024) agree and forward that burnout is an imbalance between available resources and work demands. As social workers repeatedly encounter a lack of resources, heavy paperwork requirements and clients who are not amenable to interventions, burnout builds. Human service professionals emotionally invest with clients and are vicariously exposed to clients' trauma (Tosone et al., 2012). Inadequate resources for clients and insufficient support from organizations and supervisors can result in social workers experiencing the symptoms of burnout including exhaustion and lower self-efficacy.

A history of personal trauma for the practitioner increases the risk of developing burnout when working with clients who have similar histories (Newell & MacNeil, 2010). Therefore, not only do workplace environmental factors influence the development of job burnout, but human service professionals can be "preloaded" to develop burnout. Social work professionals can be attracted to the field based on their own personal experience of trauma. For example, a human service worker who experienced abuse in her childhood may be drawn to a career in child welfare or a social worker who battled depression could be interested in providing mental health services. The preexistence of mood disorders or anxiety are other vulnerabilities to the development of burnout (Newell & MacNeil, 2010).

Initial Development of Burnout as a Concept

The term burnout has been used in psychological literature for decades and is generally used to describe a constellation of symptoms including emotional exhaustion, depersonalization, cynicism and diminished professional efficacy (Shepherd & Newell, 2020). Bradley (1969) is credited with the first published use of the expression "staff burn out" when referring to probation officers and their work in a residential center for young adult offenders. Bradley explored organizational design, staff roles and feedback and suggested a rotating staff schedule to prevent burnout.

Although Bradley was the first to mention the term burnout, the development of the concept is most closely associated with Herbert Freudenberger (Schaufeli & Enzmann, 1998). Freudenberger, a psychologist, was immersed in the Free Clinic movement of the 1960's and 1970's and his seminal work "Staff Burn-Out" was published in the Journal of Social Issues a volume focused on the topic of Free Clinics (Fontes, 2020). Free Clinics provided services without cost to indigent populations seeking care for drug abuse, infections, venereal diseases and other general medical problems. Freudenberger visited Free Clinics in Haight-Ashbury, San Francisco and volunteered at a Free Clinic in New York where he observed fellow volunteers' work trajectory move from initial enthusiasm to exhaustion and low commitment while working with drug abusers.

Freudenberger noted that volunteers, including himself, who were initially motivated to work long hours and empathetically gave of themselves gradually lost motivation (Fontes, 2020). The volunteers showed multiple physical and mental symptoms including agitation, depression and apathy. Freudenberger termed this the "burnt out syndrome", a phrase plucked from the colloquial word for chronic drug abuse – burnout. Schaufeli and Enzmann (1998) state, "His detailed description of the burnout syndrome was easily and readily recognized, particularly by those who worked in the human services" (p. 3). Indeed, Leiter (1991) described the tension between the passion that brings professionals to human services and the daily grind of the work that leads to burnout.

Burnout Around the Globe

Burnout is a global phenomenon which has been studied in Iran, China, Kenya, Australia and New Zealand (Almen & Jansson, 2021). Therefore, burnout is not a phenomenon solely known in the United States or only found in western cultures. In a 2024 Gallup poll, 41% of the global population reported daily work stress

(Gallup, 2024). Schaufeli and Enzmann (1998) report nations are concerned with researching burnout due to its negative effect on worker productivity. According to the researchers, worker burnout is estimated to cost the European Union ten percent of the GNP which is spent on absenteeism, sick-leave and other impacts.

Tan and Yeap (2022) investigated the relationship between work engagement, meaningful work and the alleviation of burnout. A study surveyed 530 social workers in New Zealand found practitioners who describe their work as meaningful also report work engagement (Tan &Yeap, 2022). The researchers forward that when social workers believe that the work is meaningful, they invest even more of themselves in the job, placing more demands on themselves and opening the potential for burnout. Thus, job burnout can occur even when the social worker considers their role to be meaningful. Tan and Yeap (2022) recommended nonprofit organizations offer programs to the social workers that reveal alignment between social workers' orientation and the agency's objectives. Doing so may link the social workers' professional identity and motivation for work to the agency's objectives and the connection could help to mitigate job burnout.

While Tan and Yeap explored social work and burnout in the Southern Hemisphere, Shinan-Altman (2024) studied social work and burnout in the Northern Hemisphere. A survey of 163 Israeli social workers reported compassion satisfaction rose with worker resilience and organizational support (Shinan-Altman, 2024). The researchers compared professional quality of life for hospital social workers and community health maintenance social workers. Similar to Tan and Yeap (2022), Shinan-Altman (2024) suggests intervention programs in the workplace will help decrease burnout.

Hu et al. (2022) researched the social work profession, burnout and turnover intention on the Eastern Hemisphere. A study collected data from 829 members of Xiehou Shegong, a social work organization in China, and found that being seeped in a social worker professional identity reduced burnout (Hu et al., 2022). According to Hu et al. (2022), the social work profession in China is in its infancy and an emphasis on social work training and education is important. Regardless of the global location, social work and reduction of burnout are being investigated.

HOW IS BURNOUT ASSESSED?

Much of the scholarly understanding for assessing burnout uses a framework developed in the pre-pandemic era (Doherty et al. 2021). Christina Maslach, a social psychologist, and Susan Jackson, a social psychologist, developed the Maslach Burnout Inventory (MBI) in 1981 and the MBI is the most often cited assessment for burnout (Lee & Ashforth, 1990). The MBI is an outgrowth of qualitative research conducted by Maslach in the early 1980's (Schaufeli & Enzmann, 1998). Maslach interviewed healthcare professionals to examine the way workers cope with stressful positions. The lived experience of study participants revealed three themes (Schaufeli & Enzmann, 1998). Theme one described healthcare workers such as physicians, psychiatrists, nurses, and counsellors report of emotional exhaustion and feeling drained from their professional practice. Theme two found that the practitioners developed cynical or caustic attitudes toward clients. Theme three reported that the healthcare participants in the study had a lower sense of professional competence caused by the emotional turmoil they felt toward clients and the field of practice.

The three qualitative themes of burnout Maslach's research described were repackaged into a survey instrument to measure burnout (Maslach & Leiter, 2016). The MBI is a 22 item, self-reported survey comprised of three subscales, emotional exhaustion (EE) having nine items, depersonalization (DP) having five items, and reduced personal accomplishment (PA) having eight items (Leiter, 1991). The inventory presents a seven-point Likert scale ranging from zero (never) to six (every day) which asks respondents to score statements. For example, respondents reflect on statements such as "I feel emotionally drained from my work" or "I feel like I'm working too hard on my job" (Almen & Jansson, 2021).

Expansion of the Maslach Burnout Inventory

The MBI was designed to measure burnout for professionals in the human service sector and has been shown to have good reliability (Doherty, 2021). According to Schaufeli (2021) the MBI is used in approximately 90% of all published burnout studies. MBI became such a popular instrument to measure burnout for human service professionals that other employment fields wanted to adopt the inventory for their disciplines. Therefore, MBI has been modified to address particular work populations and currently there are five versions of the MBI (i.e., MBI-HSS for Human Services workers; MBI-GS for General Use; MBI-HSS for Medical Personnel; MBI-ES for Educators; MBI-GSS for Students).

Since the original MBI was designed for use with human service professionals, when the MBI was used with employees not working in the human service sector differences were found (Maslach et al., 1996). Not only were the statement items made "occupation-neutral" (Maslach and Leiter, 2016), but the scales Emotional Exhaustion and Depersonalization seemed to combine. Depersonalization is specific to employee groups who work with people. For non-human service professionals, the MBI General Use was revised to assess detachment from work. Similarly, Personal Accomplishment was revised to professional efficacy (Maslach and Leiter, 2016).

Assessment of Burnout Around the Globe

The MBI is used globally in English-speaking nations and non-English speaking nations. McFadden (2015) found social workers in the United Kingdom (UK) scored moderate to high on the MBI emotional exhaustion subscale (91%), while 61% scored moderate to high on the MBI depersonalization subscale, and 91% scored high on the MBI personal accomplishment subscale. While the UK social workers' scores on emotional exhaustion and depersonalization indicate burnout, the score on the personal accomplishment subscale does not. The personal accomplishment subscale score is a favorable one since burnout is associated with a low score.

The MBI has been translated into Spanish, Italian, French, German, Dutch, Swedish, Finnish Polish, Hebrew, Japanese, and other languages (Maslach et al., 1996). The modification went beyond language translation and also accounted for cultural context. The Spanish translation of the MBI contains four subscales (enthusiasm towards the job, psychological exhaustion, indolence and guilt) (Maslach and Leiter, 2016).

Although the MBI has been used around the globe, it is not the only burnout assessment instrument. The Oldenburg Burnout Inventory, the Shirom-Melamed Burnout Questionnaire/Measure (Almen and Jansson, 2021), the Perceived Stress Scale (Evan, et al, 2021) and the Copenhagen Burnout Inventory (Childs et al., 2024) are other available instruments for measuring burnout. Burnout is a well-researched phenomenon, and we have gained useful information regarding the burnout syndrome.

WHAT CIRCUMSTANCES ARE ASSOCIATED WITH SOCIAL WORKERS EXPERIENCING BURNOUT?

Cherniss (1980) paints a picture of a social worker, Mary, beginning her work life with enthusiasm which turned to apathy and eventual bitterness after experiencing months of routine disappointments while working with clients.

> *Like most new social workers, she began with great expectations. She was idealistic, committed, and hopeful. After eight months on the job, she became discouraged and demoralized about the lack of motivation and change in so many of her clients. She wanted to do family therapy, but she could never get a whole family to come in together for treatment. ... She had expected that being a therapist and counselor in a mental health agency would be as fascinating as it seemed in the books she had read in college. But she became bored during many sessions with clients. She eventually quit ... (Cherniss, 1980, pp.14-15)*

The signs of burnout are emotional exhaustion, depersonalization and feelings of lack of personal accomplishment (Yuma, 2019). But the building blocks of burnout have been associated with terms such as compassion fatigue, vicarious trauma, secondary trauma, shared trauma, collective trauma, and trauma trigger fatigue (Logan et al., 2024; Hirschberger, 2018; Wagaman, et al., 2015; Tosone et al., 2012). The themes and terms are likely familiar to social workers and their experiences. Interestingly, the listed terms are often used interchangeably and refer to exhaustion, i.e., mental, physical and emotional, which partially define burnout (Hochschild, 2012). However, there are subtle differences between the terms. The following discussion presents an introduction to the terms and then a subsection dedicated to each term.

The term compassion fatigue reflects the emotional and psychological exhaustion social workers experience from the routine job expectation to be empathetic toward client concerns (Wagaman, et al, 2015). Social workers are driven by a passion to empower clients and remove obstacles which impede clients. On the flipside of this passion can be compassion fatigue. While social workers can experience compassion fatigue regardless of whether or not their caseloads include clients exposed to trauma, the terms secondary trauma and vicarious trauma are specific to a practitioner's exposure to clients' recounting of traumatic experiences (Stamm, 1995). Such practitioners may exhibit symptoms of posttraumatic stress disorder (PTSD) like their clients, but in a milder form (Figley, 1995). Shared trauma represents situations where the provider and client have been exposed to the same traumatic event such as a natural disaster (Asakura, 2023). Collective trauma goes a step further and implies that not just the provider and client have been exposed to the trauma, but the whole society has exposure (Hirschberger, 2018). Kranke et al. (2024) introduced the term trauma trigger fatigue "to capture the unique experiences of social workers during the pandemic" (p. 403). Many social workers are attracted to the profession due to a driving desire to help others. The passion to help others may have been sparked by the social worker's own past trauma. Kranke et al. asserts there is a need to understand social worker's past trauma as part of the contributing factors for burnout.

Therefore, there is a long list of factors which contribute to social worker burnout. The list includes organizational factors such as lack of role clarity, unfair treatment at work, unmanageable workload, unreasonable time expectations, and lack of communication and support (Childs et al., 2024). Additional factors manifest from being in a caregiver's profession, i.e., compassion fatigue, vicarious trauma, secondary trauma, shared trauma, collective trauma (Shepherd & Newell, 2020). Trauma trigger fatigue is a personal factor which can exist alongside the organizational and professional factors of burnout.

Compassion Fatigue

Compassion fatigue is a lowered ability to express compassion and empathy for clients which occurs in the context of the human service professionals feeling overwhelmed. Figley (1995) found the symptoms of sadness, depression, sleeplessness, and general anxiety can be associated with compassion fatigue. The example of the social worker, Mary, described above may have been struggling with compassion fatigue. Hansel and Saltzman (2023) suggest that compassion fatigue may be a compelling factor in choosing to leave the profession. Further, demographic factors such as being female and years of experience in the field are associated with compassion fatigue. Compassion fatigue has been dubbed the "cost of caring" (Figley, 1995). Social workers feel an urgency and passion to assist others that can turn into compassion fatigue when clients need for service seems unending (Kranke et al., 2024). According to Kranke et al. compassion fatigue is common in the social work profession. Compassion fatigue can be a contributing factor to burnout.

Secondary Trauma

Secondary trauma occurs when there is significant knowledge of a traumatizing event experienced by another person. Social workers know the narrative stories of clients' traumas. In the role of counselor, advocate, resource broker, and other roles, social workers learn the intimate details of clients' experiences with victimization, abuse, and natural disasters. Secondary trauma differs from compassion fatigue in that the former includes the human service professional experiencing PTSD like symptoms whereas the latter does not (Powell, 2019). Figley (1995) identifies that the human service professional who has secondary trauma may experience intrusive thoughts such as recollections of the event described by the primary traumatized person. The person with secondary trauma may display avoidance behaviors such as avoiding situations and becoming detached. Secondary trauma exposure may result in persistent arousal such as irritability, concentration difficulties and sleep disturbance. Holmes (2021) conducted a quantitative study using 181 social workers to measure the impact of COVID-19 on posttraumatic stress, grief, burnout and secondary trauma. Approximately 50% of study participants reported experiencing average secondary trauma, while 26% could have been diagnosed with PTSD based on meeting the criteria, and 16% reported severe grief symptoms. The consequences of exposure to secondary trauma are significant. Approximately 64% of the social workers surveyed reported burnout.

Vicarious Trauma

Powell (2019) describes that vicarious trauma, unlike secondary trauma, adds the complication of permanent change to cognitive schema or perceptions. A human service worker who experiences vicarious trauma may have a permanent change in their sense of self, perceptions of safety or spiritual beliefs after being exposed to secondary trauma. For example, social workers who are employed in the criminal justice system and have knowledge of violent actions taken by clients may find themselves more fearful of their physical safety or more vigilant about safety protocols in their personal life.

Shared Trauma

Shared trauma occurs in situations where both the human service professionals and clients are exposed to the same traumatic event (Asakure et al., 2023). A shared trauma would impact on the social worker in both personal and professional life. Shared trauma can result in heightened anxiety, fears about personal safety and well-being (Tosone et al., 2014). Discussion of shared trauma is very relevant to the 21st century. The concept of shared trauma was first used after the September 11, 2021 disaster in New York (Tosone et al., 2003). Shared trauma can be applied to the 9/11 event and the multiple hurricanes that have impacted the United States and its territories. Tosone et al. (2011) surveyed 481 Manhattan social workers to explore the relationship between the risk factors for posttraumatic stress, secondary trauma and shared traumatic stress for clinicians who survived September 11th. One of the study's hypotheses was accepted in the findings indicate that clinicians who had insecure attachments experienced higher levels of shared traumatic stress. Educational programs and professional development training should take the relationships between risk factors for posttraumatic stress, secondary trauma and shared traumatic stress into account when designing curriculum (Tosone et al., 2011). Doing so may help prevent burnout.

Collective Trauma

Collective trauma implies having a wider impact than shared trauma in that not only is the traumatic event experienced by both the human service professional and the client, but the whole society is impacted by the trauma and has a collective memory of the trauma (Hirschberger, 2018). Hirschberger argues that collective trauma is transgenerational. Individuals who do not have first-hand experience with the trauma will nonetheless possess a collective memory of the trauma. The trauma binds the group together culturally and becomes part of the group's identity. The

COVID-19 pandemic is a possible example of collective trauma (Holmes et al., 2021). Collective trauma is situational and being a social work practitioner at the time of a collective trauma such as COVID-19 can be a factor in burnout. Miller et al. (2021) surveyed 1568 mental health social workers to examine the relationships between COVID-19 distress and self-care. The participants experienced emotional and physiological distress related to the COVID-19 pandemic. For the social workers in the study the more engaged they were in self-care, the less distress they reported.

Trauma Trigger Fatigue

In the wake of the COVID-19 pandemic, trauma trigger fatigue was introduced into the literature by Kranke et al. (2024). Social workers may enter the profession with a history of personal trauma in their background. As noted earlier, social workers can be attracted to a career in advocacy due to a desire to serve an oppressed group that they personally identify as. For example, a social worker who experienced poverty and prejudice in childhood may want to work in low-income areas because of the ability to identify with and encourage the population. The social worker may have unresolved trauma from childhood. Kranke et al. (2024) suggest that the collective trauma of the COVID-19 pandemic reopened hitherto concealed wounds for social workers with a history of trauma.

> *We must be aware, appreciate, and understand where each social worker is at with their prior history of trauma as the effects of the pandemic linger and reemerge in various communities over time. Burnout is an indication that the social work profession does not have the capacity to confront the invisible wounds that led many social workers to the field in the first place (Kranke et al., 2024, p. 404).*

WHAT PREVENTION AND INTERVENTION TECHNIQUES WERE LEARNED FROM RESEARCH ON SOCIAL WORK BURNOUT IN THE PRE-PANDEMIC AND COVID-19 PANDEMIC ERAS?

Stress in the workplace can lead to burnout. In the pre-pandemic era, social workers encountered many stressful situations and events including working in a hospital during the severe acute respiratory syndrome (SARS) crisis (Gearing et al, 2007), working with new immigrants (Negi et al., 2019), and working with populations in post disaster settings (Powell et al., 2019). During the pandemic, social workers continued to function as client advocates, client resource brokers, and counselors. The onset of the COVID-19 pandemic complicated social workers job stress by adding mandatory quarantines, isolation, and fear of infection to the factors that must be navigated as practitioners delivered service to clients (Holmes et al., 2021).

We know that rates of burnout among social workers are high, and burnout can lead to job turnover (Hu et al., 2022). Therefore, the prevention of burnout in the social work profession is a worthwhile endeavor (Kranke et al, 2024). A strong professional social work identity (Hu et al., 2022) is part of a prevention strategy for burnout. Further, having a social support network, tending to self-care and practicing mindfulness are all part of intervention strategies when confronting burnout (Gearing et al, 2007; Negi et al., 2019; Powell et al., 2019). The best recommendations to thwart burnout from the pre-COVID-19 era are echoed and expanded by research on social work burnout during the pandemic.

Benefits of Professional Social Work Identity

Social workers can lean on the core values of the profession to help cope with stressful situations and burnout (Gearing et al., 2007). A qualitative study of 39 hospital social workers who practiced during the SARS crisis was conducted (Gearing et al.,2007). SARS is a coronavirus, so how social workers managed the job stress may be instructive to thinking about coping with stress caused by the COVID-19 pandemic that occurred years later. Gearing et al. found that the SARS crisis impacted on social workers both personally (emotional) and professionally (technical). The researchers uncovered two subthemes related to the emotional level of impact which are emotional awareness and coping strategies. Additionally, the subthemes related to the technical level of impact are communication, advocacy, family-centered approach, knowledge of systems and ethics.

On an emotional level, social workers in the study reported they were alert to the emotional tone of the hospital setting. As stated earlier in the discussion, one of the core social work values is the importance of human relationships. Social workers were aware of the anxious feelings of patients and staff alike. Not only did the social workers describe increasing their visibility as a way of quieting anxiety of others, but the social workers also recognized the need for self-awareness regarding their own emotional responses (Gearing et al, 2007). The hospital social workers in the study reported intentionally using coping strategies such as humor, social support systems, and self-care time as coping techniques.

On a professional level, social workers stated that open communication was pivotal, and creative strategies were used to achieve communication during SARS such as interviewing family members in cars and use of telephone versus in-person contact. Similarly, social workers found creative ways to advocate for patient families and nursing staff. Gearing et al. (2007) concluded that social workers had to balance emotional and professional aspects of practice, and the core values of the profession helped them to do so.

The call to serve and treat people with dignity and respect are among the core values and utilizing social work practice skills helps assuage burnout (Gearing et al, 2007). Wagaman et al. (2015) suggest compassion satisfaction is a salve to burnout. Compassion satisfaction draws on the positive feelings workers get from helping others and uses this altruistic sensibility to thwart burnout.

Negi et al. (2018) underlined the worth of an altruistic orientation. A qualitative study of 29 social care workers employed in a new immigrant settlement city was conducted to investigate the workers' motivations and responses to stress. An altruistic orientation was found to mitigate stress and burnout (Negi et al., 2018). Participants in the study described being called to serve Latina/o immigrants and this sense of duty outweighed the stress and frustration of lack of resources. Study participants described celebrating small victories, being inspired by the resilience of immigrants, and loving the work with immigrant communities. The altruistic orientation coupled with the positive reframing of the meaning of success buffered burnout.

Relatedly, based on research during the pandemic Hu et al. (2022) recommend social work education prioritize the development of professional identity and non-attachment. An educational focus on the development of professional social work identity provides a buffer against burnout and job turnover in a social work career (Wiles, 2017). Additionally, the education of social workers should highlight that there can be a disparity between social workers' passion for service and the realities of limited resources (Hu et al., 2022). The realistic preparation of social work students may help to alleviate burnout when they enter the profession and encounter challenges.

Therefore, Hu et al. (2022) suggests that professional identity is an important factor in easing the impacts of burnout. A quantitative survey of social workers in China explored professional identity, turnover and burnout where Hu et al. concluded professional identity should be promoted. A strong professional identity anchors social workers in the field. Social workers are taught to align themselves with the core values of the profession and the alignment of personal and professional values helps to lessen burnout (Negi, 2018; Gearing et al, 2007). Pre-pandemic

Gearing et al, (2007) and Negi et al. (2018) conclude that embracing social work values helps to lower burnout. During the pandemic Hu et al. reached the same conclusion that having a strong social work identity is a useful guard against the development of burnout.

Benefits of Social Support

Negi et al. (2019) argue that having supportive colleagues and a supportive organization allays stress and burnout. When social workers join with others in the profession who possess the same set of values, the stress and daily frustrations are buoyed by the supportive community. Powell et al. (2019) conducted research with 722 social service providers post Superstorm Sandy and concluded that social support can be a protective factor against burnout. Powell et al. examined the effectiveness of the Caregivers Journey of Hope (CJoH), a post disaster psychoeducational intervention program, utilized by social workers and counselors. CJoH presented a half-day workshop and presented information on stress, the impact of stress, coping with stress and rebuilding after a natural disaster. Participants were surveyed pre-and-post participation in the workshop. During the workshop, participants learned to recognize stress, strategies for coping with stress such as exercise, rest, and mindfulness. The pre- and post-test results indicate that participants gained knowledge. Organizations can bolster employees' protective factors against burnout by providing training, managing workloads, and encouraging peer support (Powell et al., 2019). So, if we already know a lot about burnout and self-care in the human services the question becomes, what other lessons are learned from social workers managing burnout during COVID-19 and what are the best prevention/intervention strategies?

Kranke et al. (2024) identified six themes of factors which aided social workers retention during the pandemic. Kranke et al. collected qualitative data from thirteen outpatient social workers employed by the U.S. Department of Veterans Affairs (VA) during the pandemic. Commitment to serve veterans, collegial support, leadership support, job flexibility, maintenance of normal routines and trust in science/evidence-based practices were all factors in social worker retention during the challenges of the COVID-19 pandemic.

Both Negi (2018) and Kranke et al. (2024) underscore the importance of having supportive colleagues. The team mentality of social workers cushions against succumbing to burnout. In studies conducted prior to the pandemic, researchers found having a supportive organization or agency tempered social workers experience of burnout (Gearing et al., 2007; Negi et al., 2019; Powell et al., 2019). Likewise, Kranke et al. found that having a supportive supervisor helps counter burnout. Leaders can remind social workers of the importance of self-care, provide adequate supervision and allow for flexibility in the workday. Moreover, Kranke et al. recommend permanently establishing the option of telework to help decrease social workers' attrition. The efficiency and flexibility of online, virtual and hybrid work is one of the lessons learned from the pandemic.

Finally, maintain normal routines and trusting scientific, evidence-based practices added to social workers' abilities to continue functioning in their job roles during the pandemic (Kranke et al., 2024). Normal routines can provide a sense of order or control, while trusting evidence-based practices provide a sense of safety and hope. The management of social workers' burnout during the pandemic taught the profession new lessons about coping with stress.

Benefits of Self-Care and Mindfulness

Various research studies explored the benefits of self-care and mindfulness practices to combat burnout for social workers during the pre-pandemic era (Gearing et al, 2007; Negi et al., 2019; Powell et al., 2019). Self-care is a multifaceted practice which includes activities to address physical, emotional, and spiritual well-being (Maddock & McCusker, 2022). Shepherd & Newell (2020) add that there are multiple forms of self-care which have different benefits. Spiritual self-care can bolster mental health. Physical self-care such as exercise can support vitality. Human service professionals are recommended to engage in more than one type of self-care to gain maximum benefits.

Indeed, in Gearing et al. (2007) study of hospital social workers during the SARS crisis concluded that social workers should practice the kindness and empathy that are part of the core orientation of the profession. Further, social workers do well when they focus on self-care. The recommendation for relaxation time was underscored since self-care helps to replenish the wherewithal needed to function in crisis environments (Gearing et al., 2007). A survey of 45 social workers from the southern region of the United States found the using self-care practices is associated with better emotional and physical health (Shepherd & Newell, 2020). Miller et al., (2021) conducted a larger study of 1568 licensed social workers from the southeastern United States and reported self-care assuages distress in practitioners. Not only is self-care recommended for social workers, but the concept of self-care is broadened to include improved pay scale for social workers, enhanced employee benefits and more manageable caseloads. The recommendations remove the total onus for self-care being placed on the social work practitioner. Self-care should not just occur in the social worker's personal time. Instead, employers should step into the self-care arena and provide employee training, support a healthy work environment and incorporate self-care behavior into the workday.

In fact, Maddock and McCusker (2022) developed a mindfulness-based social work and self-care (MBSWSC) programme in the United Kingdom (UK). The researchers contend that mindfulness is being intentional and attending to the present moment. Thirty social work students who were in field placement during the COVID-19 pandemic were enrolled in MBSWSC (Maddock & McCusker, 2022). For six weeks, the social work students attended the online programme which provided instruction on mindfulness practices. MBSWSC coached the social work students to develop coping skills, mindfulness, self-compassion, non-attachment, attention regulation and non-aversion. Through quantitative and qualitative analysis of participants data, MBSWSC was found to decrease burnout feelings and improve well-being.

A personal step toward mindfulness is the use of practices such as self-compassion, non-attachment, attention regulation and non-aversion (Maddock & McCusker, 2022). The ability to forgive oneself when something goes awry is self-compassion. Self-compassion requires awareness of thoughts and feelings. Attention regulation/decentering is helpful in quieting worries and anxiety. The mindfulness practice allows one to accept thoughts and continue to move forward.

Finally, the National Association of Social Workers (NASW) code of ethics contains the following statement in the Purpose section.

> *Professional self-care is paramount for competent and ethical social work practice. Professional demands, challenging workplace climates, and exposure to trauma warrant that social workers maintain personal and professional health, safety, and integrity. Social work organizations, agencies, and educational institutions are encouraged to promote organizational policies, practices, and materials to support social workers' self-care (NASW, 2021, para. 10).*

CONCLUSION

The concept of burnout first appeared in psychological literature in the 1960's (Bradley, 1969). Therefore, the notion of burnout is not new. Research on burnout was initially focused on human service professionals' experiences (Schaufeli & Enzmann, 1998). Burnout is a well-researched phenomenon. Published from 2014 through 2017, the Burnout Research journal solely focused on the exploration of burnout.

For human service professionals, burnout was defined as emotional exhaustion caused by the mismatch between the demands of human service work and the resources afforded to human service work (Powell, 2019; Kranke, et al, 2024). Further, burnout is a global phenomenon for social workers (Almen et al., 2021) and burnout is found to develop incrementally overtime (Cherniss, 1980). The stages of burnout development include social workers first experiencing stress due to lack of resources colliding with high demand for services (Cherniss, 1980). The author conjectured that inability to meet client needs leads to feelings of strain and fatigue for the practitioner. While experiencing negative emotional bombardment, social workers may withdraw or become cynical about the work. The pattern of social work burnout is similar around the globe (Almen & Jansson, 2021).

While there are several burnout assessments used around the world (e.g., the Oldenburg Burnout Inventory, the Shirom-Melamed Burnout Questionnaire/Measure, the Perceived Stress Scale, and the Copenhagen Burnout Inventory), the Maslach Burnout Inventory (MBI) is the most popular (Almen and Jansson, 2021; Evans, et al, 2022; Childs et al., 2024; Maslach, & Leiter 2016). The MBI assesses emotional exhaustion, depersonalization, and reduced personal accomplishment (Maslach, & Leiter 2016). The MBI offers subscale scores for each of these areas.

Emotional exhaustion, depersonalization and feelings of lack of personal accomplishment are the signs and symptoms of burnout which happens due to stress (Maslach, & Leiter 2016). Compassion fatigue, vicarious trauma, secondary trauma, shared trauma, collective trauma, and trauma trigger fatigue are types of stressful lived experiences which lead to burnout. When a social workers experience compassion fatigue, they are less able to offer empathy and compassion toward clients. Social workers typically experience compassion fatigue when they feel overwhelmed by heavy caseloads, lack of resources and other circumstances (Figley, 1995). Social workers can experience secondary trauma when they are exposed to the traumatic stories of clients. A social worker with secondary trauma can have PTSD symptoms like the client including intrusive thoughts, avoidance behaviors and detachment (Powell, 2019). Similar to secondary trauma, vicarious trauma occurs when a social worker is exposed to clients' traumatic narratives. However, vicarious trauma goes a step further and includes the social worker having a permanent change in their sense of self, their perception of safety or their spiritual beliefs. Social workers who experience vicarious trauma are so impacted by clients' stories that the social worker has some change in their worldview. On occasion, both the social work and the client are exposed to the same traumatic event such as the September 11th tragedy or a hurricane (Tosone et al., 2003). In instances of collective trauma, the trauma is shared not only by the social worker and client, but the trauma is experienced by the whole society (Holmes et al., 2021). The COVID-19 pandemic is an example of a collective trauma. Finally, trauma trigger fatigue occurs in the context of the social worker having a prior history of trauma and then being exposed to another trauma via client narratives (Kranke et al., 2024). Social workers encounter stressful situations that can lead to burnout both in the pre-pandemic era and during the pandemic.

Self-care and mindfulness practices are often the recommendations given to social workers who want to minimize or prevent burnout. Self-care includes physical, interpersonal, familial, professional and spiritual aspects (Shepherd & Newell, 2020). Given that the NASW code of ethics mandates social workers to pursue a self-care regimen, self-care is a requirement for the profession. Self-care can include mindfulness practices. Purposely paying attention to the current moment, feelings and body experiences is mindfulness (Hulsheger et al., 2022). Mindfulness practices can include meditation and body awareness. There are personal steps social workers can take to reduce burnout and steps organizations and agencies can take to minimize social work employees' burnout. Sometimes, the action steps cross pollenate between the worker and employer.

Understandably, personal steps include social workers focusing on their professional identity and their original reasons for joining a helping profession (Hu et al., 2022). The passion for human service attracts social workers to the field and keeps the employee motivated. In other words, professional identity solidifies commitment to the social work profession and acts as a shield against burnout. Social workers can spend time in the presence of supportive social work colleagues, attend conferences and workshops to refresh professional identity and recommit to the core values of social work.

As well as the social worker taking personal steps to combat burnout, the social work agency or organization can support the reduction of burnout. A supportive supervisor who allows flexibility in the workday helps diminish burnout (Kranke et al., 2024). Leaders can both role model and encourage mindfulness practices and self-care practices for social workers. The prevention of and/or intervention for burnout is not the sole responsibility of the individual social worker. In other words, a conclusion can be drawn that the onus to minimize burnout belongs to everyone on the team.

REFERENCES

Adam, J. (2024.). The 20 most stressful jobs | careers | U.S. news. https://money.usnews.com/careers/articles/the-most-stressful-jobs

Almén, N., & Jansson, B. (2021). The reliability and factorial validity of different versions of the shirom-melamed burnout measure/questionnaire and normative data for a general Swedish sample. *International Journal of Stress Management*, *28*(4), 314–325. DOI: 10.1037/str0000235

Asakura, K., Gheorghe, R. M., Rieger, D., Tarshis, S., Borgen, S., & D'Angiulli, A. (2023). Exploring shared trauma in the time of COVID: A simulation-based survey study of mental health clinicians. *Clinical Social Work Journal*, *51*(2), 163–174. DOI: 10.1007/s10615-022-00860-0 PMID: 36536816

Axelrad-Levy, T., Schwartz Tayri, T. M., Achdut, N., & Sarid, O. (2023). The perceived job performance of child welfare workers during the COVID-19 pandemic. *Clinical Social Work Journal*, *51*(2), 175–187. DOI: 10.1007/s10615-022-00861-z PMID: 36713302

Bakker, A. B., & Demerouti, E. (2017). Job demands–resources theory: Taking stock and looking forward. *Journal of Occupational Health Psychology*, *22*(3), 273–285. DOI: 10.1037/ocp0000056 PMID: 27732008

Berg-Weger, M. (2019). *Social work and social welfare: An invitation* (5th ed.). Routledge. DOI: 10.4324/9780429466687

Birkenmaier, J., & Berg-Weger, M. (2017). *Practicum companion for social work: Integrating class and field work* (4th ed.). Pearson.

Bradley, H. B. (1969). Community-based treatment for young adult offenders. *Crime and Delinquency*, *15*(3), 359–370. https://doi-org.uvi.idm.oclc.org/10.1177/001112876901500307. DOI: 10.1177/001112876901500307

Bride, B. E., & Figley, C. R. (2007). The fatigue of compassionate social workers: An introduction to the special issue on compassion fatigue. *Clinical Social Work Journal*, *35*(3), 151–153. DOI: 10.1007/s10615-007-0093-5

Cain, D. (2019). Best practices in disasters and disasters mental health. *Best Practices in Mental Health*, *15*(2), xii.

Carnes, S. L. (2023). "Overworked and stretched thin": Burnout and systemic failure in school social work. *Children & Schools*, *45*(3), 151–159. https://doi-org.uvi.idm.oclc.org/10.1093/cs/cdad015. DOI: 10.1093/cs/cdad015

Cherniss, C. (1980). *Staff burnout. Job stress in the human services*. Sage.

Childs, T. M., Iachini, A. L., Reitmeier, M., Browne, T., DeHart, D., Bengel, A., & Haynesworth, M. (2024). Exploring social work practitioners' perspectives on the contributors to burnout since the COVID-19 pandemic. *Social Work*, *69*(2), 142–150. https://doi-org.uvi.idm.oclc.org/10.1093/sw/swae005. DOI: 10.1093/sw/swae005 PMID: 38366254

Crawford, C. A. (2021). Studying social workers' roles in natural disasters during a global pandemic: What can we learn? *Qualitative Social Work: Research and Practice*, *20*(1–2), 456–462. DOI: 10.1177/1473325020973449 PMID: 34253986

Doherty, A. S., Mallett, J., Leiter, M. P., & McFadden, P. (2021). Measuring burnout in social work. *European Journal of Psychological Assessment*, *37*(1), 6–14. DOI: 10.1027/1015-5759/a000568

Evans, E. J., Noureddine, N., Curry, S. R., & Nam, K. (2021). COVID-19 impacts on social work and nursing now and into the future: National administration plans. *Health & Social Work*, *46*(3), 152–157. https://doi-org.uvi.idm.oclc.org/10.1093/hsw/hlab020. DOI: 10.1093/hsw/hlab020 PMID: 34255036

Figley, C. R. (1995). *Compassion fatigue: Coping with secondary traumatic stress disorder in those who treat the traumatized*. Brunner/Mazel.

Findley, P. A., Pottick, K. J., & Giordano, S. (2017). Educating graduate social work students in disaster response: A real-time case study. *Clinical Social Work Journal*, *45*(2), 159–167. DOI: 10.1007/s10615-015-0533-6

Fontes, F. (2020). Herbert J. Freudenberger and the making of burnout as a psychopathological syndrome. 37, 1-19. DOI: 10.35699/1676-1669.2020.19144

Freudenberger, H. (2010). Staff burn-out. *The Journal of Social Issues*, *30*(1), 159–165. DOI: 10.1111/j.1540-4560.1974.tb00706.x

Gallup. (2024). *State of the global workplace report*. Gallup. https://www.gallup.com/workplace/349484/state-of-the-global-workplace.aspx

Gearing, R. E., Saini, M., & McNeill, T. (2007). Experiences and implications of social workers practicing in a pediatric hospital environment affected by SARS. *Health &amp. Social Work*, *32*(1), 17–27. DOI: 10.1093/hsw/32.1.17 PMID: 17388080

Hansel, T. C., & Saltzman, L. Y. (2024). Secondary traumatic stress and burnout: The role of mental health, work experience, loneliness and other trauma in compassion fatigue in the healthcare workforces. *Traumatology*, *30*(4), 615–618. DOI: 10.1037/trm0000478

Hirschberger, G. (2018). Collective trauma and the social construction of meaning. *Frontiers in Psychology*, *9*, 1441. DOI: 10.3389/fpsyg.2018.01441 PMID: 30147669

Hochschild, A. (2012). *The managed heart: Commercialization of human feeling* (3rd ed.). University of California Press. DOI: 10.1525/9780520951853

Holmes, M. R., Robin, R. C., Korsch-Williams, A., & King, J. A. (2021). Impact of COVID-19 pandemic on posttraumatic stress, grief, burnout, and secondary trauma of social workers in the United States. *Clinical Social Work Journal*, *49*(4), 495–504. DOI: 10.1007/s10615-021-00795-y PMID: 33678920

Hu, H., Wang, E., Si, J., Sui, X., Yi, Z., Zheng, Z., & Liu, H. (2022). Professional identity and turnover intention amongst Chinese social workers: Roles of job burnout and a social work degree. *British Journal of Social Work*, *52*(3), 1703–1723. https://doi-org.uvi.idm.oclc.org/10.1093/bjsw/bcab155. DOI: 10.1093/bjsw/bcab155

Hülsheger, U. R., Yang, T., Bono, J. E., Goh, Z., & Ilies, R. (2022). Stop the spin: The role of mindfulness practices in reducing affect spin. *Journal of Occupational Health Psychology*, *27*(6), 529–543. DOI: 10.1037/ocp0000332 PMID: 35797166

HURDAT Re-analysis. (n.d.). ww.aoml.noaa.gov. https://www.aoml.noaa.gov/hrd/hurdat/All_U.S._Hurricanes.html

Katz, I., Katz, C., Andresen, S., Bérubé, A., Collin-Vezina, D., Fallon, B., Fouché, A., Haffejee, S., Masrawa, N., Muñoz, P., Priolo Filho, S. R., Tarabulsy, G., Truter, E., Varela, N., & Wekerle, C. (2021). Child maltreatment reports and child protection service responses during COVID-19: Knowledge Exchange among Australia, Brazil, Canada, Colombia, Germany, Israel, and South Africa. *Child Abuse &amp. Child Abuse & Neglect*, *116*, 105078. DOI: 10.1016/j.chiabu.2021.105078 PMID: 33931238

Kirst-Ashman, K. K., & Hull, G. H. (2018). *Understanding Generalist Practice* (8th ed.). Brooks/Cole.

Kranke, D., Kranke, B., & Der-Martirosian, C. (2024). We cannot have next year if we do not take care of today. *Health & Social Work*, *49*(3), 209–210. https://doi-org.uvi.idm.oclc.org/10.1093/hsw/hlae016. DOI: 10.1093/hsw/hlae016 PMID: 38822671

Kranke, D., Kranke, B., Milligan, S., & Dobalian, A. (2024). Introducing trauma trigger fatigue as an underlying factor of social work burnout. *Social Work*, *69*(4), 403–405. https://doi-org.uvi.idm.oclc.org/10.1093/sw/swae034. DOI: 10.1093/sw/swae034 PMID: 39013117

Kranke, D., Mudoh, Y., Weiss, E. L., Hovsepian, S., Gin, J., Dobalian, A., & Der-Martirosian, C. (2022). "Emotional preparedness": A nuanced approach to disaster readiness among social workers. *Social Work Education*, *41*(5), 860–873. https://doi-org.uvi.idm.oclc.org/10.1080/02615479.2021.1900099. DOI: 10.1080/02615479.2021.1900099

Kranke, D. A., Kranke, B., Solorzano, E., Gioia, D., & Dobalian, A. (2024). Applying a novel approach to understanding social worker job retention during the pandemic. *Social Work*, *69*(2), 151–157. https://doi-org.uvi.idm.oclc.org/10.1093/sw/swae013. DOI: 10.1093/sw/swae013 PMID: 38366959

Lee, R. T., & Ashforth, B. E. (1990). On the meaning of Maslach's three dimensions of burnout. *The Journal of Applied Psychology*, *75*(6), 743–747. DOI: 10.1037/0021-9010.75.6.743 PMID: 1981064

Leiter, M. (1991). The dream denied: Professional burnout and the constraints of human service organizations. *Canadian Psychology*, *32*(4), 547–558. DOI: 10.1037/h0079040

Logan, D. A., De King, J., Edwards, J., Saltzman, L. Y., Hansel, T. C., & Figley, C. (2024). The grit of mental health professionals: Initial conceptualization and measurement. *Traumatology*, *30*(3), 423–431. DOI: 10.1037/trm0000446

Maddock, A., & McCusker, P. (2022). Exploring the potential mechanisms of action of the mindfulness-based Social Work and self-care programme. *British Journal of Social Work*, *52*(8), 4477–4496. DOI: 10.1093/bjsw/bcac066

Manning, S., & Kushma, J. (2016). A systematic review of the international disaster case management literature in the aftermath of Hurricane Katrina. *International Journal of Emergency Management*, *12*(3), 241–262. DOI: 10.1504/IJEM.2016.079017

Maslach, C., Jackson, S. E., & Leiter, M. P. (1996). *Maslach burnout inventory manual* (3rd ed.). Consulting Psychologists Press.

Maslach, C., & Leiter, M. P. (2007). Burnout. In Fink, G. (Ed.), *Stress: Concepts, cognition, emotion, and behavior* (pp. 351–357). Elsevier Academic Press.

Maslach, C., & Leiter, M. P. (2016). Understanding the burnout experience: Recent research and its implications for psychiatry. *World Psychiatry; Official Journal of the World Psychiatric Association (WPA)*, *15*(2), 103–111. DOI: 10.1002/wps.20311 PMID: 27265691

McFadden, P. (2015). Measuring burnout among UK social workers: a Community care study, available at: https://www.qub.ac.uk/ (accessed 8 November 2024).

Miller, J. J., Barnhart, S., Robinson, T. D., Pryor, M. D., & Arnett, K. D. (2021). Assuaging covid-19 peritraumatic distress among mental health clinicians: The potential of self-care. *Clinical Social Work Journal, 49*(4), 505–514. DOI: 10.1007/s10615-021-00815-x PMID: 34728866

Moyo, O., & Moldovan, V. (2008). Lessons for social workers: Hurricane Katrina as a social disaster. *Social Development Issues, 30*(1), 1–12.

NASW. (2021). *Code of ethics*. National Association of Social Workers. https://www.socialworkers.org/About/Ethics/Code-of-Ethics/Code-of-Ethics-English

Negi, N. J., Forrester, P., Calderon, M., Esser, K., & Parrish, D. (2019). We are at full capacity: Social care workers persisting through work-related stress in a new immigrant settlement context in the United States. *Health & Social Care in the Community, 27*(5), e793–e801. https://doi-org.uvi.idm.oclc.org/10.1111/hsc.12802. DOI: 10.1111/hsc.12802 PMID: 31260160

Newell, J. M., & MacNeil, G. A. (2010). Professional burnout, vicarious trauma, secondary traumatic stress, and compassion fatigue: A review of theoretical terms, risk factors, and preventive methods for clinicians and researchers. *Best Practices in Mental Health, 6*(2), 57–68. DOI: 10.70256/607490pbruec

Powell, T. M., Wegmann, K. M., & Shin, O. J. (2019). Stress and coping in social service providers after superstorm sandy: An examination of a postdisaster psychoeducational intervention. *Traumatology, 25*(2), 96–103. DOI: 10.1037/trm0000189

Schaufeli, W. (2021). The burnout enigma solved? *Scandinavian Journal of Work, Environment & Health, 47*(3), 169–170. Advance online publication. DOI: 10.5271/sjweh.3950 PMID: 33604675

Schaufeli, W. & Enzmann, D. (1998). The burnout companion to study and practice: A critical analysis. DOI: 10.1201/9781003062745

Shepherd, M. A., & Newell, J. M. (2020). Stress and health in social workers: Implications for self-care practice. *Best Practices in Mental Health, 16*(1), 46–65. https://www.proquest.com/scholarly-journals/stress-health-social-workers-implications-self/docview/2551714261/se-2. DOI: 10.70256/994929qbhenn

Shinan-Altman, S., Rosenne, H., Chen, W., Kaofer, H., Zeevi, S., Nir-Paz, R., Daphna-Tekoah, S., Guttman, N., & Schiff, M. (2024). Professional quality of life among Israeli social workers in hospitals and a health maintenance organization (HMO) during the COVID-19 pandemic. *The American Journal of Orthopsychiatry*. Advance online publication. DOI: 10.1037/ort0000798 PMID: 39250251

Sidpra, J., Abomeli, D., Hameed, B., Baker, J., & Mankad, K. (2021). Rise in the incidence of abusive head trauma during the COVID-19 pandemic. *Archives of Disease in Childhood, 106*(3), e14–e14. DOI: 10.1136/archdischild-2020-319872 PMID: 32616522

Stamm, B. H. (1995). *The professional quality of life scale: Compassion satisfaction, burnout, & compassion fatigue/secondary trauma scales*. Sidran Press.

Substance Abuse and Mental Health Services Administration. (2022). Addressing burnout in the behavioral health workforce through organizational strategies (SAMHSA Publication No. PEP22-06-02-005). National Mental Health and Substance Use Policy Laboratory.

Swedo, E., Idaikkadar, N., Leemis, R., Dias, T., Radhakrishnan, L., Stein, Z., Chen, M., Agathis, N., & Holland, K. (2020). Trends in U.S. emergency department visits related to suspected or confirmed child abuse and neglect among children and adolescents aged <18 years before and during the COVID-19 pandemic — United States, January 2019–September 2020. *MMWR. Morbidity and Mortality Weekly Report, 69*(49), 1841–1847. DOI: 10.15585/mmwr.mm6949a1 PMID: 33301436

Tan, K., & Yeap, P. F. (2022). The impact of work engagement and meaningful work to alleviate job burnout among social workers in new zealand. *Management Decision, 60*(11), 3042–3065. DOI: 10.1108/MD-05-2021-0689

Tosone, C., Lee, M., Bialkin, L., Martinez, A., Campbell, M., Martinez, M. M., & Stefan, A. (2003). Shared trauma: Group reflections on the September 11th disaster. *Psychoanalytic Social Work, 10*(1), 57–77. 10n01_ 06DOI: 10. 1300/ J032v

Tosone, C., McTighe, J., Bauwens, J., & Naturale, A. (2011). Shared traumatic stress and the long-term impact of 9/11 on Manhattan clinicians. *Journal of Traumatic Stress, 24*(5), 546–552. DOI: 10.1002/jts.20686 PMID: 21882250

Tosone, C., Nuttman-Shwartz, O., & Stephens, T. (2012). Shared trauma: When the professional is personal. *Clinical Social Work Journal, 40*(2), 231–239. DOI: 10.1007/s10615-012-0395-0

US Department of Commerce. N. O. and A. A. (2016, April 20). *NOAA historical Hurricane Tracks*. NOAA's National Ocean Service. https://oceanservice.noaa.gov/news/historical-hurricanes/

Wagaman, M. A., Geiger, J. M., Shockley, C., & Segal, E. A. (2015). The role of empathy in burnout, compassion satisfaction, and secondary traumatic stress among social workers. *Social Work, 60*(3), 201–209. DOI: 10.1093/sw/swv014 PMID: 26173361

Wiles, F. (2017). What is professional identity and how do social workers acquire it? In Webb, S. A. (Ed.), *Professional Identity and Social Work* (pp. 35–50). Routledge Academic., https://www.routledge.com/Professional-Identity-an DOI: 10.4324/9781315306957-3

World Health Organization. (2019). *Burn-out an "Occupational phenomenon": International Classification of Diseases*. World Health Organization. Retrieved March 7, 2023, from https://www.who.int/news/item/28-05-2019-burn-out-an-occupational-phenomenon-international-classification-of-diseases

Yuma, P., Powell, T., Scott, J., & Vinton, M. (2019). Resilience and Coping for the Healthcare Community: A Post-disaster Group Work Intervention for Healthcare and Social Service Providers. *Journal of Family Strengths*, *19*(1). Advance online publication. https://library.capella.edu/login?url=https://www.proquest.com/scholarly-journals/resilience-coping-healthcare-community-post/docview/2647680412/se-2. DOI: 10.58464/2168-670X.1402

Zerden, L. de S. (2024). Social work and burnout: Everything, everywhere, all at once. *Social Work*, *69*(3), 217–219. https://doi-org.uvi.idm.oclc.org/10.1093/sw/swae021. DOI: 10.1093/sw/swae021 PMID: 38745383

KEY TERMS AND DEFINITIONS

Burnout in the Workplace: occurs when there is repeated unresolved stress caused by job demands consistently exceeding occupational resources.

Collective Trauma: occurs when a traumatic event is experienced by the society at large.

Compassion Fatigue: describes a lowered ability to express compassion and empathy for clients which occurs when practitioners feel overwhelmed.

Secondary Trauma: can occur when a practitioner has significant knowledge of a traumatizing event experienced by a client.

Shared Trauma: can occur when the practitioner and the client have experienced the same traumatic event.

Social Work: is a helping profession where the practitioner has multiple roles while working with clients. The practitioner may be an advocate, a resource broker, or a counselor.

Trauma Trigger Fatigue: can occur when practitioners have unresolved trauma from past personal experiences and the current trauma revives and exacerbates previous trauma.

Vicarious Trauma: is described as practitioners indirectly experiencing trauma via client recollections and permanently changing perceptions or sense of self based on the secondary trauma exposure.

Chapter 8
Leadership Strategies to Mitigate Public Sector Burnout:
Fostering Resilience, Employee Morale, and Organizational Wellness

Vishal Jain
https://orcid.org/0000-0003-1126-7424
Sharda University, India

Archan Mitra
https://orcid.org/0000-0002-1419-3558
Amity University Mumbai, India

P. V. Satya Prasad
NITTE University, India

ABSTRACT

This study examines the effectiveness of leadership strategies in mitigating burnout among public sector employees by fostering resilience, enhancing morale, and promoting organizational wellness. Using a mixed-methods approach, data were collected from 300 employees through surveys and 30 leaders via semi-structured interviews. Findings indicate that transformational leadership significantly reduces burnout by fostering psychological safety, motivation, and engagement, while transactional leadership exacerbates stress. Resilience emerged as a key protective factor, mediating the relationship between leadership and burnout. Additionally, organizational wellness initiatives, such as mental health support and flexible work

DOI: 10.4018/979-8-3373-0169-3.ch008

policies, complement leadership efforts in burnout mitigation. The study underscores the need for leadership development programs and policy reforms to enhance workplace well-being in the public sector.

INTRODUCTION

Background of the Study

Burnout in the public sector has become a significant concern as employees face increasing workloads, bureaucratic pressures, and resource constraints. Unlike private sector organizations, public sector employees often work under rigid administrative structures, limited budgets, and heightened public scrutiny, which contribute to high levels of job-related stress (Maslach & Leiter, 2016). Burnout is characterized by emotional exhaustion, depersonalization, and reduced personal accomplishment, which can severely impact an individual's well-being and professional effectiveness (Schaufeli et al., 2009). The prevalence of burnout among public sector employees has raised alarms due to its negative consequences on job satisfaction, work efficiency, and public service delivery.

The impact of burnout extends beyond individual employees and affects organizational performance and societal outcomes. Research indicates that chronic stress and exhaustion among public sector workers lead to decreased motivation, lower productivity, and higher absenteeism rates (Kim & Wright, 2017). Additionally, burnout is linked to high turnover rates, which further strain public resources and reduce institutional memory within organizations (Tummers et al., 2018). When employees in critical public services, such as healthcare, education, and law enforcement, experience burnout, it can lead to diminished service quality and adverse effects on the communities they serve. Consequently, addressing burnout in public sector organizations is not only essential for employee well-being but also for ensuring the effective functioning of government institutions and the provision of quality public services.

Problem Statement

Mitigating burnout in public sector organizations is a pressing challenge, given the unique stressors faced by employees in these institutions. Unlike in the private sector, where organizations have greater flexibility in implementing workplace changes, public sector entities often operate within rigid regulatory frameworks that can exacerbate stress and limit opportunities for workplace improvements (Bakker & Demerouti, 2017). The high incidence of burnout among public sector employees has been linked to reduced engagement, increased absenteeism, and a decline in overall organizational effectiveness (Hakanen et al., 2008). If left unaddressed, burnout can lead to a vicious cycle where employee dissatisfaction and turnover further deplete organizational resources, making it even more difficult to implement meaningful reforms.

Leadership plays a crucial role in addressing workplace stress and mitigating burnout in the public sector. Effective leadership strategies can help create a supportive work environment, promote resilience, and enhance employee morale (Bass & Riggio, 2006). Transformational leaders, for example, inspire employees by fostering a sense of purpose, providing support, and encouraging innovation in problem-solving (Northouse, 2019). In contrast, transactional leadership approaches that focus solely on performance and compliance without addressing employee well-being may exacerbate burnout. Therefore, exploring how leadership strategies can be leveraged to mitigate burnout is essential for developing practical solutions that enhance organizational wellness and employee retention.

Research Objective

The primary objective of this study is to examine the effectiveness of leadership strategies in mitigating burnout among public sector employees. This research will focus on how leadership approaches can foster resilience, enhance employee morale, and promote organizational wellness. By analyzing leadership interventions and their impact on employee well-being, this study aims to provide actionable insights that can be implemented to improve public sector work environments.

Research Questions

This study seeks to address the following research questions:

1. What leadership strategies are most effective in reducing burnout in the public sector?
2. How do leadership approaches influence employee resilience and morale?
3. What organizational wellness initiatives complement leadership efforts in burnout mitigation?

By answering these questions, the research will contribute to a deeper understanding of how leadership can be used as a tool to reduce burnout and improve public sector work environments.

Significance of the Study

This study holds significant implications for public sector management and policy. Given the widespread nature of burnout in government and public service institutions, identifying effective leadership strategies can help policymakers and administrators design interventions that improve employee well-being and job satisfaction (Goleman et al., 2013). By fostering a supportive work culture, public sector leaders can enhance productivity, reduce absenteeism, and improve overall organizational efficiency. Moreover, understanding the relationship between leadership and burnout can inform training programs for current and aspiring public sector leaders, equipping them with the skills necessary to manage workplace stress and promote resilience.

From a theoretical perspective, this study contributes to leadership and organizational behavior research by examining how different leadership styles impact employee well-being in high-stress environments. While existing research has extensively explored burnout in the private sector, fewer studies have focused on the unique challenges faced by public sector employees (Tummers & Knies, 2016). By bridging this gap, this study will add to the body of knowledge on public sector leadership and offer evidence-based recommendations for fostering healthier and more sustainable workplaces.

LITERATURE REVIEW

Theoretical Framework

The study of leadership strategies to mitigate public sector burnout is underpinned by several theoretical frameworks that offer insights into the relationship between workplace demands, leadership approaches, and employee well-being. The Job Demands-Resources (JD-R) Model is one of the most widely used frameworks for understanding burnout and engagement in organizational settings. According to Bakker and Demerouti (2017), the JD-R model posits that job demands, such as excessive workload and bureaucratic constraints, contribute to employee burnout, while job resources, including leadership support and autonomy, serve as protective factors that enhance employee engagement and well-being. When public sector leaders effectively manage job demands by providing resources such as training, autonomy, and emotional support, employees are more likely to exhibit resilience and maintain job satisfaction despite workplace challenges.

The effectiveness of leadership styles in burnout mitigation can also be understood through the lens of Transformational vs. Transactional Leadership. Transformational leadership, characterized by inspirational motivation, individualized consideration, intellectual stimulation, and idealized influence, has been found to positively impact employee morale and reduce burnout (Bass & Riggio, 2006). Leaders who adopt this approach create a supportive work environment that fosters engagement and professional growth. Conversely, transactional leadership, which focuses on performance-based rewards and penalties, may exacerbate stress if leaders do not incorporate supportive elements into their management style (Judge & Piccolo, 2004). In the public sector, where employees often face high workloads and bureaucratic constraints, transformational leadership has been found to be particularly effective in fostering resilience and mitigating burnout.

Additionally, Resilience Theory in Organizational Contexts provides a framework for understanding how employees cope with workplace stress and adversity. Resilience, defined as the ability to adapt and recover from stressors, plays a critical role in determining whether employees experience burnout or maintain their well-being (Luthans et al., 2006). Public sector leaders can foster resilience by promoting psychological safety, encouraging adaptability, and providing social support mechanisms (Caza & Milton, 2012). By integrating resilience-building strategies into leadership practices, organizations can enhance employees' capacity to cope with workplace challenges and sustain their motivation and job satisfaction.

Understanding Burnout in the Public Sector

Burnout in the public sector is a growing concern due to the demanding nature of government and public service roles. The causes and consequences of burnout are well-documented, with research indicating that prolonged exposure to high job demands, excessive bureaucracy, and limited organizational resources significantly contribute to employee exhaustion (Maslach & Leiter, 2016). Public sector employees often face unrealistic expectations, job insecurity, and frequent policy changes, all of which elevate stress levels and contribute to burnout. As a result, many employees experience decreased job performance, higher absenteeism, and lower levels of job satisfaction (Schaufeli et al., 2009).

Several unique stressors in public sector work environments differentiate burnout in government organizations from the private sector. Public sector employees are often expected to serve the public interest while adhering to strict regulations and budgetary constraints, which can create conflicting demands and role ambiguity (Tummers et al., 2018). Additionally, the hierarchical nature of government institutions may limit employees' autonomy and decision-making power, further exacerbating stress (Kim & Wright, 2017). The emotional labor associated with roles in healthcare, education, and law enforcement also contributes to burnout, as employees are frequently required to manage emotionally charged situations with limited support (Brotheridge & Grandey, 2002).

Leadership Strategies for Burnout Mitigation

To address burnout in the public sector, leadership strategies that prioritize employee well-being are essential. One effective approach is emotional intelligence and supportive leadership, which involves leaders demonstrating empathy, active listening, and interpersonal awareness when managing employees (Goleman et al., 2013). Leaders who exhibit high emotional intelligence can create a psychologically safe work environment where employees feel valued and supported, reducing stress and increasing job satisfaction (Barling et al., 2011).

Another critical strategy involves work-life balance initiatives and flexible policies that allow employees to manage their workloads without compromising their well-being. Research has shown that flexible work arrangements, such as remote work options and alternative scheduling, contribute to lower burnout levels and improved job satisfaction in public sector organizations (Kossek et al., 2014). Leaders who advocate for these policies play a vital role in ensuring that employees can maintain a healthy balance between professional responsibilities and personal well-being.

Employee empowerment and participatory decision-making also serve as key leadership strategies for mitigating burnout. When employees are given autonomy and a voice in decision-making, they experience greater job satisfaction and lower stress levels (Deci & Ryan, 2000). Public sector leaders who engage employees in organizational planning and policy development foster a sense of ownership and commitment, which enhances motivation and reduces burnout (Fernandez & Moldogaziev, 2015).

Fostering Resilience and Employee Morale

Building resilience and morale among public sector employees requires proactive efforts in training and workplace support. Training programs and psychological safety are essential in equipping employees with coping strategies and stress management techniques (Luthans et al., 2006). Leadership training that focuses on resilience-building skills can help employees navigate workplace challenges and reduce their susceptibility to burnout (Caza & Milton, 2012). Additionally, fostering a culture of psychological safety, where employees feel comfortable expressing concerns and seeking help, can mitigate stress and enhance overall workplace well-being (Edmondson, 2019).

Recognition, incentives, and job satisfaction also play a vital role in maintaining employee morale. Research indicates that employees who receive regular recognition for their contributions experience higher levels of engagement and motivation (Kuvaas & Dysvik, 2010). Public sector leaders can implement reward systems, such as performance-based incentives and professional development opportunities, to boost morale and reduce burnout. Creating a culture of appreciation and support can significantly enhance employee satisfaction and commitment to their roles (Tummers et al., 2018).

Organizational Wellness Approaches

In addition to leadership strategies, mental health support and employee assistance programs serve as crucial interventions in burnout prevention. Providing access to counseling services, stress management workshops, and wellness programs can help employees manage work-related stress and prevent burnout (Quick et al., 2013). Public sector organizations that invest in mental health initiatives demonstrate a commitment to employee well-being, which in turn fosters a more engaged and productive workforce (Avey et al., 2011).

Lastly, workplace culture and engagement strategies play a significant role in shaping employee experiences and reducing burnout. Organizations that prioritize open communication, collaboration, and employee engagement create a supportive environment that promotes well-being (Saks, 2006). Leaders who actively engage employees in decision-making and organizational development contribute to a culture of trust and inclusion, which enhances job satisfaction and reduces stress (Bakker & Demerouti, 2017). A strong workplace culture that values well-being and employee input ultimately leads to higher levels of motivation, productivity, and organizational success.

RESEARCH METHODOLOGY

Research Design

This study employed a mixed-methods research design, integrating both qualitative and quantitative approaches to examine the effectiveness of leadership strategies in mitigating burnout among public sector employees. This approach enabled the collection of in-depth narratives through qualitative data and statistical validation through quantitative data. A cross-sectional survey and semi-structured interviews were conducted concurrently to gather a holistic view of leadership impact on employee well-being.

Population and Sampling

The target population for this study included public sector employees and leaders from a range of government organizations such as healthcare, education, law enforcement, and administrative services across multiple regions. A stratified random sampling technique was utilized to ensure diverse representation across hierarchical levels, occupational categories, and organizational functions.

The population was stratified into subgroups based on job roles (e.g., frontline staff, middle management, senior leadership) and sectors (e.g., healthcare, education, administration). From each stratum, participants were randomly selected to ensure proportional representation. The final sample comprised 300 public sector employees who completed the quantitative survey and 30 public sector leaders who participated in in-depth interviews. Eligibility criteria required participants to have at least one year of tenure in their respective organizations to ensure familiarity with internal leadership practices and workplace conditions.

Data Collection Methods

Quantitative data were collected using a structured questionnaire composed of validated measurement instruments, each targeting specific constructs:

- Maslach Burnout Inventory (MBI): This tool measures burnout across three distinct dimensions—*emotional exhaustion*, *depersonalization*, and *reduced personal accomplishment*. In this study, responses for each subscale were analyzed separately to capture nuanced variations in burnout experiences. A composite burnout score (aggregate mean) was also computed for comparative and regression purposes to allow for an overarching analysis of burnout trends.
- Multifactor Leadership Questionnaire (MLQ): This instrument was used to assess both *transformational* and *transactional leadership* across multiple sub-dimensions (e.g., idealized influence, contingent reward). Each subscale was analyzed individually to identify which specific leadership behaviors were most strongly associated with burnout outcomes.
- Connor-Davidson Resilience Scale (CD-RISC): The full 25-item version was administered. Individual item responses and total resilience scores were both analyzed to understand the variance and consistency across participants. (Connor & Davidson, 2003)

- Utrecht Work Engagement Scale (UWES): This tool measures three components of work engagement—*vigor*, *dedication*, and *absorption*. Each dimension was reported separately, alongside a composite engagement score used in correlational and regression analyses.

Justification for Analytical Approach

Descriptive statistics (mean, standard deviation, min/max) were initially used to summarize the central tendencies and variability across the sample for each variable and subscale. These summaries provided an essential foundation for identifying general trends and guiding further inferential analysis.

While composite scores were employed in some correlational and regression analyses for parsimony and to maintain manageable model complexity, the subscale scores were also examined to capture multidimensional insights. This dual-level analysis (composite and subscale) allowed for both broad and detailed interpretations of the data.

Qualitative Data Analysis

Thematic analysis of semi-structured interviews was conducted using NVivo. Transcripts were coded inductively and deductively. Codes were informed by existing theory (e.g., transformational leadership behaviors, employee well-being themes) and emergent themes that surfaced during analysis. Triangulation with quantitative results was performed to enhance the validity and richness of the findings.

Data Analysis Techniques

- Quantitative Analysis: Data were analyzed using SPSS software. Descriptive statistics summarized burnout levels and leadership styles. Pearson correlation and multiple regression analysis identified significant relationships and predictors of burnout reduction.
- Qualitative Analysis: Interview transcripts were thematically analyzed using NVivo software. Thematic coding followed Braun and Clarke's (2006) six-step framework to identify recurring patterns and leadership themes.

Data Analysis Techniques

The quantitative data collected through surveys will be analyzed using descriptive statistics, correlation analysis, and multiple regression analysis. Descriptive statistics (means, standard deviations, and frequencies) will provide an overview of burnout levels, leadership practices, and employee well-being across different public sector organizations. Pearson's correlation analysis will be used to examine the relationships between leadership styles, burnout reduction, resilience, and morale. Multiple regression analysis will help identify the most significant predictors of burnout mitigation, thereby assessing the effectiveness of different leadership strategies. The statistical analysis will be conducted using SPSS or R software.

The qualitative data from interviews will be analyzed using thematic analysis, following Braun and Clarke's (2006) framework. This process will involve coding transcripts, identifying recurring themes, and developing insights into leadership practices that influence burnout mitigation. NVivo software will be used to manage and analyze qualitative data efficiently. Key themes expected to emerge include leadership support, emotional intelligence, empowerment strategies, and organizational wellness programs.

Ethical Considerations

This study will adhere to ethical research principles to ensure the protection and rights of all participants. Informed consent will be obtained from all respondents before their participation. Participants will be assured of confidentiality and anonymity, with all personal information anonymized in reports and publications. Ethical approval will be sought from the relevant institutional review board (IRB) before data collection begins. Additionally, interview recordings and survey data will be securely stored, and only authorized researchers will have access to the data.

Limitations of the Study

While the mixed-methods approach strengthens the study's validity, certain limitations must be acknowledged. First, self-reported data from surveys may be subject to response bias, where employees might underreport or overreport their experiences due to social desirability concerns. Second, cross-sectional design limits the ability to determine causality, as the data represents only a snapshot of burnout and leadership effectiveness at a given time. A longitudinal study would provide deeper insights into the long-term impact of leadership strategies on burnout mitigation. Finally, while the study aims to cover various public sector organizations, differences in organizational culture and governance structures may introduce contextual variations that limit the generalizability of findings.

DATA ANALYSIS

Descriptive Statistics

To understand the overall trends in burnout levels, leadership styles, and employee well-being in public sector organizations, descriptive statistical analysis was conducted. The study measured the key variables, including burnout (measured using the Maslach Burnout Inventory), leadership strategies (assessed using the Multifactor Leadership Questionnaire), resilience (measured via the Connor-Davidson Resilience Scale), and organizational wellness (evaluated using the Utrecht Work Engagement Scale). The data collected from 300 public sector employees were analyzed for mean, standard deviation, and frequency distribution.

Demographic Characteristics

To provide a comprehensive overview of the sample, descriptive statistics were calculated for the survey respondents and interviewees. Table 1 summarizes key demographic variables, including leadership level, type of public sector organization, and selected sociodemographic characteristics (e.g., age, gender, tenure).

Table 1. Demographic characteristics of survey respondents and interviewees

Variable	Category/Range	Frequency (%) / Mean (SD)
Leadership Level	Frontline Staff	40% (n = 120)
	Middle Management	35% (n = 105)
	Senior Leadership	25% (n = 75)
Type of Public Sector Organization	Healthcare	30% (n = 90)
	Education	25% (n = 75)
	Law Enforcement	20% (n = 60)
	Administrative Services	25% (n = 75)
Age	Mean (SD)	42.5 (± 8.6) years
Gender	Male	55% (n = 165)
	Female	45% (n = 135)
Tenure in Organization	Mean (SD)	8.2 (± 3.9) years

Note: Similar demographic breakdowns were observed among the 30 interviewees, with a proportional representation of leadership levels and public sector domains.

Detailed Subscale Analyses

Beyond demographic data, additional analyses were conducted on the subscales of the employed instruments. For instance, the Maslach Burnout Inventory (MBI) provided detailed scores for emotional exhaustion, depersonalization, and reduced personal accomplishment. These scores were summarized as follows:

- Emotional Exhaustion: Mean = 3.9 (SD = 0.85)
- Depersonalization: Mean = 2.8 (SD = 0.70)
- Reduced Personal Accomplishment: Mean = 3.2 (SD = 0.80)

These subscale analyses allowed us to understand the specific dimensions of burnout experienced by public sector employees, alongside composite scores used in subsequent correlation and regression analyses.

Integration with Leadership and Well-being Measures

The descriptive demographic and subscale data were then integrated with leadership and organizational wellness measures. For example, the leadership levels (as identified by the Multifactor Leadership Questionnaire subscales) were compared across demographic groups to assess whether senior leaders exhibited different patterns in leadership behaviors compared to frontline staff. These comparisons helped in identifying trends such as higher transformational leadership scores in organizations with strong employee engagement initiatives.

Table 1 presents the descriptive statistics for the key variables. The mean burnout score of participants was 3.41 (SD = 0.76), indicating moderate levels of burnout among public sector employees. The resilience scores averaged 3.78 (SD = 0.82), suggesting that employees exhibit moderate resilience despite the workplace stressors. Leadership strategies showed a mean score of 4.12 (SD = 0.69) for transformational leadership, whereas transactional leadership had a lower mean score of 2.93 (SD = 0.88), indicating that transformational leadership is more prevalent in public sector organizations.

Figure 1. Histogram representing burnout score distribution

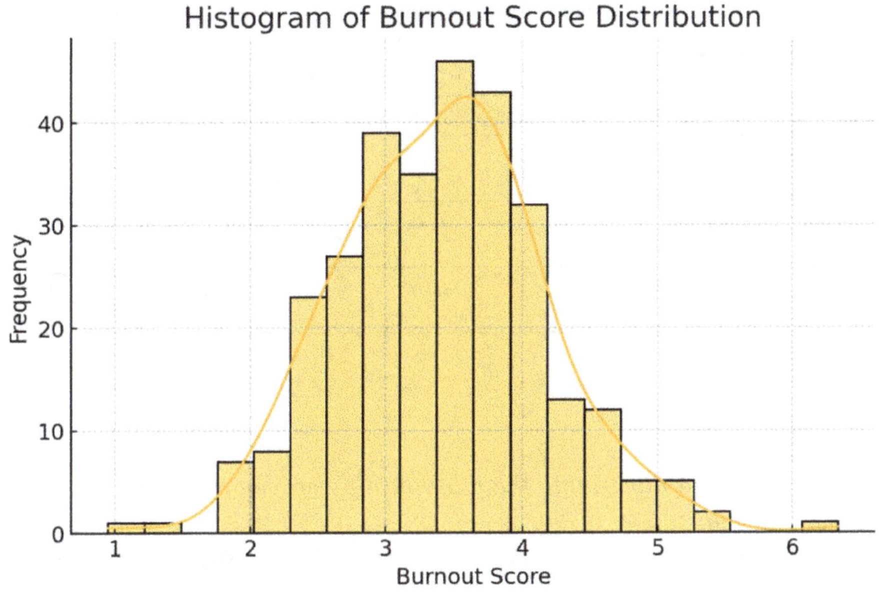

Correlation Analysis

Pearson's correlation analysis was conducted to examine the relationships between leadership strategies, burnout mitigation, resilience, and organizational wellness. The results in Table 2 show a significant negative correlation between transformational leadership and burnout ($r = -0.62$, $p < 0.01$), indicating that as transformational leadership practices increase, burnout levels tend to decrease. Additionally, transformational leadership positively correlates with resilience ($r = 0.58$, $p < 0.01$) and organizational wellness ($r = 0.65$, $p < 0.01$), suggesting that effective leadership strategies foster employee well-being and engagement. Conversely, transactional leadership exhibited a weak positive correlation with burnout ($r = 0.31$, $p < 0.05$) and a negative relationship with resilience ($r = -0.29$, $p < 0.05$), implying that transactional leadership may contribute to burnout rather than mitigate it.

Table 2. Pearson correlation matrix

Variables	Burnout	Resilience	Transformational Leadership	Transactional Leadership	Organizational Wellness
Burnout	1.00	-0.52**	-0.62**	0.31*	-0.55**
Resilience	-0.52**	1.00	0.58**	-0.29*	0.63**
Transformational Leadership	-0.62**	0.58**	1.00	-0.48**	0.65**
Transactional Leadership	0.31*	-0.29*	-0.48**	1.00	-0.22
Organizational Wellness	-0.55**	0.63**	0.65**	-0.22	1.00

$p < 0.01$ (**) $p < 0.05$ (*)

Figure 2. Scatter plot illustrating the relationship between transformational leadership and burnout

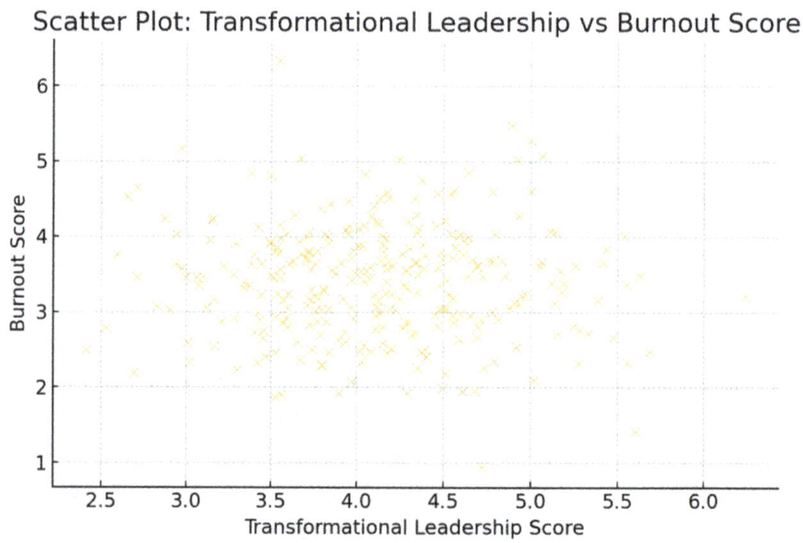

Multiple Regression Analysis

To assess the predictive impact of leadership strategies on burnout mitigation, multiple regression analysis was conducted. Burnout was used as the dependent variable, while transformational leadership, transactional leadership, resilience, and organizational wellness were used as independent variables. The model was found to be statistically significant ($F(4,295) = 21.38$, $p < 0.001$, $R^2 = 0.54$), indicating that 54% of the variance in burnout levels can be explained by the selected predictors.

Table 3 presents the results of the regression analysis. Transformational leadership emerged as a significant negative predictor of burnout ($\beta = -0.47$, $p < 0.01$), reaffirming that employees under transformational leadership experience lower burnout levels. Resilience was also a significant predictor ($\beta = -0.34$, $p < 0.05$), suggesting that employees with higher resilience experience reduced burnout. Conversely, transactional leadership showed a positive relationship with burnout ($\beta = 0.26$, $p < 0.05$), indicating that this leadership style contributes to burnout rather than alleviating it.

Table 3. Multiple regression results for burnout prediction

Predictor Variables	Beta (β)	Standard Error	t-value	p-value
Transformational Leadership	-0.47**	0.08	-5.88	<0.01
Transactional Leadership	0.26*	0.11	2.45	<0.05
Resilience	-0.34*	0.09	-3.78	<0.05
Organizational Wellness	-0.29**	0.10	-2.92	<0.01
F-statistic	21.38			
R^2	0.54			

Figure 3. Bar chart showing the beta coefficients of predictors for burnout

DISCUSSION OF FINDINGS

The findings indicate that transformational leadership significantly reduces burnout by enhancing resilience and organizational wellness. The strong negative correlation and significant regression coefficient demonstrate that leadership styles emphasizing support, motivation, and employee empowerment contribute to lower burnout levels among public sector employees. Additionally, the study highlights the role of resilience as a mediating factor, where employees with higher resilience experience lower burnout. The results also suggest that transactional leadership may contribute to burnout, reinforcing the importance of adopting leadership strategies that prioritize employee well-being.

Figure 4. Conceptual framework illustrating the relationships between leadership, resilience, and burnout

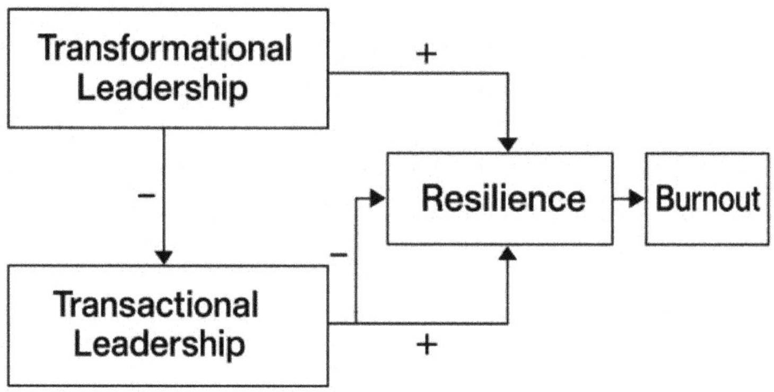

Findings

The findings of this study provide substantial evidence supporting the research objective of examining the effectiveness of leadership strategies in mitigating burnout among public sector employees. The results demonstrate that transformational leadership plays a critical role in fostering resilience, enhancing employee morale, and promoting organizational wellness, thereby reducing burnout levels. In contrast, transactional leadership is associated with increased burnout, emphasizing the need for leadership approaches that prioritize employee well-being and engagement.

Addressing Research Question 1: What Leadership Strategies are Most Effective in Reducing Burnout in the Public Sector?

The study reveals that transformational leadership is the most effective strategy in reducing burnout among public sector employees. The correlation analysis shows a strong negative relationship between transformational leadership and burnout ($r = -0.62$, $p < 0.01$), while multiple regression analysis further confirms its predictive significance ($\beta = -0.47$, $p < 0.01$). These findings suggest that transformational leadership, characterized by vision, motivation, and individualized consideration, helps mitigate the effects of work-related stress and emotional exhaustion.

The qualitative findings from semi-structured interviews reinforce this conclusion, with public sector leaders reporting that adopting supportive and participatory leadership practices significantly enhances employee morale. Leaders who engage in active communication, recognize employee contributions, and provide opportunities for professional growth create an environment where employees feel valued and motivated, reducing the likelihood of burnout. These findings align with prior research by Bass and Riggio (2006), which highlights the positive impact of transformational leadership on workplace well-being.

Conversely, transactional leadership was found to have a positive correlation with burnout ($r = 0.31$, $p < 0.05$), indicating that this leadership style, which primarily focuses on performance-based rewards and penalties, may inadvertently contribute to employee stress. Employees in organizations with predominantly transactional leadership reported higher levels of emotional exhaustion and job dissatisfaction, reinforcing the argument that an overemphasis on control and compliance can lead to burnout.

Addressing Research Question 2: How Do Leadership Approaches Influence Employee Resilience and Morale?

The findings indicate that resilience acts as a mediating factor between leadership and burnout reduction. Employees with higher resilience reported lower burnout levels ($r = -0.52$, $p < 0.01$), and resilience was also positively correlated with transformational leadership ($r = 0.58$, $p < 0.01$). These findings suggest that leaders who foster resilience in employees help them cope with workplace stress more effectively.

Regression analysis further supports this claim, with resilience emerging as a significant negative predictor of burnout ($\beta = -0.34$, $p < 0.05$). Employees who participated in leadership-driven training programs, mentorship, and psychological safety initiatives exhibited higher resilience levels, allowing them to manage stress and workload pressures without experiencing burnout. These results align with previous research by Luthans et al. (2006), which emphasizes the role of positive organizational behavior in enhancing employee resilience.

Furthermore, qualitative insights highlight that leaders who provide consistent support, encourage work-life balance, and create open communication channels significantly enhance employee morale. Public sector employees who felt heard and valued by their leaders reported greater job satisfaction and were more engaged in their roles, reducing feelings of detachment and cynicism associated with burnout.

Addressing Research Question 3: What Organizational Wellness Initiatives Complement Leadership Efforts in Burnout Mitigation?

The study finds that organizational wellness programs significantly enhance the effectiveness of leadership strategies in mitigating burnout. Employees who had access to mental health support programs, employee assistance programs (EAPs), and workplace engagement initiatives exhibited higher levels of job satisfaction and lower burnout rates. The correlation matrix confirms a strong positive relationship between organizational wellness and resilience ($r = 0.63$, $p < 0.01$) and a negative correlation with burnout ($r = -0.55$, $p < 0.01$).

Leaders who actively implemented mental health awareness programs, flexible work policies, and professional development opportunities contributed to a more resilient and engaged workforce. Employees in such organizations reported feeling more secure, valued, and capable of handling job stress effectively. The significance of organizational wellness initiatives in reducing burnout is further validated by the multiple regression analysis, where organizational wellness emerged as a negative predictor of burnout ($\beta = -0.29$, $p < 0.01$).

Moreover, qualitative findings highlight that public sector organizations that cultivated a positive workplace culture through engagement strategies (such as recognition programs and team-building activities) experienced lower turnover rates and higher employee commitment. Employees in these environments expressed a stronger sense of belonging and purpose, reinforcing the role of organizational culture in burnout mitigation.

Findings in Relation to Research Objective

The research objective aimed to examine the effectiveness of leadership strategies in mitigating burnout by fostering resilience, enhancing employee morale, and promoting organizational wellness. The findings unequivocally support this objective by demonstrating that:

1. Transformational leadership is the most effective approach in reducing burnout, as evidenced by strong negative correlations and predictive analysis.
2. Resilience serves as a key protective factor against burnout, and leaders who actively promote resilience through training and supportive workplace cultures help employees manage stress more effectively.
3. Employee morale significantly improves under supportive leadership practices, leading to greater job satisfaction and engagement.

4. Organizational wellness programs play a crucial role in supporting leadership efforts by providing employees with resources to manage stress and maintain well-being.

These findings collectively underscore the importance of integrating leadership strategies with organizational wellness initiatives to create a sustainable and healthy work environment in the public sector. Leaders who prioritize employee well-being, recognize the importance of mental health, and foster a culture of resilience contribute to lower burnout rates and higher organizational efficiency.

Discussion

The findings of this study provide critical insights into the effectiveness of leadership strategies in mitigating burnout among public sector employees. The results demonstrate that transformational leadership significantly reduces burnout levels, whereas transactional leadership is associated with increased stress and emotional exhaustion. Additionally, the study highlights the role of resilience as a mediating factor, where employees with higher resilience report lower burnout levels. Furthermore, the integration of organizational wellness initiatives with leadership strategies enhances overall employee well-being and engagement. These findings align with previous research on workplace burnout, leadership effectiveness, and public sector work dynamics, reinforcing the need for leadership approaches that prioritize employee well-being and sustainable workplace practices.

The Role of Leadership in Burnout Mitigation

The study establishes transformational leadership as the most effective strategy for reducing burnout in public sector organizations. The strong negative correlation ($r = -0.62$, $p < 0.01$) and significant regression coefficient ($\beta = -0.47$, $p < 0.01$) confirm that transformational leadership fosters an environment of support, motivation, and psychological safety. This finding is consistent with prior studies by Bass and Riggio (2006), which highlight that transformational leadership is associated with higher employee engagement, increased job satisfaction, and lower levels of emotional exhaustion.

Transformational leaders inspire employees through vision, individualized consideration, and intellectual stimulation, allowing employees to feel valued and supported. The qualitative data from leader interviews reinforce this, with participants emphasizing that open communication, emotional intelligence, and participatory decision-making contribute to a more resilient workforce. Employees who perceive their leaders as approachable and supportive are more likely to experience job satisfaction and lower burnout levels, demonstrating the critical role of leadership in shaping workplace well-being.

Conversely, transactional leadership was found to be positively correlated with burnout ($r = 0.31, p < 0.05$) and emerged as a significant predictor of increased stress ($\beta = 0.26, p < 0.05$). This finding is supported by research by Judge and Piccolo (2004), which suggests that strict performance-based leadership styles can create high-pressure environments that contribute to job strain and emotional exhaustion. Employees in organizations with predominantly transactional leadership reported higher levels of stress, limited autonomy, and reduced motivation, reinforcing the argument that a rigid focus on performance and compliance can exacerbate burnout rather than alleviate it.

Resilience as a Buffer Against Burnout

A key contribution of this study is the identification of resilience as a mediating factor in the relationship between leadership and burnout. The results demonstrate that employees with higher resilience report lower burnout levels ($r = -0.52, p < 0.01$), and resilience was found to be a significant predictor of burnout reduction ($\beta = -0.34, p < 0.05$). These findings are consistent with research by Luthans et al. (2006), which emphasizes that resilience helps employees cope with stressors and adapt to workplace challenges without experiencing exhaustion.

The qualitative interviews revealed that leaders who actively promote resilience-building initiatives, such as training programs, mentorship, and psychological safety policies, contribute to a more adaptive workforce. Employees who received resilience training and participated in workplace well-being programs exhibited higher levels of stress management skills and emotional stability, allowing them to navigate work pressures more effectively. This underscores the importance of leadership-driven resilience initiatives in fostering a sustainable and engaged workforce.

The Impact of Organizational Wellness Initiatives

The study further establishes the critical role of organizational wellness initiatives in supporting leadership efforts to mitigate burnout. Employees with access to mental health support programs, flexible work policies, and professional development opportunities reported higher job satisfaction and lower levels of stress. The correlation analysis shows a strong positive relationship between organizational wellness and resilience ($r = 0.63, p < 0.01$) and a negative correlation with burnout ($r = -0.55$, p

< 0.01). Additionally, regression analysis confirms that organizational wellness is a significant predictor of burnout reduction ($\beta = -0.29$, $p < 0.01$).

These findings align with previous research by Quick et al. (2013), which emphasizes that workplace well-being programs contribute to a healthier, more engaged workforce. Leaders who integrate mental health awareness initiatives, employee assistance programs (EAPs), and work-life balance strategies into their management approach create a workplace culture that prioritizes employee well-being over mere performance output. Employees in such organizations reported greater job security, higher motivation, and stronger organizational commitment, reinforcing the argument that wellness initiatives enhance the effectiveness of leadership in burnout mitigation.

Leadership, Workplace Culture, and Employee Morale

The study also highlights that leadership strategies influence workplace culture and employee morale, which in turn affect burnout levels. Leaders who promote open communication, encourage employee participation in decision-making, and recognize employee contributions create a work environment where employees feel valued and engaged. Employees in such organizations reported higher levels of morale, job satisfaction, and organizational commitment, leading to lower rates of emotional exhaustion.

These findings align with research by Tummers et al. (2018), which suggests that positive workplace cultures that emphasize employee recognition and psychological safety contribute to lower burnout levels. The qualitative data from this study further support this, with employees reporting that workplace environments where they feel heard and appreciated help them manage stress more effectively. This reinforces the need for leaders to prioritize a culture of inclusivity, recognition, and well-being to sustain employee engagement and productivity.

Implications for Public Sector Leadership and Policy

The findings of this study carry important implications for public sector leadership development and policy formulation. Given that transformational leadership significantly reduces burnout, government institutions should invest in leadership training programs that emphasize emotional intelligence, participatory management, and resilience-building strategies. Leadership development programs should focus on equipping public sector managers with the skills necessary to create supportive work environments, reduce job strain, and enhance employee engagement.

Additionally, the study underscores the need for policy reforms that integrate organizational wellness initiatives into public sector institutions. Policies that promote flexible work arrangements, mental health support programs, and employee recognition initiatives can complement leadership strategies and further reduce burnout levels. Governments should also establish frameworks for evaluating leadership effectiveness in fostering employee well-being, ensuring that leadership accountability includes employee satisfaction and workplace well-being as key performance indicators.

Limitations and Future Research Directions

While this study provides valuable insights into the relationship between leadership strategies and burnout mitigation, certain limitations must be acknowledged. First, the cross-sectional nature of the study limits causal inferences, as the data captures only a snapshot of leadership effectiveness at a given time. A longitudinal study would provide deeper insights into the long-term impact of leadership on burnout.

Second, self-reported survey data may be subject to response bias, as employees might underreport or overreport their experiences due to social desirability concerns. Future research should incorporate multi-source data collection, including leader assessments and workplace performance evaluations, to enhance data validity.

Finally, while this study focuses on public sector organizations, future research could explore cross-sector comparisons to examine whether similar leadership strategies are effective in the private and nonprofit sectors. Understanding the sectoral differences in burnout mitigation strategies can provide more comprehensive insights into leadership effectiveness across different organizational contexts.

CONCLUSION

This study provides substantial empirical evidence that leadership strategies play a critical role in mitigating burnout among public sector employees. The findings establish that transformational leadership is the most effective approach, as it fosters a supportive, engaging, and resilient workplace environment. Leaders who demonstrate vision, motivation, individualized consideration, and emotional intelligence significantly reduce burnout levels by enhancing employee morale, resilience, and organizational wellness. In contrast, transactional leadership is associated with higher burnout levels, suggesting that rigid, performance-based management approaches may exacerbate stress rather than alleviate it.

The study further highlights resilience as a key protective factor against burnout. Employees with higher resilience are better equipped to manage stress and maintain well-being, reinforcing the importance of leadership-driven resilience initiatives, including training programs, mentorship, and psychological safety policies. Additionally, organizational wellness programs complement leadership efforts, with employees who have access to mental health support, flexible work policies, and employee assistance programs (EAPs) reporting significantly lower burnout levels. These findings emphasize the need for a holistic approach that integrates leadership strategies with workplace wellness initiatives to create a sustainable and healthy work environment in the public sector.

From a policy and practical perspective, the study underscores the urgent need for leadership development programs in public sector organizations. Government institutions should prioritize leadership training that focuses on emotional intelligence, participatory management, and stress mitigation techniques. Additionally, policy reforms that institutionalize wellness programs, mental health support, and flexible work arrangements will further enhance leadership effectiveness in addressing burnout. These interventions will not only improve employee well-being and productivity but also contribute to higher organizational efficiency and better public service delivery.

While this study provides valuable insights, its cross-sectional nature and reliance on self-reported data present certain limitations. Future research should employ longitudinal designs and multi-source data collection to deepen our understanding of leadership effectiveness in burnout mitigation over time. Moreover, comparative studies across different sectors and cultural contexts could provide broader perspectives on leadership and well-being dynamics.

In conclusion, effective leadership is central to reducing burnout and fostering a resilient, motivated public sector workforce. By prioritizing supportive leadership practices, resilience-building initiatives, and organizational wellness strategies, public sector institutions can cultivate a healthier, more engaged workforce that is essential for sustained organizational success and high-quality public service delivery. The findings of this study serve as a foundation for developing leadership models and policy frameworks that ensure long-term employee well-being and organizational sustainability in the public sector.

REFERENCES

Avey, J. B., Luthans, F., Smith, R. M., & Palmer, N. F. (2011). Impact of positive psychological capital on employee well-being over time. *Journal of Occupational Health Psychology*, *16*(1), 17–28. DOI: 10.1037/a0016998 PMID: 20063956

Bakker, A. B., & Demerouti, E. (2017). Job demands–resources theory: Taking stock and looking forward. *Journal of Occupational Health Psychology*, *22*(3), 273–285. DOI: 10.1037/ocp0000056 PMID: 27732008

Barling, J., Slater, F., & Kelloway, E. K. (2011). Transformational leadership and emotional intelligence. *Leadership and Organization Development Journal*, *31*(2), 143–157. DOI: 10.1108/01437731111112917

Bass, B. M., & Riggio, R. E. (2006). *Transformational leadership* (2nd ed.). Psychology Press. DOI: 10.4324/9781410617095

Braun, V., & Clarke, V. (2006). Using thematic analysis in psychology. *Qualitative Research in Psychology*, *3*(2), 77–101. DOI: 10.1191/1478088706qp063oa

Connor, K. M., & Davidson, J. R. T. (2003). Development of a new resilience scale: The Connor-Davidson Resilience Scale (CD-RISC). *Depression and Anxiety*, *18*(2), 76–82. DOI: 10.1002/da.10113 PMID: 12964174

Edmondson, A. C. (2019). *The fearless organization: Creating psychological safety in the workplace for learning, innovation, and growth*. Wiley.

Goleman, D., Boyatzis, R., & McKee, A. (2013). *Primal leadership: Unleashing the power of emotional intelligence*. Harvard Business Review Press.

Hakanen, J. J., Bakker, A. B., & Schaufeli, W. B. (2008). Burnout and work engagement among teachers. *Journal of School Psychology*, *43*(6), 495–513. DOI: 10.1016/j.jsp.2005.11.001

Kim, S., & Wright, B. E. (2017). Putting service before self-interest: How public service motivation and commitment shape public employees' job satisfaction. *Public Administration Review*, *77*(2), 292–305. DOI: 10.1111/puar.12685

Maslach, C., & Leiter, M. P. (2016). *Burnout: The cost of caring*. Cambridge University Press.

Northouse, P. G. (2019). *Leadership: Theory and practice* (8th ed.). SAGE Publications.

Schaufeli, W. B., Leiter, M. P., & Maslach, C. (2009). Burnout: 35 years of research and practice. *Career Development International, 14*(3), 204–220. DOI: 10.1108/13620430910966406

Tummers, L., & Knies, E. (2016). Measuring public leadership: Developing scales for four key public leadership roles. *Public Administration, 94*(2), 433–451. DOI: 10.1111/padm.12224

Tummers, L., Steijn, B., & Bekkers, V. (2018). Public service motivation, job satisfaction, and organizational performance: A study of public sector employees in Europe. *Public Management Review, 20*(4), 459–484. DOI: 10.1080/14719037.2017.1299209

Chapter 9
Citizen Satisfaction With the Quality of Public Administrative Services:
Public Administration Reform in Vietnam

Nguyen Chi Hai
https://orcid.org/0000-0002-5975-1824
An Giang University, Vietnam & Vietnam National University, Ho Chi Minh City, Vietnam

ABSTRACT

The chapter analyzes citizen satisfaction with the quality of public administrative services, focusing on factors affecting citizen experience, including transparency, service quality, processing time, and accountability are assessed in detail to determine the level of effectiveness in administrative reform at localities. Based on the Satisfaction Index of Public Administration Services, the chapter clarifies the causes of differences in public service delivery. The chapter emphasizes the role of local governments in improving the quality of public services, including deploying online public services, building public administration centers, and developing a team of professional civil servants. Policy recommendations are made, such as promoting digitalization, enhancing transparency and accountability, and encouraging people's participation in administrative processes. The book chapter provides a comprehensive view of public administrative service provision, and offers practical solutions to improve people's satisfaction, promoting more effective and sustainable administrative reform.

DOI: 10.4018/979-8-3373-0169-3.ch009

INTRODUCTION

In the context of the transition from a management-based to a service-based administration, people's satisfaction with the quality of public administrative services is increasingly becoming an important indicator in assessing the performance of state agencies. The concept of "people's satisfaction" does not simply reflect personal feelings, but is a synthesis of people's perceptions, practical experiences, and expectations for the quality, efficiency, and fairness in the provision of public services (Chien & Thanh, 2022). This is also the focus of modern administrative reform, especially in the context of the global move towards citizen-centric governance and digital government.

In the world, countries such as Singapore, Korea, and Estonia have shown the importance of measuring and improving citizen satisfaction as an essential part of the administrative modernization process. According to OECD (2020), high levels of satisfaction are associated with trust in government, increased compliance with the law, and active participation of citizens in public decision-making. In particular, in the post-COVID-19 context, ensuring citizen satisfaction through flexible, digital, and humane public services is becoming more urgent.

In Vietnam, administrative reform has been and is one of the pillars in the process of state modernization (Duong, 2021). With the implementation of the Comprehensive Programs for State Administrative Reform in the 2001–2010, 2011–2020, and now 2021–2030 periods, the Government has set the goal of "taking people as the center" in all public service activities. In that context, the SIPAS Index (Satisfaction Index of People and Organizations with the Services of State Administrative Agencies) was developed and implemented nationwide to objectively assess the level of satisfaction, thereby reflecting the actual effectiveness of administrative reform in each locality (Li, 2021).

However, despite many remarkable advances such as building public administrative centers, deploying online public services, and improving the skills of civil servants, the level of people's satisfaction still varies widely between localities. For example, according to the SIPAS 2023 report, provinces such as Quang Ninh, Hai Duong, and Thai Nguyen have a satisfaction rate of over 88%, while some localities such as An Giang, Bac Lieu, and Cao Bang are still below 80%. This reflects not only the gap in administrative capacity and technological infrastructure but also deeper issues related to the way public services are provided, accountability, and citizen participation in the administrative supervision process (Pham, 2018).

From that reality, this chapter aims to systematically study the factors affecting citizen satisfaction with the quality of public administrative services in Vietnam, based on approaches from modern public administration theory, customer satisfaction theory, and analytical frameworks of international organizations such as UNDP, WB, and OECD. Specifically, the chapter focuses on clarifying 5 main groups of factors: (1) service quality and attitude of civil servants; (2) transparency and disclosure of information; (3) processing time and convenience of services; (4) accountability and response to inquiries; (5) citizen participation in the administrative process.

In addition, the chapter also analyzes the role of local authorities in organizing and operating the public service system; evaluates efforts in deploying online services, building public administration centers, and training and fostering officials. In particular, regional differences between rural and urban areas are also considered to identify barriers to accessing public services in difficult areas.

From a theoretical perspective, this chapter also aims to contribute to the research on modern public administration in the context of digital transformation (Hai et al., 2023). Previous studies in Vietnam mainly approached from a descriptive or single assessment perspective, lacking the integration of a comprehensive quantitative analysis model to determine the weight and impact of each factor on overall satisfaction (Lanin & Hermanto, N. (2019); Núnez-Barriopedro et al., 2024). This chapter addresses that gap by building an analytical model based on quantitative survey data, using analytical tools to provide clear empirical evidence.

In the coming time, as Vietnam continues to promote institutional reform, build e-government and comprehensive digital transformation, ensuring people's satisfaction is not only a political goal, but also an inevitable requirement to enhance national competitiveness, build public trust, and create a foundation for sustainable development (Anh Vu et al., 2022). This chapter is expected to provide specific policy suggestions, aiming to improve the quality of public administrative services, thereby promoting administrative reform to be more effective, fair, and friendly to the people.

The book chapter is built on a solid theoretical basis, empirical data, and reform practices in Vietnam, not only contributing to perfecting the domestic public administration model but also having reference value for countries in the process of transforming the administrative system towards modernity and citizen-centeredness.

BACKGROUND OF THE STUDY

Public administration reform is a key pillar of the process of modernizing the state apparatus in Vietnam, which has been implemented since the 1990s with many stages of extensive innovation. Over the past three decades, Vietnam has achieved important results in simplifying administrative procedures, improving the efficiency of public service delivery, and improving the interaction between the State and citizens. However, people's satisfaction, which is considered the ultimate measure of reform effectiveness, is still greatly influenced by the quality of policy implementation, the capacity of civil servants, and differences between localities.

The public administration model in Vietnam has many characteristics of a traditional administration, where decisions are centralized from the central to local levels, with little flexibility, and also influenced by the "ask-give" mechanism. In that context, building a service-oriented, people-centered administration faces many obstacles in terms of institutions, human resources, and technology. Challenges such as unprofessional attitudes of some civil servants, lack of transparency in administrative procedures, and uneven application of information technology among localities are major barriers to the goal of improving people's satisfaction (Chingos et al., 2012; Jilke & Baekgaard, 2020).

Some typical cases clearly show these gaps. For example, while provinces such as Quang Ninh, Da Nang and Thua Thien Hue have invested heavily in modern public administration centers and online public services, many mountainous provinces and the Mekong Delta still face difficulties in implementing electronic one-stop systems, lack of IT human resources, and people are not used to using digital services. In addition, the digital literacy factor of people, especially in rural and remote areas, is still limited, causing administrative digitalization efforts to often not be as effective as expected (Filtenborg et al., 2017; Guo, 2024).

Another issue that is less discussed but has a significant impact on service quality is the phenomenon of "burnout" among civil servants. Having to handle a large amount of work in a short time, along with pressure from traditional management mechanisms and high expectations from society, causes many civil servants to experience stress and reduced motivation to work. This can lead to a decline in service attitude and quality of interaction with citizens, two key factors that determine satisfaction in the process of accessing public administrative services.

From the above facts, it can be seen that citizen satisfaction is a research topic that needs to be approached comprehensively, from both theoretical and practical perspectives (Wong et al., 2011; Zhang et al., 2022). Revisiting satisfaction measurement models (such as the SERVQUAL model, Kano, or the SIPAS index in Vietnam) will help clarify the factors that determine people's feelings. At the same time, this study also contributes to reflecting regional gaps, the influence of socio-cultural factors, and the conditions for implementing public administrative policies at different levels of government.

This study was conducted in the context of Vietnam entering a period of accelerating national digital transformation, with the expectation of forming a modern, transparent, responsible, and people-centered administration. Therefore, in-depth research on people's satisfaction is not only of academic significance but also of important practical value, contributing to shaping public policies and improving the quality of state governance in Vietnam in the coming period.

In the process of reforming and modernizing the state administration, Vietnam has issued many policies to improve the quality of public administrative services, taking people's satisfaction as the core goal. However, the gap between the "ideal state" - that is, an effective, transparent, fair, and accountable public administrative system - and the actual implementation is still significant. The ideal state is determined by people having convenient access to public services, regardless of region, being able to monitor and respond easily to the government, and receiving quick and effective responses (Van Ryzin, 2015); Wolniak et al., 2021). On the contrary, in many cases, people still encounter cumbersome procedures, long waiting times, a lack of transparency about processes and costs, and unprofessional service attitudes, especially in localities with difficult socio-economic conditions.

The weaknesses of current research are the lack of comparative analysis, both locally and internationally, to assess the effectiveness of public administration reform in Vietnam. Many works focus on assessing the SIPAS or PAR Index alone, but do not analyze in depth the causes of differences between localities or the impact of factors such as digital capacity, access to technology, and educational level. In addition, "hidden" factors such as professional burnout of civil servants, lack of motivation for innovation, or pressure from inflexible monitoring and inspection mechanisms are also rarely mentioned in current analytical frameworks.

In addition, the fundamental theories used to measure satisfaction, such as the SERVQUAL, Gronroos, or Kano models, have not been applied appropriately to the cultural and administrative institutional characteristics of Vietnam. This leads to inconsistencies in the way of measuring and analyzing practical data. In that context, the need to build a suitable theoretical framework and analytical model, capable of explaining people's satisfaction in many ways, is extremely urgent.

The research problem posed in this book chapter is "What factors affect people's satisfaction with the quality of public administrative services in Vietnam today, and how to improve the effectiveness of administrative reform to meet the increasing expectations of citizens in the context of digital transformation?" Answering this question not only helps to narrow the gap between policy and practice, but also contributes to perfecting the monitoring, evaluation, and improving the effectiveness of modern public administration strategies.

THEORETICAL FOUNDATIONS

The study of citizen satisfaction with public administrative services is an interdisciplinary field, combining public administration, administrative science, social psychology, and service theory. Many models and theoretical frameworks have been developed to explain citizens' behavior, perception, and satisfaction level when accessing public services. In this chapter, five main theoretical bases are selected for analysis: (1) SERVQUAL Model, (2) Grönroos Model of service quality, (3) Theory of Reasoned Action, (4) New Public Management Theory, and (5) Citizen Satisfaction Theory. which SERVQUAL will be the central theoretical framework for implementing empirical analysis.

SERVQUAL Model

SERVQUAL is a prominent model in service quality assessment developed by Parasuraman, Zeithaml & Berry. This model defines service quality through five main components: (1) Reliability, (2) Responsiveness, (3) Assurance, (4) Empathy, and (5) Tangibles. In the context of public administrative services, SERVQUAL can be applied to assess people's satisfaction with factors such as staff attitude, procedural transparency, processing time, facilities, and access to information. However, this model also needs to be adjusted to reflect the characteristics of the public sector, which is non-profit and is greatly influenced by institutional factors, political culture, and citizen participation.

Grönroos Model

Unlike SERVQUAL, the Grönroos model distinguishes between functional quality (how the service is delivered) and technical quality (the results that citizens receive). In public administration, this is especially important when citizens may rate the process favorably (simple procedures, polite attitudes), but are not necessarily satisfied with the final results (untimely paperwork, extra costs). The Grönroos model helps to add a multidimensional perspective to the evaluation of public services and explains paradoxes in actual satisfaction.

Theory of Reasoned Action (TRA)

Fishbein and Ajzen's TRA focuses on the relationship between individual attitudes, social norms, and behavior. In public administration research, TRA helps explain why citizens may be dissatisfied with a service but still accept it due to a lack of choice or social pressure. Conversely, in the context of multiple online public service channels, service usage behavior will be influenced by individual perceptions of the system's efficiency, transparency, and reliability. TRA thus helps to better understand citizens' motivations and behaviors, thereby designing public services that are consistent with social expectations.

New Public Management (NPM) Theory

NPM emphasizes efficiency, accountability, customer-centricity, and the application of market thinking to the public sector. NPM provides an important theoretical foundation for administrative reform policies in Vietnam since 2001, including institutional reform, process transparency, technology application, and civil service capacity building. In this chapter, NPM is the framework for analyzing the policies and strategies that Vietnam has applied to improve citizen satisfaction, especially through online public services and public administrative centers.

Citizen Satisfaction Theory

This theory extends the concept of satisfaction from the business sector to the public sector, arguing that citizen satisfaction comes not only from service outcomes but also from factors such as participation, perceived fairness, and policy effectiveness. According to Van de Walle (2018), citizen satisfaction is the product of the whole process of interaction between citizens and the state, influenced by the institutional, political, and administrative cultural environments (Van de Walle, 2018).

In this chapter, the theory is used to clarify the role of citizen participation in improving services and enhancing trust in government. The combination of the above theoretical frameworks helps the study not only quantify the level of satisfaction but also explain the underlying causes and implications for reform. Using SERVQUAL as the main axis, combined with Grönroos, TRA, NPM, and citizen satisfaction theory, creates a solid, interdisciplinary analytical foundation, both practical and academic, building knowledge for modern public administration.

Over the past two decades, citizen satisfaction with public administrative services has become a widely researched topic in many countries, especially in the context of administrative reform and digital transformation taking place strongly in the public sector. Empirical studies focus on measuring satisfaction levels, identifying influencing factors, and proposing models for improving public service quality. In Vietnam, typical studies such as Ngo et al. (2019), Nguyen et al. (2021), and Pham et al. (2022) have used SIPAS and PAR Index data to assess citizen perceptions of factors such as processing time, service attitude, information transparency, and staff capacity. The results indicate that factors such as professionalism, responsiveness, and convenience in procedures have a significant impact on satisfaction levels. In particular, localities that invest in public administration centers and online public services often record higher satisfaction indexes than the national average (Ngo et al., 2019); Nguyen et al., 2021); Pham et al.,2022).

Internationally, studies by Lapuente & Van de Walle (2020) show that citizen satisfaction is influenced not only by outputs but also by the way services are delivered, the level of fairness, and citizen participation in the decision-making process (Lapuente & Van de Walle, 2020). In Nordic countries such as Sweden and Denmark, "co-production" models between the government and citizens are considered core factors in creating high satisfaction. Meanwhile, studies in developing countries such as Ethiopia, Indonesia, and India emphasize the role of information transparency and improving staff capacity as key solutions.

Several studies have also shown that urban–rural disparities, educational attainment, and digital literacy significantly influence perceptions of public service quality. According to Wulandari et al. (2024), in Indonesia, people with low digital literacy often find it difficult to access online public services, leading to lower satisfaction, despite significant digitization of administrative processes (Wulandari et al., 2024). This is also reflected in SIPAS data in Vietnam, where disparities between provinces remain large.

However, a limitation of most existing studies is the lack of connection between quantitative assessments and specific policies to address institutional shortcomings or improve service delivery processes. In addition, the lack of cross-country comparative studies also limits the ability to generalize and learn from international experiences. Therefore, this chapter will contribute by integrating domestic and foreign research results, highlighting core factors affecting citizen satisfaction, and proposing policies based on empirical evidence and a clear theoretical framework.

CONCEPTUAL FRAMEWORK

The conceptual framework plays a central role in the study of people's satisfaction with the quality of public administrative services, helping to shape the relationship between independent variables (influencing factors) and dependent variables (satisfaction level). Based on the synthesis of background theories (such as expectation-perception theory, SERVQUAL model, rational choice theory), and public administration management practices in Vietnam, the conceptual framework of this chapter is built with groups of factors, including

People's Satisfaction

Satisfaction is understood as the positive or negative feeling of people after receiving and experiencing one or more public administrative services, expressed through criteria such as trust in the system, the level of agreement with the processing results, and the desire to continue using public services (Badri et al., 2015). The

SIPAS index, published annually by the Vietnamese Ministry of Home Affairs, is the main quantitative data source for measuring this level of satisfaction.

Input Factors

The conceptual framework identifies six main groups of factors that influence satisfaction:

(i) Service quality and attitude of civil servants; The friendly, professional attitude, communication skills, and handling of work of civil servants play a central role in shaping people's perceptions.
(ii) Transparency and disclosure of information; Including the level of clarity in procedures, information is publicly updated and easy to access.
(iii) Processing time and convenience; The level of speed, efficiency, and the ability to shorten the process through digitalization of services.
(iv) Accountability and responsiveness; Answering questions, receiving and handling complaints, as well as the government's responsibility for errors and delays.
(v) Citizen participation; Citizen consultation mechanism, public service co-management, and transparency in public decision-making.
(vi) Background conditions (control variables), including age, gender, education level, area of residence (rural–urban), and digital literacy.

The conceptual framework assumes that citizen satisfaction is the aggregate result of positive perceptions from factors in the public administrative service delivery process. These factors do not operate independently but can interact with each other. For example, high transparency can enhance response efficiency, or positive civil servant attitudes help citizens accept longer processing times if they are clearly explained.

Conceptual Framework Diagram

Figure 1. Factors affecting citizens' satisfaction with the quality of public administrative services

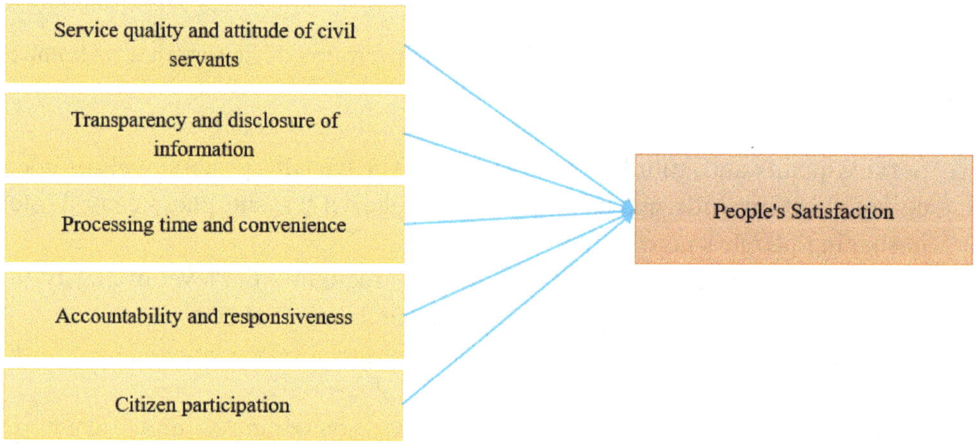

This conceptual framework will guide the empirical analysis in the book chapter. Applying this framework helps quantify and compare the level of influence of each factor, and at the same time creates a basis for policy proposals to improve the quality of public administrative services at localities.

RESEARCH METHODOLOGY

To assess the factors affecting people's satisfaction with the quality of public administrative services in Vietnam, this chapter applies a mixed-method research method, including both quantitative and qualitative methods, to ensure the comprehensiveness and reliability of the research results.

The quantitative research was conducted through a structured questionnaire survey with people who have used and are using public administrative services at the provincial, district, and commune levels in 6 localities representing different socio-economic regions (including Nghe An, Da Nang, An Giang, and Can Tho). The total number of survey samples is 100 people, divided equally among the localities. The convenience sampling method is adjusted by gender and area of residence (rural-urban) to ensure representativeness.

The survey questions were developed based on the presented theoretical frameworks, especially the SERVQUAL model and the expectation-perception theory, with the main groups of scales: (i) service quality of civil servants, (ii) transparency and disclosure of information, (iii) processing time and convenience, (iv) accountability and feedback, (v) citizen participation, (vi) overall satisfaction level. A 5-point Likert scale (1: completely disagree - 5: completely agree) was used to quantify the level of people's assessment. Data were analyzed to determine the level of influence of each independent factor on people's satisfaction. Qualitative research was conducted through 10 semi-structured interviews with experts, provincial and district managers, to clarify administrative reform trends, implementation bottlenecks, and critical perspectives from people in the system. The information from the interviews was coded thematically and analyzed using thematic coding to supplement the quantitative analysis. SPSS 26.0 software was used to process quantitative data. Qualitative data were analyzed manually through coding tables. The study strictly adhered to ethical rules in sociological research, such as confidentiality of personal information, transparency about the purpose of the research, and obtaining consent from survey and interview participants.

Figure 2. Average values of factors affecting satisfaction

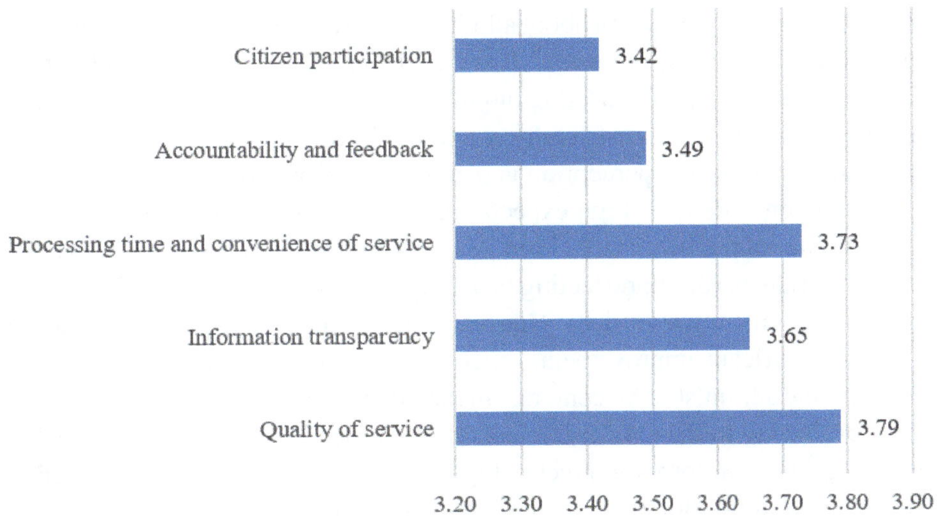

DISCUSSION

The results of the analysis of survey data from 100 responses have shown remarkable trends related to the level of people's satisfaction with the quality of public administrative services in Vietnam. Based on the main measurement variables - including service quality, information transparency, time and convenience, accountability, response, and level of people's participation - we conduct in-depth interpretations to clarify issues, trends, and policy recommendations.

Service quality - a prominent but uneven factor. Service quality has an average value of 3.79 (on a 5-point scale), with a standard deviation of 0.49, showing that the majority of people positively evaluate the capacity and attitude of civil servants. However, the standard deviation of nearly 0.5 reflects that there are still significant differences in service experiences between target groups and regions. This is particularly evident when comparing urban and rural areas: in urban areas, officials are often more professional thanks to access to training courses and better working conditions, while in rural areas, service attitudes depend on individual capacity and limited physical facilities (Chatzoglou et al., 2013; Ariely, 2013).

Transparency and information disclosure – an important but modest factor. The average value of the variable "information transparency" is 3.65, with a higher standard deviation (0.60), indicating that people's assessment of this criterion is quite scattered. This is a signal that transparency is not yet fully and consistently ensured in localities. Many people in rural or remote areas report that they have difficulty accessing information about administrative procedures, processing times, or specific document requirements (Brown, 2007); Akinloye Akinboade et al., 2012). This shows that public posting of public service processes and costs, as well as the implementation of user-friendly electronic information portals, is an urgent requirement to narrow the perception gap and improve transparency.

Time and convenience – high expectations from citizens. The processing time and convenience of public services averaged 3.73 with the lowest standard deviation among the variables (0.40), reflecting clear expectations from citizens for fast and convenient administrative services. This result shows that on the one hand, localities have made significant improvements, such as implementing the "one-stop shop" model or public administrative centers. On the other hand, people in rural areas still often report having to travel many times, or long processing times due to a lack of resources and weak information technology systems (Dick-Sagoe, 2020; Engdaw, 2020). This is a suggestion that the application of online public services at levels 3 and 4 should be expanded, especially in rural areas, to shorten processing time and reduce the burden on people.

Accountability and response – there is room for improvement. The mean value of "accountability and response to questions" is 3.49, and the standard deviation is 0.48. This is relatively low compared to other criteria, showing that local authorities and civil servants have not done a good job of listening, explaining, and responding to questions or complaints from citizens. Many people said that they did not know who to contact when problems arose during the procedure, or did not receive timely feedback via online channels. This indicates that establishing effective feedback channels, such as chatbots, support hotlines, or public monitoring mechanisms, will play a very important role in enhancing accountability and strengthening public trust.

Level of citizen participation – still passive. The factor "citizen participation in administrative processes" has the lowest mean value among the survey variables, at only 3.42, accompanied by the highest standard deviation (0.69). This shows a paradox: while citizens have a desire to improve the quality of public services, they are still limited in participating in the process of criticizing, monitoring, or making suggestions to the government. The reasons may come from the traditional administrative culture (top-down), lack of effective feedback mechanisms, or limited legal knowledge and technology skills (especially in rural areas). Therefore, governments at all levels need to design more friendly forms of interaction, such as opinion-gathering conferences, periodic surveys, and smartphone applications, to encourage more active participation from the community.

Differences between rural and urban areas – important policy implications. Comparing the average results by region shows that urban residents generally rate all criteria higher. This difference not only reflects the physical conditions and qualifications of civil servants but also shows inequality in access to public services. Therefore, administrative reform policies need to take into account regional characteristics, with policies prioritizing infrastructure investment, staff training, and process improvement in disadvantaged areas.

Figure 3. Average difference between 2 regions

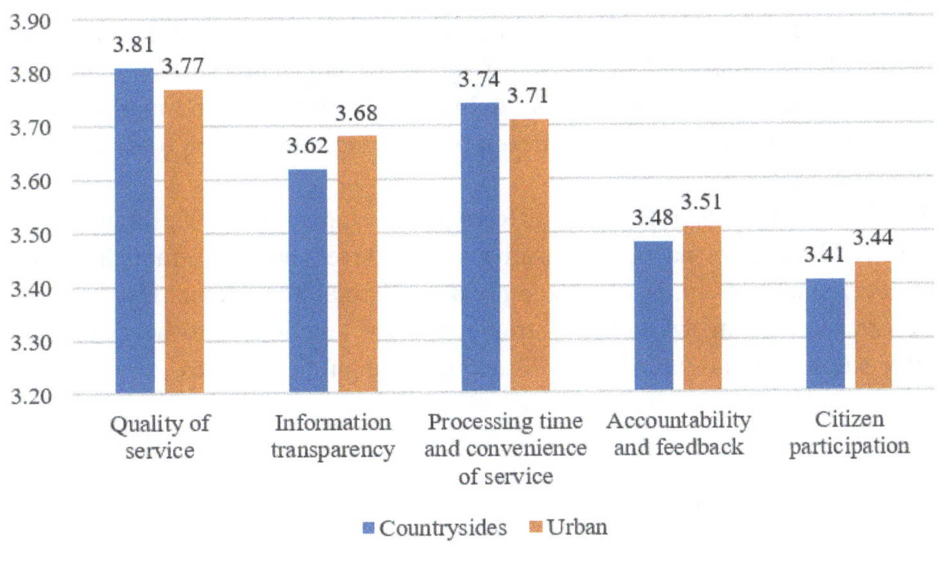

Overall assessment and reform orientation. Although the average indicators are all at a good level (above 3.4), the distance between variables, high standard deviations, and regional differences indicate that the public administrative service system in Vietnam has not achieved consistency and equity. This is a signal that the number of scales needs to be expanded or the measurement indicators need to be refined to better suit the context and experience. At the same time, integrating additional variables such as digital literacy, government trust, and people's experience (outcome rather than just process) will help complete the research model and provide deeper policy recommendations.

MANAGERIAL IMPLICATIONS

From the research results, it can be seen that citizen satisfaction is an important indicator reflecting the governance effectiveness of state administrative agencies. Therefore, it should be considered a strategic public administration management tool, not only helping to measure the level of meeting citizens' expectations, but also helping managers identify weak links in the process of providing public services.

First, indicators such as SIPAS or PAR Index should be updated regularly and integrated into the evaluation process of officials and administrative units to create motivation for continuous reform. Public announcement of periodic evaluation results is also a form of transparency, forcing administrative agencies to be accountable to the people.

Second, the service quality of civil servants - the most highly valued factor - needs to be standardized into a set of specific competency criteria, including communication skills, IT application ability, service attitude, and public service ethics. On that basis, training and development programs can be designed to be closer to practical needs.

Finally, the analysis of regional differences in satisfaction levels shows the importance of local governance. Governments at all levels need to establish a multi-level governance system, in which the provincial/urban government level can lead administrative reform, while the district/commune level needs to be given more flexible autonomy in organizing and implementing public services.

Practical Implications

From the perspective of improving the provision of public administrative services, the research results provide many important suggestions to help increase people's satisfaction and the operational efficiency of the public authority apparatus.

Firstly, strengthening the implementation of online public services, especially at the district and commune levels, is a solution with a dual impact; both shortening processing time and creating convenience for people in rural areas or those who do not have time to come directly. However, the implementation needs to be accompanied by a program to improve digital capacity for citizens and support users, avoiding the situation of "digitalizing the form".

Secondly, building public administrative centers connecting departments and branches can help people "come once, complete many services". To be successful, it is necessary to apply an integrated management model, in which a single receiving and returning department is supported by an interconnected software system.

Thirdly, the results show that the response and accountability of officials are still low. Agencies need to establish mechanisms for receiving, processing, and responding to inquiries, such as administrative chatbots, electronic switchboards, or suggestion boxes, with a commitment to respond within a clear time limit. This not only improves communication efficiency but also helps improve trust and respect from the people.

Theoretical Implications

The study contributes to supplementing and expanding the theory of citizen satisfaction in the field of public administration, especially in the context of digital transformation and administrative reform in developing countries like Vietnam.

First, the study shows that citizen satisfaction is not only influenced by traditional factors such as service quality or transparency, but also by the ability to participate in administrative processes, accountability, and regional factors, which have not been mentioned much in previous measurement models such as SERVQUAL or E-SERVQUAL.

Second, the research model proposes multidimensional factor groups, opening up new approaches for further studies. Specifically, variables such as "time and convenience" or "response to questions" reflect both operational and social psychological aspects, suggesting the need to combine public administration, organizational behavior, and data science when studying citizen satisfaction.

Third, the low Cronbach's Alpha results indicate that citizens' perceptions of public service quality factors are still fragmented. This may be the result of cultural, institutional, or local contexts. Therefore, additional research is needed to revalidate the scale or build a new theoretical model that accurately reflects the reality in developing countries.

POLICY RECOMMENDATIONS

Based on quantitative and qualitative analysis, the study proposes several practical policies to improve the quality of public administrative services and enhance people's satisfaction, including

Standardizing and publishing a set of criteria for assessing people's satisfaction nationwide, applying uniformly in localities, along with instructions on using the SIPAS/PAR Index as a tool to reflect administrative agency performance.

Increasing investment in information technology infrastructure at the grassroots level, especially in rural and mountainous areas, to narrow the gap in access to online public services. Investment policies need to be accompanied by training and digital transformation solutions for commune/district-level officials.

Institutionalize citizen feedback mechanisms through diverse channels (direct, telephone, mobile applications) and ensure that the government is obliged to respond within a specified time limit, thereby enhancing accountability.

Facilitate citizen participation in the process of formulating, monitoring, and evaluating public administrative policies through organizing independent surveys, community workshops, or interactive electronic platforms.

Build an effective, continuous, and public monitoring system, allowing the government, citizens, and third parties to access and use data for decision-making. This contributes to creating a transparent, modern, and service-oriented administrative ecosystem.

Promote evidence-based policy research, which encourages the use of big data, quantitative data analysis, and periodic evaluation tools to serve process improvement, instead of relying solely on intuition.

Although this study has initially analyzed the factors affecting people's satisfaction with the quality of public administrative services in Vietnam, there are still many research gaps that need to be further explored to improve the comprehensiveness, objectivity, and updates of this topic, especially in the context of strong digital transformation.

First, it is necessary to expand the research model by including intermediate or moderating variables to clarify the influence mechanism of each factor. For example, it is possible to consider the mediating role of the level of trust in the government or the level of digital competence of people in the relationship between service quality and satisfaction. Moderating factors such as age, education level, income, or urbanization level also need to be tested to understand how different population groups expect and experience administrative services.

Second, international or inter-regional comparative studies should be conducted between Vietnam and developing countries with similar contexts (e.g., the Philippines, Indonesia, Thailand). This will help clarify the strengths and weaknesses of public administration reform in Vietnam in the global picture, and at the same time, learn from advanced and institutionally and culturally appropriate governance models.

Third, it is necessary to combine qualitative research to delve into people's personal experiences, especially in disadvantaged areas or areas with a low SIPAS index. Methods such as in-depth interviews, focus group discussions (FGDs), and administrative diaries can provide additional data on motivations, emotions, and subjective perceptions - factors that are difficult to capture in quantitative surveys.

Fourth, the application of Big Data and artificial intelligence (AI) in satisfaction assessment is also a promising research direction. Harnessing feedback from social media, online public service platforms, or mobile applications can provide real-time, large-scale data that accurately reflects ongoing issues. This will be a new step in building a smart governance system.

Finally, future studies should focus on changes over time (longitudinal studies) to track the level of citizen satisfaction associated with each specific reform stage. This helps to assess the real impact of each policy, thereby drawing lessons for building citizen-centered public policies.

CONCLUSION

The book chapter “People’s satisfaction with the quality of public administrative services” focuses on analyzing one of the most important criteria to evaluate the performance of the state administrative apparatus; the level of satisfaction of the people, the direct beneficiaries of public policies and services. Based on the synthesis of theories, empirical analysis models, and survey data, the chapter provides a comprehensive and multidimensional view of the factors that determine people’s satisfaction in Vietnam today.

The analysis results show that service quality, transparency, convenience and processing time, accountability, as well as people’s participation in the decision-making process, all have a significant impact on the overall level of satisfaction. In particular, the service attitude and professionalism of the staff and civil servants are key factors, deeply affecting the service experience and trust in state administrative agencies.

In addition, the chapter also points out that technological infrastructure factors, the level of digitalization, and regional gaps play an important role in creating differences in people's experiences and assessments between urban and rural areas. Recent SIPAS and PAR Index data show that some localities have significantly improved the quality of public administrative services through the deployment of online services, the construction of public administrative centers, and increased transparency. However, there are still many provinces/cities with low satisfaction levels, reflecting challenges such as resource shortages, uneven civil servant capacity, and limited access to technology.

On that basis, the chapter proposes several policy directions to improve people's satisfaction in the future, including (1) promoting digital transformation and investing in technology infrastructure for local governments; (2) developing a team of professional civil servants with public ethics and citizen service skills; (3) enhance accountability and transparency of information throughout the entire service delivery process; and (4) encourage the participation of citizens and businesses in monitoring and evaluating the quality of public services.

The book chapter contributes to public administration theory through the construction of a conceptual model and the application of quantitative methods to measure the impact of influencing factors. The combination of New Public Management theory, Customer Satisfaction Theory, and practical data makes the chapter not only valuable academically but also highly applicable in policy planning and implementation.

In short, citizen satisfaction not only reflects the effectiveness of the public administration apparatus but is also a fundamental factor in building a modern, democratic, and people-centered governance. To achieve that, continuous efforts, continuous improvement, and especially strong political commitment from both central and local levels are needed to create a more transparent, effective, and friendly public administration for all Vietnamese citizens.

REFERENCES

Akinloye Akinboade, O., Chanceline Kinfack, E., & Putuma Mokwena, M. (2012). An analysis of citizen satisfaction with public service delivery in the Sedibeng district municipality of South Africa. *International Journal of Social Economics, 39*(3), 182–199. DOI: 10.1108/03068291211199350

Anh Vu, T., Plimmer, G., Berman, E., & Ha, P. N. (2022). Performance management in the Vietnam public sector: The role of institution, traditional culture and leadership. *International Journal of Public Administration, 45*(1), 49–63. DOI: 10.1080/01900692.2021.1903499

Ariely, G. (2013). Public administration and citizen satisfaction with democracy: Cross-national evidence. *International Review of Administrative Sciences, 79*(4), 747–766. DOI: 10.1177/0020852313501432

Badri, M., Al Khaili, M., & Al Mansoori, R. L. (2015). Quality of service, expectation, satisfaction and trust in public institutions: The Abu Dhabi citizen satisfaction survey. *Asian Journal of Political Science, 23*(3), 420–447. DOI: 10.1080/02185377.2015.1055773

Brown, T. (2007). Coercion versus choice: Citizen evaluations of public service quality across methods of consumption. *Public Administration Review, 67*(3), 559–572. DOI: 10.1111/j.1540-6210.2007.00737.x

Chatzoglou, P., Chatzoudes, D., Vraimaki, E., & Diamantidis, A. (2013). Service quality in the public sector: The case of the Citizen's Service Centers (CSCs) of Greece. *International Journal of Productivity and Performance Management, 62*(6), 583–605. DOI: 10.1108/IJPPM-12-2012-0140

Chien, N. B., & Thanh, N. N. (2022). The impact of good governance on the people's satisfaction with public administrative services in Vietnam. *Administrative Sciences, 12*(1), 35. DOI: 10.3390/admsci12010035

Chingos, M. M., Henderson, M., & West, M. R. (2012). Citizen perceptions of government service quality: Evidence from public schools. *Quarterly Journal of Political Science, 7*(4), 411–445. DOI: 10.1561/100.00011071

Dick-Sagoe, C. (2020). Decentralization for improving the provision of public services in developing countries: A critical review. *Cogent Economics & Finance, 8*(1), 1804036. DOI: 10.1080/23322039.2020.1804036

Duong, H. (2021). The politicization of civil service recruitment and promotion in Vietnam. *Public Administration and Development, 41*(2), 51–62. DOI: 10.1002/pad.1910

Engdaw, B. D. (2020). The impact of quality public service delivery on customer satisfaction in Bahir Dar city administration: The case of Ginbot 20 sub-city. *International Journal of Public Administration, 43*(7), 644–654. DOI: 10.1080/01900692.2019.1644520

Filtenborg, A. F., Gaardboe, F., & Sigsgaard-Rasmussen, J. (2017). Experimental replication: An experimental test of the expectancy disconfirmation theory of citizen satisfaction. *Public Management Review, 19*(9), 1235–1250. DOI: 10.1080/14719037.2017.1295099

Guo, Y. (Ed.). (2024). *Digital Government and Public Interaction: Platforms, Chatbots, and Public Satisfaction: Platforms, Chatbots, and Public Satisfaction.* IGI Global. DOI: 10.4018/979-8-3693-3665-6

Hai, N. C., Le, V. T. P., Son, N. T., & Tuan, P. V. (2023). Evaluation of citizens' satisfaction with the quality of public administrative services in the Mekong Delta, Vietnam. *GeoJournal of Tourism and Geosites*, 48(2spl), 750–770

Jilke, S., & Baekgaard, M. (2020). The political psychology of citizen satisfaction: Does functional responsibility matter? *Journal of Public Administration: Research and Theory*, *30*(1), 130–143. DOI: 10.1093/jopart/muz012

Lanin, D., & Hermanto, N. (2019). The effect of service quality toward public satisfaction and public trust on local government in Indonesia. *International Journal of Social Economics*, *46*(3), 377–392. DOI: 10.1108/IJSE-04-2017-0151

Lapuente, V., & Van de Walle, S. (2020). The effects of new public management on the quality of public services. *Governance: An International Journal of Policy, Administration and Institutions*, *33*(3), 461–475. DOI: 10.1111/gove.12502

Li, H. (2021). An empirical research on the construction of a government website public satisfaction index model in China. [JGIM]. *Journal of Global Information Management*, *29*(5), 112–137. DOI: 10.4018/JGIM.20210901.oa7

Ngo, H. V., Edelenbos, J., & Gianoli, A. (2019). Community participation and local government capacity in Vietnam: Conditions for coproduction. *Public Administration and Development*, *39*(2), 104–118. DOI: 10.1002/pad.1844

Nguyen, C. V., Giang, L. T., Tran, A. N., & Do, H. T. (2021). Do good governance and public administration improve economic growth and poverty reduction? The case of Vietnam. *International Public Management Journal, 24*(1), 131–161. DOI: 10.1080/10967494.2019.1592793

Núnez-Barriopedro, E., Penelas-Leguía, A., López-Sanz, J. M., & Loranca-Valle, M. C. (2024). A public service management model as an antecedent for citizen satisfaction and fiscal policy. *Management Decision, 62*(2), 725–739. DOI: 10.1108/MD-11-2022-1547

Pham, H. N. (2018). Leadership and public sector reform in Vietnam. In *Leadership and public sector reform in Asia* (Vol. 30, pp. 127–149). Emerald Publishing Limited. DOI: 10.1108/S2053-769720180000030006

Pham, T. H., Hoang, T. T. H., Thalassinos, E. I., & Le, H. A. (2022). The impact of quality of public administration on local economic growth in Vietnam. *Journal of Risk and Financial Management, 15*(4), 158. DOI: 10.3390/jrfm15040158

Van de Walle, S. (2018). Explaining citizen satisfaction and dissatisfaction with public services. *The Palgrave handbook of public administration and management in Europe*, 227-241.

Van Ryzin, G. G. (2015). Service quality, administrative process, and citizens' evaluation of local government in the US. *Public Management Review, 17*(3), 425–442. DOI: 10.1080/14719037.2013.841456

Wong, S. L., Liu, H. T., & Cheng, L. J. (2011). Elucidating the relationship between satisfaction and citizen involvement in public administration. *Public Management Review, 13*(4), 595–618. DOI: 10.1080/14719037.2010.525032

Wulandari, D., Hamdi, M., & Sigit, W. (2024). Analysis of the Quality of Population Administration Services in Increasing Public Satisfaction In South Tangerang City. *Journal of Science, 13*(02), 1679–1694.

Zhang, J., Chen, W., Petrovsky, N., & Walker, R. M. (2022). The expectancy-disconfirmation model and citizen satisfaction with public services: A meta-analysis and an agenda for best practice. *Public Administration Review, 82*(1), 147–159. DOI: 10.1111/puar.13368

Chapter 10
The Invisible Load: Identity Struggles and Burnout in the Public Sector

Damla Koroglu Unver
https://orcid.org/0000-0001-9749-3152
Istanbul University, Turkey

ABSTRACT

Burnout in the public sector is a complex issue influenced by systemic inequities and identity-based stressors. This chapter examines the intersection of identity and burnout, focusing on how factors such as race, gender, and sexual orientation amplify vulnerabilities in public sector workplaces. Using Social Identity Theory and Intersectionality as analytical frameworks, the chapter explores the unique challenges faced by marginalized employees and provides actionable strategies to mitigate burnout. Key solutions include inclusive leadership development, equity audits, flexible work arrangements, and mentorship programs. By addressing identity-based inequities and fostering inclusive organizational cultures, public sector organizations can enhance employee well-being, improve performance, and strengthen trust with the communities they serve.

INTRODUCTION

Burnout, characterized by emotional exhaustion, depersonalization, and diminished personal accomplishment, poses a pervasive challenge across industries. Yet, its ramifications are particularly severe in the public sector, where employees grapple with high-stress environments, constrained resources, and the moral imperatives of serving diverse populations. These factors are further compounded by systemic

DOI: 10.4018/979-8-3373-0169-3.ch010

inequities, with identity-based dynamics—such as gender, race, sexual orientation, and socioeconomic status—creating unique and layered vulnerabilities to burnout.

The intersection of identity and burnout reveals profound disparities. Women of color, individuals with marginalized sexual orientations, and those from economically disadvantaged backgrounds often face "double jeopardy" in navigating both organizational and societal biases. Public sector employees frequently contend with microaggressions, exclusionary practices, and the emotional toll of representing underrepresented groups in leadership. These compounded stressors not only undermine individual well-being but also impair organizational performance and trust with the communities served.

This chapter draws on Social Identity Theory and Intersectionality to examine how identity-based stressors contribute to burnout in the public sector. These frameworks provide insight into how identity affiliations shape self-perception and workplace experience, and how overlapping systems of oppression intensify vulnerability to burnout.

The public sector workforce, by design, reflects the diversity of the populations it serves. However, this diversity often exists within the constraints of bureaucratic structures, high emotional labor demands, and limited autonomy. These factors contribute significantly to burnout, particularly for employees from marginalized backgrounds. Research indicates that women, individuals with marginalized sexual orientations, racial and ethnic minorities, and those with intersecting identities experience burnout at disproportionately higher rates due to systemic inequities and identity-based stressors (Ashikali et al., 2021; Roberson & Perry, 2022).

By addressing burnout through the lens of identity and intersectionality, this chapter highlights not only the human and organizational costs of inaction but also the transformative potential of inclusive practices. Creating equitable workplaces in the public sector is not merely an ethical imperative—it is a strategic necessity to enhance employee resilience, foster community trust, and ensure the effective delivery of public services.

The discussion unfolds in three key sections. The first provides a theoretical grounding in burnout, emphasizing its dimensions and relevance to public sector dynamics. The second section integrates empirical research and case studies to illustrate the intersectional challenges faced by marginalized employees. Finally, the chapter presents actionable solutions, including mentorship programs, equity audits, inclusive leadership development, and policy reforms, aimed at fostering equity and reducing burnout in public sector organizations. By integrating these perspectives, the chapter seeks to:

Explore the Influence of Identity: Examine how identity-based factors, such as race, gender, and sexual orientation, shape burnout experiences in the public sector.

Address Intersectionality: Highlight the compounded challenges faced by individuals with intersecting marginalized identities, emphasizing their unique vulnerabilities to burnout.

Provide Actionable Solutions: Offer evidence-based recommendations for creating inclusive policies and practices that mitigate burnout and promote equity.

By adding these elements, the chapter not only provides a comprehensive analysis of burnout but also positions identity and intersectionality as central to understanding and addressing this pervasive issue. This approach ensures that the chapter aligns with both theoretical insights and practical applications, offering a roadmap for fostering equity and well-being in public sector workplaces.

THEORETICAL FRAMEWORK

Burnout Syndrome

Burnout was initially explored in the healthcare sector during the 1970s, primarily focusing on professionals such as doctors, nurses, and social workers. Freudenberger's groundbreaking work on burnout among clinical volunteers laid the foundation for further exploration into the syndrome. Burnout, a term first introduced by Freudenberger (1974), refers to a state of physical and emotional depletion caused by prolonged exposure to demanding work environments. Freudenberger observed this phenomenon in clinical workers and defined it as "*a condition of fatigue or frustration brought about by devotion to a cause, way of life, or relationship that failed to produce the expected reward.*"

Later, Maslach and Jackson (1981) expanded on this concept, describing burnout as a multidimensional syndrome encompassing emotional exhaustion, depersonalization, and a reduced sense of personal accomplishment. This framework became the cornerstone for understanding burnout and remains widely cited in both academic and practical discussions of workplace well-being. By the 1980s, Maslach and Jackson's development of the Maslach Burnout Inventory (MBI) provided a robust tool for assessing burnout, enabling researchers to standardize measurements across diverse populations.

In the 1990s and 2000s, research expanded to include various professions beyond healthcare, such as teaching, law enforcement, and corporate sectors. During this period, studies began to emphasize the systemic and organizational factors contributing to burnout, moving beyond individual traits and behaviors. Contemporary research continues to explore burnout's multifaceted nature, including its intersection with technology, remote work, and the evolving demands of modern workplaces. Burnout is characterized by three core dimensions:

Emotional Exhaustion

Emotional exhaustion is the primary and most evident symptom of burnout. It reflects feelings of being emotionally overextended and drained by work demands. Employees experiencing emotional exhaustion often report chronic fatigue, lack of energy, and an inability to recover from work-related stress (Maslach et al., 2001). This dimension is strongly influenced by high workload, emotional labor, and persistent stressors in the workplace. Research highlights that emotional exhaustion is not limited to physical tiredness but also affects psychological and social well-being, often leading to sleep disturbances and interpersonal conflicts. Emotional exhaustion also fosters a sense of detachment from the organization, as employees feel incapable of fulfilling job requirements. This can result in absenteeism and even complete withdrawal from the workplace.

Depersonalization (Cynicism)

This dimension involves a detached or impersonal response toward the recipients of one's work. For example, healthcare workers may begin treating patients as cases rather than individuals, developing cynical attitudes to cope with their workload. Depersonalization creates a barrier between employees and the people they serve, leading to strained relationships and reduced empathy (Maslach, 2003). This detachment often manifests as a defense mechanism to shield oneself from emotional exhaustion. Employees exhibiting high depersonalization levels may display irritability, reduced patience, and a lack of interest in collaborative work. Depersonalization also extends to colleagues and organizational culture, where employees may adopt a "bare minimum" approach, disengaging from shared goals and values.

Reduced Personal Accomplishment

Burnout affects employees' self-efficacy and competence. Workers feel they are no longer making meaningful contributions, leading to diminished motivation and satisfaction with their achievements (Schaufeli & Enzmann, 2020). This dimension erodes professional self-esteem and can trigger feelings of inadequacy and failure. Employees may experience "imposter syndrome," believing their efforts are insufficient or undervalued.

Over time, reduced personal accomplishment compounds the psychological toll of burnout, creating a vicious cycle where diminished confidence leads to lower performance and further dissatisfaction. This is particularly pronounced in professions requiring creativity or high-stakes decision-making, where perceived failures are more personal and impactful.

Burnout: Causes, Dynamics, and Its Multifaceted Impacts

Burnout is not simply synonymous with stress; it is the chronic, unmanaged progression of stress into a state of emotional collapse. Lazarus and Folkman (1984) differentiate between stress as a temporary response to external demands and burnout as the long-term consequence of stress exceeding coping resources.

Stress can be categorized into two types: Acute stress is a short-term response to specific challenges or events and typically resolves once the challenge is addressed. For instance, meeting a project deadline may be stressful but manageable with adequate resources and time. On the other hand, chronic stress results from ongoing challenges such as high workloads, poor management, or interpersonal conflicts, and when coping mechanisms are insufficient, it often becomes a precursor to burnout.

Burnout is influenced by a range of interconnected factors that affect employees' emotional and physical well-being. One of the primary contributors is workload imbalance. Prolonged exposure to excessive workloads places significant strain on individuals, leading to heightened levels of emotional exhaustion and physical fatigue. Employees in high-stress roles, such as emergency responders, educators, and healthcare professionals, are particularly susceptible to workload-related burnout due to the demanding nature of their responsibilities and the constant pressure to perform at high levels.

Another critical factor is role conflict and ambiguity. When employees face conflicting job responsibilities or unclear expectations, their stress levels are likely to escalate. This uncertainty can create feelings of inadequacy and frustration, particularly when employees perceive a lack of support or guidance from supervisors. The combination of unclear roles and insufficient direction can leave individuals feeling undervalued and overwhelmed, further intensifying symptoms of burnout.

Lack of social support also plays a significant role in exacerbating burnout. Employees who experience limited emotional or practical assistance from supervisors, colleagues, or family members often feel isolated and disconnected. This lack of support contributes to depersonalization, a core dimension of burnout characterized by a sense of detachment from work and others. On the other hand, strong social networks can act as a protective factor, buffering against the effects of stress and providing much-needed emotional reassurance and practical help.

Maslach et al. (2001) emphasize the critical role of organizational dynamics in shaping burnout experiences. Systemic factors such as workplace culture, management practices, and resource availability significantly influence employee well-being. For instance, organizations with rigid, hierarchical structures and inflexible policies often report higher burnout rates. These environments limit employees' autonomy and create a perceived lack of control over their work, fostering feelings of helplessness and dissatisfaction. Addressing these systemic issues is essential for reducing burnout and fostering healthier, more supportive workplace environments.

In addition to these systemic factors, the emotional labor often required in service-oriented professions plays a significant role in exacerbating burnout. When combined with organizational dynamics, the constant demand for emotional regulation further increases the risk of burnout among employees. Emotional labor refers to the process of managing emotions to fulfill job requirements, often seen in service-oriented professions (Hochschild, 1983). This constant regulation of emotions can lead to emotional exhaustion, a central component of burnout. Employees in roles requiring frequent emotional labor, such as healthcare professionals, social workers, and educators, are particularly vulnerable.

Employees in roles requiring frequent emotional labor may engage in surface acting, where they fake emotional expressions to meet job expectations, or deep acting, where they attempt to align their internal emotions with organizational demands. Surface acting is particularly associated with higher levels of burnout because it creates a disconnect between internal feelings and external expressions, adding to emotional strain. Additionally, in caregiving professions, constant exposure to others' suffering can lead to compassion fatigue, a state closely linked to burnout. This condition often results in professionals struggling to maintain empathy, which not only reduces the quality of care they provide but also increases their emotional exhaustion.

The emotional strain caused by frequent emotional labor, particularly surface acting and compassion fatigue, not only exacerbates burnout but also contributes to its far-reaching consequences for individuals and organizations alike. On an individual level, chronic burnout can lead to physical and mental health issues such as anxiety, depression, and cardiovascular problems (Maslach et al., 2001). Emotional exhaustion impairs cognitive functioning, decision-making, and interpersonal relationships, while individuals may also suffer from sleep disturbances, reduced immunity, and a decline in overall well-being. Prolonged burnout is further associated with substance abuse and an increased risk of suicidal ideation.

On an organizational level, high burnout rates are linked to increased absenteeism, reduced productivity, and high employee turnover, which erode workplace morale and disrupt team dynamics, ultimately diminishing organizational performance (Schaufeli et al., 2009). Burnout also results in decreased innovation and employee engagement, both critical for maintaining a competitive edge in dynamic industries. Additionally, the financial costs of burnout are considerable, as organizations face expenses related to recruitment, training, and healthcare for affected employees. Proactively addressing burnout can help mitigate these costs and promote a healthier workplace culture.

Burnout in the Public Sector: Unique Challenges

The hierarchical structure and bureaucratic processes of the public sector often create an environment where employees experience limited control over decision making. This lack of autonomy contributes to feelings of helplessness and exacerbates stress and burnout. Sarisik et al. (2019) emphasize that excessive regulation and constrained authority can lead to reduced job satisfaction and decreased motivation among public employees. Additionally, Golembiewski et al. (1998) highlight that the rigidity of public sector institutions makes it challenging for employees to adapt to evolving job demands, further amplifying burnout levels.

Public sector employees frequently face high workloads and constant exposure to crisis situations, such as natural disasters, public health emergencies, and socio-political upheavals. These conditions require sustained emotional and physical effort, often without adequate resources or support. For instance, Rajan and Engelbrecht (2018) found that healthcare professionals in public emergency centers experienced heightened levels of emotional exhaustion and depersonalization due to high patient loads and life-or-death decision-making scenarios. Addressing these challenges requires a focus on workload management and crisis preparedness initiatives.

These persistent challenges underscore that the public sector provides a unique and critical context for examining burnout due to its service-oriented nature and societal impact. Unlike private sector roles, public sector jobs are often mission-driven and directly influence community well-being. Golembiewski et al. (1998) argue that burnout in public sector roles, such as education, healthcare, and emergency services, has cascading effects on public service quality and organizational performance.

As discussed earlier, emotional labor plays a particularly acute role in public service professions. Educators, healthcare workers, and social service providers often engage in sustained emotional regulation to meet the needs of diverse populations. Pérez-Luño et al. (2022) note that the COVID-19 pandemic intensified these demands, particularly for educators transitioning to remote instruction and navigating increased expectations from parents and students. This highlights the need for targeted mental health support and training to help employees cope with the emotional aspects of their roles.

Service-oriented public sector roles demand high levels of empathy, patience, and resilience. The persistent requirement to serve vulnerable populations adds emotional strain, increasing susceptibility to burnout. Shanafelt et al. (2012) emphasize that these roles often involve significant psychological demands, which—when coupled with resource limitations—further exacerbate burnout risks.

The diversity of tasks and populations served in the public sector creates additional stressors. Managing crises while addressing the needs of marginalized groups requires employees to constantly adapt and innovate. This dynamic environment, while fulfilling, can also lead to increased stress if not supported by effective leadership and inclusive workplace cultures. Studies suggest that such environments can mitigate the adverse effects of burnout (Pérez-Luño et al., 2022).

Burnout manifests differently across various professional fields due to the unique demands and challenges associated with each sector. Understanding these distinctions is particularly important for the public sector, where the societal impact of burnout is significant, particularly in high-stakes roles such as emergency healthcare, where rapid decisions under pressure are the norm.

Healthcare: Healthcare professionals often face intense emotional labor, high patient loads, and life-or-death decision-making scenarios. These stressors make them particularly vulnerable to emotional exhaustion and depersonalization. Studies, such as Rajan and Engelbrecht (2018), highlight that over 66% of public healthcare professionals in emergency centers exhibit high levels of emotional exhaustion and depersonalization. Burnout in this sector not only affects individual well-being but also compromises patient care quality and safety, increasing medical errors and staff turnover. In public healthcare settings, limited resources and overcrowding exacerbate these challenges, necessitating systemic interventions. Research underscores the importance of improving staffing ratios and providing mental health support to mitigate burnout's impact (Dwinijanti et al., 2020).

Education: While burnout among healthcare professionals is exacerbated by resource constraints and overcrowding, educators face a different set of challenges, including excessive workloads and the emotional labor required to address diverse student needs. Teachers and educators frequently encounter burnout due to excessive workloads, large class sizes, and limited resources. Emotional labor is a significant factor, as educators must maintain patience and empathy while managing diverse student needs. Pérez-Luño et al. (2022) found that educators in public schools were particularly affected during the COVID-19 pandemic, with stressors such as adapting to remote teaching and increased demands from parents and students. Burnout in this sector often leads to high turnover rates and reduced student outcomes. Public sector educators are especially vulnerable due to bureaucratic constraints and insufficient recognition for their efforts. Addressing these issues requires a comprehensive approach, including workload management and enhanced professional development opportunities (Serin & Balkan, 2014).

Public Administration: Public administration roles come with their own distinct stressors, including job security concerns, limited autonomy, and heightened political pressures. Kim (2018) emphasizes that intrinsic motivation plays a crucial role in reducing burnout and turnover intention among public sector employees. Public administration roles are also characterized by heightened scrutiny and political pressures, which can further increase stress levels. Promoting a culture of recognition and providing flexible work options can alleviate these challenges (Sarisik et al., 2019).

Emergency Services: The high-stakes nature of emergency services—law enforcement, firefighting, and paramedics—introduces unique stressors, including exposure to traumatic events and physical danger. These conditions significantly heighten the risk of burnout. Golembiewski et al. (1998) report alarmingly high burnout rates in public emergency services. Addressing this requires access to counseling services, peer support, and resilience training initiatives tailored to the demands of these professions.

Social Work: Social workers face persistent emotional challenges from handling cases involving abuse, neglect, or poverty. These emotional demands, combined with bureaucratic constraints, make them particularly susceptible to burnout. Research indicates that public sector social workers experience higher depersonalization than their private sector counterparts due to limited resources and overwhelming caseloads (Dwinijanti et al., 2020). Effective strategies include ensuring manageable caseloads, providing regular supervision, and supporting professional growth.

Burnout in the public sector is not only a personal health issue but also a broader organizational and societal concern. Public employees in education, healthcare, law enforcement, and social services directly impact community well-being. High burnout rates in these areas can reduce service quality, increase absenteeism, and drive turnover, adding strain to already overburdened systems (Sarisik et al., 2019; Golembiewski et al., 1998).

Moreover, public sector organizations frequently operate under constrained budgets and bureaucratic structures, limiting their capacity for sweeping reform. Nevertheless, targeted interventions—such as creating supportive environments, offering mental health resources, and recognizing employee contributions—can meaningfully reduce burnout (Kim, 2018; Pérez-Luño et al., 2022). By understanding how burnout manifests across public roles, organizational leaders can develop strategies that promote well-being and ensure the sustainability of public services.

Social Identity Theory and Burnout

Social Identity Theory (SIT) was developed by Henri Tajfel and John Turner in the late 1970s as a framework to understand how individuals derive their self-concept from group memberships. This groundbreaking theory emerged as a response to the limitations of individual-centric models of intergroup behavior, which often neglected the collective dimensions of identity and social dynamics (Turner et al., 1979; Hornsey, 2008)

Tajfel's early work on the Minimal Group Paradigm demonstrated that even arbitrary group distinctions could lead to in-group favoritism and out-group discrimination. This experiment revealed that people's mere categorization into groups was sufficient to elicit biased behavior. These findings laid the foundation for SIT, which posited that group identity significantly influences self-concept and intergroup relations (Tajfel, 1970; Abrams & Hogg, 1990).

Over time, SIT evolved to include complementary frameworks, such as Self-Categorization Theory (Maines, 1989). which focuses on the cognitive processes underpinning group identification. Together, these theories form the "social identity approach," providing a robust lens to examine group behavior, intergroup dynamics, and identity-related phenomena (Trepte & Loy, 2017).

As a framework for understanding how individuals define themselves through group affiliations, SIT rests on key mechanisms such as social categorization, identification, and comparison. This cognitive process simplifies complex social interactions by creating clear boundaries between in-groups and out-groups. However, it also reinforces distinctions that can lead to biases and intergroup tensions (Turner, 1985).

Another key aspect is *social identification*, where individuals internalize the norms, values, and behaviors of their in-group. This identification strengthens group loyalty and significantly impacts self-esteem, as individuals derive a sense of pride and belonging from their association with the group (Ashforth & Mael, 1989; Islam, 2014). By adopting the identity of their group, individuals align their behaviors and attitudes with group expectations, which can influence their actions in organizational and social contexts.

Social comparison is a natural extension of identification, as individuals evaluate their in-group against relevant out-groups to maintain or enhance their self-esteem. Favorable comparisons elevate group identity, while unfavorable comparisons may prompt strategies to improve the group's status or even lead individuals to distance themselves from the group (Huddy, 2001; Knippenberg & Ellemers, 1990). This process helps explain why individuals are motivated to achieve positive distinctions for their group in competitive or hierarchical settings.

A consequence of strong group identification is in-group bias and out-group discrimination, where individuals favor members of their in-group while displaying biased or discriminatory attitudes toward out-group members. This phenomenon is central to understanding intergroup conflict, prejudice, and social hierarchies. In-group favoritism and out-group hostility have been widely observed in various social and organizational settings, contributing to the persistence of inequities and tensions (Hornsey, 2008; Hogg et al., 1995).

SIT in Organizational Contexts

In organizational contexts, SIT sheds light on how employees' identification with their organization influences their commitment, performance, and reactions to intergroup dynamics. Strong organizational identification fosters a sense of belonging and purpose, which has been shown to mitigate burnout by buffering against stressors and enhancing resilience (Ashforth & Mael, 1989; Trepte & Loy, 2017). Employees who strongly identify with their organization often exhibit higher levels of motivation and job satisfaction, as they perceive their contributions as aligned with the group's goals.

SIT is also pivotal in understanding intergroup relations and conflict. The theory explains how group identities contribute to biases such as ethnocentrism, nationalism, and workplace discrimination. By emphasizing the role of identity in shaping intergroup dynamics, SIT offers insights into reducing intergroup tensions and promoting more inclusive environments (Turner et al., 1979; Abrams & Hogg, 1990). Interventions based on SIT often focus on enhancing shared group identities to reduce divisive behaviors and foster collaboration.

For marginalized groups, SIT reveals how identity-based stressors contribute to burnout. Individuals facing systemic discrimination, microaggressions, or identity threats often experience heightened emotional exhaustion and depersonalization. For example, women in male-dominated industries or LGBTQ+ employees managing identity concealment pressures are particularly vulnerable to burnout due to the ongoing demands of social comparisons and identity management (Hornsey, 2008). These experiences highlight the need for supportive organizational policies that mitigate identity-related stress and foster inclusive environments.

Critiques and Emerging Directions

While Social Identity Theory has offered a robust framework for understanding identity and group behavior, it has also faced several critiques and limitations. One key critique involves its underemphasis on broader cultural and historical contexts. Critics argue that SIT does not fully account for how societal structures, historical legacies, and cultural norms influence identity formation and intergroup dynamics. For example, Huddy (2001) and Knippenberg & Ellemers (1990) argue that identity processes cannot be entirely disentangled from the cultural and historical environments in which they occur. This limitation points to the need for more integrative approaches that situate identity within larger societal frameworks.

Another significant challenge lies in the operationalization of social identity. Measuring subjective aspects of identity, such as salience and behavioral influence, remains complex. This difficulty limits the theory's applicability in contexts that require precise, quantifiable assessments of identity-driven behaviors (Brown, 2000). Despite its conceptual strength, SIT's practical utility can be hindered by these methodological constraints.

In response to these critiques, recent advancements in identity research have enriched SIT's explanatory power. For instance, studies on intersectionality explore how overlapping social identities—such as race, gender, and sexual orientation—shape individual experiences in multifaceted ways. Similarly, research on identity salience examines how the prominence of specific identities shifts depending on situational and contextual factors, adding depth to SIT's understanding of group dynamics.

Implications for Burnout

In the context of burnout, Social Identity Theory (SIT) offers valuable insights into how identity-related stressors amplify emotional exhaustion and depersonalization. Social identity threat arises when individuals perceive their group identity as undervalued, stereotyped, or excluded (Steele et al., 2002). This form of stress is particularly salient for marginalized groups, where systemic biases and microaggressions exacerbate psychological distress.

For instance, Hall et al. (2015) found that women in STEM fields frequently encounter subtle cues of exclusion during workplace interactions, contributing to mental exhaustion and disengagement. Similarly, marginalized individuals experiencing overlapping forms of discrimination often face heightened identity-based pressures that can compound burnout symptoms (Lammers et al., 2013). These overlapping stressors, commonly described as intersectional threats, will be explored more deeply in the next section.

Another critical factor is emotional labor—the process of managing one's emotions to meet organizational expectations. This burden disproportionately affects women and minority employees, who often feel pressure to regulate their behavior or suppress aspects of their identity to avoid confirming stereotypes (Cheng et al., 2016). Emotional labor functions as both a coping strategy and a stressor, particularly in environments where authenticity is constrained.

Nurses, for example, often engage in high levels of emotional labor to balance patient care with institutional demands. While strong professional identity can buffer against burnout, it may also intensify emotional strain when one's role is undervalued or unsupported (Cheng et al., 2016). This duality underscores the need for inclusive organizational cultures that validate diverse identities and reduce identity-based stress.

Recent large-scale surveys such as the Federal Employee Viewpoint Survey (U.S. OPM, 2022) and the UK Civil Service People Survey (UK Cabinet Office, 2021) reinforce these patterns, reporting burnout rates exceeding 60% among women, LGBTQ+ employees, and racial minorities in the public sector. These data underscore the systemic nature of identity-related burnout and validate the theoretical links discussed here.

Public sector organizational structures can also perpetuate burnout. Hierarchical rigidity, limited career advancement, and insufficient managerial support intensify emotional labor and limit autonomy (Kim & Fernandez, 2017). These institutional dynamics reinforce identity-related stress and highlight the need for structural reforms. These dynamics, especially as they intersect with multiple social identities, are elaborated in the following section.

Intersectionality Theory

Intersectionality, a concept introduced by Kimberlé Crenshaw in her seminal works "Demarginalizing the Intersection of Race and Sex" (1989) and "Mapping the Margins" (1991), critiques single-axis frameworks of discrimination that overlook how overlapping social identities—such as race, gender, class, and sexuality—interact to shape lived experiences. Crenshaw's metaphor of a traffic intersection illustrates how multiple forms of oppression can collide and intensify one another, emphasizing that analyzing identity categories in isolation is insufficient (Crenshaw, 1989; 1991).

The roots of intersectionality are grounded in Black feminist thought, including foundational contributions such as the Combahee River Collective (1977), Frances Beal's concept of "double jeopardy" (1970), and Deborah King's "multiple jeopardy" (1988), all of which underscore how interlocking systems of oppression uniquely affect Black women and other marginalized groups (Carastathis, 2014).

At its core, intersectionality provides a multidimensional framework for analyzing how structures such as patriarchy, racism, capitalism, and heteronormativity interact. One of its key principles is the simultaneity of oppressions, which posits that individuals experience multiple systems of discrimination at once, not sequentially. For instance, a Black woman in the workforce may face bias that cannot be reduced to either race or gender alone, but emerges from the interaction of both (Crenshaw, 1989; McCall, 2005).

Another foundational principle is contextual specificity, emphasizing that oppression manifests differently across social, cultural, and historical settings. For example, Afghan refugee women in Western countries face layered challenges—from racial stereotyping to cultural displacement—demonstrating the need to account for local sociopolitical contexts in intersectional analysis (Samuels & Ross-Sheriff, 2008).

Intersectionality also reveals the relational nature of power, showing that individuals may simultaneously experience both marginalization and privilege. A white, middle-class woman may encounter sexism while still benefiting from racial and economic advantages—challenging simplistic binaries of victim and oppressor (Walby et al., 2012).

Crucially, the theory emphasizes structural and systemic causes of inequality rather than attributing disadvantage to individual behavior. Institutions, cultural norms, and policies often operate together to uphold systems of exclusion, such as in hiring discrimination or the underrepresentation of certain groups in leadership (Cho et al., 2013).

Applications of Intersectionality

Through these core principles, intersectionality provides a powerful analytical framework for examining how multiple systems of oppression intersect to shape experiences in various contexts. Its applications span workplace inequality, social justice initiatives, healthcare disparities, and global human rights advocacy, highlighting the importance of addressing interconnected forms of discrimination to promote equity and inclusion. The following sections illustrate how intersectionality applies across various domains, beginning with workplace dynamics.

Workplace Inequality: One significant application of intersectionality is in understanding workplace inequality. Intersectionality reveals how race, gender, and class intersect to influence career progression, workplace experiences, and power dynamics. For example, women of color are often underrepresented in leadership roles due to systemic biases that disadvantage them based on their intersecting identities. These biases manifest in discriminatory hiring practices, limited access to mentorship opportunities, and heightened scrutiny in professional settings, which collectively hinder their career advancement (Lammers et al., 2013;). Intersectionality helps identify these overlapping barriers and provides insights into creating more equitable workplace policies and practices.

Violence Against Women: Another critical area where intersectionality has been applied is in addressing violence against women. Crenshaw (1991) highlighted how anti-domestic violence programs often failed to address the specific needs of women of color. These programs primarily focused on gender while neglecting the intersections of race and socioeconomic status, thereby marginalizing those most vulnerable to violence. For example, women of color may face unique barriers to accessing support services, including language obstacles, fear of law enforcement, or cultural stigmas. Intersectionality underscores the need for inclusive anti-violence strategies that address these compounded vulnerabilities.

Burnout and Class-Based Stress: In addition to identity-based stressors such as race and gender, class-related factors significantly influence burnout risk in the public sector. Lower-wage employees—such as administrative staff, custodians, and clerical workers—often face high workloads, limited recognition, and minimal decision-making power. Research shows that these "working poor" employees often experience economic scarcity, which impairs cognitive bandwidth, increases emotional exhaustion, and diminishes workplace performance (Meuris & Leana, 2015; Mullainathan & Shafir, 2013).

Despite being essential to daily operations, these roles are frequently excluded from organizational inclusion efforts and leadership development programs. The chronic stress of job insecurity, suppressed wages, and limited upward mobility can create a "scarcity trap"—a cycle of stress and cognitive overload that perpetuates burnout and disengagement (Haushofer & Fehr, 2014; Mullainathan & Shafir, 2013). Expanding burnout discourse to include class-based dimensions is therefore essential for designing equitable and comprehensive well-being interventions in the public sector.

Healthcare Disparities: In healthcare, intersectionality has been instrumental in understanding systemic disparities. For instance, Black women in the United States experience significantly higher rates of maternal mortality than their white counterparts, a disparity linked to the compounded effects of racial and gender discrimination. These inequities are further exacerbated by class-based barriers, such as limited access to quality healthcare and economic instability (Walby et al., 2012). Intersectional analysis in healthcare helps identify how these overlapping systems of oppression create barriers to care, guiding the development of policies and interventions that address structural inequities.

Through its structural, contextual, and relational focus, intersectionality offers a comprehensive lens for understanding the complex interplay of identity and oppression. It moves beyond single-axis models by revealing how hierarchies of power are maintained and experienced differently depending on the convergence of identities. This framework not only deepens our theoretical understanding of inequality but also provides actionable insights for crafting inclusive policies and social justice interventions.

Implications for Burnout

Intersectionality elucidates how overlapping social identities, particularly those involving marginalized statuses, intensify stressors that contribute to burnout. For instance, individuals who simultaneously navigate multiple axes of marginalization—such as a Black lesbian woman in a corporate environment—encounter compounded microaggressions, systemic biases, and isolation. These experiences accumulate as chronic stress, elevating the risk of emotional exhaustion and psychological disengagement. Research by Teshome et al. (2022) highlights that medical students with intersecting marginalized identities report significantly higher burnout rates due to a combination of mistreatment, perceived incompetence by peers, and lack of institutional support. This underscores the need to address intersectional inequities as a core strategy in mitigating burnout in diverse workplace contexts.

The compounding effects of identity-based stress are particularly evident in high-stakes professions, such as healthcare and education, where marginalized employees often face greater scrutiny. For example, women of color in these sectors frequently report being judged more harshly for mistakes or being excluded from critical decision-making processes, which exacerbates their feelings of inadequacy and isolation. Such dynamics, when left unaddressed, perpetuate a cycle of stress and disengagement, further reinforcing structural inequities.

Furthermore, the absence of inclusive organizational cultures intensifies the impact of intersecting oppressions. Organizations that fail to recognize and validate diverse experiences inadvertently contribute to identity-based stress. Incorporating intersectionality into workplace policies and practices can alleviate these challenges by fostering an environment that acknowledges and respects the complexities of identity.

One significant manifestation of the lack of recognition for diverse experiences is the prevalence of microaggressions in the workplace. Microaggressions, which are subtle yet pervasive forms of discrimination, disproportionately affect individuals with intersecting marginalized identities, amplifying their workplace stress and risk of burnout. Kim et al. (2024) found that mothers of color in professional settings endure additional workplace stress due to the dual burden of microaggressions and traditional gender role expectations, directly correlating to higher levels of emotional exhaustion.

The emotional toll of microaggressions is further intensified by the lack of acknowledgment or redress within organizational settings. When employees feel that their concerns about discriminatory behaviors are dismissed or minimized, it reinforces a sense of powerlessness and frustration. This, in turn, contributes to disengagement and reduced workplace productivity, creating a feedback loop that perpetuates burnout. Addressing the impact of microaggressions requires proactive organizational strategies, including bias awareness training, clear reporting mechanisms, and leadership accountability. By creating an environment where employees feel supported in addressing discriminatory behaviors, organizations can mitigate the psychological burden on marginalized groups and reduce burnout risk.

Another critical aspect of addressing the psychological burden on marginalized groups is recognizing the disproportionate emotional labor they undertake in navigating workplaces where their identities are undervalued or scrutinized. Emotional labor, the effort required to manage emotions and maintain professional decorum, is disproportionately shouldered by marginalized groups. Women and minority employees often engage in extensive emotional labor to navigate workplaces where their identities are undervalued or scrutinized. For example, Black women in public service roles frequently perform "identity management" behaviors, such as suppressing authentic expressions or overcompensating to counteract stereotypes. These behaviors, while often necessary for professional survival, contribute to emotional exhaustion and depersonalization.

An et al. (2024) demonstrated that Black women in local government positions engage in significantly more uncompensated extra-role behaviors, such as mentoring and advocating for equity, compared to their peers. While these efforts foster organizational improvement, they also place an additional emotional burden on individuals who are already navigating systemic biases. This dual responsibility intensifies the risk of burnout, highlighting the need for equitable workload distribution and recognition of invisible labor.

Furthermore, the intersection of emotional labor and identity is particularly evident in caregiving professions. Nurses and educators with marginalized identities report higher levels of burnout due to the compounded pressures of meeting both professional and societal expectations. By acknowledging and addressing these unique stressors, organizations can create more supportive environments that reduce the emotional burden on diverse employees.

This intersection of emotional labor and identity becomes even more pronounced in the healthcare sector, where workers with intersecting marginalized identities, such as female physicians of color, face unique challenges that exacerbate their stress levels. Healthcare workers with intersecting marginalized identities, such as female physicians of color, face unique challenges that exacerbate their stress levels. Cawcutt et al. (2021) emphasize that biases, combined with the imposter phenomenon, contribute significantly to burnout in this group. These physicians often report feelings of inadequacy despite their accomplishments, a phenomenon linked to systemic biases that undermine their professional credibility.

The intersectional burden of burnout in healthcare is particularly visible in work-life balance disparities. Many women of color manage caregiving responsibilities alongside high-pressure professional demands, leading to disproportionately high levels of emotional exhaustion. Addressing these inequities requires systemic efforts—such as flexible scheduling, inclusive mentorship opportunities, and anti-discrimination initiatives.

Moreover, organizational culture plays a pivotal role in either mitigating or amplifying identity-based stress. Healthcare institutions that actively promote diversity and inclusion tend to report lower burnout rates among underrepresented groups. Advancing equitable career pathways and cultivating inclusive leadership are essential strategies for improving workplace well-being and resilience.

INTERACTION BETWEEN BURNOUT AND IDENTITY-BASED DISCRIMINATION

Burnout and identity-based discrimination are deeply interconnected, with discrimination exacerbating the stressors that lead to emotional exhaustion, depersonalization, and reduced personal accomplishment. Marginalized employees—such as women of color, LGBTQ+ individuals, and those at the intersection of multiple minority identities—often face exclusionary practices, microaggressions, and heightened scrutiny that intensify workplace strain (Lammers et al., 2013; Kim et al., 2024).

These dynamics are particularly harmful in high-contact professions like healthcare and education, where employees manage both professional demands and identity-based vigilance. For instance, closeted LGBTQ+ staff and transgender employees in public-facing roles report high burnout levels due to identity concealment and lack of inclusive policies (Cawcutt et al., 2021; Walby et al., 2012).

A key factor is identity threat—the perception that one's identity is undervalued—which is reinforced by daily microaggressions and limited institutional support. This threat undermines belonging and leads to disengagement, especially in rigid public sector environments where conformity often overrides inclusion (Lammers et al., 2013).

Some individuals cope through overcompensation strategies such as John Henryism—a pattern of high-effort striving in response to systemic barriers—which may yield short-term success but leads to long-term emotional and physical depletion (Watson, 2024). This is particularly common among racial and gender minorities under biased scrutiny in fields like STEM and healthcare.

Systemic organizational inequities—such as lack of mentorship, inclusive leadership, and anti-discrimination protections—further entrench these stressors (Ryus et al., 2022; McCall, 2005). In the public sector, where emotional labor is already high, the absence of support mechanisms disproportionately affects marginalized employees.

Understanding burnout through an intersectional lens is therefore essential. The next sections will explore how specific identity intersections—such as gender, race, sexual orientation, immigration status, and class—shape burnout experiences and illuminate targeted strategies for change.

Gender, Race, and Emotional Labor

Burnout experiences are deeply shaped by the intersection of gender and race, particularly for women of color in leadership roles. These individuals often face heightened scrutiny and systemic barriers not encountered by their peers. In addition to overt discrimination, internalized pressure to defy stereotypes adds to the emotional burden, contributing to chronic exhaustion and depersonalization. Research in sectors such as education and refugee support highlights how systemic inequities disproportionately burden women of color, emphasizing the need for intersectionally-informed workplace training (Sagaltici et al., 2022).

These challenges are further intensified by the "double jeopardy" of racial and gender biases. Women of color in leadership are expected to perform at higher standards with less organizational support (Lammers et al., 2013; Watson, 2024). This convergence of bias amplifies emotional labor and reduces access to institutional resources, underscoring the need for structural reforms to dismantle inequities in leadership pipelines.

The burdens intensify for working mothers of color, who navigate both workplace discrimination and caregiving responsibilities. The "motherhood penalty" limits access to promotions, parental leave, and other supports, placing additional stress on women already contending with racial and gender-based exclusion (Kim et al., 2024). In contrast, fathers often benefit from the "fatherhood premium," receiving positive recognition for parenting without the same penalties. This inequity reinforces gendered workplace expectations and heightens burnout risk for mothers balancing intersecting roles (Lyonette & Crompton, 2015).

Women, especially from ethnic minority backgrounds, are also disproportionately tasked with invisible emotional labor—roles such as mentoring, mediating team conflict, or managing morale. These responsibilities, while critical to workplace cohesion, are rarely acknowledged or compensated. During the COVID-19 pandemic, for example, women healthcare workers reported significantly higher emotional exhaustion due to increased caregiving demands and systemic discrimination (Khan et al., 2021).

Traditional gender norms further exacerbate burnout by assigning emotional management tasks to women. Redistributing emotional labor more equitably and implementing policies that challenge gendered expectations are vital for alleviating stress and promoting gender equity in professional settings (Kim et al., 2024).

Sexual Orientation and Workplace Exclusion

Employees with marginalized sexual orientations face distinct challenges in the workplace, where systemic discrimination and exclusionary practices contribute significantly to burnout. One of the most persistent stressors is the pressure to conceal one's sexual identity to avoid bias. This concealment demands continuous emotional regulation, leading to psychological distress over time. Research shows that individuals who feel compelled to hide their sexual identity report higher rates of emotional exhaustion and depersonalization compared to those who feel safe expressing themselves (Kim et al., 2024).

These stressors are intensified in emotionally demanding professions such as mental health care. Sexual minority therapists, for instance, often manage client biases and workplace microaggressions while navigating their own identity-related stress. Viehl and Dispenza (2015) found that mental health professionals with marginalized sexual orientations report higher burnout levels than their heterosexual counterparts due to persistent exclusion and lack of institutional support.

Microaggressions compound burnout risk. Heteronormative assumptions and exclusion from informal professional networks create a persistent sense of alienation. In medical education, students with marginalized sexual or gender identities report elevated burnout levels due to perceived mistreatment and lack of inclusive learning environments (Ryus et al., 2022).

Structural heterosexism also plays a critical role. Organizations that fail to implement inclusive policies or protect against identity-based bias contribute to the ongoing emotional strain of professionals with marginalized sexual or gender identities. Without protections or representation in leadership, these individuals remain vulnerable to chronic stress and burnout (Watson, 2024).

Acculturative Stress, Social Class, and Immigrant Burnout

Burnout risk in the public sector is significantly shaped by both social class and migration status, which generate distinct yet often intersecting stressors. Workers in lower-income or hourly roles—such as aides, custodial staff, and administrative personnel—frequently contend with high workloads, limited recognition, and job insecurity. These employees often perform essential yet invisible labor, which is neither adequately compensated nor institutionally acknowledged. Economic scarcity erodes cognitive bandwidth, heightens emotional exhaustion, and contributes to disengagement and fatigue (Meuris & Leana, 2015; Mullainathan & Shafir, 2013). Social class disadvantage, when left unaddressed, reinforces long-term burnout trajectories by restricting access to wellness resources and advancement opportunities.

For immigrant employees, class-based stressors are intensified by acculturative stress—the psychological burden of adapting to new cultural, linguistic, and institutional environments. This dual strain is particularly evident in caregiving and education roles, where immigrant workers face both emotional labor demands and systemic exclusion. As Varma (2024) notes, navigating unfamiliar norms while receiving little institutional support leads to higher rates of depersonalization and emotional exhaustion. Language barriers, lack of recognition, and limited leadership pathways further isolate immigrant professionals, while immigrant youth in educational settings also face elevated burnout due to social marginalization and pressure to assimilate (Salmela-Aro et al., 2018).

Together, economic precarity and cultural adjustment form a compounding structure of burnout risk—one that demands intersectional and equity-driven interventions. Addressing these issues requires not only culturally competent practices but also fair compensation, workload redistribution, and meaningful opportunities for professional development.

These overlapping structural challenges underscore the urgent need for comprehensive reform. The following section presents strategic solutions designed to mitigate burnout in the public sector by confronting identity-based stressors through inclusive leadership, systemic policy changes, and supportive organizational practices.

STRATEGIC SOLUTIONS FOR BURNOUT IN THE PUBLIC SECTOR

An inclusive public sector provides significant advantages that extend beyond the workplace, positively impacting employees, organizational performance, and the communities served. By embedding inclusivity into structures and practices, public sector organizations can foster environments that prioritize equity and collaboration.

Inclusive policies play a critical role in reducing identity-based stressors, thereby decreasing burnout and improving overall mental health among employees. When employees feel valued and supported, their emotional resilience and job satisfaction increase, contributing to a healthier and more productive workforce. For instance, policies that address microaggressions and promote equity directly enhance the well-being of marginalized employees, creating a more cohesive and engaged organizational culture (Watson, 2024).

Diverse and inclusive teams drive innovation and adaptability, enabling public sector organizations to address complex societal challenges more effectively. Research shows that organizations with greater diversity are better equipped to develop creative solutions and respond to the evolving needs of the communities they serve. By leveraging the diverse perspectives and experiences of their employees, public sector institutions can improve decision-making and operational efficiency (Roberson & Perry, 2022).

Organizations that prioritize inclusivity are better positioned to build trust with the diverse communities they serve. By ensuring equitable access to public services and resources, inclusive public sector organizations demonstrate their commitment to addressing systemic inequities and promoting fairness. This trust strengthens the relationship between public institutions and the populations they serve, fostering collaboration and mutual respect (Alang et al., 2022). By adopting inclusive practices, public sector organizations not only enhance internal operations but also serve as catalysts for societal progress. These initiatives create equitable environments that benefit employees and communities alike, reinforcing the public sector's role as a model of fairness and justice. Sustained commitment to inclusivity is essential for fostering trust, collaboration, and resilience in public service.

Addressing the burnout experienced by marginalized groups requires a comprehensive understanding of intersectionality and its role in shaping workplace dynamics. Tailored interventions that promote equity, inclusion, and support for diverse identities are essential for mitigating these intersecting stressors and fostering a healthier organizational culture. Table 1 below summarizes the core strategies discussed in this section, their primary target groups, and the anticipated outcomes for mitigating burnout in the public sector workforce.

Table 1. Strategic interventions for burnout reduction in the public sector

Strategic Intervention	Target Groups	Expected Outcomes
Inclusive Leadership	All public sector employees, especially women, LGBTQ+, and ethnic minorities	Increased psychological safety, inclusion, and reduced microaggressions
Mentorship Programs	Women, racial minorities, LGBTQ+ individuals, immigrants	Enhanced career development, reduced isolation, increased resilience
Equity Audits	Organizational decision-makers	Identification of systemic barriers, pay equity, improved representation
Policy Reforms	Marginalized and underrepresented groups	Structural change, increased trust, equity in hiring and promotion
Workplace Training	All employees, with emphasis on management and leadership	Cultural competence, bias reduction, improved team dynamics
Social Support Networks	LGBTQ+, women, immigrants, racial minorities	Peer support, stronger sense of belonging, buffering of identity-related stress
Flexible Working Arrangements (FWAs)	Parents, caregivers, LGBTQ+ staff, employees with disabilities	Improved work-life balance, reduced emotional exhaustion, greater job satisfaction

Inclusive Leadership

Inclusive leadership is foundational for public organizations striving to reflect the diversity of the populations they serve. By implementing inclusive practices, public sector organizations can enhance employee well-being, improve organizational performance, and build trust with the communities they serve. Initiatives such as diversity audits, anonymous feedback systems, and targeted recruitment efforts have proven effective in reducing burnout and improving employee satisfaction (Bourke et al., 2020).

Creating an inclusive public sector is not only crucial for addressing employee burnout but also essential for ensuring equitable service delivery to diverse communities. Public sector organizations, often seen as societal role models, must lead by example in promoting inclusivity at all levels. Inclusive leadership and policies are the cornerstones of this transformation, driving organizational success by fostering trust, collaboration, and a sense of belonging among employees.

To achieve the desired outcomes of an inclusive and equitable public sector, leaders must demonstrate a sustained commitment to equity, transparency, and collaboration. This requires actionable practices such as setting measurable diversity and inclusion objectives, conducting regular equity audits, and ensuring transparency and accountability at all organizational levels. These efforts reinforce a collective commitment to equity, guide the development of equitable workplace practices, and address systemic inequities that contribute to burnout (Steffens et al., 2014; Ashikali et al., 2021).

Inclusive leadership also prioritizes collaboration by integrating diverse perspectives into decision-making processes. Cross-departmental teamwork and inclusive decision-making empower employees, enhance organizational effectiveness, and foster a shared sense of purpose. By promoting these principles, leaders can reduce burnout risks and create a workplace culture where all employees feel valued and supported.

To sustain these benefits and deepen their impact, inclusive leadership development programs are essential. Inclusive leadership development programs are critical for fostering equitable workplaces and combating identity-based burnout, particularly in the public sector. Training programs focused on building skills in empathy, cultural competence, and equity-conscious decision-making equip leaders to address systemic inequities effectively. Identity-conscious leadership strengthens team dynamics, fosters trust, and contributes to reduced stress and improved well-being within diverse teams (Cawcutt et al., 2021).

Inclusive leaders play a critical role in fostering a sense of belonging among employees, particularly those from marginalized backgrounds. Employees who feel valued and included are less likely to experience emotional exhaustion and depersonalization. Inclusive policies, such as diverse hiring practices and equity-focused team-building activities, significantly enhance employee morale and reduce stress levels.

Beyond individual benefits, fostering a culture of belonging also mitigates the challenges that cultural diversity may pose to team cohesion. For instance, studies have shown that employees in inclusive workplaces report stronger engagement and lower turnover rates, demonstrating the importance of inclusive leadership in addressing systemic inequities and fostering psychological safety (Alang et al., 2022).

However, achieving this requires addressing structural challenges, particularly in the public sector, which has often been criticized for top-down decision-making processes that limit the participation of underrepresented groups. Inclusive leadership counters this by empowering employees to actively contribute to decision-making processes. Leaders who encourage employee voice foster psychological safety, reducing feelings of frustration and alienation that often lead to burnout. Structured opportunities for employee feedback, such as town hall meetings and anonymous surveys, further enhance organizational trust and improve job satisfaction (Roberson & Perry, 2022).

Addressing systemic barriers also involves tackling microaggressions and implicit biases, which remain significant contributors to employee burnout in the public sector. Inclusive leadership directly addresses these challenges by implementing policies and training programs designed to promote cultural competence and awareness. For example, zero-tolerance policies for discriminatory behaviors, combined with ongoing education on the impact of microaggressions, help create a safer and more inclusive workplace (Watson, 2024; Hall et al., 2015).

Moreover, organizations that actively combat microaggressions report lower levels of emotional exhaustion among employees. Initiatives such as anonymous reporting systems and leadership accountability frameworks ensure that employees feel supported and respected. By fostering open communication through feedback mechanisms, organizations can proactively address workplace biases, reducing the prevalence of microaggressions and their impact on employee well-being (Jin et al., 2017; Khan et al., 2021).

By integrating these strategies—developing inclusive leadership, enhancing belongingness, amplifying employee voice, and addressing microaggressions—public sector organizations can foster equitable environments that reduce burnout and support all employees. These practices not only promote employee well-being but also enhance organizational performance and the equitable delivery of services to diverse communities.

Mentorship

Promoting mentorship opportunities is another key strategy within inclusive leadership development. By pairing experienced leaders with employees from underrepresented groups, organizations can create pathways for career advancement and professional growth. Mentorship not only enhances individual development but also strengthens the overall sense of community within the organization (McCall, 2005).

Mentorship programs are powerful tools to address systemic inequities and mitigate burnout, especially for underrepresented groups such as women, racial minorities, and LGBTQ+ individuals. Inclusive mentorship goes beyond traditional mentoring by intentionally focusing on the diverse backgrounds and unique challenges faced by mentees. This approach recognizes the mentees' cultural and professional identities as assets, fostering resilience and career advancement. For example, Addy et al. (2023) describe inclusive mentorship as culturally responsive and equity-focused, designed to enhance the holistic development of mentees. This framework has been shown to increase mentees' sense of belonging, reduce stress, and create a support system that buffers against the psychological toll of workplace inequities.

Mentorship programs are a powerful tool for fostering inclusivity, addressing systemic inequities, and reducing burnout, particularly in diverse and high-stress public sector environments. Implementing structured, peer-based, and network-driven mentorship initiatives provides employees with the guidance, support, and resources they need to navigate workplace challenges effectively.

Tailored mentorship programs designed to meet the needs of specific demographic groups, such as women of color or first-generation professionals, offer targeted support. These programs often pair mentees with mentors who understand their unique challenges, fostering a sense of shared identity and belonging (Colley, 2003). By addressing the specific barriers faced by underrepresented groups, these initiatives create an environment where mentees feel supported and valued. For example, mentorship programs in healthcare, as described by Ohue and Menta (2024), incorporate psychological interventions such as Cognitive Behavioral Therapy (CBT) to address stress and burnout among nurses. This dual approach provides professional guidance while directly addressing the emotional and mental health needs of mentees, enhancing both their professional growth and personal resilience.

Peer mentorship programs, such as the MaGE curriculum described by Pon-Barry et al. (2019), emphasize active learning and inclusion in educational and professional settings. These programs have been shown to increase retention rates and promote professional growth among mentees, particularly in fields where they are underrepresented. Peer mentorship fosters a collaborative environment where mentees learn from one another's experiences, enhancing their sense of belonging and engagement.

Establishing formal mentorship networks and support groups creates safe spaces for mentees to discuss challenges and share strategies for overcoming systemic barriers. These structured programs provide mentees with access to experienced professionals who can offer guidance and insights into career development. Informal mentorship relationships, on the other hand, foster trust and long-term professional growth by allowing mentees to build organic connections with mentors over time.

Mentorship programs play a pivotal role in reducing burnout by providing mentees with the guidance, emotional support, and practical tools needed to navigate workplace challenges effectively. One of the keyways mentorship reduces burnout is by addressing feelings of isolation. Representation burnout, often experienced by individuals who feel alone as the only person from their demographic in their workplace, can be mitigated through these programs. Mentorship initiatives create spaces where mentees can connect with others who share similar experiences and challenges. This shared understanding fosters a sense of community and belonging, helping mentees feel more supported and connected within their organizations.

Another significant benefit of mentorship programs is their ability to empower mentees. Programs that adopt asset-based approaches encourage mentees to focus on their strengths and capabilities, fostering self-efficacy and resilience. This perspective is particularly impactful for employees who face high levels of stress and discrimination, as it redirects their focus from external barriers to personal growth and potential. By highlighting the unique value that mentees bring to their organizations, these programs instill confidence and promote a sense of agency, enabling employees to navigate challenges more effectively.

Inclusive mentorship programs also improve job satisfaction by addressing underlying causes of burnout, such as lack of recognition and inadequate support. These programs provide mentees with the tools and resources to manage workplace obstacles while fostering a sense of belonging. By ensuring that mentees feel valued and supported, mentorship initiatives enhance job satisfaction and lead to improved retention rates. Employees who feel recognized and connected are more likely to remain engaged and committed to their organizations, further demonstrating the value of mentorship as a strategy for promoting well-being and reducing burnout (Jin et al., 2017).

To maximize the effectiveness of mentorship programs in public sector organizations, it is essential to implement strategies that ensure these initiatives are impactful, inclusive, and sustainable. One critical step is to develop comprehensive mentorship policies. By institutionalizing mentorship programs and embedding them within organizational frameworks, public sector organizations can make these initiatives accessible to all employees while addressing the unique needs of underrepresented groups. This approach guarantees the sustainability of mentorship programs and ensures they remain a core component of the organization's efforts to promote inclusivity and support professional development.

Another key strategy is to invest in ongoing training for mentors. Effective mentorship requires mentors to be equipped with the skills and knowledge necessary to support their mentees effectively. Training sessions focused on cultural competence and inclusivity, incorporating scenario-based learning, can help mentors navigate the unique challenges their mentees may face. For example, mentors can learn strategies for addressing identity-related stress or systemic discrimination, ensuring they are well-prepared to foster meaningful and supportive relationships with their mentees (Addy et al., 2023).

Additionally, leveraging data to measure the impact of mentorship programs is essential for evaluating their success and identifying opportunities for improvement. Regular assessments using metrics such as employee retention rates, satisfaction surveys, and career progression data provide valuable insights into the effectiveness of these initiatives. By analyzing this data, organizations can refine mentorship programs over time, ensuring they continue to meet the evolving needs of employees and contribute to a more inclusive and supportive workplace environment (Pon-Barry et al., 2019).

By adopting structured mentorship programs, fostering peer support, and building formal and informal networks, public sector organizations can create inclusive environments that empower employees and mitigate burnout. These efforts not only enhance individual well-being but also contribute to the overall effectiveness and equity of public sector operations.

Equity Audits

Conducting regular inclusivity audits ensures that leadership practices align with organizational goals of equity and diversity. These audits provide actionable insights into potential gaps in representation, pay equity, and leadership diversity, enabling organizations to address systemic barriers proactively.

Regular equity audits are critical for identifying and addressing disparities in pay, promotions, and representation within public sector organizations. These audits provide actionable insights into systemic barriers that perpetuate inequality. Research by Ashikali, Groeneveld and Kuipers (2021) highlights that organizations conducting routine equity audits experience improved employee morale and reduced turnover rates.

Regular equity audits are essential for addressing disparities in pay, promotions, and representation within public sector organizations. These audits serve as a diagnostic tool to uncover systemic barriers that perpetuate inequality, providing actionable insights for creating equitable workplaces. Studies highlight that organizations conducting equity audits not only identify gaps in diversity but also improve organizational morale and reduce turnover rates (Greenwood & Zhan, 2019).

In public sector organizations, where bureaucratic inertia and systemic inequities often intersect, equity audits play a crucial role in promoting inclusivity. The public sector faces unique challenges due to its hierarchical structure, which can exacerbate disparities in decision-making power and access to resources. Equity audits provide data-driven recommendations to dismantle these barriers, fostering a culture of fairness and accountability (McNamee & Fleming, 2007). For example, Greenwood and Zhan (2019) analyzed audit adjustments in the English National Health Service (NHS) and found that audits could mitigate management bias in financial reporting, indirectly promoting equitable resource allocation. Their findings underscore the broader applicability of audit principles to equity evaluations in public sector contexts.

Stakeholder engagement is another essential component of effective equity audits. Collaborating with employees to understand their lived experiences of inequity provides valuable qualitative insights that complement quantitative data. This engagement fosters a sense of inclusion and ensures that the voices of marginalized groups are considered when designing interventions and reforms.

Once disparities are identified, organizations move to the action planning phase. This involves developing targeted strategies, such as implementing mentorship programs for underrepresented groups or creating policies to address unconscious bias. Research shows that equity audits are most effective when supported by leadership commitment and integrated into broader organizational strategies. For example, organizations that align audit findings with policy reforms, such as implementing pay transparency measures, often report significant improvements in employee satisfaction and productivity (Salehi et al., 2020; McNamee & Fleming, 2007).

To maximize the impact of equity audits, public sector organizations should adopt several key practices. Establishing clear metrics for assessing equity, such as representation benchmarks and promotion rates, ensures that progress can be tracked over time. Transparency in audit processes and findings is equally important, as it builds trust among employees and reinforces the organization's commitment to inclusivity. Integrating equity audits into the performance review cycle ensures that equity remains a continuous organizational priority, rather than a one-time initiative. Additionally, leveraging external expertise provides unbiased analysis and actionable recommendations, enhancing the credibility and effectiveness of the audits.

By institutionalizing equity audits, public sector organizations can proactively address disparities and foster a more inclusive work environment. This approach not only aligns with broader organizational goals of promoting diversity but also strengthens public trust by demonstrating a commitment to equity and fairness in public service delivery.

Policy Reforms

Policy reforms play a pivotal role in addressing systemic inequities and reducing burnout, particularly in the public sector. Inclusive hiring practices and equity-focused policies are critical for dismantling barriers that disproportionately affect marginalized groups, creating more equitable and supportive workplaces.

Reforming recruitment and promotion processes to prioritize diversity and combat implicit biases is a crucial first step. Practices such as blind hiring, which anonymizes applications, ensure fairer evaluations by minimizing the influence of unconscious bias. Additionally, mentorship programs targeting underrepresented groups—including women, racial minorities, and LGBTQ+ individuals—offer essential professional support and clear pathways for advancement. These initiatives not only enhance organizational diversity but also foster a sense of belonging and equity among employees (Samuels & Ross-Sheriff, 2008

To further enhance diversity, recruitment strategies should actively seek candidates from underrepresented backgrounds. Public sector organizations can implement blind recruitment processes alongside outreach initiatives targeting marginalized communities. Targeted recruitment campaigns, particularly for leadership roles, can address representation gaps and strengthen organizational decision-making by incorporating diverse perspectives (Roberson & Perry, 2022).

Equity-focused policies complement these inclusive hiring practices by addressing structural inequalities that contribute to burnout. For instance, implementing pay transparency eliminates wage disparities that frequently marginalize women and employees of color, fostering a sense of fairness and equity. Similarly, establishing accountability measures for leadership diversity ensures equitable representation at decision-making levels. Research shows that organizations with diverse leadership teams benefit from improved employee morale, reduced turnover rates, and enhanced performance, further demonstrating the value of such policies (McCall, 2005; Walby et al., 2012).

By integrating inclusive hiring practices with equity-focused policies, organizations can create environments where employees feel valued, supported, and empowered. These systemic reforms not only reduce identity-based stressors but also promote organizational trust and fairness, which are essential for mitigating burnout—particularly for marginalized employees facing compounded challenges in traditional workplace structures.

Public sector organizations must also focus on engaging with the communities they serve to ensure that their policies and practices reflect the needs of diverse populations. Community engagement initiatives, such as town hall meetings and participatory budgeting, promote transparency and inclusivity, building stronger relationships between organizations and their stakeholders (Alang et al., 2022)

Policy reforms, therefore, serve as a foundation for fostering equity and well-being in the workplace, aligning organizational goals with the principles of diversity, inclusion, and social justice. They represent a tangible commitment to creating inclusive environments that support both individual and organizational success.

Workplace Training

Workplace training programs that focus on bias awareness and cultural competence are critical for fostering inclusivity and reducing identity-based stress. These initiatives aim to educate employees about the impact of unconscious biases, microaggressions, and systemic inequities, which often contribute to workplace exclusion and burnout. Bias awareness training helps individuals recognize how their behaviors and assumptions may unintentionally perpetuate discrimination, creating opportunities for meaningful change (Haslam et al., 2005). Complementary cultural competence training equips leaders with the skills needed to identify and address discriminatory behaviors, fostering a supportive workplace culture where all employees feel valued and respected (Steffens et al., 2014).

To ensure lasting impact, training programs must be ongoing and integrated into professional development frameworks. Regular workshops, scenario-based learning, and tailored training sessions embed inclusivity into organizational practices. These initiatives help organizations create equitable workplaces that support diversity, reduce stressors, and promote employee well-being. For instance, scenario-based training sessions illustrating real-life examples of microaggressions allow employees to recognize and address these behaviors effectively. Leadership accountability further reinforces these programs, ensuring that their lessons lead to meaningful cultural shifts (Hall et al., 2015).

Ongoing training programs are instrumental in equipping leaders and employees with the skills to recognize and address systemic inequities effectively. These programs emphasize strategies for building psychologically safe and inclusive workplaces, fostering cultural competence, and reducing biases. Institutionalizing these practices is critical to ensuring a sustained impact on organizational culture and employee well-being. In the public sector, such training has demonstrated significant improvements in attitudes toward underrepresented groups, particularly in settings requiring complex interpersonal interactions (Roberson & Perry, 2022; Alang et al., 2022).

Training programs specifically designed for public sector needs have shown success in various contexts. For instance, inclusive leadership training in municipal governments improved workplace inclusion perceptions among Indigenous employees, enhancing their engagement and voice. Similarly, gender equity programs have proven effective in reducing workplace inequities and creating leadership pathways for women and gender minorities, further promoting a more equitable organizational culture (López Torres & Fernández-Elías, 2024).

Effective workplace training programs play a vital role in addressing systemic inequities and fostering inclusive environments. Several key components ensure the success of these initiatives by equipping employees and managers with the tools needed to promote equity and inclusivity. Developing cultural competence is a cornerstone of effective workplace training. These programs focus on fostering cultural awareness and sensitivity, helping employees and managers understand diverse perspectives and how they shape workplace dynamics. By incorporating interactive sessions and real-life scenarios, participants can better internalize inclusive practices and apply them in their daily interactions. Research highlights that a lack of cultural competence often results in implicit biases that affect decision-making processes and workplace relationships, emphasizing the need for targeted training to mitigate these biases.

Workshops designed to uncover and address unconscious biases are essential for creating equitable workplaces. These evidence-based programs enable participants to recognize and challenge their assumptions, fostering more inclusive decision-making processes. Bias reduction initiatives have been shown to significantly reduce workplace inequities by creating a more aware and empathetic organizational culture. By targeting systemic discrimination, these workshops serve as a crucial step in mitigating identity-based stressors and promoting fairness (Lecompte et al., 2021).

Ensuring psychological safety within teams is critical for fostering an environment where employees feel valued and respected. Training programs that prioritize psychological safety focus on creating spaces where individuals can express themselves without fear of retaliation or judgment. This sense of security has been linked to lower turnover rates, increased job satisfaction, and improved team cohesion, particularly in high-stress public sector roles. Additionally, inclusive team-building activities that emphasize collaboration and mutual respect further strengthen workplace bonds and enhance organizational performance. By incorporating these components into training initiatives, organizations can address systemic inequities more comprehensively, cultivate inclusive environments, and support employee well-being and engagement.

Tailored training programs in the public sector have proven highly effective in addressing workplace inequities and fostering inclusivity. These initiatives demonstrate the importance of designing training to meet the specific needs of public sector organizations, ensuring their relevance and impact. By addressing systemic challenges unique to this sector, such as navigating bureaucratic constraints and serving diverse populations, these programs help create equitable and supportive work environments.

One notable example is diversity training in French educational institutions, where teacher training programs emphasizing inclusive education have significantly improved self-efficacy among educators working with students with disabilities. These programs not only reduce burnout but also equip educators with practical tools to create equitable learning environments. By focusing on specific challenges, such as supporting diverse student populations, these initiatives underscore the value of targeted training in achieving meaningful outcomes for both educators and their students (Rohmer et al., 2024).

Similarly, gender equity workshops in public affairs have addressed workplace inequities by fostering leadership pathways for women and gender minorities. These workshops, when combined with mentorship programs, provide ongoing support and professional development opportunities for underrepresented groups. This dual approach creates sustainable change by tackling systemic barriers and fostering inclusive leadership structures, ensuring a long-term positive impact on organizational culture (Elias et al., 2024).

In the social services sector, LGBTQ+ inclusion training has been instrumental in improving service delivery and employee retention. These programs educate staff on the unique challenges faced by LGBTQ+ employees and clients while equipping organizations with tools to address these needs effectively. Research highlights that integrating these initiatives with policy changes, such as robust anti-discrimination measures, enhances their sustainability and ensures lasting cultural transformation (Lecompte et al., 2021).

To maximize the effectiveness of these training programs, public sector organizations should adopt key policy recommendations. Mandatory training modules for diversity and inclusion should be integrated into both onboarding and continuous professional development. Making such programs a standard part of organizational practice ensures widespread participation and embeds inclusivity into the workplace culture.

Additionally, customized content tailored to public sector needs can address the unique challenges faced by employees, such as managing high-stress roles and navigating complex interpersonal interactions. Context-specific training ensures that lessons are directly applicable to real-world scenarios, enhancing both relevance and impact.

Evaluation and feedback mechanisms are essential for refining these initiatives. Collecting feedback from participants allows organizations to assess the effectiveness of training programs and make necessary improvements. Anonymous feedback systems also provide employees with a safe channel to report discrimination, microaggressions, or other workplace challenges. These mechanisms foster open communication, improve trust, and encourage engagement by addressing underlying issues that contribute to burnout (Jin et al., 2017).

By adopting these tailored training programs and policy recommendations, public sector organizations can comprehensively address systemic inequities while fostering inclusive environments. These efforts not only reduce identity-based stressors but also enhance employee well-being, organizational performance, and the equitable delivery of services. By prioritizing such comprehensive strategies, public sector organizations can cultivate a culture of equity and inclusion, driving sustainable success and societal impact.

Social Support Networks

Social support and collaboration are critical factors in reducing burnout and fostering inclusivity, particularly for marginalized employees. Peer support groups offer dedicated spaces where employees can share experiences, develop coping strategies, and build a sense of community. These networks serve as emotional resources, buffering against identity threats and enhancing individual resilience. Marginalized employees who participate in such groups often report a stronger sense of belonging and lower stress levels, demonstrating the profound impact of peer support on employee well-being (Haslam et al., 2005).

In addition to peer support groups, Employee Resource Groups (ERGs) provide formalized platforms for fostering dialogue and solidarity. Sponsored by organizations, ERGs create safe spaces for employees to discuss diversity and inclusion issues while offering opportunities for mentorship, advocacy, and professional networking. These groups strengthen organizational commitment and reduce turnover rates by ensuring that employees feel valued and supported (Lammers et al., 2013). Together, peer support groups and ERGs create collaborative environments where employees can navigate workplace challenges more effectively, reducing burnout risks and promoting overall well-being.

Promoting collaboration within diverse teams further enhances resilience against identity-related stressors. Open communication and opportunities for teamwork help build trust and encourage employees to learn from one another's unique perspectives. This approach not only strengthens team cohesion but also fosters a sense of belonging and shared purpose, which reduces identity-based stress and improves overall morale.

Team-building activities also play a crucial role in fostering collaboration and mutual support. Activities emphasizing collective problem-solving and recognizing both individual and collective achievements create a sense of shared ownership among team members. Peer mentorship programs embedded within teams enable employees to share knowledge, support one another, and develop stronger interpersonal connections, further enhancing resilience (Walby et al., 2012). These programs create a foundation for collaboration and trust, empowering employees to work cohesively in diverse environments.

Building on this foundation, addressing potential conflicts within diverse teams becomes essential to sustaining harmony and inclusivity. These sessions provide practical tools for navigating disagreements arising from cultural or identity differences, fostering mutual respect and understanding. Similarly, cross-functional projects that bring together employees from various departments or backgrounds encourage inclusivity and allow individuals to broaden their perspectives while working toward shared goals. In hybrid or remote work environments, these collaborative efforts can be effectively supported by leveraging virtual collaboration tools, such as platforms for brainstorming, team-building exercises, and open discussions, ensuring that all voices are heard and valued. Recognizing individual contributions alongside collective achievements further enhances confidence and engagement, creating a supportive and equitable workplace culture.

By integrating peer support networks, ERGs, and collaborative strategies, organizations can build environments that reduce identity-related stressors, enhance team cohesion, and improve organizational resilience. These initiatives not only promote employee well-being but also demonstrate a commitment to equity and inclusion, enabling diverse teams to thrive and succeed.

Flexible Working Arrangements

Introducing flexible work arrangements (FWAs) is a vital strategy for reducing stress and promoting overall well-being, particularly for employees juggling multiple identity-based pressures. Flexible schedules, remote work options, and childcare support empower employees to better balance their personal and professional responsibilities. These initiatives are particularly beneficial for women of color, who often face the dual challenge of caregiving responsibilities and workplace demands, further exacerbating their risk of burnout (Samuels & Ross-Sheriff, 2008).

Flexible work arrangements provide a foundation for achieving work-life balance by offering employees greater control over their schedules. This autonomy reduces emotional exhaustion and helps employees manage the competing demands of work and family more effectively. For example, remote work options enable individuals to save time otherwise spent commuting, allowing them to dedicate more energy to caregiving or personal well-being. Similarly, childcare support programs alleviate the burden on working parents, particularly those from marginalized groups who may face limited access to affordable childcare.

Work-life balance initiatives not only benefit employees but also yield significant advantages for organizations. Research highlights that employees who experience greater balance report higher job satisfaction, increased productivity, and stronger organizational commitment. Lammers et al. (2013) emphasize that such initiatives reduce burnout and turnover rates, fostering a more engaged and loyal workforce.

To ensure the effectiveness of these programs, organizations must actively assess and address barriers to implementation. For instance, leaders should engage in open dialogue with employees to understand their needs and tailor flexible work policies accordingly. By prioritizing employee well-being through flexible work arrangements and supportive policies, organizations can create inclusive environments that promote resilience, productivity, and long-term success.

FWAs are especially beneficial for marginalized groups who face unique workplace challenges. Women, particularly those balancing caregiving responsibilities, experience relief from the double burden of professional and domestic duties when flexible scheduling is available. Such policies promote retention and reduce burnout, particularly for women in leadership roles who often face heightened pressures. Studies emphasize that women provided with adaptable work options are more likely to remain in their positions and thrive professionally (Özbilgin et al., 2011).

LGBTQ+ employees, who frequently encounter stressors like identity concealment and workplace microaggressions, also benefit significantly from FWAs. Remote work provides a psychological buffer, allowing these employees to work in environments where they feel safer and more authentic. Research shows that LGBTQ+ employees with access to remote work report lower levels of emotional exhaustion and higher job satisfaction, underscoring the importance of these arrangements in fostering inclusivity (Lee et al., 2024).

Similarly, employees with disabilities face unique challenges, including physical accessibility and accommodation barriers. FWAs, such as telecommuting, help eliminate these obstacles, enabling employees to manage their health needs while remaining professionally productive. Studies indicate that FWAs reduce absenteeism and improve overall productivity, creating a more inclusive workplace environment for employees with disabilities (Booth & Lup, 2024).

While FWAs offer numerous advantages, their implementation in the public sector is not without challenges. Perceived inequities can arise when employees in non-flexible roles or those without caregiving responsibilities feel excluded. Transparent communication about eligibility criteria and equitable access can help address these concerns (Lee et al., 2024). Additionally, some managers resist FWAs due to concerns about productivity or team cohesion. Providing training on managing remote teams and leveraging performance metrics can alleviate these fears and foster acceptance of flexible work policies (Michielsens et al., 2013).

To maximize the benefits of FWAs, public sector organizations must adopt a comprehensive approach to their implementation. First, organizations should formalize FWAs into clear policies that outline eligibility, processes, and expectations.

These policies must address intersectional challenges and prioritize equity to ensure access for all employees (Almer & Kaplan, 2002)

Leadership commitment is equally essential. Leaders should model flexible work behaviors and communicate the benefits of FWAs for employee well-being and organizational performance. Promoting organizational culture change around FWAs helps normalize these practices and reduces stigma (Proctor, 2024). Moreover, investing in robust technological infrastructure is crucial for supporting seamless remote work. Tools for virtual meetings, document sharing, and real-time communication enhance collaboration and productivity in flexible work environments.

Case studies demonstrate the effectiveness of FWAs in reducing burnout and promoting inclusivity. For instance, a study on local governments implementing FWAs revealed a 25% reduction in burnout and significant improvements in work-life balance. Women and caregivers particularly benefited, citing increased job satisfaction and reduced stress levels (Michielsens et al., 2013). In another example, LGBTQ+ employees in a federal agency pilot program for telecommuting reported feeling safer and more productive while working remotely. The program's success led to its adoption across multiple departments, illustrating the scalability of FWAs in diverse public sector contexts (Lee et al., 2024).

By adopting flexible work arrangements, public sector organizations can address systemic inequities, reduce burnout, and foster an inclusive workplace culture. These policies not only enhance employee well-being but also improve organizational performance, making them an essential component of modern workforce strategies.

CONCLUSION

Burnout in the public sector extends beyond individual challenges, reflecting broader systemic issues shaped by identity, societal structures, and organizational dynamics. The role of identity and gender in burnout is particularly critical, as they intersect with systemic inequities to create compounded stressors for marginalized employees. Individuals from historically marginalized backgrounds—such as women, people with marginalized sexual orientations, and racial or ethnic minorities—often encounter distinct challenges in the workplace, including subtle forms of bias, exclusion from decision-making processes, and increased performance scrutiny. These intersecting stressors amplify emotional exhaustion, depersonalization, and feelings of reduced personal accomplishment, making targeted interventions essential.

Theoretical insights, particularly from Social Identity Theory and Intersectionality, provide a nuanced understanding of how identity-based stressors manifest in the workplace. Social Identity Theory highlights the importance of belonging and group dynamics, while Intersectionality emphasizes the overlapping systems of oppression that shape the lived experiences of marginalized employees. Together, these frameworks underscore the systemic roots of burnout, moving beyond individual factors to address structural inequities and organizational cultures.

For public sector organizations, the implications are clear and far-reaching:

Inclusive Leadership and Policies: Leadership plays a pivotal role in driving equity and inclusion. Leaders must actively champion diversity through transparent policies, targeted recruitment efforts, and representation in decision-making. Inclusive leadership not only addresses systemic inequities but also fosters trust, collaboration, and organizational cohesion.

Comprehensive Training Programs: Addressing burnout requires equipping employees and leaders with the tools to recognize and mitigate systemic inequities. Ongoing training in cultural competence, bias awareness, and psychological safety creates a supportive workplace culture where all employees feel valued and respected.

Systemic Reforms: Structural changes, such as implementing pay transparency, conducting equity audits, and creating flexible work arrangements, are essential for reducing identity-based stressors. These reforms ensure that inclusivity is embedded into the fabric of organizational practices, benefiting both employees and the communities they serve.

Empowering Marginalized Employees: Mentorship programs, peer support networks, and Employee Resource Groups (ERGs) provide platforms for marginalized employees to share experiences, develop coping strategies, and advance professionally. These initiatives not only reduce feelings of isolation but also enhance individual and organizational resilience.

The central message of this chapter is that addressing burnout in the public sector is both a moral and strategic imperative. Public sector organizations, as societal role models, have the unique opportunity to lead by example, demonstrating how inclusive practices can transform workplaces. By prioritizing equity and addressing identity-based inequities, these organizations can create environments where all employees can thrive.

The journey toward an equitable public sector requires sustained commitment and continuous improvement. By integrating theoretical insights with actionable solutions, public sector leaders can reduce burnout, improve employee well-being, and enhance organizational performance. Most importantly, these efforts strengthen the sector's ability to serve diverse communities equitably, fostering trust and collaboration while building a more inclusive society.

REFERENCES

Abrams, D. E., & Hogg, M. A. (1990). *Social identity theory: Constructive and critical advances*. Springer-Verlag Publishing.

Addy, T. M., Addy, N. A., Hendrickson, B., & Mitchell, K. A. (2023). Supporting mentees through inclusive mentorship. *New Directions for Teaching and Learning*, *2023*(175), 11–19. DOI: 10.1002/tl.20554

Alang, T., Stanton, P., & Rose, M. (2022). Enhancing employee voice and inclusion through inclusive leadership in public sector organizations. *Public Personnel Management*, *51*(3), 309–329. DOI: 10.1177/00910260221085583

Almer, E. D., & Kaplan, S. E. (2002). The effects of flexible work arrangements on stressors, burnout, and behavioral job outcomes in public accounting. *Behavioral Research in Accounting*, *14*(1), 1–34. DOI: 10.2308/bria.2002.14.1.1

An, B. Y., Barboza-Wilkes, C. J., & Resh, W. G. (2024). Applying an intersectional understanding of extra work behavior and emotional exhaustion in local public service. *Public Administration*, *102*(4), 1578–1603. DOI: 10.1111/padm.12989

Ashforth, B. E., & Mael, F. (1989). Social identity theory and the organization. *Academy of Management Review*, *14*(1), 20–39. DOI: 10.2307/258189

Ashikali, T., Groeneveld, S., & Kuipers, B. (2021). The role of inclusive leadership in supporting an inclusive climate in diverse public sector teams. *Review of Public Personnel Administration*, *41*(3), 497–519. DOI: 10.1177/0734371X19899722

Booth, J. E., & Lup, D. (2024). Enabling inclusion: An analysis of positive and negative outcomes of discretionary work arrangements for employees with disabilities. *British Journal of Industrial Relations*, bjir.12862. DOI: 10.1111/bjir.12862

Bourke, J., Titus, A., & Espedido, A. (2020). The key to inclusive leadership. *Harvard Business Review, 6*, H05GLB.

Brown, R. (2000). Social identity theory: Past achievements, current problems and future challenges. *European Journal of Social Psychology*, *30*(6), 745–778. DOI: 10.1002/1099-0992(200011/12)30:6<745::AID-EJSP24>3.0.CO;2-O

Carastathis, A. (2014). The concept of intersectionality in feminist theory. *Philosophy Compass*, *9*(5), 304–314. DOI: 10.1111/phc3.12129

Cawcutt, K. A., Clance, P., & Jain, S. (2021). Bias, burnout, and imposter phenomenon: The negative impact of under-recognized Intersectionality. *Women's Health Reports (New Rochelle, N.Y.)*, *2*(1), 643–647. DOI: 10.1089/whr.2021.0138 PMID: 35141712

Cheng, C., Bartram, T., Karimi, L., & Leggat, S. (2016). Transformational leadership and social identity as predictors of team climate, perceived quality of care, burnout and turnover intention among nurses. *Personnel Review*, *45*(6), 1200–1216. DOI: 10.1108/PR-05-2015-0118

Cho, S., Crenshaw, K. W., & McCall, L. (2013). Toward a field of intersectionality studies: Theory, applications, and praxis. *Signs (Chicago, Ill.)*, *38*(4), 785–810. DOI: 10.1086/669608

Colley, H. (2003). *Mentoring for social inclusion: A critical approach to nurturing mentor relationships*. Routledge. DOI: 10.4324/9780203458310

Crenshaw, K. (1989). Demarginalizing the intersection of race and sex: A black feminist critique of antidiscrimination doctrine, feminist theory and antiracist politics. In *Feminist legal theories* (pp. 23–51). Routledge.

Crenshaw, K. W. (1991). Mapping the margins: Intersectionality, identity politics, and violence against women of color. In *The public nature of private violence* (pp. 93–118). Routledge.

Dwinijanti, L., Adhikara, M. A., & Kusumapradja, R. (2020). Job satisfaction and turnover intention among public sector nurses: Is workload and burnout the issue? *JEMA: Jurnal Ilmiah Bidang Akuntansi Dan Manajemen*, *17*(1), 67–77. DOI: 10.31106/jema.v17i1.4951

Freudenberger, H. J. (1974). Staff burn-out. *The Journal of Social Issues*, *30*(1), 159–165. DOI: 10.1111/j.1540-4560.1974.tb00706.x

Golembiewski, R. T., Boudreau, R. A., Sun, B. C., & Luo, H. (1998). Estimates of burnout in public agencies: Worldwide, how many employees have which degrees of burnout, and with what consequences? *Public Administration Review*, *58*(1), 59–65. DOI: 10.2307/976890

Greenwood, M., & Zhan, R. (2019). Audit adjustments and public sector audit quality. *Abacus*, *55*(3), 511–534. DOI: 10.1111/abac.12165

Hall, W. M., Schmader, T., & Croft, E. (2015). Engineering exchanges: Daily social identity threat predicts burnout among female engineers. *Social Psychological & Personality Science*, *6*(5), 528–534. DOI: 10.1177/1948550615572637

Haslam, S. A., O'Brien, A., Jetten, J., Vormedal, K., & Penna, S. (2005). Taking the strain: Social identity, social support, and the experience of stress. *British Journal of Social Psychology*, *44*(3), 355–370. DOI: 10.1348/014466605X37468 PMID: 16238844

Haushofer, J., & Fehr, E. (2014). On the psychology of poverty. *science, 344*(6186), 862-867.

Hochschild, A. R. (1983). *The Managed Heart: Commercialization of Human Feeling*. University of California Press.

Hogg, M. A., Terry, D. J., & White, K. M. (1995). A tale of two theories: A critical comparison of identity theory with social identity theory. *Social Psychology Quarterly*, *58*(4), 255–269. DOI: 10.2307/2787127

Hornsey, M. J. (2008). Social identity theory and self-categorization theory: A historical review. *Social and Personality Psychology Compass*, *2*(1), 204–222. DOI: 10.1111/j.1751-9004.2007.00066.x

Huddy, L. (2001). From social to political identity: A critical examination of social identity theory. *Political Psychology*, *22*(1), 127–156. DOI: 10.1111/0162-895X.00230

Islam, G. (2014). Social identity theory. *Journal of Personality and Social Psychology*, *67*(1), 741–763.

Jin, M., Lee, J., & Lee, M. (2017). Does leadership matter in diversity management? Assessing the relative impact of diversity policy and inclusive leadership in the public sector. *Leadership and Organization Development Journal*, *38*(2), 303–319. DOI: 10.1108/LODJ-07-2015-0151

Khan, N., Palepu, A., Dodek, P., Salmon, A., Leitch, H., Ruzycki, S., Townson, A., & Lacaille, D. (2021). Cross-sectional survey on physician burnout during the COVID-19 pandemic in Vancouver, Canada: The role of gender, ethnicity and sexual orientation. *BMJ Open*, *11*(5), e050380. DOI: 10.1136/bmjopen-2021-050380 PMID: 33972345

Kim, J. (2018). The contrary effects of intrinsic and extrinsic motivations on burnout and turnover intention in the public sector. *International Journal of Manpower*, *39*(3), 486–500. DOI: 10.1108/IJM-03-2017-0053

Kim, S., & Fernandez, S. (2017). Employee empowerment and turnover intention in the U.S. federal bureaucracy. *American Review of Public Administration*, *47*(1), 4–22. DOI: 10.1177/0275074015583712

Kim, S., Kantamneni, N., Ahmad Ridzuan, N. H., & Miramonti, A. A. (2024). Work-Family Conflict and Burnout for Mothers of Color: Exploring the Role of Microaggressions and Gender Role Beliefs. *Journal of Career Assessment*, •••, 10690727241307957. DOI: 10.1177/10690727241307957

Knippenberg, A. V., & Ellemers, N. (1990). Social identity and intergroup differentiation processes. *European Review of Social Psychology*, *1*(1), 137–169. DOI: 10.1080/14792779108401860

Lammers, J. C., Atouba, Y. L., & Carlson, E. J. (2013). Which identities matter? A mixed-method study of group, organizational, and professional identities and their relationship to burnout. *Management Communication Quarterly*, *27*(4), 503–536. DOI: 10.1177/0893318913498824

Lazarus, R. S., & Folkman, S. (1984). *Stress, Appraisal, and Coping*. Springer.

Lecompte, M., Ducharme, J., Beauchamp, J., & Couture, M. (2021). Inclusive practices toward LGBT older adults in healthcare and social services: A scoping review of quantitative and qualitative evidence. *Clinical Gerontologist*, *44*(3), 210–221. DOI: 10.1080/07317115.2020.1862946 PMID: 33357121

Lee, H. J., Probst, T. M., Bettac, E. L., Jenkins, M. R., & Bazzoli, A. (2024). The use of flexible work arrangements: Examining experiences of perceived backlash through the lens of diversity. *Group & Organization Management*, *49*(5), 1159–1198. DOI: 10.1177/10596011221150025

López Torres, O., & Fernández-Elías, V. E. (2024). Training and Nutrition for Performance: Males, Females, and Gender Differences. *Nutrients*, *16*(23), 3979. DOI: 10.3390/nu16233979 PMID: 39683373

Lyonette, C., & Crompton, R. (2015). Sharing the load? Partners' relative earnings and the division of domestic labour. *Work, Employment and Society*, *29*(1), 23–40. DOI: 10.1177/0950017014523661

Maines, D. R. (1989). Rediscovering the social group: A self-categorization theory.

Maslach, C. (2003). *Burnout: The Cost of Caring*. Prentice-Hall.

Maslach, C., & Jackson, S. E. (1981). The measurement of experienced burnout. *Journal of Organizational Behavior*, *2*(2), 99–113. DOI: 10.1002/job.4030020205

Maslach, C., Schaufeli, W. B., & Leiter, M. P. (2001). Job burnout. *Annual Review of Psychology*, *52*(1), 397–422. DOI: 10.1146/annurev.psych.52.1.397 PMID: 11148311

McCall, L. (2005). The complexity of intersectionality. *Signs (Chicago, Ill.)*, *30*(3), 1771–1800. DOI: 10.1086/426800

McNamee, M. J., & Fleming, S. (2007). Ethics audits and corporate governance: The case of public sector sports organizations. *Journal of Business Ethics, 73*(4), 425–437. DOI: 10.1007/s10551-006-9216-0

Meuris, J., & Leana, C. R. (2015). The high cost of low wages: Economic scarcity effects in organizations. *Research in Organizational Behavior, 35*, 143–158. DOI: 10.1016/j.riob.2015.07.001

Michielsens, E., Bingham, C., & Clarke, L. (2013). Managing diversity through flexible work arrangements: Management perspectives. *Employee Relations, 36*(1), 49–69. DOI: 10.1108/ER-06-2012-0048

Mullainathan, S., & Shafir, E. (2013). *Scarcity: Why having too little means so much.* Macmillan.

Ohue, T., & Menta, M. (2024). Effectiveness of Mentorship Using Cognitive Behavior Therapy to Reduce Burnout and Turnover among Nurses: Intervention Impact on Mentees. *Nursing Reports, 14*(2), 1026–1036. DOI: 10.3390/nursrep14020077 PMID: 38804410

Özbilgin, M. F., Beauregard, T. A., Tatli, A., & Bell, M. P. (2011). Work–life, diversity and intersectionality: A critical review and research agenda. *International Journal of Management Reviews, 13*(2), 177–198. DOI: 10.1111/j.1468-2370.2010.00291.x

Pérez-Luño, A., Díez Piñol, M., & Dolan, S. L. (2022). Exploring high vs. low burnout amongst public sector educators: COVID-19 antecedents and profiles. *International Journal of Environmental Research and Public Health, 19*(2), 780. DOI: 10.3390/ijerph19020780 PMID: 35055602

Pon-Barry, H., St. John, A., Packard, B. W. L., & Rotundo, B. (2019, February). A flexible curriculum for promoting inclusion through peer mentorship. In *Proceedings of the 50th ACM technical symposium on computer science education* (pp. 1116-1122). DOI: 10.1145/3287324.3287434

Proctor, E. B. (2024). *Employee Engagement Among Intersectional Identifying Employees: Considering Flexible Work Arrangements in the Era of Increased Remote and Hybrid Work*(Doctoral dissertation).

Rajan, S., & Engelbrecht, A. (2018). A cross-sectional survey of burnout amongst doctors in a cohort of public sector emergency centres in Gauteng, South Africa. *African Journal of Emergency Medicine : Revue Africaine de la Médecine d'Urgence, 8*(3), 95–99. DOI: 10.1016/j.afjem.2018.04.001 PMID: 30456156

Roberson, Q., & Perry, J. L. (2022). Inclusive leadership in thought and action: A thematic analysis. *Group & Organization Management*, *47*(4), 755–778. DOI: 10.1177/10596011211013161

Rohmer, O., Palomares, E. A., & Popa-Roch, M. (2024). Attitudes towards disability and burnout among teachers in inclusive schools in France. *International Journal of Disability Development and Education*, *71*(1), 83–100. DOI: 10.1080/1034912X.2022.2092078

Ryus, C. R., Samuels, E. A., Wong, A. H., Hill, K. A., Huot, S., & Boatright, D. (2022). Burnout and perception of medical school learning environments among gay, lesbian, and bisexual medical students. *JAMA Network Open*, *5*(4), e229596–e229596. DOI: 10.1001/jamanetworkopen.2022.9596 PMID: 35486396

Sagaltici, E., Cetinkaya, M., Nielsen, S. Y., Sahin, S. K., Gulen, B., & Altindag, A. (2022). Identified predictors and levels of burnout among staff workers in a refugee camp of first immigrant group: A cross-sectional study. *Medicine*, *11*(1), 135–141. PMID: 35440085

Salehi, M., Seyyed, F., & Farhangdoust, S. (2020). The impact of personal characteristics, quality of working life and psychological well-being on job burnout among Iranian external auditors. *International Journal of Organization Theory and Behavior*, *23*(3), 189–205. DOI: 10.1108/IJOTB-09-2018-0104

Salmela-Aro, K., Read, S., Minkkinen, J., Kinnunen, J. M., & Rimpelä, A. (2018). Immigrant status, gender, and school burnout in Finnish lower secondary school students: A longitudinal study. *International Journal of Behavioral Development*, *42*(2), 225–236. DOI: 10.1177/0165025417690264

Samuels, G. M., & Ross-Sheriff, F. (2008). Identity, oppression, and power: Feminisms and intersectionality theory. *Affilia*, *23*(1), 5–9. DOI: 10.1177/0886109907310475

Sarisik, M., Bogan, E., Zengin, B., & Dedeoglu, B. B. (2019). The impact of burnout on organizational commitment: A study of public sector employees in Turkey. *Journal of global business insights,* *4*(2), 106-118.

Schaufeli, W. B., & Enzmann, D. (2020). *The Burnout Companion to Study and Practice: A Critical Analysis*. CRC press. DOI: 10.1201/9781003062745

Schaufeli, W. B., Leiter, M. P., & Maslach, C. (2009). Burnout: 35 years of research and practice. *Career Development International*, *14*(3), 204–220. DOI: 10.1108/13620430910966406

Serin, A. E., & Balkan, M. O. (2014). Burnout: The effects of demographic factors on staff burnout: An application at public sector. *International Business Research, 7*(4), 151–159. DOI: 10.5539/ibr.v7n4p151

Shanafelt, T. D., Boone, S., Tan, L., Dyrbye, L. N., Sotile, W., Satele, D., West, C. P., Sloan, J., & Oreskovich, M. R. (2012). Burnout and satisfaction with work-life balance among US physicians relative to the general US population. *Archives of Internal Medicine, 172*(18), 1377–1385. DOI: 10.1001/archinternmed.2012.3199 PMID: 22911330

Steele, C. M., Spencer, S. J., & Aronson, J. (2002). Contending with group image: The psychology of stereotype and social identity threat. In Vol. 34, pp. 379–440). Advances in experimental social psychology. Academic Press. DOI: 10.1016/S0065-2601(02)80009-0

Steffens, N. K., Haslam, S. A., Kerschreiter, R., Schuh, S. C., & van Dick, R. (2014). Leaders enhance group members' work engagement and reduce their burnout by crafting social identity. *German Journal of Human Resource Management, 28*(1-2), 173–194. DOI: 10.1177/239700221402800110

Tajfel, H. (1970). Experiments in intergroup discrimination. *Scientific American, 223*(5), 96–103. DOI: 10.1038/scientificamerican1170-96 PMID: 5482577

Teshome, B. G., Desai, M. M., Gross, C. P., Hill, K. A., Li, F., Samuels, E. A., ... & Boatright, D. H. (2022). Marginalized identities, mistreatment, discrimination, and burnout among US medical students: cross sectional survey and retrospective cohort study. *bmj, 376*.

Trepte, S., & Loy, L. S. (2017). Social identity theory and self-categorization theory. *The international encyclopedia of media effects*, 1-13.

Turner, J. C. (1985). Social categorization and the self-concept: A social cognitive theory of group behaviour. In E. J. U.S. Office of Personnel Management. (2022). *Federal Employee Viewpoint Survey Results.*https://www.opm.gov/fevs/

Turner, J. C., Brown, R. J., & Tajfel, H. (1979). Social comparison and group interest in ingroup favouritism. *European Journal of Social Psychology, 9*(2), 187–204. DOI: 10.1002/ejsp.2420090207

UK Cabinet Office. (2021). *Civil Service People Survey 2021: Summary of Findings.*https://www.gov.uk/government/publications/civil-service-people-survey-2021-results

Varma, P. (2024). Burnout in immigrant early childhood educators.

Viehl, C., & Dispenza, F. (2015). Burnout and coping: An exploratory comparative study of heterosexual and sexual minority mental health practitioners. *Journal of LGBT Issues in Counseling*, *9*(4), 311–328. DOI: 10.1080/15538605.2015.1112337

Walby, S., Armstrong, J., & Strid, S. (2012). Intersectionality: Multiple inequalities in social theory. *Sociology*, *46*(2), 224–240. DOI: 10.1177/0038038511416164

Watson, D. L. (2024). Burnout Among Sexual and Gender Minority Physicians—From Recognition to Intervention. *JAMA Network Open*, *7*(11), e2443891–e2443891. DOI: 10.1001/jamanetworkopen.2024.43891 PMID: 39535802

KEY TERMS AND DEFINITIONS

Burnout: Burnout refers to a psychological state characterized by emotional exhaustion, depersonalization, and a diminished sense of personal accomplishment. It often arises from prolonged exposure to workplace stress, particularly in roles with high emotional demands and limited support systems.

Social Identity Theory: A theoretical framework that explains how individuals derive self-esteem and belonging from their membership in social groups. This theory highlights the impact of group affiliations on behaviors, attitudes, and workplace dynamics.

Intersectionality: A framework for understanding how overlapping social identities, such as race, gender, and sexual orientation, interact with systemic oppression and privilege. It emphasizes the compounded challenges faced by individuals with multiple marginalized identities.

Inclusive Leadership: A leadership approach that prioritizes equity, diversity, and inclusion by actively engaging with diverse teams, fostering collaboration, and addressing systemic inequities. Inclusive leaders create environments where all employees feel valued and supported.

Microaggressions: Subtle, often unintentional, behaviors or statements that convey bias or discrimination against marginalized groups. These actions contribute to workplace exclusion and identity-based stress, exacerbating burnout.

Equity Audits: Systematic evaluations of organizational policies and practices aimed at identifying and addressing disparities in areas such as recruitment, pay, and promotion. Equity audits help organizations build more inclusive and equitable workplaces.

Cultural Competence: The ability of individuals and organizations to understand, respect, and effectively engage with diverse cultural perspectives. Cultural competence is critical for reducing biases and fostering inclusivity in professional settings.

Employee Resource Groups (ERGs): Voluntary, employee-led groups that provide support, advocacy, and networking opportunities for individuals who share common identities or experiences. ERGs play a significant role in fostering belonging and reducing burnout.

Identity-Based Stressors: Workplace challenges and pressures that stem from an individual's social identity, such as race, gender, or sexual orientation. These stressors often manifest as microaggressions, exclusionary practices, or systemic inequities.

Workplace Inclusivity: The creation of organizational environments where employees of all backgrounds feel valued, respected, and supported. Inclusivity involves equitable practices, diverse representation, and intentional efforts to eliminate systemic barriers.

Chapter 11
Job-Related and Life-Related Stress

P. Selvakumar
https://orcid.org/0000-0002-3650-4548
Department of Science and Humanities, Nehru Institute of Technology, Coimbatore, India

Vijay Uprikar
https://orcid.org/0000-0003-2546-8307
Datta Meghe Institute of Management Studies, India

Supriya Bhagat
MIT School of Management, MIT ADT University, India

Ravi Kishor Agrawal
https://orcid.org/0009-0001-2768-4946
MATS University, India

Nimita Srivastava Nimkar
Sri Balaji University, India

T. C. Manjunath
https://orcid.org/0000-0003-2545-9160
Rajarajeswari College of Engineering, India

ABSTRACT

Stress is a multifaceted n from psychologists, medical professionals, and researchers due to its profound effects on mental and physical well-being. Stress refers to the body's response to any demand or challenge, often perceived as a threat or strain on an individual's resources. It can be caused by external factors, This article explores the definitions, causes, and consequences of stress, emphasizing its complexity and pervasive impact. Definitions changes that require adjustment or action. Hans Selye, a pioneering endocrinologist, described stress as the "nonspecific response of the body to any demand." This definition highlights that stress is not inherently negative; instead, it is a general reaction, such as preparing for an important exam or competing in a sports event. Conversely, distress, or "negative stress," occurs when demands exceed an individual's coping abilities, potentially leading to harmful consequences.

DOI: 10.4018/979-8-3373-0169-3.ch011

UNDERSTANDING STRESS: DEFINITIONS, CAUSES, AND CONSEQUENCES

Psychologically, stress is viewed through the lens of cognitive appraisal theories, which suggest that stress results from an individual's perception of a situation emphasizes the dynamic interaction between individuals and their environment. They argue that stress this perception-based understanding underscores the subjective nature of stress, varying widely among individuals based on personality traits, past experiences, and cultural backgrounds. Causes of Stress Common external stressors are work-related pressures, financial difficulties, relationship conflicts, major life events (e.g., divorce, bereavement, or relocation), and traumatic experiences. For example, high job demands, tight deadlines, and lack of control at work are significant contributors to occupational stress, which affects millions worldwide. Internal stressors are rooted in an individual's thoughts, emotions, and physical state. These may include unrealistic expectations, perfectionism, self-doubt, or fear of failure. Negative thinking patterns, such as catastrophizing or overgeneralization, can amplify stress levels. Additionally, physiological conditions like chronic illness, sleep deprivation, or hormonal imbalances can predispose individuals to heightened stress responses.

Importantly, the interaction between internal and external stressors often determines the severity and impact of stress. Stress can also be acute or chronic. Acute stress arises from immediate, short-term challenges, such as narrowly avoiding a car accident or meeting a tight deadline. While acute stress is temporary and often resolves once the situation is over, chronic stress persists over extended periods. Chronic stress, such as living in stress-response system activated for prolonged durations. Consequences of Stress The effects of stress are extensive, influencing physical health, mental well-being, and social relationships. Physiologically, stress activates the body's "fight or flight" response, releasing hormones like adrenaline and cortisol. While this response is beneficial for short-term survival, chronic activation can lead to adverse health outcomes. Long-term stress is associated with cardiovascular problems, such as hypertension and heart disease, weakened immune function, digestive disorders, and metabolic imbalances. For instance, chronic stress can increase the risk of obesity by promoting unhealthy eating habits or altering fat storage patterns. Psychologically, stress is a leading contributor to mental health disorders, including anxiety, depression, and burnout. It can impair cognitive functions like memory, attention, and decision-making, and decreased motivation, which can interfere with daily functioning and personal goals. For example, a student experiencing academic stress may struggle to concentrate, leading to poor performance and heightened anxiety. Stress also takes a toll on social and interpersonal relationships. Individuals under stress may become withdrawn, impatient, or argumentative, straining their connections with friends, family, and colleagues. Over time, this can lead to isolation and a lack of social support, which exacerbates stress levels. On the other hand, unresolved stress within relationships, such as persistent conflicts or communication breakdowns, can perpetuate a cycle of emotional distress for all parties involved.

THE IMPACT OF STRESS ON PHYSICAL AND MENTAL HEALTH

This discussion delves into the profound effects of stress on physical and mental well-being, highlighting the mechanisms through which it impacts health, the conditions it exacerbates, and the importance of addressing it effectively. When an individual encounters a stressor, the body initiates the "fight or flight"(Abel et al., 2007) response, a survival mechanism designed to handle immediate threats. This response involves the release of stress hormones such as adrenaline and cortisol, which trigger physiological changes like increased heart rate, heightened alertness, and a surge of energy. While these changes are helpful in acute situations, prolonged activation of the stress response can lead to adverse effects oǹ physical health. raises blood pressure and keeps the heart working harder than necessary, increasing the risk of arterial damage. Over time, this can lead to the buildup of plaque in the arteries, contributing to conditions like atherosclerosis. Stress also triggers unhealthy coping behaviors, such as smoking, overeating, and alcohol consumption, which further exacerbate cardiovascular risks (Sameer Babu, M., et al. 2025). Immune System Dysregulation has been shown to slow wound healing, increase the severity of autoimmune diseases, and weaken resistance to common infections like colds Metabolic and Endocrine Health Prolonged stress alters metabolism and hormonal balance, contributing to conditions such as obesity and diabetes. Stress can also disrupt blood sugar regulation, leading to insulin resistance and heightened susceptibility to type 2 diabetes (Avendano et al., 2009). Furthermore, stress often interferes with appetite control, leading to unhealthy eating patterns like binge eating or loss of appetite. Gastrointestinal Health The gut is highly sensitive to stress, with the brain-gut axis playing a central role in this interaction. Persistent stress may lead to abdominal pain, nausea, and changes in bowel habits, further affecting quality of life Musculoskeletal and Neurological Effects(Backé et al., 2012)Physical stress often manifests as tension in the muscles, leading to headaches, back pain, and neck stiffness. Chronic stress can also contribute to migraines and exacerbate conditions like fibromyalgia. Neurologically, stress affects the central nervous system, contributing to conditions like chronic fatigue syndrome and insomnia, which impair the body's ability to recover and rejuvenate. Stress and the Mind: Mental Health Impacts The psychological effects of stress are equally, if not more, concerning.

Prolonged stress disrupts brain function, emotional regulation, and overall mental health. It plays a significant role in the onset and progression of various mental health disorders. Anxiety and Depression Stress is a major contributor to anxiety and depression, two of the most common mental health conditions.

Persistent stress causes hyperactivation of the amygdala, the brain's fear-processing center, leading to heightened feelings of worry and unease. Simultaneously, stress can suppress the activity of the prefrontal cortex, impairing decision-making and emotional regulation. Chronic stress also reduces levels of neurotransmitters like serotonin and dopamine, which are vital for mood regulation, increasing the risk of depression memory formation, leading to forgetfulness and difficulty concentrating. Stress also interferes with the ability to process information, make decisions, and plan effectively a direct consequence of chronic stress. It is particularly prevalent in high-stress professions and caregiving roles. Individuals experiencing burnout often feel detached, overwhelmed, and unable to meet their obligations, which can lead to decreased job Severe stress, particularly from traumatic events, can lead to PTSD, a condition characterized by intrusive memories, flashbacks, and hypervigilance. PTSD profoundly affects an individual's mental health, relationships, and quality of life. It highlights the long-lasting effects that acute stressors can have on mental well-being (Subramanian, M., et al. 2025). Substance Abuse and Addiction Stress often drives individuals to unhealthy coping mechanisms, including substance abuse. The temporary relief offered by alcohol, drugs, or other addictive behaviors creates a dangerous cycle of dependency, further worsening mental health. Chronic stress alters brain reward pathways, increasing vulnerability to addiction. Social and Interpersonal Strains Stress affects social relationships by increasing irritability, withdrawal, and communication difficulties. This can lead to isolation, reduced social support, and feelings of loneliness, which further exacerbate mental health challenges. Family conflicts and strained friendships are common consequences of unaddressed stress.

THE INTERPLAY BETWEEN JOB-RELATED AND LIFE-RELATED STRESS

Among its many sources, job-related and life-related stress are the most pervasive, often intersecting in ways that amplify their effects. Job-related stress arises from professional demands, responsibilities, and workplace dynamics, while life-related stress originates from recognizing their combined impact on individuals and for developing effective strategies to mitigate their adverse. Sources and Effects Job-related stress, also known as occupational stress, stems from various aspects of the professional environment. High workloads, tight deadlines, lack of autonomy, and unclear expectations are common stressors. Additionally, factors like job insecurity, workplace conflicts, and poor organizational support contribute to heightened stress levels (Bakker & Demerouti, 2007). For instance, employees in fast-paced industries may experience pressure to meet performance targets, leading to chronic stress and burnout. (Bakker & Geurts, 2004) Specific professions are particularly susceptible to job-related stress. Healthcare workers, educators, law enforcement officers, and customer service personnel often face unique stressors, such as emotional labor, exposure to trauma, and dealing with difficult clients or patients. Over time, these stressors can result in physical and psychological consequences, including fatigue, anxiety, depression, and reduced job satisfaction. Furthermore, workplace stress affects organizational outcomes. It also creates a toxic work environment, which perpetuates stress for all team members. Life-Related Stress: Sources and Effects Life-related stress encompasses challenges that arise in personal and social domains. These r life transitions, such as marriage, divorce, or relocation. Unlike job-related stress, which is often confined to work hours, life-related stress can persist 24/7, making it harder to escape or manage. Family-related stress is a significant component of life stress. Balancing the demands of raising children, managing household responsibilities, and maintaining healthy relationships can be overwhelming. For example, a single parent juggling multiple roles may experience feelings of inadequacy and exhaustion, compounded by a lack of social support.

Similarly, individuals caring for elderly relatives often face emotional and financial strain, leading to chronic stress. The Interplay Between Job-Related and Life-Related Stress Job-related and life-related stress are deeply interconnected, with one often influencing the other. Stress from the workplace can spill over into personal life, a phenomenon known as "work-to-home spillover." For instance, a demanding job that requires long hours may reduce the time available for family, leading to conflicts and feelings of neglect. Similarly, unresolved workplace conflicts or job insecurity can increase irritability and strain personal relationships. Conversely, life-related stress can affect job performance, referred to as "home-to-work spillover." An individual dealing with a family crisis, financial hardship, or health issue may find it challenging to focus at work, leading to decreased productivity and increased absenteeism (Shende, A. D., et al. 2025). This bidirectional relationship creates a cycle where stress in one domain exacerbates stress in the other. Work-life balance, or the lack thereof, plays a critical role in this interplay. Inadequate boundaries between professional and personal life can blur the lines between the two, making it harder to compartmentalize stress. The advent of remote work, while offering flexibility, has also intensified this challenge. Employees working from home often struggle to separate work tasks from household (Cartwright & Boyes, 2000). Socially, the combined stress can strain relationships with family, friends, and colleagues, leading to isolation and reduced social support. For example, an overworked employee who is also dealing with personal problems may withdraw from social interactions, further compounding feelings of loneliness and stress. This dual burden of stress can also lead to maladaptive coping mechanisms, such as substance abuse, overeating, or excessive screen time. These behaviors provide temporary relief but ultimately worsen the situation, creating a vicious cycle. Strategies for Managing Job-Related and Life-Related Stress Stress Management Techniques Stress management practices, such as mindfulness, meditation, and physical activity, are effective for reducing stress levels. Regular exercise, for instance, releases endorphins that counteract the negative effects of stress hormones. Deep breathing exercises and progressive muscle relaxation can also provide immediate relief during stressful moments. Financial and Time Management practical strategies, such as budgeting and time management, can reduce the burden of financial and time-related stressors. Learning help individuals manage their workload effectively. Professional Help in cases of severe stress, seeking professional assistance is vital. Therapists and counselors can provide coping strategies tailored to an individual's unique situation, while doctors can address physical symptoms related to stress.

SOURCES OF JOB-RELATED STRESS: WORKLOAD, TIME PRESSURE, AND CONFLICT

Job-related stress, a growing concern in modern workplaces, is fueled by various factors that challenge employees' physical, emotional, and mental well-being. Among the most prominent sources are excessive workload, relentless time pressure, and interpersonal conflicts. Each of these stressors contributes to a significant deterioration in job satisfaction, performance, and overall health, making them critical areas of focus for both employees and employers. This exploration highlights the origins, dynamics, and consequences of these stressors, offering insights into their impact and strategies for effective management. Workload: The Burden of Excessive Expectations Workload is one of the most cited causes of job-related stress. Excessive workload often stems from organizational demands, understaffing, or the expectation to "do more with less." Employees in such situations frequently find themselves juggling multiple responsibilities without adequate resources or support. (Choi et al., 2011) For example, a teacher required to handle oversized classrooms with insufficient teaching aids faces an overwhelming burden, leading to frustration and burnout. The effects of heavy workloads are multifaceted. Physically, employees may experience fatigue, sleep disturbances, and increased susceptibility to illness.

Mentally, overwhelming workloads can lead long working hours and insufficient breaks exacerbate stress, leaving little time for recovery or personal pursuits.

The Race Against the Clock Time pressure, or the need to complete tasks within tight deadlines, is another significant source of employees are often expected to deliver results promptly, regardless of the complexity or feasibility of the task. For instance, professionals in the tech industry may face unyielding deadlines for product launches, forcing them to work long hours under immense pressure. The constant rush to meet deadlines triggers a sense of urgency that can compromise decision-making and attention to detail. (Code & Langan-Fox, 2001) Employees under time pressure may resort to shortcuts, increasing the likelihood of errors and reducing overall work quality. Furthermore, the inability to meet tight deadlines fosters a fear of failure, which can erode self-confidence and job satisfaction. Time pressure also disrupts work-life balance, as employees sacrifice personal time to keep up with demands. This leads to chronic stress, fatigue, and resentment toward the organization. Over time, the cumulative effects of time-related stress can result in burnout, characterized by emotional exhaustion, detachment, and diminished productivity. To alleviate time pressure, employers must establish realistic timelines, encourage prioritization, and provide training in time management skills. Conflict: Navigating Interpersonal Challenges Workplace conflict, whether between colleagues, supervisors, or teams, is a potent source of job-related stress. The presence of conflict can erode organizational culture, leading to increased turnover rates and reputational damage. Effective conflict resolution strategies, such as mediation, clear communication channels, and fostering a culture of respect, are essential for mitigating the stress caused by workplace disagreements. The Interconnected Nature of Workload, Time Pressure, and Conflict These sources of job-related stress are often interrelated, compounding their effects on employees. For instance, an excessive workload can lead to time pressure, as employees struggle to complete their tasks within unrealistic deadlines. Similarly, time pressure can heighten workplace tensions, increasing the likelihood of conflicts. Moreover, job-related stress affects organizational outcomes, including decreased productivity, higher absenteeism, and increased employee turnover. (Dewe & Kompier, 2008) Stress-related illnesses drive up healthcare costs and disrupt workplace continuity, creating a significant burden on employers. Stress Reduction Program Introduce wellness programs, such as mindfulness training and exercise initiatives (Ranjitha P. K., et al. 2025). Provide access to mental health resources, including counseling and employee assistance programs. Encourage open dialogue about stress and mental health to reduce stigma. Leadership Development Train managers to recognize and address sources of stress in their teams. Foster a leadership style that emphasizes empathy, transparency, and support.ConclusionWorkload, time pressure, and conflict are significant sources of job-related stress, with far-reaching implications for both employees and organizations. Understanding the dynamics of these stressors and their interconnected nature is crucial for developing effective strategies to mitigate their impact healthier, more sustainable workplaces.

THE EFFECTS OF JOB-RELATED STRESS ON PERFORMANCE AND PRODUCTIVITY

Job-related stress is a pervasive issue in modern workplaces, significantly influencing employee performance and organizational productivity. As businesses strive to meet competitive demands, employees often encounter stressors such as heavy workloads, time pressure, and workplace conflicts. While short-term stress can sometimes enhance focus and motivation, chronic stress has detrimental effects on an individual's ability to perform effectively. This discussion explores the multifaceted ways in which job-related stress impacts performance and productivity, both at the individual and organizational levels, and highlights strategies to mitigate these effects. Individual Performance: The Cognitive and Behavioral Impact Chronic stress disrupts cognitive functions critical for workplace performance, such as attention, memory, and decision-making. Prolonged exposure to stress hormones, particularly cortisol, impairs the prefrontal cortex, the brain region responsible for planning and problem-solving. Employees experiencing stress may struggle to prioritize tasks, process information accurately, and make sound decisions. For example, a project manager under significant stress might overlook key details, leading to errors and delays in project delivery. (Dragano & Wahrendorf, 2014)Behaviorally, stress often manifests in reduced motivation and engagement. Employees burdened by stress may exhibit procrastination, avoidance behaviors, or a decline in work quality.

Figure 1. Major causes of work stress

These issues can spiral, as the inability to meet expectations further exacerbates stress, Emotional and Social Effects on Workplace Performance. The emotional toll of job-related stress affects interpersonal relationships and teamwork, both of which are critical to organizational success. Stressed employees often experience irritability, mood swings, and reduced tolerance for frustration. These emotional responses can strain relationships with colleagues, leading to conflicts, miscommunication, and a breakdown of collaboration. For example, a team member under stress might react defensively to feedback, hindering constructive discussions and problem-solving efforts. embrace change, further limiting their effectiveness. In high-stress environments, employees may become (Ferrie et al., 2005). The Broader Impact of Stress at the organizational level, the cumulative effects of job-related stress significantly impact productivity. higher absenteeism rates. Empathetic leadership, where managers demonstrate understanding and support, fosters trust and reduces stress among team members. Encouraging Collaboration and Social Support Building a sense of community within the workplace helps employees feel valued and supported. Team-building activities, peer support programs, and open forums for discussing challenges encourage collaboration and reduce feelings of isolation. For example, a mentorship program can provide guidance and alleviate stress for employees facing complex tasks. Monitoring and Evaluating Stress Levels Regular assessments of workplace stress levels through surveys, feedback sessions, or performance reviews help organizations identify and address stressors early. Data-driven insights enable targeted interventions, ensuring that stress management initiatives are effective and responsive to employees' needs.

MANAGING JOB-RELATED STRESS: STRATEGIES FOR EMPLOYEES AND ORGANIZATIONS

Job-organizations. While stress can sometimes drive performance in short bursts, chronic and unmanaged stress has detrimental effects on mental and physical health, productivity, and overall job satisfaction. As stress impacts individual well-being and organizational efficiency, adopting effective strategies to manage it is essential. Both employees and organizations play a critical role in mitigating stress, and a collaborative approach can foster a healthier, more productive work environment. Employee Strategies for Managing Job-Related Stress Time Management and Prioritization effective time management is a cornerstone of stress management for employees. By organizing tasks and setting priorities, employees can reduce feelings of being overwhelmed. Techniques such as the Eisenhower Matrix, which categorizes tasks by urgency and importance, or time-blocking schedules help employees focus on high-priority activities. Delegating tasks where possible and breaking large projects into smaller, manageable steps can also ease the burden of a heavy workload (Mehta, A. K., et al. 2025). Building Emotional Resilience Emotional resilience allows employees to navigate workplace challenges without becoming overwhelmed. Strategies include cultivating a growth mindset, focusing on what can be controlled, and reframing negative thoughts into constructive ones. Seeking professional counselling Employees should establish clear boundaries, such as avoiding work-related communications after hours, and take advantage of vacation days to recharge.

Pursuing personal goals and spending time with family or friends ensures that work does not dominate one's life. Seeking Support when stress becomes unmanageable, reaching out for support is vital. Employees can confide in trusted colleagues, mentors, or supervisors to discuss stressors and potential solutions. Accessing provides additional professional help for managing stress-related challenges. Organizational Strategies for Managing Job-Related Stress Creating a Supportive Work Environment Organizations must prioritize employee well-being by fostering a positive and inclusive workplace culture. Transparent communication. Ensuring open-door policies where employees can express concerns without fear of retaliation encourages a sense of trust. prevents burnout and maintains long-term productivity. Managing Workloads Employers must ensure that workloads are realistic and achievable. (Firth-Cozens, 2003) Overburdened employees leading to decreased productivity and higher turnover rates. For instance, organizations with robust EAPs see better engagement and lower turnover rates as employees feel supported in addressing their challenges Empowering Leadership to Address Stress managers and leaders play a critical role in stress management. Leadership training on recognizing signs of employee stress and providing appropriate support ensures a proactive approach. Empathetic leadership that prioritizes employee well-being fosters trust and reduces workplace tension. encouraging open communication. Monitoring and Evaluating Workplace Stress Organizations should regularly assess stress levels through employee surveys, feedback sessions, or performance reviews. This data helps identify stressors, monitor the effectiveness of implemented strategies, and make necessary adjustments. For example, organizations that track metrics like absenteeism, turnover, and engagement levels can pinpoint areas needing improvement and take corrective action.

SOURCES OF LIFE-RELATED STRESS: FAMILY, FINANCES, AND HEALTH

Life-related stress is an inevitable part of the human experience, often arising from significant domains such as family, finances, and health. While these areas are vital for personal well-being and stability, they can also serve as major stressors, influencing individuals' emotional, f responsibilities, uncertainties, and external pressures in these aspects of life creates challenges that can feel overwhelming. Understanding the roots and impact of stress from family obligations, financial concerns, and health issues is crucial for managing its effects and fostering resilience. Family as a Source of Stress Family relationships, while often a source of support and love, can also contribute significantly to life-related stress. The complexities of familial dynamics, caregiving responsibilities, and life changes such as marriage, divorce, or the birth of a child create emotional and logistical challenges.(Garhammer, 2004) Interpersonal Conflicts: Disputes or unresolved tensions among family members can lead to chronic stress. Differences in values, communication styles, or expectations may result in frequent arguments and strained relationships. For instance, a parent and adolescent child may clash over issues such as independence and discipline, creating a cycle of frustration for both. The constant worry about paying bills or managing expenses can lead to chronic stress, anxiety, and even depression. Job Insecurity and Unemployment: Uncertainty about employment stability or the loss of a job contributes heavily to financial stress. The fear of losing a steady income affects not only the individual but also their dependents. Prolonged unemployment often erodes self-esteem and creates a sense of hopelessness. Planning for the Future: Concerns about saving for retirement, funding education, or covering healthcare costs add long-term stress. For instance, parents saving for their children's college education may feel overwhelmed by the rising costs of tuition, while simultaneously trying to secure their own retirement plans.(Glanz & Schwartz, 2008)Health as a Source of Stress Health-related issues, whether concerning one's own well-being or that of loved ones, are a profound source of stress. Physical illnesses, mental health conditions, and concerns about access to healthcare compound emotional burdens. The high cost of medical care, coupled with the uncertainty of navigating insurance systems, adds significant stress. Many individuals delay seeking treatment due to financial constraints, worsening their health outcomes and increasing their anxiety about the future. The Interconnected Nature of Family, Finances, and Health (Hershcovis, 2011). The sources of life-related stress often intersect, amplifying their impact. For instance, a family member's serious illness can create financial strain due to medical expenses, while also introducing emotional stress from caregiving responsibilities. Similarly, financial difficulties can strain familial relationships, leading to conflicts and reduced emotional support. A proactive approach to managing stress fosters not only personal well-being but also stronger, more harmonious communities.

THE IMPACT OF LIFE-RELATED STRESS ON WELL-BEING AND RELATIONSHIPS

Life-related stress, stemming from personal, financial, or health challenges, significantly impacts individuals' overall well-being and their relationships. Whether triggered by demanding family dynamics, economic uncertainty, or chronic health issues, stress disrupts emotional balance, mental clarity, and physical health. Furthermore, the effects of life-related stress extend beyond the individual, influencing interactions with loved ones, friends, and colleagues. Understanding these impacts is crucial to fostering resilience, maintaining strong relationships, and promoting a higher quality of life. Effects on Well-Being Physical Health Consequences Stress also disrupts sleep patterns, resulting in insomnia or poor-quality sleep. Sleep deprivation exacerbates physical exhaustion and diminishes the body's ability to repair and recharge, creating a vicious cycle of declining health. Social Isolation and Loneliness Stress often isolates individuals, as they withdraw from social interactions to cope with overwhelming responsibilities or emotional burdens. This self-imposed isolation deprives them of the support systems necessary for stress relief and exacerbates feelings of loneliness (Hobfoll, 2001). For example, someone dealing with a chronic illness may feel disconnected from friends or family who cannot fully understand their struggles, deepening their sense of alienation. Effects on Relationships. Increased Conflict and Communication Challenges Life-related stress frequently causes strain in personal relationships, as individuals under stress may become irritable, impatient, or withdrawn. Poor communication fueled by emotional exhaustion often leads to misunderstandings and conflicts (Athavale, V. A., et al. 2025). For instance, financial stress can trigger arguments between partners over spending habits or budgeting priorities. Similarly, caregiving stress may lead to feelings of resentment or frustration within families if responsibilities are perceived as unequally distributed. Stress also reduces the ability to listen actively or empathize with others, making it harder to resolve disagreements constructively.

Over time, unresolved conflicts weaken trust and intimacy in relationships, potentially leading to emotional distancing or separation. Caregiving Strain When life-related stress stems from caregiving responsibilities, the emotional and physical demands can strain relationships between caregivers and care recipients. For example, an adult child caring for an aging parent with dementia may experience guilt, frustration, and sadness, while the parent may feel a loss of independence and dignity. These dynamics can create tension, even in loving relationships. Moreover, caregivers often neglect their own well-being, leading to burnout that further impacts their ability to provide effective care. This can create a cycle of mutual frustration and guilt, eroding the quality of the relationship. Impact on Parenting and Family Dynamics Parental stress affects not only the parent's well-being but also the emotional and developmental outcomes of children. Stressed parents may unintentionally project their frustrations onto their children, leading to strained parent-child relationships. (Jacobshagen & Rigotti, 2008). Coping with the Impact of Life-Related Stress Addressing the effects of stress on well-being and relationships requires a combination of self-care strategies, social support, and professional resources. Building Emotional Resilience (Jungbauer-Gans & Gross, 2009) Practicing mindfulness, meditation, or deep-breathing exercises helps individuals manage stress and regain emotional balance. For instance, financial advisors can help individuals manage debt, while family therapists can mediate conflicts and strengthen relationships Conclusion Life-related stress profoundly affects both individual well-being and interpersonal relationships. Its impact on physical health, mental stability, and social connections underscores the importance of proactive stress management.

By building resilience, fostering —such as healthcare access, economic stability, and family support systems—are essential for creating environments that promote collective well-being. With a collaborative approach, it is possible to transform the challenges of life-related stress into opportunities for growth and connection.

COPING WITH LIFE-RELATED STRESS: PERSONAL AND SOCIAL RESOURCES

Life-related stress is a universal challenge that stems from diverse sources, such as family responsibilities, financial pressures, and health concerns. well-being. Coping involves a combination of personal resilience and the use of social resources, creating a comprehensive approach to managing stress and fostering a sense of control. By leveraging internal strengths and external support systems, individuals can navigate stressful circumstances more effectively Personal Resources for Coping Personal managing stress, as they empower individuals to develop resilience and maintain balance amidst life's challenges. Emotional Resilience and Mindset motional resilience is the ability to adapt to adversity and recover from setbacks. Developing a positive mindset helps individuals view challenges as opportunities for growth rather than insurmountable obstacles. Practices such as reframing negative thoughts, focusing on solutions, and celebrating small victories build confidence and reduce the emotional burden of stress. Flexible work arrangements, access to Employee Assistance Programs (EAPs), and a supportive workplace culture help employees balance professional and personal responsibilities. For example, a flexible schedule allows an employee to attend to family matters without compromising their job performance. Community and Faith-Based Resources Community organizations and faith-based groups provide additional avenues of support. Resources such as food banks, (Kauffeld & Hoppe, 2011) childcare services, or financial assistance programs reduce practical stressors. Faith-based communities also offer spiritual guidance and a sense of hope, helping individuals find meaning and purpose during challenging times. Integrating Personal and Social Resources The most effective coping strategies combine personal resilience with social support. For instance, an individual facing a health crisis might use mindfulness practices to manage immediate anxiety while relying on family for emotional encouragement and a healthcare team for professional guidance. Similarly, someone experiencing financial stress can adopt budgeting tools for personal management while seeking advice from a financial counselor. Collaboration between personal and social resources fosters a holistic approach to stress management. While personal resources build internal strength, social resources provide external validation and assistance, creating a balance that supports overall well-being. Benefits of Effective Coping with life-related stress effectively yields numerous benefits for physical, emotional, and social well-being.

STRESS MANAGEMENT TECHNIQUES: RELAXATION, MINDFULNESS, AND EXERCISE

Each technique offers unique benefits and can be adapted to fit individual preferences and lifestyles. Relaxation Techniques: Promoting Calm and Restorative States Relaxation techniques are designed (Lampert et al., 2005). The practice of relaxation is essential for calming the mind, reducing muscle tension, and promoting rest. Several relaxation techniques are commonly used to manage stress, each with distinct benefits. can be used in moments of acute stress to quickly activate a relaxation response. Over time, autogenic training can lead to improved stress resilience and reduced physiological signs of stress, such as high blood pressure and heart rate and reduce stress (Pradeep, E., et al. 2025). This practice helps anchor the individual in the present moment and counteracts the "fight-or-flight" stress response. Mindful breathing can be done in any setting, making it a practical tool for managing stress throughout the day. To practice mindful breathing, individuals can focus on each breath, paying attention to the sensation of air entering and leaving the body. Both practices emphasize the connection between the mind and body, helping individuals focus on the present moment and release physical and mental tension. Research suggests that regular participation in yoga and Pilates can lead to significant reductions in perceived stress, enhanced mood, and improved mental clarity. Group Exercise Classes Participating in group exercise classes, such as dance, aerobics, or martial arts, offers both physical and social benefits (Lampert et al., 2016). Exercise in a group setting promotes a sense of community and belonging, stay motivated, and build positive relationships. Conclusion relaxation practices, mindfulness, and exercise are powerful tools for coping with the challenges of life.

BUILDING RESILIENCE: DEVELOPING COPING SKILLS AND ADAPTABILITY

Building resilience is crucial for managing life's inevitable stressors and setbacks, from personal losses and health issues to work pressures and financial difficulties. The ability to adapt to change, overcome obstacles, and maintain a positive outlook can significantly improve one's mental, emotional, and physical well-being. Developing resilience is an ongoing process that involves strengthening coping skills, fostering adaptability, and building supportive relationships. These elements work together to create a robust foundation for navigating adversity and can help individuals not only survive stressful situations but also grow through them. Understanding Resilience Resilience is often misunderstood as a trait that some people are born with, but it is, in fact, a dynamic skill set that anyone can develop with practice and intention. It is an internal resource that allows individuals to recover from setbacks, adapt to change, and maintain a sense of control during turbulent times. Research in psychology emphasizes that resilience is not about avoiding stress or adversity but about learning how to respond to and manage these challenges in a healthy way. This involves recognizing and leveraging personal strengths, developing coping strategies, and engaging with external resources like support networks. While some people may naturally demonstrate more resilience due to personality traits or early life experiences, resilience can be learned by practicing certain strategies that enhance emotional regulation, problem-solving abilities, and social connections. Building resilience involves cultivating mental toughness, but also knowing when to seek support, practice self-compassion, and take care of one's mental and physical health. Coping Skills: Tools for Managing Stress and Adversity people to manage their reactions to stressors and reduce their impact on well-being. Effective coping strategies are essential for building resilience because they provide (Law et al., 2020) the emotional and psychological tools to navigate difficulties.

They identify potential solutions, weigh the pros and cons, and take actionable steps toward resolving the issue. Effective problem-solving reduces the feeling of helplessness that often accompanies stress and helps maintain a sense of control, (Nerdinger et al., 2008) For example, if a person is experiencing financial difficulties, they may create a budget, explore ways to cut expenses, and research additional sources of income to improve their situation. Emotional Regulation Emotional regulation involves managing one's emotional responses to stressors in a way that minimizes negative reactions and enhances positive ones. This skill is particularly important for building resilience because it allows individuals to by a work deadline, a person may practice deep breathing to calm their nervous system before taking focused, methodical action.. Stress Management Techniques In addition to emotional regulation, effective stress management is crucial for coping with life's challenges. Techniques like relaxation exercises, meditation, and physical activities such as yoga or walking can help reduce the physiological and psychological effects of stress. By managing their time effectively, resilient individuals can prioritize tasks, can help balance responsibilities and reduce stress levels. Effective time management provides a sense of accomplishment, which in turn supports feelings of competence and control. (Peters & O'Connor, 1980) Adaptability: Embracing Change and Uncertainty. It is a cornerstone of resilience because life is inherently unpredictable, and being able to cope with change is essential for overcoming challenges. Conclusion

Building resilience is a continuous process that involves developing coping skills, fostering adaptability, and cultivating social support.

PROMOTING WELLBEING: SELF-CARE, SOCIAL SUPPORT, AND WORK-LIFE BALANCE

Wellbeing is a holistic concept that encompasses physical, mental, and emotional health. It is, the constant pace of digital life, and personal responsibilities, it is essential to prioritize and nurture one's health in order to lead a fulfilling and balanced life. Promoting wellbeing involves adopting practices that proactive approach to wellbeing by regularly addressing one's needs, whether through diet, exercise, sleep, relaxation, or mindfulness. Self-care is not just about occasional indulgence, such as taking a spa day or treating oneself to a favorite activity, but about consistently prioritizing one's health, both in terms of prevention and recovery. Stabilize energy levels and improve long-term health. Mental and Emotional Self-Care: Supporting Emotional Health Mental and emotional self-care involves taking intentional steps to nurture one's emotional health and cognitive wellbeing. Managing stress, practicing self-compassion, and engaging in activities that promote mental clarity and relaxation are crucial for emotional resilience. individuals can better cope with stress and improve their emotional wellbeing. of difficulty. It helps individuals cope with failure, disappointment, or difficult emotions by fostering an attitude of understanding and patience. Practicing self-compassion can reduce self-criticism and promote a more balanced and healthier outlook on life, book or a favorite show provides individuals with time for self-expression and relaxation. These activities help to reduce stress and promote a sense of fulfillment and enjoyment, which are integral to emotional wellbeing.

Socializing regularly helps prevent feelings of loneliness and isolation, which have been linked to depression and anxiety. Engaging in shared activities, such as having meals with loved ones or participating in community events, helps individuals feel connected and supported. Setting Boundaries: Healthy boundaries are critical for maintaining balanced relationships and personal wellbeing. Being able to say "no" when necessary and setting limits on time and energy helps prevent burnout. Healthy boundaries also allow individuals to protect their emotional space and engage in self-care without feeling overwhelmed or taken advantage of. Social Support: The Role of Relationships in Wellbeing It plays a significant role in promoting wellbeing, as supportive relationships act as a buffer against stress and adversity. Whether it is family, friends, colleagues, or a support group, having people who provide empathy, encouragement, and help during difficult times contributes to improved emotional resilience and mental health. Emotional support involves receiving empathy, understanding, and validation from others. Having someone to listen without judgment or offering comfort during difficult moments can reduce the psychological burden of stress and enhance emotional wellbeing. Emotional support. Support Instrumental support refers to the practical help or assistance individuals receive from their social network. This may involve tangible help, such as assistance with tasks, financial support, or caregiving. Knowing that one can rely on others for practical assistance can significantly reduce feelings of overwhelm, especially during times of illness or stress. Informational support involves receiving advice, guidance, or resources from others to help solve problems or cope with challenges. The pressure to succeed in both spheres can lead to stress, burnout, and physical and emotional exhaustion. A balanced approach to work and life, where individuals prioritize both their careers and personal wellbeing, is essential for long-term health and happiness (Pfeiffer, 2007). Setting boundaries at work is crucial to prevent burnout and maintain personal wellbeing. This includes establishing clear limits on working hours, avoiding excessive overtime, and resisting the temptation to check emails or work-related tasks during personal time. By maintaining boundaries, individuals can protect their personal life from encroaching work demands and ensure that they have the time and space to recharge. Flexible Work Arrangements Many organizations are increasingly offering flexible work arrangements, such as remote work options or flexible hours, to help employees manage their professional and personal responsibilities (Rigotti et al., 2014).

MANAGING STRESS IN SPECIFIC PROFESSIONS: HEALTHCARE, EDUCATION, AND EMERGENCY SERVICES

Healthcare, education, and emergency services are three such fields where stress is a constant companion. In these professions, managing stress effectively is not only crucial for the wellbeing of the employees but also for the quality of care, learning, and emergency response provided. Effective stress management in these high-pressure professions involves understanding the unique stressors they face, recognizing the impact of stress on both personal and professional lives, and implementing tailored strategies to mitigate its harmful effects. Healthcare professionals are constantly exposed to stressful situations, from life-or-death decision-making to long hours, understaffed teams, and emotional exhaustion. The nature of healthcare work, whether in hospitals, clinics, or caregiving settings, often requires professionals to be present during times of intense emotional and physical distress for patients and their families. Healthcare workers are expected to maintain high standards of care while balancing administrative tasks, dealing with the trauma of patients' conditions, and managing the expectations of families, colleagues, and superiors. Stress in Education: Balancing Teaching and Administrative Demands Teachers and educators are often tasked with managing classrooms filled with students, ensuring effective lesson delivery, handling administrative duties, and meeting the expectations of parents, school boards, and the broader community. These pressures are compounded by the increasing demand for standardized testing, the need for individualized learning plans, and the emotional labor of supporting students' mental and emotional needs. Educational professionals frequently report higher levels of stress, which can lead to burnout, levels of energy, patience, and adaptability. (Schieman et al., 2006) The emotional labor involved in teaching—especially for educators who work with students facing socio-economic hardships, behavioral issues, or mental health challenges—can also contribute to stress.

Teachers often take on the role of counselor or caregiver, providing emotional support to students who may be dealing with trauma, bullying, or family problems. Over time, this emotional involvement can lead to emotional exhaustion and burnout. Administrative Pressures and Workload In addition to the demands of teaching, educators are often burdened with administrative tasks such as grading, lesson planning, attending meetings, and adhering to curriculum standards. With large class sizes, limited resources, and the growing expectation to meet academic standards set by testing agencies, teachers are often stretched thin. These administrative pressures can create a feeling of being overwhelmed, which directly impacts the quality of teaching and the educator's wellbeing. Time constraints and a lack of professional development opportunities also contribute to high stress levels among teachers. Stress Management Strategies for Educators For educators, stress management strategies must include both personal coping mechanisms and institutional support. Self-care practices such as setting boundaries, taking breaks during the day, engaging in physical activities, and practicing mindfulness can help manage classroom-related stress. Furthermore, schools should foster a supportive environment by providing professional development programs, reducing unnecessary administrative tasks, and offering mentoring or peer support groups for teachers. A culture of openness and collaboration among colleagues can help educators share the emotional and psychological challenges they face. Schools should also offer resources such as counseling services and access to mental health support to help educators cope with emotional stress. Stress in Emergency Services: Coping with Crisis and Life-or-Death situations Emergency service workers, such as paramedics, firefighters, police officers, and dispatchers, are exposed to some of the most high-stress environments imaginable. These professionals often work in life-or-death situations, responding to accidents, medical emergencies, criminal incidents, and natural disasters. The emotional and physical demands of emergency services can cause significant stress, affecting both the mental health of employees and their performance in the field. Physical Demands and Fatigue (Schmidt et al., 2012). The impact of stress on professionals in these fields can be profound, affecting both their personal health and the quality of service they provide. However, with effective stress management strategies tailored to the specific needs of each profession, it is possible to mitigate the negative effects of stress. By prioritizing self-care, promoting organizational support, fostering teamwork and peer support, and providing access to mental health resources, professionals in these fields can improve their resilience, job satisfaction, and overall wellbeing. Managing stress is not only vital for the individuals working in these professions but also for ensuring that the essential services they provide continue to be delivered with empathy, competence, and efficiency.

STRESS AND TECHNOLOGY: THE IMPACT OF DIGITAL COMMUNICATION AND SOCIAL MEDIA

The rise of digital communication and social media has led to an increasingly connected world, but this constant connectivity comes at a cost. The continuous flow of information, the pressures of online interactions, and the pervasive nature of social media have contributed to heightened stress levels, particularly among individuals who struggle to manage The Ubiquity of Digital Communication and Its Effects on Stressit has also contributed to stress in several ways. The constant availability of communication tools means that individuals are rarely "off the clock" and are expected to respond to messages and notifications at all times of day or night.. Information Overload and Cognitive Strain One of the most significant contributors to digital stress is information overload. With a constant barrage of emails, texts, social media updates, and news articles, individuals often find themselves overwhelmed by the sheer volume of information they are expected to process. The inability to "switch off" from work-related tasks can create a sense of perpetual urgency and a feeling of being constantly on call, contributing to heightened stress levels (Zapf & Semmer, 2004). Fear of Missing Out (FOMO) and Social IsolationFOMO is a psychological phenomenon that is especially prevalent in the digital age, where people feel the need to stay connected to everything happening on social media. The constant flow of updates, photos, and posts can create a sense of urgency, as individuals feel compelled to be a part of every trend, event, or conversation. This pressure can lead to stress as people attempt to keep up with the ever-changing online landscape, often to the detriment of their real-life relationships and wellbeing. Ironically, while social media is designed to connect people, it can also contribute to feelings of social isolation. When individuals see others engaging in social activities or experiences they are not a part of, it can create a sense of exclusion and loneliness, further contributing to stress and negative mental health outcomes.

Digital Addiction and Its Contribution to Stress The pervasive nature of digital communication and social media has also led to a rise in digital addiction, where individuals feel compelled to check their devices constantly, even when it is unnecessary. This addiction is fueled by the dopamine-driven rewards system, where notifications, likes, comments, and messages trigger pleasurable feelings, encouraging people to continue engaging with their devices. The constant need for validation and the desire for social approval contribute to the compulsive use of digital devices, which can lead to stress when individuals feel disconnected or anxious when they are unable to check their devices. As a result, individuals who engage with digital devices late at night may experience difficulty falling asleep or maintaining restful sleep, which can contribute to physical and mental exhaustion. Poor sleep, in turn, leads to heightened stress levels, reduced cognitive function, and diminished emotional resilience. Disconnection from the Present Moment. The constant use of digital devices also contributes to a disconnection from the present moment. As individuals are engrossed in their screens, they often miss out on real-life interactions and experiences, which can lead to feelings of disconnection and dissatisfaction. The inability to be fully present in one's environment—whether at home, work, or social gatherings—can increase stress and anxiety, as individuals may feel that they are constantly "missing out" or that they are not truly engaging with the world around them.

CULTURAL AND DIVERSITY FACTORS IN STRESS MANAGEMENT

Cultural factors influence not only how stress is triggered but also how it is processed and alleviated, with varying approaches to coping strategies, social support, and professional interventions. By examining the cultural dimensions of stress and stress management, we can better understand the complex ways in which stress impacts individuals and identify tailored approaches that are culturally sensitive and effective. The Role of Culture in In contrast, individualist cultures, such as those in many Western societies, place a higher value on personal autonomy and individual responsibility. In these cultures, stress is often seen as a personal challenge to be overcome through self-reliance, problem-solving, and individual coping strategies (Tepper & Henle, 2011). Individuals in these societies may be more likely to address stress through private means, such as seeking therapy or engaging in solo activities like exercise or meditation. While personal achievements and self-sufficiency are highly valued in individualist cultures, the emphasis on individual responsibility can sometimes lead to feelings of isolation or inadequacy when stress becomes overwhelming. In some cultures, expressing emotions openly, especially negative emotions like frustration or sadness, is discouraged or seen as a sign of weakness. For example, in many East Asian cultures, emotional restraint is often valued, and showing vulnerability in the face of stress may be considered inappropriate or shameful. In these cultures, individuals may be more likely to suppress their feelings or internalize their stress, which can lead to physical manifestations of stress, such as headaches, gastrointestinal issues, or sleep disturbances contrast, cultures that encourage open emotional expression, such as many Western societies, may have a greater acceptance of discussing stress and seeking emotional support through social networks or professional help. However, this openness can sometimes lead to a tendency to ruminate on stressors or to share emotional burdens in ways that may not always lead to effective solutions.

In cultures that place a high value on emotional restraint or social harmony, emotion-focused coping may be preferred, but it can take on different forms. In some Asian cultures, for example, individuals might turn to spiritual practices, such as prayer, meditation, or engaging in religious rituals, to help alleviate stress. These practices offer a way to calm the mind, reflect on personal challenges, and restore a sense of balance without openly expressing distress. Similarly, in many Latin American and African cultures, emotional support from close-knit family units is a key coping mechanism, where individuals share their feelings in a safe and empathetic environment. In Western cultures, emotion-focused coping may include activities such as journaling, therapy, or mindfulness practices like meditation and yoga, which allow individuals to process their emotions in a private and reflective manner (Voßemer et al., 2018). These practices are often centered around individual emotional growth and self-regulation. The emphasis in these societies is often on empowering individuals to manage their stress independently, which may include using coping tools, such as cognitive-behavioral techniques or stress reduction exercises. However, this individualistic approach can sometimes be at odds with the collectivist orientation of many other cultures, where the sharing of emotional burdens within the family or community is more conclusion more effective, culturally sensitive approaches to supporting individuals in managing stress. Whether through collective support networks, emotion-focused practices, or individualized approaches to problem-solving (Uchino, 2006) stress management must be adaptable to the cultural context in which it occurs. A deeper understanding of cultural diversity in stress management can promote healthier, more inclusive environments and ensure that individuals from all backgrounds have the tools and support they need to cope with stress effectively

FUTURE DIRECTIONS FOR STRESS MANAGEMENT RESEARCH AND PRACTICE

Stress, a universal response to both external and internal demands, has long been studied within the fields of psychology, medicine, and sociology. However, as society evolves, so too does the nature of stress and the ways it affects individuals. The increasing complexity of modern life, accelerated by rapid technological advancements, social changes, and global interconnectedness, presents new challenges for both understanding and managing stress. As such, the future of stress management research and practice holds tremendous potential for improving individual well-being, enhancing mental and physical health, and promoting healthier societies. This direction will involve refining existing models of stress, exploring the unique challenges posed by contemporary stressors, and leveraging new methodologies and interdisciplinary approaches to develop more effective, personalized(Ulich & Wülser, 2010). This could range from specific exercises and relaxation techniques to tailored mental health treatments based on one's neurobiological makeup. Additionally, advances in psychophysiology, which looks at the relationship between the mind and body, could also play a crucial role. Understanding how factors like heart rate variability, hormonal response, and the nervous system influence stress responses will allow for more personalized stress management practices. Furthermore, the rise of digital health technologies, including wearable devices and health apps, allows for real-time monitoring of stress levels, which can be personalized to provide immediate feedback. These technologies can measure physiological markers such as heart rate, skin conductivity, and even cortisol levels, offering individuals insights into their stress triggers and providing immediate suggestions for managing their responses. With the help of machine learning algorithms, these devices can learn from a user's past experiences to predict stress patterns and offer tailored recommendations for stress management, such as breathing exercises, mindfulness practices, or even scheduling relaxation periods.

CONCLUSION

This type of predictive analytics could revolutionize the way we understand and manage stress, providing personalized and anticipatory interventions. Cultural Sensitivity and Diversity in Stress Management. As globalization continues to shape the interconnectedness of societies, it is increasingly important to ensure that stress management strategies are culturally sensitive and inclusive. Cultural norms, values, and expectations influence how stress is perceived, expressed, and managed. The future of stress management must account for these cultural differences, ensuring that stress interventions are adaptable and effective across diverse populations. Future research should focus on developing culturally relevant models of stress management that reflect the unique needs of different communities. The Role of Workplace and Organizational Interventions Given the increasing prevalence of workplace stress, especially in high-demand environments, the future of stress management will also involve comprehensive workplace interventions that support employee well-being. Companies are already beginning to implement stress management programs, but there is significant room for growth. In the future, organizations should adopt a more holistic approach to employee well-being, integrating stress management into their corporate cultures. Additionally, longitudinal studies will help establish a clearer understanding of the long-term effects of chronic stress and the most effective interventions for mitigating these effects over time. Furthermore, interdisciplinary collaboration between psychologists, neuroscientists, sociologists, and medical professionals will be essential for developing a holistic approach to stress management. As research continues to evolve, integrating different perspectives will allow for the creation of more innovative and effective strategies for stress reduction. The future of stress management research and practice holds immense promise for improving the way we understand, experience, and cope with stress.

REFERENCES

Abel, T., Duetz-Schmuck, M., & Huwiler-Müntener, K. (2007). Sozialmedizin und Gesundheitssoziologie. In Gutzwiller, F., & Paccaud, F. (Eds.), *Sozial- und Präventivmedizin. Public Health* (3rd ed., pp. 23–34). Huber.

Athavale, V. A., Selvakumar, P., Poorani, S., Anand, T., & Rathore, D. S. (2025). Designing Chatbots for Educational Leadership. In Musundire, A. (Ed.), *Chatbots in Educational Leadership and Management* (pp. 181–204). IGI Global Scientific Publishing., DOI: 10.4018/979-8-3693-8734-4.ch008

Avendano, M., Jürges, H., & Mackenbach, J. P. (2009). Educational level and changes in health across Europe: Longitudinal results from SHARE. *Journal of European Social Policy*, *19*(4), 301–316. DOI: 10.1177/1350506809341512

Backé, E. M., Seidler, A., Latza, U., Rossnagel, K., & Schumann, B. (2012). The role of psychosocial stress at work for the development of cardiovascular diseases: A systematic review. *International Archives of Occupational and Environmental Health*, *85*(1), 67–79. DOI: 10.1007/s00420-011-0643-6 PMID: 21584721

Bakker, A. B., & Demerouti, E. (2007). The Job-Demands-Resources Model: State of the art. *Journal of Managerial Psychology*, *22*(3), 309–328. DOI: 10.1108/02683940710733115

Bakker, A. B., & Geurts, S. A. E. (2004). Toward a dual-process model of work-home interference. *Work and Occupations*, *31*(3), 345–366. DOI: 10.1177/0730888404266349

Cartwright, S., & Boyes, R. F. (2000). Taking the pulse of executive health in the UK. *The Academy of Management Perspectives*, *14*(2), 16–24. DOI: 10.5465/ame.2000.3819301

Choi, A. I., Weekley, C. C., Cheng Chen, S., Li, S., Kurella Tamura, M., Norris, K. C., & Shlipak, M. G. (2011). Association of educational attainment with chronic disease and mortality: The Kidney Early Evaluation Program (KEEP). *American Journal of Kidney Diseases*, *58*(2), 228–234. DOI: 10.1053/j.ajkd.2011.02.388 PMID: 21601328

Code, S., & Langan-Fox, J. (2001). Motivation, cognitions and traits: Predicting occupational health, well-being and performance. *Stress and Health*, *17*(3), 159–174. DOI: 10.1002/smi.897

Dewe, P., & Kompier, M. (2008). *Foresight mental capital and wellbeing project: wellbeing and work: future challenges*. The Government Office for Science.

Dragano, N., & Wahrendorf, M. (2014). Consistent health inequalities in Europe: The importance of labour market disadvantage. *Journal of Epidemiology and Community Health, 68*(4), 293–294. DOI: 10.1136/jech-2013-203655 PMID: 24419233

Ferrie, J. E., Shipley, M. J., Newman, K., Stansfeld, S. A., & Marmot, M. (2005). Selfreported job insecurity and health in the Whitehall II study: Potential explanations of the relationship. *Social Science & Medicine, 60*(7), 1593–1602. DOI: 10.1016/j.socscimed.2004.08.006 PMID: 15652690

Firth-Cozens, J. (2003). Doctors, their wellbeing, and their stress: It's time to be proactive about stress — and prevent it. *BMJ (Clinical Research Ed.), 326*(7391), 670–671. DOI: 10.1136/bmj.326.7391.670 PMID: 12663377

Garhammer, M. (2004). Auswirkungen neuer Arbeitsformen auf Stress und Lebensqualität. In Badura, B., Schellschmidt, H., & Vetter, C. (Eds.), *Fehlzeiten-Report 2003*. Springer-Verlag. DOI: 10.1007/978-3-662-07193-9_3

Glanz, K., & Schwartz, M. D. (2008). Stress, coping, and health behavior. In Glanz, K., Rimer, B. K., & Viswanath, K. (Eds.), *Health behavior and health education: Theory, research, and practice* (pp. 211–223). Jossey-Bass.

Hershcovis, M. (2011). 'Incivility, social undermining, bullying ... oh my!': A call to reconcile constructs within workplace aggression research. *Journal of Organizational Behavior, 32*(3), 499–519. DOI: 10.1002/job.689

Hobfoll, S. E. (2001). The influence of culture, community, and the nested-self in the stress process: Advancing conservation of resources theory. *Applied Psychology, 50*(3), 337–421. DOI: 10.1111/1464-0597.00062

Jacobshagen, N., & Rigotti, T. (2008). Voll der Stress? Stress bei Adoleszenten in den letzten Schuljahren. In Krause, A., Schüpbach, H., Ulich, E., & Wülser, M. (Eds.), *Arbeitsort Schule* (pp. 289–308). Betriebswirtschaftlicher Verlag Dr. Th. Gabler. DOI: 10.1007/978-3-8349-9551-3_11

Jungbauer-Gans, M., & Gross, C. (2009). Erklärungsansätze sozial differenzierter Gesundheitschancen. In Richter, M., & Hurrelmann, K. (Eds.), *Gesundheitliche Ungleichheit* (pp. 77–98). Grundlagen, Probleme, Perspektiven. VS Verlag für Sozialwissenschaften. DOI: 10.1007/978-3-531-91643-9_4

Kauffeld, S., & Hoppe, D. (2011). Arbeit und Gesundheit. In Kauffeld, S. (Ed.), *Arbeits-, Organisations- und Personalpsychologie für Bachelor* (pp. 223–244). Springer-Verlag. DOI: 10.1007/978-3-642-16999-1_12

Lampert, T., Kuntz, B., Hoebel, J., Müters, S., & Kroll, L. E. (2016) Bildung als Ressource für Gesundheit. Datenreport 2016. bpb, Bonn

Lampert, T., Saß, A. C., Häfelinger, M., & Ziese, T. (2005). Armut, soziale Ungleichheit und Gesundheit. Expertise des Robert Koch-Instituts zum 2. Armuts- und Reichtumsbericht der Bundesregierung. In Koch-Institut, R. (Ed.), *Beiträge zur Gesundheitsberichterstattung des Bundes*. RKI.

Law, P. C. F., Too, L. S., Butterworth, P., Witt, K., Reavley, N., & Milner, A. J. (2020). A systematic review on the effect of work-related stressors on mental health of young workers. *International Archives of Occupational and Environmental Health*, *93*(5), 611–622. DOI: 10.1007/s00420-020-01516-7 PMID: 31932956

Mehta, A. K., Yashoda, L., Selvakumar, P., Mishra, B. R., Das, A., & C. T. C., M. (2025). Teaching Methods: Techniques for Disadvantaged Learners. In S. Hai-Jew (Ed.), Mitigating Learner Disadvantages in Teaching and Learning (pp. 181-206). IGI Global Scientific Publishing. DOI: 10.4018/979-8-3693-8623-1.ch007

Nerdinger, F. W., Blickle, G., & Schaper, N. (2008). *Arbeits- und Organisationspsychologie*. Springer.

Peters, L. H., & O'Connor, E. J. (1980). Situational constraints and work outcomes: The influence of a frequently overlooked construct. *Academy of Management Review*, *5*(3), 391–397. DOI: 10.2307/257114

Pfeiffer, S. (2007). *Montage und Erfahrung. Warum ganzheitliche Produktionssysteme menschliches Arbeitsvermögen brauchen*. Rainer Hampp Verlag.

Pradeep, E., Mukherjee, S. K., Selvakumar, P., Koppaka, A. K., Chandel, P. S., & Vats, C. (2025). Empowering Social Media Users With Ethical AI. In Chakraborty, S. (Ed.), *Ethical AI Solutions for Addressing Social Media Influence and Hate Speech* (pp. 91–118). IGI Global Scientific Publishing., DOI: 10.4018/979-8-3693-9904-0.ch005

Ranjitha, P. K., Selvakumar, P., Anute, N., Manjunath, T., Sureshkrishna, G., & Pougajendy, S. (2025). Transportation Challenges In Islands Tourism. In Hassan, V. (Ed.), *Navigating Mass Tourism to Island Destinations: Preservation and Cultural Heritage Challenges* (pp. 287–312). IGI Global Scientific Publishing., DOI: 10.4018/979-8-3693-9107-5.ch011

Rigotti, T, Holstad, T, Mohr, G, Stempel, C, Hansen, E, Loeb, C, Isaksson, K, Otto, K, Kinnunen, U, & Perko, K (2014)

Sameer Babu, M., Karunakaran, N. B., Selvakumar, P., Sethumadhavan, R., & Chandel, P. S. (2025). The Role of Chatbots in Educational Leadership. In Musundire, A. (Ed.), *Chatbots in Educational Leadership and Management* (pp. 321–346). IGI Global Scientific Publishing., DOI: 10.4018/979-8-3693-8734-4.ch013

Schieman, S., Whitestone, Y. K., & Van Gundy, K. (2006). The nature of work and the stress of higher status. *Journal of Health and Social Behavior*, *47*(3), 242–257. DOI: 10.1177/002214650604700304 PMID: 17066775

Schmidt, S., Petermann, F., & Brähler, E. (2012). Bildungsniveau, körperliche und psychische Gesundheit – Zusammenhänge aus der Makro- und Mikroperspektive. In Brähler, E., Kiess, J., Schubert, C., & Kiess, W. (Eds.), *Gesund und gebildet –Voraussetzungen für eine moderne Gesellschaft* (pp. 74–90). Vandenhoeck & Ruprecht.

Shende, A. D., Tekade, S. A., Deshmukh, A. A., Tembhurkar, S. P., & Selvakumar, P. (2025). Water Quality Monitoring and Control With AI. In Ruiz-Vanoye, J., & Díaz-Parra, O. (Eds.), *Smart Water Technology for Sustainable Management in Modern Cities* (pp. 51–80). IGI Global Scientific Publishing., DOI: 10.4018/979-8-3693-8074-1.ch003

Subramanian, M., Portia, R., Mishra, B. R. R., & Selvakumar, P. PV, R., & TC, M. (2025). Assessment and Evaluation in Personalized STEAM Education. In Integrating Personalized Learning Methods Into STEAM Education (pp. 103-122). IGI Global Scientific Publishing.

Tepper, B. J., & Henle, C. A. (2011). A case for recognizing distinctions among constructs that capture interpersonal mistreatment in work organizations. *Journal of Organizational Behavior*, *32*(3), 487–498. DOI: 10.1002/job.688

Uchino, B. N. (2006). Social support and health: A review of physiological processes potentially underlying links to disease outcomes. *Journal of Behavioral Medicine*, *29*(4), 377–387. DOI: 10.1007/s10865-006-9056-5 PMID: 16758315

Ulich, E., & Wülser, M. (2010). *Gesundheitsmanagement in Unternehmen. Arbeitspsychologische Perspektiven* (4th ed.). Springer Gabler. DOI: 10.1007/978-3-8349-8979-6

Voßemer, J., Gebel, M., Täht, K., Unt, M., Högberg, B., & Strandh, M. (2018). The effects of unemployment and insecure jobs on well-being and health: The moderating role of labor market policies. *Social Indicators Research*, *138*(3), 1229–1257. DOI: 10.1007/s11205-017-1697-y

Zapf, D., & Semmer, N. (2004). Stress und Gesundheit in Organisationen. In Schuler, H. (Ed.), *Enzyklopädie der Psychologie-Organisationspsychologie* (pp. 1007–1112). Hogrefe.

Chapter 12

Impact of Organizational Climate on Teacher Burnout:

Family Conflict as a Mediating Factor

Ankur Nandi
https://orcid.org/0009-0008-3459-3429
Kalyani University, India

Shishupal Gorain
https://orcid.org/0000-0001-5901-1415
Rajiv Gandhi University, India

Kislay Kishor Mirgank
https://orcid.org/0009-0002-8890-2692
Rajiv Gandhi University, India

Tapash Das
https://orcid.org/0000-0003-4619-0009
Kazi Nazrul University, India

Tarini Halder
https://orcid.org/0009-0007-8807-7182
University of Kalyani, India

ABSTRACT

This chapter aims to explore the impact of organizational climate on teacher burnout and explore the mediating role of family conflict in this relationship. The study was

DOI: 10.4018/979-8-3373-0169-3.ch012

done by using the survey method followed by quantitative analysis and the cross-sectional method. The researchers used the Organizational Climate Scale, Maslach Burnout Inventory, and Family Conflict Sale for data collection from 200 teachers from 10 government secondary schools. Multiple regression analyses were conducted to assess the effect of organizational climate on teachers' burnout. The mediating role of family conflict in the link between organizational climate and teacher burnout was investigated using Bootstrap methodology. The findings highlighted that organizational climate significantly contributes to burnout, corroborating prior research. Key dimensions of organizational climate, such as involvement, control, autonomy, and physical comfort, were identified as influential factors. Family conflict was found to moderate the impact of organizational involvement and autonomy on burnout.

INTRODUCTION

Teachers play a crucial role in shaping the future of society by educating the next generation. However, the teaching profession is often associated with high levels of stress and burnout, which can have detrimental effects on both teachers' well-being and the quality of education they provide. One significant factor that contributes to teacher burnout is the organizational climate of their school environment.

Organizational climate refers to the prevailing atmosphere or "feel" of a work setting, including factors such as leadership style, communication patterns and the degree of support and recognition provided to employees (Schneider et al. 2013). A good work environment makes teachers feel like they belong, have freedom, and trust each other. But a bad environment with lots of conflict, little support and strict rules can make employees feel stressed, frustrated, and burned out. (Kuenzi. & Schminke. 2009). Several studies have examined the relationship between organizational climate and teacher burnout, consistently finding that a supportive and positive organizational climate is associated with lower levels of burnout among teachers (Maslach & Leiter, 1999; Collie et al. 2012). However, the mechanisms through which organizational climate influences teacher burnout are not fully understood. One potential mediator of this relationship is family conflict. Teachers, akin to all professionals, bear numerous roles and responsibilities beyond their workplace, encompassing family obligations and relationships. When teacher endure elevated stress levels and burnout in their workplace, often attributed to a detrimental organizational atmosphere, they are prone to carrying these adverse emotions home, potentially resulting in conflicts within their families (Wayne, Musisca, & Fleeson, 2004). Conversely, a positive organizational climate may buffer against stress and burnout, reducing the likelihood of family conflict (Bakker et al. 2014).

The inter-relationship among organizational climate, teachers' burnout and family conflict is complex and multi-faceted. Maslach & Leiter. (2016), said a positive organization climate, characterized by support, fairness and collaboration are the important factors of teacher burnout. Family conflict refers to disagreements, tension, or discord within the family unit, which can result from various sources such as work-family conflict, marital issues, and parenting challenges. When teachers experience conflict in their family lives, it can spill over into their work environment, exacerbating feelings of burnout and reducing their capacity to cope with job demands (Leiter & Maslach, 2005). Moreover, According to Maslach (2005), family conflict can act as a mediator between organization climate and teachers' burnout by influencing the relationship between these two factors. For example, a negative organization climate characterized by high job demands and low support may contribute to increased family conflict as teachers struggle to balance work and family responsibilities. Conversely, a positive organization climate that fosters work-life balance and provides support for employees' personal needs may help mitigate family conflict and reduce the likelihood of burnout.

This study aims to explore the impact of organizational climate on teacher burnout and explore the mediating role of family conflict in this relationship. It aims to clarify how a positive or negative work environment influences burnout and how family dynamics contribute to this process.

THEORITICAL BACKGROUND

Organization Climate and Teachers Burnout

Research from multiple contexts supports the significant correlations between organizational climate and teacher burnout. Several studies found correlation between OC and burnout (Cordes et al., 1997; Dincbutun et al., 2020; Kaya et al., 2010; Lubranska, 2011; Maidaniuc Chirila & Constantin, 2015; Martinussen et al., 2007; Yildirim & Dinc, 2019; Vallen, 1993). Research has consistently shown a significant correlation between organizational commitment and burnout across different sectors. For instance, Lubranska (2011) highlighted a strong correlation between organization climate and burnout in the service sector. Similarly, Pecino et al. (2019) found a strong negative correlation between organization climate and burnout in public organizations. Examining specific dimensions of organization climate and their impact on burnout levels, Cordes et al. (1997) identified several factors. These include strained subordinate-manager relationships, attempts to achieve success in roles with inadequate resources, and problems with management and coordination, all contributing to emotional exhaustion and depersonalization.

Studies by Anbar & Eker (2008), Maidaniuc-Chirila & Constantin (2016), and Taka et al. (2016) underscore this negative connection, emphasizing the importance of organizational commitment in mitigating burnout among academic staff. Recent research on auditors has highlighted the significant impact of organizational climate on both audit quality and performance. Gorain & Pal (2021) underscored that a positive organizational climate correlates negatively with these outcomes, suggesting a critical role of organizational factors in influencing burnout and overall effectiveness within the auditing profession. Maslach and Leiter (2022) further argue that burnout often stems from a mismatch between individuals and their work environment across six key dimensions: workload, control, fairness, reward, community, and values. These factors collectively contribute to the development of burnout, emphasizing the importance of addressing organizational dynamics to mitigate its effects. These findings underscore the critical role of organizational climate in influencing levels of teacher burnout. Previous research has shown a negative relationship between organizational climate and audit burnout, highlighting how organizational factors impact burnout and overall performance in the auditing field. Therefore, on the basis on previous research finding the following hypotheses are;

Hypothesis 1: Organization Climate has a significant effect on Burnout.

Inter-Relation Among Organization Climate, Burnout, and Family Conflict

Organizational climate plays a crucial role in influencing burnout and work-family conflict among various professions. Studies have shown that dimensions of organizational climate such as involvement, control, autonomy, task orientation, and physical comfort are significantly associated with burnout and family conflict (Silva et al., 2022; Dongying, 2020). Additionally, organizational climate and work-family conflict have been found to positively affect burnout, highlighting the interconnectedness of these factors (Ford et al., 2007). Work-family conflict has been identified as a mediator in the relationship between organizational climate and burnout, with family interfering with work showing a stronger mediating effect than work interfering with family (Margareth & Satrya, 2022). These findings underscore the importance of considering organizational climate and work-family conflict in addressing burnout issues among educators, emphasizing the need for supportive work environments and effective strategies to manage work-family balance. Family conflict mediates the relationship between job demands and burnout among primary government school teachers (Chirila, 2015). Work-family conflict not only impacts burnout but is also significantly affected by organizational climate. Furthermore, some studies have suggested that work-family conflict might mediate the relationship between work demands and turnover intention (Geurts et al., 2008 & Denison, 2016). Ford et al. (2007) performed a meta-analysis of Frone's Work Family Conflict Model and found that family conflict partially mediated the relationship between antecedents of work factors and family satisfaction. However, some studies suggest that family conflicts do not mediate the relationship between organizational climate and burnout among university employees (Raja et al., 2015). Additionally, Mehmet and Kayode (2023) found a mediated path through family conflict in the relationship between burnout and organization behaviour. Although, previous literature suggests that family conflict is a significant moderating factor between organizational climate and burnout in teachers. It emphasizes the importance of supportive work environments and work-family balance strategies to mitigate these effects. Therefore, based on the provided literature review and the identified relationships between organizational climate, work-family conflict, and burnout, the following hypotheses can be proposed;

The inclusion of family conflict as a mediating factor is grounded in work-family conflict theory (Greenhaus & Beutell, 1985), which suggests that stress originating from organizational demands can disrupt family roles and relationships. Unlike other potential mediators such as emotional exhaustion or perceived organizational support, family conflict uniquely bridges the interface between personal and professional spheres-particularly salient for teachers whose work often extends beyond the school day.

Empirical evidence supports this pathway. Studies (e.g., Netemeyer et al., 1996; Carlson et al., 2000) reveal that adverse organizational climates exacerbate work-family conflict, which, in turn, increases burnout. Therefore, this study situates family conflict within a well-established mediation framework and aims to offer deeper insight into how workplace conditions indirectly impact teacher well-being through familial strain.

> Hypothesis 2: Family Conflict has a significant mediate between organizational climate and teacher burnout.

While previous research has explored the direct effects of organizational climate on teacher burnout and family conflict separately, few studies have examined the mediating role of family conflict in the relationship between organizational climate and teacher burnout. Mediation analysis allows for a more nuanced understanding of the underlying processes linking these variables, shedding light on potential pathways through which organizational factors influence teacher well-being. Findings from this study can inform the development of targeted interventions aimed at improving organizational practices within secondary schools to mitigate teacher burnout and reduce family conflict. In summary, this study aims to investigate the relationship between organizational climate, teacher burnout and family conflict among secondary school teachers, with a particular focus on exploring the mediating role of family conflict.

METHODOLOGY

This section presents the method used for the study. This study is cross-sectional in nature. Following the purpose of the study researchers used a quantitative approach followed by a survey method and.

Population & Sample

This study focuses on the "selected government secondary school teachers, West Bengal." The "Purulia Distract of West Bengal in India" was the target population of the study. A total of 207 questionnaires were administered to the secondary teachers, of which 200 were returned, indicating a response rate of 90.8%. These 200 responses formed the final sample. Researchers did not conduct pilot study before collecting the data, directly goes to the field and collected hand to hand data by hard copy questionnaires. For this study, random sampling technique was used at that time when ever collected data and the researchers collected data only on 10 schools from Purulia in West Bengal.

Instruments

Basically, the researchers three scandalized Tools have used for the present study, namely; Organization Climate Scale (Bandhu, 2008), Maslach Burnout Inventory (develop by Maslach & Jackson, 1981) and Family Conflict Scale (develop by Netemeyer et al. 2012). As per suggestions of the experts, these two Tools are bitterly repetitive to this study and did not adopt by the researchers before collecting the data.

Organizational Climate Scale: was used for this study check the organizational climate and this scale were developed by Bandhu (2008). In this tool total four key elements: involvement, consistency, adaptability, and mission with consisting 50 statements. The nature of the instrument was from really occurs (0) to very frequently occurs (4) with range.

The Maslach Burnout Inventory (1987), was used for assess burnout among secondary school teachers. This inventory consisting of 22 items includes three dimensions: emotional exhaustion, depersonalization, and personal accomplishment. Each item was rated on a 7-point Likert scale, ranging from 1 (Never) to 7 (Always). Additionally, items 4, 7, 8, 9, 12, 14, 17, 18, and 19 were reverse-scored.

Family Conflict Sale: The Teacher Family Conflict Scale was also employed, developed by Netemeyer et al. (2012) with consisting 10 items questionnaire. Comprising 10 items, respondents rated each item on a 5-point Likert-type scale ranging from 1 (strongly disagree) to 5 (strongly agree). Elevated scores denote heightened levels of work–family conflict. The validity of the scale has been verified in Chinese research (Li & Zhao, 2009), where it demonstrated a Cronbach's alpha of 0.90.

Data Analysis

The analyzed the data SPSS 24 version software to used. Multiple regression analyses were conducted to assess the effect of organizational climate on teachers' burnout. Furthermore, the potential mediating role of family conflict in the link between organizational climate and teacher burnout was investigated using Bootstrap methodology. A re-sampling size of 1,000 was employed, indicating that the indirect effect of the mediation path was calculated across 1,000 bootstrapped samples. (Je, & Yeu 2020).

RESULTS

In the present study, the researchers conducted a systematic analysis of the data by the selected hypotheses. However, it is noteworthy that in this study, researchers focused solely on analyzing and interpreting variables rather than examining dimensions individually. The results of the study are given below:

Table 1. Demographic data of the secondary school teachers

Variable	Categories	Frequency	Percentage
Gender	Male	110	55
	Female	90	45
	Total	200	100
Location of School	Rural	85	42.5
	Urban	115	57.5
	Total	200	100
Experiences	Below 8 Year	60	30
	9-16 Yeats	85	42.4
	Above 16 Year	55	27.5
	Total	200	100

Demographic data for the secondary school teachers are presented in Table 1. The results show that 55% were males while 45% were females. For the school location, 57.5% work in urban areas as opposed to 42.5% who work in rural. With teaching experience, 30% have less than 8 years of teaching experience while 42.4% fall within the 9-16 years category, and 27.5% with more than 16 years of teaching experience. The sample is described by descriptive statistics, showing the distribution of the sample by gender, school location, and teaching experience. Indeed, it allegedly shows the composition of the secondary school teaching staff in the study.

Table 2. Descriptive statistics & mean difference in organizational climate, burnout, and family conflict with different background

Variables	Types	Organizational Climate		Burnout		Family Conflict	
Variables		M	SD	M	SD	M	SD
Gender	Male (N=110)	5.23	0.91	6.65	1.02	7.65	1.43
	Female (N= 90)	4.24	0.76	5.53	0.98	6.54	1.23
	t	4.23		3.45		3.23	
Locality	Rural (85)	6.43	1.54	6.45	1.54	6.45	1.76
	Urban (115)	6.98	1.56	6.23	1.65	5.76	1.54
	t	6.43		0.65		1.65	
Experiences	Low (60)	4.45	0.65	5.12	0.98	6.11	1.34
	Medium (85)	5.67	0.98	4.86	1.12	5.45	1.76
	High (55)	6.12	1.12	4.45	0.87	5.23	1.87
	t	2.67		2.11		1.99	

Table 2 showed that the distribution of the organization climate, burnout, and family conflict in the secondary school teacher sample contained these different characteristics. If taken concerning gender, males scored higher in organization climate, burnout, and family conflict compared to females, with statistical significance. The results on gender were that males had an Organizational Climate score of 5.23 with an SD of 0.91, burnout was 6.65 with an SD of 1.02, and Family Conflict at 7.65 with an SD of 1.43. Female respondents returned lower means on all three variables: their organizational climate stood at 4.24 with an SD of 0.76, the burnout was 5.53 with an SD of 0.98, and the family conflict was 6.54 with an SD of 1.23. The t-values for Gender difference are 4.23 in Organizational Climate, 3.45 in Burnout, and 3.23 in Family Conflict.

On the dimension of locality, those of rural origin give mean scores in Organizational Climate of 6.43 with a standard deviation of 1.54, for Burnout 6.45 and a standard deviation of 1.54, and for Family Conflict 6.45 and a standard deviation of 1.76. In contrast, those of urban origin had a higher score on Organizational Climate at 6.98 with a standard deviation of 1.56, with lower scores on Burnout at 6.23 with a standard deviation of 1.65, and on Family Conflict at 5.76 with a standard deviation of 1.54. These are the following t-values for differences by locality: Organizational Climate 6.43, Burnout 0.65, and Family Conflict 1.65. There are differences regarding Organizational Climate and Family Conflict. The experience: for those participants with low experience, N=60, the mean score is 4.45, SD=0.65 regarding Organizational Climate, 5.12, SD=0.98 for Burnout, and 6.11, SD=1.34 for Family Conflict. For medium experience, N=85, the score in Organizational Climate is high with 5.67 and SD=0.98, but low in Burnout and Family Conflict with means of 4.86 and 5.45, and standard deviations of 1.12 and 1.76, respectively. For high experience, respondents N=55, it has the highest mean score for Organizational Climate with 6.12 and an SD=1.12, and their scores for Burnout and Family Conflict were the lowest at 4.45 and 5.23, with standard deviations of 0.87 and 1.87, respectively. The t-values with respect to experience differences are: Organizational Climate, 2.67; Burnout, 2.11; Family Conflict, 1.99-all significant.

Table 3. Direct and indirect effect between involvement and burnout dimensions with mediating variables family conflict

Variables	Effect (β)	SE	t	p
Involvement- Emotional Exhaustion	.63	.323	2.46	.00
Involvement- Depersonalization	.54	.312	2.32	.00
Involvement- Personal Accomplishment	.73	.413	1.99	.02
Involvement- Family Conflict - Emotional Exhaustion	.43	.223	2.15	.02
Involvement- Family Conflict - Depersonalization	.34	.198	1.99	.04
Involvement- Family Conflict - Personal Accomplishment	.43	.214	2.34	.01

Table 3 shows the direct and moderating effects between organizational climate's dimension of involvement and burnout, where family behavior acts as a mediating role player between the two variables. A significant impact has been found for involvement with emotional exhaustion, the β coefficient being .63, SE = .323, $p < 0.01$. Additionally, depersonalization and personal accomplishment have impacted by teachers' involvement, the calculated analysis value is respectively, β = .54; SE = .312; t = 2.32; $p < .01$, for depersonalization and β = .73; SE = .413; t = 1.99; p = .02 for personal accomplishment. More so, moderating variables family conflict has not impacted between teachers' involvement and emotional exhaustion (β = .43, SE = .223, t = 2.15, p = .02), similarly, not impact depersonalization (β = .34, SE = .198, t = 1.99, p = .04) and personal accomplishment (β = .43, SE = .214, t

= 2.34, p = .01). Hence, results highlight the organizational climate' dimension of involvement directly inspects to overall burnout in secondary school teachers but family conflict do not play any contribution role between these two variables i.e. involvement and burnout.

Table 4. Direct and indirect effect between consistency and burnout dimensions with mediating variables family conflict

Variables	Effect (β)	SE	t	p
Consistency- Emotional Exhaustion	.54	.301	2.23	.00
Consistency- Depersonalization	.65	.312	2.34	.00
Consistency- Personal Accomplishment	.47	.285	2.11	.00
Consistency- Family Conflict - Emotional Exhaustion	.09	.009	0.23	.23
Consistency- Family Conflict - Depersonalization	.07	.008	0.17	.36
Consistency- Family Conflict - Personal Accomplishment	.05	.007	0.24	.27

Table 4 shows direct and moderating effects between the organizational climate dimension of consistency and burnout dimensions were family conflict plays a mediating role. Consistency of secondary teachers generates significant influence on emotional exhaustion with the value β =.54, SE = .301, at significance level of $p < .01$; depersonalization with the influence value of β = .65, SE = .312, at a significance level of $p < .01$; personal accomplishment with an influence value of β =.47, at standard error of SE = .285, at a significance level of $p < .01$. These moderating effects through family conflict, however, were not influences to emotional exhaustion, depersonalization, and personal accomplishment. As such, consistency has a direct impact on dimensions of burnout, while family conflicts do not mediate significantly between organizational climate Stress and burnout.

Table 5. Direct and indirect effect between adaptability and burnout dimensions with mediating variables family conflict

Variables	Effect (β)	SE	t	p
Adaptability- Emotional Exhaustion	.53	.297	2.03	.00
Adaptability- Depersonalization	.71	.345	2.67	.00
Adaptability- Personal Accomplishment	.32	.231	1.99	.03
Adaptability- Family Conflict - Emotional Exhaustion	.23	.176	2.11	.03
Adaptability- Family Conflict - Depersonalization	.34	.198	2.43	.02
Adaptability- Family Conflict - Personal Accomplishment	.37	.187	2.33	.02

Table 5 presents the direct and moderating effects of teachers' involving adaptability and burnout dimensions (emotional exhaustion, depersonalization, personal accomplishment), and the mediating variable of family conflict. The results suggest the teacher's adaptability is significantly affected to overall burnout syndrome, indicated by β values are 0.53, 0.71 & 0.32. Conversely, while checking the moderating effect between teachers' adaptability and burnout, the less effect is found among them. The analysis values are respectively (adaptability- family conflict- emotional exhaustion = β = 0.23; adaptability- family conflict- depersonalization = β = 0.34; adaptability- family conflict- personal accomplishment = 0.37), Therefore, teacher's adaptability has directly and indirectly affected to burnout, however, the less indirect effect is founding between these two variables.

Table 6. Direct and indirect effect between mission and burnout dimensions with mediating variables family conflict

Variables	Effect (β)	SE	t	p
Mission- Emotional Exhaustion	.43	.261	2.11	.02
Mission- Depersonalization	.54	.276	2.24	.01
Mission- Personal Accomplishment	.57	.266	2.45	.00
Mission- Family Conflict - Emotional Exhaustion	.09	.110	0.74	.76
Mission- Family Conflict - Depersonalization	.04	.051	0.23	.32
Mission- Family Conflict - Personal Accomplishment	.10	.120	1.84	.08

Table 6 indicates the direct effects between teachers' mission and overall burnout, with a moderating variable of family conflict. The results indicate a significant impact between teachers' mission and burnout while checking the direct effect between them and the β values 0.43, 0.54 & .57 respectively for personal accomplishment, depersonalization, and personal accomplishment. Conversantly, while checking the indict effect with the help of family conflict there no impact is found between teachers' mission and burnout, (β value are 0.09 for teachers' mission- family conflict- emotional exhaustion; β = 0.04 for teachers' mission- depersonalization- family conflict; 0.10 for teachers' mission- personal accomplishment- family conflict). Thus, results highlight the teachers' mission has an impact on overall secondary school teachers' burnout, however, indirectly does not impact burnout while family conflict is moderator.

DISCUSSION

The Relationship Between Organization Climate and Burnout

The findings indicating that organizational climate positively affects burnout are consistent with numerous past studies (Brotheridge & Grandey, 2002; Grandey, 2017; & Montgomery et al., 2010). Yu et al. (2015) and Bilai (2017) reported that a non-supportive school organizational climate significantly impacts burnout, with higher degrees associated with increased teacher stress and burnout. This effect is further corroborated by Gorain (2014), who found that organizational climate is significantly associated with burnout, aligning with the broader literature. Maslach and Leiter (2016) emphasize that an inclusive and supportive work environment enhances employee well-being and reduces burnout rates. In the educational sector, Silva (2020) identified specific dimensions of organizational climate, such as involvement, control, autonomy, and physical comfort, which correlate with burnout. Notably, physical comfort and autonomy climates were found to reduce burnout through decreased work-family conflict. Similarly, Aryee et al., (2005) noted that individuals with greater autonomy spend less time at work, possess greater occupational self-efficacy, and experience less burnout.

The present study's results are consistent with those of Maslach et al. (2017) and Maslach and Leiter (1997), who showed that insincerity within organizational values and ethical conflicts lead to employee stress and burnout. Ayub et al. (2022) highlighted that unethical organizational practices can increase employee burnout, a finding supported by Mulki et al. (2007). Organizational climate refers to the absolute amount of work required and the time frame for completion (Cooper et al., 2001). Ghodsy (2008) indicated that a positive climate can reduce job stress and burnout, thereby enhancing retention. Employees with a positive perception of the organizational climate demonstrate higher commitment and a reduced intention to leave. Pacheco & Webber (1994) found that participation in decision-making significantly correlates with perceived accomplishment among South African academics, which is consistent with the findings of this study. Dinibutun et al. (2020) found similar results in their comparative study, highlighting that a positive organizational climate for teachers leads to job satisfaction, increased productivity, and reduced burnout. Organizational climate, encompassing shared perceptions of policies, practices, and procedures, substantially impacts employees' stress levels and overall job satisfaction. A positive organizational climate, including supportive leadership, recognition, and professional growth opportunities, mitigates the risk of burnout by fostering a sense of belonging and purpose (Bakker & Demerouti, 2007).

The Mediating Role of Family Conflicts between Organization Climate and Burnout

The results of the study showed that the organizational climate dimensions of Involvement and Adaptability indirectly affect burnout, while family conflict plays a moderating role. This result aligns with previous studies by Ji & Yue (2020) and Lingard & Francis (2006). According to Lingard & Francis (2006), perceived organizational support (POS) can alter the relationship between work-family conflict (WFC) and emotional exhaustion, with high POS serving as a protective buffer against burnout. Similarly, an adaptable climate, which is flexible and open to change, can reduce stress by providing a supportive environment that helps employees manage uncertainties and challenges (Denison, 1996). However, the study found that the role of teacher adaptability is consistent across different types of burnouts. Previous research indicates that organizational support helps enhance work flexibility (Ferguson et al., 2016). Barnett et al. (2012) found that family conflict fully mediated the effect of work demands on distress, emphasizing that diligent effort is key to family happiness and meeting familial obligations. Gemlik and Ayanoglu-Şişman (2010) found that work-family conflict significantly affects burnout and reduces performance in subject knowledge. They identified joint family dynamics, childcare responsibilities, and overloaded class schedules as major factors contributing to burnout in academic life.

Interestingly, the Consistency and Mission dimensions of organizational climate did not show an indirect effect on secondary school teachers' overall burnout when considering family conflicts. While these dimensions are crucial for job satisfaction and engagement, they may not mitigate the stress and exhaustion caused by personal life conflicts. Maslach and Leiter (2016) suggest that burnout is a complex syndrome influenced by work environment, personal traits, and external stressors. This finding aligns with Kinnunen et al. (2006), who indicated that family-work conflicts significantly contribute to employee stress and burnout, regardless of workplace support structures. Although the study did not explicitly mention the Consistency and Mission dimensions, it emphasized the importance of factors like involvement, control, autonomy, task orientation, physical comfort, innovation, and professional growth in influencing burnout and work-family conflict (Zhao et al., 2022; Kamarul. 2018). According to Leung & Zhang (2017), excessive consistency can interfere with teachers' development needs, leading to stress and burnout as they struggle to meet job demands.

The results of this study can help schools create a friendly and healthy workplace, guiding school principals on improving their organizational climates to reduce job stress and burnout among teachers. This, in turn, enhances the quality of teaching and medication safety, ultimately improving teachers' work environment and retention.

PRACTICAL IMPLICATION AND RECOMMENDATIONS

This study highlights the organizational climate that impact secondary teachers' burnout, suggesting initiatives such as providing support and resources for teachers, promoting a positive work environment, and fostering open communication between administration and staff. Educational institution should consider implementing strategies to support work-life balance and address work-family conflict to help reduce burnout among teachers. Although many creational studies have examined the relationship between organizational climate and burnout (Bronkhorst et al., 2015; Idris & Dollard, 2014; Kaya et al., 2010; Lee et al., 2013; Lubranska, 2011), there has been a gap in linking specific dimensions of organizational climate to burnout levels. This study aims to fill these gaps in the literature. It indicates that various dimensions of organizational climate are significant predictors of burnout. Effective training and socialization, including involving family members, can minimize teachers' organizational stress (Dinibutun, 2020). Silva and Freire (2020) suggested that school managers should promote the necessary autonomy for teachers to carry out their work proactively and fulfill pedagogical goals while minimizing the impact on education. These initiatives could help promote a physically comfortable climate, so teachers do not feel discomfort inherent in poor work environments. Nevertheless, it is essential to emphasize that stimulating cohesion among colleagues can be beneficial to a certain extent, as it can lead to a higher level of work-family conflict (WFC). Therefore, some control from management can help teachers fulfill their pedagogic goals, monitor their task performance, and prevent WFC to a certain extent (Lopez et al., 2021).

The study's results reveal that family conflict mediates the relationship between the organizational climate dimensions of involvement and adaptability, and secondary teachers' burnout. Consequently, it is recommended that the government implement family-friendly policies to support work-life balance for teachers. These policies could include flexible work schedules, parental leave, and support for childcare services. Adaptability within the organizational climate allows for a more flexible approach to addressing teachers' needs, potentially reducing work-related stressors that spill over into family life. As Lambert et al. (2006) suggest, addressing work-family conflict through organizational support can lead to reduced burnout and improved overall well-being for teachers. To control family conflict, promoting greater awareness of the importance of sharing responsibilities between partners is crucial. Encouraging husbands to play a more equal role at home can reduce the burden of work-family conflict on their wives (Noor & Zainuddin, 2011). This study also reveals that female teachers experience more family conflict than male teachers, which mediates burnout and organizational climate. Therefore, institutions should provide daycare facilities for female teachers to manage work-family conflict and its various outcomes, such as stress, burnout, and deviant behavior at work (Buric & Kim, 2020). Finally, enhancing organizational climates, promoting shared family responsibilities, and implementing supportive policies can significantly reduce burnout and improve the well-being of secondary teachers.

This study underscores the critical need for educational institutions to address organizational climate factors-such as support, autonomy, and collegiality-given their profound and far-reaching impact on teachers' professional and personal well-being. Prolonged exposure to a toxic organizational climate not only heightens the risk of burnout but also strains family relationships, perpetuating a cycle of emotional exhaustion. To mitigate these challenges, institutions should implement targeted professional development programs that enhance communication and reduce role ambiguity, establish flexible scheduling policies that support family responsibilities, introduce wellness initiatives that promote work-life balance and mental health, and develop systems for early detection and intervention of teacher burnout.

LIMITATION

The present study, limited to a single district and selected a mediation design, aimed to determine the directional effect between variables. However, employing longitudinal or experimental designs would provide a more robust framework for understanding the temporal sequence of events and potential causal relationships. The study collected a sample of 200 participants from selected schools in the Purulia district of India. The selection of this specific geographic region or government secondary schools was primarily due to time constraints faced by the researchers. Furthermore, a pilot study was not conducted prior to administering the questionnaires; instead, researchers directly applied tools and collected data based on expert suggestions and previous literature.

FUTURE RESEARCH DIRECTION

- Future studies should focus on more extensive and diverse samples, with schools from different sectors and regions, to make the findings more generalizable.
- Future studies should include more districts or regions to ascertain greater generalizability of the findings across very diverse educational environments.
- Other variables that could mediate or moderate may have to be researched before an in-depth view of the relationship between organizational climate and teacher burnout can be embraced.

- Such designs would allow studying the causal relationships between organizational climate, family conflict, and burnout of teachers more profoundly.
- The study can target other variables that could influence the outcome of the results in future research, including socio-economic background and school policies.

CONCLUSION

In conclusion, this study examined the significant impact of organizational climate on secondary teachers' burnout, emphasizing dimensions such as involvement, autonomy, physical comfort, and memory. The findings indicate that a positive organizational climate reduces burnout by fostering a supportive and inclusive work environment. Family conflict mediates this relationship, highlighting the importance of work-life balance in mitigating burnout. Practical implications suggest that schools should implement strategies to enhance organizational climate, support work-life balance, and address work-family conflicts. Additionally, promoting family-friendly policies and shared family responsibilities can further reduce burnout and improve teacher well-being. Moving forward, further research should delve into the specific mechanisms underlying these relationships and explore effective strategies for fostering supportive environments in both spheres of teachers' lives. This study highlights the interconnectedness of organizational climate, family dynamics, and teacher well-being. By identifying family conflict as a critical mediator, it offers new directions for institutional policy and human resource management in education. Future research should consider longitudinal designs and examine cross-cultural variations to generalize findings more broadly.

REFERENCES

Anbar, A., & Eker, M. (2008). An examination of the relationship between burnout and job satisfaction among Turkish accounting and finance academicians. *European Journal of Economic and Political Studies*, *1*(1), 46–67.

Aryee, S., Srinivas, E. S., & Tan, H. H. (2005). Rhythms of Life: Antecedents and outcomes of work-family balance in employed parents. *The Journal of Applied Psychology*, *90*(1), 132–146. DOI: 10.1037/0021-9010.90.1.132 PMID: 15641894

Ayub, N., Ahmad, M. S., & Jabeen, Z. (2022). Impact of unethical organizational practices on employee burnout: A study of the banking sector. *Journal of Business Ethics*, *170*(3), 517–536.

Bakker, A. B., & Demerouti, E. (2007). The Job Demands-Resources model: State of the art. *Journal of Managerial Psychology*, *22*(3), 309–328. DOI: 10.1108/02683940710733115

Bakker, A. B., Demerouti, E., & Sanz-Vergel, A. I. (2014). Burnout and work engagement: The JD–R approach. *Annual Review of Organizational Psychology and Organizational Behavior*, *1*(1), 389–411. DOI: 10.1146/annurev-orgpsych-031413-091235

Brotheridge, C. M., & Grandey, A. A. (2002). Emotional labor and burnout: Comparing two perspectives of "people work.". *Journal of Vocational Behavior*, *60*(1), 17–39. DOI: 10.1006/jvbe.2001.1815

Buric, I., & Kim, L. E. (2020). Teacher self-efficacy, instructional quality, and student motivational beliefs: An analysis using multilevel structural equation modeling. *Learning and Instruction*, *66*, 101302. Advance online publication. DOI: 10.1016/j.learninstruc.2019.101302

Carlson, D. S., Kacmar, K. M., & Williams, L. J. (2000). Construction and initial validation of a multidimensional measure of work-family conflict. *Journal of Vocational Behavior*, *56*(2), 249–276. DOI: 10.1006/jvbe.1999.1713

Chirila, T. (2015). A multi-mediation model of the relationship among workplace bullying, coping strategies, resilience, and employees' strain: Insights for a training program. *Psihologia Resurselor Umane Revista Asociatiei de Psihologie Industriala si Organizaţionala*, *13*(1), 63–82.

Collie, R. J., Shapka, J. D., & Perry, N. E. (2012). School climate and social-emotional learning: Predicting teacher stress, job satisfaction, and teaching efficacy. *Journal of Educational Psychology*, *104*(4), 1189–1204. DOI: 10.1037/a0029356

Cooper, C. L., Dewe, P., & O'Driscoll, M. P. (2001). Organizational Stress: A Review and Critique of Theory, Research, and Applications. *Sage (Atlanta, Ga.)*. Advance online publication. DOI: 10.4135/9781452231235

Denison, D. R. (1996). What is the difference between organizational culture and organizational climate? A native's point of view on a decade of paradigm wars. *Academy of Management Review*, *21*(3), 619–654. DOI: 10.2307/258997

Dinibutun, S. R. (2020). Factors associated with burnout among physicians: An evaluation during a period of COVID-19 pandemic. *Journal of Healthcare Leadership*, *12*, 85–94. DOI: 10.2147/JHL.S270440 PMID: 32982532

Dinibutun, S. R., Kuzey, C., & Dinc, M. S. (2020). The effect of organizational climate on faculty burnout at state and private universities: A comparative analysis. *Journal of Educational and Social Research*, *10*(1), 56–74. DOI: 10.1177/2158244020979175

Ferguson, M., Carlson, D., Kacmar, K. M., & Halbesleben, J. R. B. (2016). The supportive spouse at work: Does being work-linked help? *Journal of Occupational Health Psychology*, *21*(1), 37–50. DOI: 10.1037/a0039538 PMID: 26236955

Ford, M. T., Heinen, B. A., & Langkamer, K. L. (2007). Work and family satisfaction and conflict: A meta-analysis of cross-domain relations. *The Journal of Applied Psychology*, *92*(1), 57–80. DOI: 10.1037/0021-9010.92.1.57 PMID: 17227151

Gemlik, N., Ayanoglu Sisman, F., & Unsal, S. (2010). The relationship between burnout and organizational commitment among health sector staff in Turkey. *Journal of Global Strategic Management*, *4*(2), 137–149. DOI: 10.20460/JGSM.2010415831

Geurts, S. A. E., Taris, T., Kompier, M. A. J., Lagerveld, S., & Blonk, R. W. B. (2008). My love, my life, and my everything: Work-home interaction among self-employed. *The individual in the changing working life* (pp. 147-168). DOI: 10.1017/CBO9780511490064.008

Ghodsy, A. (2008). The role of school organizational climate in occupational stress among secondary school teachers in Tehran. *International Journal of Occupational Medicine and Environmental Health*, *21*(4), 319–329. DOI: 10.2478/v10001008000188 PMID: 19228578

Gorain, S., & Pal, S. (2021). Satisfaction of online education of college students during pandemic situation. *International Journal of Applied Research*, *7*(2), 157–160.

Grandey, A. A. (2017). When "The Show Must Go On": Surface acting and deep acting as determinants of emotional exhaustion and peer-rated service delivery. *Academy of Management Journal*, *46*(1), 1–23. DOI: 10.5465/30040678

Greenhaus, J. H., & Beutell, N. J. (1985). Sources of conflict between work and family roles. *Academy of Management Review, 10*(1), 76–88. DOI: 10.2307/258214

Idris, M. A., Dollard, M. F., & Yulita, . (2014). Psychosocial safety climate, emotional demands, burnout, and depression: A longitudinal multilevel study in the Malaysian private sector. *Journal of Occupational Health Psychology, 19*(3), 291–302. DOI: 10.1037/a0036599 PMID: 24802994

Ji, D., & Yue, Y. (2020). Relationship between kindergarten organizational climate and teacher burnout: Work–family conflict as a mediator. *Frontiers in Psychiatry, 11*, 408–422. DOI: 10.3389/fpsyt.2020.00408 PMID: 32499727

Kaya, A., Sen, S., & Dogan, E. (2010). Organizational climate and burnout: A research on employees in Turkish educational institutions. *Procedia: Social and Behavioral Sciences, 9*, 161–169.

Khalid, M., Hassani, D., & Bilal, M. (2017). Identification of oral cavity bio-film forming bacteria and determination of their growth inhibition medicinal plants. *Archives of Oral Biology, 81*, 175–185. DOI: 10.1016/j.archoralbio.2017.05.011 PMID: 28549260

Kinnunen, U., Feldt, T., Geurts, S., & Pulkkinen, L. (2006). Types of work-family interface: Well-being correlates of negative and positive spillover between work and family. *Scandinavian Journal of Psychology, 47*(2), 149–162. DOI: 10.1111/j.1467-9450.2006.00502.x PMID: 16542357

Kuenzi, M., & Schminke, M. (2009). Assembling fragments into a lens: A review, critique, and proposed research agenda for the organizational work climate literature. *Journal of Management, 35*(3), 634–717. DOI: 10.1177/0149206308330559

Lambert, S. J., & Haley-Lock, A. (2006). The organizational stratification of opportunities for work-life balance: Addressing issues of equality and social justice in the workplace. *Community Work & Family, 9*(3), 303–318. DOI: 10.1080/13668800600743518

Leiter, M. P., & Maslach, C. (2005). *Banishing burnout: Six strategies for improving your relationship with work*. John Wiley & Sons.

Leiter, M. P., & Maslach, C. (2017). Motivation, competence, and job burnout. In Elliot, A. J., Dweck, C. S., & Yeager, D. S. (Eds.), *Handbook of competence and motivation: Theory and application* (2nd ed., pp. 370–384). The Guilford Press.

Leiter, M. P., & Maslach, C. (2024). Job burnout. *Handbook of occupational health psychology* (3rd ed., pp. 291-307). DOI: 10.1037/0000331-015

Leung, D. Y., & Zhang, L. W. (2017). Teachers' development needs and stress: The role of excessive consistency in organizational climate. *Teaching and Teacher Education*, *64*, 117–126.

Leung, L., & Zhang, R. (2017). Mapping ICT use at home and telecommuting practices: A perspective from work/family border theory. *Telematics and Informatics*, *34*(1), 385–396. DOI: 10.1016/j.tele.2016.06.001

Lingard, H., & Francis, V. (2006). Does work-family conflict mediate the relationship between job schedule demands and burnout in male construction professionals and managers? *Construction Management and Economics*, *24*(6), 617–628.

Lopez, S. P., Peon, J. M. M., & Ordas, C. J. V. (2021). Organizational culture as a mediator between leadership behavior and organizational commitment. *Journal of Organizational Change Management*, *34*(1), 123–138. DOI: 10.1108/JOCM-10-2020-0321

Lubranska, A. (2011). Organizational climate and burnout syndrome. *Medicine Pharmacy*, *62*(6), 623–631. PMID: 22312954

Ma, P., Zhang, L., Dong, H., & Yu, J. (2023). The relationships between teachers' emotional labor and display rules, trait emotions, exhaustion, and classroom emotional climate. *Frontiers in Psychology*, *14*, 957856. Advance online publication. DOI: 10.3389/fpsyg.2023.957856 PMID: 36923140

Maidaniuc-Chirila, T. (2015). A multi-mediation model of the relationship among workplace bullying, coping strategies, resilience, and employees' strain: Insights for a training programme. *Psihologia Resurselor Umane Revista Asociaţiei de Psihologie Industriala si Organizaţionala*, *13*(1), 63–82. DOI: 10.1037/%20t55271-000

Margareth, M., & Satrya, A. (2021). Work-family conflict as a mediator between organizational interventions for work-life balance and job satisfaction. In *Proceedings of the 4th International Conference on Economics, Business and Economic Education Science, (ICE-BEES 2021)*. DOI: 10.4108/eai.27-7-2021.2316893

Martinussen, M., Richardsen, A. M., & Burke, R. J. (2007). Job demands, job resources, and burnout among police officers. *Journal of Criminal Justice*, *35*(3), 239–249. DOI: 10.1016/j.jcrimjus.2007.03.001

Maslach, C., & Leiter, M. P. (1997). *The Truth about Burnout: How Organizations Cause Personal Stress and What to do about It*. Jossey-Bass.

Maslach, C., & Leiter, M. P. (1999). Teacher burnout: A research agenda. In Vandenberghe, R., & Huberman, A. M. (Eds.), *Understanding and Preventing Teacher Burnout: A Sourcebook of International Research and Practice* (pp. 295–303). Cambridge University Press. DOI: 10.1017/CBO9780511527784.021

Maslach, C., & Leiter, M. P. (2016). Understanding the burnout experience: Recent research and its implications for psychiatry. *World Psychiatry; Official Journal of the World Psychiatric Association (WPA), 15*(2), 103–111. DOI: 10.1002/wps.20311 PMID: 27265691

Montgomery, C., Maslach, C., & Leiter, M. P. (2006). Burnout in the teaching profession: A study of the relationship between teachers' job demands and burnout. *The Journal of Applied Psychology, 91*(4), 103–113.

Mulki, J. P., Jaramillo, F., & Locander, W. B. (2006). Effects of ethical climate and supervisory trust on salesperson's job attitudes and intentions to quit. *Journal of Personal Selling & Sales Management, 26*(1), 19–26. DOI: 10.2753/PSS0885-3134260102

Netemeyer, R. G., Boles, J. S., & McMurrian, R. (1996). Development and validation of work–family conflict and family–work conflict scales. *The Journal of Applied Psychology, 81*(4), 400–410. DOI: 10.1037/0021-9010.81.4.400

Pacheco, G., & Webber, D. J. (n.d.). *Participative decision-making and job satisfaction.* Department of Economics, Auckland University of Technology. DOI: 10.1108/PR-04-2014-0088

Pecino, V., Manas, M. A., Díaz-Funez, P. A., Aguilar-Parra, J. M., Padilla-Gongora, D., & Lopez-Liria, R. (2019). Organizational climate, role stress, and public employees' job satisfaction. *International Journal of Environmental Research and Public Health, 16*(10), 1792. Advance online publication. DOI: 10.3390/ijerph16101792 PMID: 31117168

Raja, U., Johns, G., & Ntalianis, F. (2015). The impact of personality on psychological contracts. *Academy of Management Journal, 47*(3), 350–367. DOI: 10.2307/20159586

Schneider, B., Ehrhart, M. G., & Macey, W. H. (2013). Organizational climate and culture. *Annual Review of Psychology, 64*(1), 361–388. DOI: 10.1146/annurev-psych-113011-143809 PMID: 22856467

Shien, L. (2023). Organizational climate and its impact on auditor performance: A meta-analysis. *Journal of Accounting and Economics, 65*(2), 210–225.

Shirom, A. (2003). Job-related burnout: A review. In Quick, J. C., & Tetrick, L. E. (Eds.), *Handbook of occupational health psychology* (pp. 245–264). American Psychological Association., DOI: 10.1037/10474-012

Silva, A., & Freire, M. (2022). The role of organizational climate, and work–family conflict in burnout: The case of teachers. *Sustainability*, *14*(21), 138–171. DOI: 10.3390/su142113871

Steeger, C. M., & Gondoli, D. M. (2013). Mother adolescent conflict as a mediator between adolescent problem behaviors and maternal psychological control. *Developmental Psychology*, *49*(4), 804–814. DOI: 10.1037/a0028599 PMID: 22612432

Taka, F., Ozcelik, G., & Avci, O. (2016). Exploring the impact of organizational climate on burnout and job satisfaction: Evidence from Turkish universities. *Journal of Higher Education Policy and Management*, *38*(3), 233–250.

Vallen, G. (1993). Organizational climate and burnout. *The Cornell Hotel and Restaurant Administration Quarterly*, *34*(1), 54–60. DOI: 10.1177/001088049303400110

Yildirim, F., & Dinc, M. S. (2019). Factors influencing burnout of the principals: A pilot study in Flemish schools of Belgium. *Ekonomska Istrazivanja*, *32*(1), 3538–3553. DOI: 10.1080/1331677X.2019.1660200

Zhang, Y., Zhang, H., Ma, X., & Di, Q. (2020). Mental health problems during the COVID-19 pandemics and the mitigation effects of exercise: A longitudinal study of college students in China. *International Journal of Environmental Research and Public Health*, *17*(10), 3722. DOI: 10.3390/ijerph17103722 PMID: 32466163

Zhao, M., & Tian, J.-L. (2022). Recent advances on the structure identification of components in food. *eFood*, *3*(6), 1–6. DOI: 10.1002/efd2.51

Zhao, W., Liao, X., Li, Q., Jiang, W., & Ding, W. (2021). The relationship between teacher job stress and burnout: A moderated mediation model. *Frontiers in Psychology*, *12*, 784–243. DOI: 10.3389/fpsyg.2021.784243 PMID: 35145457

Zhou, Y. J. (2015). The influence of organizational climate perception on job burnout in tumor hospital nurses. *The Journal of Nursing Administration*, *15*(2), 96–97.

KEY TERMS AND DEFINITIONS

Bootstrap Testing: A resampling method used to estimate the precision of sample statistics by drawing samples with replacement.

Family Conflict: A situation arising between family members due to the disagreement of views, roles, responsibilities, or emotional needs, leading towards tension or strain. Causes of such conflicts may be from almost any source and include financial problems, issues of work-life imbalance, communication problems, or parenting style.

Mediating Factor: Known as a mediator, it is the variable that explains the mechanism or process by which one variable influence another. For instance, the relationship between organizational climate and teacher burnout is family conflict as a mediator which would explain the indirect influence of the organizational environment on burnout through the dynamics in their families.

Organizational Climate: Organizational climate refers to the total atmosphere surrounding an organization and determines employee behavior, motivation, and job satisfaction.

Structural Equation Modeling (SEM): A multivariate statistical technique used to analyze structural relationships between measured variables and latent constructs.

Teacher Burnout: Teacher burnout refers to a state of emotional, physical, and mental exhaustion resulting from prolonged stress or pressure in one's job as a teacher.

Compilation of References

Abareshi, F., Salimi, F., Farnia, F., Fallahi, M., & Rastaghi, S. (2022). The impact of mental workload, work-related and socio-demographic factors on job burnout among emergency medical staff. *Work (Reading, Mass.)*, *72*(4), 1269–1277. DOI: 10.3233/WOR-210001 PMID: 35723141

Abdallah, R., AbdelGaber, S. A., & Sayed, H. A. (2024, March). Disease Outbreak/Epidemic in Public Health Sector. In *2024 6th International Conference on Computing and Informatics (ICCI)* (pp. 203-216). IEEE.

Abdul-Messie, L. (2023). "Trying to feel the right feeling for the job": The emotional labour of English language teachers in state secondary schools in Italy. *Social Sciences & Humanities Open*, *8*(1), 100582. DOI: 10.1016/j.ssaho.2023.100582

Abel, T., Duetz-Schmuck, M., & Huwiler-Müntener, K. (2007). Sozialmedizin und Gesundheitssoziologie. In Gutzwiller, F., & Paccaud, F. (Eds.), *Sozial- und Präventivmedizin. Public Health* (3rd ed., pp. 23–34). Huber.

Abrams, D. E., & Hogg, M. A. (1990). *Social identity theory: Constructive and critical advances*. Springer-Verlag Publishing.

Acheson, K., Taylor, J., & Luna, K. (2016). The burnout spiral: The emotion labor of five rural US foreign language teachers. *Modern Language Journal*, *100*(2), 522–537. DOI: 10.1111/modl.12333

Adam, J. (2024.). The 20 most stressful jobs | careers | U.S. news. https://money.usnews.com/careers/articles/the-most-stressful-jobs

Addy, T. M., Addy, N. A., Hendrickson, B., & Mitchell, K. A. (2023). Supporting mentees through inclusive mentorship. *New Directions for Teaching and Learning*, *2023*(175), 11–19. DOI: 10.1002/tl.20554

Adriaenssens, J., De Gucht, V., & Maes, S. (2015). Determinants and prevalence of burnout in emergency nurses: A systematic review of 25 years of research. *International Journal of Nursing Studies*, *52*(2), 649–661. DOI: 10.1016/j.ijnurstu.2014.11.004 PMID: 25468279

Afrahi, B., Blenkinsopp, J., de Arroyabe, J. C. F., & Karim, M. S. (2022). Work disengagement: A review of the literature. *Human Resource Management Review*, *32*(2), 100822. DOI: 10.1016/j.hrmr.2021.100822

Akinloye Akinboade, O., Chanceline Kinfack, E., & Putuma Mokwena, M. (2012). An analysis of citizen satisfaction with public service delivery in the Sedibeng district municipality of South Africa. *International Journal of Social Economics*, *39*(3), 182–199. DOI: 10.1108/03068291211199350

Alang, T., Stanton, P., & Rose, M. (2022). Enhancing employee voice and inclusion through inclusive leadership in public sector organizations. *Public Personnel Management*, *51*(3), 309–329. DOI: 10.1177/00910260221085583

Alden, L. E., Matthews, L. R., Wagner, S., Fyfe, T., Randall, C., Regehr, C., White, M., Buys, N., Carey, M. G., Corneil, W., White, N., Fraess-Phillips, A., & Krutop, E. (2021). Systematic literature review of psychological interventions for first responders. *Work and Stress*, *35*(2), 193–215. DOI: 10.1080/02678373.2020.1758833

Allam, F. C., & Martin, M. M. (2021). Issues and Challenges in Special Education: A Qualitative Analysis from Teacher's Perspective. *Southeast Asia Early Childhood*, 10(1), 37-49. https://eric.ed.gov/?id=EJ1296259

Allan, J., Olcon, K., Everingham, R., Fox, M., Pai, P., Mackay, M., & Keevers, L. (2023). Leading wellness in healthcare: A qualitative study of leadership practices for wellness in hospital settings. *PLoS One*, *18*(7), e0285103. DOI: 10.1371/journal.pone.0285103 PMID: 37467299

Allison, E. E. (2024). *Does Structural Empowerment Mitigate Organizational Burnout? A Qualitative Exploration of the Relationship Between Managerialism and Burnout Among Middle Managers in Two Nonprofit Human Service Agencies* (Order No. 31236335). [Doctoral dissertation, San Diego State University]. ProQuest Dissertations & Theses Global. http://libproxy.tulane.edu:2048/login?url=https://www.proquest.com/dissertations-theses/does-structural-empowerment-mitigate/docview/3040227374/se-2

Almén, N., & Jansson, B. (2021). The reliability and factorial validity of different versions of the shirom-melamed burnout measure/questionnaire and normative data for a general Swedish sample. *International Journal of Stress Management*, *28*(4), 314–325. DOI: 10.1037/str0000235

Almer, E. D., & Kaplan, S. E. (2002). The effects of flexible work arrangements on stressors, burnout, and behavioral job outcomes in public accounting. *Behavioral Research in Accounting*, *14*(1), 1–34. DOI: 10.2308/bria.2002.14.1.1

Alves, L., Abreo, L., Petkari, E., & Pinto da Costa, M. (2023). Psychosocial risk and protective factors associated with burnout in police officers: A systematic review. *Journal of Affective Disorders*, *332*, 283–298. DOI: 10.1016/j.jad.2023.03.081 PMID: 36972850

Alvesson, M. (2002). *Understanding Organizational Culture*. SAGE Publications Ltd. DOI: 10.4135/9781446280072

An, B. Y., Barboza-Wilkes, C. J., & Resh, W. G. (2024). Applying an intersectional understanding of extra work behavior and emotional exhaustion in local public service. *Public Administration*, *102*(4), 1578–1603. DOI: 10.1111/padm.12989

Anbar, A., & Eker, M. (2008). An examination of the relationship between burnout and job satisfaction among Turkish accounting and finance academicians. *European Journal of Economic and Political Studies*, *1*(1), 46–67.

Andruszkiewicz, F. (2019). Professional burnout as a source of an early school education teachers' career destabilization. *Szkoła-Zawód-Praca*, (18), 111–121.

Anh Vu, T., Plimmer, G., Berman, E., & Ha, P. N. (2022). Performance management in the Vietnam public sector: The role of institution, traditional culture and leadership. *International Journal of Public Administration*, *45*(1), 49–63. DOI: 10.1080/01900692.2021.1903499

Arañas, J. Q. (2023). Tasks Beyond Instruction: A Case Study on Teachers' Ancillary Functions. *International Journal of Educational Innovation and Research*, *2*(2), 179–186. DOI: 10.31949/ijeir.v2i2.5740

Aras, F. M., & Gümüssoy, S. (2024). Emotional burnout, job satisfaction, and intention to leave among pre-hospital emergency healthcare workers during the COVID-19 pandemic. *Work (Reading, Mass.)*, *79*(1), 47–59.

Arcay, N.Jr, Rebucas, J. N., & Aparece, R. (2024). The Attrition and Migration of Bohol Association of Catholic Schools Teachers of The Diocese of Tagbilaran. *University of Bohol Multidisciplinary Research Journal*, *12*(1), 77–93. DOI: 10.15631/ppmzak16

Ariely, G. (2013). Public administration and citizen satisfaction with democracy: Cross-national evidence. *International Review of Administrative Sciences*, *79*(4), 747–766. DOI: 10.1177/0020852313501432

Armenakis, A. A., Harris, S. G., & Mossholder, K. W. (1993). Creating Readiness for Organizational Change. *Human Relations*, *46*(6), 681–703. DOI: 10.1177/001872679304600601

Aryee, S., Srinivas, E. S., & Tan, H. H. (2005). Rhythms of Life: Antecedents and outcomes of work-family balance in employed parents. *The Journal of Applied Psychology*, *90*(1), 132–146. DOI: 10.1037/0021-9010.90.1.132 PMID: 15641894

Asakura, K., Gheorghe, R. M., Rieger, D., Tarshis, S., Borgen, S., & D'Angiulli, A. (2023). Exploring shared trauma in the time of COVID: A simulation-based survey study of mental health clinicians. *Clinical Social Work Journal*, *51*(2), 163–174. DOI: 10.1007/s10615-022-00860-0 PMID: 36536816

Ashforth, B. E., & Humphrey, R. H. (1993). Emotional Labor in Service Roles: The Influence of Identity. *Academy of Management Review*, *18*(1), 88–115. DOI: 10.2307/258824

Ashforth, B. E., & Mael, F. (1989). Social identity theory and the organization. *Academy of Management Review*, *14*(1), 20–39. DOI: 10.2307/258189

Ashikali, T., Groeneveld, S., & Kuipers, B. (2021). The role of inclusive leadership in supporting an inclusive climate in diverse public sector teams. *Review of Public Personnel Administration*, *41*(3), 497–519. DOI: 10.1177/0734371X19899722

Asplund, J., & Tatel, C. (2023, March 22). *Fighting burnout with strengths*. CliftonStrengths. https://www.gallup.com/cliftonstrengths/en/472067/fighting-burnout-strengths.aspx

Asuncion, R. A. (2021). An Exploratory Study on Emotional Labor: The 'Invisible' Work of Teachers. *Philippine Journal of Labor and Industrial Relations*, *34*, 80–113. https://www.journals.upd.edu.ph/index.php/pjlir/article/view/ 7704/6712

Athavale, V. A., Selvakumar, P., Poorani, S., Anand, T., & Rathore, D. S. (2025). Designing Chatbots for Educational Leadership. In Musundire, A. (Ed.), *Chatbots in Educational Leadership and Management* (pp. 181–204). IGI Global Scientific Publishing., DOI: 10.4018/979-8-3693-8734-4.ch008

Auger, G. A., & Formentin, M. J. (2021). This is depressing: The emotional labor of teaching during the pandemic spring 2020. *Journalism & Mass Communication Educator*, *76*(4), 376–393. DOI: 10.1177/10776958211012900

Auld, M. E., Allen, M. P., Hampton, C., Montes, J. H., Sherry, C., Mickalide, A. D., Logan, R. A., Alvarado-Little, W., & Parson, K. (2020). Health literacy and health education in schools: Collaboration for action. *NAM Perspectives*. Advance online publication. DOI: 10.31478/202007b

Austin, Z., & Gregory, P. (2020). Resilience in the time of pandemic: The experience of community pharmacists during COVID-19. *Research in Social & Administrative Pharmacy, 17*(1), 1867.

Avendano, M., Jürges, H., & Mackenbach, J. P. (2009). Educational level and changes in health across Europe: Longitudinal results from SHARE. *Journal of European Social Policy, 19*(4), 301–316. DOI: 10.1177/1350506809341512

Avey, J. B., Luthans, F., Smith, R. M., & Palmer, N. F. (2011). Impact of positive psychological capital on employee well-being over time. *Journal of Occupational Health Psychology, 16*(1), 17–28. DOI: 10.1037/a0016998 PMID: 20063956

Axelrad-Levy, T., Schwartz Tayri, T. M., Achdut, N., & Sarid, O. (2023). The perceived job performance of child welfare workers during the COVID-19 pandemic. *Clinical Social Work Journal, 51*(2), 175–187. DOI: 10.1007/s10615-022-00861-z PMID: 36713302

Ayub, N., Ahmad, M. S., & Jabeen, Z. (2022). Impact of unethical organizational practices on employee burnout: A study of the banking sector. *Journal of Business Ethics, 170*(3), 517–536.

Backé, E. M., Seidler, A., Latza, U., Rossnagel, K., & Schumann, B. (2012). The role of psychosocial stress at work for the development of cardiovascular diseases: A systematic review. *International Archives of Occupational and Environmental Health, 85*(1), 67–79. DOI: 10.1007/s00420-011-0643-6 PMID: 21584721

Badri, M., Al Khaili, M., & Al Mansoori, R. L. (2015). Quality of service, expectation, satisfaction and trust in public institutions: The Abu Dhabi citizen satisfaction survey. *Asian Journal of Political Science, 23*(3), 420–447. DOI: 10.1080/02185377.2015.1055773

Bakker, A. B., & de Vries, J. D. (2021). Job Demands–Resources theory and self-regulation: New explanations and remedies for job burnout. *Anxiety, Stress, and Coping, 34*(1), 1–21. DOI: 10.1080/10615806.2020.1797695 PMID: 32856957

Bakker, A. B., & Demerouti, E. (2007). The Job-Demands-Resources Model: State of the art. *Journal of Managerial Psychology, 22*(3), 309–328. DOI: 10.1108/02683940710733115

Bakker, A. B., & Demerouti, E. (2017). Job demands–resources theory: Taking stock and looking forward. *Journal of Occupational Health Psychology, 22*(3), 273–285. DOI: 10.1037/ocp0000056 PMID: 27732008

Bakker, A. B., & Demerouti, E. (2018). Multiple levels in job demands-resources theory: implications for employee well-being and performance. In Diener, E., Oishi, S., & Tay, L. (Eds.), *Handbook of well-being*. DEF Publishers., https://research.tue.nl/files/116456879/Multiple_Levels_in_Job_Demands_Resources_Theory_Implications_for_Employee_Well_being_and_Performance.pdf

Bakker, A. B., Demerouti, E., & Sanz-Vergel, A. I. (2014). Burnout and work engagement: The JD–R approach. *Annual Review of Organizational Psychology and Organizational Behavior*, *1*(1), 389–411. DOI: 10.1146/annurev-orgpsych-031413-091235

Bakker, A. B., & Geurts, S. A. E. (2004). Toward a dual-process model of work-home interference. *Work and Occupations*, *31*(3), 345–366. DOI: 10.1177/0730888404266349

Bakker, A. B., Killmer, C. H., Siegrist, J., & Schaufeli, W. B. (2000). Effort-reward imbalance and burnout among nurses. *Journal of Advanced Nursing*, *31*(4), 884–891. DOI: 10.1046/j.1365-2648.2000.01361.x PMID: 10759985

Bakker, A. B., Schaufeli, W. B., Sixma, H. J., & Bosveld, W. (2001). Burnout contagion among general practitioners. *Journal of Social and Clinical Psychology*, *20*(1), 82–98. DOI: 10.1521/jscp.20.1.82.22251

Bandura, A. (1977). Self-efficacy: Toward a unifying theory of behavioral change. *Psychological Review*, *84*(2), 191–215. DOI: 10.1037/0033-295X.84.2.191 PMID: 847061

Bang, K. M. (2022). Occupational epidemiology. *Modern Occupational Diseases: Diagnosis, Epidemiology, Management and Prevention*, 25-40.

Banks, J., Lopez, V., Sahay, A., & Cleary, M. (2024). A scoping review of compassion fatigue among oncology nurses caring for adult patients. *Cancer Nursing*, *47*(4), E213–E225. DOI: 10.1097/NCC.0000000000001226 PMID: 36944157

Barboza-Wilkes, C., Gonzalez, E., Resh, W., & Wong, S. (2024). The emotional toll of the COVID-19 crisis on local government workers. *Review of Public Personnel Administration*, *44*(1), 60–85. DOI: 10.1177/0734371X221108501

Bardach, L., Klassen, R. M., & Perry, N. E. (2022). Teachers' psychological characteristics: Do they matter for teacher effectiveness, teachers' well-being, retention, and interpersonal relations? An integrative review. *Educational Psychology Review*, *34*(1), 259–300. DOI: 10.1007/s10648-021-09614-9

Barling, J., Slater, F., & Kelloway, E. K. (2011). Transformational leadership and emotional intelligence. *Leadership and Organization Development Journal*, *31*(2), 143–157. DOI: 10.1108/01437731111112917

Barry, D. P. (2023). Self-Compassion practice to mitigate teachers' empathy fatigue and burnout. In *Developing Trauma-Informed Teachers: Creating* Classrooms That Foster Equity, Resiliency, and Asset-Based Approaches, 49-70. USA: Information Age Publishing.

Basilio, K. C. L. (2024). *Philippine Students are in Deep Trouble*. Retrieved from https://www.bworldonline.com/special-reports/2024/09/09/619447/philippin e-students-are-in-deep-trouble/

Bass, B. M., & Riggio, R. E. (2006). *Transformational leadership* (2nd ed.). Psychology Press. DOI: 10.4324/9781410617095

Bellas, M. L. (1999). Emotional labor in academia: The case of professors. *The Annals of the American Academy of Political and Social Science*, *561*(1), 96–110. DOI: 10.1177/000271629956100107

Bennis, W., & Nanus, B. (2012). *Leaders: strategies for taking charge [Second edition]* 9780061762505, 0061762504. Dokumen.pub. https://dokumen.pub/leaders-strategies-for-taking-charge-second-edition-9780061762505-0061762504.html

Benveniste, T., Smith, D. R., Gupta, C. C., Chappel, S. E., & Sprajcer, M. (2024). Compassion Fatigue in Out of Home Care Workers: A Systematic Review. *Residential Treatment for Children & Youth*, *42*(1), 51–79. DOI: 10.1080/0886571X.2024.2310583

Berg-Weger, M. (2019). *Social work and social welfare: An invitation* (5th ed.). Routledge. DOI: 10.4324/9780429466687

Beyer, J. M., & Hannah, D. R. (2002). Building on the past: Enacting established personal identities in a new work setting. *Organization Science*, *13*(6), 636–652. DOI: 10.1287/orsc.13.6.636.495

Bhugra, D. (2025). Compassion fatigue: Result or cause of burnout? And do doctors get it? *Journal of the Royal Society of Medicine*, *118*(4), 138–140. DOI: 10.1177/01410768251320166 PMID: 39946213

Bianchi, R., & Schonfeld, I. S. (2023). Examining the evidence base for burnout. *Bulletin of the World Health Organization*, *101*(11), 743–745. DOI: 10.2471/BLT.23.289996 PMID: 37961064

Bianchi, R., & Schonfeld, I. S. (2024). Beliefs about burnout. *Work and Stress*, •••, 1–19. DOI: 10.1080/02678373.2024.2364590

Birkenmaier, J., & Berg-Weger, M. (2017). *Practicum companion for social work: Integrating class and field work* (4th ed.). Pearson.

Biyela, B. N. (2019). *Leading teaching and learning in an overcrowded* classroom: experiences of four teachers in two secondary schools. Unpublished Master's Thesis, University of Kwazulu-Natal, South Africa. Retrieved from https://researchspace.ukzn.ac.za/server/api/core/bitstreams/beea2023-cd42-4f49-83a2-b38a37375c02/content

Blanco-Donoso, L. M., Moreno-Jiménez, J., Hernández-Hurtado, M., Cifri-Gavela, J. L., Jacobs, S., & Garrosa, E. (2021). Daily Work-Family Conflict and Burnout to Explain the Leaving Intentions and Vitality Levels of Healthcare Workers: Interactive Effects Using an Experience-Sampling Method. *International Journal of Environmental Research and Public Health, 18*(4), 1932. DOI: 10.3390/ijerph18041932 PMID: 33671211

Bodjrenou, K., & Xu, M. (2018). Review of recent developments in leadership theories. *Open Journal of Social Sciences, 6*(7), 180–188. DOI: 10.4236/jss.2018.67014

Booth, J. E., & Lup, D. (2024). Enabling inclusion: An analysis of positive and negative outcomes of discretionary work arrangements for employees with disabilities. *British Journal of Industrial Relations*, bjir.12862. DOI: 10.1111/bjir.12862

Borrell, L. N., & Kapadia, F. (2021, August). Social Justice for Marginalized Communities. *American Journal of Public Health, 111*(8), 1366. DOI: 10.2105.AJPH.2021.306426

Bourke, J., Titus, A., & Espedido, A. (2020). The key to inclusive leadership. *Harvard Business Review, 6*, H05GLB.

Bowman, M. E. (2022). Child welfare worker wellness: An ethical imperative in the service of children. *Child Abuse Review, 31*(5), e2758. DOI: 10.1002/car.2758

Bradley, H. B. (1969). Community-based treatment for young adult offenders. *Crime and Delinquency, 15*(3), 359–370. https://doi-org.uvi.idm.oclc.org/10.1177/001112876901500307. DOI: 10.1177/001112876901500307

Brandert, K., Alperin, M., Lloyd, L. M., Rose, B., Bekemeier, B., Rogers, M., & Grimm, B. (2022). Learning to lead: 3 Models to support public health leadership development. *Journal of Public Health Management and Practice, 28*(S5), S203–S211. DOI: 10.1097/PHH.0000000000001519 PMID: 35867490

Braun, V., & Clarke, V. (2006). Using thematic analysis in psychology. *Qualitative Research in Psychology, 3*(2), 77–101. DOI: 10.1191/1478088706qp063oa

Breevaart, K., & Bakker, A. B. (2018). Daily job demands and employee work engagement: The role of daily transformational leadership behavior. *Journal of Occupational Health Psychology, 23*(3), 338–349. DOI: 10.1037/ocp0000082 PMID: 28358569

Breevaart, K., Bakker, A. B., Demerouti, E., Sleebos, D. M., & Maduro, V. (2014a). Uncovering the underlying relationship between transformational leaders and followers' task performance. *Journal of Personnel Psychology*, *13*(4), 194–203. DOI: 10.1027/1866-5888/a000118

Breevaart, K., Bakker, A. B., Hetland, J., Demerouti, E., Kjellevoldd-Olsen, O., & Espevik, R. (2014b). Daily transactional and transformational leadership and daily employee engagement. *Journal of Occupational and Organizational Psychology*, *87*(1), 138–157. DOI: 10.1111/joop.12041

Brewer, J. D. (2000). *Ethnography*. Open University Press.

Bride, B. E., & Figley, C. R. (2007). The fatigue of compassionate social workers: An introduction to the special issue on compassion fatigue. *Clinical Social Work Journal*, *35*(3), 151–153. DOI: 10.1007/s10615-007-0093-5

Bridgeman, P. J., Bridgeman, M. B., & Barone, J. (2018). Burnout syndrome among healthcar professionals. *Bulletin - American Society of Hospital Pharmacists*, *75*(3), 147–152.

Broadbent, J., & Guthrie, J. (1992). Changes in the Public Sector: A Review of 'Alternative' Accounting Research. *Accounting, Auditing & Accountability Journal*, *5*(3), 3–31. DOI: 10.1108/09513579210011835

Brotheridge, C. M., & Grandey, A. A. (2002). Emotional labor and burnout: Comparing two perspectives of "people work.". *Journal of Vocational Behavior*, *60*(1), 17–39. DOI: 10.1006/jvbe.2001.1815

Brown, E. L., Stark, K., Vesely, C., & Choe, J. (2023). "Acting often and everywhere:" Teachers' emotional labor across professional interactions and responsibilities. *Teaching and Teacher Education*, *132*, 104227. Advance online publication. DOI: 10.1016/j.tate.2023.104227

Brown, R. (2000). Social identity theory: Past achievements, current problems and future challenges. *European Journal of Social Psychology*, *30*(6), 745–778. DOI: 10.1002/1099-0992(200011/12)30:6<745::AID-EJSP24>3.0.CO;2-O

Brown, T. (2007). Coercion versus choice: Citizen evaluations of public service quality across methods of consumption. *Public Administration Review*, *67*(3), 559–572. DOI: 10.1111/j.1540-6210.2007.00737.x

Buric, I., & Kim, L. E. (2020). Teacher self-efficacy, instructional quality, and student motivational beliefs: An analysis using multilevel structural equation modeling. *Learning and Instruction*, *66*, 101302. Advance online publication. DOI: 10.1016/j.learninstruc.2019.101302

Buriel, M. C., Cachero, K. C., Padua, S. G., Palmeda, M. A., & Vergara, E. M. (2021). A comparative study of compassion fatigue between selected public and private junior and senior high school educators.*GreenPrints*. https://greenprints.dlshsi.edu.ph/grade_12/242

Buttigieg, S. C., Daher, P., Cassar, V., & Guillaume, Y. (2023). Under the shadow of looming change: Linking employees' appraisals of organisational change as a job demand and transformational leadership to engagement and burnout. *Work and Stress*, *37*(2), 148–170. DOI: 10.1080/02678373.2022.2120560

Cain, D. (2019). Best practices in disasters and disasters mental health. *Best Practices in Mental Health*, *15*(2), xii.

Cai, Q., Feng, H., Huang, J., Wang, M., Wang, Q., Lu, X., Xie, Y., Wang, X., Liu, Z., Hou, B., Ouyang, K., Pan, J., Li, Q., Fu, B., Deng, Y., & Liu, Y. (2020). The mental health of frontline and non-frontline medical workers during the coronavirus disease 2019 (COVID-19) outbreak in China: A case-control study. *Journal of Affective Disorders*. Advance online publication. DOI: 10.1016/j.jad.2020.06.031

Calcaterra, G., Bassareo, P., Barilla, F., Romeo, F., de Gregorio, C., Mehta, P., & Mehta, J. L. (2022). Syndemic: A Synergistic Anthropological Approach to the COVID-19 Pandemic. *Encyclopedia*, *2*(3), 1344–1356. DOI: 10.3390/encyclopedia2030090

Carastathis, A. (2014). The concept of intersectionality in feminist theory. *Philosophy Compass*, *9*(5), 304–314. DOI: 10.1111/phc3.12129

Cardarelli, R. (2023). Challenges facing educators and displaced students during emergencies: Implications for higher education. In *Higher Education in Emergencies: Best Practices and Benchmarking* (pp. 67-81). Emerald Publishing Limited. https://doi.org/DOI: 10.1108/S2055-364120230000053005

Carlotto, M. S., & Câmara, S. G. (2019). Burnout syndrome in public servants: Prevalence and association with occupational stressors. *Psico-USF*, *24*(3), 425–435. DOI: 10.1590/1413-82712019240302

Carlson, D. S., Kacmar, K. M., & Williams, L. J. (2000). Construction and initial validation of a multidimensional measure of work-family conflict. *Journal of Vocational Behavior*, *56*(2), 249–276. DOI: 10.1006/jvbe.1999.1713

Carnes, S. L. (2023). "Overworked and stretched thin": Burnout and systemic failure in school social work. *Children & Schools*, *45*(3), 151–159. https://doi-org.uvi.idm.oclc.org/10.1093/cs/cdad015. DOI: 10.1093/cs/cdad015

Carod-Artal, F. J., & Vázquez-Cabrera, C. (2013). Burnout Syndrome in an International Setting. In Bährer-Kohler, S. (Ed.), *Burnout for Experts: Prevention in the Context of Living and Working* (pp. 15–35). Springer. [1], https://link.springer.com/chapter/10.1007/978-1-4614-4391-9_2 DOI: 10.1007/978-1-4614-4391-9_2

Cartwright, S., & Boyes, R. F. (2000). Taking the pulse of executive health in the UK. *The Academy of Management Perspectives*, *14*(2), 16–24. DOI: 10.5465/ame.2000.3819301

Castro Schepers, O. (2023). Exploring the demographics of teachers who experience secondary traumatic stress. *BMC Psychology*, *11*(1), 181. DOI: 10.1186/s40359-023-01217-z PMID: 37322560

Catubig, C. G. H., Alas, A. F. D., Danganon, A. C., & Cagape, W. E. (2024). Elementary Teachers Lived Experiences in Handling Learners with Behavioral Difficulties. *International Journal of Research Publications*, *149*(1), 19–19. DOI: 10.47119/IJRP1001491520246548

Cavanaugh, C. (2024). #EMLowPay: Is America Investing Enough In The Salaries Of Non-Federal Emergency Managers? National Emergency Management Advanced Academy. https://www.usfa.fema.gov/library/

Cavanaugh, M. A., Boswell, W. R., Roehling, M. V., & Boudreau, J. W. (2000). An empirical examination of self-reported work stress among US managers. *The Journal of Applied Psychology*, *85*(1), 65–74. DOI: 10.1037/0021-9010.85.1.65 PMID: 10740957

Cawcutt, K. A., Clance, P., & Jain, S. (2021). Bias, burnout, and imposter phenomenon: The negative impact of under-recognized Intersectionality. *Women's Health Reports (New Rochelle, N.Y.)*, *2*(1), 643–647. DOI: 10.1089/whr.2021.0138 PMID: 35141712

Chatzoglou, P., Chatzoudes, D., Vraimaki, E., & Diamantidis, A. (2013). Service quality in the public sector: The case of the Citizen's Service Centers (CSCs) of Greece. *International Journal of Productivity and Performance Management*, *62*(6), 583–605. DOI: 10.1108/IJPPM-12-2012-0140

Cheng, C., Bartram, T., Karimi, L., & Leggat, S. (2016). Transformational leadership and social identity as predictors of team climate, perceived quality of care, burnout and turnover intention among nurses. *Personnel Review*, *45*(6), 1200–1216. DOI: 10.1108/PR-05-2015-0118

Cherniss, C. (1980). *Staff burnout. Job stress in the human services*. Sage.

Chesser, S., Porter, M. M., & Tuckett, A. G. (2019). Cultivating citizen science for all: Ethical considerations for research projects involving diverse and marginalized populations. *International Journal of Social Research Methodology*, *23*(5), 497–508. DOI: 10.1080/13645579.2019.1704355

Cheung, F. Y., & Lun, V. M. C. (2015). Relation between emotional labor and organizational citizenship behavior: An investigation among Chinese teaching professionals. *The Journal of General Psychology*, *142*(4), 253–272. DOI: 10.1080/00221309.2015.1091764 PMID: 26649924

Chien, N. B., & Thanh, N. N. (2022). The impact of good governance on the people's satisfaction with public administrative services in Vietnam. *Administrative Sciences*, *12*(1), 35. DOI: 10.3390/admsci12010035

ChildHope Philippines. (2023). *Breaking the Cycle: Children Poverty in the Philippines.* Retrieved from https://childhope.org.ph/children-in-poverty/

Childs, T. M., Iachini, A. L., Reitmeier, M., Browne, T., DeHart, D., Bengel, A., & Haynesworth, M. (2024). Exploring social work practitioners' perspectives on the contributors to burnout since the COVID-19 pandemic. *Social Work*, *69*(2), 142–150. https://doi-org.uvi.idm.oclc.org/10.1093/sw/swae005. DOI: 10.1093/sw/swae005 PMID: 38366254

Ching, G. S., Malabanan, J. C., & Canete, J. J. O. (2025). Adapting to online education: Social and emotional learning and teaching efficacy among Filipino teachers post-pandemic. *International Journal of Research*, *14*(3), 1–16. DOI: 10.5861/ijrse.2025.25801

Chingos, M. M., Henderson, M., & West, M. R. (2012). Citizen perceptions of government service quality: Evidence from public schools. *Quarterly Journal of Political Science*, *7*(4), 411–445. DOI: 10.1561/100.00011071

Chirila, T. (2015). A multi-mediation model of the relationship among workplace bullying, coping strategies, resilience, and employees' strain: Insights for a training program. *Psihologia Resurselor Umane Revista Asociatiei de Psihologie Industriala si Organizaţionala*, *13*(1), 63–82.

Chlap, N., & Brown, R. (2022). Relationships between workplace characteristics, psychological stress, affective distress, burnout and empathy in lawyers. *International Journal of the Legal Profession*, *29*(2), 159–180. DOI: 10.1080/09695958.2022.2032082

Choi, R., Chowdhary, S., Erdmann, D., & Ward, T. (2023, March 17). Bridging the talent gap in state government postpandemic. *McKinsey & Company*. https://www.mckinsey.com/industries/public-sector/our-insights/bridging-the-talent-gap-in-state-government-postpandemic

Choi, A. I., Weekley, C. C., Cheng Chen, S., Li, S., Kurella Tamura, M., Norris, K. C., & Shlipak, M. G. (2011). Association of educational attainment with chronic disease and mortality: The Kidney Early Evaluation Program (KEEP). *American Journal of Kidney Diseases*, *58*(2), 228–234. DOI: 10.1053/j.ajkd.2011.02.388 PMID: 21601328

Cho, S., Crenshaw, K. W., & McCall, L. (2013). Toward a field of intersectionality studies: Theory, applications, and praxis. *Signs (Chicago, Ill.)*, *38*(4), 785–810. DOI: 10.1086/669608

Christian-Brandt, A. S., Santacrose, D. E., & Barnett, M. L. (2020). In the trauma-informed care trenches: Teacher compassion satisfaction, secondary traumatic stress, burnout, and intent to leave education within underserved elementary schools. *Child Abuse & Neglect*, *110*, 104437. DOI: 10.1016/j.chiabu.2020.104437 PMID: 32151429

Cinite, I., Duxbury, L. E., & Higgins, C. (2009). Measurement of Perceived Organizational Readiness for Change in the Public Sector. *British Journal of Management*, *20*(2), 265–277. DOI: 10.1111/j.1467-8551.2008.00582.x

Clarke, J. J., Rees, C. S., Breen, L. J., & Heritage, B. (2021). The perceived effects of emotional labor in psychologists providing individual psychotherapy. *Psychotherapy (Chicago, Ill.)*, *58*(3), 414–424. DOI: 10.1037/pst0000351 PMID: 33271050

Clarke, J. J., Rees, C. S., Mancini, V. O., & Breen, L. J. (2024). Emotional labor and emotional exhaustion in psychologists: Preliminary evidence for the protective role of self-compassion and psychological flexibility. *Journal of Contextual Behavioral Science*, *31*, 100724. DOI: 10.1016/j.jcbs.2024.100724

Cochran-Smith, M. (2021). Rethinking teacher education: The trouble with accountability. *Oxford Review of Education*, *47*(1), 8–24. DOI: 10.1080/03054985.2020.1842181

Code, S., & Langan-Fox, J. (2001). Motivation, cognitions and traits: Predicting occupational health, well-being and performance. *Stress and Health*, *17*(3), 159–174. DOI: 10.1002/smi.897

Coelho, E., Amaral, A. P., Rocha, C., Cruz, R., & Brito-Costa, S. (2022). Burnout in pharmacy professionals during COVID-19 outbreak. *Acta Biomedica*, *93*(6), e2022281. DOI: 10.23750/abm.v93i6.13386

Colley, H. (2003). *Mentoring for social inclusion: A critical approach to nurturing mentor relationships*. Routledge. DOI: 10.4324/9780203458310

Collie, R. J., Shapka, J. D., & Perry, N. E. (2012). School climate and social-emotional learning: Predicting teacher stress, job satisfaction, and teaching efficacy. *Journal of Educational Psychology, 104*(4), 1189–1204. DOI: 10.1037/a0029356

Colquitt, J. A., Lepine, J. A., Zapata, C. P., & Wild, R. E. (2011). Trust in Typical and High-Reliability Contexts: Building and Reacting to Trust Among Firefighters. *Academy of Management Journal, 54*(5), 999–1015. DOI: 10.5465/amj.2006.0241

Conner, K. O., Abusuampeh, D. K., Kosyluk, K., Tran, J. T., Davis-Cotton, D., Hill, A. M., & Brown, A. P. (2024). Mitigating the stigma of mental illness: The impact of story telling in the black community. *International Journal of Environmental Research and Public Health, 21*(11), 1473.

Conner, K. O., Kosyluk, K., Tran, J. T., Anderson, E., Davis-Cotton, D., & Hill, A. M. (2023). The impact of a culturally meaningful storytelling intervention on stigma and attitudes about mental health treatment. *The Journal of Nervous and Mental Disease, 211*(6), 419–426.

Connor, K. M., & Davidson, J. R. T. (2003). Development of a new resilience scale: The Connor-Davidson Resilience Scale (CD-RISC). *Depression and Anxiety, 18*(2), 76–82. DOI: 10.1002/da.10113 PMID: 12964174

Cooper, C. L., Dewe, P., & O'Driscoll, M. P. (2001). Organizational Stress: A Review and Critique of Theory, Research, and Applications. *Sage (Atlanta, Ga.)*. Advance online publication. DOI: 10.4135/9781452231235

Cordaro, M. (2020). Pouring from an Empty Cup: The Case for Compassion Fatigue in Higher Education. *Building Healthy Academic Communities Journal, 4*(2), 17–28. DOI: 10.18061/bhac.v4i2.7618

Costin, A., Roman, A. F., & Balica, R. S. (2023). Remote work burnout, professional job stress, and employee emotional exhaustion during the COVID-19 pandemic. *Frontiers in Psychology, 14*, 1193854. DOI: 10.3389/fpsyg.2023.1193854 PMID: 37325768

Crawford, C. A. (2021). Studying social workers' roles in natural disasters during a global pandemic: What can we learn? *Qualitative Social Work: Research and Practice, 20*(1–2), 456–462. DOI: 10.1177/1473325020973449 PMID: 34253986

Crenshaw, K. (1989). Demarginalizing the intersection of race and sex: A black feminist critique of antidiscrimination doctrine, feminist theory and antiracist politics. In *Feminist legal theories* (pp. 23–51). Routledge.

Crenshaw, K. W. (1991). Mapping the margins: Intersectionality, identity politics, and violence against women of color. In *The public nature of private violence* (pp. 93–118). Routledge.

Crosby, B. C., & Bryson, J. M. (2017). Why leadership of public leadership research matters: And what to do about it. *Public Management Review*, *20*(9), 1265–1286. DOI: 10.1080/14719037.2017.1348731

Cuadra, J. M. (2023). Uncovering the Complexities of Coping: A Qualitative Study on the Challenges Faced by Special Education Teachers in the Sandwich Generation. *Philippine Social Science Journal*, *6*(1), 41–51. DOI: 10.52006/main.v6i1.646

Cui, L. (2022). The role of teacher–student relationships in predicting teachers' occupational wellbeing, emotional exhaustion, and enthusiasm. *Frontiers in Psychology*, *13*, 896813. DOI: 10.3389/fpsyg.2022.896813 PMID: 35664194

da Silva Menguer, L., Pereira, E. V., da Silva, A. C. R., & de Farias, J. M. (2024). Burnout syndrome and job satisfaction in community health workers. *Revista Brasileira de Medicina do Trabalho : Publicacao Oficial da Associacao Nacional de Medicina do Trabalho-ANAMT*, *21*(4), e2021903. PMID: 39132269

Dada, D., Djiometio, J. N., McFadden, S. M., Demeke, J., Vlahov, D., Wilton, L., & Nelson, L. E. (2022). Strategies that promote equity in COVID-19 vaccine uptake for black communities: A review. *Journal of Urban Health*, *99*(1), 15–27.

Dahles, H., & Van Hees, E. (2004). Firefighters across frontiers: Two fire brigades cooperating in the Dutch–German borderland. *Culture and Organization*, *10*(4), 315–328. DOI: 10.1080/1475955042000313759

Dandalt, E. (2024). Government-level public leadership development in the United States. *Australian Journal of Public Administration*, 1467-8500.12670. Advance online publication. DOI: 10.1111/1467-8500.12670

Daniel, C., Gentina, E., & Mesmer-Magnus, J. (2022). Mindfulness buffers the deleterious effects of workaholism for work-family conflict. *Social Science & Medicine*, *306*, 115118. Advance online publication. DOI: 10.1016/j.socscimed.2022.115118 PMID: 35696778

Dankwa-Mullan, I., Pérez-Stable, E. J., Gardner, K. L., Zhang, X., & Rosario, A. M. (2021). *The Science of Health Disparities Research*. John Wiley & Sons., DOI: 10.1002/9781119374855

Darawsheh, S. R., Asha, I. K. K., AbuSaif, R., Alhejoj, A. F., & Khasawneh, M. A. S. (2023). An Outline of the Professional Quality of Teachers who Teach Children with Special Needs. *Journal of Education and e-learning Research, 10*(3), 358–363. https://eric.ed.gov/?id=EJ1408079. DOI: 10.20448/jeelr.v10i3.4711

Dave, G., Frerichs, L., Jones, J., Kim, M., Schaal, J., Vassar, S., Varma, D., Striley, C., Ruktanonchai, C., Black, A., Hankins, J., Lovelady, N., Cene, C., Green, M., Young, T., Tiwari, S., Cheney, A., Cottler, L., Sullivan, G., & Corbie-Smith, G. (2018). Conceptualizing trust in community-academic research partnerships using concept mapping approach: A multi-CTSA study. *Evaluation and Program Planning, 66*, 70–78. DOI: 10.1016/j.evalprogplan.2017.10.007

Davis, K., & Palladino, J. (2011).*Compassion Fatigue among Secondary Special* Education Teachers: A Case Study about Job Stress and Burnout. Retrieved from https://eric.ed.gov/?id=ED522807

Day, D. V., Fleenor, J. W., Atwater, L. E., Sturm, R. E., & McKee, R. A. (2014). Advances in leader and leadership development: A review of 25 years of research and theory. *The Leadership Quarterly, 25*(1), 63–82. DOI: 10.1016/j.leaqua.2013.11.004

De Clercq, M., Watt, H. M. G., & Richardson, P. W. (2022). Profiles of teachers' striving and wellbeing: Evolution and relations with context factors, retention, and professional engagement. *Journal of Educational Psychology, 114*(3), 637–655. DOI: 10.1037/edu0000702

De Smet, A., Dowling, B., Hancock, B., & Schaninger, B. (2022, July 13). The Great Attrition is making hiring harder. Are you searching the right talent pools? *McKinsey & Company*. https://www.mckinsey.com/capabilities/people-and-organizational-performance/our-insights/the-great-attrition-is-making-hiring-harder-are-you-searching-the-right-talent-pools

Deci, E. L., & Ryan, R. M. (1985). *Intrinsic motivation and self-determination in human behavior*. Plenum. DOI: 10.1007/978-1-4899-2271-7

Del Ben, K. S., Scotti, J. R., Chen, Y.-C., & Fortson, B. L. (2006). Prevalence of posttraumatic stress disorder symptoms in firefighters. *Work and Stress, 20*(1), 37–48. DOI: 10.1080/02678370600679512

Denison, D. R. (1996). What is the difference between organizational culture and organizational climate? A native's point of view on a decade of paradigm wars. *Academy of Management Review, 21*(3), 619–654. DOI: 10.2307/258997

Derycke, H., Vlerick, P., Burnay, N., Decleire, C., D'Hoore, W., Hasselhorn, H. M., & Braeckman, L. (2010). Impact of the effort-reward imbalance model on intent to leave among Belgian health care workers: A prospective study. *Journal of Occupational and Organizational Psychology, 83*(4), 879–893. DOI: 10.1348/096317909X477594

Dewe, P., & Kompier, M. (2008). *Foresight mental capital and wellbeing project: wellbeing and work: future challenges*. The Government Office for Science.

Dewe, P., O' Driscoll, M., & Cooper, C. (2010). *Coping with Work Stress: A Review and Critique*. Wiley-Blackwell. DOI: 10.1002/9780470711712

Di Tella, M., Tesio, V., Bertholet, J., Gasnier, A., Del Portillo, E. G., Spalek, M., & Franco, P. (2020). Professional quality of life and burnout among medical physicists working in radiation oncology: The role of alexithymia and empathy. *Physics and Imaging in Radiation Oncology, 15*, 38–43. DOI: 10.1016/j.phro.2020.07.001 PMID: 33458324

Dick-Sagoe, C. (2020). Decentralization for improving the provision of public services in developing countries: A critical review. *Cogent Economics & Finance, 8*(1), 1804036. DOI: 10.1080/23322039.2020.1804036

Dierdorff, E. C., & Ellington, K. (2008). It's the nature of work: Examining behavior-based sources of work- family conflict across occupations. *The Journal of Applied Psychology, 93*(4), 883–892. DOI: 10.1037/0021-9010.93.4.883 PMID: 18642990

Dierdorff, E. C., & Morgeson, F. P. (2007). Consensus in work role requirements: The influence of discrete occupational context on role expectations. *The Journal of Applied Psychology, 92*(5), 1228–1241. DOI: 10.1037/0021-9010.92.5.1228 PMID: 17845082

Dierdorff, E. C., Rubin, R. S., & Morgeson, F. P. (2009). The milieu of managerial work: An integrative framework linking work context to role requirements. *The Journal of Applied Psychology, 94*(4), 972–988. DOI: 10.1037/a0015456 PMID: 19594238

Dik, B. J., & Duffy, R. D. (2009). Calling and Vocation at Work: Definitions and Prospects for Research and Practice. *The Counseling Psychologist, 37*(3), 424–450. DOI: 10.1177/0011000008316430

Dinibutun, S. R. (2020). Factors associated with burnout among physicians: An evaluation during a period of COVID-19 pandemic. *Journal of Healthcare Leadership, 12*, 85–94. DOI: 10.2147/JHL.S270440 PMID: 32982532

Dinibutun, S. R., Kuzey, C., & Dinc, M. S. (2020). The effect of organizational climate on faculty burnout at state and private universities: A comparative analysis. *Journal of Educational and Social Research, 10*(1), 56–74. DOI: 10.1177/2158244020979175

Doherty, A. S., Mallett, J., Leiter, M. P., & McFadden, P. (2021). Measuring burnout in social work. *European Journal of Psychological Assessment, 37*(1), 6–14. DOI: 10.1027/1015-5759/a000568

Dollard, M. F., & Bailey, T. (2021). Building psychosocial safety climate in turbulent times: The case of COVID-19. *The Journal of Applied Psychology, 106*(7), 951–964. DOI: 10.1037/apl0000939 PMID: 34383511

Dominic, C., Gopal, D. P., & Sidhu, A. (2021). 'It's like juggling fire daily': Well-being, workload and burnout in the British NHS - A survey of 721 physicians. *Work (Reading, Mass.), 70*(2), 395–403. DOI: 10.3233/WOR-205337 PMID: 34633337

Dowling, F., Genet, B., & Moynihan, G. (2005). A Confidential Peer-Based Assistance Program for Police Officers. *Psychiatric Services (Washington, D.C.), 56*(7), 870–871. DOI: 10.1176/appi.ps.56.7.870 PMID: 16020823

Dragano, N., & Wahrendorf, M. (2014). Consistent health inequalities in Europe: The importance of labour market disadvantage. *Journal of Epidemiology and Community Health, 68*(4), 293–294. DOI: 10.1136/jech-2013-203655 PMID: 24419233

Dreer, B. (2021). Teachers' well-being and job satisfaction: The important role of positive emotions in the workplace. *Educational Studies, 50*(1), 61–77. DOI: 10.1080/03055698.2021.1940872

DuBois, A. L., & Mistretta, M. A. (2019). *Overcoming burnout and compassion fatigue in schools: A guide for counselors, administrators, and educators*. Routledge. DOI: 10.4324/9781351030021

Dudau, A., & Brunetto, Y. (2020). Debate: Managing emotional labour in the public sector. *Public Money & Management, 40*(1), 11–13. DOI: 10.1080/09540962.2019.1665912

Duong, H. (2021). The politicization of civil service recruitment and promotion in Vietnam. *Public Administration and Development, 41*(2), 51–62. DOI: 10.1002/pad.1910

Durand, A.-C., Bompard, C., Sportiello, J., Michelet, P., & Gentile, S. (2019). Stress and burnout among professionals working in the emergency department in a French university hospital: Prevalence and associated factors. *Work (Reading, Mass.), 63*(1), 57–67. DOI: 10.3233/WOR-192908 PMID: 31127745

Dwinijanti, L., Adhikara, M. A., & Kusumapradja, R. (2020). Job satisfaction and turnover intention among public sector nurses: Is workload and burnout the issue? *JEMA: Jurnal Ilmiah Bidang Akuntansi Dan Manajemen, 17*(1), 67–77. DOI: 10.31106/jema.v17i1.4951

Dy-Zulueta, D. (2024, January 5). *Filipino teachers overworked by 400 unpaid hours annually — Study*. PhilStar Global. Retrieved June 7, 2025, from https://www.philstar.com/lifestyle/on-the-radar/2024/01/05/2297929/filipino-t eachers-overworked-400-unpaid-hours-annually-study

Eastwood, C., & Ecklund, K. (2008). Compassion Fatigue Risk and Self-Care Practices among Residential Treatment Center Childcare Workers. *Residential Treatment for Children & Youth, 25*(2), 103–122. DOI: 10.1080/08865710802309972

Eckleberry-Hunt, J., Kirkpatrick, H., & Barbera, T. (2018). The problems with burnout research. *Academic Medicine, 93*(3), 367–370. DOI: 10.1097/ACM.0000000000001890 PMID: 28817432

Eder, L. L., & Meyer, B. (2022). Self-endangering: A qualitative study on psychological mechanisms underlying nurses' burnout in long-term care. *International Journal of Nursing Sciences, 9*(1), 36–48. DOI: 10.1016/j.ijnss.2021.12.001 PMID: 35079603

Edmondson, A. C. (2019). *The fearless organization: Creating psychological safety in the workplace for learning, innovation, and growth*. Wiley.

Edú-Valsania, S., Laguía, A., & Moriano, J. A. (2022). Burnout: A review of theory and measurement. *International Journal of Environmental Research and Public Health,* 19 (1780), 1-27. https://doi.org/DOI: 10.3390/ijerph19031780

Ehrlich, H., McKenney, M., & Elkbuli, A. (2020). Defending the front lines during the COVID-19 pandemic: Protecting our first responders and emergency medical service personnel. *The American Journal of Emergency Medicine, 40*, 213–214. DOI: 10.1016/j.ajem.2020.05.068 PMID: 32513453

Eisen, E. A., Elser, H., & Picciotto, S. (2022). Working: The role of occupational epidemiology. *American Journal of Epidemiology, 191*(2), 237–240. DOI: 10.1093/aje/kwab243 PMID: 34613355

Emmons, R. S. (2019). Burnout No More: How to Push Back Against the Toxic Medical Workplace. *Journal of American Physicians and Surgeons, 24*(4), 114–119.

Engdaw, B. D. (2020). The impact of quality public service delivery on customer satisfaction in Bahir Dar city administration: The case of Ginbot 20 sub-city. *International Journal of Public Administration, 43*(7), 644–654. DOI: 10.1080/01900692.2019.1644520

EREnvision Resolution A Wellness Movement. https://ermovement.com/

Escalante, L., & Maisonnave, H. (2021). The impact of the COVID-19 pandemic on women's welfare and domestic burdens in Bolivia. HAL Archives. hal-03118060.

Escalante, E., Golden, R. L., & Mason, D. J. (2021). Social isolation and loneliness: Imperatives for health care in a post-COVID world. *Journal of the American Medical Association, 325*(6), 520–521.

Esguerra, D. J. (2024). *PBBM OKs law to arrest 'alarming' mental health concerns among youth.* Retrieved from https://www.pna.gov.ph/articles/1239528

Eva, A. L. (2022). *Surviving teacher burnout: A weekly guide to build resilience, deal with emotional exhaustion, and stay inspired in the classroom.* New Harbinger Publications.

Evans, E. J., Noureddine, N., Curry, S. R., & Nam, K. (2021). COVID-19 impacts on social work and nursing now and into the future: National administration plans. *Health & Social Work, 46*(3), 152–157. https://doi-org.uvi.idm.oclc.org/10.1093/hsw/hlab020. DOI: 10.1093/hsw/hlab020 PMID: 34255036

Fabelico, F., & Afalla, B. (2020). Perseverance and passion in the teaching profession: Teachers' grit, self-efficacy, burnout, and performance. *Journal of Critical Reviews, 7*(11), 108–119. DOI: 10.31838/jcr.07.03.05

Fabella, F. E. T., & Paz-Aler, R. A. D. (2023). Optimism as a mitigator of burnout: The relationship between optimism and burnout among selected teachers. *International Research Journal of Modernization in Engineering Technology and Science, 5*(02), 414–420.

Fardous, N., & Afzal, M. T. (2022). Contribution of emotional exhaustion towards depersonalization among teachers. *Journal of Positive School Psychology, 6*(8), 5265–5274.

Fazackerley, A. (2024). *Schools in England boost maternity pay to stem exodus of female teachers in their 30s*. Retrieved from https://www.theguardian.com /teacher-network/2024/nov/02/uk-schools-boost-maternity-pay-to-stem-exo dus-of-female-teachers-in-their-30s

Federal Emergency Management Agency. (2020). *Peer-to-Peer Mentoring at FEMA: The What, Why, and How of Getting Involved: Monday Minute for June 22, 2020.* https://content.govdelivery.com/accounts/USDHSFEMA/bulletins/2920b4e

Feng, H., Zhang, M., Li, X., Shen, Y., & Li, X. (2024). The Level and Outcomes of Emotional Labor in Nurses: A Scoping Review. *Journal of Nursing Management, 2024*(1), 5317359. DOI: 10.1155/2024/5317359 PMID: 40224865

Ferguson, M., Carlson, D., Kacmar, K. M., & Halbesleben, J. R. B. (2016). The supportive spouse at work: Does being work-linked help? *Journal of Occupational Health Psychology*, *21*(1), 37–50. DOI: 10.1037/a0039538 PMID: 26236955

Ferlie, E., Hartley, J., & Martin, S. (2003). Changing Public Service Organisations: Current Perspectives and Future Prospects. *British Journal of Management, 14*(s1), 1–14. DOI: 10.1111/j.1467-8551.2003.00389.x

Fernet, C., Trépanier, S.-G., Austin, S., Gagné, M., & Forest, J. (2015). Transformational leadership and optimal functioning at work: On the mediating role of employees' perceived job characteristics and motivation. *Work and Stress*, *29*(1), 11–31. DOI: 10.1080/02678373.2014.1003998

Ferrer, J. C. (2024). Academic Performance and Predictors of the Licensure Examination for Teachers of the Bachelor of Elementary Education. [MJSSH]. *Malaysian Journal of Social Sciences and Humanities*, *9*(11), e003091–e003091. DOI: 10.47405/mjssh.v9i11.3091

Ferrie, J. E., Shipley, M. J., Newman, K., Stansfeld, S. A., & Marmot, M. (2005). Selfreported job insecurity and health in the Whitehall II study: Potential explanations of the relationship. *Social Science & Medicine*, *60*(7), 1593–1602. DOI: 10.1016/j.socscimed.2004.08.006 PMID: 15652690

Figley, C. R. (1995). *Compassion fatigue: Coping with secondary traumatic stress disorder in those who treat the traumatized.* Brunner/Mazel.

Figley, C. R. (1995). Compassion fatigue: Toward a new understanding of the costs of caring. In Stamm, B. H. (Ed.), *Secondary traumatic stress: Self-care issues for clinicians, researchers, and educators* (pp. 3–28). The Sidran Press.

Figley, C. R. (2002). Compassion fatigue: Psychotherapists' chronic lack of self care. *Journal of Clinical Psychology*, *58*(11), 1433–1441. DOI: 10.1002/jclp.10090 PMID: 12412153

Filtenborg, A. F., Gaardboe, F., & Sigsgaard-Rasmussen, J. (2017). Experimental replication: An experimental test of the expectancy disconfirmation theory of citizen satisfaction. *Public Management Review*, *19*(9), 1235–1250. DOI: 10.1080/14719037.2017.1295099

Findley, P. A., Pottick, K. J., & Giordano, S. (2017). Educating graduate social work students in disaster response: A real-time case study. *Clinical Social Work Journal, 45*(2), 159–167. DOI: 10.1007/s10615-015-0533-6

Firth-Cozens, J. (2003). Doctors, their wellbeing, and their stress: It's time to be proactive about stress — and prevent it. *BMJ (Clinical Research Ed.), 326*(7391), 670–671. DOI: 10.1136/bmj.326.7391.670 PMID: 12663377

Fleuren, B. P., Nübold, A., Uitdewilligen, S., Verduyn, P., & Hülsheger, U. R. (2023). Troubles on troubled minds: An intensive longitudinal diary study on the role of burnout in the resilience process following acute stressor exposure. *European Journal of Work and Organizational Psychology, 32*(3), 373–388. DOI: 10.1080/1359432X.2022.2161369

Floyd, K. K., Horn, A., & Sherfinski, M. (2024). Compassion Fatigue, Resilience, and Endurance of Special Educators in Rural P–12 and Higher Education. *Rural Special Education Quarterly, 43*(2), 104–116. DOI: 10.1177/87568705241244576

Fontes, F. (2020). Herbert J. Freudenberger and the making of burnout as a psychopathological syndrome. 37, 1-19. DOI: 10.35699/1676-1669.2020.19144

Ford, M. T. (2012). Job-occupation misfit as an occupational stressor. *Journal of Vocational Behavior, 80*(2), 412–421. DOI: 10.1016/j.jvb.2011.10.004

Ford, M. T., Heinen, B. A., & Langkamer, K. L. (2007). Work and family satisfaction and conflict: A meta-analysis of cross-domain relations. *The Journal of Applied Psychology, 92*(1), 57–80. DOI: 10.1037/0021-9010.92.1.57 PMID: 17227151

Fortich, J., & Jaspe, M. (2022). Teachers' Emotional Labor in Relation to Classroom Management Practices of University of Bohol, Tagbilaran City, Bohol. *ACADEME University of Bohol, Graduate School and Professional Studies*, 20(1), 88-97.DOI: 10.15631/aubgsps.v20i1.181

Foster, D. (2024). How to create a successful leadership development program. *Harvard Business Publishing*. https://www.harvardbusiness.org/how-to-create-a-successful-leadership-development-program/

Francis, K., Clavier, N., & Hendrickson, K. (2021). *Frontline Government Workers: Assessing Post-Disaster Burnout and Quality of Life* (Natural Hazards Center Public Health Disaster Research Report Series, Report 8). Natural Hazards Center, University of Colorado Boulder. https://hazards.colorado.edu/public-health-disaster-research/frontline-government-workers-assessing-post-disaster-burnout-and-quality-of-life

Freedy, J. R., & Hobfoll, S. E. (1994). Stress inoculation for reduction of burnout: A conservation of resources approach. *Anxiety, Stress, and Coping*, *6*(4), 311–325. DOI: 10.1080/10615809408248805

Frérot, M., Lefebvre, A., Aho, S., Callier, P., Astruc, K., & Aho Glélé, L. S. (2018). What is epidemiology? Changing definitions of epidemiology 1978-2017. *PLoS One*, *13*(12), e0208442. DOI: 10.1371/journal.pone.0208442 PMID: 30532230

Freudenberger, H. (2010). Staff burn-out. *The Journal of Social Issues*, *30*(1), 159–165. DOI: 10.1111/j.1540-4560.1974.tb00706.x

Fute, A., Sun, B., & Oubibi, M. (2022). Assessing teaching compassion, work engagement, and compassion fatigue among teachers during the pandemic. *Psychology Research and Behavior Management*, *15*, 2561–2571. DOI: 10.2147/PRBM.S383292 PMID: 36124334

Gaastra, G. F., Groen, Y., Tucha, L., & Tucha, O. (2020). Unknown, unloved? Teachers' reported use and effectiveness of classroom management strategies for students with symptoms of ADHD. In *Child & Youth Care Forum* (Vol. 49, pp. 1-22). Springer US.DOI: 10.1007/s10566-019-09515-7

Galanis, P., Fragkou, D., & Katsoulas, T. A. (2021). Risk factors for stress among police officers: A systematic literature review. *Work (Reading, Mass.)*, *68*(4), 1255–1272. DOI: 10.3233/WOR-213455 PMID: 33867384

Gallup. (2024). *State of the global workplace report*. Gallup. https://www.gallup.com/workplace/349484/state-of-the-global-workplace.aspx

Garhammer, M. (2004). Auswirkungen neuer Arbeitsformen auf Stress und Lebensqualität. In Badura, B., Schellschmidt, H., & Vetter, C. (Eds.), *Fehlzeiten-Report 2003*. Springer-Verlag. DOI: 10.1007/978-3-662-07193-9_3

Garnett, A., Hui, L., Oleynikov, C., & Boamah, S. (2023). Compassion fatigue in healthcare providers: A scoping review. *BMC Health Services Research*, *23*(1), 1336. DOI: 10.1186/s12913-023-10356-3 PMID: 38041097

Gearing, R. E., Saini, M., & McNeill, T. (2007). Experiences and implications of social workers practicing in a pediatric hospital environment affected by SARS. *Health &amp. Social Work*, *32*(1), 17–27. DOI: 10.1093/hsw/32.1.17 PMID: 17388080

Geiger, D., Danner-Schröder, A., & Kremser, W. (2021). Getting Ahead of Time—Performing Temporal Boundaries to Coordinate Routines under Temporal Uncertainty. *Administrative Science Quarterly*, *66*(1), 220–264. DOI: 10.1177/0001839220941010

Gembalska-Kwiecień, A. (2019). *Occupational burnout-characteristics of the phenomenon and methods of counteracting*. Zeszyty Naukowe. Organizacja i Zarządzanie/ Politechnika Śląska. DOI: 10.29119/1641-3466.2019.134.3

Gemlik, N., Ayanoglu Sisman, F., & Unsal, S. (2010). The relationship between burnout and organizational commitment among health sector staff in Turkey. *Journal of Global Strategic Management*, *4*(2), 137–149. DOI: 10.20460/JGSM.2010415831

Geng, F., Yu, S., & Yuan, R. E. (2023). Exploring L2 writing teachers' feeling rules, emotional labor and regulation strategies. *System*, *119*, 103160. DOI: 10.1016/j.system.2023.103160

Geurts, S. A. E., Taris, T., Kompier, M. A. J., Lagerveld, S., & Blonk, R. W. B. (2008). My love, my life, and my everything: Work-home interaction among self-employed. *The individual in the changing working life* (pp. 147-168). DOI: 10.1017/CBO9780511490064.008

Ghodsy, A. (2008). The role of school organizational climate in occupational stress among secondary school teachers in Tehran. *International Journal of Occupational Medicine and Environmental Health*, *21*(4), 319–329. DOI: 10.2478/v1000100800188 PMID: 19228578

Gibbons, C. (2024). Stress, Coping, burnout and mental health in the Irish Police Force. *Journal of Police and Criminal Psychology*, *39*(2), 348–357. DOI: 10.1007/s11896-023-09638-7

Gilin, D. A., Anderson, G. G., Etezad, S., Lee-Baggley, D., Cooper, A. M., & Preston, R. K. (2023). Impact of a Wellness Leadership Intervention on the Empathy, Burnout, and Resting Heart Rate of Medical Faculty. *Mayo Clinic Proceedings. Innovations, Quality & Outcomes*, *7*(6), 545–555. DOI: 10.1016/j.mayocpiqo.2023.09.005 PMID: 38075429

Gillis, C., Montenigro, P., Nejati, M., & Maserejian, N. (2023). Estimating prevalence of early Alzheimer's disease in the United States, accounting for racial and ethnic diversity. *Alzheimer's & Dementia*, *19*(5), 1841–1848. DOI: 10.1002/alz.12822

Gilmour, A. F., & Wehby, J. H. (2020). The association between teaching students with disabilities and teacher turnover. *Journal of Educational Psychology*, *112*(5), 1042–1060. DOI: 10.1037/edu0000394

Ginevra, M. C., Di Maggio, I., Valbusa, I., Santilli, S., & Nota, L. (2022). Teachers' attitudes towards students with disabilities: The role of the type of information provided in the students' profiles of children with disabilities. *European Journal of Special Needs Education*, *37*(3), 357–370. DOI: 10.1080/08856257.2021.1878658

Giray, L., Asuncion, M. K. C., Edem, J., Gumalin, D. L., Jacob, J., & Lucero, S. M. (2023). Positive and Negative Lessons from Hidden Curriculum at a Philippine State University.*Educational Process: International Journal*, 12(1), 71-93. https://www.ceeol.com/search/article-detail?id=1109519

Glanz, K., & Schwartz, M. D. (2008). Stress, coping, and health behavior. In Glanz, K., Rimer, B. K., & Viswanath, K. (Eds.), *Health behavior and health education: Theory, research, and practice* (pp. 211–223). Jossey-Bass.

Glasmeier, A. (2025). *Living Wage Calculator*. Https://Livingwage.Mit.Edu. https://livingwage.mit.edu./

Glickman, C., & Burns, R. W. (2021). Supervision and teacher wellness: An essential component for improving classroom practice. *Journal of Educational Supervision, 4*(1), 18.https://doi.org/https://doi.org/10. 31045/jes.4.1.3

Goff, D. A., Ashiru-Oredope, D., Cairns, K. A., Eljaaly, K., Gauthier, T. P., Langford, B. J., & Schellack, N. (2020). Global contributions of pharmacists during the COVID-19 pandemic. *Journal of the American College of Clinical Pharmacy: JAACP*, *3*(8), 1480–1492.

Goleman, D., Boyatzis, R., & McKee, A. (2013). *Primal leadership: Unleashing the power of emotional intelligence*. Harvard Business Review Press.

Golembiewski, R. T., Boudreau, R. A., Sun, B. C., & Luo, H. (1998). Estimates of burnout in public agencies: Worldwide, how many employees have which degrees of burnout, and with what consequences? *Public Administration Review*, *58*(1), 59–65. DOI: 10.2307/976890

Go, M. B., Golbin, R. A.Jr, Velos, S. P., & Bate, G. P. (2020). Filipino Teachers' Compartmentalization Ability, Emotional Intelligence, and Teaching Performance. *Asian Journal of University Education*, *16*(3), 27–42. https://eric.ed.gov/?id=EJ1274296. DOI: 10.24191/ajue.v16i3.7912

Gomes, G. P., Ribeiro, N., & Gomes, D. R. (2022). The Impact of Burnout on Police Officers' Performance and Turnover Intention: The Moderating Role of Compassion Satisfaction. *Administrative Sciences*, *12*(3), 1–18. DOI: 10.3390/admsci12030092

Gomez, S. L., Llera, A., Neuhausen, S. L., Newman, L., Nguyen, T., Palmer, J. R., Palmer, N. R., & Fejerman, L. (2021). Cancer health disparities in racial/ethnic minorities in the United States. *British Journal of Cancer*, *124*, 315–332. 10.1038s41416-020-01038-6

Gorain, S., & Pal, S. (2021). Satisfaction of online education of college students during pandemic situation. *International Journal of Applied Research*, *7*(2), 157–160.

Grandey, A. A. (2017). When "The Show Must Go On": Surface acting and deep acting as determinants of emotional exhaustion and peer-rated service delivery. *Academy of Management Journal*, *46*(1), 1–23. DOI: 10.5465/30040678

Greene, P., Kane, D., Christ, G., Lynch, S., & Corrigan, M. (2006). *FDNY Crisis Counselling: Innovative Responses to 9/11 Firefighters, Families and Communities*. John Wiley & Sons.

Greenhaus, J. H., & Beutell, N. J. (1985). Sources of conflict between work and family roles. *Academy of Management Review*, *10*(1), 76–88. DOI: 10.2307/258214

Greenwood, M., & Zhan, R. (2019). Audit adjustments and public sector audit quality. *Abacus*, *55*(3), 511–534. DOI: 10.1111/abac.12165

Grønstad, A., Kjekshus, L. E., Tjerbo, T., & Bernstrøm, V. H. (2019). Organizational change and the risk of sickness absence: A longitudinal multilevel analysis of organizational unit-level change in hospitals. *BMC Health Services Research*, *19*(1), 895. DOI: 10.1186/s12913-019-4745-2 PMID: 31771576

Grzebyk, M., Pierścieniak, A., & Ohimor, J. (2018). PROFESSIONAL BURNOUT OF EMPLOYEES IN LOCAL PUBLIC ADMINISTRATION–KNOWLEDGE, CAUSES AND PREVENTION. *ZESZYTY NAUKOWE POLITECHNIKI CZĘSTOCHOWSKIEJ RESEARCH REVIEWS OF CZESTOCHOWA UNIVERSITY OF TECHNOLOGY*, 131.

Gualano, M. R., Sinigaglia, T., Lo Moro, G., Rousset, S., Cremona, A., Bert, F., & Siliquini, R. (2021). The burden of burnout among healthcare professionals of intensive care units and emergency departments during the COVID-19 pandemic: A systematic review. *International Journal of Environmental Research and Public Health*, *18*(15), 8172.

Guo, Y. (Ed.). (2024). *Digital Government and Public Interaction: Platforms, Chatbots, and Public Satisfaction: Platforms, Chatbots, and Public Satisfaction*. IGI Global. DOI: 10.4018/979-8-3693-3665-6

Haan, K. (2022, November 22). *Employee Benefits In 2025: The Ultimate Guide*. Forbes Advisor. https://www.forbes.com/advisor/business/emp

Hai, N. C., Le, V. T. P., Son, N. T., & Tuan, P. V. (2023). Evaluation of citizens' satisfaction with the quality of public administrative services in the Mekong Delta, Vietnam. *GeoJournal of Tourism and Geosites*, 48(2spl), 750–770

Hakanen, J. J., Bakker, A. B., & Schaufeli, W. B. (2008). Burnout and work engagement among teachers. *Journal of School Psychology*, *43*(6), 495–513. DOI: 10.1016/j.jsp.2005.11.001

Halbesleben, J. R. B., & Buckley, M. R. (2004). Burnout in Organizational Life. *Journal of Management, 30*(6), 859–879. DOI: 10.1016/j.jm.2004.06.004

Halbesleben, J. R. B., Neveu, J.-P., Paustian-Underdahl, S. C., & Westman, M. (2014). Getting to the "COR": Understanding the Role of Resources in Conservation of Resources Theory. *Journal of Management, 40*(5), 1334–1364. DOI: 10.1177/0149206314527130

Hällgren, M., Rouleau, L., & de Rond, M. (2018). A matter of life or death: How extreme context research matters for management and organization studies. *The Academy of Management Annals, 12*(1), 111–153. DOI: 10.5465/annals.2016.0017

Hall, W. M., Schmader, T., & Croft, E. (2015). Engineering exchanges: Daily social identity threat predicts burnout among female engineers. *Social Psychological & Personality Science, 6*(5), 528–534. DOI: 10.1177/1948550615572637

Hansel, T. C., & Saltzman, L. Y. (2024). Secondary traumatic stress and burnout: The role of mental health, work experience, loneliness and other trauma in compassion fatigue in the healthcare workforces. *Traumatology, 30*(4), 615–618. DOI: 10.1037/trm0000478

Hartigan-Go, K., Castillo, A. F., & Prieto, M. L. (2024, January 28). *Hungry children do not make good students*. Rappler. Retrieved June 2, 2025, from https://www.rappler.com/voices/imho/opinion-hungry-children-do-not-make-good-students/

Haslam, C., & Mallon, K. (2003). A preliminary investigation of post-traumatic stress symptoms among firefighters. *Work and Stress, 17*(3), 277–285. DOI: 10.1080/02678370310001625649

Haslam, S. A., O'Brien, A., Jetten, J., Vormedal, K., & Penna, S. (2005). Taking the strain: Social identity, social support, and the experience of stress. *British Journal of Social Psychology, 44*(3), 355–370. DOI: 10.1348/014466605X37468 PMID: 16238844

Haushofer, J., & Fehr, E. (2014). On the psychology of poverty. *science, 344*(6186), 862-867.

Headley, A. M., Remington, C., Witkowski, K., Contreras, S. L., & Ganapati, N. E. (2023). The impact of COVID-19 on first responders in the United States of America. *International Journal of Emergency Services, 12*(2), 243–251. DOI: 10.1108/IJES-12-2022-0071

Hechanova, M. R. M. (2011). Deconstructing Emotional Labor. *Philippine Journal of Psychology, 44*(1), 1–1.

Heffernan, A., Bright, D., Kim, M., Longmuir, F., & Magyar, B. (2022). 'I cannot sustain the workload and the emotional toll': Reasons behind Australian teachers' intentions to leave the profession. *Australian Journal of Education*, *66*(2), 196–209. DOI: 10.1177/00049441221086654

Helm-Murtagh, P. C., & Erwin, P. C. (2024). Building a new generation of public health leaders forged in a public health crisis. *American Journal of Public Health*, *114*(6), 626–632. DOI: 10.2105/AJPH.2024.307633 PMID: 38603662

Henson, J. S. (2020). Burnout or compassion fatigue: A comparison of concepts. *Medsurg Nursing*, *29*(2).

Hershcovis, M. (2011). 'Incivility, social undermining, bullying ... oh my!': A call to reconcile constructs within workplace aggression research. *Journal of Organizational Behavior*, *32*(3), 499–519. DOI: 10.1002/job.689

Hess, D. W. (2020, June 22-26). *Technical Leadership Skills Development Through Interactive Workshops* [Conference session]. ASEE Virtual Conference. https://peer.asee.org/35288

Hetzel-Riggin, M. D., Swords, B. A., Tuang, H. L., Deck, J. M., & Spurgeon, N. S. (2020). Work Engagement and Resiliency Impact the Relationship Between Nursing Stress and Burnout. *Psychological Reports*, *123*(5), 1835–1853. DOI: 10.1177/0033294119876076 PMID: 31510876

Hinds, T. S., & Giardino, A. P. (2020). Compassion fatigue, burnout, and coping strategies among child-serving professionals. Child Sexual Abuse: Current Evidence, Clinical Practice, and Policy *Directions*, 95-102.DOI: 10.1007/978-3-030-52549-1_4

Hirschberger, G. (2018). Collective trauma and the social construction of meaning. *Frontiers in Psychology*, *9*, 1441. DOI: 10.3389/fpsyg.2018.01441 PMID: 30147669

Hirsch, S. E., Bruhn, A. L., McDaniel, S., & Mathews, H. M. (2021). A Survey of Educators Serving Students With Emotional and Behavioral Disorders During the Covid-19 Pandemic. *Behavioral Disorders*, *47*(2), 95–107. DOI: 10.1177/01987429211016780

Hobfoll, S. E. (1989). Conservation of resources: A new attempt at conceptualizing stress. *The American Psychologist*, *44*(3), 513–524. DOI: 10.1037/0003-066X.44.3.513 PMID: 2648906

Hobfoll, S. E. (2001). The influence of culture, community, and the nested-self in the stress process: Advancing conservation of resources theory. *Applied Psychology*, *50*(3), 337–421. DOI: 10.1111/1464-0597.00062

Hochschild, A. R. (1983). *The managed heart: Commercialization of human feeling*. University of California Press.

Hochschild, A. R. (1983). *The Managed Heart: Commercialization of Human Feeling*. University of California Press.

Hofmeyer, A., Taylor, R., & Kennedy, K. (2020). Fostering compassion and reducing burnout: How can health system leaders respond in the Covid-19 pandemic and beyond? *Nurse Education Today*, *94*, 104502. DOI: 10.1016/j.nedt.2020.104502 PMID: 32980180

Hogg, M. A., Terry, D. J., & White, K. M. (1995). A tale of two theories: A critical comparison of identity theory with social identity theory. *Social Psychology Quarterly*, *58*(4), 255–269. DOI: 10.2307/2787127

Holmes, M. R., Robin, R. C., Korsch-Williams, A., & King, J. A. (2021). Impact of COVID-19 pandemic on posttraumatic stress, grief, burnout, and secondary trauma of social workers in the United States. *Clinical Social Work Journal*, *49*(4), 495–504. DOI: 10.1007/s10615-021-00795-y PMID: 33678920

Horner, C. G., Brown, E. L., Mehta, S., & Scanlon, C. L. (2020). Feeling and acting like a teacher: Reconceptualizing teachers' emotional labor. *Teachers College Record*, *122*(5), 1–36. DOI: 10.1177/016146812012200502

Hornsey, M. J. (2008). Social identity theory and self-categorization theory: A historical review. *Social and Personality Psychology Compass*, *2*(1), 204–222. DOI: 10.1111/j.1751-9004.2007.00066.x

Hou, Y., & Zheng, J. (2021). The Relationship Between Bob Burnout and Emotional Labor among College Counselors: Mediating Effect of General Self-Efficacy. *In7th International Conference on Social Science and Higher Education (ICSSHE 2021)* (pp. 616-621). Atlantis Press.DOI: 10.2991/assehr.k.211122.167

Huddy, L. (2001). From social to political identity: A critical examination of social identity theory. *Political Psychology*, *22*(1), 127–156. DOI: 10.1111/0162-895X.00230

Hughes, H. E., Edeghere, O., O'Brien, S. J., Vivancos, R., & Elliot, A. J. (2020). Emergency department syndromic surveillance systems: A systematic review. *BMC Public Health*, *20*(1), 1–15. DOI: 10.1186/s12889-020-09949-y PMID: 33298000

Hu, H., Wang, E., Si, J., Sui, X., Yi, Z., Zheng, Z., & Liu, H. (2022). Professional identity and turnover intention amongst Chinese social workers: Roles of job burnout and a social work degree. *British Journal of Social Work*, *52*(3), 1703–1723. https://doi-org.uvi.idm.oclc.org/10.1093/bjsw/bcab155. DOI: 10.1093/bjsw/bcab155

Hülsheger, U. R., Yang, T., Bono, J. E., Goh, Z., & Ilies, R. (2022). Stop the spin: The role of mindfulness practices in reducing affect spin. *Journal of Occupational Health Psychology, 27*(6), 529–543. DOI: 10.1037/ocp0000332 PMID: 35797166

Humphrey, N. M. (2021). Emotional labor and employee outcomes: A meta-analysis. *Public Administration, 101*(2), 422–446. DOI: 10.1111/padm.12818

HURDAT Re-analysis. (n.d.). ww.aoml.noaa.gov. https://www.aoml.noaa.gov/hrd/hurdat/All_U.S._Hurricanes.html

Hyndman, N., & McGeough, F. (2008). NPM and performance measurement: A comparative study of the public sectors in Ireland and the UK. *Irish Accounting Review, 15*(2), 5–46. DOI: 10.52399/001c.26982

Idris, M. A., Dollard, M. F., & Yulita, . (2014). Psychosocial safety climate, emotional demands, burnout, and depression: A longitudinal multilevel study in the Malaysian private sector. *Journal of Occupational Health Psychology, 19*(3), 291–302. DOI: 10.1037/a0036599 PMID: 24802994

Ignacio, T. D., & Allit, K. J. N. I. (2023). Attitudes of university faculty toward inclusion of students with special education needs. *Erudio Journal of Educational Innovation, 10*(1), 1–11. DOI: 10.5281/zenodo.8105178

Ilies, R., Nahrgang, J. D., & Morgeson, F. P. (2007). Leader-member exchange and citizenship behaviors: A meta-analysis. *The Journal of Applied Psychology, 92*(1), 269–277. DOI: 10.1037/0021-9010.92.1.269 PMID: 17227168

Inbar, L., & Shiri, S.-A. (2021). Managing the emotional aspects of compassion fatigue among teachers in Israel: A qualitative study. *Journal of Education for Teaching, 47*(4), 562–575. DOI: 10.1080/02607476.2021.1929876

Isenberg, E., Max, J., Gleason, P., & Deutsch, J. (2021). Do Low-Income Students Have Equal Access to Effective Teachers? *Educational Evaluation and Policy Analysis, 44*(2), 234–256. DOI: 10.3102/01623737211040511

Islam, G. (2014). Social identity theory. *Journal of Personality and Social Psychology, 67*(1), 741–763.

Ivanić, D., Adam, V. N., Srzić, I., Stepić, A., & Pintarić, H. (2017). Burnout syndrome in emergency medicine. *Hong Kong Journal of Emergency Medicine, 24*(6), 290–297. DOI: 10.1177/1024907917740094

Izard-Carroll, M. (2016). Public Sector Leaders' Strategies to Improve Employee Retention. *Walden Dissertations and Doctoral Studies*. https://scholarworks.waldenu.edu/dissertations/2157

Jacobs, M. (2021). *The influence of leadership development and psychological capital on burnout and turnover* [Doctoral dissertation, Liberty University]. https://digitalcommons.liberty.edu/cgi/viewcontent.cgi?article=4045&context=doctoral

Jacobshagen, N., & Rigotti, T. (2008). Voll der Stress? Stress bei Adoleszenten in den letzten Schuljahren. In Krause, A., Schüpbach, H., Ulich, E., & Wülser, M. (Eds.), *Arbeitsort Schule* (pp. 289–308). Betriebswirtschaftlicher Verlag Dr. Th. Gabler. DOI: 10.1007/978-3-8349-9551-3_11

Jahnke, S. A., Poston, W. S. C., Haddock, C. K., & Murphy, B. (2016). Firefighting and mental health: Experiences of repeated exposure to trauma. *Work (Reading, Mass.)*, *53*(4), 737–744. DOI: 10.3233/WOR-162255 PMID: 26890595

Jalili, M., Niroomand, M., Hadavand, F., Zeinali, K., & Fotouhi, A. (2021). Burnout among healthcare professionals during COVID-19 pandemic: A cross-sectional study. *International Archives of Occupational and Environmental Health*, *94*, 1345–1352.

Jennings, P. A., & Min, H. H. (2023). Transforming empathy-based stress to compassion: Skillful means to preventing teacher burnout. *Mindfulness*, *14*(10), 2311–2322. DOI: 10.1007/s12671-023-02115-6 PMID: 37362185

Ji, D., & Yue, Y. (2020). Relationship between kindergarten organizational climate and teacher burnout: Work–family conflict as a mediator. *Frontiers in Psychiatry*, *11*, 408–422. DOI: 10.3389/fpsyt.2020.00408 PMID: 32499727

Jilke, S., & Baekgaard, M. (2020). The political psychology of citizen satisfaction: Does functional responsibility matter? *Journal of Public Administration: Research and Theory*, *30*(1), 130–143. DOI: 10.1093/jopart/muz012

Jin, M., Lee, J., & Lee, M. (2017). Does leadership matter in diversity management? Assessing the relative impact of diversity policy and inclusive leadership in the public sector. *Leadership and Organization Development Journal*, *38*(2), 303–319. DOI: 10.1108/LODJ-07-2015-0151

Joffe, A. D., & Peters, L. (2024). The association between emotional labour, affective symptoms, and burnout in Australian psychologists. *Australian Psychologist*, *59*(4), 1–13. DOI: 10.1080/00050067.2023.2299668

Johnson, H. A., & Goodhart, A. L. (2021). The pharmacists behind the front lines: One year later. *Journal of the American Pharmacists Association*, *61*(6), 648.

Johnston, K., O'Reilly, C. L., Scholz, B., Georgousopoulou, E. N., & Mitchell, I. (2021). Burnout and the challenges facing pharmacists during COVID-19: Results of a national survey. *International Journal of Clinical Pharmacy*, *43*(3), 716–725.

Jones, A. M., Clark, J. S., & Mohammad, R. A. (2021). Burnout and secondary traumatic stress in health-system pharmacists during the COVID-19 pandemic. *American Journal of Health-System Pharmacy*, *78*(9), 818–824.

Juárez, S. W., & Becton, A. B. (2024). A Self-Care and Wellness Framework in Educator Preparation to Address Burnout, Compassion Fatigue, and Secondary Traumatic Stress. *Action in Teacher Education*, *46*(2), 168–186. DOI: 10.1080/01626620.2024.2319294

Judge, T. A., & Piccolo, R. F. (2004). Transformational and transactional leadership: A meta-analytic test of their relative validity. *The Journal of Applied Psychology*, *89*(5), 755–768. DOI: 10.1037/0021-9010.89.5.755 PMID: 15506858

Jungbauer-Gans, M., & Gross, C. (2009). Erklärungsansätze sozial differenzierter Gesundheitschancen. In Richter, M., & Hurrelmann, K. (Eds.), *Gesundheitliche Ungleichheit* (pp. 77–98). Grundlagen, Probleme, Perspektiven. VS Verlag für Sozialwissenschaften. DOI: 10.1007/978-3-531-91643-9_4

Kalogiannidis, S. (2021). IMPACT OF EMPLOYEE MOTIVATION ON ORGANIZATIONAL PERFORMANCE. A SCOPING REVIEW PAPER FOR PUBLIC SECTOR. *Strategic Journal of Business & Change Management*, *8*(3). Advance online publication. DOI: 10.61426/sjbcm.v8i3.2064

Kapucu, N., & Van Wart, M. (2008). Making matters worse: An anatomy of leadership failures in managing catastrophic events. *Administration & Society*, *40*(7), 711–740. DOI: 10.1177/0095399708323143

Karakus, M., Toprak, M., Caliskan, O., & Crawford, M. (2024). Teachers' affective and physical well-being: Emotional intelligence, emotional labour and implications for leadership. *International Journal of Educational Management*, *38*(2), 469–485. DOI: 10.1108/IJEM-07-2023-0335

Kariou, A., Koutsimani, P., Montgomery, A., & Lainidi, O. (2021). Emotional Labor and Burnout among Teachers: A Systematic Review. *International Journal of Environmental Research and Public Health*, *18*(23), 12760. DOI: 10.3390/ijerph182312760 PMID: 34886485

Katz, I., Katz, C., Andresen, S., Bérubé, A., Collin-Vezina, D., Fallon, B., Fouché, A., Haffejee, S., Masrawa, N., Muñoz, P., Priolo Filho, S. R., Tarabulsy, G., Truter, E., Varela, N., & Wekerle, C. (2021). Child maltreatment reports and child protection service responses during COVID-19: Knowledge Exchange among Australia, Brazil, Canada, Colombia, Germany, Israel, and South Africa. *Child Abuse &amp. Child Abuse & Neglect*, *116*, 105078. DOI: 10.1016/j.chiabu.2021.105078 PMID: 33931238

Kauffeld, S., & Hoppe, D. (2011). Arbeit und Gesundheit. In Kauffeld, S. (Ed.), *Arbeits-, Organisations- und Personalpsychologie für Bachelor* (pp. 223–244). Springer-Verlag. DOI: 10.1007/978-3-642-16999-1_12

Kaya, A., Sen, S., & Dogan, E. (2010). Organizational climate and burnout: A research on employees in Turkish educational institutions. *Procedia: Social and Behavioral Sciences*, *9*, 161–169.

Keller, M. M., Becker, E. S., Frenzel, A. C., & Taxer, J. L. (2018). When teacher enthusiasm is authentic or inauthentic: Lesson profiles of teacher enthusiasm and relations to students' emotions. *AERA Open*, *4*(2), 2332858418782967. DOI: 10.1177/2332858418782967

Khalid, M., Hassani, D., & Bilal, M. (2017). Identification of oral cavity bio-film forming bacteria and determination of their growth inhibition medicinal plants. *Archives of Oral Biology*, *81*, 175–185. DOI: 10.1016/j.archoralbio.2017.05.011 PMID: 28549260

Khan, N., Palepu, A., Dodek, P., Salmon, A., Leitch, H., Ruzycki, S., Townson, A., & Lacaille, D. (2021). Cross-sectional survey on physician burnout during the COVID-19 pandemic in Vancouver, Canada: The role of gender, ethnicity and sexual orientation. *BMJ Open*, *11*(5), e050380. DOI: 10.1136/bmjopen-2021-050380 PMID: 33972345

Kim, Y. (2016). *Emotional labour and burnout among public middle school teachers in South Korea*. Unpublished Master's Thesis, University of Jyväskylä. https://urn.fi/URN:NBN:fi:jyu-201604262318

Kim, J. (2018). The contrary effects of intrinsic and extrinsic motivations on burnout and turnover intention in the public sector. *International Journal of Manpower*, *39*(3), 486–500. DOI: 10.1108/IJM-03-2017-0053

Kim, R., Hee Ha, J., & Jue, J. (2020). The moderating effect of compassion fatigue in the relationship between firefighters' burnout and risk factors in working environment. *Journal of Risk Research*, *23*(22), 1491–1503. DOI: 10.1080/13669877.2020.1738529

Kim, S., & Fernandez, S. (2017). Employee empowerment and turnover intention in the U.S. federal bureaucracy. *American Review of Public Administration*, *47*(1), 4–22. DOI: 10.1177/0275074015583712

Kim, S., Kantamneni, N., Ahmad Ridzuan, N. H., & Miramonti, A. A. (2024). Work-Family Conflict and Burnout for Mothers of Color: Exploring the Role of Microaggressions and Gender Role Beliefs. *Journal of Career Assessment*, •••, 10690727241307957. DOI: 10.1177/10690727241307957

Kim, S., & Wang, J. (2018). The Role of Job Demands–Resources (JDR) between Service Workers' Emotional Labor and Burnout: New Directions for Labor Policy at Local Government. *International Journal of Environmental Research and Public Health, 15*(12), 2894. DOI: 10.3390/ijerph15122894 PMID: 30562995

Kim, S., & Wright, B. E. (2017). Putting service before self-interest: How public service motivation and commitment shape public employees' job satisfaction. *Public Administration Review, 77*(2), 292–305. DOI: 10.1111/puar.12685

Kinman, G. (2016). Effort-reward imbalance and overcommitment in UK academics: Implications for mental health, satisfaction and retention. *Journal of Higher Education Policy and Management, 38*(5), 504–518. DOI: 10.1080/1360080X.2016.1181884

Kinnunen, U., Feldt, T., Geurts, S., & Pulkkinen, L. (2006). Types of work-family interface: Well-being correlates of negative and positive spillover between work and family. *Scandinavian Journal of Psychology, 47*(2), 149–162. DOI: 10.1111/j.1467-9450.2006.00502.x PMID: 16542357

Kirst-Ashman, K. K., & Hull, G. H. (2018). *Understanding Generalist Practice* (8th ed.). Brooks/Cole.

Kishimoto, K., & Asano, K. (2024). The relationships among factors affecting compassion fatigue, compassion satisfaction, and burnout in Japanese nurses: A cross-sectional study. *Japan Journal of Nursing Science, 21*(4), e12617. DOI: 10.1111/jjns.12617 PMID: 39148343

Knippenberg, A. V., & Ellemers, N. (1990). Social identity and intergroup differentiation processes. *European Review of Social Psychology, 1*(1), 137–169. DOI: 10.1080/14792779108401860

Koenig, A., Rodger, S., & Specht, J. (2018). Educator burnout and compassion fatigue: A pilot study. *Canadian Journal of School Psychology, 33*(4), 259–278. DOI: 10.1177/0829573516685017

Kokkinos, C. M. (2006). Factor structure and psychometric properties of the Maslach Burnout Inventory-Educators Survey among elementary and secondary school teachers in Cyprus. *Stress and Health, 22*(1), 25–33. DOI: 10.1002/smi.1079

Kolman, S. (2024). State actions to bolster the public health workforce. *National Conference of State Legislatures*. https://www.ncsl.org/health/state-actions-to-bolster-the-public-health-workforce

Kovaka, K. (2021). Evaluating community science. *Studies in History and Philosophy of Science, 88*, 102–109.

Kranke, D. A., Kranke, B., Solorzano, E., Gioia, D., & Dobalian, A. (2024). Applying a novel approach to understanding social worker job retention during the pandemic. *Social Work, 69*(2), 151–157. https://doi-org.uvi.idm.oclc.org/10.1093/sw/swae013. DOI: 10.1093/sw/swae013 PMID: 38366959

Kranke, D., Kranke, B., & Der-Martirosian, C. (2024). We cannot have next year if we do not take care of today. *Health & Social Work, 49*(3), 209–210. https://doi-org.uvi.idm.oclc.org/10.1093/hsw/hlae016. DOI: 10.1093/hsw/hlae016 PMID: 38822671

Kranke, D., Kranke, B., Milligan, S., & Dobalian, A. (2024). Introducing trauma trigger fatigue as an underlying factor of social work burnout. *Social Work, 69*(4), 403–405. https://doi-org.uvi.idm.oclc.org/10.1093/sw/swae034. DOI: 10.1093/sw/swae034 PMID: 39013117

Kranke, D., Mudoh, Y., Weiss, E. L., Hovsepian, S., Gin, J., Dobalian, A., & Der-Martirosian, C. (2022). "Emotional preparedness": A nuanced approach to disaster readiness among social workers. *Social Work Education, 41*(5), 860–873. https://doi-org.uvi.idm.oclc.org/10.1080/02615479.2021.1900099. DOI: 10.1080/02615479.2021.1900099

Krishnapriya, R. B. (2023). BURN OUT AMONG NURSES DURING COVID-19 PANDEMIC.

Kristensen, T. S., Borritz, M., Villadsen, E., & Christensen, K. B. (2007). The Copenhagen Burnout Inventory: A new tool for the assessment of burnout. *Work and Stress, 19*(3), 192–207. DOI: 10.1080/02678370500297720

Kuenzi, M., & Schminke, M. (2009). Assembling fragments into a lens: A review, critique, and proposed research agenda for the organizational work climate literature. *Journal of Management, 35*(3), 634–717. DOI: 10.1177/0149206308330559

Kumar, A., & Narula, S. (2021). Quantitative Demands, Burnout, and Applied Outcomes for Indian Police Officers. *Fortune Institute of International Business. Business Review, 10*(1), 74–85. DOI: 10.1177/2319714521999136

Lacerenza, C. N., Reyes, D. L., Marlow, S. L., Joseph, D. L., & Salas, E. (2017). Leadership training design, delivery, and implementation: A meta-analysis. *The Journal of Applied Psychology, 102*(12), 1686–1718. DOI: 10.1037/apl0000241 PMID: 28749153

LaFontaine, A. (2024). One element of the emergency department nurse burnout epidemic – who can help? Based on a qualitative exploratory case study. *International Journal of Healthcare Management, 18(*1), 141-153, 1–12. DOI: 10.1080/20479700.2024.2405324

Lambert, S. J., & Haley-Lock, A. (2006). The organizational stratification of opportunities for work-life balance: Addressing issues of equality and social justice in the workplace. *Community Work & Family*, *9*(3), 303–318. DOI: 10.1080/13668800600743518

Lammers, J. C., Atouba, Y. L., & Carlson, E. J. (2013). Which identities matter? A mixed-method study of group, organizational, and professional identities and their relationship to burnout. *Management Communication Quarterly*, *27*(4), 503–536. DOI: 10.1177/0893318913498824

Lamontagne, A. D., Keegel, T., Louie, A. M., Ostry, A., & Landsbergis, P. A. (2007). A Systematic Review of the Job-stress Intervention Evaluation Literature, 1990–2005. *International Journal of Occupational and Environmental Health*, *13*(3), 268–280. DOI: 10.1179/oeh.2007.13.3.268 PMID: 17915541

Lampert, T., Kuntz, B., Hoebel, J., Müters, S., & Kroll, L. E. (2016) Bildung als Ressource für Gesundheit. Datenreport 2016. bpb, Bonn

Lampert, T., Saß, A. C., Häfelinger, M., & Ziese, T. (2005). Armut, soziale Ungleichheit und Gesundheit. Expertise des Robert Koch-Instituts zum 2. Armuts- und Reichtumsbericht der Bundesregierung. In Koch-Institut, R. (Ed.), *Beiträge zur Gesundheitsberichterstattung des Bundes*. RKI.

Lanin, D., & Hermanto, N. (2019). The effect of service quality toward public satisfaction and public trust on local government in Indonesia. *International Journal of Social Economics*, *46*(3), 377–392. DOI: 10.1108/IJSE-04-2017-0151

Lapuente, V., & Van de Walle, S. (2020). The effects of new public management on the quality of public services. *Governance: An International Journal of Policy, Administration and Institutions*, *33*(3), 461–475. DOI: 10.1111/gove.12502

Łaskawiec-Żuławińska, D., Grajek, M., Krupa-Kotara, K., Szlacheta, P., Karacan, H., Roszak, M., Łabuz-Roszak, B., & Korzonek-Szlacheta, I. (2024). Burnout and Life Satisfaction among Healthcare Workers Related to the COVID-19 Pandemic (Silesia, Poland). *Behavioural Neurology*, *2024*(1), 9945392. DOI: 10.1155/2024/9945392 PMID: 38725562

Lavy, S., & Eshet, R. (2018). Spiral effects of teachers' emotions and emotion regulation strategies: Evidence from a daily diary study. *Teaching and Teacher Education*, *73*, 151–161. DOI: 10.1016/j.tate.2018.04.001

Law, P. C. F., Too, L. S., Butterworth, P., Witt, K., Reavley, N., & Milner, A. J. (2020). A systematic review on the effect of work-related stressors on mental health of young workers. *International Archives of Occupational and Environmental Health*, *93*(5), 611–622. DOI: 10.1007/s00420-020-01516-7 PMID: 31932956

Lazarus, R. S., & Folkman, S. (1984). *Stress, Appraisal, and Coping*. Springer.

Lecompte, M., Ducharme, J., Beauchamp, J., & Couture, M. (2021). Inclusive practices toward LGBT older adults in healthcare and social services: A scoping review of quantitative and qualitative evidence. *Clinical Gerontologist, 44*(3), 210–221. DOI: 10.1080/07317115.2020.1862946 PMID: 33357121

Lee, H. J., Probst, T. M., Bettac, E. L., Jenkins, M. R., & Bazzoli, A. (2024). The use of flexible work arrangements: Examining experiences of perceived backlash through the lens of diversity. *Group & Organization Management, 49*(5), 1159–1198. DOI: 10.1177/10596011221150025

Lee, M., & Van Vlack, S. (2018). Teachers' emotional labour, discrete emotions, and classroom management self-efficacy. *Educational Psychology, 38*(5), 669–686. DOI: 10.1080/01443410.2017.1399199

Lee, R. T., & Ashforth, B. E. (1990). On the meaning of Maslach's three dimensions of burnout. *The Journal of Applied Psychology, 75*(6), 743–747. DOI: 10.1037/0021-9010.75.6.743 PMID: 1981064

Lee, S.-H., & Olshfski, D. (2002). Employee Commitment and Firefighters: It's My Job. *Public Administration Review, 62*(s1), 108–114. DOI: 10.1111/1540-6210.62.s1.19

Lee-Spiewak, D. (2012). *Core vs. Program Functions* [Professional Organization]. Https://Www.Iaem.Org/Certification/CEM_Corner/Core-vs-Program-Functions. https://www.iaem.org/certification/CEM_Corner/core-vs-program-functions

Leider, J. P., Yeager, V. A., Kirkland, C., Krasna, H., Hare Bork, R., & Resnick, B. (2023). The state of the US public health workforce: Ongoing challenges and future directions. *Annual Review of Public Health, 44*(1), 323–341. DOI: 10.1146/annurev-publhealth-071421-032830 PMID: 36692395

Leiter, M. P., & Maslach, C. (2024). Job burnout. *Handbook of occupational health psychology* (3rd ed., pp. 291-307). DOI: 10.1037/0000331-015

Leiter, M. (1991). The dream denied: Professional burnout and the constraints of human service organizations. *Canadian Psychology, 32*(4), 547–558. DOI: 10.1037/h0079040

Leiter, M. P., & Maslach, C. (1999). Six areas of worklife: A model of the organizational context of burnout. *Journal of Health and Human Services Administration, 21*(4), 472–489. PMID: 10621016

Leiter, M. P., & Maslach, C. (2005). *Banishing burnout: Six strategies for improving your relationship with work*. John Wiley & Sons.

Leiter, M. P., & Maslach, C. (2017). Motivation, competence, and job burnout. In Elliot, A. J., Dweck, C. S., & Yeager, D. S. (Eds.), *Handbook of competence and motivation: Theory and application* (2nd ed., pp. 370–384). The Guilford Press.

Leung, D. Y., & Zhang, L. W. (2017). Teachers' development needs and stress: The role of excessive consistency in organizational climate. *Teaching and Teacher Education*, *64*, 117–126.

Leung, L., & Zhang, R. (2017). Mapping ICT use at home and telecommuting practices: A perspective from work/family border theory. *Telematics and Informatics*, *34*(1), 385–396. DOI: 10.1016/j.tele.2016.06.001

Levkovich, I., & Gada, A. (2020). The weight falls on my shoulders": Perceptions of compassion fatigue among Israeli preschool teachers. *Asia-Pacific Journal of Research in Early Childhood Education*, *14*(3), 91–112. DOI: 10.17206/apjrece.2020.14

Li, H. (2021). An empirical research on the construction of a government website public satisfaction index model in China. [JGIM]. *Journal of Global Information Management*, *29*(5), 112–137. DOI: 10.4018/JGIM.20210901.oa7

Li, H., Chen, J., Wei, Q., & Chen, H. (2025). Knowledge, attitudes, and practices of vocational college teachers towards occupational burnout. *Frontiers in Public Health, 13*, 1513170. López-Cabarcos, M. Á., López-Carballeira, A., & Ferro-Soto, C. (2019). The role of emotional exhaustion among public healthcare professionals. *Journal of Health Organization and Management*, *33*(6), 649–655.

Lim, H., Lee, T. J., Weng, C., & Lee, S. M. (2025). Effects of surface acting on exhaustion of Korean school counselors. *Journal of Counseling and Development*, *103*(1), 49–59. DOI: 10.1002/jcad.12536

Lindstrom Johnson, S., Johnson, B., Meléndez Guevara, A. M., & Fillhouer, M. (2024). The Life of a School Mental Health Professional: A Daily Diary of School Counselor and Social Worker Tasks. *School Mental Health*, •••, 1–13. DOI: 10.1007/s12310-024-09733-y

Lingard, H., & Francis, V. (2006). Does work-family conflict mediate the relationship between job schedule demands and burnout in male construction professionals and managers? *Construction Management and Economics*, *24*(6), 617–628.

Linos, E., & Ruffini, K. (2019). Belonging affirmation reduces employee burnout and resignations in front line workers. *ResearchGate*. https://doi.org/DOI: 10.13140/RG.2.2.21546.36801

Linos, E., Ruffini, K., & Wilcoxen, S. (2022). Reducing burnout and resignations among frontline workers: A field experiment. *Journal of Public Administration: Research and Theory*, *32*(3), 473–488. DOI: 10.1093/jopart/muab042

Listopad, I. W., Michaelsen, M. M., Werdecker, L., & Esch, T. (2021). Bio-psycho-socio-Spirito-cultural factors of burnout: A systematic narrative review of the literature. *Frontiers in Psychology*, *12*, 722862. DOI: 10.3389/fpsyg.2021.722862 PMID: 34925130

Liu, C., Wang, D., Liu, C., Jiang, J., Wang, X., Chen, H., Ju, X., & Zhang, X. (2020). What is the meaning of health literacy? A systematic review and qualitative synthesis. *Family Medicine and Community Health*, *8*(2), e000351. DOI: 10.1136/fmch-2020-000351

Logan, D. A., De King, J., Edwards, J., Saltzman, L. Y., Hansel, T. C., & Figley, C. (2024). The grit of mental health professionals: Initial conceptualization and measurement. *Traumatology*, *30*(3), 423–431. DOI: 10.1037/trm0000446

López Torres, O., & Fernández-Elías, V. E. (2024). Training and Nutrition for Performance: Males, Females, and Gender Differences. *Nutrients*, *16*(23), 3979. DOI: 10.3390/nu16233979 PMID: 39683373

López-Cabarcos, M. Á., López-Carballeira, A., & Ferro-Soto, C. (2019). The role of emotional exhaustion among public healthcare professionals. *Journal of Health Organization and Management*, *33*(6), 649–655. DOI: 10.1108/JHOM-04-2019-0091 PMID: 31625822

Lopez, S. P., Peon, J. M. M., & Ordas, C. J. V. (2021). Organizational culture as a mediator between leadership behavior and organizational commitment. *Journal of Organizational Change Management*, *34*(1), 123–138. DOI: 10.1108/JOCM-10-2020-0321

Lubranska, A. (2011). Organizational climate and burnout syndrome. *Medicine Pharmacy*, *62*(6), 623–631. PMID: 22312954

Lu, Y., Wu, W., Mei, G., Zhao, S., Zhou, H., Li, D., & Pan, D. (2019). Surface Acting or Deep Acting, Who Need More Effortful? A Study on Emotional Labor Using Functional Near-Infrared Spectroscopy. *Frontiers in Human Neuroscience*, *13*, 419957. DOI: 10.3389/fnhum.2019.00151 PMID: 31133836

Lyonette, C., & Crompton, R. (2015). Sharing the load? Partners' relative earnings and the division of domestic labour. *Work, Employment and Society*, *29*(1), 23–40. DOI: 10.1177/0950017014523661

Maddock, A., & McCusker, P. (2022). Exploring the potential mechanisms of action of the mindfulness-based Social Work and self-care programme. *British Journal of Social Work, 52*(8), 4477–4496. DOI: 10.1093/bjsw/bcac066

Maidaniuc-Chirila, T. (2015). A multi-mediation model of the relationship among workplace bullying, coping strategies, resilience, and employees' strain: Insights for a training programme. *Psihologia Resurselor Umane Revista Asociaţiei de Psihologie Industriala si Organizaţionala, 13*(1), 63–82. DOI: 10.1037/%20t55271-000

Maines, D. R. (1989). Rediscovering the social group: A self-categorization theory.

Malquisto, I. R., Casinillo, L. F., & Salabao, A. A. (2023). Burnout among secondary teachers amid the new normal: Case in Ormoc City, Philippines. Journal of Research, Policy & Practice of Teachers & Teacher. *Education, 13*(2). Advance online publication. DOI: 10.37134/jrpptte.vol13.2.2.2023

Manning, S., & Kushma, J. (2016). A systematic review of the international disaster case management literature in the aftermath of Hurricane Katrina. *International Journal of Emergency Management, 12*(3), 241–262. DOI: 10.1504/IJEM.2016.079017

Ma, P., Zhang, L., Dong, H., & Yu, J. (2023). The relationships between teachers' emotional labor and display rules, trait emotions, exhaustion, and classroom emotional climate. *Frontiers in Psychology, 14*, 957856. Advance online publication. DOI: 10.3389/fpsyg.2023.957856 PMID: 36923140

Margareth, M., & Satrya, A. (2021). Work-family conflict as a mediator between organizational interventions for work-life balance and job satisfaction. In *Proceedings of the 4th International Conference on Economics, Business and Economic Education Science, (ICE-BEES 2021)*. DOI: 10.4108/eai.27-7-2021.2316893

Martinussen, M., Richardsen, A. M., & Burke, R. J. (2007). Job demands, job resources, and burnout among police officers. *Journal of Criminal Justice, 35*(3), 239–249. DOI: 10.1016/j.jcrimjus.2007.03.001

Maslach, C. (1982). *Burnout: The cost of caring*. Prentice Hall.

Maslach, C. (2003). *Burnout: The Cost of Caring*. Prentice-Hall.

Maslach, C., & Jackson, S. E. (1981). The measurement of experienced burnout. *Journal of Organizational Behavior, 2*(2), 99–113. DOI: 10.1002/job.4030020205

Maslach, C., Jackson, S. E., & Leiter, M. P. (1996). *Maslach burnout inventory manual* (3rd ed.). Consulting Psychologists Press.

Maslach, C., & Leiter, M. P. (1997). *The Truth about Burnout*. Jossey-Bass.

Maslach, C., & Leiter, M. P. (1997). *The Truth about Burnout: How Organizations Cause Personal Stress and What to do about It*. Jossey-Bass.

Maslach, C., & Leiter, M. P. (1999). Teacher burnout: A research agenda. In Vandenberghe, R., & Huberman, A. M. (Eds.), *Understanding and Preventing Teacher Burnout: A Sourcebook of International Research and Practice* (pp. 295–303). Cambridge University Press. DOI: 10.1017/CBO9780511527784.021

Maslach, C., & Leiter, M. P. (2007). Burnout. In Fink, G. (Ed.), *Stress: Concepts, cognition, emotion, and behavior* (pp. 351–357). Elsevier Academic Press.

Maslach, C., & Leiter, M. P. (2016). Understanding the burnout experience: Recent research and its implications for psychiatry. *World Psychiatry; Official Journal of the World Psychiatric Association (WPA)*, *15*(2), 103–111. DOI: 10.1002/wps.20311 PMID: 27265691

Maslach, C., Leiter, M. P., & Schaufeli, W. (2009). Measuring Burnout. In Cartwright, S., & Cooper, C. L. (Eds.), *The Oxford Handbook of Organizational Well Being*. Academic., DOI: 10.1093/oxfordhb/9780199211913.003.0005

Maslach, C., & Schaufeli, W. (1993). Historical and Conceptual Development of Burnout. In Schaufeli, W., Maslach, C., & Marek, T. (Eds.), *Professional Burnout: Recent Developments in Theory and Research* (pp. 1–16). Taylor & Francis.

Maslach, C., Schaufeli, W. B., & Leiter, M. P. (2001). Job Burnout. *Annual Review of Psychology*, *52*(1), 397–422. DOI: 10.1146/annurev.psych.52.1.397 PMID: 11148311

Maslow, A. H. (1943). A THEORY OF HUMAN MOTIVATION. *Psychological Review*, *50*(4), 370–396. DOI: 10.1037/h0054346

Mason-Williams, L., Bettini, E., Morris Mathews, H., Boveda, M., & Rodgers, W. (2022). Disparities in Teachers' Access to Schools' Collective Social Assets Based on Role, Race, and Poverty. *Remedial and Special Education*, *44*(1), 3–15. DOI: 10.1177/07419325211068170

Mazzetti, A. S. (2019). *To Tape or Not to Tape? Reflections on the Complexities of Taping Ethnographic Interviews*. SAGE Research Methods., DOI: 10.4135/9781526477347

Mazzola, J. J., & Disselhorst, R. (2019). Should we be "challenging" employees? A critical review and meta-analysis of the challenge-hindrance model of stress. *Journal of Organizational Behavior*, *40*(8), 949–961. DOI: 10.1002/job.2412

Mazzucato, M., & Kattel, R. (2020). COVID-19 and public-sector capacity. *Oxford Review of Economic Policy*, *36*(Supplement_1), graa031. Advance online publication. DOI: 10.1093/oxrep/graa031 PMID: 40504220

McCall, L. (2005). The complexity of intersectionality. *Signs (Chicago, Ill.)*, *30*(3), 1771–1800. DOI: 10.1086/426800

McDonald, R., Conant, D., & Marshall, A. (2020, April 20). A non-partisan model for developing public-service leaders. *Harvard Business Review*. https://hbr.org/2020/04/a-nonpartisan-model-for-developing-public-service-leadership

McFadden, P. (2015). Measuring burnout among UK social workers: a Community care study, available at: https://www.qub.ac.uk/ (accessed 8 November 2024).

McGlinchey, D., Roebuck, B. S., Sakauye, P., Lalonde, C., Ferns, A., & Killian, K. (2024). "Increasing Demands and Competing Priorities": How Organizational Structure Affects Worker Well-Being in the Victim Services Field. *Human Service Organizations: Management, Leadership & Governance*, 49(2), 152–169.https://doi.org/. 2024.2417785DOI: 10.1080/23303131

McNamee, M. J., & Fleming, S. (2007). Ethics audits and corporate governance: The case of public sector sports organizations. *Journal of Business Ethics*, *73*(4), 425–437. DOI: 10.1007/s10551-006-9216-0

Meeusen, V., Gatt, S. P., Barach, P., & van Zundert, A. (2023). Occupational well-being, resilience, burnout, and job satisfaction of surgical teams. In Sanchez, J. A., Higgins, R. S., & Kent, P. S. (Eds.), *Handbook of perioperative and procedural patient safety* (pp. 205–229). Elsevier.

Mehta, A. K., Yashoda, L., Selvakumar, P., Mishra, B. R., Das, A., & C. T. C., M. (2025). Teaching Methods: Techniques for Disadvantaged Learners. In S. Hai-Jew (Ed.), Mitigating Learner Disadvantages in Teaching and Learning (pp. 181-206). IGI Global Scientific Publishing. DOI: 10.4018/979-8-3693-8623-1.ch007

Mendenhall, E., Newfield, T., & Tsai, A. C. (2021). Syndemic theory, methods, and data. *Social Science & Medicine (1982)*, *295*, 114656.

Mendoza, M. (2020). The Lived Experiences of Beginning Teachers: An Odyssey. *JPAIR Multidisciplinary Research*, *41*(1), 1–15. DOI: 10.7719/jpair.v41i1.787

Meuris, J., & Leana, C. R. (2015). The high cost of low wages: Economic scarcity effects in organizations. *Research in Organizational Behavior*, *35*, 143–158. DOI: 10.1016/j.riob.2015.07.001

Michielsens, E., Bingham, C., & Clarke, L. (2013). Managing diversity through flexible work arrangements: Management perspectives. *Employee Relations*, *36*(1), 49–69. DOI: 10.1108/ER-06-2012-0048

Microsoft. (2022). *Hybrid Work Is Just Work. Are We Doing It Wrong?*https://www.microsoft.com/en-us/worklab/work-trend-index/hybrid-work-is-just-work

Mika-Lude, K. M., Degges-White, S., & Isawi, D. (2023). Under fire: Meta-dehumanization and burnout among first responders. *Journal of Employment Counseling*, *60*(3), 144–158. DOI: 10.1002/joec.12208

Miller, J. J., Barnhart, S., Robinson, T. D., Pryor, M. D., & Arnett, K. D. (2021). Assuaging covid-19 peritraumatic distress among mental health clinicians: The potential of self-care. *Clinical Social Work Journal*, *49*(4), 505–514. DOI: 10.1007/s10615-021-00815-x PMID: 34728866

Mind Garden. (n.d.). *List of psychological assessments*. https://www.mindgarden.com/14-our-products

Mitchell, U. A., Nishida, A., Fletcher, F. E., & Molina, Y. (2021). The long arm of oppression: How structural stigma against marginalized communities perpetuates within-group health disparities. *Health Education & Behavior*, *48*(3), 342–351.

Monroe, M., Morse, E., & Price, J. M. (2020). The relationship between critical care work environment and professional quality of life. *American Journal of Critical Care*, *29*(2), 145–149. DOI: 10.4037/ajcc2020406 PMID: 32114615

Montgomery, C., Maslach, C., & Leiter, M. P. (2006). Burnout in the teaching profession: A study of the relationship between teachers' job demands and burnout. *The Journal of Applied Psychology*, *91*(4), 103–113.

Morgan, K. (2024). *'The extra shift': The unpaid emotional labour expected of women at work*. Retrieved from https://www.bbc.com/worklife/article /20240313-invisible-emotional-labour-women-in-workplace

Moyo, O., & Moldovan, V. (2008). Lessons for social workers: Hurricane Katrina as a social disaster. *Social Development Issues*, *30*(1), 1–12.

Mulki, J. P., Jaramillo, F., & Locander, W. B. (2006). Effects of ethical climate and supervisory trust on salesperson's job attitudes and intentions to quit. *Journal of Personal Selling & Sales Management*, *26*(1), 19–26. DOI: 10.2753/PSS0885-3134260102

Mullainathan, S., & Shafir, E. (2013). *Scarcity: Why having too little means so much*. Macmillan.

Murphy, E., & Dingwall, R. (2001). The Ethics of Ethnography. In Atkinson, P., Coffey, A., Delamont, S., Lofland, J., & Lofland, L. (Eds.), *Handbook of Ethnography*. SAGE Publications Ltd. DOI: 10.4135/9781848608337.n23

NACCHO. (2022). 2020 forces of change: The COVID-19 edition. https://www.naccho.org/uploads/downloadable-resources/2020-Forces-of-Change-The-COVID-19-Edition.pdf

Nalipay, M. J. N., King, R. B., Haw, J. Y., Mordeno, I. G., & Rosa, E. D. D. (2021). Teachers who believe that emotions are changeable are more positive and engaged: The role of emotion mindset among in-and preservice teachers. *Learning and Individual Differences*, *92*, 102050. DOI: 10.1016/j.lindif.2021.102050

Nana-Sinkam, P., Kraschnewski, J., Sacco, R., Chavez, J., Fouad, M., Gal, T., & Behar-Zusman, V. (2021). Health disparities and equity in the era of COVID-19. *Journal of Clinical and Translational Science*, *5*(1), 99. DOI: 10.1017/cts.2021.23

Naparan, G., Deloria, O., & Naparan, J. (2025). Special Education Teachers' Challenges and Coping Mechanisms in Behavior Management of Learners with Autism. *International Journal of Social Sciences & Educational Studies*, *12*(2), 37–53.

NASW. (2021). *Code of ethics*. National Association of Social Workers. https://www.socialworkers.org/About/Ethics/Code-of-Ethics/Code-of-Ethics-English

Navarro Moya, P., Villar Hozb, E., & Gonzalez Carrasco, M. (2020). How medical transport service professionals perceive risk/protective factors with regard to occupational burnout syndrome: Differences and similarities between an Anglo-American and Franco-German model. *Work (Reading, Mass.)*, *67*(2), 295–312. DOI: 10.3233/WOR-203280 PMID: 33044211

Naz, V., Raza, M. A., & Ali, R. (2024). An analysis of female teachers' emotional labor and work-life conflicts at the secondary level. *International Journal of Academic Research for Humanities*, *4*(3), 85–95. https://jar.bwo-researches .com/index.php/jarh/article/view/438

Negi, N. J., Forrester, P., Calderon, M., Esser, K., & Parrish, D. (2019). We are at full capacity: Social care workers persisting through work-related stress in a new immigrant settlement context in the United States. *Health & Social Care in the Community*, *27*(5), e793–e801. https://doi-org.uvi.idm.oclc.org/10.1111/hsc.12802. DOI: 10.1111/hsc.12802 PMID: 31260160

Nerdinger, F. W., Blickle, G., & Schaper, N. (2008). *Arbeits- und Organisationspsychologie*. Springer.

Netemeyer, R. G., Boles, J. S., & McMurrian, R. (1996). Development and validation of work–family conflict and family–work conflict scales. *The Journal of Applied Psychology*, *81*(4), 400–410. DOI: 10.1037/0021-9010.81.4.400

Newell, J. M., & MacNeil, G. A. (2010). Professional burnout, vicarious trauma, secondary traumatic stress, and compassion fatigue: A review of theoretical terms, risk factors, and preventive methods for clinicians and researchers. *Best Practices in Mental Health*, *6*(2), 57–68. DOI: 10.70256/607490pbruec

Newhouse, S. M. (2024). Burnout among government workers is decreasing but still high, according to new pulse survey data. https://www.govexec.com/workforce/2024/06/burnout-among-government-workers-decreasing-still-high/397392/

Ngo, H. V., Edelenbos, J., & Gianoli, A. (2019). Community participation and local government capacity in Vietnam: Conditions for coproduction. *Public Administration and Development*, *39*(2), 104–118. DOI: 10.1002/pad.1844

Nguyen Van, H., Dinh Le, M., Nguyen Van, T., Nguyen Ngoc, D., Tran Thi Ngoc, A., & Nguyen The, P. (2018). A systematic review of effort-reward imbalance among health workers. *The International Journal of Health Planning and Management*, *33*(3), 674–695. DOI: 10.1002/hpm.2541 PMID: 29722057

Nguyen, C. V., Giang, L. T., Tran, A. N., & Do, H. T. (2021). Do good governance and public administration improve economic growth and poverty reduction? The case of Vietnam. *International Public Management Journal*, *24*(1), 131–161. DOI: 10.1080/10967494.2019.1592793

Nnubia, U. I., & Nwobi, C. A. FO, O. F. O., & Eke, B. A. (2022). Assessment of Compassion Fatigue and Psychological Well-Being of Special Needs Children's Educators in Enugu State. *Journal For Family & Society Research*, 1(2).https://jfsr .afass.org.ng/index.php/JFSR/article/ view/18

Noblet, A., & LaMontagne, A. (2006). The role of workplace health promotion in addressing job stress. *Health Promotion International*, *21*(4), 346–353. DOI: 10.1093/heapro/dal029 PMID: 16880197

Noblet, A., Rodwell, J., & McWilliams, J. (2006). Organizational change in the public sector: Augmenting the demand control model to predict employee outcomes under New Public Management. *Work and Stress*, *20*(4), 335–352. DOI: 10.1080/02678370601050648

Noor, N. M., & Zainuddin, M. (2011). Emotional labor and burnout among female teachers: Work–family conflict as mediator. *Asian Journal of Social Psychology*, 14(4), 283-293.https://doi.org/. 01349.xDOI: 10.1111/j.1467-839X.2011

Noorollahi, A., Pordelan, N., Khalijian, S., Koohi, A. H., & Abbasi, M. (2022). Investigating the Relationship between Sleep Quality and Career Adaptability with Occupational Burnout among Employees. *Journal of Sleep sciences*.

Northouse, G. Peter. (2022). *Leadership: Theory and practice* (9th Edition). Thousand Oaks: SAGE Publications.

Northouse, P. G. (2019). *Leadership: Theory and practice* (8th ed.). SAGE Publications.

Núnez-Barriopedro, E., Penelas-Leguía, A., López-Sanz, J. M., & Loranca-Valle, M. C. (2024). A public service management model as an antecedent for citizen satisfaction and fiscal policy. *Management Decision*, *62*(2), 725–739. DOI: 10.1108/MD-11-2022-1547

Nytr, Ø. (2000). An appraisal of key factors in the implementation of occupational stress interventions. *Work and Stress*, *14*(3), 213–225. DOI: 10.1080/02678370010024749

O' Reilly, K. (2008). *Key concepts in ethnography*. SAGE Publications Ltd.

O'Toole, C., & Dobutowitsch, M. (2023). The Courage to Care: Teacher Compassion Predicts More Positive Attitudes Toward Trauma-Informed Practice. *Journal of Child & Adolescent Trauma*, *16*(1), 123–133. DOI: 10.1007/s40653-022-00486-x PMID: 36157295

Oberg, G., Carroll, A., & Macmahon, S. (2023, March). Compassion fatigue and secondary traumatic stress in teachers: How they contribute to burnout and how they are related to trauma-awareness. In *Frontiers in Education* (Vol. 8, p. 1128618). Frontiers Media SA.https://doi.org/. 1128618DOI: 10.3389/feduc.2023

Ocbian, M. M., & Dischoso, M. A. (2015). Empowering Secondary School Teachers through Administrative Tasks. *Asia Pacific Journal of Multidisciplinary Research*, *3*(4), 19–27.

Office of Disease Prevention. Healthy People 2030 https://odphp.health.gov/our-work/national-health-initiatives/healthy-people/healthy-people 2030#:~:text=Healthy%20People%202030%20includes%20355%20core%20%E2%80%94%20or,and%20prioritize%20the%20most%20pressing%20public%20health%20issues

Office of Personnel Management. (2021). Handbook on Pay and Leave Benefits for Federal Employees Affected by Severe Weather Conditions or Other Emergency Situations.

Ohue, T., & Menta, M. (2024). Effectiveness of Mentorship Using Cognitive Behavior Therapy to Reduce Burnout and Turnover among Nurses: Intervention Impact on Mentees. *Nursing Reports*, *14*(2), 1026–1036. DOI: 10.3390/nursrep14020077 PMID: 38804410

Ombay, G. (2025). *Bullying still a 'silent, persistent' problem in schools – EDCOM*. Retrieved from https://www.gmanetwork.com/news/topstories/nation/ 934485/ bullying-still-a-silent-persistent-problem-in-schools-edcom/story/

Ondrejková, N., & Halamová, J. (2022a). Prevalence of compassion fatigue among helping professions and relationship to compassion for others, self-compassion and self-criticism. *Health & Social Care in the Community*, *30*(5), 1680–1694. DOI: 10.1111/hsc.13741 PMID: 35133041

Ondrejková, N., & Halamová, J. (2022b). Stressful factors, experiences of compassion fatigue and self-care strategies in police officers. *Journal of Police and Criminal Psychology*, *37*(4), 892–903. DOI: 10.1007/s11896-022-09538-2 PMID: 35874902

Orgambídez-Ramos, A., & Borrego-Alés, Y. (2014). Empowering employees: Structural empowerment as antecedent of job satisfaction in university settings. *Psychological Thought*, *7*(1), 28–36. DOI: 10.5964/psyct.v7i1.88

Ormiston, H. E., Nygaard, M. A., & Apgar, S. (2022). A systematic review of secondary traumatic stress and compassion fatigue in teachers. *School Mental Health*, *14*(4), 802–817. DOI: 10.1007/s12310-022-09525-2 PMID: 35694002

Orr, J. M., & Leider, J. P. (2023). Voluntary separations and COVID-19: A snapshot of turnover intention in the federal workforce in the first year of the pandemic. *Journal of Public Health Management and Practice*, *29*(4), 442–445. DOI: 10.1097/ PHH.0000000000001720 PMID: 36693625

Owen, C., Scott, C., Adams, R., & Parsons, D. (2015). Leadership in crisis: Developing beyond command and control. *Australian Journal of Emergency Management*, *30*(3), 15–19. https://hdl.handle.net/102.100.100/541400

Özbilgin, M. F., Beauregard, T. A., Tatli, A., & Bell, M. P. (2011). Work–life, diversity and intersectionality: A critical review and research agenda. *International Journal of Management Reviews*, *13*(2), 177–198. DOI: 10.1111/j.1468-2370.2010.00291.x

Pacheco, G., & Webber, D. J. (n.d.). *Participative decision-making and job satisfaction*. Department of Economics, Auckland University of Technology. DOI: 10.1108/PR-04-2014-0088

Palatino, M. (2023). *The Philippines' Basic Education Crisis*. Retrieved from https:// thediplomat.com/2023/02/the-philippines-basic-education-crisis/

Palazoğlu, C. A., & Koç, Z. (2019). Ethical Sensitivity, Burnout and Job Satisfaction in Emergency Nurses. *Nursing Ethics*, *26*(3), 809–822. DOI: 10.1177/0969733017720846 PMID: 28814140

Pálfi, K., Major, J., Horváth-Sarródi, A., Deák, A., Fehér, G., & Gács, B. (2024). Adaptive emotion regulation might prevent burnout in emergency healthcare professionals: An exploratory study. *BMC Public Health*, *24*(1), 3136. DOI: 10.1186/s12889-024-20547-0 PMID: 39533222

Pallewaththa, P., & Wijesiri, B. (2021). Occupational health: The impact of occupational stressors on job productivity. *Sri Lanka Journal of Social Sciences*, *44*(2), 149–164. DOI: 10.4038/sljss.v44i2.8229

Park, J., & Ahn, Y. (2022). Government employees' experience and expectation of COVID-19 hardships: The moderating role of gender and race in the United States. *American Review of Public Administration*, *52*(1), 15–35. DOI: 10.1177/02750740211049280

Partnership for Public Service. (n.d.a) *Public Service Leadership Model*. https://ourpublicservice.org/public-service-leadership-institute/public-service-leadership-model/

Partnership for Public Service. (n.d.b). *Senior Executive Service: Trends over 25 years*. https://ourpublicservice.org/fed-figures/senior-executive-service-trends-over-25-years/

Partnership for Public Service. (n.d.c). *Public Service Leadership Model: Engaging others*. https://ourpublicservice.org/public-service-leadership-institute/public-service-leadership-model/engaging-others/

Patel, S. S., Guevara, K., Hollar, T. L., Richard, A., DeVito, J., & Erickson, T. B. (2023). Surveying mental health stressors of emergency management professionals: Factors in recruiting and retaining emergency managers in an era of disasters and pandemics. *Journal of Emergency Management (Weston, Mass.)*, *21*(5), 375–384. DOI: 10.5055/jem.0820 PMID: 37932942

Paulsrud, D., & Nilholm, C. (2020). Teaching for inclusion – a review of research on the cooperation between regular teachers and special educators in the work with students in need of special support. *International Journal of Inclusive Education*, *27*(4), 541–555. DOI: 10.1080/13603116.2020.1846799

Peat, A., & Ridge, E. (2023). Introduction: Imagining and Reimagining Emotional Labour. *Women a Cultural Review*, *34*(4), 259–270. DOI: 10.1080/09574042.2023.2278261

Pecino, V., Manas, M. A., Díaz-Funez, P. A., Aguilar-Parra, J. M., Padilla-Gongora, D., & Lopez-Liria, R. (2019). Organizational climate, role stress, and public employees' job satisfaction. *International Journal of Environmental Research and Public Health, 16*(10), 1792. Advance online publication. DOI: 10.3390/ijerph16101792 PMID: 31117168

Pehlivan, T., & Güner, P. (2018). Compassion fatigue: The known and unknown. Journal of Psychiatric Nursing/Psikiyatri Hemsireleri Dernegi, 9(2).DOI: 10.14744/phd.2017.25582

Penfold, C., Lewis, J., & Tennant, R. (2009). *Attendance Management in the Fire and Rescue Service: Managing sickness absence and managing and supporting attendance*. National Centre for Social Research.

PennState. (2024). *What is Emotional Labor?* Retrieved from https://weld.la.psu.edu/what-is-emotional-labor/#:~:text=Emotional%20labor%20is% 20a%20workhanbooks%2C%20training%2C%20financial%20goals.

Penz, M., Wekenborg, M. K., Pieper, L., Beesdo-Baum, K., Walther, A., Miller, R., Stalder, T., & Kirschbaum, C. (2018). The Dresden Burnout Study: Protocol of a prospective cohort study for the bio-psychological investigation of burnout. *International Journal of Methods in Psychiatric Research, 27*(2), e1613. DOI: 10.1002/mpr.1613 PMID: 29611872

Pérez-Luño, A., Díez Piñol, M., & Dolan, S. L. (2022). Exploring high vs. low burnout amongst public sector educators: COVID-19 antecedents and profiles. *International Journal of Environmental Research and Public Health, 19*(2), 780. DOI: 10.3390/ijerph19020780 PMID: 35055602

Perez, R. J., & Bettencourt, G. M. (2023). Exploring Compassion Fatigue and Community Care in Student Affairs. *Journal of Student Affairs Research and Practice, 61*(2), 266–278. DOI: 10.1080/19496591.2023.2176774

Perry, J. L., & Wise, L. R. (1990). The Motivational Bases of Public Service. *Public Administration Review, 50*(3), 367–373. DOI: 10.2307/976618

Peters, L. H., & O'Connor, E. J. (1980). Situational constraints and work outcomes: The influence of a frequently overlooked construct. *Academy of Management Review, 5*(3), 391–397. DOI: 10.2307/257114

Petrucelli, L., & Ritz, M. (2024, March 25). *What is driving federal government burnout?* Gallup. https://www.gallup.com/workplace/612518/driving-federal-government-burnout.aspx

Pfeiffer, S. (2007). *Montage und Erfahrung. Warum ganzheitliche Produktionssysteme menschliches Arbeitsvermögen brauchen*. Rainer Hampp Verlag.

Pham, H. N. (2018). Leadership and public sector reform in Vietnam. In *Leadership and public sector reform in Asia* (Vol. 30, pp. 127–149). Emerald Publishing Limited. DOI: 10.1108/S2053-769720180000030006

Pham, T. H., Hoang, T. T. H., Thalassinos, E. I., & Le, H. A. (2022). The impact of quality of public administration on local economic growth in Vietnam. *Journal of Risk and Financial Management*, *15*(4), 158. DOI: 10.3390/jrfm15040158

Phan, H., Mills, A. R., & Fleming, J. (2021). Perceived wellness among pharmacy residents during COVID-19. *Journal of the American Pharmacists Association*, *61*(6), e52–e59.

Pharris, A. B., Munoz, R. T., & Hellman, C. M. (2022). Hope and resilience as protective factors linked to lower burnout among child welfare workers. *Children and Youth Services Review*, *136*, 106424. DOI: 10.1016/j.childyouth.2022.106424

Philippine Congress. (1966). Magna Carta for Public School Teachers. Retrieved from https://lawphil.net/statutes/repacts/ra1966/ ra_4670_1966.html

Philippine Congress. (1995).*Fair and Equitable Access to Education Act*. Retrieved from https://lawphil.net/statutes/repacts/ra1995/ra _7880_1995.html

Pladdys, J. (2024). Mitigating workplace burnout through transformational leadership and employee participation in recovery experiences. *HCA Healthcare Journal of Medicine*, *5*(3). Advance online publication. DOI: 10.36518/2689-0216.1783 PMID: 39015600

Pluut, H., Ilies, R., Curşeu, P. L., & Liu, Y. (2018). Social support at work and at home: Dual-buffering effects in the work-family conflict process. *Organizational Behavior and Human Decision Processes*, *146*, 1–13. DOI: 10.1016/j.obhdp.2018.02.001

Pon-Barry, H., St. John, A., Packard, B. W. L., & Rotundo, B. (2019, February). A flexible curriculum for promoting inclusion through peer mentorship. In *Proceedings of the 50th ACM technical symposium on computer science education* (pp. 1116-1122). DOI: 10.1145/3287324.3287434

Powell, T. M., Wegmann, K. M., & Shin, O. J. (2019). Stress and coping in social service providers after superstorm sandy: An examination of a postdisaster psychoeducational intervention. *Traumatology*, *25*(2), 96–103. DOI: 10.1037/trm0000189

Pradeep, E., Mukherjee, S. K., Selvakumar, P., Koppaka, A. K., Chandel, P. S., & Vats, C. (2025). Empowering Social Media Users With Ethical AI. In Chakraborty, S. (Ed.), *Ethical AI Solutions for Addressing Social Media Influence and Hate Speech* (pp. 91–118). IGI Global Scientific Publishing., DOI: 10.4018/979-8-3693-9904-0.ch005

Prati, G., & Pietrantoni, L. (2010). The relation of perceived and received social support to mental health among first responders: A meta-analytic review. *Journal of Community Psychology*, *38*(3), 403–417. DOI: 10.1002/jcop.20371

Proctor, E. B. (2024). *Employee Engagement Among Intersectional Identifying Employees: Considering Flexible Work Arrangements in the Era of Increased Remote and Hybrid Work*(Doctoral dissertation).

Prosen, M. (2020). Social stigma in the time of coronavirus (COVID-19): an epidemic we must not remain silent about. Obzornik zdravstvene nege, 54(2), 100-103.

Qi, X., Ji, S., Zhang, J., Lu, W., Sluiter, J. K., & Deng, H. (2017). Correlation of - emotional labor and cortisol concentration in hair among female kindergarten teachers. *International Archives of Occupational and Environmental Health*, *90*(1), 117–122. DOI: 10.1007/s00420-016-1179-6 PMID: 27804039

Rabbing, L., Lau, B., Fostervold, K. I., Blenkinsopp, J., & Bjørkelo, B. (2023). Enhancing Self-Reported Assessment of Working Conditions in Policing: Revisiting the Psychometric Properties and Applications of the Police Stress Questionnaire. *Psychological Reports*, *0*(0), 00332941231207957. Advance online publication. DOI: 10.1177/00332941231207957 PMID: 37902227

Rafferty, A. E. (2021). Organizational Change and Employee Health and Well-Being: A Review and Recommendations for Future Research. In P. Brough, E. Gardiner & K. Daniels (Eds), *Handbook on Management and Employment Practices*. Handbook Series in Occupational Health Sciences. Springer. pp.1-21. https://doi.org/DOI: 10.1007/978-3-030-24936-6_11-1

Rajan, S., & Engelbrecht, A. (2018). A cross-sectional survey of burnout amongst doctors in a cohort of public sector emergency centres in Gauteng, South Africa. *African Journal of Emergency Medicine : Revue Africaine de la Médecine d'Urgence*, *8*(3), 95–99. DOI: 10.1016/j.afjem.2018.04.001 PMID: 30456156

Raja, U., Johns, G., & Ntalianis, F. (2015). The impact of personality on psychological contracts. *Academy of Management Journal*, *47*(3), 350–367. DOI: 10.2307/20159586

Rami, F., Thompson, L., & Solis-Cortes, L. (2023). Healthcare disparities: vulnerable and marginalized populations. In Searight, H. R. (Ed.), *Covid-19: Health Disparities and Ethical Challenges Across the Globe*. Springer., DOI: 10.1007/978-3-031-26200-5_6

Ranjitha, P. K., Selvakumar, P., Anute, N., Manjunath, T., Sureshkrishna, G., & Pougajendy, S. (2025). Transportation Challenges In Islands Tourism. In Hassan, V. (Ed.), *Navigating Mass Tourism to Island Destinations: Preservation and Cultural Heritage Challenges* (pp. 287–312). IGI Global Scientific Publishing., DOI: 10.4018/979-8-3693-9107-5.ch011

Raudenská, J., Steinerová, V., Javůrková, A., Urits, I., Kaye, A. D., Viswanath, O., & Varrassi, G. (2019). Occupational burnout syndrome and post-traumatic stress among healthcare professionals during the novel coronavirus disease 2019 (COVID-19) pandemic. *Best Practice & Research. Clinical Anaesthesiology*, *34*(3), 553–560. DOI: 10.1016/j.bpa.2020.07.008 PMID: 33004166

Rauf, Z., & Saba, M. (2024). Compassion fatigue and professional quality of life among health professionals: Moderating role of professional resilience. *Wah Academia Journal of Social Sciences*, *3*(2), 427–449.

Raver, C., Ledford, A., Norton, M. (2022). A strategic organizational approach to developing leadership developers. Journal of Character and Leadership Development, 10(1), 15-28. - http://dx.doi.org/DOI: 10.58315/jcld.v10.253

Recede, R. A. A. (2025, April 29). *Restoring discipline and moral values among Filipino learners*. Philippine Daily Inquirer. Retrieved June 8, 2025, from https://opinion.inquirer.net/182799/restoring-discipline-and-moral-values-a mong-filipino-learners

Redillas, S. (2020). Filipino Teachers' Identity: Framed by Community Engagements, Challenges for Citizenship Education. *The Palgrave Handbook of Citizenship and Education*, 275-295. DOI: 10.1007/978-3-319-67828-3_11

Regehr, C., & Bober, T. (2005). *In the Line of Fire: Trauma in Emergency Services*. Oxford University Press. DOI: 10.1093/acprof:oso/9780195165029.001.0001

Remington, C. L. (2016). Emotional Labor. In Farazmand, A. (Ed.), *Global Encyclopedia of Public Administration, Public Policy, and Governance*. Springer., DOI: 10.1007/978-3-319-31816-5_2779-1

Remington, C. L., Witkowski, K., Ganapati, N. E., Headley, A. M., & Contreras, S. L. (2024). First Responders and the COVID-19 Pandemic: How Organizational Strategies Can Promote Workforce Retention. *American Review of Public Administration, 54*(1), 33–56. DOI: 10.1177/02750740231192968

Renkiewicz, G. K., & Hubble, M. W. (2021). Secondary Traumatic Stress in Emergency Services Systems (STRESS) Project: Quantifying and Predicting Compassion Fatigue in Emergency Medical Services Personnel. *Prehospital Emergency Care, 26*(5), 652–663. DOI: 10.1080/10903127.2021.1943578 PMID: 34128453

Resnik, D. B. (2015). Bioethical issues in providing financial incentives to research participants. *Medicolegal and Bioethics*, •••, 35–41. DOI: 10.2147/MB.S70416 PMID: 26807399

Restrepo, J., & Lemos, M. (2021). Addressing psychosocial work-related stress interventions: A systematic review. *Work (Reading, Mass.), 70*(1), 53–62. DOI: 10.3233/WOR-213577 PMID: 34511476

Reyes, R. O. (2024). *Overworked, underpaid Filipino teachers leaving for bigger paychecks abroad.* Retrieved from https://www.sunstar.com.ph/tacloban /overworked-underpaid-filipino-teachers-leaving-for-bigger-paychecks-abro ad

Richardson, K. (2023). Quality Check: How Good is Your Emergency Management Program? [Dissertation]. West Chester University. https://digitalcommons.wcupa .edu/all_doctoral/229/

Richardson, K. M., & Rothstein, H. R. (2008). Effects of Occupational Stress Management Intervention Programs: A Meta-Analysis. *Journal of Occupational Health Psychology, 13*(1), 69–93. DOI: 10.1037/1076-8998.13.1.69 PMID: 18211170

Rigotti, T, Holstad, T, Mohr, G, Stempel, C, Hansen, E, Loeb, C, Isaksson, K, Otto, K, Kinnunen, U, & Perko, K (2014)

Roberson, Q., & Perry, J. L. (2022). Inclusive leadership in thought and action: A thematic analysis. *Group & Organization Management, 47*(4), 755–778. DOI: 10.1177/10596011211013161

Robosa, J., Paras, N., Perante, L., Alvez, T., & Tus, J. (2021). The experiences and challenges faced of the public school teachers amidst the COVID-19 pandemic: A phenomenological study in the Philippines. *International Journal of Advance Research and Innovative Ideas in Education, 7*(1), 1342–1361.

Rodrigues, L. A., Rodrigues, A. M., Brunetti, M. N., Michels, M., Abatti, M., Indalecio, A., Rocha, L. B., & Dal Pizzol, F. (2024). Association between occupational stress, markers of inflammation, and oxidative stress in intensive care unit workers: A cross-sectional study. *Revista Brasileira de Medicina do Trabalho : Publicacao Oficial da Associacao Nacional de Medicina do Trabalho-ANAMT*, *22*(2), 1–11. DOI: 10.47626/1679-4435-2022-1049 PMID: 39371284

Rohmer, O., Palomares, E. A., & Popa-Roch, M. (2024). Attitudes towards disability and burnout among teachers in inclusive schools in France. *International Journal of Disability Development and Education*, *71*(1), 83–100. DOI: 10.1080/1034912X.2022.2092078

Rozo, J. A., Olson, D. M., Thu, H., & Stutzman, S. E. (2017). Situational Factors Associated With Burnout Among Emergency Department Nurses. *Workplace Health & Safety*, *65*(6), 262–265. DOI: 10.1177/2165079917705669 PMID: 28557637

Ruiz-Fernández, M. D., Pérez-García, E., & Ortega-Galán, Á. M. (2020). Quality of Life in Nursing Professionals: Burnout, Fatigue, and Compassion Satisfaction. *International Journal of Environmental Research and Public Health*, *17*(4), 1253. DOI: 10.3390/ijerph17041253 PMID: 32075252

Ryus, C. R., Samuels, E. A., Wong, A. H., Hill, K. A., Huot, S., & Boatright, D. (2022). Burnout and perception of medical school learning environments among gay, lesbian, and bisexual medical students. *JAMA Network Open*, *5*(4), e229596–e229596. DOI: 10.1001/jamanetworkopen.2022.9596 PMID: 35486396

Saaed, H. K., Raheemah, S. H., & Shaalan, U. H. (2019). The Effect of Organizational Silence on Occupational Burnout. *Opción: Revista de Ciencias Humanas y Sociales*, (22), 875–891.

Sagaltici, E., Cetinkaya, M., Nielsen, S. Y., Sahin, S. K., Gulen, B., & Altindag, A. (2022). Identified predictors and levels of burnout among staff workers in a refugee camp of first immigrant group: A cross-sectional study. *Medicine*, *11*(1), 135–141. PMID: 35440085

Sagaltici, E., Saydam, R. B., Cetinkaya, M., Şahin, Ş. K., Küçük, S. H., & Müslümanoğlu, A. Y. (2022). Burnout and psychological symptoms in healthcare workers during the COVID-19 pandemic: Comparisons of different medical professions in a regional hospital in Turkey. *Work (Reading, Mass.)*, *72*(3), 1077–1085. DOI: 10.3233/WOR-210517 PMID: 35634831

Sahin, E. B., Homberg, F., Sahin, E. B., & Homberg, F. (2024). *How to Reduce Burnout in Public Service Organizations during Times of Crisis? A Review of (Promising) Interventions*. IntechOpen., DOI: 10.5772/intechopen.1006691

Salehi, M., Seyyed, F., & Farhangdoust, S. (2020). The impact of personal characteristics, quality of working life and psychological well-being on job burnout among Iranian external auditors. *International Journal of Organization Theory and Behavior, 23*(3), 189–205. DOI: 10.1108/IJOTB-09-2018-0104

Salmela-Aro, K., Read, S., Minkkinen, J., Kinnunen, J. M., & Rimpelä, A. (2018). Immigrant status, gender, and school burnout in Finnish lower secondary school students: A longitudinal study. *International Journal of Behavioral Development, 42*(2), 225–236. DOI: 10.1177/0165025417690264

Salmela, L., Woehrle, T., Marleau, E., & Kitch, L. (2020). Implementation of a "Serenity Room": Promoting Resiliency in the ED. *Nursing, 50*(10), 58–63. DOI: 10.1097/01.NURSE.0000697160.77297.06 PMID: 32976304

Samuels, G. M., & Ross-Sheriff, F. (2008). Identity, oppression, and power: Feminisms and intersectionality theory. *Affilia, 23*(1), 5–9. DOI: 10.1177/0886109907310475

Sarabia, A., & Collantes, L. M. . (2020). Work-Related Stress and Teaching Performance of Teachers in Selected School in the Philippines. *Indonesian Research Journal in Education |IRJE|*, 4(1), 6–27. DOI: 10.22437/irje.v4i1.8084

Sarisik, M., Bogan, E., Zengin, B., & Dedeoglu, B. B. (2019). The impact of burnout on organizational commitment: A study of public sector employees in Turkey. *Journal of global business insights, 4*(2), 106-118.

Saud, J., & Rice, J. (2024). Stress, Teamwork, and Wellbeing Policies: A Synergistic Approach to Reducing Burnout in Public Sector Organizations. *Administrative Sciences, 14*(319), 1–19. DOI: 10.3390/admsci14120319

Savellano, J. M. (1999). Teacher education in the Philippines. *Philippine Studies, 47*(2), 253–268. https://www.jstor.org/stable/42634316

Schaufeli, W. & Enzmann, D. (1998). The burnout companion to study and practice: A critical analysis. DOI: 10.1201/9781003062745

Schaufeli, W. B., & Buunk, B. P. (2003). *Burnout: An Overview of 25 Years of Research and Theorizing*. https://www.wilmarschaufeli.nl/publications/Schaufeli/181.pdf

Schaufeli, W. B., Enzmann, D., & Girault, N. (2017). Measurement of burnout: A review. *Professional burnout*, 199-215.

Schaufeli, W. (2021). The burnout enigma solved? *Scandinavian Journal of Work, Environment & Health, 47*(3), 169–170. Advance online publication. DOI: 10.5271/sjweh.3950 PMID: 33604675

Schaufeli, W. B. (2017). Applying the Job Demands-Resources model: A 'how to' guide to measuring and tackling work engagement and burnout. *Organizational Dynamics*, *46*(2), 120–132. DOI: 10.1016/j.orgdyn.2017.04.008

Schaufeli, W. B., Leiter, M. P., & Maslach, C. (2009). Burnout: 35 years of research and practice. *Career Development International*, *14*(3), 204–220. DOI: 10.1108/13620430910966406

Schieman, S., Whitestone, Y. K., & Van Gundy, K. (2006). The nature of work and the stress of higher status. *Journal of Health and Social Behavior*, *47*(3), 242–257. DOI: 10.1177/002214650604700304 PMID: 17066775

Schmidt, S., Petermann, F., & Brähler, E. (2012). Bildungsniveau, körperliche und psychische Gesundheit – Zusammenhänge aus der Makro- und Mikroperspektive. In Brähler, E., Kiess, J., Schubert, C., & Kiess, W. (Eds.), *Gesund und gebildet –Voraussetzungen für eine moderne Gesellschaft* (pp. 74–90). Vandenhoeck & Ruprecht.

Schneider, B., Ehrhart, M. G., & Macey, W. H. (2013). Organizational climate and culture. *Annual Review of Psychology*, *64*(1), 361–388. DOI: 10.1146/annurev-psych-113011-143809 PMID: 22856467

Schwab, D., Napolitano, N., Chevalier, K., & Pettorini-D'Amico, S. (2016). Hidden Grief and Lasting Emotions in Emergency Department Nurses. *Creative Nursing*, *22*(4), 249–253. DOI: 10.1891/1078-4535.22.4.249 PMID: 29195538

Scott, C., & Myers, K. K. (2005). The Socialization of Emotion: Learning Emotion Management at the Fire Station. *Journal of Applied Communication Research*, *33*(1), 67–92. DOI: 10.1080/0090988042000318521

Scott, T. (2007). Expression of humour by emergency personnel involved in sudden deathwork. *Mortality*, *12*(4), 350–364. DOI: 10.1080/13576270701609766

Seifert, R., & Sibley, T. (2005). *'United They Stood': The Story of the UK Firefighters' Dispute, 2002-2004*. Lawrence and Wishart.

Sekar, R. R., Herrel, L. A., & Stensland, K. D. (2024). Social Determinants of Health and the Availability of Cancer Clinical Trials in the United States. *JAMA Network Open*, *7*(5), e2410162. DOI: 10.1001/jamanetworkopen.2024.10162

Seo, E., Kim, H., Sim, Y., Ha, M.-S., Kim, U., & Kim, H. (2022). Burnout, Presenteeism and Workplace Conditions of Korean Taekwondo Coaches of High-Performance Athletes. *International Journal of Environmental Research and Public Health*, *19*(10), 5912. DOI: 10.3390/ijerph19105912 PMID: 35627449

Serin, A. E., & Balkan, M. O. (2014). Burnout: The effects of demographic factors on staff burnout: An application at public sector. *International Business Research, 7*(4), 151–159. DOI: 10.5539/ibr.v7n4p151

Sever, M. S., Ortiz, A., Maggiore, U., Bac-García, E., & Vanholder, R. (2021). Mass disasters and burnout in nephrology personnel: From earthquakes and hurricanes to COVID-19 pandemic. *Clinical Journal of the American Society of Nephrology; CJASN, 16*(5), 829–837. DOI: 10.2215/CJN.08400520 PMID: 33414153

Sexton, B., Levine, L. K., & Flores, D. (2021). An Analysis of Nurse Burnout in the Emergency Department. *Journal of Business and Behavioral Sciences, 33*(1), 94–108.

Sezen-Gultekin, G., Bayrakcı, M., & Limon, I. (2021). The mediating role of organizational commitment on the relationship between emotional labor and work engagement of teachers. *Frontiers in Psychology, 12*, 648404. DOI: 10.3389/fpsyg.2021.648404 PMID: 34290645

Shanafelt, T. (2011). Burnout in anesthesiology: A call to action. *Anesthesiology, 114*(1), 1–2. DOI: 10.1097/ALN.0b013e318201cf92 PMID: 21139497

Shanafelt, T. D., Boone, S., Tan, L., Dyrbye, L. N., Sotile, W., Satele, D., West, C. P., Sloan, J., & Oreskovich, M. R. (2012). Burnout and satisfaction with work-life balance among US physicians relative to the general US population. *Archives of Internal Medicine, 172*(18), 1377–1385. DOI: 10.1001/archinternmed.2012.3199 PMID: 22911330

Sharifi, Y., Ebrahimpur, M., Payab, M., & Larijani, B. (2022). The Syndemic Theory, the COVID-19 Pandemic, and The Epidemics of Non-Communicable Diseases (NCDs). *Medical Journal of the Islamic Republic of Iran, 36*, 177. DOI: 10.47176/mjiri.36.177 PMID: 36919009

Shawe, R., & McAndrew, I. R. (2023). Theories of leadership and emergency management. *Modern Economy, 14*(6), 738–750. DOI: 10.4236/me.2023.146040

Shende, A. D., Tekade, S. A., Deshmukh, A. A., Tembhurkar, S. P., & Selvakumar, P. (2025). Water Quality Monitoring and Control With AI. In Ruiz-Vanoye, J., & Díaz-Parra, O. (Eds.), *Smart Water Technology for Sustainable Management in Modern Cities* (pp. 51–80). IGI Global Scientific Publishing., DOI: 10.4018/979-8-3693-8074-1.ch003

Shepherd, M. A., & Newell, J. M. (2020). Stress and health in social workers: Implications for self-care practice. *Best Practices in Mental Health, 16*(1), 46–65. https://www.proquest.com/scholarly-journals/stress-health-social-workers-implications-self/docview/2551714261/se-2. DOI: 10.70256/994929qbhenn

Shien, L. (2023). Organizational climate and its impact on auditor performance: A meta-analysis. *Journal of Accounting and Economics, 65*(2), 210–225.

Shi, L., Van Veldhoven, M., Kooij, D., Van De Voorde, K., & Karanika-Murray, M. (2024). High-performance work systems and individual performance: A longitudinal study of the differential roles of happiness and health well-being. *Frontiers in Psychology, 14*, 1261564. Advance online publication. DOI: 10.3389/fpsyg.2023.1261564 PMID: 38298369

Shim, R. S., & Starks, S. M. (2021). COVID-19, structural racism, and mental health inequities: Policy implications for an emerging syndemic. *Psychiatric Services (Washington, D.C.), 72*(10), 1193–1198.

Shinan-Altman, S., Rosenne, H., Chen, W., Kaofer, H., Zeevi, S., Nir-Paz, R., Daphna-Tekoah, S., Guttman, N., & Schiff, M. (2024). Professional quality of life among Israeli social workers in hospitals and a health maintenance organization (HMO) during the COVID-19 pandemic. *The American Journal of Orthopsychiatry*. Advance online publication. DOI: 10.1037/ort0000798 PMID: 39250251

Shirom, A. (2003). Job-related burnout: A review. In Quick, J. C., & Tetrick, L. E. (Eds.), *Handbook of occupational health psychology* (pp. 245–264). American Psychological Association., DOI: 10.1037/10474-012

Sidpra, J., Abomeli, D., Hameed, B., Baker, J., & Mankad, K. (2021). Rise in the incidence of abusive head trauma during the COVID-19 pandemic. *Archives of Disease in Childhood, 106*(3), e14–e14. DOI: 10.1136/archdischild-2020-319872 PMID: 32616522

Siegrist, J. (1996). Adverse health effects of high effort–low reward conditions at work. *Journal of Occupational Health Psychology, 1*(1), 27–41. DOI: 10.1037/1076-8998.1.1.27 PMID: 9547031

Siegrist, J. (2001). A theory of occupational stress. In Dunham, J. (Ed.), *Stress in the workplace: Past, present and future*. Whurr Publishers.

Siegrist, J. (2016). Effort-Reward Imbalance Model. In Fink, G. (Ed.), *Stress: Concepts, Cognition, Emotion, and Behavior* (pp. 81–86). Academic Press.

Siegrist, J. (2017). The Effort–Reward Imbalance Model. In Cooper, C. L., & Quick, J. C. (Eds.), *The Handbook of Stress and Health* (pp. 24–35)., DOI: 10.1002/9781118993811.ch2

Siegrist, J., Starke, D., Chandola, T., Godin, I., Marmot, M., Niedhammer, I., & Peter, R. (2004). The measurement of effort–reward imbalance at work: European comparisons. *Social Science & Medicine*, *58*(8), 1483–1499. DOI: 10.1016/S0277-9536(03)00351-4 PMID: 14759692

Siekkinen, T., Pekkola, E., & Carvalho, T. (2020). Change and continuity in the academic profession: Finnish universities as living labs. *Higher Education*, *79*(3), 533–551. DOI: 10.1007/s10734-019-00422-3

Silva, A., & Freire, M. (2022). The role of organizational climate, and work–family conflict in burnout: The case of teachers. *Sustainability*, *14*(21), 138–171. DOI: 10.3390/su142113871

Sinclair, S., Raffin-Bouchal, S., Venturato, L., Mijovic-Kondejewski, J., & Smith-MacDonald, L. (2017). Compassion fatigue: A meta-narrative review of the health-care literature. *International Journal of Nursing Studies*, *69*, 9–24. DOI: 10.1016/j.ijnurstu.2017.01.003 PMID: 28119163

Skipton, L. H., & Lang, F. (2010). Leadership Development via Action Learning. *Advances in Developing Human Resources*, *12*(2), 225–240. DOI: 10.1177/1523422310367800

Smith, T. D. (2021). Teaching through trauma: Compassion fatigue, burnout, or secondary traumatic stress? In *Trauma And Resilience In Music Education* (pp. 49–63). Routledge. DOI: 10.4324/9781003124207-3

Soeker, M. S. (2022). Healthcare professionals' perceptions and experiences of the influence of the COVID-19 pandemic on their personal and work performance. *Work (Reading, Mass.)*, *73*(3), 787–798. DOI: 10.3233/WOR-211143 PMID: 35988253

Sogunro, O. A. (1997). Impact of training on leadership development. *Evaluation Review*, *21*(6), 713–737. DOI: 10.1177/0193841X9702100605

Song, X., Fu, W., Liu, X., Luo, Z., Wang, R., Zhou, N., Yan, S., & Lv, C. (2020). Mental health status of medical staff in emergency departments during the Coronavirus disease 2019 epidemic in China. Brain, behavior, and immunity, S0889-1591(20)30962-4. Advance online publication. https://doi.org/DOI: 10.1016/j.bbi.2020.06.002

Sousa, J. (2021). A new and old pandemic–the burnout syndrome. *MOJ Gerontol Geriatr*, *6*(1), 22–26. DOI: 10.15406/mojgg.2021.06.00262

Stamm, B. H. (2010). The Concise ProQOL Manual. 2010. Pocatello, ID: ProQOL.org. http://ProQOL.org/uploads/ProQOL_Concise_2ndEd_12-2010.pd

Stamm, B. H. (1995). *The professional quality of life scale: Compassion satisfaction, burnout, & compassion fatigue/secondary trauma scales*. Sidran Press.

Stang-Rabrig, J., Brüggemann, T., Lorenz, R., & McElvany, N. (2022). Teachers' occupational well-being during the COVID-19 pandemic: The role of resources and demands. *Teaching and Teacher Education*, *117*, 103803. DOI: 10.1016/j.tate.2022.103803 PMID: 35761972

Stanley, S., & Sebastine, A. J. (2024). Predictors of Compassion Fatigue and Compassion Satisfaction in Social Workers (A Quantitative Study from India). *Human Service Organizations: Management, Leadership & Governance*, 48(5), 540–554. https://doi.org/. 2319210DOI: 10.1080/23303131.2024

Stark, K., & Bettini, E. (2021). Teachers' perceptions of emotional display rules in schools: A systematic review. *Teaching and Teacher Education*, *104*, 103388. Advance online publication. DOI: 10.1016/j.tate.2021.103388

Steeger, C. M., & Gondoli, D. M. (2013). Mother adolescent conflict as a mediator between adolescent problem behaviors and maternal psychological control. *Developmental Psychology*, *49*(4), 804–814. DOI: 10.1037/a0028599 PMID: 22612432

Steele, C. M., Spencer, S. J., & Aronson, J. (2002). Contending with group image: The psychology of stereotype and social identity threat. In Vol. 34, pp. 379–440). Advances in experimental social psychology. Academic Press. DOI: 10.1016/S0065-2601(02)80009-0

Steffens, N. K., Haslam, S. A., Kerschreiter, R., Schuh, S. C., & van Dick, R. (2014). Leaders enhance group members' work engagement and reduce their burnout by crafting social identity. *German Journal of Human Resource Management*, *28*(1-2), 173–194. DOI: 10.1177/239700221402800110

Stevens, K., & Al-Abbadey, M. (2024). Compassion fatigue and global compassion fatigue in practitioner psychologists: A qualitative study. *Current Psychology (New Brunswick, N.J.)*, *43*(8), 7259–7274. DOI: 10.1007/s12144-023-04908-3

Stoves, D. (2014). *Compelled to Act: The Negotiation of Compassion Fatigue among Student Affairs Professionals*. Unpublished Doctor of Education Dissertation, University of Corpus Christi. Retrieved from https://www.proquest.com/openview/ec869e694e7be8574dbafa131e973fb 9/1?pq-origsite=gscholar&cbl= 8750

Subramanian, M., Portia, R., Mishra, B. R. R., & Selvakumar, P. PV, R., & TC, M. (2025). Assessment and Evaluation in Personalized STEAM Education. In Integrating Personalized Learning Methods Into STEAM Education (pp. 103-122). IGI Global Scientific Publishing.

Substance Abuse and Mental Health Services Administration. (2022). Addressing burnout in the behavioral health workforce through organizational strategies (SAMHSA Publication No. PEP22-06-02-005). National Mental Health and Substance Use Policy Laboratory.

Swedo, E., Idaikkadar, N., Leemis, R., Dias, T., Radhakrishnan, L., Stein, Z., Chen, M., Agathis, N., & Holland, K. (2020). Trends in U.S. emergency department visits related to suspected or confirmed child abuse and neglect among children and adolescents aged <18 years before and during the COVID-19 pandemic — United States, January 2019–September 2020. *MMWR. Morbidity and Mortality Weekly Report*, *69*(49), 1841–1847. DOI: 10.15585/mmwr.mm6949a1 PMID: 33301436

Sy, J. M., & Hernandez, R. A. (2023). *Teachers, Precarity and State Violence in the Philippines*. Retrieved from https://labourreview.org/teachers-precarity -violence/

Tajfel, H. (1970). Experiments in intergroup discrimination. *Scientific American*, *223*(5), 96–103. DOI: 10.1038/scientificamerican1170-96 PMID: 5482577

Taka, F., Ozcelik, G., & Avci, O. (2016). Exploring the impact of organizational climate on burnout and job satisfaction: Evidence from Turkish universities. *Journal of Higher Education Policy and Management*, *38*(3), 233–250.

Tan, K., & Yeap, P. F. (2022). The impact of work engagement and meaningful work to alleviate job burnout among social workers in new zealand. *Management Decision*, *60*(11), 3042–3065. DOI: 10.1108/MD-05-2021-0689

Taranu, S. M., Ilie, A. C., Turcu, A. M., Stefaniu, R., Sandu, I. A., Pislaru, A. I., & Alexa-Stratulat, T. (2022). Factors associated with burnout in healthcare professionals. *International Journal of Environmental Research and Public Health*, *19*(22), 14701.

Tarcan, G. Y., Tarcan, M., & Top, M. (2016). An analysis of relationship between burnout and job satisfaction among emergency health professionals. *Total Quality Management & Business Excellence*, *28*(11–12), 1339–1356. DOI: 10.1080/14783363.2016.1141659

Tarraya, H. (2023). Teachers' Workload Policy: Its Impact on Philippine Public School Teachers. *Puissant*, 4. https://puissant.stepacademic.net/

Tavella, G., Hadzi-Pavlovic, D., & Parker, G. (2021). Burnout: Redefining its key symptoms. *Psychiatry Research*, *302*, 114023. DOI: 10.1016/j.psychres.2021.114023 PMID: 34052460

Tepper, B. J., & Henle, C. A. (2011). A case for recognizing distinctions among constructs that capture interpersonal mistreatment in work organizations. *Journal of Organizational Behavior*, *32*(3), 487–498. DOI: 10.1002/job.688

Teshome, B. G., Desai, M. M., Gross, C. P., Hill, K. A., Li, F., Samuels, E. A., ... & Boatright, D. H. (2022). Marginalized identities, mistreatment, discrimination, and burnout among US medical students: cross sectional survey and retrospective cohort study. *bmj, 376*.

Thamrin, S., Sariwulan, T., Suryatni, M., Ridlo, M., Qamarius, I., & Capnary, M. C. (2022). The impact of work from home (WFH) during covid-19 pandemic period on job expectations: The case of the state civil apparatus. *Journal of Management Information and Decision Sciences*, *25*(S2).

Tham, T. L., Alfes, K., Holland, P., Thynne, L., & Vieceli, J. (2023). Extreme work in extraordinary times: The impact of COVID-stress on the resilience and burnout of frontline paramedic workers – the importance of perceived organisational support. *International Journal of Human Resource Management*, *35*(10), 1739–1762. DOI: 10.1080/09585192.2023.2237871

The White House. (2025, February 11). *Fact Sheet: President Donald J. Trump Works to Remake America's Federal Workforce*. The White House. https://www.whitehouse.gov/fact-sheets/2025/02/fact-sheet-president-donald-j-trump-works-to-remake-americas-federal-workforce/

Todaro-Franceschi, V. (2024). *Compassion fatigue and burnout in nursing: Enhancing professional quality of life*. Springer Publishing Company. DOI: 10.1891/9780826155290

Töre, E. (2022). Investigation of Emotional Labor in Teaching. *International Journal of Psychology and Educational Studies*, *8*(3), 51–62. DOI: 10.52380/ijpes.2021.8.3.225

Tosone, C., Lee, M., Bialkin, L., Martinez, A., Campbell, M., Martinez, M. M., & Stefan, A. (2003). Shared trauma: Group reflections on the September 11th disaster. *Psychoanalytic Social Work, 10*(1), 57–77. 10n01_ 06DOI: 10. 1300/ J032v

Tosone, C., McTighe, J., Bauwens, J., & Naturale, A. (2011). Shared traumatic stress and the long-term impact of 9/11 on Manhattan clinicians. *Journal of Traumatic Stress*, *24*(5), 546–552. DOI: 10.1002/jts.20686 PMID: 21882250

Tosone, C., Nuttman-Shwartz, O., & Stephens, T. (2012). Shared trauma: When the professional is personal. *Clinical Social Work Journal*, *40*(2), 231–239. DOI: 10.1007/s10615-012-0395-0

Treluyer, L., & Tourneux, P. (2021). Burnout among paediatric residents during the COVID-19 outbreak in France. *European Journal of Pediatrics*, *180*(2), 627–633. DOI: 10.1007/s00431-020-03907-x PMID: 33410942

Trepte, S., & Loy, L. S. (2017). Social identity theory and self-categorization theory. *The international encyclopedia of media effects*, 1-13.

Triviño-Amigo, N., Mendoza-Muñoz, D. M., Mayordomo-Pinilla, N., Barrios-Fernández, S., Contreras-Barraza, N., Gil-Marín, M., Castillo, D., Galán-Arroyo, C., & Rojo-Ramos, J. (2022). Inclusive Education in Primary and Secondary School: Perception of Teacher Training. *International Journal of Environmental Research and Public Health*, *19*(23), 15451. DOI: 10.3390/ijerph192315451 PMID: 36497523

Truglia, H. (2024). *Testing the effectiveness of the ImpACT Me burnout intervention for leaders*. https://library2.smu.ca/bitstream/handle/01/31963/Truglia_Holly_MASTERS_2024.pdf

Trummers, L. G., & Bakker, A. B. (2021). Leadership and Job Demands-Resources theory: A systematic review. *Frontiers in Psychology*, *12*, 722080. Advance online publication. DOI: 10.3389/fpsyg.2021.722080 PMID: 34659034

Tuchinda, N. (2020). The imperative for trauma-responsive special education. *NYUL Rev.*, *95*, 766. Retrieved from https://heinonline.org/HOL/Landing Page?handle=hein.journals/nylr95&div=18&id=&page=

Tuckey, D., Winwood, P., & Dollard, M. (2012). Psychological culture and pathways to psychological injury within policing. *Police Practice and Research*, *13*(3), 224–240. DOI: 10.1080/15614263.2011.574072

Tummers, L., & Knies, E. (2016). Measuring public leadership: Developing scales for four key public leadership roles. *Public Administration*, *94*(2), 433–451. DOI: 10.1111/padm.12224

Tummers, L., Steijn, B., & Bekkers, V. (2018). Public service motivation, job satisfaction, and organizational performance: A study of public sector employees in Europe. *Public Management Review*, *20*(4), 459–484. DOI: 10.1080/14719037.2017.1299209

Turner, J. C. (1985). Social categorization and the self-concept: A social cognitive theory of group behaviour. In E. J. U.S. Office of Personnel Management. (2022). *Federal Employee Viewpoint Survey Results*.https://www.opm.gov/fevs/

Turner, J. C., Brown, R. J., & Tajfel, H. (1979). Social comparison and group interest in ingroup favouritism. *European Journal of Social Psychology*, *9*(2), 187–204. DOI: 10.1002/ejsp.2420090207

U.S. Dept of Labor. (1993). *The Family and Medical Leave Act of 1993*. The Family and Medical Leave Act of 1993. https://www.dol.gov/agencies/whd/laws-and-regulations/laws/fmla

Uchino, B. N. (2006). Social support and health: A review of physiological processes potentially underlying links to disease outcomes. *Journal of Behavioral Medicine, 29*(4), 377–387. DOI: 10.1007/s10865-006-9056-5 PMID: 16758315

Ugwu, L. E., & Idemudia, E. S. (2024). Burnout and Post-traumatic Stress Disorders in Police Officers: Systematic Review and Meta-analysis. *Journal of Police and Criminal Psychology*. Advance online publication. DOI: 10.1007/s11896-024-09713-7

UK Cabinet Office. (2021). *Civil Service People Survey 2021: Summary of Findings*.https://www.gov.uk/government/publications/civil-service-people-survey-2021-results

Ulich, E., & Wülser, M. (2010). *Gesundheitsmanagement in Unternehmen. Arbeitspsychologische Perspektiven* (4th ed.). Springer Gabler. DOI: 10.1007/978-3-8349-8979-6

University of South Florida Pocket Fact Book. (2019-20). [Infographic]. Retrieved from https:www.usf.edu/ods/documents/system-facts/usf-system-facts-2019-20.pdf

University of South Florida Pocket Fact Book. (2022-23). [Infographic]. Retrieved December 9, 2022 from https://www.usf.edu/ods/documents/factbook-2022-23-final.pdf

University of South Florida Taneja College of Pharmacy. https://health.usf.edu/pharmacy

University of South Florida. (n.d.) About USF overview, [Webpage]. Retrieved August 17, 2021 from https://www.usf.edu/about-usf/

US Department of Commerce. N. O. and A. A. (2016, April 20). *NOAA historical Hurricane Tracks*. NOAA's National Ocean Service. https://oceanservice.noaa.gov/news/historical-hurricanes/

USF College of Public Health. https://health.usf.edu/publichealth/research/calm/overview

Vallen, G. (1993). Organizational climate and burnout. *The Cornell Hotel and Restaurant Administration Quarterly, 34*(1), 54–60. DOI: 10.1177/001088049303400110

Van de Walle, S. (2018). Explaining citizen satisfaction and dissatisfaction with public services. *The Palgrave handbook of public administration and management in Europe*, 227-241.

Van Der Kolk, B. A. (2014). *The Body Keeps the Score*. https://www.penguinrandomhouse.com/books/313183/the-body-keeps-the-score-by-bessel-van-der-kolk-md/

Van Ryzin, G. G. (2015). Service quality, administrative process, and citizens' evaluation of local government in the US. *Public Management Review*, *17*(3), 425–442. DOI: 10.1080/14719037.2013.841456

Van Wart, M. (2003). A comprehensive model of organizational leadership: The Leadership Action Cycle. *International Journal of Organization Theory and Behavior*, *7*(2), 173–208. DOI: 10.1108/IJOTB-07-02-2004-B002

Varma, P. (2024). Burnout in immigrant early childhood educators.

Vaughn, T. (2023). *Reducing Burnout using Emergency Planning: A Literature Review*.

VIBER. (2024). 2023 U.S. VIRGIN ISLANDS ECONOMY. https://usviber.org/wp-content/uploads/2024/10/ECON-REVIEW-9-16-24.pdf

Viehl, C., & Dispenza, F. (2015). Burnout and coping: An exploratory comparative study of heterosexual and sexual minority mental health practitioners. *Journal of LGBT Issues in Counseling*, *9*(4), 311–328. DOI: 10.1080/15538605.2015.1112337

Villarejo, F. B., Mamburao, R. S., & Lumapenet, H. T. (2022). Work demands and occupational burnout among public school teachers in the Philippines. *International Journal of Advance Research and Innovative Ideas in Education*, *8*(3), 4923–4926.

VIOMB (2024). United States Virgin Islands Recovery Plan. Microsoft Word - DRAFT_USVI 2024 Recovery Plan_7.25.2024.docx

VIOMB. US Recovery Plan. https://arpa.vi.gov/wp-content/uploads/2024/08/USVI-2024-Recovery-Plan-1.pdf

Voßemer, J., Gebel, M., Täht, K., Unt, M., Högberg, B., & Strandh, M. (2018). The effects of unemployment and insecure jobs on well-being and health: The moderating role of labor market policies. *Social Indicators Research*, *138*(3), 1229–1257. DOI: 10.1007/s11205-017-1697-y

Voth Schrag, R. J., Wood, L. G., Wachter, K., & Kulkarni, S. (2021). Compassion Fatigue Among the Intimate Partner Violence and Sexual Assault Workforce: Enhancing Organizational Practice. *Violence Against Women*, *28*(1), 277–297. DOI: 10.1177/1077801220988351 PMID: 33596785

Vranjes, I., Notelaers, G., & Salin, D. (2021). Putting workplace bullying in context: The role of high-involvement work practices in the relationship between job demands, job resources, and bullying exposure. *Journal of Occupational Health Psychology*, *27*(1), 136–151. DOI: 10.1037/ocp0000315 PMID: 34968115

Vučinić, V., Stanimirovic, D., Gligorović, M., Jablan, B., & Marinović, M. (2020). Stress and Empathy in Teachers at General and Special Education Schools. *International Journal of Disability Development and Education*, *69*(2), 533–549. DOI: 10.1080/1034912X.2020.1727421

Wagaman, M. A., Geiger, J. M., Shockley, C., & Segal, E. A. (2015). The role of empathy in burnout, compassion satisfaction, and secondary traumatic stress among social workers. *Social Work*, *60*(3), 201–209. DOI: 10.1093/sw/swv014 PMID: 26173361

Walby, S., Armstrong, J., & Strid, S. (2012). Intersectionality: Multiple inequalities in social theory. *Sociology*, *46*(2), 224–240. DOI: 10.1177/0038038511416164

Walker, T. (2018). *'Education is Political': Neutrality in the Classroom Shortchanges Students*. Retrieved from https://www.nea.org/nea-today /all-news-articles/education-political-neutrality-classroom-shortchanges-stu dents

Waller, S. N., Wozencroft, A. J., & Scott, J. L. (2016). Compassion fatigue among disability camp staff: An exploratory study. *Annals of Leisure Research*, *20*(2), 206–221. DOI: 10.1080/11745398.2016.1162724

Waters, J., & Ussery, W. (2007). Police stress: History, contributing factors, symptoms and interventions. *Policing*, *30*(2), 169–188. DOI: 10.1108/13639510710753199

Watson, D. L. (2024). Burnout Among Sexual and Gender Minority Physicians—From Recognition to Intervention. *JAMA Network Open*, *7*(11), e2443891–e2443891. DOI: 10.1001/jamanetworkopen.2024.43891 PMID: 39535802

What is preeminence and why it matters to you. (2020, September 17). In Wikipedia. https:admissions.usf.edu/blog/what-is-preeminence-and-why-it-matters-to-you

Wiles, F. (2017). What is professional identity and how do social workers acquire it? In Webb, S. A. (Ed.), *Professional Identity and Social Work* (pp. 35–50). Routledge Academic., https://www.routledge.com/Professional-Identity-an DOI: 10.4324/9781315306957-3

Willgerodt, M. A., Abu-Rish Blakeney, E., Summerside, N., Vogel, M. T., Liner, D. A., & Zierler, B. (2020). Impact of leadership development workshops in facilitating team-based practice transformation. *Journal of Interprofessional Care*, *34*(1), 76–86. DOI: 10.1080/13561820.2019.1604496 PMID: 31039647

Williamson, G. (2024). Healthcare access disparities among marginalized communities. Global Perspectives in Health. *Medicine and Nursing*, *3*(1), 11–22.

Wilson, C. A., & Britt, T. W. (2021). Living to work: The role of occupational calling in response to challenge and hindrance stressors. *Work and Stress*, *35*(2), 111–131. DOI: 10.1080/02678373.2020.1743791

Wiszniewska, M., Rybacki, M., Lipińska-Ojrzanowska, A., Szkiela, M., & Walusiak-Skorupa, J. (2023). Recognition COVID-19 as an occupational disease in Poland–definition, criteria and recommendation. *Medycyna Pracy*, *74*(5), 435–442. DOI: 10.13075/mp.5893.01427 PMID: 38104343

Wong, S. L., Liu, H. T., & Cheng, L. J. (2011). Elucidating the relationship between satisfaction and citizen involvement in public administration. *Public Management Review*, *13*(4), 595–618. DOI: 10.1080/14719037.2010.525032

World Health Organization. (2019). *Burn-out an "Occupational phenomenon": International Classification of Diseases*. World Health Organization. Retrieved March 7, 2023, from https://www.who.int/news/item/28-05-2019-burn-out-an-occupational-phenomenon-international-classification-of-diseases

Wulandari, D., Hamdi, M., & Sigit, W. (2024). Analysis of the Quality of Population Administration Services in Increasing Public Satisfaction In South Tangerang City. *Journal of Science*, *13*(02), 1679–1694.

Wu, Q., Cao, H., & Du, H. (2023). Work Stress, Work-Related Rumination, and Depressive Symptoms in University Teachers: Buffering Effect of Self-Compassion. *Psychology Research and Behavior Management*, *16*, 1557–1569. DOI: 10.2147/PRBM.S403744 PMID: 37151906

Xie, S., Liang, L., & Li, H. (2022). Emotional labor and professional identity in Chinese early childhood teachers: The gendered moderation models. *Sustainability (Basel)*, *14*(11), 6856. DOI: 10.3390/su14116856

Xu, Y. W., & Fan, L. (2023). Emotional labor and job satisfaction among nurses: The mediating effect of nurse–patient relationship. *Frontiers in Psychology*, *14*, 1094358. Advance online publication. DOI: 10.3389/fpsyg.2023.1094358 PMID: 37342648

Yanay, N., & Shahar, G. (1998). Professional Feelings as Emotional Labor. *Journal of Contemporary Ethnography*, *27*(3), 346–373. DOI: 10.1177/089124198027003003

Yang, C., & Chen, A. (2021). Emotional labor: A comprehensive literature review. *Human Systems Management*, *40*(4), 479–501. DOI: 10.3233/HSM-200937

Yang, C., Chen, Y., & Zhao, X. (2019). Emotional Labor: Scale Development and Validation in the Chinese Context. *Frontiers in Psychology*, *10*, 486277. DOI: 10.3389/fpsyg.2019.02095 PMID: 31620048

Yang, C., Greenstein, J. E., Manchanda, S., Golshirazi, M., & Yabiku, T. (2023). Preventing compassion fatigue among educators: an educator resiliency study during the COVID-19 pandemic. In *School Violence and Primary Prevention* (pp. 653–686). Springer International Publishing., DOI: 10.1007/978-3-031-13134-9_26

Yang, C., Manchanda, S., & Greenstein, J. (2021). Educators' online teaching self-efficacy and compassion fatigue during the COVID-19 pandemic: The dual roles of "connect". *School Psychology*, *36*(6), 504–515. DOI: 10.1037/spq0000475 PMID: 34766814

Yemiscigil, A., Born, D., Snook, S., & Pate, E. (2022). Authentic leader(ship) development and leaders' psychological well-being: An outcome-wide analysis. *Leadership and Organization Development Journal*, *43*(8), 1287–1307. DOI: 10.1108/LODJ-11-2021-0525

Yildirim, F., & Dinc, M. S. (2019). Factors influencing burnout of the principals: A pilot study in Flemish schools of Belgium. *Ekonomska Istrazivanja*, *32*(1), 3538–3553. DOI: 10.1080/1331677X.2019.1660200

Yin, H. (2016). Knife-like mouth and tofu-like heart: Emotion regulation by Chinese teachers in classroom teaching. *Social Psychology of Education*, *19*(1), 1–22. DOI: 10.1007/s11218-015-9319-5

Yu, H., Jiang, A., & Shen, J. (2016). Prevalence and predictors of compassion fatigue, burnout and compassion satisfaction among oncology nurses: A cross-sectional survey. *International Journal of Nursing Studies*, *57*, 28–38. DOI: 10.1016/j.ijnurstu.2016.01.012 PMID: 27045562

Yuma, P., Powell, T., Scott, J., & Vinton, M. (2019). Resilience and Coping for the Healthcare Community: A Post-disaster Group Work Intervention for Healthcare and Social Service Providers. *Journal of Family Strengths*, *19*(1). Advance online publication. https://library.capella.edu/login?url=https://www.proquest.com/scholarly-journals/resilience-coping-healthcare-community-post/docview/2647680412/se-2. DOI: 10.58464/2168-670X.1402

Yurt, Y. (2023). Work-Related and Occupational Liver Diseases. *EURASIAN JOURNAL OF MEDICAL ADVANCES*, *3*(2), 51–55. DOI: 10.14744/ejma.2023.74046

Yu, X., Sun, C., Sun, B., Yuan, X., Ding, F., & Zhang, M. (2022). The cost of caring: Compassion fatigue is a special form of teacher burnout. *Sustainability (Basel)*, *14*(10), 6071. DOI: 10.3390/su14106071

Zaghini, F., Biagioli, V., Proietti, M., Badolamenti, S., Fiorini, J., & Sili, A. (2020). The role of occupational stress in the association between emotional labor and burnout in nurses: A cross-sectional study. *Applied Nursing Research*, *54*, 151277. DOI: 10.1016/j.apnr.2020.151277 PMID: 32650898

Zakeri, M. A., Bazmandegan, G., Ganjeh, H., Zakeri, M., Mollaahmadi, S., Anbariyan, A., & Kamiab, Z. (2021). Is nurses' clinical competence associated with their compassion satisfaction, burnout and secondary traumatic stress? A cross-sectional study. *Nursing Open*, *8*(1), 354–363. DOI: 10.1002/nop2.636 PMID: 33318843

Zapf, D., & Semmer, N. (2004). Stress und Gesundheit in Organisationen. In Schuler, H. (Ed.), *Enzyklopädie der Psychologie-Organisationspsychologie* (pp. 1007–1112). Hogrefe.

Zavala, V.A., Bracci, P.M., Carethers, J.M., Carvajal-Carmona, L., Coggins, N.B., Cruz-Correa, M.R., Davis, M., de Smith, A.J., Dutil, J., Figueiredo, J.C., Fox, R., & Graves, K.D.,

Zembylas, M. (2003). Emotions and teacher identity: A poststructural perspective. *Teachers and Teaching*, *9*(3), 213–238. DOI: 10.1080/13540600309378

Zerden, L. de S. (2024). Social work and burnout: Everything, everywhere, all at once. *Social Work*, *69*(3), 217–219. https://doi-org.uvi.idm.oclc.org/10.1093/sw/swae021. DOI: 10.1093/sw/swae021 PMID: 38745383

Zhang, J., Chen, W., Petrovsky, N., & Walker, R. M. (2022). The expectancy-disconfirmation model and citizen satisfaction with public services: A meta-analysis and an agenda for best practice. *Public Administration Review*, *82*(1), 147–159. DOI: 10.1111/puar.13368

Zhang, Q., & Zhu, W. (2008). Exploring emotion in teaching: Emotional labor, burnout, and satisfaction in Chinese higher education. *Communication Education*, *57*(1), 105–122. DOI: 10.1080/03634520701586310

Zhang, Y., Zhang, H., Ma, X., & Di, Q. (2020). Mental health problems during the COVID-19 pandemics and the mitigation effects of exercise: A longitudinal study of college students in China. *International Journal of Environmental Research and Public Health*, *17*(10), 3722. DOI: 10.3390/ijerph17103722 PMID: 32466163

Zhang, Y., & Zhang, L. J. (2024). "Good for me to leave it for good": A longitudinal study on how emotion labor in teaching contributes to a beginning EFL teacher's resignation. *TESOL Quarterly*, *58*(4), 1460–1492. DOI: 10.1002/tesq.3289

Zhao, M., & Tian, J.-L. (2022). Recent advances on the structure identification of components in food. *eFood*, *3*(6), 1–6. DOI: 10.1002/efd2.51

Zhao, W., Liao, X., Li, Q., Jiang, W., & Ding, W. (2021). The relationship between teacher job stress and burnout: A moderated mediation model. *Frontiers in Psychology, 12*, 784–243. DOI: 10.3389/fpsyg.2021.784243 PMID: 35145457

Zhou, Y. J. (2015). The influence of organizational climate perception on job burnout in tumor hospital nurses. *The Journal of Nursing Administration, 15*(2), 96–97.

Zou, Y., Lu, Y., Zhou, F., Liu, X., Ngoubene-Atioky, A. J., Xu, K., Hong, L., Shen, G., Wu, H., Cai, Z., Liu, Y., Chen, L., & Bao, D. (2022). Three Mental Health Symptoms of Frontline Medical Staff Associated With Occupational Stressors During the COVID-19 Peak Outbreak in China: The Mediation of Perceived Stress and the Moderation of Social Support. *Frontiers in Psychology, 13*, 888000. DOI: 10.3389/fpsyg.2022.888000 PMID: 35712133

About the Contributors

Kenny A. Hendrickson is a Professor of Public Administration and Social Sciences, and Interim Dean of Graduate Studies at the University of the Virgin Islands. He holds a Doctor of Philosophy in Urban Studies and Public Affairs from the University of Akron in Ohio. Dr. Hendrickson's current research interests and publications focus on public administration, leadership, disaster management, burnout, STEM education, public health, caring, professional quality of life and public trust. In 2021, Dr. Hendrickson was part of an investigative team that completed a research project, entitled "Frontline Government Workers: Assessing Post-Disaster Burnout and Quality of Life". This project was funded by the Natural Hazards Center, University of Colorado Boulder. The project examined the relationship between post-disaster burnout of US Virgin Islands frontline government employees and their professional quality of life. The following year, Dr. Hendrickson was the principal investigator of a research project, entitled "Public Trust, Community Resilience, and Disaster Response in the U.S. Virgin Islands". This project was also funded by the Natural Hazards Center, University of Colorado Boulder. The project examined the relationship between territorial public trust in public health emergency response (PHER) and community resilience.

Kula A. Francis is an Associate Professor of Political Science in the College of Liberal Arts and Social Sciences at the University of the Virgin Islands. She holds a Doctor of Philosophy in Urban Studies and Public Affairs from the University of Akron in Ohio. Her current research interests are social equity in public organizations, evaluation, international relations, history, politics, and public administration. In 2021, Dr. Francis was principal investigator was on an investigative team that completed a research project, entitled "Frontline Government Workers: Assessing Post-Disaster Burnout and Quality of Life". This project was funded by the Natural Hazards Center, University of Colorado Boulder. The project examined the relationship between post-disaster burnout of US Virgin Islands frontline government employees and their professional quality of life. The following year, Dr. Francis was also part of a research project, entitled "Public Trust, Community Resilience, and Disaster Response in the U.S. Virgin Islands". This project was also funded by the Natural Hazards Center, University of Colorado Boulder. The project examined the relationship between territorial public trust in public health emergency response (PHER) and community resilience.

***

Ravi Kishor Agrawal is a seasoned academic and industry professional with over 14 years of experience spanning both sectors. He is currently associated with the Department of MSMSR at MATS University, Raipur, Chhattisgarh. His expertise bridges theoretical knowledge and practical application, contributing significantly to academic development and industry-oriented learning.

Carolyn Allen received her PHD in African American Studies from Temple University. She also received a Master of Arts in African American Studies from Temple University and a Master of Social Service degree from Bryn Mawr College. Dr. Allen has 28 years of teaching experience at the university level in both brick-and-mortar and online programs. She is currently Associate Professor of Social Work at the University of the Virgin Islands. Dr. Allen has a personal and academic commitment to the area of Diversity Studies. She has published, delivered a number of professional presentations and developed courses in this area.

Kristy Andre is an IT Relationship Manager for the Morsani College of Medicine in the Department of Medical Education. She leads adoption and change management campaigns for emerging and new technologies and facilitate completion of project implementation.

Deborah A. Austin, whose professional goals included having one foot in the community and the other in the academy, was part of the federal Central Hillsborough Healthy Start Project and REACHUP, Inc. for 24 years. REACHUP, Inc, is a community non-profit whose focus is advocating for and mobilizing resources to help communities achieve equality in healthcare and positive health for families. She is one of three co-founders of the maternal and child health non-profit and recently retired as Director of Community Engagement. As Director of Community Engagement, Dr. Austin provided oversight to the community outreach, faith initiative, male involvement, and advertising and marketing components of the organization; supervised graduate student interns from various universities across Florida and the southeastern United States; and conducted workshops and trainings on implicit/unconscious bias and appreciative inquiry. With expertise in qualitative methods and community-engaged research, she served as principal liaison between REACHUP, Inc. and its partners conducting research which required community engagement and mobilization.

Savannah Baus, MPH Disaster Management Student at the Tulane Celia Scott Weatherhead School of Public Health and Tropical Medicine.

Supriya Bhagat holds a Master's in HRM, SET in Management, and a PGDIMM. With over 13 years of academic experience, she brings deep expertise in HRM, Marketing, and General Management. Her teaching and research interests span across core HR practices, strategic marketing, and management principles, fostering holistic student development through domain-focused learning and practical application.

John Blenkinsopp is Professor of Organisational Psychology at Oslo New University College. His research focuses on whistleblowing & silence and the future of work, with an underlying interest in how people make sense of work and the impact on their health and well-being. He has held posts at Northumbria University, Newcastle University, Teesside University and Hull University (all in the UK) as well as visiting professor roles at Galway University in Ireland and the University of Kuwait. He has published over 50 peer reviewed articles, collaborating with researchers on every continent.

Colby Cavanaugh is a public sector Emergency Manager for a city of 50,000 in the United States. He holds a Master of Professional Studies in Emergency and Disaster Management from Georgetown University, where his research focused on enhancing community resilience and deepening the understanding of the wildland-urban interface. Colby also holds a Bachelor of Arts in Communication from Washington State University, with a concentration in Public Relations and Comparative Ethnic Studies. An active member of the International Association of Emergency Managers, he maintains the Certified Emergency Manager (CEM) designation. With a strong background in planning and operations, Colby has successfully addressed challenges at both the local and state levels in the U.S., as well as within higher education. His work and research are shaped by personal experiences responding to large-scale disasters, including the Oso Landslide (2014), the 2015 Wildfire Season in Washington State, and the COVID-19 pandemic. Colby is passionate about advancing the field of emergency management, exploring innovative ideas, and harnessing the power of community to build resilience in both professional and personal settings.

Feng Cheng is a computational biologist. He received systematic training in bioinformatics at Chinese Academy of Science, University of Illinois at Urbana Champaign, University of Virginia, and Yale University. His research is mainly focused on applications of bioinformatics methods for the identification of drug–drug interactions (DDIs) and for drug repositioning by analyzing Big Data from public resources. He is also interested in computer-aided drug design. Dr. Cheng has published about 100 research papers in prestigious journals including Nature, Neuron, Journal of the American Chemical Society, and Journal of Alzheimer's Disease. His work has been cited more than 5,000 times. Dr. Cheng has been serving as an editorial member of several journals.

Nguyen Chi Hai, corresponding Author 1 Dr. Nguyen Chi Hai, An Giang University, Vietnam National University Ho Chi Minh City (nchai@agu.edu.vn) No 18, Ung Van Khiem street, Dong Xuyen ward Long Xuyen, An Giang 90100, VN Nguyen Chi Hai, Dr., Political Science Lecturer, An Giang University, Vietnam National University Ho Chi Minh City. He teaches and conducts research at An Giang University, Vietnam National University, Ho Chi Minh City, Vietnam. His research interests and areas of research include Education, Indigenous Culture, Public Policy, Public Management, Social Sciences, and Humanities. Address: No 18, Ung Van Khiem street, Dong Xuyen ward, Long Xuyen city, An Giang province. Phone +(84) 965 118 318. Email: nchai@agu.edu.vn

John E. Clark is Associate Professor in the Department of Pharmacotherapeutics and Clinical Research and Director of Culture and Climate Programs at the University of South Florida (USF) Taneja College of Pharmacy. He also holds a joint appointment as Assistant Professor in the Department of Family Medicine at the Morsani College of Medicine at the University of South Florida in Tampa, Florida. Clark is also a Clinical Pharmacist and Faculty Preceptor in Ambulatory Care at the USF Morsani Health Center BRIDGE Healthcare Clinic. The BRIDGE Healthcare Clinic is a student-run, multidisciplinary, non-profit clinic that services uninsured and underinsured patients in the Tampa area. Clark oversees the development and provision of pharmacy services, including medication reconciliation, patient education and counseling, and disease and medication management services. Clark earned a B.S. in Pharmacy from Texas Southern University College of Pharmacy and a Pharm.D. from Florida A&M University. He earned a M.S. in Pharmaceutical Administration from Wayne State University and completed his residency training at Detroit General Hospital.

Kyaien Conner, Ph.D., LSW, MPH is a Full Professor and Donald M. Henderson Endowed Chair at the University of Pittsburgh School of Social Work where she directs the Center on Race and Social Problems (CRSP). She also serves as the Associate Dean for Justice, Equity, Diversity and Inclusion for the school of social work. Dr. Conner is a clinical social worker by profession, and her research investigates the factors that influence disparities in health and mental health service utilization and treatment outcomes for racial and ethnic minorities. She focuses on the development and evaluation of culturally meaningful approaches to improving behavioral health for older African Americans. She further studies the adaptation of evidence-based intervention, to include culturally relevant components (e.g., cultural dance and music) to address mental health concerns in communities of color. The overarching goal of her research and praxis is health equity and social justice. Dr. Conner has received over 5 million dollars in funding for her research on behavioral health disparities. She has received many awards for her work including Distinguished Alumni Award, Chancellors Award for Excellence in Civic and Community Engagement, and Black Faculty Member of the year. Dr. Conner presents nationally on issues regarding Diversity, Equity and Inclusion, anti-racism and race-based trauma. Dr. Conner wrote a bill that was signed into law on 6/17/2021 to restructure the Florida State Office of Minority Health and Health Equity (Senate Bill 404 sponsored by State Senator Darryl Rouson Senate Bill 404 (2021) - The Florida Senate (flsenate.gov)). The overarching goal of her research and praxis is health equity and social justice.

Tapash Das is now serving as Assistant Professor in the Department of Education at Kazi Nazrul University, Asansol, West Bengal, India with more than six years of teaching experience. He has done M.A, M.Phil. and Ph.D. in Education from University of Kalyani, Nadia, West Bengal, India and qualified UGC NET & SET in Education. He has authored many chapters in National and International edited volumes as well as many articles in a number of reputable peer-reviewed Journals with high impact factors. The author has participated in various National and International conferences and seminars, where he has delivered papers also.

Antionette Davis is the founder and CEO of EnVision Resolution and the EnVision Resolution Foundation. She is known for being a community activist and change agent who works with others in the community to achieve common objectives. Antionette is a strong forward-thinking leader who listens, and has experience not only collaborating and advocating, but uses her God-given abilities to strategically get results. She is guilty of doing the hard and heart work of being a fierce advocate for change, justice ministry leader, community health educator, and collaborator. She thinks globally and act locally to bring the best ideas to Hillsborough County going to where the people are. She is an entrepreneur and homemaker, a retired homeschool educator, and the former Director of Justice

Ministry at Bible-Based Fellowship Church in Carrollwood, FL for an 8-year tenure. She is a champion of grassroots organizing and a true testament of how hard work, faithfulness, and passion can pay off. A University of South Florida alumna with a Bachelor's Degree in Accounting.

Joseph Diamond is a PharmD candidate at the University of South Florida Taneja College of Pharmacy (USF TCOP) with a Bachelor of Science in Biology from North Carolina State University. Passionate about pharmaceutical innovation and community health, Joseph has led impactful initiatives and research projects. As Lead Student Ambassador for the Workgroup Enhancing Community Advocacy and Research Engagement (WE-CARE) Program, he educated the Tampa community on critical health issues and led different initiatives like a social media cancer awareness campaign and a drive-thru COVID-19 vaccination clinic. His research at USF includes implementing a standardized medication reconciliation tool to enhance patient safety and analyzing academic data to better support student progression. Joseph also served as Vice President of Membership for the Innovation Technology and Entrepreneurship in Health Care (ITEHC), leading its transition to the Industry Pharmacists Organization (IPhO). As a Student Delegate for USF TCOP, he contributed to the admissions committee and coordinated recruitment and school events. With experience as a Quality Governance and Strategy Intern at Johnson & Johnson, Joseph aims to bridge the gap between pharmaceutical innovation and patient care while advocating for community health and student development.

Marie Grace A. Gomez is Professor 4 at the Counselor Education Area, College of Education, University of the Philippines-Diliman. She teaches counseling and research courses at the undergraduate and graduate levels. She has a bachelor's degree in Political Science, a Master of Arts in Education (Guidance) degree, a Doctor of Philosophy degree in Guidance, and another doctorate in Special Education. She has served as a classroom teacher, guidance counselor, and administrator in the basic and tertiary education settings. Her community extension projects involve counseling and assessment of children, persons with disabilities, children in conflict with the law, drug surrenderees, development of sexual health literacy programs for teens with disabilities, sexually abused children, medical personnel, women with mental health issues in institutional settings, and persons affected by COVID-19. She has led test development endeavors on various DepEd projects in coordination with the National Council on Disability Affairs and Leonard Cheshire Philippines. She has been the lead researcher for the Philippines in a UNESCO research led by Leonard Cheshire UK on Comprehensive Sexuality Education for persons with disabilities. She has received the 2022 Most Outstanding Professional Teacher Award in the field of Academe and Research from the Philippine Federation for Professional

Associations. Recently, she won the UP Centennial Professorial Chair for publication and mentoring students to publish in refereed journals.

Sishupal Gorain is now acting as a Senior Research Fellow (Ph.D.) in the Department of Education at Rajiv Gandhi University, Arunachalpradesh India. He has done B.A. (Hons) & M.A. in Education. He qualified UGC NET/JRF & SET in Education. He has authored many chapters in National and International edited volumes as well as many articles in a number of reputable peer-reviewed Journals.

Tanya M. Grant is an Assistant Professor of Criminal Justice at St. Mary's University in San Antonio, TX, USA. . Dr. Grant holds a Ph.D. in Criminal Justice from Capella University, a Master of Science in Criminal Justice from The University of New Haven and a Bachelor of Arts in Psychology from Fairfield University. She has extensive field experience in juvenile justice, corrections, and domestic violence/ sexual violence advocacy. Her areas of research interest are domestic violence, specifically advocate burnout, law enforcement response to victims of domestic violence, and agency / department culture as an impact on victim service delivery. Her teaching interests include domestic and sexual violence and mass shooting events, particularly in schools/ school settings. Dr. Grant is a member of the Academy of Criminal Justice Sciences and The World Social Science Association.

Hiram Green has been a staple in the USF Community for over 40 years. He is an alumnus who returned to the University as the Assistant Athletic Director, and worked in Alumni Affairs, as the Director of Ambassador Program, and started the revenue generating programs for the USF Alumni Association. He also started an endowment for Embracing Legacy (through Revealing Truth Ministries) to provide financial support to students attending USF. He served as the Director of Development for the College of Medicine and in that capacity, he started the alumni association. He is currently the Director of Community Engagement for USF Health and Director of Public Relations for the Taneja College of Pharmacy. Part of his duties include work as a member of WE-CARE where he is a part of a team that helps promote diversity in clinical trial participation and initiatives to help close the gap in health disparities. Beyond the University, but to the University's benefit, he has served on the Board of Directors of the American Heart Association, ALS, and East Tampa Partnership, and still is an active board member with the Salvation Army. He also coordinated the Florida Classic for four year with the Florida Classic Association.

Anniken Grønstad works as Associate Professor at Oslo New University College. Her research revolves around work environment, leadership, organizational change, remote and hybrid work, employee health and well-being, sexual harassment at work, and whistleblowing.

Tarini Halder is working as a Professor in the Department of Education, University of Kalyani, Kalyani, Nadia, West Bengal, India. He obtained an M.A. in History and Education, and a Ph.D. in Education from the University of Kalyani, West Bengal, India. He has qualified for NET and SET in education. He has acted as a resource person in many national and international seminars and conferences and presented many research his research work at many universities, state, national, and international level seminars, and conferences. He has published more than 50 papers in peer-reviewed national and international journals and more than 20 book chapters in edited books. Along with these publications he also published more than 10 textbooks for different higher education level courses. Under his supervision, many scholars were awarded M.Phil. and Ph.D. degrees.

Angela M. Hill is a professor, Associate Dean of Clinical Affairs and the Project Director for WE-CARE at the Taneja College of Pharmacy at the University of South Florida. She received her doctorate in pharmacy from Florida A&M University, and completed a post-graduate residency in neurology from the Neuroscience Research Foundation, Inc. of Florida. Throughout her career, she has helped patients with neurological and psychiatric disorders through her work in community and hospital pharmacy practice, specialty clinics and community boards. She has provided pharmacy services to patients being screened, treated, or involved in clinical research with Alzheimer's disease and other dementias for the last 25+ years, and is one of the pioneering pharmacists to be involved in Memory Disorder Clinics in the State of Florida and was acknowledged by the Department of Elder Affairs and the Alzheimer's Resource Association for her pioneering work. Dr. Hill is the project manager for WE-CARE where she does work in clinical trial recruitment and health disparities. Dr. Hill has done research and published on a variety of topics related to her specialty areas, which includes pharmacogenomic principles in psychiatric and neurologic disorders. Her work and training of pharmacists spans from the United States to other countries like Nigeria, Trinidad, Panama, and most recently Canada. She is currently practicing at Dr. Tracy's House, an innovative holistic health primary care practice that serves underrepresented and marginalized populations in Tampa, Florida.

Vishal Jain is presently working as Professor at the Department of Computer Science and Engineering, School of Engineering and Technology, Sharda University, Greater Noida, India. Before that, he worked for several years as an Associate Professor at Bharati Vidyapeeth's Institute of Computer Applications and

Management (BVICAM), New Delhi. He has more than 18 years of experience in the academics. He has earned degrees: Ph.D (CSE), M.Tech (CSE), MBA (HR), MCA, MCP, and CCNA. He has more than 2200 research citations with Google Scholar (h-index score 24 and i-10 index 55) and has authored more than 150 research papers in professional journals and conferences. He has authored and edited more than 60 books (most of them are indexed at the Scopus) with various reputed publishers, including Elsevier, Springer, IET, Apple Academic Press, CRC, Taylor and Francis Group, Scrivener, Wiley, Emerald, NOVA Science, River Publishers, IGI-Global and Bentham Science. He has more than 200 Scopus publications. His research areas include machine learning, information retrieval, semantic web, ontology engineering, data mining, ad hoc networks, sensor networks and network security.

Kazi Kutubuddin Sayyad Liyakat has completed his B.E., M.E., and Ph.D. in E&TC Engineering and is nowadays working as a Professor & Head of Department, E&TC Engineering Department and was Dean R&D. He is Post-Doctoral Fellow working on "IoT in Healthcare Applications". His area of Interest is IoT, AI and ML. He has published more than 110+ papers in various Journals. Also published 11 books in the field of Engineering. He has published 15 Indian Patents, 2 South African Grant Patent, 2 Indian Copyright Patents and 8 UK Grant Patent. He worked as a Reviewer for Scopus Conferences and Journal. Also work as Editorial Board Member for various Journals. He got 2 Best Researcher Award, Best Faculty Award and Appreciation Letter from MoE's Innovation Cell, Govt. of India.

Damla Köroğlu Ünver completed her double major in Business Administration and Psychology at Hacettepe University in 2014. Since 2015, she has been serving as a lecturer at Istanbul University's School of Business, conducting academic research in behavioral finance, organizational behavior, gender studies, and strategic management. Through her academic publications and participation in national and international conferences, she contributes to the knowledge base in business and management. Her work integrates insights from both psychology and business disciplines, offering an interdisciplinary perspective. Köroğlu's academic contributions focus on advancing new approaches and methodologies in the field of Management and Organization, supporting innovation and development within the discipline.

Judette Louis is the Chair of the Department of OB/GYN at the University of South Florida. She has a joint faculty appointment in both the College of Public Health and the College of Medicine. She is a specialist in Maternal Fetal Medicine. She is a past president of the Society for Women's Health Research. She has authored numerous scientific articles and book chapters on sleep apnea and maternal morbidity/mortality. She is a member of the Society for Women's Health Research Interdisciplinary Network on Sleep, which worked to bring attention to sleep health issues in women and to enhance discussions between health care providers and patients to better address women's sleep needs. Through her work as a clinical leader for the Florida Perinatal Quality Collaborative, Dr. Louis has led statewide programs to improve management of obstetric emergencies in the State of Florida. She is passionate about making pregnancy safer for all women and in particular, improving maternal health across the lifespan.

Karia MacAulay has a PhD in Business Administration and her dissertation focused on identity in the workplace and its role in change management within the government sector. Before obtaining her PhD, she worked as an HR Practitioner and Director in both for profit and non-profit organizations. Throughout her career she has worked to and studied how to make organizations more effective and inclusive places to work. She has worked with for-profit, non-profit, and higher education organizations to help them cope with the stress and complexities of our current reality. She has also worked predominately in diversity, equity, and inclusion with a goal of ensuring employees are working in a civil and productive environment. She is currently a Professor of Instruction for the Information Systems and Management Department in the Muma College of Business.

T.C. Manjunath was born on 6th February 1967. He did his BE from RV College of Engg. in 1989, ME in Robotics & Automation from LD College of Engg. in 1992 with First Rank and PhD in Systems & Control Engg. from IIT Bombay in the year 2007. He is currently working as the Dean Research R D and as Professor in the Dept. of Computer Science & Engineering with specialization in IoT, Cyber Security & Blockchain Technology in Rajarajeswari College of Engineering, Bengaluru, Karnataka. He has completed B.E. Degree from R.V. College of Engg., M.E. Govt.'s LD College of Engg., Gujarat Univ., Ahmedabad in First Rank and Ph.D. in Systems and Control Engineering from the Indian Institute of Technology Bombay IIT Bombay He has got a teaching academic, research and administrative experience of more than 35+ years 10 years as Principal, 8 years as HoD rest as faculty and has published more than 1200+ research papers in various national & international journals and conferences, with 175+ patents, 25 book-chapters, 25 awards and also published 25 text books in various field of science, engineering and technology, completed projects worth Rs. 9 Crores till date apart from guiding 10 PhD scholars. He is a member of 30 Professional Society Chapters and is a fellow of IE, IETE, AMIEE and a chartered engineer. He got the best research scholar award in 2006 in IIT Bombay amongst all the research scholars of the institute. He has got 10 awards in academics and research activities.

Angela Mazzetti is interested in how our 'personal ecology' (defined as the unique embeddedness of embodied individuals in dynamic socio-cultural and multi-sensorial environments that shift and evolve over time) influences what we consider to be stressful and the coping strategies and behaviours we adopt to deal with stressful conditions. Through her research, she has explored themes such as adaptation and resilience; trauma, coping resources and reserves; recourse to intervention strategies; how stress is conceptualised and discussed; readiness and resistance to change; the long-term impact of career disruptions; and how stressful encounters are remembered and narrated.

Archan Mitra is an Assistant Professor at NICO, NITTE University, Mangalore. He is the author of two book "Cases for Classroom Media and Entertainment Business" and "Multiverse and Media", he also has other several edited books to his credit. He has done his doctorate from Visva-Bharati Santiniketan, West Bengal in the field of "environmental informatics and communication for sustainability". In addition to that he is a certified Science Communicator and Journalism from Indian Science Communication Society (ISCOS), certified Corporate Trainer with Amity Institute of Training and Development, Certified Social Media Network Analyst. He has a strong interest in environmental communication. He was awarded certificate of merit by PRSI, Kolkata Chapter and Medal of Honor by Journalistic Club of Kolkata. He was working as a research assistant with the World Bank's "Environmental Capacity Building in Southeast Asia" project at IIM Kashipur. He was instrumental in launching the World Bank's Green MBA MOOC, he has also assisted in the research project on Uttarakhand disaster mitigation by ICSSR, the leading research on Uttarakhand disaster.

Thea Moore is an associate professor in the Department of Pharmacotherapeutics and Clinical Research at the University of South Florida, Taneja College of Pharmacy. She is a graduate of University of Michigan College of Pharmacy, and licensed as a registered pharmacist in the State of Florida. She completed a residency and fellowship in psychiatric pharmacy in Kansas City, MO and is a board certified psychiatric pharmacist (BCPP.) During her career as a pharmacist, Dr. Moore has published several articles, and participated in numerous research projects in the area of psychiatry. She has trained many pharmacy residents and pharmacy students and collaborated in obtaining funding for research and other clinical activities. She was faculty at Florida A&M University and most recently worked at Lakeland Regional Medical Center as a pharmacotherapy specialist prior to joining the University of South Florida. She has a joint appointment with the Morsani College of Medicine in the Department of Psychiatry and Behavioral Neurosciences and collaborates with other clinicians at University Psychiatry Center to provide patient education, medication reviews, consultation and research assistance. Dr. Moore has had a sustained interest in assisting underrepresented groups to access and excel in pharmacy. She has been the faculty advisor for Student National Pharmaceutical Association (SNPhA) since 2012. She has also volunteered as a mentor and has enjoyed working with students to expose them to more aspects of pharmacy in programs like Upward Bound and Pre-Health Scholars Program. Dr. Moore has presented webinars on Faith and Pharmacy to expand community knowledge about what pharmacists can do and how they can serve the community. Dr. Moore's professional interests include nutritional psychiatry, complementary and alternative medicine and wellness. Dr. Moore recently received a certificate as an Integrative Pharmacy Specialist and an ASHP WellBeing Ambassador certificate. Dr. Moore is an active member of National Alliance on Mental Illness (NAMI).

Michael Morgan is the Community Engagement and Outreach manager for REACHUP Incorporated. Mr. Morgan coordinates the Affirming Fatherhood Conference, and supports the USF/WE CARE Maternal Health events.

Stephen Murphy leads Tulane's Weatherhead's SPHTM Health Security Masters of Science degree program, leveraging his 20+ years of practice-based experience shaping and implementing local, state, federal, and private sector public health emergency preparedness, homeland security, health security, and disaster management and resilience programs. His experience includes developing and managing preparedness plans, exercises, and operational responses for major metropolitan jurisdictions addressing health threats such as COVID-19, Ebola Virus Disease, hurricane evacuation, pandemic influenza, and coastal oil spills, as well as planning for high-threat events of national significance such as the Super Bowl and other large-scale mass gatherings. He has served on numerous state-wide advisory boards in Louisiana and was the former Chief of Planning and Preparedness for New Orleans Office of Homeland Security & Emergency Preparedness in the years following Hurricane Katrina. Dr. Murphy's research is at the intersection of health security strategies, translation and implementation science, and workforce development. He is passionate about teaching and typically leads multiple graduate courses and an undergraduate course each year.

Ankur Nandi is now acting as a Senior Research Fellow (Ph.D.) in the Department of Education at University of Kalyani, Nadia, West Bengal, India. He has done B.A. (Hons) & M.A. in Education, M.Phil. in Education, and done B.Ed. also. He qualified UGC NET/JRF & SET in Education. He has authored many chapters in National and International edited volumes as well as many articles in a number of reputable peer-reviewed Journals.

Nimita Srivastava Nimkar is an Associate Professor at the Balaji Institute of Management and Human Resource Development (BIMHRD), Sri Balaji University, Pune. With a strong academic background and extensive experience in management education, she specializes in areas related to human resource management and organizational development. Dr. Nimkar is known for her commitment to academic excellence, research, and mentoring future business leaders. Her contributions to teaching and thought leadership continue to enrich the academic community at Sri Balaji University.

Victor Obi is a pharmacist, entrepreneur and philanthropist with 29 years of experience in the Medical and Pharmacy industries. Mr. Obi's career spans Retail Pharmacy, Specialty Pharmacy, Pharmaceutical Consulting, Project Management, Medical Management and Business development, with a proven track record of success. Mr. Obi holds a degree in Pharmacy and Business Management. Mr. Obi established Superior Specialty Pharmacy and Tampa Bay professional Pharmacy Group, which expanded to five stores with over 100 employees. He later sold the business and founded Brent Cross Consulting, focusing on third-party credentialing, new Pharmacy set up, and Specialty Pharmacy management. Mr. Obi also established an Occupational health clinic, dedicated to preventing and treating work-related injuries and illnesses. Additionally, he serves as CEO of WBS Medical Clinic, a pioneering facility specializing in Anti-Aging and Regenerative Medicine. Throughout his career, Mr. Obi has developed himself in Executive Leadership Strategies, Project Management, Medical and Pharmaceutical investment. He serves as the liaison for the Pharmaceutical Society of Nigeria. His passion for giving back led him to establish two charity organizations in Nigeria, providing health services, education, and economic empowerment to widows, the poor, and the infirm. These charities are THEEE INITIATIVE (theeeinitiative.org) & VICTOR & HILDA OBI FOUNDATION. In the United States, Mr. Obi also founded Bayside Foundation,(BaysideHustle.org) hosting annual 5K run/walk events through the Bayside Hustle 5K Charity Run/Walk which aims to raise funds for organizations like Shriners Hospital for Children and the Nigerian Association of Pharmacists and Pharmaceutical Scientists (NAPPSA).

P. Selvakumar is currently an Associate Professor in the Department of Science and Humanities at Nehru Institute of Technology, Coimbatore, Tamil Nadu, India. Since 2023, he has served as the Department IQAC Coordinator at the institute. Prior to joining Nehru Institute of Technology, he held positions as an Assistant Professor in the Department of Science and Humanities various engineering colleges in Coimbatore, Tamil Nadu, India, spanning from 2011 to 2023. Dr.P. Selvakumar's academic and research interests lie primarily in the field of phytochemistry. He has made significant contributions to his field, with an impressive record that includes 30 journal publications, 12 patents, and 20 conference papers. Additionally, he has organized 5 seminars and conferences, further demonstrating his commitment to academic and scientific exchange. Throughout his career, Dr. P.Selvakumar has been recognized for his dedication and excellence in teaching, having been honored with several awards, including the Best Teacher Awards. He holds a prominent position in the academic community, contributing actively to research.

Kesley Richardson is a U.S. Virgin Islands Native, scholar, public speaker, researcher, and practitioner in Emergency Management. Recently identified In the top 40 under 40 and as the USA Rising star for the International Association of Emergency Managers, he is currently an Adjunct professor at Loyola University in Chicago, Texas Southern University, and Nova Southeastern University. He is part of organizations such as the International Association of Emergency Managers(IAEM), Black Emergency Managers Association (BEMA), Florida Public Health Association (FPHA), and Florida Emergency Preparedness Association (FEPA) to make an actionable change and cultivate action-based research.

Janet Roman's life's work involves improving outcomes for heart failure patients and promoting the use of palliative care and hospice. Dr. Roman is currently serving as the Special Advisor to Diversity, Equity, and Inclusion at the University of South Florida and the Director of Cardiac Services at Empath Health and has dedicated a large portion of her nursing practice to those suffering with heart failure. As a board-certified Acute Care Nurse Practitioner, Certified Heart Failure Nurse, and Advanced Certified Hospice & Palliative Care Nurse, she has been the Principal Investigator in a plethora of studies to advance the use of palliative care in the heart failure population. Other research interests include heart failure across the continuum, the reduction of symptom burden through comprehensive heart failure care, improving self-care through remote patient monitoring and simulation education. Dr. Roman's clinical experience expands across many concentrations including cardio-thoracic surgery, mechanical circulatory support, cardiac transplant, cardiac, medical, and surgical intensive care, emergency medicine, homecare and hospice.

Natasha Rubie is a Community Partnership Specialist responsible for promoting Empath Health's vision and mission in the African American community and generating inquiries and referrals into our range of services to increase the level of services provided to the African American community. I conduct a variety of outreach activities, build strategic relationships based on the needs and requirements of the organization and the community, and represents the organization to the

African American population as needed to increase awareness of our mission and utilization of our services.

Kevin B. Sneed is a tenured Professor and the founding Dean of the University of South Florida Taneja College of Pharmacy. He also serves as a Senior Associate Vice-President for USF Health. Dr. Sneed earned his Bachelor of Science Degree in Biology with a concentration in Microbiology from the University of Central Florida. He received his Doctor of Pharmacy from Xavier University of Louisiana College of Pharmacy. He completed an Ambulatory Care Pharmacy Practice Specialty Residency at Bay Pines Veteran's Administration Medical Center. He has received numerous clinical and leadership awards and most recently received the Distinguished Fellow National Academies of Practice award from the National Academies of Practice, Chauncey I. Cooper Medal from the National Pharmaceutical Association, and the National Pharmaceutical Association Fellow from the National Pharmaceutical Association. Dr. Sneed serves on the board of several organizations and participates in many community endeavors.

Maisha N. Standifer is the Director of Population Health in the Satcher Health Leadership Institute at Morehouse School of Medicine. In her role, Dr. Standifer conducts population-based health studies and administers evidence-based prevention initiatives that effectively employ tailored strategies to reduce negative health outcomes throughout under-resourced, racial and ethnic, and medically vulnerable populations. Her public health career expertise spans across the fields of health program administration, evaluation, implementation and dissemination, health policy development and analysis, mixed methods research and examining drivers of social and political determinants of health. Dr. Standifer is also an Assistant Professor, Principal investigator and a Co-Investigator on multiple private, sponsored and federally funded studies. Her research portfolio furthers production in implementation science and health services research, along with community-based participatory research to create culturally-tailored interventions which empowers disenfranchised populations to make healthy and informed decisions. She is a community-based engaged researcher who has extensive training and project implementation expertise in reducing cancer disparities, substance abuse, sexual health and transmission of HIV in marginalized populations at high risk for traumatic stress and health equity. Dr. Standifer received her Bachelor's degree at Spelman College, her Master's degree in Public Health from Rollins School of Public Health at Emory University, and a doctorate in Applied Anthropology with a concentration in Medical Anthropology from the University of South Florida.

Samantha Thompson's education and research background reflected a dedication to assessing the major health gaps to underserved communities in ambulatory care and mental health advocacy. After completing her Doctor of Pharmacy at Florida A&M University College of Pharmacy and Pharmaceutical Sciences, she successfully completed her an Academic Pharmacy Research Fellow in 2018. Her primary patient base consisted of underserved minority members of the community that were being treated for hypertension, type II diabetes, gout, cancer, HIV, and other infectious diseases. From 2018-2021 she was the clinical HIV pharmacist at the Florida Department of Health-Duval. In 2021 she was invited to be a tenure track Assistant Professor of Advanced Pharmacy Practice at Florida A&M University College of Pharmacy in Duval County, Florida. As an Assistant Professor, she has continued to nurture national research interest in care in filling healthcare gaps in underserved minority patients, especially in urban areas. She currently conducts yearly research examining the mental health touch points of pharmacists and pharmacy technicians during and post COVID-19 pandemic as well as possible resources to fill those gaps of care.

Vijay Uprikar A passionate Marketing Faculty at Datta Meghe Institute of Management Studies, Nagpur. With over 20 years of blended experience in academics and pharmaceutical industry, having a unique blend of corporate insights and academic expertise to the world of marketing education. A firm believer in innovative pedagogy, have developed study materials that hold six copyrights, designed to enhance conceptual clarity in marketing management. His interdisciplinary research explores Mahatma Jotirao Phule's contributions to Entrepreneurial Social Responsibility (ESR), integrating historical and social perspectives into contemporary management frameworks.

Kenith B. Villaruel is the Guidance Counselor II at the Guidance Services Center, Northern Iloilo State University-Barotac Viejo Campus. He earned his bachelor's degree in Nursing and master's degree in Guidance and Counseling both from Central Philippine University, Iloilo City. As a guidance counselor, his research interests are mostly aligned with mental health, gender and development, positive education, bullying, student welfare, and program development. Aside from guidance work, he serves as a professional lecturer and an adviser to student organizations. He is also an active member of the Philippine Guidance and Counseling Association (PGCA) and is currently pursuing his PhD in Education (Guidance) at the Counselor Education Area, College of Education, University of the Philippines-Diliman.

Deanna J. Wathington, MD, MPH, FAAFP currently serves as president-elect of the American Public Health Association (APHA). She is the clinical director at

REACHUP, Inc., an affiliate professor at the University of South Florida College of Public Health and the executive director of the Consortium of African American Public Health Programs. She previously served as the founding dean of the Bethune-Cookman University College of Health Sciences, associate dean for Academic and Student Affairs at the USF College of Public Health, founding associate dean for Academic Enrichment at the USF College of Medicine and as the director of the Office of Minority Health at the Florida Department of Health.

Index

A

B

C

D

E

F

H

I

J

L

M

O

P

R

S

T

U

V

W

www.ingramcontent.com/pod-product-compliance
Lightning Source LLC
LaVergne TN
LVHW081248011026
849162LV00004BA/658

* 9 7 9 8 3 3 7 3 0 1 6 9 3 *